Academic Assessment and Intervention

Serving students with academic deficiencies necessitates communication and collaboration among professionals from several disciplines. *Academic Assessment and Intervention* brings together divergent approaches in order to demonstrate that scientific evidence, rather than biases or previous practice, must determine assessment practices that are selected and used for particular purposes.

Similar to a handbook in its comprehensive topical coverage, this edited collection provides a contextual foundation for academic assessment and intervention; describes both norm-referenced and curriculum-based assessment/measurement in detail; considers the implications of both of these assessments on ethnically diverse populations; provides a clear link between assessment, evidence-based interventions, and the RTI model; and considers other important topics related to this area such as teacher behavior. Intended primarily for graduate-level courses in education, school psychology, or child clinical psychology, it will also be of interest to practicing professionals in these fields.

Steven G. Little is Professor in the Clinical Psychology program at Walden University, US.

Angeleque Akin-Little is President of Akin-Little & Little Behavioral Psychology Consultants based in northern New York, US.

Academic Assessment and Intervention

Edited by Steven G. Little
and Angeleque Akin-Little

Routledge
Taylor & Francis Group

NEW YORK AND LONDON

First published 2014
by Routledge
711 Third Avenue, New York, NY 10017

and by Routledge
2 Park Square, Milton Park, Abingdon, Oxon OX14 4RN

Routledge is an imprint of the Taylor & Francis Group, an informa business

© 2014 Taylor & Francis

Library of Congress Cataloging-in-Publication Data
Academic assessment and intervention / edited by Steven G. Little, Angeleque Akin-Little.
    pages cm
  Includes bibliographical references and index.
  1. Academic achievement.   2. Educational tests and measurements.
I. Little, Steven G.   II. Akin-Little, Angeleque.
    LB1061.A23 2014
    371.26'2—dc23
    2013028086

ISBN: 978-0-415-53919-7 (hbk)
ISBN: 978-0-415-53921-0 (pbk)
ISBN: 978-0-203-10845-1 (ebk)

Typeset in Minion
by Apex CoVantage, LLC

Printed and bound in the United States of America by Publishers Graphics, LLC on sustainably sourced paper.

This book is dedicated to our fathers, Raymond F. Akin and George E. Little. Both men were committed to helping those less fortunate than themselves. They also had a strong belief in the importance of educating their children. Their influence, even in their absence, continues to be felt.

Contents

Acknowledgments

We are extremely grateful to all of the contributing authors. Each and every one of you made our job incredibly easy. We were thrilled when you agreed, some of you for a second time, to work with us. You were prompt with your submissions and revisions, and you wrote excellent manuscripts. We gave you the opportunity to structure the chapter as you saw fit—you are the expert, after all—and you did not let us down. We think we have created a book that will provide important information for psychologists, particularly those working within the educational milieu.

We also thank the editors and publishers at Routledge for taking an interest in and encouraging us to submit a proposal for this book. Lane Akers was our initial contact at Routledge. His keen insight and ideas for what the book could and should be were excellent. His dogged encouragement made this book a reality. We hope he is enjoying his retirement! His replacement, Rebecca Novack, and her assistant, Andrew Weckenmann, were most helpful in reviewing final chapters, offering feedback, and helping with minor details. While this is indeed our second edited book, we are still somewhat neophytes at this process. Thank you, Lane, Rebecca, and Andrew for your incredible professionalism, knowledge, kindness, and support as we traversed this territory of editing a book again.

For many years, and especially with the increased use of Curriculum-Based Measurements and the advent of Response to Intervention, we felt there was not one individual book that encompassed all areas of academic assessment and intervention. We think we have provided such a book here, with sections on both norm-referenced assessment and the use of CBM. Further, there is a focus on how results from each type of assessment can lead to effective intervention. We thank all of you for joining us in this process. We feel very strongly that the end product is something of which we can all be very proud and which will, hopefully, provide better learning opportunities for children.

Part I
Foundations of Academic Assessment and Intervention

1

Methods of Academic Assessment

Steven G. Little and Angeleque Akin-Little

Assessing students' academic performance, both individual and as a group, is a vital part of the education process and has been a component of education for as long as formal education has been a part of civilization. Academic assessment can be defined as the process of observing and measuring learning. The rationale for evaluating students' achievement levels is ultimately to improve student learning by monitoring students' acquisition of knowledge and progress in mastering the curriculum. Academic assessment can take many forms and can be either formative (non-evaluative, designed to monitor student progress, and guide education decisions) or summative (evaluative, used to assign grades or determine if some predetermined criteria has been met). This chapter will discuss purposes of academic assessment and then summarize the characteristics and uses of norm-referenced tests of academic achievement and curriculum-based measures of academic achievement, each of which will also be discussed in more depth in subsequent chapters.

[handwritten margin notes: formative / progress / summative / outcome]

Purpose of Academic Assessment

Salvia and Ysseldyke (1995) identified the main purposes of academic assessment as specifying and verifying problems and to make decisions. While these purposes certainly continue to exist today, Lawrence (2013) better clarifies the purpose of academic assessment as (a) Identifying student strengths and weaknesses, (b) Monitoring student progress, and (c) Assessing student prior knowledge. In addition, the *No Child Left Behind* (No Child Left Behind [NCLB], 2002) legislation mandated that every child in every public and charter school in the country be tested in reading and math in Grades 3 through 8 and at least once in Grades 10 to 12, with science assessments administered at least once during Grades 3 to 5; 6 to 9; and 10 to 12. The need for academic assessments to fulfill the requirements of NCLB has therefore increased since the law's implementation. These "high stakes" assessments will be discussed in more detail in Chapter 6.

Academic assessment can be focused on an individual or a group. When the focus is on an individual student, the purpose of the assessment tends to be on the individual needs of that student, such as identifying strengths and weaknesses, measuring acquisition or retention of knowledge or skills, and evaluating performance relative to expected levels of performance (Shapiro, 2000). When the focus is on a group, such as a classroom, school, or district, the purpose of the assessment is more on evaluating whether the school or district is meeting certain objectives, either self-identified objectives or ones mandated by NCLB or other legislation. The type of assessment used for the purpose of assessing the individual may be either norm-referenced or curriculum-based. Group assessments tend to be exclusively norm-referenced.

Norm-Referenced Tests of Academic Achievement

Norm-referenced assessment is an assessment where student performance or the collective performance of multiple students is compared to a larger group. Usually, the larger group or "norm group" is a national sample that is selected to be representative of the population of the country. Individual students, classrooms, schools, school districts, and states are compared or rank-ordered in relation to the norm group. The comparison being made is generally with same-age peers from the test's norm group. An examinee's test score is compared to that of a norm group by converting the examinee's raw scores into derived or scaled scores (e.g., standard scores, percentile ranks, age-equivalent scores, grade-equivalent scores) that correspond to the normal curve, thus providing an interpretive framework for those who were administered the norm-referenced test. While the majority of commercially successful norm-referenced tests of academic achievement are standardized on a norm group, representative of the population of children from the United States (i.e., a national norm group), it can consist of a smaller, more-limited population, such as all children in an individual school or school district (i.e., a local norm group).

Ornstein (1993) presented a number of strengths of norm-referenced test including: (a) they generally maintain adequate statistical rigor and are reliable (i.e., dependable and stable) and valid (i.e., measure what they are reported to measure); (b) test items are generally of high quality as they are developed by test experts, piloted, and undergo revision before they are included in the test; and (c) administration procedures are standardized and the test items are designed to rank examinees for the purpose of placing them in specific programs or instructional groups. Using local norms also has specific advantages. Stewart and Kaminski (2002) reported that local norms have the added advantage of providing meaningful information regarding average performance in a particular school or school district. Other advantages of using local norms include a decrease in the probability of bias in educational decision-making, because individual test performance is compared to others who share similar demographic and background factors. They also allow school systems the option of comparing data on students' educational outcomes to the curriculum to which students have been exposed. Finally, local norms help in the identification of students at highest risk for academic failure as the comparison is being made to similar students who have been exposed to the same curriculum.

The most common criticism of norm-referenced academic assessment is that their content is most likely not aligned with curricular content taught in any specific school or district (i.e., content validity). Ideally, the content of the items on a norm-referenced test should closely match the content of the curriculum taught in a classroom. The greater the mismatch between test content and curricular content, the more difficult it becomes to design efficacious interventions for students in need. Norm-referenced tests also do not allow for a close monitoring of academic progress over an extended period of time. They only provide a measure of achievement in comparison to a norm group at one specific point in time (Shapiro, 2011).

Subsequent chapters discuss norm-referenced assessment of academic achievement in more detail. Flanagan, Alfonso, and Dixon (Chapter 4) discuss salient features of academic achievement batteries and provide information on nine achievement batteries along a number of different dimensions. Riccio, Dennison, and Bowman-Perrott (Chapter 5) review measures used in the individual assessment of academic skills, with specific emphasis on the areas of reading, written expression, and mathematics. Little and Akin-Little (Chapter 6) review selected published group academic assessment batteries that have been used in states and districts throughout the country and discuss their use with regard to requirements of NCLB and other legislation. Finally, Clinton and Olvera (Chapter 7) discuss norm-referenced assessment with regard to bilingual populations. Specifically, they address second language acquisition processes, important factors in the assessment of ELL students as well as discussing specific norm-referenced measures and their uses and limitations for this population.

Curriculum-Based Measures of Academic Achievement

The term curriculum-based assessment (CBA) refers to measurement that uses direct observation and recording of a student's performance in the local curriculum as a basis for gathering information to make instructional decisions (Deno, 2003). While there may be different models of CBA, they all share the basic assumption that testing should correspond to what is taught. CBA emphasizes the direct, repeated assessment of academic behaviors via probes (e.g., brief reading passages, short spelling lists, math item) from books or materials that make up the child's curriculum. The focus is, therefore, on how well a student performs on the materials that are being used in the classroom. The rationale is that if data are collected frequently, the student's progress with the curriculum can be monitored and teaching modifications can be made as needed to improve academic performance (Witt, Elliot, Daly, Gresham, & Kramer, 1998). According to Hintze, Christ, and Methe (2006), most forms of CBA rely on global curriculum being broken down into a set of ordered subskills from which assessment material is constructed.

The most obvious advantage of CBA is that it is aligned with the curriculum (i.e., the student is being tested on what is being taught). CBA is also easy to develop, quickly administered, and easy to score and monitor. In addition, studies have found high correlations between CBA scores on reading and math and achievement levels on high-stakes. For example, Good, Simmons, and Kame'enui (2001) found that students who, at the beginning of third grade, were able to read more than 110 words correctly in one minute were likely to pass the Oregon statewide test. Other advantages include continuous measurement, as CBAs are administered frequently; they are sensitive to short-term gains in academic skills; teachers can quickly determine whether a child's academic skills are delayed, comparable to, or ahead of classmates; and they help plan and monitor the effectiveness of interventions (McLane, 2006). It is hard to identify specific disadvantages to curriculum-based assessment. It is possible that teaching might be narrowed to focus only on those areas being assessed, but good teaching practices should help avoid this issue. It is also possible that teacher evaluations could be tied to student progress as measured by the CBA process. Further, one disadvantage is finding adequately trained educational personnel to administer these assessments, as they do require more expertise than the administration of a norm-referenced tool. Again, this is not so much a disadvantage of CBA but, rather, a more systemic issue in schools, and one that is not limited to CBA.

Subsequent chapters discuss curriculum-based assessment of academic achievement in more detail. Christ, Keller-Margulis, and Marcotte (Chapter 8) discuss the underlying assumptions and critical features of CBA. They also examine prominent methods of CBA, including Curriculum-Based Measurement (CBM), Brief Experimental Analysis (BEA), Curriculum-Based Assessment for Instructional Design (CBA-ID), Curriculum-Based Assessment Criterion Referenced (CBA-CR), and Curriculum-Based Evaluation (CBE). Phillips, Shinn, and Ditkowsky (Chapter 9) summarize the history and current use of technology in published CBM products. Brown, Steege, and Bickford (Chapter 10) provide an overview of Response to Intervention/Multi-Tier Systems of Support (RTI/MTSS), and discuss how they can be used to implement effective assessment practices in schools. Finally, Vanderwood, Tung, and Hickey (Chapter 11) discuss the challenges faced when using CBA procedures with culturally and linguistically diverse students and how to overcome these challenges.

Conclusions

Assessing academic performance is a critical aspect of the education process for all students. This chapter discusses the general purposes of academic assessment, summarizes the characteristics and uses of norm-referenced tests of academic achievement and curriculum-based measures of academic achievement, discusses the strengths and weakness of each type of assessment, and summarizes subsequent chapters that discuss these tests and issues associated with these tests in more detail.

References

Deno, S. L. (2003). Developments in curriculum-based measurement. *Journal of Special Education, 37,* 184–192.

Good, R. H., Simmons, D. C., & Kame'enui, E. J. (2001). The importance and decision-making utility of a continuum of fluency-based indicators of foundational reading skills for third-grade high-stakes outcomes. *Scientific Studies of Reading, 5,* 257–288.

Hintze, J. M., Christ, T. J., & Methe, S. A. (2006). Curriculum-based assessment. *Psychology in the Schools, 43,* 45–56.

Lawrence, B. M. (2013). What is the purpose of classroom assessments? Retrieved from http://www.ehow.com/facts_7651703_purpose-classroom-assessments.html#ixzz2UbwxvTEh

McLane, K. (2006). Curriculum-based measurement and statewide assessments. Retrieved from http://www.studentprogress.org/

Ornstein, A. C. (1993). Norm referenced and criterion referenced tests: An overview. *NASSP Bulletin, 77*(555), 28–39. (Reprinted from H. Torrance (Ed.), (2012). *Educational assessment and evaluation.* New York, NY: Routledge.)

Salvia, J., & Ysseldyke, J. E. (1995). *Assessment is special and remedial education.* Boston, MA: Houghton Mifflin.

Shapiro, E. S. (2000). Academic assessment of performance. In A. E. Kazdin (Ed.), *Encyclopedia of psychology, Vol. 1* (pp. 10–14). Washington, DC: APA Press.

Shapiro, E. S. (2011). *Academic skills problems* (4th ed.). New York, NY: Guilford Press.

Stewart, L. H., & Kaminski, R. (2002). Best practices in developing local norms for academic problem solving. In A. Thomas & J. Grimes (Eds.), *Best practices in school psychology IV* (pp. 737–752). Bethesda, MD: National Association of School Psychologists.

Witt, J. C., Elliot, S. N., Daly, E. J., Gresham, F. M., & Kramer, J. J. (1998). *Assessment of at-risk and special needs children* (2nd ed.). Boston, MA: McGraw-Hill.

2
A General Case Framework for Academic Intervention

George H. Noell and Kristin A. Gansle

Academic expectations are a central developmental reality for children living in industrial and information age societies. Academic expectations are set in a social context that emphasizes normative rates of progress and comparative levels of achievement for keystone skills and performance on high-stakes assessments (Ditkowsky & Koonce, 2010). It can be argued reasonably that students do not have academic performance deficits in any absolute sense. All students are performing at the level one should expect, given their genetic endowment, motivation, prior skills, the quality of instruction they receive, and their family/community support. Viewed from this perspective, behavior *per se* is neither wrong nor right, but is the expression of one's cumulative experiences (Skinner, 1953). Academic deficits are a mismatch between students' current levels of academic performance and expectations for peers. The large number of children who are identified as exhibiting academic deficits is a foreseeable feature of any developmental system that sets expectations based on normative comparisons at specific points in time and normative expectations for rates of progress between those times (Nese, Park, Alonzo, & Tindal, 2011; Zigmond & Kloo, 2009). By definition, one in 10 students will always be in the bottom 10% of performers, and half of all students will always be behind the average student in acquiring any skill. These normative statistical realities are evident throughout our educational landscape in areas such as the rate of referral to special education (Office of Special Education and Rehabilitative Services [OSERS], December 2011).

The description above is not intended as an argument against standards, but as an acknowledgement that the way we traditionally have set standards ensures that some group of students will always be identified as failing to meet them. It is also intended to highlight that what we call an academic deficit is a mismatch between expectations and performance, rather than an absolute feature of either performance or students. This reality should cause us to be thoughtful and cautious in making consequential decisions about children, especially when the standards are normative, comparative, and arbitrary. It is also worth noting that standards that are informal, as in teacher referral, or statistically defined, as in standardized test performance, have different but substantive limitations (Hibel, Farkas, & Morgan,

2010; Shapiro, 2011). Although the bulk of this chapter ultimately focuses on how one thinks about student academic behavior and how educators can change that behavior, it is worth recognizing at the outset that we should be just as careful about the standards we are using to define who has a problem as we are about how to address those problems.

Academic standards can serve a variety of useful functions for students, educators, and schools. In the best of circumstances, they would be orienting, motivating, and challenging, and represent substantive markers toward success after K–12 education (Meyer, McClure, Walkey, Weir, & McKenzie, 2009). A standard based on evidence showing that achieving a particular level of literacy by third grade was necessary for a student to have a high probability of graduating from high school would be a substantive standard. Similarly, a standard demonstrating what level of mathematics proficiency high school students must demonstrate in order to compete effectively in the workplace would be a substantive standard (e.g., Falbo & Glover, 1999). Unfortunately, outcomes-driven criteria are rarely what drive referral in schools. In essence, students are referred for not being average "enough" in some formal or informal comparison. This reality is not the result of educators acting in bad faith, but is an artifact of the information systems at hand. It is highly salient to a third-grade teacher that two students are chronically behind their peers in reading skills despite efforts to help them catch up. It may be completely unclear whether they are on track to hit key readiness milestones for high school, or whether they and half of their peers are all off of a trajectory for high school readiness due to ineffective classroom instruction (Fuchs, Fuchs, & Speece, 2002). Similarly, even when we have outcome-informed standards data available, there is no guarantee that the information will penetrate to the educators on the front lines (Harris, 2012). When we lack substantive criterion-based standards or do not get the critical information to educators, we are reduced to using rules of thumb that are based on typical outcomes; it will be necessary to make decisions based on the information that is at hand.

Although standard setting is a critical component of education and of identifying students for intervention support, it is not the central focus of this chapter (see Chapter 18 this volume for an extended consideration). Similarly, this chapter is not focused on detailed descriptions of specific interventions for the diverse array of referral concerns, such as reading decoding, written expression, and mathematics skills (see Chapters 12 through 16 this volume). This chapter presents a general case problem-solving framework for providing academic intervention to referred students. The framework is based on four critical action steps that are necessary for effective intervention. The first step is moving from a referral concern to clear instructional targets and goals. The second step is assessing the referral concern in a way that is relevant to intervention design. The third step is devising an instructional intervention that is appropriate to the goals and guided by the assessment data. Finally, assuring implementation in a comprehensive way can be a particularly challenging step (Noell & Gansle, 2006; Noell & Gansle, in press). This will include assuring implementation, measuring progress, and adjusting procedures as informed by the progress monitoring data.

Identifying Instructional Targets

Academic intervention commonly begins with a referral concern. The events that trigger referrals typically do not contain enough information to allow an educator to plan a relevant intervention. For example, learning that a student is receiving failing grades in mathematics should cause concern, but does not provide the person receiving the referral any information about expectations, current instruction, instructional demands, student skills, student work habits, or student motivation. Similarly, a student failing the reading portion of the state-mandated standardized reading assessment will likely raise alarm, but is not sufficient information for educators to know what specific aspects of which behavior or behaviors need to be addressed, or how to provide relevant support (Shapiro, 2011; Yen, Konold, & McDermott, 2004).

Instructional targets are developed through an assessment process that includes interviews of the referral source, teacher(s), and target student, as well as review of current work products and direct assessment of academic skills. Several chapters in this volume are devoted entirely to the topic of academic assessment and obviously that information will not be repeated here. However, development of a general case model for instructional intervention requires defining what the outcome of the assessment process is. One outcome of the initial assessment process is the specification of an *instructional target*. An instructional target is the behavior that the intervention is designed to change. It should be stated in objective, observable terms with a measurable goal. Goal setting and measurement against that goal has repeatedly been found to be an effective component of intervention (e.g., Codding, Chan-Iannetta, Palmer, & Lukito, 2009; Fuchs, Fuchs, & Hamlett, 1989; Jenkins & Terjeson, 2011; Morgan, Sideridis, & Hua, 2012; Morisano, Hirsh, Peterson, Pihl, Shore, 2010). Table 2.1 provides examples of poor instructional targets and strong alternatives, with a short description of why the strong alternative is an improvement over the weak example.

Almost any behavior potentially could become an instructional target. This diversity is both inspiring, when one considers the range of human abilities with which educators have the opportunity to engage, and overwhelming. In order to frame a general case approach to academic intervention, we must recognize a few types of instructional targets that imply different instructional needs. Although types of instructional targets can be organized in a number of ways, the organization presented here is intended to highlight differences that are intuitive, easily distinguished, and have clear relevance to how we design instructional intervention. The general framework described below proceeds from simple behaviors to more complex and is built on four basic distinctions. Although students generally will progress from the simpler to the more complex targets within a domain as they advance through

Table 2.1 Examples of Poor and Sound Instructional Targets

Poor Instructional Target	Strong Instructional Target	Contrast
Jeremy's reading skills will improve.	Jeremy will read a median of 100 words per minute on a 3rd-grade reading probe.	The first goal is stated so broadly that it can't be measured and it lacks a specific goal.
Sandra will earn Bs on math quizzes.	Sandra will complete mixed math addition fact probes with 100% accuracy at 40 digits correct per minute.	The first goal doesn't clarify what the skills are that the student will work on.
Malik will follow conventions in paragraph writing with 90% accuracy.	90% of Malik's sentences will include correct capitalization, punctuation, and subject/verb agreement on writing probes.	While the first target has a goal level, it is too vague to be measured.
Tom will understand the functioning of the cell.	Tom will correctly identify the function of the nine primary cell structures provided on the syllabus, with 100% accuracy.	The first target lacks a performance goal.

curriculum, it is important to recognize that students will continue to have learning needs at both the simpler and more complex levels throughout their lives. The importance of this fact is touched on below.

The first type of target, *stimulus control*, is the simplest. Stimulus control occurs when students reliably make the correct response when presented with a stimulus that requires a response (Cooper, Heron, & Heward, 1987). Stimulus control relationships are common across the academic curriculum. They include academic tasks such as naming letters, producing letter sounds, reading words, defining vocabulary terms, translating languages, and solving math facts. Stimulus control learning provides a basic building block upon which more complex skills and knowledge are built across the curriculum.

The critical point for the current discussion is that stimulus control is evident when students can *see* or *hear* an instructional prompt and *respond* with the correct response. For example, a student seeing the printed word "cat" who can then say the word "cat" has exhibited stimulus control. That student has demonstrated an understanding that both the spoken word and the printed word represent the same thing. Similarly, the student who can see "4 + 2 = " and respond with "six," whether orally, in writing, or on a multiple-choice test, has exhibited stimulus control. Some sources will describe stimulus control as a lower form of learning, or as relevant only for early instruction. Those arguments gloss over the fact that human beings continue to acquire new stimulus-response relationships over the course of their entire lives. A graduate student acquires new reading and spoken vocabulary, a surgeon learns to recognize organs first observed in drawings, and everyone learns the names of new acquaintances. This type of learning occurs across the life span.

The second type of instructional target to consider is the *behavioral chain*. A behavioral chain is a sequence of behaviors in which completion of each behavior serves as a stimulus to complete the next behavior. When viewed in their entireties, behavioral chains normally appear as coherent units that produce an end. Washing one's hands is an example of a behavioral chain. It requires a series of steps that have to be performed in the correct order to complete the task. Common behavioral chains for academic responses include completing long division or spelling tasks. Behavioral chains, sometimes described as procedural knowledge, are a common feature of life in technological and information age cultures (Kuhn, Lerman, Vorndran, & Addison, 2006; Phillips & Vollmer, 2012).

The third type of instructional target to consider is *schema development*. A schema in this context is an organized representation of knowledge. It commonly includes relationships, inferences, and connections between related ideas. A schema can contain relatively concrete factual information, such as how photosynthesis works at the cellular level, or it can be somewhat abstract and inferential, such as students' interpretations of the main themes of *Hamlet*. Such a large portion of K–12 education focuses on the development of these organized bodies of knowledge that it often can appear at first observation that this is the focus of instruction and education.

The final type of instructional target to consider is *strategic behavior*. Strategic behavior integrates knowledge and skills across multiple domains to produce an end product or result (Noell, Call, & Ardoin, 2011). Although we may not commonly think of it in this way, the use of strategic behavior is often necessary in schools. For example, a student who is asked to write a persuasive essay about the importance of economic factors at the onset of the American Revolution must integrate knowledge and skills from a number of domains, including information about the content, persuasive communication, and writing skills. Similarly, solving typical mathematics applications problems provided in text (i.e., word problems) is a complex strategic task. Students must read and comprehend the question, devise a mathematical representation of the problem, solve computational problems, and represent the mathematical answer. These steps comprise a multifaceted, planned task that often requires strategic instruction.

Critical Contextual Considerations

Once the instructional target has been identified, information about three factors that set the context for the concern will be needed. These are (1) the nature and quality of current instruction, (2) the degree to which the referral concern is specific versus representative of many students, and (3) the target student's motivation to perform the academic task. The nature of what an educator learns about these contextual factors can substantially shift what intervention is provided or how that intervention is designed. The following section briefly touches on what the intervention design implications are for each issue before turning to how to design academic interventions for stimulus control, chained behavior, schema development, and strategic behaviors.

Motivational issues. To state what hopefully is obvious, but frequently is salient when confronted with a referral concern, it is perfectly possible that the student possesses the skills necessary to complete the instructional target. Indeed, the fact that students produce unacceptable academic products does not necessarily mean that they do not know how to produce them (e.g., Duhon et al., 2004). It may well be the case that the student has the necessary skills, but that engaging in other behaviors is more reinforcing, or there is simply no consequence that motivates the student to do the work (e.g., Martens & Houk, 1989). Research has demonstrated relatively simple, quick procedures for examining the possibility that poor performance is the result of poor motivation (Noell, Freeland, Witt, & Gansle, 2001). A sample of academic performance is obtained under typical or standardized conditions, and followed by an assessment with equivalent materials but which provides a powerful reward contingency for improved performance. Researchers have found that some, but not all, students' performance will improve substantially under reward conditions, suggesting primarily a motivational issue rather than a deficit of skills (Noell et al., 2001). Additionally, the study demonstrated that brief assessments of motivational issues did a good job in predicting which student would respond favorably to a motivational intervention rather than an instructional one (Noell et al., 2001).

To state the obvious, it makes little sense to teach students to do something they already know how to do. If the problem is motivational, an instructional intervention may look like it is producing great gains because it includes some motivational components, when in fact it is the motivational part that is producing all of the gains. It can also emerge that an instructional intervention that does not address motivational problems, when they are the core issue, can simply further frustrate the student and educators. Effective intervention design requires examining motivation and intervening on motivation when it is at the core of the concern. The procedures for intervening with motivational problems are relatively straightforward. They include defining the target behavior, setting the standard of performance that will earn reinforcement, identifying an effective reinforcer, devising the schedule of reinforcement, and implementing the plan. A comprehensive discussion of how to devise systematic reinforcement plans is beyond the scope of this chapter, but extensive consideration is available from other sources (see Cooper et al., 1987; or Sulzer-Azaroff & Mayer, 1991).

Problem prevalence. An additional issue that is fundamental to devising reasonable interventions, but is often overlooked, is considering the prevalence of the problem (VanDerHeyden, Witt, & Gilbertson, 2007). In some cases, a student is referred who is the only student in the class who exhibits the target concern. In this case, a traditional student-focused intervention is an appropriate course of action. However, it is not uncommon on further examination to learn that the referred student is one among several, many, or an entire class exhibiting essentially the same concern (e.g., VanDerHeyden et al., 2007). It obviously makes no sense to design an intervention for one student when the concern is relevant to a group of students or to the whole class. The intervention principles described below are as applicable to groups of students as they are to individuals. However, the critical consideration is getting the target group right so that all of the students who need the intervention are getting it in the most time- and resource-efficient manner practical. In many cases, the same intervention elements can be implemented in a one-to-one, small group, or whole group context with appropriate modifications. Far too often in education, interventionists accept referral concerns for individuals without examining the possibility that the problem is actually widespread (VanDerHeyden et al., 2007). In these cases, the limited available resources are consumed with helping one student when the same resources could have helped many students. Further, there are likely to be economies of scale in providing the intervention to multiple students at the same time; the sum of the marginal cost for providing the same intervention to each additional student is considerably smaller than multiplying the cost for one student by the total number of students. Predictably, another student is likely to be referred for the same concern as soon as or even before the target student improves, especially if the intervention is having positive effects on the target student. Additionally, the narrow focus on the poorest-performing student in isolation can prevent educators from recognizing and acting on systemic problems, such as curricula that are poorly matched to students' educational needs, or teachers whose own instructional skill sets need development.

Current instruction. Obviously, intervention design should be informed by examination of current instruction (Kelley, Reitman, & Noell, 2002; Shapiro, 2011). If the target skill is part of current instruction, it may be possible to integrate the intervention into ongoing instruction in a way that reduces resource demands, meets the target student's needs, and benefits additional students. If the target student needs support for skills that are no longer being instructed, intervention must then be a separate activity. Additionally, it is important to recognize that teachers vary widely in their instructional effectiveness (Aaronson, Barrow, & Sander, 2007; Boyd, Lankford, Loeb, Rockoff, & Wyckoff, 2008; Gansle, Noell, & Burns, 2012; Kane, Rockoff, & Staiger, 2008; Rivkin, Hanushek, & Kain, 2005; Rockoff, 2004; Sanders & Rivers, 1996). The pre-intervention assessment should minimally examine the degree to which teachers are emotionally supportive of students, effectively organize their class routines to maximize learning, and provide effective instructional supports (Burchinal, Peisner-Feinberg, Pianta, & Howes, 2002). A few standardized assessments of instructional practice with normative data and standards are available (Danielson Group, 2013; Pianta & Hamre, 2009).

Obviously, if observation and assessment of instruction reveal that the core problem is poor general instruction, intervening with an individual student is a bit like bailing water on the RMS *Titanic* after she is struck by the iceberg. It might do a little good, but it is not going to change the ultimate outcome. The student may catch up on the targeted skill in the short term, but ineffective instruction will ultimately result in that student and his or her peers gradually slipping further and further behind. Research suggests that students who are exposed to ineffective teaching for 3 consecutive years experience losses so great that they never catch up (Sanders & Rivers, 1996). Metaphorically, they slip below the surface. Although the intervention elements below can be incorporated into effective instruction, truly supporting educators to shift from ineffective to effective emotional engagement with students, classroom management, and instructional support is a complex undertaking that is beyond the scope of this chapter.

General Design Issues in Academic Intervention

Several general issues are relevant to the design of academic intervention across the different types of instructional targets described below. Rather than reexamine those issues again in each section, we will consider these crosscutting issues here. These critical concerns include: (1) who will provide the intervention, (2) how often will it be provided, (3) how much new material will be taught at one time, and (4) what will keep the student(s) motivated. The issue of who will provide the intervention is of critical importance in schools, because educators are a scarce resource. There are many ways to provide intervention in an efficient manner. Interventions can be folded into ongoing instruction or provided in small group sessions rather than individually (see Begeny, Yeager, & Martinez, 2012; Foorman & Torgesen, 2001; Jitendra et al., 2013, for examples). Students can be taught to provide peer tutoring in both strong-skill to weaker-skill formats or even, more promisingly, in a reciprocal format (Fantuzzo, Polite, & Grayson, 1990; Sutherland & Snyder, 2007). Similarly, for a number of instructional targets, software is available that can provide instruction (e.g., Intelligent Tutor, Carlson, 1995; ClickN Read Phonics, Nelson, 2003). This chapter focuses on the content of the instructional intervention and what will happen, rather than on who will provide the intervention. Although the authors recognize that who provides instruction is a critical consideration, making this decision is an extremely context-driven issue, dependent on the resources at hand.

The issues of how often instruction is provided and how much new material is introduced within each teaching session are important design decisions, but ones for which a limited research basis is available. For example, it is unlikely that students will learn if practice occasions are spaced too widely apart. If a student receives instruction on their math facts or a foreign language only once a month, they may not make any measurable progress. However, there is no clear scientific basis for choosing between intervention every other day, daily, or twice a day (Dempster, 1989), and the variables that might determine which choice is likely to lead to the best results are as yet poorly understood. However, a few simple rules of thumb may prove useful. More frequent practice is likely to be more effective than infrequent practice, as long as the practice does not become massed (Dempster, 1989). A sound strategy typically would call for making practice as frequent as is practical (e.g., daily) and then making adjustments as needed, based on practical considerations and progress monitoring data. Deciding on the amount of new material to provide at one time is essentially an art rather than a science at this time. Some students can practice 25 new multiplication facts at one time and make good progress, while others may be overwhelmed by that amount of material. Making decisions about how much new material to provide at one time typically has to be made informally by observing how the student responds in the instructional session and by evaluating progress-monitoring data.

A final intervention design concern that cuts across targets and intervention procedures is how to motivate students. In some instances, learning can be fun; it is hard work in others. There is abundant literature demonstrating that incorporating reinforcement into instructional interventions makes them more effective (e.g., Pipkin, Winters, & Diller, 2007). While the design of reinforcement systems is a topic that could consume this entire chapter, recognizing some fundamental principles will allow educators to address many common situations. The first principle is that what is reinforcing for individuals differs across them (Sulzer-Azaroff & Mayer, 1991). Some students may work hard for stickers, while others do not respond to them at all. Similarly, while many students might work hard for teacher attention, others may be more strongly motivated by free time. The critical design consideration is what motivates this particular student. Asking students what they would like to work for is preferable to picking reinforcers arbitrarily, but direct assessments where students are able to choose among reinforcers have been found to be even more effective (Northup, 2000; Northup, Jones, Broussard, & George, 1995).

A second critical consideration is what the student must do to earn the reinforcer: What is the criterion for reinforcement? There is a fairly substantial literature demonstrating that beginning with a modest criterion, a student can achieve and make contact with reinforcement; adjusting that criterion as progress is made is an effective design principle (Galbicka, 1994). Another consideration in designing the motivational system is how long the student must wait to receive the earned reinforcer (e.g., immediately, at the end of the day, at the end of the week, etc.). The literature is overwhelmingly clear on this point: although most students can benefit and can learn to benefit from delayed reinforcement, the more immediate it is, the more effective it is likely to be (Sy & Vollmer, 2012). A final consideration is how to design the reinforcement schedule. The schedule describes the rules that govern when reinforcement will be provided (e.g., after each correct response or after 10 correct responses). Schedules of reinforcement that build in some variability, but provide the opportunity to earn reinforcement at any time by continuing to work (variable ratio schedules) have been demonstrated to support high sustained rates of work (Mazur, 2006).

Teaching Students Discrete Responses

Stimulus control occurs when students reliably make the correct response when presented with a stimulus that requires a response. Generally, tightly stimulus-controlled skills serve as building blocks for more complicated skills. For example, math facts are critical skills for solving application problems, as is the knowledge of sight words to reading fluently. Educators commonly teach academic skills that call for stimulus control by providing students with complete learning trials. A *complete learning trial* occurs when an instructional demand (sometimes called an antecedent) is presented and is followed by a response that is, in turn, followed by a consequence. Feedback about the accuracy of the answer or response is often an effective consequence for helping students develop stimulus control. Praise or other reinforcers can also be used to help develop stimulus control (e.g., Chafouleas, Martens, Dobson, Weinstein, & Gardner, 2004; Rosen & Rosen, 1983).

Despite ubiquitous demands for students to develop responses that are tightly controlled by academic stimuli and the consequential amount of time devoted formally and informally to teaching these relationships by parents and teachers, many students struggle developing them. These difficulties are often evident in basic tool skills of mathematics and reading as students struggle to learn critical fundamental relations (e.g., letter sounds, sight words, or math facts) that interfere with their ability to engage with more complex academic demands (Andersson, 2010; Roberts & Norwich, 2010). The reasons that students struggle with some relationships is frequently unclear. It may be that instruction was inconsistently delivered or implemented, that feedback and/or consequences were not provided in an effective manner, that too few practice opportunities were provided, or that instruction moved on to new topics before the student had mastered the content (Daly, Witt, Martens, & Dool, 1997). It is also important to recognize that individual differences in students may play a role.

When assessment determines that these fundamental stimulus-response relationships are appropriate instructional targets, the goal is to provide students with a structured instructional experience that will help them master the skill in the most time efficient manner possible. Typically, educators focus on how to provide effective complete learning trials frequently enough, with sufficiently strong motivational design that students make excellent progress. The key term here is "effective." "Effective" in this context means providing students with instructional supports that allow them quickly to make correct responses so those responses can be reinforced, and that allow them to become independent in making those responses as quickly as is practical. Typically, this is accomplished with either shaping or a prompting strategy.

Shaping

Shaping is a process by which reinforcement is provided for responses that approximate the target behavior. The criteria for reinforcement are systematically increased so that responses must increasingly closely match the end target to obtain reinforcement. Shaping is an instructional approach that is particularly important for students who cannot exhibit the target response even with prompts or models. For example, a student with autism may not have language sufficient to say "Mommy," even with prompts or models. Shaping would begin by reinforcing making a sound in response to the request "Say 'Mommy.'" The criterion might then shift to the sound being "m," then "ma," then "mom," and finally "Mommy." The process of shaping gradually transforms one behavior into the target behavior by shifting the reinforcement criterion as the student begins to approximate the desired response. Shaping has been used successively to teach a wide range of skills (Cooper et al., 1987).

Shaping is the attempt to use reinforcement and extinction (withholding reinforcement) to gradually shift how behavior is expressed, so that the target response begins to occur and to occur reliably (Galbicka, 1994). Several factors affect the probability of successfully using shaping. First, does the student make a response that can be gradually transformed into the target response? Second, can that behavior be occasioned often enough to establish an initial teaching history of reinforcement? Third, is there some variability in the student's approximation so that reinforcement can be provided for responses that more closely approximate the target, and withheld for those that are not?

Shaping can be a challenging teaching strategy. It requires careful attention to student responses, and making frequent small adjustments in what behavior is reinforced. This can readily lead to frustration for teachers and students when mistakes are made. For example, when reinforcement is provided for the same approximation for too long, the student may find it more difficult to move on to a different approximation (Foxx, 1982). It can also occur when the jump to the next approximation is too large and the student loses access to reinforcement (Galbicka, 1994). Shaping for the purpose of establishing stimulus control is likely to be limited to students with relatively severe needs, because of how challenging it is to implement properly.

Prompting

Using prompting strategies is appropriate when a prompt can be identified that will result in the student producing the correct answer, but the student does not currently do so when presented with the relevant instructional demand (Noell et al., 2011). In a simple sense, the prompt can consist of showing the student the correct answer, as in saying "five" when presenting a "2 + 3 = " flash card. When the student repeats the correct answer, the teacher, tutor, or software has the opportunity to provide reinforcement for the correct answer (e.g., praise), making it more likely to occur again in the future. Stimulus prompts are materials that are provided with the instructional demand that cue the student to the correct response. This might include printing the correct answer on a flash card. Response prompts are provided by the instructors, such as saying the correct answer as a prompt (Wolery & Gast, 1984).

Although prompting is an effective way to occasion correct responding for students, the goal is for students to make correct responses without needing prompts. Much of the research about prompting strategies has examined ways to efficiently prompt correct responding, while quickly fading those prompts so that responding becomes independent (Schoen, 1986; Wolery & Gast, 1984). Fading of stimulus prompts typically is accomplished by making the prompt less and less salient. For example, the prompt may be printed more and more faintly or in a smaller and smaller font. A more comprehensive review of stimulus fading can be found in Ault, Wolery, Doyle, and Gast (1989).

Research has examined three primary types of instructor delivered prompts: time-delayed, most-to-least, and least-to-most. In least-to-most prompting, also known as the system of least prompts, a student is initially provided with the opportunity to respond after the instructional demand (Cooper et al., 1987; Schoen, 1986). If the student does not respond, a series of increasingly intrusive prompts are provided until the student makes the correct response. The system of least prompts can be used to teach phonics skills. For example, the word to be read aloud would be presented. If the student did not respond correctly, the teacher might provide the initial sound. If that did not lead to correct responding, the teacher could model sounding out the first syllable. If that was not successful, the teacher could model sounding out the entire word. The progression to more complete prompts would progress at a standard pace (e.g., every 3 seconds). If the student makes an incorrect response at any point, accuracy feedback would be provided along with the most intrusive model (Wolery & Gast, 1984). Two advantages of least-to-most prompt fading are that its implementation is intuitive and the student is responding as independently as possible. It has been argued that the higher level of learner independence and the natural prompt fading built into least-to-most prompting are substantive advantages over other strategies (Billingsley & Romer, 1983).

Most-to-least prompting reverses the progression of least-to-most. It begins with the most intrusive prompt and gradually decreases prompt intensity as students respond independently (Billingsley & Romer, 1983). In the phonics example above, prompting would begin with modeling the whole word. After several complete correct responses, prompts would drop down to modeling the initial syllable. The strength of most-to-least is that it typically results in fewer error responses by students, and can provide for more complete learning trials if many prompts are needed under least-to-most to obtain the correct response. The critical challenges with most-to-least prompt fading are that the student may become dependent on the prompts, and that it is not necessarily clear when to move to a less intrusive prompt (Wolery & Gast, 1984).

Time-delay prompting strategies fade out prompt supports through the use of timing rather than changing the nature of the prompt that is provided. Instruction begins with one or several trials in which the prompt is provided immediately after the instructional demand. The flash card is presented and the answer is provided immediately so that the student can imitate the model (Snell & Gast, 1981). Prompt fading has been achieved with strategies described as constant and progressive (Walker, 2008). In constant time-delay prompting, subsequent prompts are delayed for a fixed number of seconds (typically in the range of 5–10 seconds) after the presentation of the instructional demand (Walker, 2008). In progressive time-delay, the delay between the presentation of the instructional demand and prompt is gradually increased as a function of a specific number of correct responses (Heckaman, Alber, Hooper, & Heward, 1998).

Time-delay procedures generally result in low error rates for students and are easily implemented (Wolery & Gast, 1984; Walker, 2008). The ease of implementation has allowed the use of peers and siblings as tutors (e.g., Tekin & Kircaali-Iftar, 2002). Overall, reviews have generally favored constant time-delay as being more efficient than other prompting strategies (Wolery & Gast, 1984), with some exceptions providing equivocal results for more complex behaviors (Schuster et al., 1998) or favoring progressive delay for children with autism (Walker, 2008).

Teaching Students Skills That Require Sequences of Behavior

Behavioral chains are series of behaviors that must be completed in the correct order to produce a desired effect, such as washing one's hands or completing a long division problem. When behavioral chains are established, they are sequences of behaviors in which completion of each behavior serves as a stimulus to complete the next behavior (Mazur, 2006). Generally, the procedures described above are used to teach the individual steps in the chain. Technically, completion of each step serves as a conditioned reinforcer for the previous behavior and a discriminative stimulus for the next one (Mazur, 2006). Teaching a behavioral chain begins with a task analysis of the steps needed to complete the task. Instruction itself is normally accomplished through procedures described as forward chaining, backward chaining, or whole task instruction.

In forward chaining, students are taught the first step and once they complete that step independently, instruction moves to the first two steps and so on through the entire task. One could argue that this is the most intuitive approach. In backward chaining, students are taught the last step alone and once they complete this step successfully, they learn to execute the last two steps and so forth until they can complete the entire task. It has been proposed that backward chaining is desirable because each instructional trial ends with the task being completed and the possibility of delivering the natural consequence for task completion (Smith, 1999). Whole task chain instruction consists of teaching all steps in the task on each trial. It has been argued that whole task instruction will be most effective, because each instructional trial will include all steps with the opportunity for the entire sequence to be experienced and reinforced on every trial. In contrast, concerns regarding whole task have been raised regarding an increased teaching time for practicing all steps and the possibility of students struggling due to an overwhelming level of instructional demand (i.e., too many unknown steps instructed at once).

Comparisons of forward, backward, and whole task chain instruction have produced decidedly mixed results (Hur & Osborne, 1993; Smith, 1999; Walls, Zane, & Ellis, 1981;

Watters, 1992). Although it is not clear why this is the case at present, variations in the students, skills, and measures used to judge effectiveness have varied widely across studies. It is likely the case that the instructional method deemed most effective may depend on a combination of the student characteristics and the skill being instructed. For example, it may be difficult to meaningfully teach addition with regrouping skills in anything other than whole task. At present, practitioners are likely to have to rely on knowledge of the task they are teaching, and their students to make a best professional choice of the initial teaching method to apply. It is important to keep in mind that if progress-monitoring data suggest disappointing results, then the availability of three alternative methods provides the opportunity to try a different approach.

Teachings Students Structured Bodies of Knowledge

Supporting students in developing organized systems of knowledge or schemas is such an extensive area of inquiry and professional endeavor that comprehensive coverage is beyond the scope of any single chapter. Generally, instruction designed to help students develop coherent, organized content knowledge involves them learning to retain a body of information, organizing that information in a way that is meaningful, and interacting with the information in substantive ways (Pressley & Woloshyn, 1995). It remains important to acknowledge the important role that tool skills in domains such as reading, writing, speaking, listening, and mathematics play in allowing students to access and contribute to content knowledge.

A defining feature of content knowledge is the ability to demonstrate comprehension on relatively complex tasks that demonstrate mastery of meaning and functional connections between proximal and distal ideas within the domain. Although there are many potential ways to begin developing this understanding, a logical and pivotal place to begin is with vocabulary development. Obviously, it is immensely helpful in mastering a content area to understand its terms. Meta-analytic synthesis has found a large effect for vocabulary instruction on reading comprehension for passages containing the target words and a moderate effect size for reading comprehension generally (Stahl & Fairbanks, 1986). The most effective vocabulary instruction included both definitions and contextual information, required deeper processing of information, mnemonic devices, and more than two learning exposures to the words.

A number of instructional approaches are available that when used effectively, improve the probability that students will be able to understand, organize, and retain new information (Lenz, Bulgren, & Hudson, 1990). Essentially, they are activities or objects that teachers use to help their students organize, remember, and understand content. Devices vary according to how they are used and the way in which they are presented (Mercer, Mercer, & Pullen, 2011). They aid in five areas: (1) organizing information, (2) promoting understanding, (3) describing, (4) demonstrating, and (5) promoting recall. Each increases students' contact with the content in ways that are designed to enhance meaning, organization, and recall.

Deshler, Ellis, and Lenz (1996) describe examples of these devices. First, summarization, chunking, and advance organizers allow teachers to organize information verbally in ways that students are likely to remember. These tools help students retain more information by reducing demand on working memory, creating fewer larger bites of information to encode and recall. Visual cues such as outlines, tables, and flowcharts serve similar purposes. For example, an advance organizer is presented before the lesson, and it cues students to attend to important aspects of the lesson. Generally, the use of graphic organizers has been found to be associated with increased vocabulary and factual comprehension in science education (Dexter, Park, & Hughes, 2011). These can include student-completed representations as well as teacher-provided pictures, models, and diagrams that help students visualize relationships between concepts. Similarly, study guides, which often include semantic and graphic organizers, can provide an effective intervention for students who struggle.

Teacher-provided analogies, synonyms, examples, and similes are common strategies to facilitate students making connections between prior knowledge and new material (Deshler et al., 1996). Mnemonics can be designed to help students remember content by capturing critical aspects of that content and promoting those as the information to be studied, with the expectation that the underlying content will be easy to remember once the mnemonic is remembered. Classic mnemonics such as *PEMDAS* (or Parentheses, Exponents, Multiplication, Division, Addition, and Subtraction) describe the order of operations for multiple mathematics operations problems. Also, descriptions can be provided verbally using current or historical events, hypothetical stories, or visually using films or videos. These descriptions provide additional experience with the concepts and content. Fourth, demonstrations can be done through role-play or dramatic example. Fifth, recall can be promoted using acronyms or keywords, sketches or images on paper.

Teaching routines are described by Bulgren and Lenz (1996) as instructional activities that help students develop, acquire, and apply devices. These teaching devices are repeatedly embedded in instructional procedures and become a routine (Mercer et al., 2011). An example is the Concept Anchoring Routine (Bulgren, Schumaker, & Deshler, 1994). The teacher uses a table or device called an "anchoring table." This table displays new information about a topic, but ties it to a familiar topic that shares features with the new one, allowing students to access prior knowledge to facilitate organizing and encoding new information. Similarly, instructional procedures that give students hands-on experiences with the material and allow them to work in collaborative teams have been found to support educational gains in conceptually challenging content material (Springer, Stanne, & Donovan, 1999). Not surprisingly, structuring activities in which students must analyze information, construct arguments favoring a position/conclusion, and defend that argument against critique is not only a core element of most content disciplines, but is also a powerful teaching tool in and of itself (Osborne, 2010).

Teaching Students Strategic Behaviors

Educational, vocational, and life success requires that students engage in strategic behavior in addition to specific skills. Strategic behavior requires substantial planning, plan monitoring, and plan revision that has been described as "executive control" (Pennington & Ozonoff, 1996) and self-management (Gureasko-Moore, DuPaul, & White, 2006). Strategy use can be described as an overarching organizational behavior that guides the selection, ordering, and evaluation of the steps directed toward achieving a larger goal (Alexander, Graham, & Harris, 1998). Strategic behavior is remarkably common in both everyday life and academic tasks. It is evident in tasks as simple as shopping for groceries. In an academic context, a task as simple as completing a mathematics word problem or writing a book report requires that students plan, develop solutions, implement those solutions, and evaluate their products. Students who possess all of the requisite tool skills may still struggle when they do not know how to organize and manage those behaviors to produce a complete product.

Strategy instruction emphasizes teaching the student how to combine previously mastered skills in a coherent process to solve new problems (Howell & Nolet, 2000). Strategy instruction frequently includes "verbal mediation," in which the students learn to talk themselves through the process of solving the problem (Fish & Mendola, 1986). Strategy instruction has been employed with diverse learners across a variety of skills to provide students with the organizational and mediational expertise needed to solve complex problems (Harris et al., 2012; Howell & Nolet, 2000; Pressley & Woloshyn, 1995). Frequently, strategy instruction is similar to self-monitoring, in that it emphasizes providing students with behavioral tools to support the use of other skills they have previously developed (Harris, Friedlander, Saddler, Frizzelle, & Graham, 2005). Strategy instruction commonly focuses on the same set of core steps: assessing the task, planning a solution, monitoring progress toward completion of the solution, and checking the quality of the solution (Harris et al., 2012; Howell & Nolet, 2000; Pressley & Woloshyn, 1995). In specific instances, strategies may include additional elements such as planned self-talk or use of organizational tools to guide implementation. It is important to recognize that students should be reasonably fluent with the underlying tool skills to successfully engage with more strategic task demands. For example, it has been argued that younger children rarely engage in the strategic elements of writing (e.g., planning, revising, or considering audience), because the act of writing the text is so effortful that they attend to little else (McCutchen, 1996).

Academic intervention to teach students strategic behavior varies in its details across models, but includes a number of consistent elements. These include providing students with necessary prerequisite skills before initiating strategy instruction, explaining the value of the strategy, explaining the strategy, overtly modeling strategy use, and coaching the student through initial strategy use. For example, Self-Regulated Strategy Development (SRSD) is an empirically supported curriculum for teaching writing strategies, which includes explaining to students how effective writers use various specific strategy elements to achieve specific ends (Harris et al., 2012). Teachers using SRSD then model the strategy for students by writing essays while asking themselves questions aloud, followed by modeling self-instruction procedures (e.g., self-evaluation and self-reinforcement).

Sound strategy instruction also provides students with a planned sequence of opportunities to practice exemplars that move from simple to more complex (Harris et al., 2012; Swanson, Kehler, & Jerman, 2010). This allows students to experience success and to consolidate initial skill gains before moving on to more challenging problems. Effective strategy instruction commonly includes corrective feedback, reinforcement, and many models, allowing students to practice skills collaboratively. Collaborative practice, where possible, enables teachers to support students while gradually providing them with greater independence (Harris et al., 2012; Swanson et al., 2010). To foster independence and generalization, students are also often provided with mnemonics for remembering steps to the strategies, as well as self-monitoring and/or prompt cards. These steps are practiced verbally until students memorize the steps of the strategy. Efforts to promote generalization and adaptation of strategies also include providing students with opportunities to practice a strategy using various types of materials (Pressley & Woloshyn, 1995).

Behaving strategically is effortful. As a result, strategy instruction curricula commonly include motivational elements, such as teaching students to self-monitor, self-assess, and self-reinforce (Fish & Mendola, 1986). In order to teach these types of self-regulatory behaviors, teachers typically guide students to review prior work, establish goals, and plan for self-reinforcement. Teaching students self-regulatory behaviors has been shown to increase their understanding of the connection between academic effort and outcomes. Ideally, this success and connection motivates them to use strategic behavior in academic, vocational, and everyday life situations. Evidence of students making this connection has been provided through studies that have demonstrated that students explicitly taught to use self-regulatory behaviors experience greater acquisition, maintenance, and generalization of SRSD strategies (De La Paz, 1999; Pressley & Levin, 1987)

Conclusion: Assuring That Academic Interventions Benefit Students

Although the processes described in the preceding sections for identifying instructional targets and devising instructional interventions that are matched to students' needs are effortful, in many educational contexts this truly represents the easy part of the work. Often, the most challenging part of the task is assuring implementation of the plan (Noell et al., 2005; Sanetti, Gritter, & Dobey, 2011). It is far too common a reality in schools that plans are devised but not implemented substantively enough to make any difference in students' lives (Gilbertson, Witt, Singletary, & VanDerHeyden, 2007). An emerging line of research on intervention plan implementation in schools clearly demonstrates that unless intervention implementation is actively planned, and structured follow-up is provided, the usual course of events is poor and deteriorating plan implementation (DiGennaro, Martens, & Kleinmann, 2007; Noell et al., 2005). The critical elements for successful plan implementation appear to be objective measurement of whether the plan is being implemented, combined with some form of very brief formal follow-up to review the data (DiGennaro et. al, 2007; Noell et al., 2005). The follow-up meetings typically have been described as performance feedback meetings, but some variation in the content of successful follow-up meetings is evident. In order for academic interventions to make any difference for students, they must be implemented with a reasonable level of integrity.

Once the intervention is implemented, this naturally raises the issue of whether it is working. Numerous studies have demonstrated that monitoring student performance across time and making instructional decisions based upon those data result in greater academic gains for students than when teachers do not have access to or use progress monitoring data (Stecker & Fuchs, 2000). These research findings point to an important practical reality. All interventions need to be modified once they are deployed for any reasonable length of time. The obvious possibility is that the student is not making adequate progress, which should occasion a revisiting of the assessment and design process. It may be the case that any of several revisions to the instructional plan would yield success. The other instance in which revision will be needed is if the intervention is successful. In this instance, revision will be needed to move the student to new skills, shift to a focus on generalization, or decide when the intervention is no longer needed. The critical consideration is that none of these decisions can be made in a systematic way without student progress and intervention implementation data.

References

Aaronson, D., Barrow, L., & Sander, W. (2007). Teachers and student achievement in the Chicago public schools. *Journal of Labor Economics, 25*, 95–135. doi: 10.1086/508733

Alexander, P. A., Graham, S., & Harris, K. R. (1998). A perspective on strategy research: Progress and prospects. *Educational Psychology Review, 10*, 129–154.

Andersson, U. (2010). Skill development in different components of arithmetic and basic cognitive functions: Findings from a 3-year longitudinal study of children with different types of learning difficulties. *Journal of Educational Psychology, 102,* 115–134. doi: 10.1037/a0016838

Ault, M. J., Wolery, M., Doyle, P. M., & Gast, D. L. (1989). Review of comparative studies in the instruction of students with moderate and severe handicaps. *Exceptional Children, 55,* 346–356.

Begeny, J. C., Yeager, A., & Martínez, R. S. (2012). Effects of small-group and one-on-one reading fluency interventions with second grade, low-performing Spanish readers. *Journal of Behavioral Education, 21,* 58–79. doi: 10.1007/s10864–011–9141-x

Billingsley, F. F., & Romer, L. T. (1983). Response prompting and the transfer of stimulus control: Methods, research, and a conceptual framework. *Journal of the Association for the Severely Handicapped, 8,* 3–12.

Boyd, D., Lankford, H., Loeb, S., Rockoff, J., & Wyckoff, J. (2008). Narrowing the gap in New York City teacher qualifications and its implications for student achievement in high-poverty schools. *Journal of Policy Analysis and Management, 27,* 793–818. doi: 10.1002/pam.20377

Bulgren, J. A., & Lenz, B. K. (1996). Strategic instruction in the content areas. In D. D. Deshler, E. S. Ellis, & B. K. Lenz (Eds.), *Teaching adolescents with learning disabilities: Strategies and methods* (2nd ed., pp. 409–473). Denver, CO: Love.

Bulgren, J. A., Schumaker, J. B., & Deshler, D. D. (1994). The effects of a recall enhancement routine on the test performance of secondary students with and without learning disabilities. *Learning Disabilities Research & Practice, 9,* 2–11.

Burchinal, M. R., Peisner-Feinberg, E., Pianta, R., & Howes, C. (2002). Development of academic skills from preschool through second grade: Family and classroom predictors of developmental trajectories. *Journal of School Psychology, 40,* 415–436. doi: 10.1016/S0022–4405(02)00107–3

Carlson, N. (1995). *Intelligent tutor.* [Software]. Retrieved from http://www.mathtutor.com/

Chafouleas, S. M., Martens, B. K., Dobson, R. L., Weinstein, K. S., & Gardner, K. B. (2004). Fluent reading as the improvement of stimulus control: Additive effects of performance-based interventions to repeated reading on students' reading and error rates. *Journal of Behavioral Education, 13,* 67–81. doi: 10.1023/B:JOBE.00000 23656.45233.6f

Codding, R. S., Chan-Iannetta, L., Palmer, M., & Lukito, G. (2009). Examining a classwide application of cover-copy-compare with and without goal setting to enhance mathematics fluency. *School Psychology Quarterly, 24,* 173–185. doi: 10.1037/a0017192

Cooper, J. O., Heron, T. E., & Heward, W. L. (1987). *Applied behavior analysis.* Columbus, OH: Merrill Publishing Co.

Daly, E., Witt, J. C., Martens, B. K., & Dool, E. J. (1997). A model for conducting a functional analysis of academic performance problems. *School Psychology Review, 26,* 554–574.

Danielson Group. (2013). *The Framework for Teaching evaluation instrument.* Princeton, NJ: The Danielson Group.

De La Paz, S. (1999). Self-regulated strategy instruction in regular education settings: Improving outcomes for students with and without learning disabilities. *Learning Disabilities Research and Practice, 14,* 92.

Dempster, F. N. (1989). Spacing effects and their implications for theory and practice. *Educational Psychology Review, 1,* 309–330. doi: 10.1007/BF01320097

Deshler, D. D., Ellis, E. S., & Lenz, B. K. (1996). *Teaching adolescents with learning disabilities: Strategies and methods* (2nd ed.). Denver, CO: Love.

Dexter, D. D., Park, Y. J., & Hughs, C. A. (2011). A meta-analytic review of graphic organizers and science instruction for adolescents with learning disabilities: Implications for the intermediate and secondary science classroom. *Learning Disabilities Research & Practice, 4,* 204–213. doi: 10.1111/j.1540–5826.2011.00341.x

DiGennaro, F. D., Martens, B. K., & Kleinmann, A. E. (2007). A comparison of performance feedback on teachers' treatment implementation integrity and students' inappropriate behavior in special education classrooms. *Journal of Applied Behavior Analysis, 40,* 447–461. doi: 10.1901/jaba.2007.40-447

Ditkowsky, B., & Koonce, D. A. (2010). Predicting performance on high stakes assessment for proficient students and students at risk with oral reading fluency growth. *Assessment for Effective Intervention, 35,* 159–167. doi: 10.1177/1534508409333345

Duhon, G. J., Noell, G. H., Witt, J. C., Freeland, J. T., Dufrene, B. A., & Gilbertson, D. N. (2004). Identifying academic skill and performance deficits: The experimental analysis of brief assessments of academic skills. *School Psychology Review, 33,* 429–443.

Falbo, T., & Glover, R. W. (1999). Promoting excellence in American adolescents. In A. J. Reynolds, H. J. Walberg, & R. P. Weissberg (Eds.), *Promoting positive outcomes* (pp. 229–251). Washington, DC: Child Welfare League of America.

Fantuzzo, J. W., Polite, K., & Grayson, N. (1990). An evaluation of reciprocal peer tutoring across elementary school settings. *Journal of School Psychology, 28,* 309–323. doi: 10.1016/0022–4405(90)90021-X

Fish, M. C., & Mendola, L. R. (1986). The effect of self-instruction training on homework completion in an elementary special education class. *School Psychology Review, 15,* 268–276.

Foorman, B. R., & Torgesen, J. (2001). Critical elements of classroom and small-group instruction promote reading success in all children. *Learning Disabilities Research & Practice, 16,* 203–212. doi: 10.1111/0938–8982.00020

Foxx, R. M. (1982). *Decreasing behaviors of severely retarded and autistic persons.* Champaign, IL: Research Press.

Fuchs, L. S., Fuchs, D., & Hamlett, C. L. (1989). Monitoring reading growth using student recalls: Effects of two teacher feedback systems. *Journal of Educational Research, 83,* 103–110.

Fuchs, L. S., Fuchs, D., & Speece, D. L. (2002). Treatment validity as a unifying construct for identifying learning disabilities. *Learning Disability Quarterly, 25,* 33–45. doi: 10.2307/1511189

Galbicka, G. (1994). Shaping in the 21st century: Moving percentile schedules into applied settings. *Journal of Applied Behavior Analysis, 27,* 739–760. doi: 10.1901/jaba.1994.27–739

Gansle, K. A., Noell, G. H., & Burns, J. M. (2012). Do student achievement outcomes differ across teacher preparation programs? An analysis of teacher education in Louisiana. *Journal of Teacher Education, 63,* 304–317. doi: 10.1177/0022487112439894

Gilbertson, D., Witt, J. C., Singletary, L. L., & VanDerHeyden, A. (2007). Supporting teacher use of interventions: Effects of response dependent performance feedback on teacher implementation of a math intervention. *Journal of Behavioral Education, 16,* 311–326. doi: 10.1007/s10864–007–9043–0

Gureasko-Moore, S., DuPaul, G. J., & White, G. P. (2006). The effects of self-management in general education classrooms on the organizational skills of adolescents with ADHD. *Behavior Modification, 30,* 159–183.

Harris, D. M. (2012). Varying teacher expectations and standards: Curriculum differentiation in the age of standards-based reform. *Education and Urban Society, 44,* 128–150. doi: 10.1177/0013124511431568

Harris, K. R., Friedlander, B., Saddler, B., Frizzelle, R., & Graham, S. (2005). Self-monitoring of attention versus self-monitoring of academic performance: Effects among students with ADHD in the general education classroom. *The Journal of Special Education, 39,* 145–156. doi: 10.1177/00224669050390030201

Harris, K. R., Lane, K., Driscoll, S. A., Graham, S., Wilson, K., Sandmel, K., Brindle, M., & Schatschneider, C. (2012). Tier 1, teacher-implemented self-regulated strategy development for students with and without behavioral challenges. *The Elementary School Journal, 113,* 160–191. doi: 10.1086/667403

Heckaman, K. A., Alber, S., Hooper, S., & Heward, W. L. (1998). A comparison of least-to-most prompts and progressive time delay on the disruptive behavior of students with autism. *Journal of Behavioral Education, 8,* 171–201. doi: 10.1023/A:1022883523915

Hibel, J., Farkas, G., & Morgan, P. L. (2010). Who is placed into special education? *Sociology of Education, 83,* 312–332. doi: 10.1177/0038040710383518

Howell, K. W., & Nolet, V. (2000). *Curriculum-based evaluation: Teaching and decision making* (3rd ed.). Atlanta, GA: Wadsworth.

Hur, J. A., & Osborne, S. (1993). A comparison of forward and backward chaining methods used in teaching corsage making skills to mentally retarded adults. *British Journal of Developmental Disabilities, 39,* 108–117.

Jenkins, J., & Terjeson, K. J. (2011). Monitoring reading growth: Goal setting, measurement frequency, and methods of evaluation. *Learning Disabilities Research & Practice, 26,* 28–35. doi: 10.1111/j.1540–5826.2010.00322.x

Jitendra, A. K., Rodriguez, M., Kanive, R., Huang, J., Church, C., Corroy, K. A., & Zaslofsky, A. (2013). Impact of small-group tutoring interventions on the mathematical problem solving and achievement of third-grade students with mathematics difficulties. *Learning Disability Quarterly, 36,* 21–35. doi: 10.1177/0731948712457561

Kane, T. J., Rockoff, J. E., & Staiger, D. O. (2008). What does certification tell us about teacher effectiveness? Evidence from New York City. *Economics of Education Review, 27,* 615–631. doi: 10.1016/j.econedurev.2007.05.005

Kelley, M. L., Reitman, D., & Noell, G. H. (2002). *Practitioner's guide to empirically based measures of school behavior.* New York, NY: Kluwer Academic/Plenum Publishers.

Kuhn, S. A. C., Lerman, D. C., Vorndran, C. M., & Addison, L. (2006). Analysis of factors that affect responding in a two-response chain in children with developmental disabilities. *Journal of Applied Behavior Analysis, 39,* 263–280. doi: 10.1901/jaba.2006.118–05

Lenz, B. K., Bulgren, J. A., & Hudson, P. (1990). Content enhancement: A model for promoting the acquisition of content by individuals with learning disabilities. In T. Scruggs & B. Wong (Eds.), *Intervention research in learning disabilities* (pp. 122–165). New York, NY: Springer-Verlag.

Martens, B. K., & Houk, J. L. (1989). The application of Herrnstein's law of effect to disruptive and on-task behavior of a retarded adolescent girl. *Journal of the Experimental Analysis of Behavior, 51,* 17–27. doi: 10.1901/jeab.1989.51–17

Mazur, J. E. (2006). *Learning and behavior* (6th ed.). Upper Saddle River, NJ: Pearson Prentice Hall.

McCutchen, D. (1996). A capacity theory of writing: Working memory in composition. *Educational Psychology Review, 8,* 299–325.

Mercer, C. D., Mercer, A. R., & Pullen, P. C. (2011). *Teaching students with learning problems* (8th ed.). Upper Saddle River, NJ: Pearson Education, Inc.

Meyer, L. H., McClure, J., Walkey, F., Weir, K. F., & McKenzie, L. (2009). Secondary student motivation orientations and standards-based achievement outcomes. *British Journal of Educational Psychology, 79,* 273–293. doi: 10.1348/000709908X354591

Morgan, P. L., Sideridis, G., & Hua, Y. (2012). Initial and over-time effects of fluency interventions for students with or at risk for disabilities. *Journal of Special Education, 46,* 94–116. doi: 10.1177/0022466910398016

Morisano, D., Hirsh, J. B., Peterson, J. B., Pihl, R. O., & Shore, B. M. (2010). Setting, elaborating, and reflecting on personal goals improves academic performance. *Journal of Applied Psychology, 95,* 255–264. doi: 10.1037/a0018478

Nelson, J. R. (2003). *ClickN read phonics.* [Software]. Retrieved from https://www.clicknkids.com/cnk_lp/cnr-reading-program/

Nese, J. T., Park, B., Alonzo, J., & Tindal, G. (2011). Applied curriculum-based measurement as a predictor of high-stakes assessment: Implications for researchers and teachers. *The Elementary School Journal, 111,* 608–624. doi: 10.1086/659034

Noell, G. H., & Gansle, K. A. (in press). Research examining the relationships among consultation process, treatment integrity, and outcomes. In W. P. Erchul & S. M. Sheridan (Eds.), *Handbook of research in school consultation: Empirical foundations for the field* (2nd ed.). Mahwah, NJ: Lawrence Erlbaum Associates, Inc.

Noell, G. H., & Gansle, K. A. (2006). Assuring the form has substance: Treatment plan implementation as the foundation of assessing response to intervention. *Assessment for Effective Intervention, 32,* 32–39. doi: 10.1177/15345084060320010501

Noell, G. H., Call, N. A., & Ardoin, S. P. (2011). Building complex repertoires from discrete behaviors by establishing stimulus control, behavioral chains, and strategic behavior. In W. W. Fisher, C. C. Piazza, H. S. Roane (Eds.), *Handbook of applied behavior analysis* (pp. 250–269). New York, NY: Guilford Press.

Noell, G. H., Freeland, J. T., Witt, J. C., & Gansle, K. A. (2001). Using brief assessments to identify effective interventions for individual students. *Journal of School Psychology, 39,* 335–355. doi: 10.1016/S0022–4405(01)00072–3

Noell, G. H., Witt, J. C., Slider, N. J., Connell, J. E., Gatti, S. L., Williams, K. L., . . . Duhon, G. J. (2005). Treatment implementation following behavioral consultation in schools: A comparison of three follow-up strategies. *School Psychology Review, 34,* 87–106.

Northup, J. (2000). Further evaluation of the accuracy of reinforcer surveys: A systematic replication. *Journal of Applied Behavior Analysis, 33,* 335–338. doi: 10.1901/jaba.2000.33–335

Northup, J., Jones, K., Broussard, C., & George, T. (1995). A preliminary comparison of reinforcer assessment methods for children with attention deficit hyperactivity disorder. *Journal of Applied Behavior Analysis, 28,* 99–100. doi: 10.1901/jaba.1995.28–99

Office of Special Education and Rehabilitative Services (OSERS), U.S. Department of Education (2011). *30th annual report to Congress on the implementation of the* Individuals with Disabilities Education Act, *2008.*

Osborne, J. (2010). Arguing to learn science: The role of collaborative, critical discourse. *Science, 328,* 463–466. doi: 10.1126/science.1183944

Pennington, B. F., & Ozonoff, S. (1996). Executive functions and developmental psychopathology. *Journal of Child Psychology and Psychiatry, 37,* 51–87.

Phillips, C. L., & Vollmer, T. R. (2012). Generalized instruction following with pictorial prompts. *Journal of Applied Behavior Analysis, 45,* 37–54. doi: 10.1901/jaba.2012.45–37

Pianta, R. C., & Hamre, B. K. (2009). Conceptualization, measurement, and improvement of classroom processes: Standardized observation can leverage capacity. *Educational Researcher, 38,* 109–119. doi: 10.3102/0013189X09332374

Pipkin, C., Winters, S. M., & Diller, J. W. (2007). Effects of instruction, goals, and reinforcement on academic behavior: Assessing skill versus reinforcement deficits. *Journal of Early and Intensive Behavior Intervention, 4,* 648–657.

Pressley, M., & Levin, J. R. (1987). Elaborative learning strategies for the inefficient learner. In S. J. Ceci (Ed.), *Handbook of cognitive, social, and neuropsychological aspects of learning disabilities* (pp. 175–212). Hillsdale, NY: Erlbaum.

Pressley, M. E., & Woloshyn, V. E. (1995). *Cognitive strategy instruction that really improves children's academic performance. Cognitive strategy training series* (2nd ed.). Cambridge, MA: Brookline Books.

Rivkin, S. G., Hanushek, E. A., & Kain, J. F. (2005). Teachers, schools, and academic achievement. *Econometrica, 73,* 417–458. doi: 10.1111/j.1468–0262.2005.00584.x

Roberts, W., & Norwich, B. (2010). Using precision teaching to enhance the word reading skills and academic self-concept of secondary school students: A role for professional educational psychologists. *Educational Psychology in Practice, 26,* 279–298. doi: 10.1080/02667363.2010.495215

Rockoff, J. (2004). The impact of individual teachers on student achievement: Evidence from panel data. *American Economic Review, 94,* 247–252. doi: 10.1257/0002828041302244

Rosen, H. S., & Rosen, L. (1983). Eliminating stealing: Use of stimulus control with an elementary student. *Behavior Modification, 7,* 56–63. doi: 10.1177/01454455830071004

Sanders, W. L., & Rivers, J. C. (1996). *Research project report: Cumulative and residual effects of teachers on future student academic achievement.* Knoxville, TN: University of Tennessee Value-Added Research and Assessment Center.

Sanetti, L., Gritter, K. L., & Dobey, L. M. (2011). Treatment integrity of interventions with children in the school psychology literature from 1995 to 2008. *School Psychology Review, 40,* 72–84.

Schoen, S. F. (1986). Assistance procedures to facilitate the transfer of stimulus control: Review and analysis. *Education and Training of the Mentally Retarded, 21,* 62–74.

Schuster, J. W., Morse, T. E., Ault, M. J., Doyle, P. M., Crawford, M. R., & Wolery, M. (1998). Constant time delay with chained tasks: A review of the literature. *Education and Treatment of Children, 21,* 74–106.

Shapiro, E. S. (2011). *Academic skills problems* (4th ed.). New York, NY: Guilford Press.

Skinner, B. F. (1953). *Science and human behavior.* New York, NY: Macmillan.

Smith, G. J. (1999). Teaching a long sequence of a behavior using whole task training, forward chaining, and backward chaining. *Perceptual and Motor Skills, 89,* 951–965.

Snell, M. E., & Gast, D. L. (1981). Applying time delay procedure to the instruction of the severely handicapped. *Journal of the Association for the Severely Handicapped, 6,* 3–14.

Springer, L., Stanne, M. E., & Donovan, S. S. (1999). Effects of small-group learning on undergraduates in science, mathematics, engineering, and technology: A meta-analysis. *Review of Educational Research, 69,* 21–51. doi: 10.3102/00346543069001021

Stahl, S. A., & Fairbanks, M. M. (1986). The effects of vocabulary instruction: A model-based meta-analysis. *Review of Educational Research, 56,* 72–110. doi: 10.3102/00346543056001072

Stecker, P. M., & Fuchs, L. S. (2000). Effecting superior achievement using curriculum-based measurement: The importance of individual progress monitoring. *Learning Disabilities Research & Practice, 15,* 128–134. doi: 10.1207/SLDRP1503_2

Sulzer-Azaroff, B., & Mayer, G. R. (1991). *Behavior analysis for lasting change.* Fort Worth, TX: Holt, Rinehart, & Winston.

Sutherland, K. S., & Snyder, A. (2007). Effects of reciprocal peer tutoring and self-graphing on reading fluency and classroom behavior of middle school students with emotional or behavioral disorders. *Journal of Emotional & Behavioral Disorders, 15,* 103–118.

Swanson, H., Kehler, P., & Jerman, O. (2010). Working memory, strategy knowledge, and strategy instruction in children with reading disabilities. *Journal of Learning Disabilities, 43,* 24–47. doi: 10.1177/002221940338743

Sy, J. R., & Vollmer, T. R. (2012). Discrimination acquisition in children with developmental disabilities under immediate and delayed reinforcement. *Journal of Applied Behavior Analysis, 45,* 667–684.

Tekin, E., & Kircaali-Iftar, G. (2002). Comparison of the effectiveness and efficiency of two response prompting procedures delivered by sibling tutors. *Education & Training in Mental Retardation & Developmental Disabilities, 37*(3), 283–299.

VanDerHeyden, A. M., Witt, J. C., & Gilbertson, D. (2007). A multi-year evaluation of the effects of a response to intervention (RTI) model on identification of children for special education. *Journal of School Psychology, 45,* 225–256.

Walker, G. (2008). Constant and progressive time delay procedures for teaching children with autism: A literature review. *Journal of Autism And Developmental Disorders, 38,* 261–275. doi: 10.1007/s10803–007–0390–4

Walls, R. T., Zane, T., & Ellis, W. D. (1981). Forward and backward chaining, and whole task methods: Training assembly tasks in vocational rehabilitation. *Behavior Modification, 5,* 61–74. doi: 10.1177/014544558151005

Watters, J. K. (1992). Retention of human sequenced behavior following forward chaining, backward chaining, and whole task training procedures. *Journal of Human Movement Studies, 22,* 117–129.

Wolery, M., & Gast, D. L. (1984). Effective and efficient procedures for the transfer of stimulus control. *Topics in Early Childhood Special Education, 4,* 52–77. doi: 10.1177/027112148400400305

Yen, C., Konold, T. R., & McDermott, P. A. (2004). Does learning behavior augment cognitive ability as an indicator of academic achievement? *Journal of School Psychology, 42,* 157–169. doi: 10.1016/j.jsp.2003.12.001

Zigmond, N., & Kloo, A. (2009). The "Two percent students": Considerations and consequences of eligibility decisions. *Peabody Journal of Education, 84,* 478–495. doi: 10.1080/01619560903240855

3

Linking Assessment and Intervention

Steven G. Little and Angeleque Akin-Little

Assessment and intervention are closely intertwined (Sattler, 2008). More than a quarter of a century ago, calls were being made for broadening the concept of assessment by stressing the link between assessment and intervention to better make instructional decisions (Meyers, Pfeffer, & Erlbaum, 1985). The American Psychological Association (APA, 2005), in their Policy Statement on Evidence-Based Practice in Psychology, recognizes the close relationship that assessment must have with intervention, as does the National Association of School Psychologists (NASP, 2009) in their position statement on "School Psychologists Involvement with Assessment." This link between assessment and intervention was also an integral part of the Response to Intervention (RTI) movement that was introduced in the 2001 No Child Left Behind (NCLB) Act (No Child Left Behind, 2001) and the 2004 reauthorization of the Individuals with Disabilities Education Improvement Act (IDEIA; Individuals with Disabilities Education Improvement Act, 2004). It is not clear, however, that this imperative from professional organizations and research has been translated into a link between assessment and intervention in practice.

Fuchs (2000) indicated that there are seven criteria needed to maximize the academic assessment–intervention link. She detailed that assessment methods must provide teachers with information (a) on student acquisition of skills and learning strategies, (b) on students' ability to apply and integrate skills and strategies in novel contexts, and (c) about student growth to aid in the formative evaluation of instruction and help determine modifications in instructional programming. In addition, assessment methods (d) need to produce a detailed analysis of student performance linked to specific instructional actions; (e) allow routine administration, scoring, and interpretation; (f) communicate the specifics of what is important to learn to both teachers and student; and (g) produce information meeting acceptable standards for accuracy and meaningfulness.

Assessment–Intervention Link and Norm-Referenced Assessment

Traditionally, norm-referenced tests of academic achievement were and are less likely to meet the criteria set forth by Fuchs (2000) than are curriculum-based approaches, although there has been an increased effort to clarify this link since the passage of NCLB in 2001 and IDEIA in 2004. While there is little to examine in the empirical literature discussing the link between norm-referenced assessments and intervention, test publishers, particularly post-RTI, have attempted to provide specific materials supporting the link between their materials and intervention. For example, Pearson Assessment has attempted to tie their group tests of academic achievement (e.g., Stanford Achievement Tests) to the Common Core State Standards Initiative, a state-led initiative to provide teachers and parents with a common understanding of what students are expected to learn. The standards (a) focus on English, Language Arts, and Mathematics; (b) are aligned with college and work expectations; (c) are curriculum standards meant to serve as the base on which to build a broader set of assessment standards; (d) are clear, understandable, and consistent; (e) include rigorous content and application of knowledge through higher-order thinking skills; (f) build on strengths and lessons of current state standards; (g) are informed by other top performing countries, so that all students are prepared to succeed in our global economy and society; and (h) are evidence-based (Council of Chief State School Officers (CCSSO) and National Governors Association Center for Best Practices, 2012). The complete version of the Common Core State Standards is available at www.corestandards.org. Tying test results to the curriculum does not in itself, however, guarantee a link between assessment and intervention practices. Another attempt Pearson uses to tie test results to the curriculum is via "Lexile Measures," which identify students' specific reading levels and books that correspond to those reading levels. In the area of assessment of individually administered tests of academic achievement, Pearson also makes notice of the need for an assessment–intervention link in stating that results of the Wechsler Individual Achievement Test, Third Edition (WIAT-III) are supposed to help "design instructional objectives and plan interventions" (https://www.pearsonassessments.com/HAIWEB/Cultures/en-us/Productdetail.htm?Pid=015–8984–609). In a more direct attempt to link assessment results to intervention, Pearson Assessment has recognized the role of RTI in schools and has made an attempt to tie their assessments into the RTI framework. They even offer a handout to psychologists and educators on "The Role of Assessment in RTI" (http://psychcorp.pearsonassessments.com/hai/images/ca/rti/RTI_role.htm). In this handout, they describe the three-tier model and detail how assessment fits in at each level. They state, "Whether you need to identify students at risk, pinpoint strengths and weaknesses, monitor progress, or identify SLD, we have the solution." Riverside Publishing, publisher of the *Woodcock-Johnson III Tests of Achievement,* makes similar claims and also provides access to information on how their instruments fit into the RTI framework (http://www.riversidepublishing.com/rti/index.html). The link of assessment to intervention with norm-referenced approaches is discussed in greater detail later in this book (i.e., Chapters 4–7.)

Assessment–Intervention Link and Curriculum-Based Assessment

Curriculum-based assessment (CBA) uses direct observation and recording of a student's performance with the local curriculum as a basis for gathering information to make instructional decisions (Deno, 2003). With a focus on how well a student performs on materials being used in the classroom and frequent collection of data, the student's progress with the curriculum can be monitored and teaching modifications can be made as needed to improve academic performance (Witt, Elliot, Daly, Gresham, &

Kramer, 1998). Therefore, the assessment–intervention link becomes a fundamental part of the procedure.

Burns (2002) proposes using Gickling's model of curriculum-based assessment (Gickling & Havertape, 1981) in developing instructional modifications, by examining the discrepancy between curriculum and student performance. Specifically, this model proposes that the optimal learning occurs at the instructional level, operationalized as 93% to 96% words correct for reading and 70% to 85% known for drill tasks (Burns, 2002), and that by providing instruction at this level significantly improves performance. In reading, interventions based on this model involve measuring the percentage of words read correctly in his/her curriculum via CBA probes and then teaching unknown words at a known word rate less than 93% with a drill task containing 70% to 85% known words (Burns, 2002). Both Burns and Fuchs (2000) emphasize that CBA measurement presents very manageable demands on teachers in the classroom setting, because the assessments are brief and the focus of assessment, both within and between students, remains relatively constant for extended periods of time. The link of assessment to intervention with curriculum-based approaches is discussed in greater detail, in Chapters 8–11.

Summary

The importance of linking assessment to intervention is obvious and one that has been formalized in legislation, policy statements from professional organizations, and publishers of test materials. How widely this has been put into practice is still open for debate, but with the implementation of responsive assessment and instruction practices (see Chapter 10), the link is becoming more common. Treatment validity refers to the relationship between an assessment and treatment outcome (Gresham & Gansle, 1992), thus, an assessment has treatment validity if it leads to effective instruction for all students administered the assessment. Any assessment use is, therefore, only as good as its outcome (i.e., effective intervention to meet the student's needs).

References

APA (2005). *Policy statement on evidence-based practice.* Washington, DC: Author. Retrieved from http://www.apa.org/practice/resources/evidence/evidence-based-statement.pdf

Burns, M. K. (2002). Comprehensive system of assessment to intervention using curriculum-based assessments. *Intervention in School and Clinic, 38,* 8–13.

Council of Chief State School Officers (CCSSO) and National Governors Association Center for Best Practices (2012). Common core state standards initiative. Retrieved from http://www.corestandards.org/

Deno, S. L. (2003). Developments in curriculum-based measurement. *Journal of Special Education, 37,* 184–192.

Fuchs, L. S. (2000). Academic assessment-intervention link. In A. E. Kazdin (Ed.), *Encyclopedia of psychology, Vol. 1* (pp. 7–10). Washington, DC: American Psychological Association.

Gickling, E. E., & Havertape, S. (1981). *Curriculum-based assessment.* Minneapolis, MN: School Psychology Inservice Training Network.

Gresham, F. M., & Gansle, K. A. (1992). Misguided assumptions of DSM-III-R: Implications for school psychological practice. *School Psychology Quarterly, 7,* 79–95.

Individuals with Disabilities Education Improvement Act of 2004, Pub. L. No.108-446, 20 U.S.C. 1400 (2004).

Meyers, J. P., Pfeffer, J., & Erlbaum, V. (1985). Process assessment: A model for broadening assessment. *The Journal of Special Education, 19,* 73–89.

NASP (2009). *School psychologists' involvement with assessment.* Bethesda, MD: Author. Retrieved from http://www.nasponline.org/about_nasp/positionpapers/involvement_in_assessment.pdf

National Governors Association Center for Best Practices. (2012). *Common core state standards*. Retrieved from http://nga.org/cms/center/edu

No Child Left Behind (NCLB) Act of 2001, Pub. L. No. 107-110, § 115, Stat. 1425 (2002).

Sattler, J. M. (2008). *Assessment of children: Cognitive foundations* (5th ed.). San Diego, CA: Jerome M. Sattler, Publisher.

Witt, J. C., Elliott, S. N., Daly, E. J., Gresham, F. M., & Kramer, J. J. (1998). *Assessment of at-risk and special needs children* (2nd ed.). Boston: McGraw-Hill.

Part II
Norm-Referenced Assessment

4
Academic Achievement Batteries

Dawn P. Flanagan, Vincent C. Alfonso, and Shauna G. Dixon

Introduction

Academic achievement batteries are necessary to assess the specific skills of students who have learning difficulties and those who are suspected of having specific learning disabilities (SLD). According to the Individuals with Disabilities Education Improvement Act (IDEIA, 2004), SLD may manifest in one or more academic areas, including basic reading skills, reading fluency, reading comprehension, math calculation, math problem solving, written expression, listening comprehension, and oral expression. Given the importance of understanding academic skill acquisition and development in students who struggle in the learning process, it is necessary to select instruments carefully based on reason for referral, academic area(s) of concern, the appropriateness of the instrument given the student's developmental level, and the psychometric integrity of the battery.

The purpose of this chapter is to provide practitioners with some of the most salient features of academic achievement batteries that ought to be considered when measuring the academic capabilities and skill levels of all students, including those who struggle to learn. We provide information on nine achievement batteries along a number of different dimensions, including (a) interpretation features, such as the ability constructs measured by achievement tests based on the Cattell-Horn-Carroll (CHC) theory (e.g., Flanagan, Ortiz, & Alfonso, 2013); (b) specific IDEIA academic area (from the SLD definition) associated with achievement subtests; (c) variation in task demands and task characteristics of each subtest on each battery; and (d) other qualitative and quantitative characteristics, such as content features, administration procedures, and technical properties. The nine achievement batteries included in this chapter are listed below.

- CELF-4 = Clinical Evaluation of Language Fundamentals-Fourth Edition
- CTOPP-2 = Comprehensive Test of Phonological Processing-Second Edition
- GORT-5 = Gray Oral Reading Tests-Fifth Edition
- KTEA-II = Kaufman Test of Educational Achievement-Second Edition
- KM3 = KeyMath-Third Edition

- TOWL-4 = Test of Written Language-Fourth Edition
- WIAT-III = Wechsler Individual Achievement Test-Third Edition
- WJ III NU ACH = Woodcock-Johnson Third Edition Normative Update Tests of Achievement
- WRMT-3 = Woodcock Reading Mastery Test-Third Edition

These instruments were selected because they either measure a broad range of academic skills (i.e., reading, math, writing, language) or they measure a particular academic area, such as reading, comprehensively. Moreover, the batteries selected for inclusion in this chapter are current (i.e., published or re-normed within the past 10 years), and appear to be among the most frequently used individually administered, norm-referenced achievement batteries. A description of the subtests that comprise each of the nine batteries listed above is found in Table 4.1.

Table 4.1 Descriptions of Subtests on Selected Achievement Batteries

Battery	Subtest	Description
CELF-4	Concepts and Following Directions	The examinee is required to point to objects in a stimulus book in response to oral directions stated by the examiner.
	Expressive Vocabulary	The examinee is required to name illustrations of people, objects, and actions.
	Familiar Sequences	The examinee is required to manipulate and sequence auditory/verbal information, including but not limited to counting forward and backward, saying the alphabet, counting by 4s, and saying the months of the year backward as quickly as possible.
	Formulated Sentences	The examinee is shown a picture and then is required to make up (and say out loud) a sentence about the picture, using target words or phrases.
	Number Repetition-Backward	The examinee is required to repeat number sequences stated by the examiner of graduated length backward.
	Number Repetition-Forward	The examinee is required to repeat number sequences stated by the examiner of graduated length forward.
	Phonological Awareness	The examinee is asked to rhyme words and segments, to blend, and to identify sounds and syllables in words.
	Rapid Automatic Naming	The examinee is required to name colors, shapes, and shape-color combinations as quickly as possible.
	Recalling Sentences	The examinee is required to repeat a sentence stated by the examiner verbatim.
	Semantic Relationships	The examinee is required to select from the four choices shown in the stimulus booklet the two correct answers to a sentence stated by the examiner that contains a missing part.
	Sentence Assembly	The examinee is required to produce two semantically and grammatically correct sentences from visually and orally presented words or groups of words presented by the examiner and in a stimulus book.
	Sentence Structure	The examinee is required to point to the picture that best depicts a sentence stated by the examiner.
	Understanding Spoken Paragraphs	The examinee is required to provide a response to inferential questions about a paragraph that is read by the examiner.
	Word Associations	The examinee is given 60 seconds to name as many things as he or she can that go with a particular topic.
	Word Classes-Expressive	The examinee is required to express the relationship between the two words chosen in Word Classes-Receptive.
	Word Classes-Receptive	The examinee is required to name the two words that go together after the examiner reads aloud three or four words.

Battery	Subtest	Description
	Word Definitions	The examinee is required to define words stated that are presented in isolation and in a sentence by the examiner.
	Word Structure	The examinee is required to use the contents of a picture and an incomplete sentence stated by the examiner to write the missing word or words in that sentence.
CTOPP-2	Blending Nonwords	The examinee is required to combine separate sounds to form a non-word after listening to a series of tape-recorded separate sounds.
	Blending Words	The examinee is required to combine separate sounds to make a whole word after listening to a series of tape-recorded separate sounds.
	Elision	The examinee is required to repeat a compound word stated by the examiner and then say the word that remains after dropping (deleting) one of the compound words. Then the examinee is required to repeat a word spoken by the examiner, and then say the word that remains after dropping (deleting) a specific sound.
	Memory for Digits	The examinee is required to listen to a series of tape-recorded numbers, presented at a rate of 2 per second, and then sequentially repeat the numbers.
	Nonword Repetition	The examinee is required to listen to a tape-recorded nonword and then repeat it verbatim.
	Phoneme Isolation	The examinee is required to repeat a word and then to say it one sound at a time.
	Rapid Color Naming	The examinee is required to name the colors of a series of different colored blocks printed on two pages as quickly as possible.
	Rapid Digit Naming	The examinee is required to name the numbers printed on two pages as quickly as possible.
	Rapid Letter Naming	The examinee is required to name the letters printed on two pages as quickly as possible.
	Rapid Object Naming	The examinee is required to name a series of objects printed on two pages as quickly as possible.
	Segmenting Nonwords	The examinee is required to repeat each nonword and then say it one sound at a timeafter listening to a tape-recorded series of nonwords.
	Sound Matching	For the first 10 items, the examinee is required to point to the picture that corresponds to the word that starts with the same sound as the first word the examiner says aloud. For the last 10 items, the same procedure is used, except the examinee is asked to point to the picture of the word that ends with the same last sound as the first word.
GORT-5	Accuracy	The student is asked to read a passage with as few deviations from print as possible.
	Comprehension	The examinee is asked to answer questions about a passage he or she has read.
	Fluency	The examinee is required to read aloud each passage as quickly as possible after listening to a corresponding prompt presented orally by the examiner. The examinee is then required to answer multiple-choice questions aloud as presented orally by the examiner. The fluency score is the sum of the rate and accuracy scores.
	Rate	The examinee is required to read aloud each passage as quickly as possible after listening to a corresponding prompt presented orally by the examiner. The examinee is then required to answer multiple-choice questions aloud as presented orally by the examiner. The rate score is a converted value that is based on the time it takes the child to read the story.

(Continued)

Table 4.1 (Continued)

Battery	Subtest	Description
KM3	Addition and Subtraction	The examinee is required to determine the total of two sets, count to determine a total, match representing with number sentences, and complete facts. In the second domain, the examinee is required to add two- and three-digit numbers without regrouping, with regrouping ones, with regrouping ones and tens, and in column addition. For one item, the examinee is required to add positive and negative integers. In the third domain, the examinee is required to add monetary values, other decimals with same and different place values, and fractions with like and unlike denominators. The examinee is required to solve problems involving all modalities of subtraction. The examinee is then required to solve problems involving matching representations and completing facts. In the second domain, the examinee is required to solve problems involving subtracting from two- and three-digit numbers without regrouping, with regrouping tens, with regrouping across hundreds, tens, and ones, and with subtracting positive and negative integers. In the second domain, the examinee is required to solve problems involving subtracting monetary values, other decimals with same and different place values, and fractions with like and unlike denominators.
	Algebra	The examinee is required to complete tasks that involve sorting, classifying, and ordering based on various attributes or categories. He or she is also required to recognize and describe patterns and functions, and work with number sentences, operational properties, equations, expressions, variables, and functions, and represent mathematical relationships.
	Applied Problem Solving	The examinee is required to interpret problems set in a context and to apply his or her computational skills and conceptual knowledge to come up with solutions.
	Data Analysis and Probability	The examinee is required to collect, display, and interpret data. He or she must also show understanding of concepts that are associated with chance and probability (i.e., an activity that an individual is likely to get hurt doing).
	Geometry	The examinee is required to analyze, describe, compare, and classify two- and three-dimensional shapes.
	Foundations of Problem Solving	The examinee is required to identify the various elements, operations, and strategies that are necessary to solve math problems, with emphasis placed on his or her ability to explore different strategies to facilitate solutions.
	Measurement	The examinee is required to solve problems involving comparing and ordering heights, lengths, weights, sizes, temperature, and perceived container capacity. In the second domain, the examinee is required to solve problems involving non-standard units addressing length, area, capacity, weight, and parameters. In the third domain, the examinee is required to solve problems involving standard units associated with linear scales and progresses to area and temperature measurement. In the fourth domain, the examinee is required to solve problems involving weight and capacity.
	Mental Computation and Estimation	The examinee is required to solve problems involving the oral presentation of computation chains. In the second domain, the examinee is required to solve problems involving visually presented items. In the third domain, the examinee is required to solve problems involving rational numbers, subtracting a fraction from a whole number, adding a whole number to a mixed number, multiplying by a decimal that can be easily converted to a fraction, determining percent, and multiplying a decimal value by tens. For all domains, the examinee is not permitted to use pencil and paper. The examinee is required to solve problems involving whole numbers, rational numbers, measurement, and computation.

Battery	Subtest	Description
	Multiplication and Division	The examinee is required to solve problems involving multiple sets and arrays associating a representation with a number sentence. In the second domain, the examinee is required to multiply two- and three-digit numbers by a one- or two-digit multiplier. In the third domain, the examinee is required to solve problems involving multiplying monetary values, other decimal values, fractions, and mixed numbers. The examinee is required to solve problems involving the determination of how many equal-sized sets, the size of a given number of sets, and how many are left over after units are separated into sets of given sizes. The examinee is also required to associate representation with a number sentence and completes facts. In the second domain, the examinee is required to divide with one- and two-digit divisors. In the third domain, the examinee is required to solve problems involving division with decimal values, fractions, and mixed numbers.
	Numeration	The examinee is required to solve problems involving concepts including correspondence, rational counting, reading and sequencing numbers, and ordinal positions. In the second domain, the examinee is required to solve problems involving the concepts of place value (tens and ones); reading, comparing, sequencing, and renaming numbers; and skip counting. In the third domain, the examinee is required to solve problems involving the concepts of place value; representing, comparing, sequencing, renaming numbers; and rounding numbers. In the fourth domain, the examinee is required to solve problems involving multi-digit numbers and advanced numeration as well as problems that require the comparing, sequencing, and rounding of multi-digit numbers.
TOWL-4	Contextual Conventions	The examinee is asked to write a story, paying attention to punctuation, spelling, and capitalization.
	Logical Sentences	The examinee is asked to correct incorrect sentences.
	Punctuation	The examinee orally presents some sentences and the examinee is required to write them in a booklet, while paying special attention to punctuation (and spelling and capitalization). The examinee receives a separate score for punctuation.
	Sentence Combining	The examinee is asked to combine target sentences into one sentence.
	Spelling	The examinee is asked to write down sentences presented verbally by the examiner.
	Story Composition	The examinee is asked to write a story, paying attention to the use of prose, action, sequencing, and theme.
	Vocabulary	The examinee is asked to write a sentence using a given word.
WRMT-3	Listening Comprehension	A passage is read aloud (either by the examiner or on a CD) to the examinee, who is then required to answer a question about its content.
	Oral Reading Fluency	The examinee is required to read one or two passages that range in length from approximately 80 words (for a first grader) to 200 words (for an adult), while the examiner records any errors made.
	Passage Comprehension	The examinee is required to read passages and their corresponding items silently. He/she must then respond orally to the items by providing single-word responses within 30 seconds after finishing reading the passages.

(Continued)

Table 4.1 (Continued)

Battery	Subtest	Description
	Phonological Awareness	This subtest consists of five portions: First Sound Matching, Last Sound Matching, Rhyme Production, Blending, and Deletion. In First Sound Matching, the examiner first points to and names a stimulus word, which is also depicted in a picture shown to the examinee. The examiner then names two or three more items and the examinee is required to name or point to an item that has the same first sound as the main picture. In the Last Sound Matching task, which is similar, the examinee is required to name or point to the picture that has the same last sound as the main picture. The Rhyme Production task requires the examinee to name a real or made-up word that rhymes with a word given by the examiner. The Deletion task requires the examinee to say the word that is created when one syllable or phoneme is removed from the beginning or end of a word given by the examiner.
	Rapid Automatic Naming	The examinee is required to complete one of two tasks, depending on age. Examinees who are in pre-kindergarten are asked to complete Object and Color Naming, while those in kindergarten through Grade 2 must complete a Number and Letter Naming task. These tasks involve the use of Rapid Automatic Naming Stimulus cards.
	Word Attack	The examinee is required to read aloud letter combinations that are linguistically logical in English (but that do not form actual words), or words that occur with low frequency in the English language.
	Word Comprehension	This section consists of three portions. In the Synonyms part, the examinee is required to read a word and then state another word that has the same meaning. The Antonyms part requires the examinee to read a word and then state another word with the opposite meaning. In the Analogies section, the examinee is required to read a pair of words, understand the relationship between the two words, then read the first word of a second word pair and state a second word that would complete the analogy.
	Word Identification	The examinee is required to read and pronounce words in order of increasing difficulty.
KTEA-II	Associational Fluency	The examinee is required to retrieve words that belong to a semantic category (semantic; ages 4–6 to 25–11) and words that start with a given sound (semantic + phonological; ages 6–0 to 25–11) in 30 seconds for each of two trials per category.
	Decoding Fluency	The examinee is required to read the list of words from the Nonsense Word, Decoding subtest as fast as possible in 1 minute.
	Editing	The examinee is required to identify and correct errors in spelling, punctuation, capitalization, or words used in a short passage.
	Letter and Word Recognition	The examinee is required to point to letters, say the name or sound of a letter, and read regular and irregular words.
	Listening Comprehension	The examinee is required to listen to passages on an audiorecording and answer questions spoken by the examiner.
	Math Computation	The examinee is required to solve written computational problems using the four basic operations.
	Math Concepts and Application	The examinee is required to solve math problems involving reasoning (e.g., analytical geometry, trigonometry, logarithms, algebra, calculus, and probability) and mathematical concepts (e.g., biggest, fourth, and less than).
	Naming Facility	The examinee is required to name objects and colors (ages 4–6 to 25–11) and letters (ages 6–0 to 25–11). Each task contains six or eight distinct stimuli, randomly ordered in five or six rows, for a total of 36 or 40 stimuli per task.
	Nonsense Word Decoding	The examinee is required to read nonsense words.

Battery	Subtest	Description
	Oral Expression	The examinee is required to say things that characters would say via a series of related incidents involving a continuing set of characters. Items include pragmatic tasks, such as expressing greetings, questions, descriptions of events or sequences, or persuasion and syntactical and grammatical tasks such as forming plurals and possessives, and constructing sentences that combine ideas or that include particular words.
	Phonological Awareness	The examinee is required to rhyme (via production and odd-one-out), match sounds (using illustrations), blend and segment sounds (using a hand puppet), and manipulate phonemes (omitting the beginning or ending sound of a word, dropping a beginning phoneme, and deleting an internal phoneme).
	Punctuation & Capitalization	The examinee is required to use correct punctuation and capitalization in writing orally dictated words and phrases.
	Reading Comprehension	The examinee is required to look at a word and point to the picture that illustrates the word, read short sentences that direct him/her to perform a certain physical action or say a certain thing, and to answer question after reading a passage.
	Spelling	The examinee is required to spell words via dictation by the examiner.
	Word Recognition Fluency	The examinee is required to read the list of words from the letter and word recognition subtest as fast as possible in 1 minute.
	Written Expression	The examinee is required to write letters, words, and sentences, and edit text with correct punctuation and capitalization via a storybook format. In addition, the examinee has to provide a writing sample that tells a story based on a verbal or picture prompt.
WIAT-III	Alphabet Writing Fluency	The examinee is required to write as many letters of the alphabet as he or she can, working as quickly as possible. He or she is given 30 seconds to complete this task.
	Early Reading Skills	The items on this subtest require the examinee to state the names of letters that are shown in a stimulus book, and state the sounds made by letters shown. Some items require him or her to determine whether certain words rhyme, as well as provide a word that rhymes with a given word. Some items require the examinee to come up with words that begin with the same sounds as a word spoken by the examiner. Other items require the examinee to come up with a letter group that makes a particular sound in a word (i.e., Which letter group makes the \st\ sound in *stop*?). Still other items require the examinee to read a word and point to a picture that depicts the word.
	Essay Composition	The examinee is required to write an essay on a given topic (i.e., write about a favorite video game and include at least three reasons why he or she likes it) and is encouraged to write a full page. The examinee is given 10 minutes to complete this task.
	Listening Comprehension	The examinee is required to point to a picture (out of a choice of several on a page in a stimulus book) that depicts a word spoken by the examiner.
	Math Fluency-Addition	The examinee is required to use a pencil without an eraser to solve addition problems as quickly as possible within 1 minute.
	Math Fluency-Multiplication	The examinee is required to use a pencil without an eraser to solve multiplication problems as quickly as possible within 1 minute.
	Math Fluency-Subtraction	The examinee is required to use a pencil without an eraser to solve subtraction problems as quickly as possible within 1 minute.
	Math Problem Solving	The examiner reads questions to the examinee, who simultaneously views a problem written on a page in a Stimulus Book. The examinee is required to provide answers to the questions and may use paper and pencil to work out a problem. The problems increase in difficulty as the examinee progresses through the items.

(Continued)

Table 4.1 (Continued)

Battery	Subtest	Description
	Numerical Operations	The examinee is asked to identify and write numbers, count, and solve written calculations and equations using mathematical operations.
	Oral Expression	The examiner describes something that could be an object, a component of an object, an animal or living thing, a place, an action, a person with particular attributes, or a person performing a particular action or job. The examinee is required to orally express a word that means whatever the examiner is describing.
	Oral Reading Fluency	The examinee is instructed to read stories out loud and is then required to answer questions pertaining to what he or she read.
	Pseudoword Decoding	The examinee is asked to read a list of nonwords from a list.
	Sentence Composition	The examinee is required to read two sentences and write one good sentence that combines the two.
	Spelling	The examinee is required to write dictated letters, letter blends, and words.
	Reading Comprehension	The examinee is asked to read sentences without error, read passages and answer questions, and define vocabulary from context.
	Word Reading	The examinee is asked to name letters, identify and generate rhymes, identify the beginning and ending sounds of words, blend sounds, and match sounds with letter and letter blends.
WJ III NU ACH	Academic Knowledge	The examinee is required to answer questions in the sciences, history, geography, government, economics, art, music, and literature.
	Applied Problems	The examinee is required to analyze and solve practical problems in mathematics by deciding on the appropriate mathematical operations to use.
	Calculation	The examinee is required to perform mathematical operations (addition, subtraction, multiplication, division, and combinations of these basic operation, as well as geometric, trigonometric, logarithmic, and calculus operations) involving decimals, fractions, and whole numbers.
	Letter-Word Identification	The examinee is required to identify letters and words correctly.
	Math Fluency	The examinee is required to solve simple addition, subtraction, and multiplication facts quickly.
	Oral Comprehension	The examinee is required to comprehend a short audio-recorded passage and then supply the missing word using syntactic and semantic cues.
	Passage Comprehension	The examinee is required to point to pictures represented by a phrase and read a short passage to identify a missing key word that makes sense in the context of that passage.
	Picture Vocabulary	The examinee is required to identify pictured objects.
	Quantitative Concepts	The examinee is required to demonstrate knowledge of math concepts, such as writing numbers, clocks and telling time, money, and rounding numbers.
	Reading Fluency	The examinee is required to read printed statements as quickly as possible, and decide whether the statement is true or false.
	Reading Vocabulary	A three-part subtest. In Part I, the examinee is required to state a one-word response similar in meaning to the word presented. In Part II, the examinee is required to state a one-word response opposite in meaning to the word presented. In Part III, the examinee is required to read three words of an analogy and provide the fourth word to complete the analogy.
	Spelling	The examinee is required to spell words presented orally by the examiner.
	Spelling of Sounds	The examinee is required to write single letters of sounds and to listen to an audio recording to spell letter combinations that are regular patterns in English spelling.

Battery	Subtest	Description
	Story Recall	The examinee is required to recall increasingly complex stories that are presented using an audio recording.
	Story Recall-Delayed	The examinee is required to recall, after 30 or more minutes on the same day or up to 8 days after the administration, the story elements presented in Story Recall.
	Sound Awareness	The examinee is required to provide a word that rhymes with a stimulus word that is presented orally, remove part of a compound word or a letter sound from a word to make a new word, substitute a word, a word ending, or a letter sound to create a new word, and to reverse parts of compound words, as well as reverse letter sounds of words to create new words.
	Understanding Directions	The examinee is required to listen to a sequence of audio-recorded instructions and then follow the directions by pointing to various objects.
	Word Attack	The examinee is required to read aloud letter combinations that are linguistically logical in English (but that do not form actual words), or words that occur with low frequency in the English language.
	Writing Fluency	The examinee is required to formulate and write a simple sentence by using a set of three words that relates to a given stimulus picture.
	Writing Samples	The examinee is required to write down sentences in response to different demands.

Notes: CELF-4 = Clinical Evaluation of Language Fundamentals–Fourth Edition; CTOPP-2 = Comprehensive Test of Phonological Processing–Second Edition; GORT-5 = Gray Oral Reading Tests–Fifth Edition; KM3 = KeyMath–Third Edition; TOWL-4 = Test of Written Language–Fourth Edition; WRMT-3 = Woodcock Reading Mastery Test–Third Edition; KTEA-II = Kaufman Test of Educational Achievement–Second Edition; WIAT-III = Wechsler Individual Achievement Test–Third Edition; WJ III NU ACH = Woodcock-Johnson–Third Edition Normative Update Tests of Achievement.

From Flanagan, Ortiz, and Alfonso (2013), *Essentials of cross-battery assessment* (3rd ed.). Copyright 2013 by John Wiley & Sons. Adapted by permission.

Academic Achievement Defined According to Contemporary CHC Theory

Assessment of academic abilities or achievement in areas such as reading, mathematics, written expression, oral expression, and listening comprehension is typically accomplished through the use of one or more individually administered and standardized, norm-referenced tests of achievement. However, depending on the specific instruments chosen for assessment, certain academic abilities appear to be measured by *cognitive* (or intelligence) tests whereas certain cognitive abilities appear to be measured by *achievement* tests. For example, it is common to find tests that measure an individual's knowledge of vocabulary—an "ability" that is typically associated with schooling and, therefore, considered an academic achievement—comfortably located within the context of a major cognitive battery. Similarly, it is not unusual to find tests that measure an individual's ability to reason contained in many comprehensive batteries of achievement. For example, many applied problems or math reasoning tests require an individual to reason inductively and deductively using numbers. This type of *quantitative reasoning* ability is typically considered to be more cognitive than academic in nature. Thus, there is confusion surrounding the precise definitions of ability and achievement and indeed controversy with regard to which tests ought to be used (i.e., cognitive or achievement) in the assessment of individuals referred for an SLD evaluation.

The phrase "cognitive ability" is most often associated with intelligence tests (e.g., the Wechsler Intelligence Scale for Children-Fourth Edition [WISC-IV]; Wechsler, 2003) whereas the phrase "academic achievement" is generally linked to achievement tests (e.g., the

Woodcock-Johnson III Tests of Achievement [WJ III ACH], Woodcock, McGrew, & Mather, 2001 and Woodcock-Johnson III Normative Update Tests of Achievement [WJ III NU ACH] Woodcock, Schrank, Mather, & McGrew, 2007). If asked to provide a definition of each of these terms, many practitioners would likely offer two relatively *distinct* descriptions. However, as unusual as it may seem, cognitive ability and academic achievement need not be conceptualized as dichotomous concepts. In fact, an ability-achievement *dichotomy* is seldom recognized or supported in the cognitive psychology literature (Carroll, 1993). The differences that are often made between cognitive ability and academic achievement are the result of popular *verbal* distinctions that are not supported from either an empirical or theoretical standpoint (Flanagan, Ortiz, Alfonso, & Mascolo, 2002).

According to Horn (1988), "cognitive abilities are measures of achievements, and measures of achievements are just as surely measures of cognitive abilities" (p. 655). Carroll (1993) echoed this conceptualization when he stated,

> It is hard to draw the line between . . . cognitive abilities and . . . cognitive achievements. Some will argue that *all* cognitive abilities are in reality learned achievements of one kind or another. Such an argument is difficult to counter, because it is obvious that the performances required on even the most general tests of intelligence depend on at least some learnings—learnings of language and its uses, of commonly used symbols such as numbers and digits, or of procedures for solving various kinds of problems. (p. 510)

Thus, rather than conceiving of cognitive abilities and academic achievements as mutually exclusive, they may be better thought of as lying on an *ability continuum* that has the most general types of abilities at one end and the most specialized types of knowledge at the other (Carroll, 1993). Because CHC theory is well validated (Schneider & McGrew, 2012) and because its structure is well suited for the organization and interpretation of psychometric instruments (such as cognitive and achievement tests) (Carroll, 1998; Flanagan et al., 2013), it is the theoretical framework around which this chapter is organized.

CHC Theory: A Continuum of Abilities

The CHC theory of cognitive abilities is the most comprehensive and empirically supported psychometric theory of the structure of cognitive abilities to date. It represents the integrated works of Raymond Cattell, John Horn, and John Carroll (Alfonso, Flanagan, & Radwan, 2005; Horn & Blankson, 2005; McGrew, 2005; Schneider & McGrew, 2012). Because it has an impressive body of empirical support in the research literature (e.g., developmental, neuro-cognitive, outcome-criterion), it is used extensively as the foundation for selecting, organizing, and interpreting tests of intelligence and cognitive abilities (e.g., Flanagan, Alfonso, & Ortiz, 2012). Most recently, it has been used for classifying intelligence and achievement batteries as well as neuropsychological tests to: (a) facilitate interpretation of cognitive performance, and (b) provide a foundation for organizing assessments for individuals suspected of having a learning disability (Flanagan, Alfonso, Mascolo, & Sotelo-Dynega, 2012; Flanagan, Alfonso, Ortiz, & Dynda, 2010; Flanagan et al., 2013). Additionally, CHC theory is the foundation on which most new and recently revised cognitive batteries were based (see Flanagan & Harrison, 2012, for comprehensive coverage of these batteries) and from which most achievement batteries have been classified (Flanagan et al., 2002, 2007, 2013).

In recent years, CHC theory was described as encompassing 16 broad cognitive abilities, including Fluid Reasoning (Gf) and Crystallized Intelligence (Gc), and more than 80 narrow

Table 4.2 Definitions of Broad and Narrow Cattell-Horn-Carroll (CHC) Abilities Associated with Achievement Batteries

Broad stratum II name (code) Narrow stratum I name (code)	Definition
Fluid Intelligence (*Gf*)	The deliberate but flexible control of attention to solve novel, "on-the-spot" problems that cannot be performed by relying exclusively on previously learned habits, schemas, and scripts.
Quantitative Reasoning (RQ)	The ability to reason, either with induction or deduction, with numbers, mathematical relations, and operators.
Crystallized Intelligence (*Gc*)	The depth and breadth of knowledge and skills that are valued by one's culture.
Communication Ability (CM)	The ability to use speech to communicate one's thoughts clearly.
Grammatical Sensitivity (MY)	Awareness of the formal rules of grammar and morphology of words in speech.
Language Development (LD)	General understanding of spoken language at the level of words, idioms, and sentences.
Lexical Knowledge (VL)	Extent of vocabulary that can be understood in terms of correct word meanings.
Listening Ability (LS)	The ability to understand speech.
Quantitative Knowledge (*Gq*)	The depth and breadth of knowledge related to mathematics.
Mathematical Achievement (A3)	Measured (tested) mathematics achievement.
Mathematical Knowledge (KM)	Range of general knowledge about mathematics, not the performance of mathematical operations or the solving of math problems.
Auditory Processing (*Ga*)	The ability to detect and process meaningful nonverbal information in sound.
Phonetic Coding (PC)	The ability to hear phonemes distinctly.
Processing Speed (*Gs*)	The ability to perform simple, repetitive cognitive tasks quickly and fluently.
Number Facility (N)	The speed at which basic arithmetic operations are performed accurately.
Reading and Writing (*Grw*)	The depth and breadth of knowledge and skills related to written language.
Reading Comprehension (RC)	The ability to understand written discourse.
Reading Decoding (RD)	The ability to identify words from text.
Spelling Ability (SG)	The ability to spell words.
Writing Ability (WA)	The ability to use text to communicate ideas clearly.
English Usage Knowledge (EU)	Knowledge of the mechanics of writing (e.g., capitalization, punctuation, and word usage).
Reading Speed (RS)	The rate at which a person can read connected discourse with full comprehension.
Writing Speed (WS)	The ability to copy or generate text quickly.

Note: Most definitions were reported in Carroll (1993) and Schneider and McGrew (2012).

abilities (e.g., Schneider & McGrew, 2012). It is beyond the scope of this chapter to describe CHC theory in detail. The interested reader is referred to Flanagan and colleagues (2013) and Schneider and McGrew for a comprehensive description of the theory (see also Carroll, 1997; and Horn & Blankson, 2005). Table 4.2 includes a description of several broad and narrow CHC abilities, specifically those that are measured most consistently by achievement batteries.

Carroll (1993) conceptualized the broad CHC abilities (both cognitive and academic) as lying on a continuum that extends from "the most general abilities to the most specialized types of knowledges" (p. 510), the latter of which develops more through an individual's instructional and educational experiences. Based on an understanding of the main broad CHC ability definitions, it is likely that most practitioners would agree that Quantitative

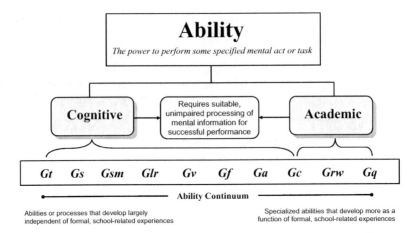

Figure 4.1 Ability Continuum

From Flanagan, Ortiz, Alfonso, and Mascolo (2002), *The achievement test desk reference: A guide to learning disability identification* (2nd ed.). Copyright 2006 by John Wiley & Sons. Adapted by permission.

Knowledge (*Gq*) and Reading/Writing (*Grw*) abilities are more influenced by school-based, experiential factors (such as direct classroom instruction) than are Visual Processing (*Gv*) and Fluid Reasoning (*Gf*) abilities, for example. It is also likely that practitioners would agree that *Gq* and *Grw* represent specialized types of knowledge bases, whereas *Gv* and *Gf* represent mental processing or "thinking" abilities. Therefore, rather than being mutually exclusive, academic and cognitive abilities may best be conceived of as lying on a continuum with those abilities that develop largely through formal education and direct learning and instruction (i.e., abilities that reflect more specialized types of knowledge, like reading and math) at one end and abilities that develop as a result of informal, incidental learning and real-world experiences (i.e., processing or thinking abilities) at the other end (see Figure 4.1).

Although the precise order of the abilities along the continuum in Figure 4.1 has not been validated, an examination of the developmental growth curves of the broad CHC abilities (McGrew, Werder, and Woodcock, 1991; McGrew & Woodcock, 2001) provided some empirical evidence that was used to guide placement of abilities on this ability continuum. A growth curve is essentially a graphical representation of the phase or phases in development that occurs for a particular cognitive ability as a function of age. Examination of growth curves related to the stores of acquired knowledge that typically reflect achievement abilities (e.g., *Gq*, *Grw*) are seen to be quite distinct from the growth curves of the process oriented abilities (e.g., *Gt* (reaction and decision speed), *Gs* (processing speed), *Gsm* (short-term memory)). For example, CHC ability growth curves that are characterized by relatively little change with age represent those abilities that are believed to be much less influenced by formal educational training, acculturation, and learning (McGrew et al., 1991). Abilities that tend to show similar and rather characteristically flat growth patterns across the life span are depicted on the left side of the ability continuum in Figure 4.1. Conversely, those abilities that tend to show a marked increase in the rate of developmental change, coinciding roughly with the school-age years, are depicted as falling to the right side of the ability continuum. The rate of growth for the abilities on the right side of the continuum is greater than the rate of development associated with the abilities that fall to the left side, precisely because of the introduction of formal, school-based training, education, and classroom learning experiences.

Because abilities such as *Gq* and *Grw* represent more specialized types of knowledge that have been accumulated primarily through formal educational experiences, they are logically referred to as *academic abilities* (or achievements), rather than cognitive abilities. Conversely, because the abilities at the opposite end of this continuum reflect those that develop, in part, through real world learning or informal, general life experiences, they are more appropriately referred to as *cognitive abilities*. However, Figure 4.1 shows that the distinction is not discrete, especially as it applies to the abilities that fall toward the center of the continuum. Interestingly, it is precisely these abilities (e.g., *Gc, Gf*) that are measured consistently by cognitive and achievement batteries. As such, there are times that specific *Gc* abilities, for example, are conceived of as cognitive in nature (e.g., verbal ability as represented by a Wechsler Verbal Comprehension Index) and, at other times, academic (e.g., vocabulary knowledge). It is important to remember that the differentiation in factors (or broad abilities) within the CHC model is evident, in part, because of the varying experiences of individuals. However, it is likely that genetic factors also influence this differentiation (Carroll, 1993; Horn & Blankson, 2005). According to Snow (1994), "Most abilities develop from extensive experience across learning history . . . And ability differences are influenced by genetic factors as well as by experience" (p. 4).

Correspondence Between IDEIA Achievement Categories and CHC Theory

The previous section used CHC theory to provide clarity regarding the nature of abilities measured by cognitive and achievement tests. With a better understanding of cognitive and academic abilities within the context of contemporary psychometric theory, evaluation of individuals with learning difficulties can focus more on measuring the *specific abilities* necessary to address referral concerns, rather than being mired in questions related to the *type of test* to be used (i.e., cognitive or achievement). Nevertheless, there is not a one-to-one correspondence between the eight achievement areas listed in IDEIA and academic abilities that are part of CHC theory.

Unlike the broad and narrow abilities specified by CHC theory, most of the eight areas of SLD are not theoretical constructs, nor were they derived through any empirical method. Rather, they tend to represent descriptions of particular areas of academic functioning relevant to the educational setting. In our opinion, they more closely resemble "clinical clusters" or composites formed by an aggregate of relatively distinct abilities that are necessary in combination for successful performance or acquisition of some skill or behavior. From the CHC perspective, such composites are often "messy," in that they are usually represented by abilities that reflect more than one distinct construct. In this section, we provide a description of the eight areas of SLD according to the empirically supported CHC theoretical constructs.

To document a strength or weakness in Basic Reading Skills, for example, it would likely be necessary to assess more than just Reading Decoding (*Grw*-RD) ability. There are other narrow CHC abilities that contribute to an understanding of Basic Reading Skills, most notably Phonetic Coding (*Ga*-PC, an aspect of phonological processing) and Rate-of-Test-Taking (*Gs*-R9, measured by tests of reading rate). Note that these abilities represent aspects of three different CHC broad abilities (i.e., *Grw, Gs,* and auditory processing, *Ga,*). Therefore, when documentation of an individual's Basic Reading Skills is warranted, a test of RD should be augmented with tests of PC and reading rate to achieve a more comprehensive evaluation of this academic domain.

In addition to Basic Reading Skills, most of the remaining SLD areas that correspond to the academic descriptors listed in the federal definition of SLD (i.e., Math Calculation, Math Problem Solving, Written Expression, Listening Comprehension, Oral Expression) can be assessed by three or four CHC narrow abilities. The specific correspondence between the eight areas of SLD and CHC narrow abilities is shown in Table 4.3.

Table 4.3 Correspondence Between Learning Disability Academic Areas in the Federal Definition (i.e., IDEIA) and Cattell-Horn-Carroll (CHC) Abilities

Learning Disability Assessment Area	Corresponding CHC Abilities
Basic Reading Skills	Phonetic Coding (*Ga*-PC) Reading Decoding (*Grw*-RD) Rate-of-Test-Taking (*Gs*-R9)
Reading Comprehension	Reading Comprehension (*Grw*-RC)
Reading Fluency	Reading Speed (*Grw*-RS)
Written Expression	English Usage Knowledge (*Grw*-EU) Spelling Ability (*Grw*-SG) Writing Ability (*Grw*-WA) Writing Speed (*Grw*-WS)
Math Calculation	Math Achievement (*Gq*-A3) Math Knowledge (*Gq*-KM) Number Facility (*Gs*-N)
Math Problem Solving	Math Achievement (*Gq*-A3) Math Knowledge (*Gq*-KM) Quantitative Reasoning (*Gf*-RQ)
Listening Comprehension	Grammatical Sensitivity (*Gc*-MY) Language Development (*Gc*-LD) Lexical Knowledge (*Gc*-VL) Listening Ability (*Gc*-LS)
Oral Expression	Communication Ability (*Gc*-CM) Grammatical Sensitivity (*Gc*-MY) Language Development (*Gc*-LD) Lexical Knowledge (*Gc*-VL)

Note: The narrow abilities listed in this table are considered primary, meaning that they have the most direct correspondence with the academic areas listed in the Federal Definition of specific learning disability.

This table should be used to identify the CHC abilities that contribute to an understanding of the eight academic achievement areas that are assessed routinely in SLD evaluations. For example, Table 4.3 shows that English Usage Knowledge (EU), Spelling Ability (SG), Writing Ability (WA), and Writing Speed (WS) are qualitatively different aspects of *Grw,* all of which are relevant to the academic area of Written Expression. Prior to concluding that an individual has a strength or weakness in Written Expression, practitioners should ensure that this academic area was assessed comprehensively. In general, when an academic area corresponds to more than one CHC narrow ability, tests that measure at least two of these narrow abilities should be administered to ensure adequate measurement of the academic domain in question. Of course, when a student is suspected of having an SLD in a particular academic area (e.g., Written Expression), measures of all corresponding CHC narrow abilities should be administered.

There are only a few sources that provide a comprehensive list of tests that measure the narrow abilities listed in Table 4.3 (e.g., Flanagan et al., 2007, 2013). These sources should be consulted when there is a need to assess academic achievement areas that are represented by multiple CHC abilities (e.g., Written Expression), particularly when the core academic achievement battery used in an evaluation falls short of assessing these abilities. For an understanding of what CHC abilities are measured by the commonly used achievement batteries included in this chapter, see Table 4.4.

Table 4.4 CHC Classifications of Achievement Subtests by IDEIA SLD Area

	Comprehensive Achievement Batteries							
	Basic Reading Skills	Reading Comprehension	Reading Fluency	Math Calculation	Math Problem Solving	Oral Expression	Listening Comprehension	Written Expression
KTEA-II	Letter and Word Recognition (*Grw*-RD) Nonsense Word Decoding (*Grw*-RD) Phonological Awareness (*Ga*-PC)	Reading Comprehension (*Grw*-RC)	Decoding Fluency (*Grw*-RD) Word Recognition Fluency (*Grw*-RD; *Gs*-R9)	Math Concepts and Applications (*Gq*-A3; *Gf*-RQ) Mathematics Computation (*Gq*-A3)	Math Concepts and Applications (*Gq*-A3; *Gf*-RQ)	Associational Fluency (*Glr*-FI, FW) Oral Expression (*Gc*-CM, MY)	Listening Comprehension (*Gc*-LS)	Spelling (*Grw*-SG) Written Expression (*Grw*-EU, WA)
WIAT-III	Early Reading Skills (*Ga*-PC; *Grw*-RD) Pseudoword Decoding (*Grw*-RD) Word Reading (*Grw*-RD)	Reading Comprehension (*Grw*-RC)	Oral Reading Fluency (*Grw*-RS)	Math Fluency Addition (*Gs*-N) Math Fluency Multiplication (*Gs*-N) Math Fluency Subtraction (*Gs*-N) Numerical Operations (*Gq*-A3)	Mathematics Problem Solving (*Gf*-RQ)	Oral Expression (*Gc*-VL; *Glr*-FI)	Listening Comprehension (*Gc*-VL, LS)	Alphabet Writing Fluency (*Grw*-WS) Essay Composition (*Grw*-WA, EU) Sentence Composition (*Grw*-EU, WA) Spelling (*Grw*-SG)
WJ III NU ACH	Letter-Word Identification (*Grw*-RD) Sound Awareness (*Ga*-PC) Word Attack (*Grw*-RD)	Passage Comprehension (*Grw*-RC)	Reading Fluency (*Grw*-RS)	Calculation (*Gq*-A3) Math Fluency (*Gs*-N) Quantitative Concepts (*Gf*-RQ; *Gq*-KM, A3)	Applied Problems (*Gf*-RQ; *Gq*-A3)	Picture Vocabulary (*Gc*-VL)	Oral Comprehension (*Gc*-LS) Understanding Directions (*Gc*-LS; *Gsm*-MW)	Editing (*Grw*-EU) Punctuation & Capitaliz. (*Grw*-EU) Spelling (*Grw*-SG) Spelling of Sounds (*Grw*-SG; *Ga*-PC) Writing Fluency (*Grw*-WS) Writing Samples (*Grw*-WA)

(Continued)

Table 4.4 (Continued)

| | Comprehensive Achievement Batteries | | | | | | | |
	Basic Reading Skills	Reading Comprehension	Reading Fluency	Math Calculation	Math Problem Solving	Oral Expression	Listening Comprehension	Written Expression
CELF-4	Phonological Awareness (Ga-PC)					Expressive Vocabulary (Gc-VL) Formulated Sentences (Gc-CM) Sentence Assembly (Gc-LD, MY) Word Associations (Glr-FI) Word Classes-Expressive (Gc-VL; Gf-I) Word Definitions (Gc-VL)	Concepts and Following Directions (Gc-LS) Semantic Relationships (Gc-LS, Gf-I) Sentence Structure (Gc-LS) Understanding Spoken Paragraphs (Gc-LS, Gf-I) Word Classes-Receptive (Gc-VL, Gf-I) Word Structure (Gc-LS, MY)	
CTOPP-2	Elision (Ga-PC) Blending Words (Ga-PC) Sound Matching (Ga-PC) Phoneme Isolation (Ga-PC) Blending Nonwords (Ga-PC) Segmenting Nonwords (Ga-PC)					Rapid Digit Naming (Glr-NA) Rapid Letter Naming (Glr-NA) Rapid Color Naming (Glr-NA) Rapid Object Naming (Glr-NA)	Memory for Digits (Gsm-MS) Nonword Repetition (Gsm-MS)	

	Accuracy (*Grw*-RD) Rate (*Gs*-R9)	Comprehension (*Grw*-RC)	Fluency (*Grw*-RD)	
GORT-5				
KM3	Addition and Subtraction (*Gq*-A3) Algebra (A3, KM) Geometry (*Gq*-KM, A3; *Gv*-VZ) Measurement (*Gq*-A3, KM) Mental Comp. and Est. (*Gq*-A3) Mult. And Div. (*Gq*-A3) Numeration (*Gq*-A3)	Applied Problem Solving (*Gf*-RQ) Data Analysis and Probability (*Gq*-KM, A3; *Gf*-RQ) Foundations of Problem Solving (*Gq*-A3; *Gf*-RQ)		
TOWL-4	Contextual Conventions (*Grw*-EU) Logical Sentences (*Grw*-EU) Punctuation (*Grw*-EU) Sentence Combining (*Grw*-WA, EU) Spelling (*Grw*-SG) Story Composition (*Grw*-WA) Vocabulary (*Gc*-VL; *Grw*-WA)			

(*Continued*)

Table 4.4 (Continued)

	Comprehensive Achievement Batteries							
	Basic Reading Skills	Reading Comprehension	Reading Fluency	Math Calculation	Math Problem Solving	Oral Expression	Listening Comprehension	Written Expression
WRMT-3	Letter Identification Phonological Awareness (Ga-PC) Word Attack (Grw-RD) Word Comprehension (Grw-RD; Gc-VL) Word Identification (Grw-RD)	Passage Comprehension (Grw-RC)	Oral Reading Fluency (Grw-RS)				Listening Comprehension (Gc-LS)	

Notes: CELF-4 = Clinical Evaluation of Language Fundamentals–Fourth Edition; CTOPP-2 = Comprehensive Test of Phonological Processing–Second Edition; GORT-5 = Gray Oral Reading Tests–Fifth Edition; KM3 = KeyMath–Third Edition; KTEA-II = Kaufman Test of Educational Achievement–Second Edition; TOWL-4 = Test of Written Language–Fourth Edition; WIAT-III = Wechsler Individual Achievement Test–Third Edition; WJ III NU ACH = Woodcock-Johnson III Normative Update Tests of Achievement; WRMT 3 = Woodcock Reading Mastery Test–Third Edition; Ga = Auditory Processing; Gc = Crystallized Intelligence; Gf = Fluid Intelligence; Gq = Quantitative Knowledge; Grw = Reading and Writing; Gs = Processing Speed; Gv = Visual Processing; A3 = Mathematical Achievement; CM = Phonetic Coding; RC = Reading Comprehension; RD = Reading Decoding; RQ = Quantitative Reasoning; RS = Reading Speed; SG = Spelling Ability; VL = Lexical Knowledge; WA = Writing Ability; WS = Writing Speed; Glr = Long-Term Storage and Retrieval; Gsm = Short-Term Memory; CM = Communication ability; MY = Grammatical Sensitivity; N = Number Facility; NA = Naming Facility; FI = Ideational Fluency; FW = Word Fluency; LS = Listening Ability; MW = Working Memory Capacity; EU = English Usage; WA = Writing Ability; LD = Language Development; I = Induction; MS = Memory Span; R9 = Rate-of-Test-Taking; VZ = Visualization.

This table shows, for example, that the WIAT-III and WJ III NU ACH measure Written Expression more comprehensively than does the KTEA-II. Therefore, when the KTEA-II is used as the achievement battery for a referral involving difficulties with written language, it should be supplemented with a test of Writing Speed (WS). Likewise, Table 4.4 shows that, not surprisingly, the CELF-4 measures Oral Expression far more comprehensively than does any of the other achievement batteries listed in the table. As such, it is highly unlikely that a single measure of Oral Expression, such as Picture Vocabulary on the WJ III NU ACH, forms a sufficient basis from which to infer a student's ability to use language via syntax, semantics, phonology, morphology, and pragmatics (Flanagan et al., 2007; Mercer, 1997). However, if practitioners use subtests that correspond to the CHC abilities associated with Oral Expression (Table 4.3), they are more likely to assess all of the components of language. For example, the CELF-4 contains subtests that measure all of the CHC abilities associated with Oral Expression, namely Communication Ability (*Gc*-CM), Grammatical Sensitivity (*Gc*-MY), Language Development (*Gc*-LD), and Lexical Knowledge (*Gc*-VL).

Close inspection of Table 4.4 shows that the comprehensive achievement batteries (i.e., KTEA-II, WIAT-III, and WJ III NU ACH) often have a single subtest representing an IDEIA achievement domain. For example, each battery includes one subtest that purports to measure Reading Comprehension (RC) and each one of these subtests has been classified in the literature as a measure of the *Grw* narrow ability of Reading Comprehension (RC). However, as most practitioners have probably already experienced, a student may perform average on one measure of reading comprehension and well below average on another. Disparate performance on tests that purport to measure the same construct—reading comprehension in this example—although unexpected may be explained by variation in the specific characteristics of the test and the requirements or demands of the test (Flanagan et al., 2007; Mascolo, 2013).

Variation in Achievement Test Characteristics and Task Demands

Knowledge of the specific characteristics and task demands of achievement subtests can assist practitioners in determining why two or more tests that purport to measure the same construct yield scores that differ significantly. Table 4.5 is organized according to the eight achievement areas listed in IDEIA. The subtests from the nine achievement batteries included in this chapter are listed in their respective achievement area in this table. For example, all reading comprehension subtests are listed in the Reading Comprehension area; all applied problems subtests are listed in the Math Problem Solving area. The vertical columns in Table 4.5 list various subtest characteristics and task demands. A review of the reading comprehension subtests listed in this table shows that they have different characteristics (e.g., cloze format, open-ended questions, multiple-choice questions) and task demands (e.g., literal vs. inferential questions, silent vs. oral reading). Thus, while all the reading comprehension tests in Table 4.5 measure the theoretical construct of RC, they do so using different formats, stimuli, and response requirements.

There are many uses for the information in Table 4.5, including test selection, test interpretation, and identifying targets for remediation. To use Table 4.5 in test selection, identify the skill area of concern based on referral information. Next, review the task characteristics and task demands in the vertical columns of the table to determine which tests align best with the type of information needed to address the referral concerns. For instance, the Basic Reading Skills section of the table includes characteristics such as "real words," "pseudowords," "isolated stimuli (letters, words, sounds, pictures)," and so forth. Based on what is known

Table 4.5 Variation in Task Characteristics and Task Demands on Achievement Subtests by IDEIA Achievement Area

Basic Reading Skills and Reading Fluency					
Battery Subtest	Real Words	Pseudowords	Isolated Stimuli (letters, words, sounds, pictures)	Connected Text	Time Limit
Comprehensive Test of Phonological Processing-Second Edition (CTOPP-2)					
Blending Nonwords		✓	✓		
Blending Words	✓		✓		
Elision	✓'		✓'		
Phoneme Isolation	✓				
Segmenting Nonwords		✓	✓		
Sound Matching	✓		✓		
Rapid Color			✓		✓
Rapid Digit			✓		✓
Rapid Letter			✓		✓
Rapid Object			✓		✓
Gray Oral Reading Tests-Fifth Edition (GORT-5)					
Accuracy, Fluency, Rate	✓			✓	✓
Kaufman Test of Educational Achievement-Second Edition (KTEA-II)					
Decoding Fluency		✓	✓		✓
Letter and Word Recognition	✓		✓		
Nonsense Word Decoding		✓	✓		
Word Recognition Fluency	✓		✓		✓
Wechsler Individual Achievement Test-Third Edition (WIAT-III)					
Early Reading Skills	✓		✓		
Oral Reading Fluency	✓				
Pseudoword Decoding		✓	✓		
Word Reading	✓		✓		
Woodcock-Johnson III Normative Update Tests of Achievement (WJ III NU ACH)					
Letter-Word Identification	✓		✓		
Reading Fluency	✓			✓	✓
Reading Vocabulary	✓		✓		
Sound Awareness	✓		✓		
Word Attack		✓	✓		
Woodcock Reading Mastery Tests-Third Edition (WRMT-3)					
Oral Reading Fluency	✓			✓	✓
Phonological Awareness	✓				
Rapid Automatic Naming			✓		✓
Word Attack		✓	✓		
Word Comprehension	✓		✓		
Word Identification	✓		✓		

Reading Comprehension

Battery / Subtest	Cloze Format	Open-Ended Questions	Multiple Choice	Literal Questions	Inferential Questions	Silent Reading	Oral Reading	Examiner Reads	Examinee Reads	Examiner/ Examinee Read	Time Limit	Examinee can refer back to text
Gray Oral Reading Tests-Fifth Edition (GORT-5)												
Reading Comprehension			✓	✓	✓							
Kaufman Test of Educational Achievement-Second Edition (KTEA-II)												
Reading Comprehension		✓		✓	✓	✓			✓			✓
Wechsler Individual Achievement Test-Third Edition (WIAT-III)												
Reading Comprehension		✓		✓	✓	✓	✓			✓		✓
Woodcock-Johnson III Normative Update Tests of Achievement (WJ III NU ACH)												
Passage Comprehension	✓					✓				✓		✓
Woodcock Reading Mastery Tests-Third Edition (WRMT-3)												
Passage Comprehension	✓					✓				✓		✓

Written Expression

Battery / Subtest	Dictated Spelling (Isolation)	Dictated Spelling (Context)	Multiple Choice	Real Words	Nonsense Words	Isolated Response (e.g., letters, single words)	Connected Response (e.g., sentences, phrases)	Writing Mechanics Assessed (punct., cap., usage)	Proofing/Editing Required	Time Limit	Picture Prompt	Oral Prompt	Written Prompt
Clinical Evaluation of Language Fundamentals-Fourth Edition (CELF-4)													
Word Structure			✓			✓	✓				✓	✓	
Kaufman Test of Educational Achievement-Second Edition (KTEA-II)													
Spelling	✓			✓		✓						✓	
Written Expression				✓		✓	✓	✓		✓	✓	✓	✓

(Continued)

Table 4.5 (Continued)

Battery / Subtest	Dictated Spelling (Isolation)	Dictated Spelling (Context)	Multiple Choice	Real Words	Nonsense Words	Isolated Response (e.g., letters, single words)	Connected Response (e.g., sentences, phrases)	Writing Mechanics Assessed (punct., cap., usage)	Proofing/Editing Required	Time Limit	Picture Prompt	Oral Prompt	Written Prompt
Test of Written Language–Fourth Edition (TOWL-4)													
Contextual Conventions				✓			✓	✓		✓	✓	✓	
Logical Sentences				✓		✓	✓						✓
Punctuation		✓		✓			✓	✓				✓	
Sentence Combining				✓			✓						✓
Spelling		✓		✓			✓	✓				✓	
Story Composition				✓			✓			✓	✓	✓	
Vocabulary				✓			✓					✓	
Wechsler Individual Achievement Test–Third Edition (WIAT-III)													
Alphabet Writing Fluency						✓				✓		✓	
Essay Composition				✓			✓	✓		✓		✓	
Sentence Composition				✓			✓	✓					✓
Spelling		✓		✓		✓		✓				✓	
Woodcock-Johnson III Normative Update Tests of Achievement (WJ III NU ACH)													
Editing				✓		✓		✓	✓				✓
Punctuation and Capitalization				✓		✓		✓	✓				
Spelling	✓			✓		✓		✓				✓	
Spelling of Sounds	✓			✓		✓						✓	
Writing Fluency				✓			✓			✓	✓		
Writing Samples				✓			✓	✓					

	Math Calculation									
Battery Subtest	Uses Worksheet	Easel Format	Time Limit	Mental Computations	Paper/Pencil Computations	Scrap Paper Allowed	Multiple Choice	Examiner Reads	Examinee Reads	Examiner/ Examinee Read
Kaufman Test of Educational Achievement-Second Edition (KTEA-II)										
Math Computation	✓				✓				✓	
Math Concepts and Applications¹		✓			✓		✓	✓		
Wechsler Individual Achievement Test-Third Edition (WIAT-III)										
Math Fluency-Addition	✓		✓		✓				✓	
Math Fluency-Subtraction	✓		✓		✓				✓	
Math Fluency-Multiplication	✓		✓		✓				✓	
Numerical Operations	✓				✓	✓			✓	
Woodcock-Johnson III Normative Update Tests of Achievement (WJ III NU ACH)										
Applied Problems	✓	✓			✓	✓		✓		
Calculation	✓				✓	✓			✓	
Math Fluency	✓		✓		✓				✓	
Quantitative Concepts								✓		
KeyMath-3 (KM3)										
Addition and Subtraction	✓				✓			✓		
Algebra		✓		✓				✓		
Applied Problem Solving		✓		✓				✓		
Data Analysis and Probability		✓		✓						✓
Foundations of Problem Solving		✓		✓				✓		
Geometry		✓		✓				✓		
Measurement		✓		✓						✓
Mental Computation and Estimation		✓		✓						✓
Multiplication and Division	✓				✓			✓		
Numeration		✓		✓						

¹ Scrap paper is allowed after item #34 on this subtest.

(Continued)

Table 4.5 (Continued)

Math Problem Solving

Battery Subtest	Uses Worksheet	Easel Format	Time Limit	Mental Computations	Paper/Pencil Computations	Scrap Paper Allowed	Uses Visual Stimuli	Word Problems	Multiple Choice	Examiner Reads	Examinee Reads	Examiner/ Examinee Read
Kaufman Test of Educational Achievement-Second Edition (KTEA-II)												
Math Concepts and Applications¹		✓		✓		✓	✓			✓		
KeyMath-3 (KM3)												
Algebra		✓	✓					✓		✓		
Applied Problem Solving		✓	✓					✓	✓	✓		
Data Analysis and Probability		✓	✓					✓	✓	✓		
Foundations of Problem Solving		✓	✓					✓	✓	✓		
Wechsler Individual Achievement Test-Third Edition (WIAT-III)												
Math Problem Solving		✓			✓	✓	✓	✓		✓		
Woodcock-Johnson III Normative Update Tests of Achievement (WJ III NU ACH)												
Applied Problems				✓				✓		✓		

¹ Scrap paper is allowed after item #34 on this subtest.

Listening Comprehension

Battery Subtest	Use of Tape Recorder/CD	Examiner Reads	Requires Verbatim Repetition	Multiple Choice	Dichotomous Response (e.g., True/False)	Requires Examinee to Perform Action Based on What He/She Hears	Use of Pictures	Motor Response Required (pointing, writing, drawing)	Oral Response Required	Single-Word Response	Multi-Word Response	Isolated Stimuli (e.g., single words, numbers, sounds, pictures)	Connected Stimuli (phrase, sentences, stories)
Clinical Evaluation of Language Fundamentals- Fourth Edition (CELF-4)													
Concepts and Following Directions	✓						✓	✓					✓

Understanding Spoken Paragraphs		✓						✓		✓		✓
Semantic Relationships		✓		✓				✓		✓		✓
Sentence Structure		✓		✓		✓	✓					✓
Word Classes-Receptive		✓						✓	✓		✓	
Word Structure		✓				✓		✓	✓	✓		✓
Comprehensive Test of Phonological Processing-Second Edition (CTOPP-2)												
Memory for Digits	✓		✓					✓		✓		✓
Nonword repetition	✓		✓					✓	✓		✓	
Kaufman Test of Educational Achievement-Second Edition (KTEA-II)												
Phonological Awareness		✓			✓	✓		✓	✓		✓	
Listening Comprehension	✓			✓				✓	✓	✓	✓	
Wechsler Individual Achievment Test-Third Edition (WIAT-III)												
Listening Comprehension		✓				✓	✓	✓		✓	✓	✓
Woodcock-Johnson III Normative Update Tests of Achievement (WJ III NU ACH)												
Story Recall	✓							✓		✓		✓
Understandng Directions	✓				✓	✓	✓					✓
Story Recall-Delayed	✓							✓		✓		✓
Oral Comprehension	✓							✓	✓			✓
Woodcock Reading Mastery Test-Third Edition (WRMT-3)												
Listening Comprehension	✓	✓						✓	✓	✓		✓

Oral Expression

Battery Subtest	Multiword Response	Single Word Response	Time Limit	Visual Stimuli	Examiner Reads	Examinee Reads	Examiner/Examinee Read
Clinical Evaluation of Language Fundamentals-Fourth Edition (CELF-4)							
Expressive Vocabulary		✓		✓			
Formulated Sentences	✓			✓	✓		
Sentence Assembly	✓			✓	✓		
Word Associations		✓	✓	✓			
Word Classes-Expressive	✓			✓			
Word Definitions	✓			✓			

(Continued)

Table 4.5 (Continued)

Battery Subtest	Oral Expression						
	Multiword Response	Single Word Response	Time Limit	Visual Stimuli	Examiner Reads	Examinee Reads	Examiner/ Examinee Read
Kaufman Test of Educational Achievement-Second Edition (KTEA-II)							
Associational Fluency		✓	✓		✓		
Oral Expression	✓			✓	✓		
Woodcock-Johnson III Normative Update Tests of Achievement (WJ III NU ACH)							
Picture Vocabulary			✓	✓			
Wechsler Individual Achievement Test-Third Edition (WIAT-III)							
Oral Expression	✓	✓	✓		✓		

From Flanagan, Ortiz, and Alfonso (2013) *Essentials of cross-battery assessment* (3rd ed.). Copyright 2013 by John Wiley & Sons. Adapted by permission.

about the examinee's difficulties, identify those characteristics important to include in an evaluation. For example, if a student can decode words in isolation, but struggles to decode words in the context of reading passages, use a measure that assesses word reading in the context of "connected stimuli (sentences, paragraphs)."

To use Table 4.5 in test interpretation, identify the two similar subtests on which the student's scores differed significantly. For example, suppose a student performed significantly higher on TOWL-4 Story Composition as compared to WIAT-III Essay Composition, both of which measure Writing Ability (WA) and are associated with the IDEIA area of Written Expression Based on the information about these subtests provided in Table 4.5, it might be hypothesized that the use of a picture prompt on the Story Composition subtest provided support and primed the student for writing as compared to the simpler, oral prompt on the Essay Composition subtest.

To use Table 4.5 to assist in identifying targets for remediation, you will need to conduct an error analysis. For example, suppose a student obtained a very low score on the KTEA-II Reading Comprehension subtest. Table 4.5 indicates that this subtest contains literal and inferential questions. If an examination of errors reveals that most literal questions were answered correctly and all inferential questions were answered incorrectly, then *drawing inferences from text* should be a target for intervention, particularly if it is supported by cognitive testing that reveals *Gf* difficulties. For example, a student with difficulty drawing inferences from text may benefit from reciprocal teaching. This method of teaching involves a dialogue between teacher and student that is structured around four strategies that aid comprehension of text: summarizing, question generating, clarifying, and predicting.

In sum, academic abilities and cognitive abilities are not mutually exclusive. Rather, they lie on a continuum, separated mainly by the extent to which they develop as a function of direct instruction and formal education. Abilities that develop largely as a function of schooling are those that are measured typically by achievement tests (i.e., reading, math, and writing abilities). The most popular comprehensive achievement batteries measure academic abilities that correspond to the eight areas of achievement listed in the IDEIA definition of SLD (i.e., Basic Reading Skill, Reading Comprehension, Reading Fluency, Math Calculation, Math Problem Solving, Written Expression, Oral Expression, and Listening Comprehension). Because these achievement areas are largely atheoretical, CHC theory was used to link achievement subtests to empirically supported constructs. These constructs (i.e., narrow CHC abilities) correspond to the eight areas of achievement in the federal definition of SLD. Knowledge of the narrow abilities that comprise each of the eight areas of achievement provides practitioners with a theoretical and empirical basis for evaluating these achievement domains. Because all measures (subtests) of a particular ability (e.g., Reading Comprehension) are not created equal, there is often a need to examine subtest characteristics and task demands to aid in test selection, interpretation, and identifying targets for intervention.

In addition to the information on the theoretical constructs measured by achievement batteries and how they differ in terms of their subtest characteristics and task demands, it is important to understand other aspects of these measures prior to using them. For example, achievement batteries have different content and administration features (e.g., alternate forms available), technical features (e.g., weighted norms), and psychometric properties (e.g., reliability). The next section of this chapter describes the most salient qualitative and quantitative features of the achievement batteries included herein.

Qualitative and Quantitative Characteristics of Achievement Batteries

Practitioners may benefit from a reference that compares quantitative and qualitative characteristics of achievement batteries, particularly for the selection of tests that best address specific referral concerns. The information provided in this section allows practitioners to compare the content, administration, and technical features of nine achievement batteries.

Content and Administration Features

Table 4.6 provides basic information about the age range of the batteries as well as the breadth of the independent lower-order composites yielded by each instrument. As may be seen in Table 4.6, some content features are unique to certain batteries. For example, five of the nine achievement batteries have procedures for conducting error analysis (e.g., CELF-4, GORT-5, KTEA-II, WIAT-III, and WRMT-3), which is important for intervention planning. Similarly, all achievement batteries have alternate forms except CELF-4, CTOPP-2, and WIAT-III. Achievement batteries with alternate forms are useful for measuring student progress, including response to intervention.

Table 4.6 also highlights important administration features of achievement batteries. For example, some batteries include a CD to allow for standardized administration of listening ability, auditory processing, and/or memory tests. The majority of achievement batteries emphasize the principle of selective testing by assessment purpose. This feature provides practitioners with the flexibility to design a battery that addresses the *unique* referral concerns of the individual and it is time efficient. The utility of selective testing procedures is apparent in the cross-battery assessment approach (see Flanagan & Ortiz, 2001; Flanagan, Ortiz, Alfonso, & Mascolo, 2002; Flanagan, et al., 2013, and McGrew & Flanagan, 1998), and has always been part and parcel of neuropsychological assessment.

Table 4.6 Content and Administration Features of Selected Achievement Batteries

Content and Administration Features	CELF-4 (2003)	CTOPP-2 (2013)	GORT-5 (2012)
Content Features			
Age range of battery	5–0 to 21–11	4–0 to 24–11	6–0 to 23–11
Composites available	Core Language Score Receptive Language Index Expressive Language Index Language Content Index Language Structure Index Language Memory Index Working Memory Index	Phonological Awareness Phonological Memory Rapid Symbolic Naming Rapid Non-Symbolic Naming Alternate Phonological Awareness	Oral Reading Index
Contains procedures for conducting error analysis	Yes	No	Yes
Alternate forms available	No	No	Yes
Administration Features			
Tests of listening ability, auditory processing and/or memory taped for standardized administration	No	Yes	N/A
Principle of selective testing by assessment purpose emphasized[a]	Yes	Yes	No
Comprehensive manual includes examiner training activities[b]	Yes (CD)	Yes	No
Administration time	Core: 30–45 minutes	30–40 minutes	15–45 minutes
Achievement Battery			

Content and Administration Features	KTEA-II (2004)	KM3 (2007)	TOWL-4 (2009)
Content Features			
Age range of battery	4–6 to 25–11	4–6 to 21–0	9–0 to 17–11
Composites available	Comprehensive Achievement Composite Reading Mathematics Written Language Oral Language	Total Test Basic Concepts Operations Applications	Contrived Writing Spontaneous Writing Overall Writing
Contains procedures for conducting error analysis	Yes	No	No
Alternate forms available	Yes	Yes	Yes

Content and Administration Features	KTEA-II (2004)	KM3 (2007)	TOWL-4 (2009)
Administration Features			
Tests of listening ability, auditory processing and/ or memory taped for standardized administration	Yes	N/A	N/A
Principle of selective testing by assessment purpose emphasized[a]	Yes	Yes	No
Comprehensive manual includes examiner training activities[b]	No	No	Yes
Administration time	30 to 85 minutes	30–90 minutes	60–90 minutes
Achievement Battery			

Content and Administration Features	WIAT-III (2009)*	WJ III NU ACH (2001, 2007)	WRMT-3 (2011)
Content Features			
Age range of battery	4–0 to 19–11	2–0 to 90+	4–6 to 79–11
Composites available	Total Achievement Oral Language Total Reading Basic Reading Reading Comp and Fluency Written Expression Mathematics Math Fluency	Total Achievement Broad Reading Basic Reading Skills Reading Comprehension Oral Language–Standard Oral Language–Extended Listening Comprehension Oral Expression Broad Math	Readiness Basic Skills Reading Comprehension Total Reading
		Math Calculation Skills Math Reasoning Broad Written Language Basic Writing Skills Written Expression Academic Knowledge Academic Skills Academic Fluency Academic Applications Phoneme/Grapheme Knowledge	
Contains procedures for conducting error analysis	Yes	No	Yes
Alternate forms available	No	Yes	Yes

(*Continued*)

Table 4.6 (Continued)

Content and Administration Features	WIAT-III (2009)*	WJ III NU ACH (2001, 2007)	WRMT-3 (2011)
	Administration Features		
Tests of listening ability, auditory processing and/or memory taped for standardized administration	Yes	Yes	Yes
Principle of selective testing by assessment purpose emphasized[a]	No	Yes	Yes
Comprehensive manual includes examiner training activities[b]	Yes	Yes	No
Administration time	35–105 minutes	Standard + Extended Batteries (varies by purpose): 75–120 minutes	15–45 minutes

Note: N/A = Not Applicable.

CELF-4 = Clinical Evaluation of Language Fundamentals–Fourth Edition; CTOPP-2 = Comprehensive Test of Phonological Processing–Second Edition; GORT-5 = Gray Oral Reading Tests–Fifth Edition; KM3 = KeyMath–Third Edition; KTEA-II = Kaufman Test of Educational Achievement–Second Edition; TOWL-4 = Test of Written Language–Fourth Edition; WIAT-III = Wechsler Individual Achievement Test–Third Edition; WJ III NU ACH = Woodcock-Johnson III Normative Update Tests of Achievement; WRMT-3 = Woodcock Reading Mastery Test–Third Edition.

[a] The phrase "selective testing" means that the test author's intent was not necessarily to require examiners to administer the entire battery, but rather to have them tailor the battery to referral concerns.

[b] Examiner training activities include an examiner training checklist, an observation checklist, scoring workbook, and so forth.

* Information based on Technical Manual, which does not provide the more recent adult norms.

Technical Features

Table 4.7 presents many technical characteristics of achievement tests. For example, most tests used the Rasch model for item analysis and scaling, which is not surprising, as it has become more widespread in test development. In addition, the technical manuals of most tests include both age- and grade-based norm tables, as well as the results of bias analyses conducted with minority samples. Table 4.7 also includes norming characteristics of achievement tests, which are described briefly below.

Norming characteristics. Test developers seek to draw individuals from the population on whom the test will be used in an effort to create a sample that is representative of the larger population. Typically, the adequacy of the standardization sample of any given test can be effectively gauged through an examination of the following characteristics: (1) size of the norming sample, (2) recency of the normative data as reflected by the date when the data were collected (and not necessarily the publication date), (3) average number of individuals per age/grade interval included in the standardization sample, (4) size of the age blocks used in the norm tables across the entire age range of the test, and (5) number and types of variables included in the norming plan (Bracken, 1987; Flanagan & Alfonso, 1995; Hammill, Brown, & Bryant, 1992; McGrew & Woodcock, 2001). This information is included in Table 4.7. While we do not render an opinion with regard to the adequacy of each achievement battery's standardization sample, we provide details about standardization characteristics below that are helpful for making this determination.

Table 4.7 Technical Features of Selected Achievement Batteries

	Achievement Battery		
Technical Features	CELF-4 (2003)	CTOPP-2	GORT-5 (2012)
Rasch model used for item analysis and scaling	No	Yes	No
Person variables in norming plan	Age Gender Race/Ethnicity Parent Education Level	Age Gender Ethnicity Hispanic Status Exceptionality Status Family Income Education Level of Parents	Age Gender Race/Hispanic Status Parental Education Household Income
Community variables in norming plan	Geographic Region	Geographic Region	Geographic Region
Size of norming sample	2,650	1,900	2,556
Norms weighted to correct sample mismatch to population	No	No	No
Age blocks in norm tables[a]	6 months: 5–0 to 6–11 1 year: 7–0 to 16–11 5 years: 17–0 to 21–11	4 months: 4–0 to 4–11 6 months: 5–0 to 7–11 1 year: 8–0 to 14–11 10 years: 15–0 to 24–11	6 months: 6–0 to 13–11 1 year: 14–0 to 18–11 5 years: 19–0 to 23–11
Grade-based norm tables available	No	No	No
Bias analyses conducted with minority samples	Yes	Yes	Yes
Lowest age at which floor is adequate by test in years and months	Concepts and Following Directions: 5–0 Word Structure: 5–0 Recalling Sentences: 5–0 Formulated Sentences: 5–6 Word Classes 1-Rec.: 5–0 Word Classes 1-Exp.: 5–6 Word Classes 2-Rec.: 8–0 Word Classes 2-Exp.: 9–0 Sentence Structure: 5–0 Expressive Vocabulary: 5–0 Word Definitions: 10–0 Understanding Spoken Paragraphs: 5–6 Semantic Relationships: 9–0 Sentence Assembly: 10–0 Phon. Awareness: N/A Rapid Auto. Naming: N/A	Elision: 6–6 Blending Words: 6–0 Phoneme Isolation: 7–0 Sound Matching: 6–0 Memory for Digits: 4–0 Nonword Repetition: 4–0 Rapid Digit Naming: 4–0 Rapid Letter Naming: 5–0 Rapid Color Naming: 4–0 Rapid Object Naming: 4–0 Blending Nonwords: 6–0 Segmenting Nonwords: 7–0	Rate: 7–6 (Form A); 8–0 (Form B) Accuracy: 8–0 Fluency: 7–6 Comprehension: 7–0 (Form A); 7–6 (Form B)

(Continued)

Table 4.7 (Continued)

Achievement Battery		
Technical Features	**CELF-4 (2003)**	**CTOPP-2**	**GORT-5 (2012)**
---	---	---	---
Highest age at which ceiling is adequate by test in years and months	Word Associations: N/A Number Rep. Total: 5–0 Familiar Sequences: 5–6 Concepts and Following Directions: 7–11 Word Structure: 6–5 Recalling Sentences: 12–11 Formulated Sentences: 9–11 Word Classes 1-Rec.: None Word Classes 1-Exp.: 6–5 Word Classes 2-Rec.: 12–11 Word Classes 2-Exp.: 15–11 Sentence Structure: 5–5 Expressive Vocabulary: 8–11 Word Definitions: 21–11 Understanding Spoken Paragraphs: 5–11 Semantic Relationships: None Sentence Assembly: 10–11 Phon. Awareness: N/A Rapid Auto. Naming: N/A Word Associations: N/A Number Rep. Total: 21–11 Familiar Sequences: 21–11	Elision: 7–6 Blending Words: 24–11 Phoneme Isolation: 7–0 Sound Matching: 5–6 Memory for Digits: 24–11 Nonword Repetition: 24–11 Rapid Digit Naming: 24–11 Rapid Letter Naming: 24–11 Rapid Color Naming: 6–11 Rapid Object Naming: 6–11 Blending Nonwords: 24–11 Segmenting Nonwords: 24–11	Rate: 15–11 (Form A); 14–11 (Form B) Accuracy: 15–11 Fluency: 14–11 Comprehension: 17–11
Subtest scores reported on a scale having a mean of 100 and a standard deviation of 15	No (10:3)	No (10:3)	No (10:3)
Composites reported on a scale having a mean of 100 and a standard deviation of 15	Yes	Yes	Yes

Achievement Battery		
Technical Features	**KTEA-II (2004)**	**KM3 (2007)**	**TOWL-4 (2009)**
---	---	---	---
Rasch model used for item analysis and scaling	Yes	Yes	No
Person variables in norming plan	Age Grade Gender Race/Ethnicity Parent Education Educational Placement	Age Sex Race/Ethnicity SES (mother/caregiver education level) Special Education Status	Age Gender Race/Ethnicity Household Income Education Level of Parents Disability Classification
Community variables in norming plan	Geographic Region	Geographic Region	Geographic Region
Size of norming sample	2,400 (Grade-based) 3,000 (Age-based)	3,630	2,205

	Achievement Battery		
Technical Features	KTEA-II (2004)	KM3 (2007)	TOWL-4 (2009)
Norms weighted to correct sample mismatch to population	No	No	No
Age blocks in norm tables[a]	3 months: 4–6 to 5–11 4 months: 6–0 to 14–11 6 months: 15–0 to 18–11 2 years: 19–0 to 20–11 5 years: 21–0 to 25–11	3 months (4–6 to 18–11) 5 months (19–0 to 19–11) 1 year (20–0 to 21–11)	1 year (9–0 to 17–11)
Grade-based norm tables available	Yes	Yes	Yes
Bias analyses conducted with minority samples	Yes	Yes	Yes
Lowest age at which floor is adequate by test in years and months	Letter & Word Rec: 6–0 Reading Comp: 6–8 (Form A); 8–0 (Form B) Math Con and App: 4–6 Math Computation: 6–8 Written Expression: 4–6 Spelling: 6–8 Listening Comp: 6–0 Oral Expression: 4–9 (Form A); 4–6 (Form B) Phonological Awareness Long: 6–0 Phonological Awareness Short: 7–0 Nonsense Word Decoding: 9–4 (Form A); 9–8 (Form B) Word Rec Fluency: 8–0 Decoding Fluency: 8–8 Associational Fluency (Semantic): 5–6 Associational Fluency (Sem+Phono): 6–0 Naming Facility (Objects+Color): 6–8 Naming Facility (Obj, Col, Let): 6–0	Numeration: 5–3 Algebra: 6–6 (Form A); 6–9 (Form B) Geometry: 5–3 (Form A); 5–6 (Form B) Measurement: 7–3 Data An. and Prob.: 5–9 Mental Comp. and Est.: 7–3 Add. and Sub.: 7–0 Mult. and Div.: 10–0 Foundations of Probl. Solv.: 6–0 (Form A); 6–9 (Form B) Applied Prob. Solv.: 6–9 (Form A); 6–3 (Form B)	Vocabulary: 9–0 Spelling: 10–0 (Form B); 11–0 (Form A) Punctuation: 17–0 (Form B); none for Form A Logical Sentences: 9–0 (Form B); 10–0 (Form A) Sentence Combining: None Context. Conventions: 9–0 Story Composition: 10–0
Highest age at which ceiling is adequate by test in years and months	Letter and Word Rec: 25–11 Reading Comp: 25–11 Math Con and App: 25–11 Math Computation: 25–11 Written Expression: 25–11 Spelling: 20–11(Form A); and 18–5 (Form B) Listening Comp: 25–11 Oral Expression: 25–11 Phonological Awareness Long: 8–0 Phonological Awareness	Numeration: 21–11 Algebra: 18–8 Geometry: 16–11 (Form A); 17–11 (Form B) Measurement: 17–11 (Form A); 16–11 (Form B) Data An. and Prob.: 21–11 Mental Comp. and Est.: 21–11 Add. and Sub.: 17–11 (Form A); 15–11 (Form B) Mult. And Div.: 21–11	Vocabulary: 16–11 (Form B); 15–11 (Form A) Spelling: 11–11 (Form B); 10–11 (Form A) Punctuation: 15–11 (Form B); 11–11 (Form A) Logical Sentences: 17–11 Sentence Combining: 17–11 Context. Conventions: 17–11

(Continued)

Table 4.7 (Continued)

Achievement Battery			
Technical Features	**KTEA-II (2004)**	**KM3 (2007)**	**TOWL-4 (2009)**
	Short: 7–3 (Form A); 6–3 (Form B) Nonsense Word: 25–11 Word Rec Fluency: 25–11 Decoding Fluency: 25–11 Associational Fluency (Semantic): 25–11 Associational Fluency (Sem+Phono): 17–5 Naming Facility (Objects+Color): 14–3 Naming Facility (Obj, Col, Let): 12–7	Foundations of Probl. Solv.: 15–11 (Form A); 14–11 (Form B) Applied Prob. Solv: 21–11	Story Composition: 17–11
Subtest scores reported on a scale having a mean of 100 and a standard deviation of 15	Yes	No (10:3)	No (10:3)
Composites reported on a scale having a mean of 100 and a standard deviation of 15	Yes	Yes	Yes

Achievement Battery			
Technical Features	**WIAT-III (2009)**	**WJ III NU ACH (2001, 2007)***	**WRMT-3 (2011)**
Rasch model used for item analysis and scaling	Yes	Yes	Yes
Person variables in norming plan	Age Grade Gender Race/Ethnicity Parent Education Level	Age Gender Race/Ethnicity SES Type of School/College/University	Age Grade Sex Education Level and Season Race/Ethnicity Parent Education Level
Community variables in norming plan	Geographic Region	Geographic Region Residence	Geographic Region
Size of norming sample	1,400 (Fall Grade-based) 1,375 (Spring Grade-based) 1,826 (Age-based)	8,782	5,000+
Norms weighted to correct sample mismatch to population	No	Yes	No

Technical Features	Achievement Battery		
	WIAT-III (2009)	WJ III NU ACH (2001, 2007)*	WRMT-3 (2011)
Age blocks in norm tables[a]	4 months: 4–0 to 13–11 1 year: 14–0 to 16–11 3 years: 17–0 to 19–11	1 month: 2–0 to 19–11 1 year: 20–0 to 89–11 > 1 year: 90+	2 months: 4–6 to 6–11 4 months: 7–0 to 13–11 1 year: 14–0 to 18–11 19–0 to 25–11 26–0 to 30–11 31–0 to 40–11 41–0 to 55–11 56+
Grade-based norm tables available	Yes	Yes	Yes
Bias analyses conducted with minority samples	Yes	Yes	Yes
Lowest age at which floor is adequate by test in years and months	Word Reading: 7–4 Reading Comp: 6–8 Early Reading Skills: 4–8 Pseudoword Decoding: 8–0 Oral Reading Fluency: 6–0 Numerical Operations: 5–8 Math Problem Solving: 4–0 Spelling: 6–0 Alphabet Writing Fl.: 6–0 Receptive Vocab: 5–8 Oral Discourse Comp.: 5–4 Sentence Comb.: 9–0 Sentence Building: 8–0 Essay Composition: 8–0 Math Fluency – Add: 6–8 Math Fluency – Sub: 7–8 Math Fluency – Mult: 9–4	Letter-Word Id.: 4–1 Reading Fluency: 7–1 Story Recall: 5–7 Understanding Directs.: 3–7 Calculation: 6–7 Math Fluency: 7–1 Spelling: 3–7 Writing Fluency: 8–1 Passage Comp.:5–7 Applied Problems: 3–1 Writing Samples: 6–1 Story Recall-Delayed: 3–0 Word Attack: 6–1 Picture Vocabulary: 2–7 Oral Comp.: 5–7 Editing: 9–1 Reading Vocabulary: 8–7 Quantitative Concepts: 4–7 Academic Knowledge: 2–7 Spelling of Sounds: 6–1 Sound Awareness: 5–7 Punct. & Capital.: 6–1	Letter Identification: 5–4 Phonological Awareness: 4–8 Rapid Auto. Naming: 4–6 Word Identification: 6–10 Word Attack: 8–0 Listening Comp.: 6–0 Word Comp.: 7–4 Passage Comp.: 7–0 Oral Reading Fluency: 6–6
Highest age at which ceiling is adequate by test in years and months	Word Reading: 13–7 Reading Comp: 19–11 Early Reading Skills: 5–7 Pseudoword Decoding: 19–11 Oral Reading Fluency: 19–11 Numerical Operations: 19–11 Math Problem Solving: 19–11 Spelling: 19–11 Alphabet Writing Fl: 8–7 Receptive Vocab: 19–11 Oral Discourse Comp.: 19–11 Sentence Comb.: 19–11 Sentence Building: 10–11 Essay Composition: 19–11	Letter-Word Id.: 17–11 Reading Fluency: 90+ Story Recall: 90+ Understanding Directs.: 90+ Calculation: 90+ Math Fluency: 90+ Spelling: 90+ Writing Fluency: 90+ Passage Comp.: 90+ Applied Problems: 90+ Writing Samples: 90+ Story Recall-Delayed: 90+ Word Attack: 11–11	Letter Identification: None Phonological Awareness: 6–5 Rapid Auto. Naming: 8–11 Word Identification: 18–11 Word Attack: 10–11 Listening Comp.: 14–11 Word Comp.: 56–0+ Passage Comp.: 17–11 Oral Reading Fluency: 56–0+

(Continued)

Table 4.7 (Continued)

| | Achievement Battery | | |
Technical Features	WIAT-III (2009)	WJ III NU ACH (2001, 2007)*	WRMT-3 (2011)
	Math Fluency–Add: 11–11 Math Fluency–Sub: 13–3 Math Fluency–Mult: 12–11	Picture Vocabulary: 90+ Oral Comp.: 90+ Editing: 90+ Reading Vocabulary: 90+ Quantitative Concepts: 90+ Academic Knowledge: 90+ Spelling of Sounds: 90+ Sound Awareness: 90+ Punct. & Capital.: 90+ **5.0**	
Subtest scores reported on a scale having a mean of 100 and a standard deviation of 15	Yes	Yes	Yes
Composites reported on a scale having a mean of 100 and a standard deviation of 15	Yes	Yes	Yes

CELF-4 = Clinical Evaluation of Language Fundamentals–Fourth Edition; CTOPP-2 = Comprehensive Test of Phonological Processing–Second Edition; GORT-5 = Gray Oral Reading Tests–Fifth Edition; KM3 = KeyMath–Third Edition; KTEA-II = Kaufman Test of Educational Achievement–Second Edition; TOWL-4 = Test of Written Language–Fourth Edition; WIAT-III = Wechsler Individual Achievement Test–Third Edition; WJ III NU ACH = Woodcock-Johnson III Normative Update Tests of Achievement; WRMT-3 = Woodcock Reading Mastery Test–Third Edition.

ᵃ In most cases age blocks represent linear interpolations.
* Information based on Normative Update whenever possible.

The adequacy of the *size of the normative group* is dependent on the adequacy of its component parts. Although it is true that the larger the sample size, the more likely it is to be a better estimate of performance of the population as a whole, it is important to note that size alone is an insufficient indicator of norm sample adequacy. A carefully constructed small sample may in fact provide a closer match or correspondence with the population than a larger sample that is collected with less care or attention. Thus, evaluation of a standardization sample's component parts provides additional important indicators regarding the appropriateness of the overall sample size. In general, it is reasonable to assume that when the component characteristics of a standardization sample are adequate, the size of the normative sample is probably large enough to ensure stable values that are representative of the population under consideration (Anastasi & Urbina, 1997, p. 69).

Review and evaluation of the *average number of participants at each age/grade interval* in the normative sample provides important information about the generalizability of the sample. For instance, suppose that a particular battery was normed on 6,000 individuals ages 2 to 85 years. Relative to the size of most norm groups, 6,000 is quite large and, therefore, would appear to represent adequately the true performance of the general population of individuals from ages 2 to 85 years. However, suppose that a careful examination of the number of individuals included at every 1-year age interval revealed that only 50 individuals comprised the "3 years, 0 months, to 3 years, 11 months" interval, whereas all other 1-year age intervals included 200 individuals. The small number of 3-year-olds in this example suggests that this test does not adequately represent all 3-year-olds to whom this test might be given. To ensure that norms at a particular age (e.g., age 3) may be generalized to all individuals of that same age in the general population, practitioners should ensure that the average number of participants at the age level corresponding to the age of the individual being tested is adequate. In this regard, Alfonso and Flanagan (2009) and Flanagan and Alfonso (1995) recommended that there should be at least 200 individuals per each 1-year age interval and at least 2,000 individuals overall in the standardization sample.

Evaluation of the *recency* of the normative data for instruments is also important, because up-to-date normative comparisons must be made to ensure accurate interpretation of an individual's obtained score. For example, the use of outdated norms (i.e., more than 10 years old) may lead to overestimates of young children's functioning. In the vast majority of cases, normative information for any given instrument is gathered typically within 1 to 3 years of the instrument's date of publication. However, not all normative data are as recent as might be implied by the publication date of the instrument. Therefore, careful reading of an instrument's technical manual is important.

The *age divisions of norm tables* are also important, particularly for very young children. An age division or block in a norm table contains the data from a selected age range of the normative sample against which an individual's performance is compared. Age blocks can range from 1-month intervals to 1-, 5-, or even 10-year intervals. Although it is possible, and even desirable, to provide norms for every specific age (e.g., 3 years, 1 month; 3 years, 2 months, etc.), the dramatic increase in the number of individuals needed to develop such norms makes this task impractical. Therefore, authors and publishers of tests that are appropriate for young children generally attempt to ensure that the age divisions are small enough to yield valid estimates of functioning relative to similar same-aged peers in the general population. Norms for ages or grades that were not sampled directly are derived by interpolation. Naturally, age blocks at the youngest age range (e.g., ages 2–5 years) of the test should typically be quite small (e.g., 1-month intervals), due to the rapid rate of growth along the ability dimensions measured by the instrument. Conversely, age divisions at the upper end of the test's age range (e.g., 75–95 years) may be rather large (e.g., 5-year age blocks), due to slower and less variable growth rates of older individuals along the ability dimensions measured by the test.

Also important to understanding the overall adequacy of a test's standardization is the *match of the demographic characteristics of the normative group to the U.S. population*. According to the *Standards for Educational and Psychological Testing*, the demographic characteristics of a standardization sample are important variables that play a role in the test selection process. Specifically, "selecting a test with demographically appropriate normative groups relevant for the [individual] being tested is important to the generalizability of the inferences that the [practitioner] seeks to make" (American Educational Research Association, American Psychological Association, American Council on Measurement [AERA, APA, NCME], 1999, p. 120). Therefore, the variables included in the norming plan provide information about the representativeness of the norm sample, or how well the characteristics of the norm sample reflect the characteristics of the general population.

Evaluation of the variables included in the norming plan, and hence the representativeness of the norm sample relative to the general population, is particularly important because "the validity of norm-referenced interpretations depends in part on the appropriateness of the reference group to which test scores are compared" (AERA et al., 1999, p. 51). Therefore, the standardization sample on which the norms of an instrument are based should be appropriately representative of the individuals on whom the instrument will be used. Appropriate representation is achieved primarily through consideration of both the *number* and *type* of variables included in the norming plan.

Typically, test developers look to establish as much correspondence between their norm sample and the general population on the basis of stratification of a wide variety of characteristics that typically include gender, race, ethnicity, socioeconomic status (SES), geographic region, and residence location. The greater the stratification of a norm sample on the basis of these and other variables, assuming that a close correspondence with the true proportion of these variables in the general population was achieved, the more likely the norm sample provides a reliable and accurate estimate of the performance of the population as a whole. For example, SES may be represented by a single variable, such as parental income. But more frequently, it is represented by a combination of subcategories in addition to parental income, such as occupation and educational attainment. Going to such lengths to represent SES, for example, is important because this variable has been found to be a strong predictor of a number of outcomes, including overall cognitive ability and academic achievement (Collier, 1992; Gould, 1981; Neisser et al., 1996; Thomas & Collier, 1997).

Because it is impractical to achieve an exact match between the standardization sample and the U.S. population characteristics through a purely random sampling method, weighting procedures have become routine (see McGrew et al., 1991). In general, tests that have relatively large standardization samples (e.g., 2,000 participants or greater) and that possess adequate component characteristics will likely have norm groups that closely match the general population characteristics. This will not, of course, be true in every case; therefore, practitioners should pay close attention to the number and type of demographic variables included in the norming plan. Norm groups that are considered appropriate typically represent the U.S. population on five or more important demographic variables, including SES (Alfonso & Flanagan, 2009; Flanagan & Alfonso, 1995).

Subtest floors and ceilings. Table 4.7 includes the lowest and highest ages at which individual subtest floors and ceilings are adequate, respectively. Tests with adequate floors and ceilings will yield scores that effectively discriminate among various degrees of functioning at the extremes of an ability continuum. A test with an *inadequate floor,* or an insufficient number of easy items, may not distinguish adequately between individuals functioning in the average, low average, and deficient ranges of ability. Likewise, a test with an *inadequate ceiling,* or an insufficient number of difficult items, may not distinguish adequately between individuals who function in the average, high average, and superior ranges of ability. Thus, a test that does not have adequate floors or ceilings may not provide information with sufficient precision for diagnostic, classification or placement decisions, especially with individuals functioning at or near the extreme ranges of the ability continuum.

For test floors, subtests in which a raw score of 1 was associated with a standard score that was *more than* 2 standard deviations below the normative mean of the test were considered adequate. If this condition was not met, the subtest floor was considered inadequate. Similarly, for test ceilings, the maximum raw score for the test had to be associated with a standard score that was *more than* 2 standard deviations above the normative mean of the test to be considered adequate. Failure to meet this criterion resulted in a test ceiling being considered inadequate. To simplify the presentation of this information, Table 4.7 lists only the lowest age at which a subtest floor is adequate and the highest age at which a subtest ceiling is adequate.

Reliability. *Reliability* refers to "the consistency of scores obtained by the same persons when they are reexamined with the same test on different occasions, or with different sets of equivalent items, or under other variable examining conditions" (Anastasi & Urbina, 1997, p. 84). The reliability of a scale affects practitioners' interpretations of the test results because it guides decisions regarding the range of scores (i.e., standard error of measurement) likely to occur as the result of factors that are not directly relevant to actual ability or performance (e.g., measurement error, chance, etc.). Test reliability, in its broadest sense, indicates the extent to which individual differences can be attributed to true differences in the characteristics under investigation or to error or chance (Anastasi & Urbina). The degree of confidence a practitioner can place in the precision of a test score is related directly to the estimated reliability of the test score. Unreliable test scores can contribute to misdiagnosis and inappropriate placement and treatment. This potential problem can be reduced significantly by selecting tests that have good reliability and, thus, fewer errors associated with their scores or by combining individual test scores into composites. In the latter case, measurement of the same or highly related abilities provides information that converges toward true performance, thereby increasing reliability. For in-depth treatment of reliability concepts, the reader is referred to Anastasi and Urbina, Crocker and Algina (1986), Lord and Novick (1968), Nunnally (1978), Salvia and Ysseldyke (1991), and Sattler (2001).

Given the importance of this characteristic as related to both test selection and interpretation, the individual mean internal consistency reliability coefficients for each subtest and composite of each achievement battery are reported in Table 4.8. In general, reliability coefficients of .90 and above are considered *high*, coefficients of .80 to .89 are considered *moderate*, and coefficients that are less than .80 are considered *low*. These descriptors provide an indication of the degree of confidence that can be placed in test score interpretation. Specifically, tests with high reliability yield scores that are sufficiently reliable for use in diagnostic decision-making when supported with converging data sources. Tests with moderate reliability are used most appropriately to make screening decisions. It is possible, however, to combine tests with moderate reliability with other similar measures to form a more reliable and stable composite. Tests with low reliability yield scores that are insufficiently reliable for most purposes and, therefore, should not be used to make either screening or diagnostic decisions.

Validity. Much like the variable and complex nature of norm samples, validity is not an "all-or-nothing" condition, and the validity of one test is dependent on the validity of the criterion measure to which it is being compared (Bracken, 1987, p. 317). Because the concept of validity itself is more abstract than is the concept of reliability, for example, it is difficult to agree on specific criteria that are appropriate for evaluating the adequacy of the validity evidence reported for any given test (Hammill et al., 1992). The criteria that currently exist for specifying the conditions under which an instrument is determined to be valid are rather arbitrary and confusing. Therefore, we do not review test validity here.

The *Standards for Educational and Psychological Testing* state that practitioners are responsible for familiarizing themselves with the validity evidence "for the intended use and purposes of the tests and inventories selected" (AERA et al., 1999, p. 120). Therefore, it is incumbent on practitioners to review the types of validity evidence that are available for the achievement batteries they use. Typically, a standardized norm-referenced test should include in its technical manual at least 3–5 strands of validity evidence (Alfonso & Flangan, 2009; Flanagan & Alfonso, 1995). For further discussion of validity concepts, the reader is referred to AERA and associates (1999), Aiken (2000), Anastasi and Urbina (1997), Gregory (2000), Salvia and Ysseldyke (1991), and Sattler (2001).

Table 4.8 Reliability of Selected Achievement Batteries

Subtest Composite	CELF-4[a]	CTOPP-2[a]	GORT-5[a]	KTEA-II[a]	KM3[b]	TOWL-4[a]	WIAT-III[a]	WJ III NU ACH[c]	WRMT-3[a]
CELF-4 Expressive Vocabulary	.83								
CELF-4 Formulated Sentences	.81								
CELF-4 Sentence Assembly	.85								
CELF-4 Word Classes-Expressive	.82								
CELF-4 Word Definitions	.86								
CELF-4 Concepts and Following Directions	.87								
CELF-4 Semantic Relationships	.82								
CELF-4 Sentence Structure	.70								
CELF-4 Understanding Spoken Paragraph	.69								
CELF-4 Word Classes-Receptive	.82								
CELF-4 Word Structure	.83								
CELF-4 Recalling Sentences	.91								
CELF-4 Familiar Sequences	.84								
CELF-4 Number Repetition Forward	.80								
CELF-4 Number Repetition Backward	.78								
CELF-4 Core Language Score	**.95**								
CELF-4 Receptive Language Index	**.89**								
CELF-4 Expressive Language Index	**.93**								
CELF-4 Language Content Index	**.92**								
CELF-4 Language Structure Index	**.93**								
CELF-4 Language Memory Index	**.91**								
CELF-4 Working Memory Index	**.87**								
CTOPP-2 Elision		.91[a]							
CTOPP-2 Blending Words		.86							
CTOPP-2 Phoneme Isolation		.88							
CTOPP-2 Sound Matching		.93							
CTOPP-2 Memory for Digits		.81							
CTOPP-2 Nonword Repetition		.77							
CTOPP-2 Blending Nonwords		.83							
CTOPP-2 Segmenting Nonwords		.90							
CTOPP-2 Phonological Awareness		**.92**							
CTOPP-2 Phonological Memory		**.85**							
CTOPP-2 Alt. Phonological Awareness		**.93**							
GORT-5 Accuracy			.91 (A)[a] .92 (B)						
GORT-5 Comprehension			.94 .94						

Subtest Composite	CELF-4[a]	CTOPP-2[a]	GORT-5[a]	KTEA-II	KM3[b]	TOWL-4[a]	WIAT-III[a]	WJ III NU ACH[c]	WRMT-3[a]
GORT-5 Rate			.92 .92						
GORT-5 Fluency			.93 .93						
GORT-5 Oral Reading Index			**.96** .97						
KTEA-II Letter and Word Recognition				.97[a]					
KTEA-II Nonsense Word Decoding				.94					
KTEA-II Phonological Awareness				.88					
KTEA-II Reading Comprehension				.93					
KTEA-II Naming Facility				.89					
KTEA-II Math Concepts and Applications				.93					
KTEA-II Math Computation				.94					
KTEA-II Associational Fluency				.72					
KTEA-II Oral Expression				.79					
KTEA-II Listening Comprehension				.85					
KTEA-II Spelling				.94					
KTEA-II Written Expression				.87					
KTEA-II Reading				**.97**					
KTEA-II Mathematics				**.96**					
KTEA-II Written Language				**.94**					
KTEA-II Oral Language				**.87**					
KM3 Addition and Subtraction					.86[b] .86				
KM3 Numeration					.87 .89				
KM3 Algebra					.84 .85				
KM3 Geometry					.79 .81				
KM3 Measurement					.85 .86				
KM3 Mental Computation and Estimation					.90 .91				
KM3 Multiplication and Division					.91 .91				
KM3 Applied Problem Solving					.87 .86				
KM3 Data Analysis and Probability					.83 .82				

(Continued)

Table 4.8 (Continued)

Subtest Composite	CELF-4[a]	CTOPP-2[a]	GORT-5[a]	KTEA-II[a]	KM3[b]	TOWL-4[a]	WIAT-III[a]	WJ III NU ACH[c]	WRMT-3[a]
KM3 Foundations and Problem Solving					.79				
					.79				
KM3 Basic Concepts					**.94**				
					.94				
KM3 Operations					**.93**				
					.93				
KM3 Applications					**.87**				
					.87				
KM3 Total Test					**.96**				
					.96				
TOWL-4 Contextual Conventions						.80[a]			
TOWL-4 Logical Sentences						.77			
TOWL-4 Punctuation						.92			
TOWL-4 Sentence Combining						.87			
TOWL-4 Spelling						.91			
TOWL-4 Story Composition						.74			
TOWL-4 Vocabulary						.90			
TOWL-4 Contrived Writing						**.96**			
TOWL-4 Spontaneous Writing						**.84**			
TOWL-4 Overall Writing						**.96**			
WIAT-III Word Reading							.97[a]		
WIAT-III Reading Comprehension							.86		
WIAT-III Early Reading Skills							.90		
WIAT-III Pseudoword Decoding							.97		
WIAT-III Oral Reading Fluency							.93		
WIAT-III Numerical Operations							.93		
WIAT-III Math Problem Solving							.91		
WIAT-III Spelling							.95		
WIAT-III Alphabet Writing Fluency							.69		
WIAT-III Sentence Composition							.87		
WIAT-III Essay Composition							.88		
WIAT-III Listening Comprehension							.83		
WIAT-III Oral Expression							.87		
WIAT-III Oral Language							**.91**		
WIAT-III Total Reading							**.97**		
WIAT-III Basic Reading							**.98**		
WIAT-III Reading Comp and Fluency							**.92**		
WIAT-III Written Expression							**.94**		
WIAT-III Mathematics							**.96**		

Subtest Composite	CELF-4[a]	CTOPP-2[a]	GORT-5[a]	KTEA-II[a]	KM3[b]	TOWL-4[a]	WIAT-III[a]	WJ III NU ACH[c]	WRMT-3[a]
WIAT-III Math Fluency							.95		
WIAT-III Total Achievement							.98		
WJ III NU ACH Letter/Word Identification								.94[c]	
WJ III NU ACH Reading Fluency								.95	
WJ III NU ACH Calculation								.86	
WJ III NU ACH Story Recall								.87	
WJ III NU ACH Understanding Directions								.83	
WJ III NU ACH Math Fluency								.98	
WJ III NU ACH Spelling								.90	
WJ III NU ACH Writing Fluency								.83	
WJ III NU ACH Passage Comprehension								.88	
WJ III NU ACH Applied Problems								.93	
WJ III NU ACH Writing Samples								.75	
WJ III NU ACH Story Recall-Delayed								.81	
WJ III NU ACH Word Attack								.87	
WJ III NU ACH Picture Vocabulary								.81	
WJ III NU ACH Oral Comprehension								.85	
WJ III NU ACH Editing								.90	
WJ III NU ACH Reading Vocabulary								.90	
WJ III NU ACH Quantitative Concepts								.91	
WJ III NU ACH Academic Knowledge								.90	
WJ III NU ACH Spelling of Sounds								.76	
WJ III NU ACH Sound Awareness								.81	
WJ III NU ACH Punctuation and Capitalization								.79	
WJ III NU ACH Total Achievement								.98	
WJ III NU ACH Broad Reading								.96	
WJ III NU ACH Basic Reading Skills								.95	
WJ III NU ACH Reading Comprehension								.93	
WJ III NU ACH Oral Language Standard								.87	
WJ III NU ACH Oral Language Extended								.92	
WJ III NU ACH Listening Comprehension								.89	
WJ III NU ACH Oral Expression								.85	
WJ III NU ACH Broad Math								.95	
WJ III NU ACH Math Calculation Skills								.91	
WJ III NU ACH Math Reasoning								.95	
WJ III NU ACH Broad Written Language								.92	
WJ III NU ACH Basic Writing Skills								.94	
WJ III NU ACH Written Expression								.85	

(*Continued*)

Table 4.8 (Continued)

Subtest Composite	CELF-4[a]	CTOPP-2[a]	GORT-5[a]	KTEA-II[a]	KM3[b]	TOWL-4[a]	WIAT-III[a]	WJ III NU ACH[c]	WRMT-3[a]
WJ III NU ACH Academic Skills								.96	
WJ III NU ACH Academic Fluency								.96	
WJ III NU ACH Academic Applications								.94	
WJ III NU ACH Phoneme/Grapheme Knowledge								.90	
WRMT-3 Letter Identification									.83[a]
									.87
WRMT-3 Phonological Awareness									.88
									.91
WRMT-3 Rapid Automatic Naming (Object + Color)									.83
									.83
WRMT-3 Rapid Automatic Naming (Number + Letter)									.88
									.88
WRMT-3 Word Attack									.89
									.88
WRMT-3 Word Comprehension									.94
									.94
WRMT-3 Word Identification									.91
									.92
WRMT-3 Passage Comprehension									.88
									.87
WRMT-3 Oral Reading Fluency									.95
									.93
WRMT-3 Listening Comprehension									.88
									.87
WRMT-3 Readiness with RAN O+C									.93
									.95
WRMT-3 Readiness with RAN N+L									.93
									.93
WRMT-3 Basic Skills									.94
									.94
WRMT-3 Reading Comprehension									.95
									.94
WRMT-3 Total Reading									.97
									.97

[a] Internal consistency reliability average computed with Fisher's z transformations.

[b] Internal consistency reliability computed by averaging age-based coefficient alphas.

[c] Internal consistency reliability reported as the median.

CELF-4 = Clinical Evaluation of Language Fundamentals–Fourth Edition; CTOPP-2 = Comprehensive Test of Phonological Processing–Second Edition; GORT-5 = Gray Oral Reading Tests–Fifth Edition; KM3 = KeyMath–Third Edition; KTEA-II = Kaufman Test of Educational Achievement–Second Edition; TOWL-4 = Test of Written Language–Fourth Edition; WIAT-III = Wechsler Individual Achievement Test–Third Edition; WJ III NU ACH = Woodcock-Johnson III Normative Update Tests of Achievement; WRMT-3 = Woodcock Reading Mastery Test–Third Edition.

Summary

The purpose of this chapter was to provide practitioners with what we believe to be some of the most salient features of academic achievement batteries that should be considered when measuring the academic capabilities and skill levels of all students. We provided detailed information on nine achievement batteries along with a number of different dimensions, including interpretation features, specific IDEIA academic areas (from the SLD definition) associated with achievement subtests, variation in task demands and task characteristics of each subtest on each battery, and qualitative and quantitative characteristics, such as content features, administration procedures, and technical properties. Practitioners may apply the information provided here for the nine selected achievement batteries to any achievement battery so that they may make informed decisions regarding test selection, generate interpretations that are theoretically and psychometrically defensible, and assist with intervention planning.

References

Aiken, L. R. (2000). *Psychological testing and assessment* (10th ed.). Boston: Allyn and Bacon.

Alfonso, V. C., & Flanagan, D. P. (2009). Assessment of preschool children. In B. A. Mowder, F. Rubinson, & A. Yasik (Eds.), *Evidence-based practice in infant and early childhood Psychology* (pp. 129–166). New York, NY: John Wiley and Sons.

Alfonso, V. C., Flanagan, D. P., & Radwan, S. W. (2005). The impact of Cattell-Horn-Carroll theory on test development and interpretation of cognitive and academic abilities. In D. P. Flanagan & P. L. Harrison (Eds.), *Contemporary intellectual assessment: Theories, tests, and issues* (2nd ed., pp. 185–202). New York, NY: Guilford.

American Educational Research Association, American Psychological Association, American Council on Measurement (AERA, APA, NCME). (1999). *Standards for educational and psychological testing*. Washington, DC: American Educational Research Association.

Anastasi, A., & Urbina, S. (1997). *Psychological testing* (7th ed.). Upper Saddle River, NJ: Prentice Hall.

Bracken, B. A. (1987). Limitations of preschool instruments and standards for minimal levels of technical adequacy. *Journal of Psychoeducational Assessment, 4,* 313–326.

Carroll, J. B. (1993). *Human cognitive abilities: A survey of factor-analytic studies.* Cambridge, UK: Cambridge University Press.

Carroll, J. B. (1997). The three-stratum theory of cognitive abilities. In D. P. Flanagan, J. L. Genshaft, & P. L. Harrison (Eds.), *Contemporary intellectual assessment: Theories, tests, and issues* (pp. 122–130). New York, NY: Guilford.

Carroll, J. B. (1998). Foreword. In K. S. McGrew & D. P. Flanagan, *The intelligence test desk reference (ITDR): Gf-Gc cross-battery assessment* (pp. xi–xii). Boston, MA: Allyn & Bacon.

Collier, V. P. (1992). A synthesis of studies examining long-term language minority student data on academic achievement. *Bilingual Research Journal, 16,* 187–212.

Connolly, A. J. (2007). KeyMath-3. Bloomington, MN: Pearson Assessment.

Crocker, L., & Algina, J. (1986). *Introduction to classical and modern test theory.* New York, NY: Holt, Rinehart, & Winston.

Flanagan, D. P., & Alfonso, V. C. (1995). A critical review of the technical characteristics of new and recently revised intelligence tests for preschool children. *Journal of Psychoeducational Assessment, 13,* 66–90.

Flanagan, D. P., Alfonso, V. C., Mascolo, J. T., & Sotelo-Dynega, M. (2012). Use of ability tests in the identification of specific learning disabilities within the context of an operational definition. In D. P. Flanagan & P. L. Harrison (Eds.), *Contemporary intellectual assessment: Theories, tests, and issues* (3rd ed., pp. 643–669). New York, NY: Guilford Press.

Flanagan, D. P., Alfonso, V. C., & Ortiz, S. O. (2012). The cross-battery assessment approach: An overview, historical perspective, and current directions. In D. P. Flanagan & P. L. Harrison (Eds.), *Contemporary intellectual assessment: Theories, tests, and issues* (3rd ed., pp. 459–483). New York, NY: Guilford Press.

Flanagan, D. P., Alfonso, V. C., Ortiz, S. O., & Dynda, A. (2010). Integrating cognitive assessment in school neuropsychological evaluations. In D.C. Miller (Ed.), *Best practices in school neuropsychology: Guidelines for effective practice, assessment, and evidence-based intervention* (pp. 101–140). Hoboken, NJ: John Wiley & Sons.

Flanagan, D. P., & Harrison, P. (2012). *Contemporary intellectual assessment: Theories, tests, and issues* (3rd ed., pp. 820–838). New York, NY: Guilford Press.

Flanagan, D. P., & Ortiz, S. O. (2001). *Essentials of cross-battery assessment.* New York, NY: Wiley.

Flanagan, D. P., Ortiz, S. O., & Alfonso, V. C. (2007). *Essentials of cross-battery assessment* (2nd ed.). Hoboken, NJ: John Wiley & Sons.

Flanagan, D. P., Ortiz, S. O., & Alfonso, V. C. (2013). *Essentials of cross-battery assessment* (3rd ed.). Hoboken, NJ: John Wiley & Sons.

Flanagan, D. P., Ortiz, S., Alfonso, V. C., & Mascolo, J. (2002). *The achievement test desk reference (ATDR): Comprehensive assessment and learning disabilities.* New York, NY: Allyn & Bacon.

Flanagan, D. P., Ortiz, S., Alfonso, V. C., & Mascolo, J. (2006). *The achievement test desk reference: A guide to learning disability identification* (2nd ed.). John Wiley & Sons, Inc., Hoboken, New Jersey.

Gould, S. J. (1981). *The mismeasure of man.* New York, NY: W. W. Norton.

Gregory, R. J. (2000). *Psychological testing: History, principles, and applications* (3rd ed.). Boston, MA: Allyn & Bacon.

Hammill, D. D., Brown, & Bryant, B. R. (1992). *A consumer's guide to tests in print.* Austin, TX: Pro-Ed.

Hammill, D. D., & Larsen, S. C. (2009). Test of Written Language. (4th ed.). Austin, TX: Pro-Ed.

Horn, J. L. (1988). Thinking about human abilities. In J. R. Nesselroade & R. B. Cattell (Eds.), *Handbook of multivariate psychology* (Rev. ed., pp. 645–685). New York, NY: Academic Press.

Horn, J. L., & Blankson, N. (2005). Foundations for better understanding of cognitive abilities. In D. P. Flanagan, J. L. Genshaft, & P. L. Harrison (Eds.), *Contemporary intellectual assessment: Theories, tests, and issues* (2nd ed., pp. 41–68). New York, NY: Guilford.

Individuals With Disabilities Education Improvement Act of 2004 (IDEIA) P.L. 108–446, 118 Stat. 2647 (2004). (Amending U.S.C. §§ 1400 et. seq.).

Kaufman, A. S., & Kaufman, N. L. (2004). Kaufman Test of Educational Achievement—Second Edition. Circle Pines, MN: AGS.

Lord, F., & Novick, M. (1968). *Statistical theories of mental test scores.* Reading, MA: Addison Wesley Publishing.

Mascolo, J. T. (2013). Variation in task demands and task characteristics of subtest on achievement batteries by IDEA academic area. In D. P. Flanagan, S. O. Ortiz, & V. C. Alfonso (Eds.), *Essentials of cross-battery assessment* (3rd ed., p. 439). Hoboken, NJ: John Wiley & Sons.

McGrew, K. S. (2005). The Cattell-Horn-Carroll theory of cognitive abilities: Past, present, and future. In D. P. Flanagan & P. L. Harrison (Eds.), *Contemporary intellectual assessment: Theories, tests, and issues* (2nd ed., pp. 136–182). New York, NY: Guilford.

McGrew, K. S., & Flanagan, D. P. (1998). *The Intelligence Test Desk Reference (ITDR): Gf-Gc cross-battery assessment.* Boston, MA: Allyn & Bacon.

McGrew, K. S., Werder, J. K., & Woodcock, R. W. (1991). *Woodcock-Johnson Psycho-Educational Battery—Revised technical manual.* Chicago, IL: Riverside.

McGrew, K. S., & Woodcock, R. W. (2001). *Technical manual: Woodcock-Johnson III.* Itasca, IL: Riverside.

Mercer, C. D. (1997). *Students with learning disabilities* (5th ed.). Upper Saddle River, NJ: Prentice Hall.

Neisser, U., Boodoo, G., Bouchard, T. J., Boykin, A. W., Brody, N., Ceci, S. J., . . . Urbina, S. (1996). Intelligence: Knowns and unknowns. *American Psychologist, 51,* 77–101.

Nunnally, J. S. (1978). *Psychometric theories.* New York, NY: McGraw-Hill.

Salvia, J., & Ysseldyke, J. (1991). *Assessment in special and remedial education* (5th ed.). Boston, MA: Houghton-Mifflin.

Sattler, J. M. (2001). *Assessment of children: Cognitive applications* (4th ed.). La Mesa, CA: Jerome M. Sattler.

Schneider, J. W., & McGrew, K. S. (2012). The Cattell-Horn-Carroll model of intelligence. In D. P. Flanagan & P. L. Harrison (Eds.), *Contemporary intellectual assessment: Theories, tests, and issues* (3rd ed., pp. 99–144). New York, NY: Guilford Press.

Semel, E., Wiig, E. H., & Secord, W. A. (2003). *Clinical evaluation of language fundamentals, fourth edition* (CELF-4). Toronto, Canada: The Psychological Corporation/A Harcourt Assessment Company.

Snow, R. E. (1994). Abilities and aptitudes. In R. J. Sternberg (Eds.), *Encyclopedia of human intelligence* (pp. 3–5). New York, NY: Macmillan.

Thomas, W. P., & Collier, V. P. (1997). *School effectiveness for language minority students.* Washington, DC: National Clearinghouse on Bilingual Education.

Wagner, R. K., Torgesen, J. K., Rashotte, C. A., & Pearson, N. A. (2013). Comprehensive test of phonological processing. Austin, TX: PRO-ED.

Wechsler, D. (2003). *Wechsler Intelligence Scale for Children* (4th ed.). San Antonio, TX: Psychological Corporation.

Wiederholt, L., & Bryant, B. R. (2012). Gray Oral Reading Tests—Fifth Edition (GORT-5). Austin, TX: Pro-Ed.

Woodcock, R. W. (2011). Woodcock reading mastery tests (3rd ed.) Boston: Pearson.

Woodcock, R. W., McGrew, K. S., & Mather, N. (2001). *Woodcock-Johnson III Tests of Achievement.* Itasca, IL: Riverside.

Woodcock, R. W., Schrank, F. A., Mather, N., & McGrew, K. S. (2007). *Woodcock-Johnson III: Normative update.* Rolling Meadows, IL: Riverside Publishing.

5

Individual Assessment of Specific Academic Areas

Cynthia A. Riccio, Andrea Dennison, and Lisa Bowman-Perrott

Concern with academic achievement has resulted in state and federal legislation intended to improve student educational outcomes. With this concern, there has been increased emphasis on curriculum-based and class-wide assessment of basic academic skills (see Section III of this volume). The information obtained from these measures as part of the accountability and benchmarking process can be used to determine students who are in need of intensive intervention, commonly referred to as Tier 2 within the Response to Intervention (RTI) framework. In some situations, a student continues to struggle despite Tier 2 intervention (Brown-Chidsey, 2008; Fuchs & Fuchs, 2002). More in-depth individual assessment of specific skills may be needed, and the student may be referred for a comprehensive or "full individual initial evaluation" (FIE; Individuals with Disabilities Education Improvement Act [IDEIA], 2004).

The FIE typically includes review of existing evaluation data, sociological/cultural and health history, sensory and motor skills, cognitive processes, speech and language development, current academic skills, adaptive skills, personality and behavior, and consideration of assistive technology, yielding a summary of findings and recommendations. For the academic skills component, the student is administered standardized, norm-referenced measures of achievement, with the intent to provide information on pattern of academic strengths and weaknesses of the student (PSW; e.g., Compton, Fuchs, Fuchs, Lambert, & Hamlett, 2012; Hale & Fiorello, 2004; Mather, Wendling, Naglieri, & Goldstein, 2009). Additional assessment of underlying cognitive processes (e.g., phonological processes, processing speed) in the deficit areas links cognitive and academic PSW (Fuchs, Hale, & Kearns, 2011). With PSW, it is important to not only consider the skill set(s) of concern (e.g., reading fluency), but also those that are not identified as concern.

Selection of the measure(s) used in the assessment of achievement should meet psychometric standards and be consistent with the presenting concerns (i.e., Trina doesn't understand what she reads), as well as meeting the requirements of special educational law for determination of eligibility. For the first of these, standards for tests and measurement have been established (American Educational Research Association, American Psychological Association, & National Council on Measurement in Education [AERA, APA, & NCME], 1999). Standards include reliability and validity, as well as consideration of basic measurement issues. For culturally and linguistically diverse learners, the cultural and linguistic load of the tests should be considered (AERA et al., 1999; Ortiz, 2008). There are currently no batteries that have been normed on bilingual students. Therefore, assessors must always keep in mind that the norms against which dual language learners are compared do not reflect their unique academic and linguistic experiences.

The second consideration, related to the more specific concerns of the individual child, looks at the type and formats used to assess the academic skill sets. This chapter reviews some of the measures that are frequently used in the individual assessment of academic skills in relation to curricular areas of reading, written expression, and mathematics. The discussion includes not only the achievement batteries, but also examples of measures of specific academic skills, and, when appropriate, less-formalized approaches to individual assessment of specific academic skills. Individual assessment of specific skills is more complex when considering cultural and linguistic differences. Following the discussion of individual achievement measures by specific skill area is a discussion of the availability of measures for the English language learner (ELL). The discussion here is not intended to serve as a critical review of measures or an endorsement of their use.

Assessment of achievement, however approached, is one component of a problem-solving, data-based decision-making model (Brown-Chidsey, 2008). The purpose of the FIE is to provide meaningful information that will inform intervention planning and improve student outcomes, as well as determination of eligibility for services. The process of hypothesis generation and confirmation in academic assessment, as in behavioral assessment, contributes to the likelihood that the interventions used with the individual student are appropriate for that student's level of competency and address the target skill (Batsche, Castillo, Dixon, & Forde, 2008). Although measures often provide composite scores, it is important to consider the various subskills that comprise such a composite score to identify which skill set(s) must be targeted for intervention. With the end goal of intervention for identified problems, the chapter will end by connecting assessment of specific academic skills to one approach to class-wide intervention.

Achievement Batteries

In consideration of comprehensive academic assessment, practitioners often will use one of the published batteries discussed in Chapter 4. Available batteries include the Kaufman Test of Educational Achievement, second edition (KTEA-II; Kaufman & Kaufman, 2004a), the Peabody Individual Achievement Test—Revised/Normative Update (PIAT-R/NU; Markwardt, 1998), the Wechsler Individual Achievement Test, third edition (WIAT-III; Wechsler, 2009), and the Woodcock Johnson, third edition—Tests of Achievement, normative update (WJ-III Achieve; Woodcock, McGrew, & Mather, 2007a). Each of these includes multiple subtests, each addressing a specific academic skill or subskill. These batteries are most often used to get a complete picture of achievement, as well as to identify the individual's PSW. Individual subtest scores as well as composite scores generated align with the academic skills areas specified in IDEIA for determination of specific learning disability (SLD), as well as others. Abbreviated versions of these batteries, intended for screening, are also available. These include the KTEA-II Brief (Kaufman & Kaufman, 2004b), and the Wide Range Achievement Test, fourth edition (Wilkinson &

Robertson, 2006) among others. The manner and scope with which each battery assesses academic skills differs. Further, there are additional measures of specific academic skills available.

Individual Assessment of Reading Skills

It has long been recognized that reading is a not a unitary task, but in fact requires the integration of multiple skills (National Institute of Child Health and Human Development [NICHD], 2000) with simple and more complex models proposed for reading (e.g., Joshi & Aaron, 2000). These component skills are often considered in terms of decoding, word recognition, reading vocabulary, reading comprehension at literal and inferential levels, and reading fluency. As such, when someone is struggling in reading, any of these, or a combination, may be deficient. There are a number of measures of reading available, but the extent to which each measures the various skills varies (see Table 5.1).

Table 5.1 Matrix of Reading Components and Measures

Battery/Test	Decoding Pseudowords	Letter/Word Recognition	Vocabulary	General Knowledge	Comprehension: Text	Comprehension: Cloze/Maze Task	Reading Fluency
DAB-3		◆	◆		◆		
KTEA-II	◆	◆			◆		◆
PIAT-R/NU		◆			◆		
WIAT-III	◆	◆			◆		◆
WJ-III Achieve/ Batería-III (Standard)		◆				◆	◆
WJ-III Achieve/ Batería-III (Extended)	◆		◆	◆			
GDRT-2	◆	◆	◆		◆		
GORT-5					◆		◆
GSRT					◆		
OWLS-2					◆		
TORC-4			◆		◆	◆	◆
TOWRE	◆	◆					◆
WRMT-III	◆	◆	◆			◆	
WRAT-4		◆				◆	
WMLS-R/NU		◆	◆			◆	
YCAT/PHAI		◆		◆	◆		

Notes: Bateria-III = Batería, third edition—*Woodcock Muñoz Pruebas de Aprovechamiento*; DAB-3 = Diagnostic Achievement Battery, third edition (Newcomer, 2001); GDRT-2 = Gray Diagnostic Reading Tests, second edition; GORT-5 = Gray Oral Reading Tests, fifth edition; GSRT = Gray Silent Reading Test, fourth edition; KTEA-II = Kaufman Test of Educational Achievement, second edition; TORC-4 = Test of Reading Comprehension, fourth edition; TOWRE = Test of Word Reading Efficiency; WRAT-4 = Wide Range Achievement Test, fourth edition; WRMT-III = Woodcock Reading Mastery Tests, third edition; PHAI = *Pruebas de Habilidades Académicas Iniciales*; YCAT = Young Children's Achievement Test; PIAT-R/NU = Peabody Individual Achievement Test—Revised/ Normative Update; WIAT-III = Wechsler Individual Achievement Test, third edition; WJ-III Achieve = Woodcock Johnson Tests of Achievement, third edition—Normative Update; OWLS-2 = Oral and Written Language Scales, second edition (Carrow-Woolfolk, 2011); WMLS-R/ NU = Woodcock-Muñoz Language Survey—Revised/Normative Update.

Basic Reading Skills

Phonological processing, which includes the ability to apply phonological skills to decode words or pseudowords, and letter/word recognition, which involves the accurate recognition of printed text as meaningful, are viewed as the foundations for literacy (Ehri, 2005). These skills require basic recognition of the sound-symbol system (phonology) and the recognition of the visual configuration (orthography) of words in language. Reading skills progress from the effortful task of applying sound-symbol relations to the quicker task of word recognition (Ehri, 2005). Because both decoding and recognition are needed for reading, it is important that both skills be included in the assessment process.

Almost all of the achievement batteries include a subtest that is comprised of letter and word recognition; however, fewer measures include a pseudoword decoding task as part of the standard battery (see Table 5.1), despite the critical role of sound-symbol relations in reading. Some batteries, for example, the WJ-III Achieve, include this type of task as supplemental. Notably, the underlying processes for decoding and recognition are different, with the former dependent on phonological processing and the latter on the ability to connect a word to a visual cue and to remember that connection over time. When deficits are identified in decoding skills, aspects of phonological processing and auditory abilities can then be explored using the Sound Awareness subtest (WJ-III Achieve), the various phonological subtests of the Woodcock Reading Mastery Tests—third edition (WRMT-III, Woodcock, 2011), or the Comprehensive Test of Phonological Processing (CTOPP, Wagner, Torgesen, & Rashotte, 1999). Alternatively, the ability to form associations between auditory and visual information can be assessed with the visual-auditory subtest on the Woodcock Johnston, third edition Tests of Cognitive Ability, normative update (Woodcock et al., 2007b), as well as short-term visual and auditory memory from other cognitive measures.

Reading Fluency

From both a theoretical and empirical base, mastery of basic decoding and recognition skills leads to automatized processing of print and increased reading fluency by freeing up capacity for higher-level comprehension (LaBerge & Samuels, 1974). In effect, as individuals master the decoding process and increase the number of words that are in their visual memory bank, reading is no longer a letter-by-letter or word-by-word process, but is automatic. Many have argued that comprehension and fluency are bidirectional, such that the connections among ideas in text (i.e., comprehension) contribute to fluency (Fuchs, Fuchs, Hosp, & Jenkins, 2001; Samuels, 2006).

Although many measures yield a fluency score or reading rate (see Table 5.1), the tasks that are used may vary. For example, the task may be to read a list of words and then determine the number of words read correctly in one minute; to read a passage aloud or silently for one minute and then determine the number of words read; to read a passage aloud or silently with the time to completion as the variable of interest; to read a series of sentences and for each sentence to then determine if the statement is true or false; or to read a passage silently with time to completion, as well as comprehension, considered. The comprehension component may affect the fluency score; however, including comprehension may provide a better measure of reading performance overall (Fuchs et al., 2001), particularly at younger ages (Valencia et al., 2010). Another potential confound to fluency is the underlying cognitive tempo or processing speed of the individual being assessed that is not necessarily specific to reading. Use of a rapid naming task (e.g., naming of objects, colors, numbers, letters), can determine if low fluency is a function of the "reading" process or the "retrieval" process, or a combination given the established relationship between naming speed and reading (e.g., Compton, Olson, DeFries, & Pennington, 2002). The KTEA-II, WRMT-III, and the Gray Diagnostic Reading Tests—second edition (GDRT-2; Bryant, Wiederholt, & Bryant, 2004) include rapid-naming tasks for this reason.

Reading Comprehension

Vocabulary and Contextual Knowledge. Reading comprehension incorporates the ability to recognize or decode words, fluency, vocabulary, and contextual knowledge. Of these basic skills, vocabulary and contextual knowledge are the least often considered as part of individualized achievement testing. In fact, few of the standardized individual measures of reading achievement include tasks tapping these two skill areas (see Table 5.1). This is of concern given that vocabulary knowledge explained unique variance in reading comprehension beyond that explained by listening comprehension across studies (Tannenbaum, Torgesen, & Wagner, 2006; Verhoeven & van Leeuwe, 2008). As part of the extended battery, the WJ-III Achieve includes subtests of reading vocabulary (antonyms, synonyms, analogies), as well as general knowledge (science, social studies, humanities). The GRDT-2, and Test of Reading Comprehension—fourth edition (TORC-4; Brown, Hammill, & Weiderholt, 2009) also include specific subtests for reading vocabulary.

Comprehension. Reading comprehension is the highest order of reading skills. Passage reading or cloze tasks are the major approaches used in the assessment of reading comprehension. Cloze formats have received the most attention for use with school-age children (Brown-Chidsey, Davis, & Maya, 2003; Wiley & Deno, 2005). A cloze test may be open-ended or use a multiple-choice format (i.e., maze format), such that the student must complete a sentence by filling in the word. Silent reading tasks followed by questions about the text read is the most frequent format for most group-administered (e.g., high stakes) tests for both children and adults (Williams, Ari, & Santamaria, 2011). Questions that follow the text may be literal and directly located in the task (e.g., Who went to the store?) or inferential (e.g., Why did Joe go to that particular store?). There are also differences in the extent to which questions following text are literal or inferential. Notably, differing formats have been found to place varying demands on the reader, thus affecting the assessment and diagnosis of reading difficulties (Kendeou, Papadopoulos, & Spanoudis, 2012). As can be seen from Table 5.1, the WJ-III, WRMT-III, and TORC-4 include a cloze or maze task. The TORC-4 also includes literal text comprehension, as do the WIAT-III, KTEA-II, and PIAT-R/NU.

Informal reading inventories (IRIs; see Nilsson, 2008, for a review) can be used to determine the extent to which the problem is in the "reading" or the "comprehension." Most IRIs include two passages that are considered to be of similar level of difficulty, and passages of increasing levels of difficulty; unlike normative measures, these tasks are intended to identify independent, instructional, and frustration reading levels. Passages range in reading level from preprimer to middle or high school (Paris & Carpenter, 2003). The individual's comprehension is measured by having the student read passages and answer questions until reaching frustration level. The alternative passage(s) are then read to the individual, followed by questions until the student reaches frustration a second time. The difference in reading comprehension (student reading) can then be compared to their level of listening comprehension (examiner reading). While not norm-referenced, the use of an IRI can be helpful in tailoring individual educational plans (Flippo, Holland, McCarthy, & Swinning, 2009; Paris & Carpenter, 2003).

Reading Assessment and the English Language Learner (ELL)

Assessment of reading achievement among English Language Learners (ELLs) must include the same types of measures and processes that are used with native English speakers. A key difference in the assessment approach for ELLs is the need for assessment of oral language skills in English, as well as the home language, as a preliminary step. This informs the examiner of the appropriate method and language for cognitive testing and helps the examiner discern whether the difficulty or deficit constitutes a true disability or is part of the normal process of acquiring a second language.

Oral language abilities in kindergarten, in both Spanish and English, contribute to the variance in English reading skills (Kieffer, 2012); as such, both should be assessed, at least in the early grades. Performance on receptive and expressive tests of picture vocabulary in both languages can provide useful comparisons. The use of the Bilingual Verbal Ability Test (BVAT; Muñoz-Sandoval, Cummins, Alvarado, & Ruef, 1998) can serve as a tool for estimating the child's native language proficiency and dominance in 18 languages (Alvarado, 2010). In addition, this test battery can help determine whether difficulty reading in English reflects their language proficiency, rather than their reading skills. Moreover, all academically relevant experiences that the child has encountered, including history of instruction, age at immigration and school attendance, must be considered as these may significantly shape the student's experience (Alvarado & the Bilingual Special Education Network of Texas, 2011).

As with language, reading abilities in the home language, if they are present, should be assessed and compared to performance in English. Some Spanish-language measures are available for this purpose. For young children, the *Pruebas de Habilidades Académicas Iniciales* (PHAI; Ramos, Hresko, & Ramos, 2006), a Spanish version of the Young Children's Achievement Test (YCAT; Hresko, Peak, Herron, & Bridges, 2000) can be used to assess early reading skills, spoken language, and general knowledge. Though the English and Spanish versions are not co-normed, nor equivalent, the use of one or both tests can provide information about how young ELLs compare to their monolingual peers.

For school-age and older individuals, the *Batería III Woodcock-Muñoz Pruebas de Aprovechamiento* (Batería-III; Muñoz-Sandoval, Woodcock, McGrew, & Mather, 2005) is the gold standard for the assessment of academic skills for Spanish speakers. The Batería-III is co-normed and statistically equivalent to the WJ-III Achieve. As such, the Batería-III provides the same coverage of reading skills as does the WJ-III Achieve. In addition, the Woodcock Muñoz Language Survey–Revised, normative update (WMLS-R/NU; Woodcock & Muñoz-Sandoval, 2011) includes measures of vocabulary, word recognition, and comprehension. It is important to note that the relation between reading fluency and comprehension differs with ELLs (Crosson & Lesaux, 2010; Quirk & Beem, 2012). Findings of both studies suggest that for a substantial proportion of ELLs, there is a significant gap between fluency and comprehension skills in English. A student may be able to decode even complex words, but may not know the meaning of those words if they lack the requisite vocabulary, with potential for under-identification of reading problems when there is a reliance on fluency measures for ELLs. As with native English speakers, rapid-naming tasks may add to explaining reading deficits. If decoding is a concern, the Test of Phonological Awareness in Spanish (TPAS; Riccio, Imhoff, Hasbrouck, & Davis, 2004) is available.

There are also some criterion-referenced or informal measures available in Spanish. The Comprehensive Reading Inventory (Cooter, Flynt, & Cooter, 2007) and Spanish Reading Inventory (Johns & Daniel, 2010) are IRIs that have Spanish as well as English passages. An informal battery that is available in English and Spanish that may be more suitable for young or very low-performing students is the Brigance Diagnostic Assessment of Basic Skills—Revised, Spanish Edition (ABS-R, Spanish; Brigance & Messer, 1984). These are criterion-referenced measures rather than norm-referenced, and as such should be interpreted with caution.

Unfortunately, Spanish is the only language other than English in which academic skills can be comprehensively and validly assessed, yet many ELLs speak languages other than Spanish. Translation of English instruments by a trained interpreter is a viable option, but may not yield reliable, valid, or generalizable results. As an alternative approach, examiners can employ a variety of strategies, such as using data from the child's school in his/her home country, work samples, curriculum-based assessment, comparison to local norms, or consulting with cultural agents from the child's language community regarding the differences between two languages and cultures and how these might affect academic skills (Rhodes, Ochoa & Ortiz, 2005).

Individual Assessment of Written Expression

As with reading, written expression is not a unitary skill, but involves the integration of linguistic and conceptual skills (McLoughlin & Lewis, 2008). Written expression requires the ability to generate and expand on ideas, to express those ideas using appropriate vocabulary and content knowledge, and to translate those ideas from oral language to print, adhering to spelling and written mechanics (Pierangelo & Giuliani, 2012). Specific components for assessment may include spelling, sentence construction, thematic development or text/paragraph construction, and editing/proofing. Potentially, the type of task used to assess written expression will result in differing diagnostic decisions, with some indication that essay or story construction may be more sensitive (Mayes, Calhoun, & Lane, 2005). Additionally, as noted with reading, consideration of vocabulary and content knowledge may be appropriate. Specific measures of written expression are provided in Table 5.2. Only the Test of Written Language, fourth edition (TOWL-4; Hammill & Larsen, 2009) includes all aspects of written expression for children and adolescents (McCrimmon & Climie, 2011).

Spelling/Encoding. Spelling requires analogous skills to decoding and word recognition in reading, but in spelling, the input is auditory/linguistic, while the output is most often in written (visual) form. The speller either identifies the letters associated with the spoken word (i.e., uses sound–symbol relations) or retrieves the correct spelling from memory. Across tests, the most common format is for the examiner to say the word, use the word in a sentence, and then say the word again; the written word is the response. Most spelling tasks combine those words that are spelled phonetically and those that do not follow rules. Spelling tasks are included on the WJ-III Achieve, the WIAT-III, the KTEA-II, and the KTEA-II Brief, as well as the WRAT-4 and the Test of Written Spelling, fourth edition (TWS-4; Larsen, Hammill, & Moats, 1999) using the dictation format. Subtests like the Spelling of Sounds from the WJ-III Achieve also may help with identifying problems with the translation of sound to orthography.

Sentence Writing. The next level of written expression is the generation of a sentence. Depending on the test, the task may be to use a specific word or words in a sentence, or it may be to write a sentence that makes sense and follows from sentence prompts. In some cases, the prompt is pictorial; in others it is provided orally and/or in written form. The student's level of expressive vocabulary and their knowledge related to the prompt provided can impact their performance. The extent to which spelling, punctuation, capitalization, syntax, and pragmatics are considered in the scoring process varies. Only the TOWL-4 assesses the ability to combine sentences or use more complex structures in sentence generation, as well as the ability to modify a sentence so that it makes sense.

Table 5.2 Matrix of Written Expression Components and Measures

Battery/Test	Spelling	Capitalization, Punctuation	Grammar, Syntax	Sentence Construction	Paragraph/Story/ Essay Construction	Writing Fluency
DAB-3	◆	◆			◆	
KTEA-II	◆			◆	◆	
PIAT-R/NU	◆				◆	
WIAT-III	◆			◆	◆	
WJ-III Achieve/ Batería-III (Standard)	◆			◆		◆
WJ-III Achieve/ Batería-III (Extended)		◆	◆			
KTEA-II Brief	◆			◆	◆	
OWLS-2	◆	◆	◆	◆	◆	
TEWL-2	◆	◆		◆	◆	
TOWL-4	◆	◆		◆	◆	
WRAT-4	◆					
WMLS-R/NU				◆		

Notes: Batería-III = Batería—third edition = *Woodcock-Muñoz Pruebas de Aprovechamiento*; DAB-3 = Diagnostic Achievement Battery, third edition; KTEA-II = Kaufman Tests of Educational Achievement—second edition; WRAT-4 = Wide Range Achievement Test—fourth edition; PIAT-R/NU = Peabody Individual Achievement Test—Revised/Normative Update; WIAT-III = Wechsler Individual Achievement Test, third edition; WJ-III Achieve = Woodcock Johnson Tests of Achievement, third edition—Normative Update; OWLS-2 = Oral and Written Language Scales—second edition; WMLS-R/ NU = Woodcock-Muñoz Language Survey—Revised/Normative Update.

Mechanics and Style. Use of punctuation, capitalization, and syntax may be included in the scoring of sentence or essay tasks (e.g., on the TOWL-4). Specific scores for punctuation are generated from the TOWL-4 with a separate task (i.e., Punctuation). The WJ-III Achieve also includes a subtest specific to punctuation and capitalization, based on production of dictated letters and sentences or adding punctuation to text. An alternate approach to assessment of mechanics and style is to have the individual identify an error in a sample provided and indicate how to correct the error (e.g., Editing on the WJ-III Achieve).

Essay/Thematic Writing. As children progress through school, the struggle may not be at the word or sentence level, but in expository writing. Tests that include this component may or may not include a picture or other visual stimulus, in addition to verbal directions. Some scoring systems include consideration of number of words written, punctuation, noun-verb agreement, spelling, and syntax (e.g., Contextual Conventions of the TOWL-4), while others emphasize composition aspects. For example, the WIAT-III, KTEA-II, and the TOWL-4 Story Composition include scoring for thematic development, plot, vocabulary, and complexity. Notably, the KTEA-II uses differing prompts based on grade level for the written expression tasks.

As with sentence production, the results can be affected by the student's vocabulary, as well as their contextual knowledge, depending on the prompt. For these reasons, it is important to consider the extent to which low scores obtained in written expression reflect low language abilities or contextual knowledge, as opposed to the ability to express what the student knows in written format. With the potential for metacognitive skills and logical sequencing skills to underlie problems in thematic development, the Test of Early Written Language, third edition (TEWL; Hresko, Herron, Peak, & Hicks, 2012) and the TORC-4 include subtests to specifically look at these skills.

Writing Fluency

As with reading fluency, the intent of measuring fluency in written expression would be to determine the extent to which the process of writing words, sentences, or text has become automatized (i.e., does the student have to think about spelling each word or producing each grapheme). The WJ-III Achieve includes a measure of writing fluency, with the student required to write short sentences using target words. The number of correctly written sentences in seven minutes is then used as the indicator of fluency. As with reading, it is important to consider not only the processing speed and language issues, but also the impact of motor production.

Written Expression and English Language Learners

When considering writing skills in English, it is important to note that common errors, likely attributable to learning English as a second language, often include the omission of articles, lack of noun-verb agreement, and, with some first languages, misuse of pronouns. If the first language is highly phonologic (also referred to as having a transparent orthography), as is Spanish, spelling may be adequate for words that are predictable, but deficient for words that are not predictable. A longer, expository sample, may take them longer if English is not fluent; the individual may write less and use more simple sentence structure in English than they are able to do in their first language. For this reason, it is always advised to compare the student's performance in English with their performance in their home language. Written language conventions may vary greatly in other countries. Commonly accepted writing practices, such as using ordinal descriptors (first, second, third, etc.) or avoiding run-on sentences, may not be taught or expected.

The Batería-III includes coverage of the same subskills related to written expression as does the WJ-III Achieve. Similarly, the WMLS-R/NU provides a measure of writing skills in Spanish and English. These test batteries allow the student to demonstrate the skills of assembling meaningful sentences using visual context cues. For young children, the PHAI includes a measure of early writing skills in Spanish.

Individual Assessment of Math Skills

Mathematics has not had the same level of emphasis historically as reading, but this has changed in recent years (Clark, Baker, & Chard, 2008; Floyd, Evans, & McGrew, 2003). Mathematics is also multifaceted, with two broad abilities underpinning math achievement—arithmetic skill and math reasoning (Nunes, Bryant, Barros, & Sylva, 2012). For this reason, both of these domains must be considered. In addition, math achievement also relies on the conceptual understanding of numbers and their relation to time and space. Difficulties in math can stem from deficits in understanding of the language and concepts in math (e.g., the number line), failure to master basic math skills at a level to foster automaticity, the arithmetic process of basic operations, or in the application of basic math skills to everyday situations. In addition, some tasks may tap procedural knowledge, conceptual understanding, or both (Ketterlin-Geller, Baker, & Chard, 2008), as well as nonverbal reasoning and oral language (e.g., Fuchs et al., 2012). The KeyMath-3 Diagnostic Assessment (Connolly, 2007) is a comprehensive standardized measure of math skills across component areas of concepts, operations, and applications.

Math Vocabulary and Concepts

An underlying construct in mathematics involves some sense of the number system used in comparing size and quantity, as well as order/sequence. Geary, Hoard, Byrd-Craven, and DeSoto (2004) suggested that understanding of number sets is a key component to the use of problem-solving skills in mathematics, with others identifying the importance of the linear representation system (i.e., the number line). At early ages, this begins with the ideas of one-to-one correspondence, ordering/sequencing, and association of a word tag with a stable quantity. The WJ-III Achieve includes a subtest to look at quantitative concepts. The KeyMath-3 includes coverage of numeration, including topics of number awareness, place value, rounding, and so on. In addition, there is coverage of the ability to classify and order elements by attributes, using terms to describe vertical and horizontal relationships, symbolic representation, and identification of two- and three-dimensional figures.

Math Calculation/Operations

Measures of math achievement include basic facts; algorithms with whole numbers and rational numbers; and coverage of fractions, ratios, and decimals across the four operations of addition, subtraction, multiplication, and division (see Table 5.3). Generally, the calculation or math operations task provides problems of increasing difficulty, yielding a single score. The KTEA-II provides guidance for task analysis to determine specific skills (e.g., subtraction with regrouping) that the student may need to work on. Alternatively, it is up to the examiner to determine if there is a pattern of errors or one or more specific skill sets that is/are deficient. When calculation deficits are identified, it may be appropriate

Table 5.3 Matrix of Math Components and Measures

Battery/Test	Math Vocabulary	Basic Math Concepts	Computation Skills	Math Reasoning/ Applied Skills	Math Fluency	Composite Skills
DAB-3			◆	◆		
KTEA-II			◆	◆		
PIAT-R/NU		◆				
WIAT-III			◆	◆	◆	
WJ-III Achieve, Batería-III (Standard)			◆	◆	◆	
WJ-III Achieve, Batería-III (Extended)		◆				
KTEA-II Brief			◆	◆		
Key Math		◆	◆	◆		
TEMA 2	◆	◆	◆	◆		
WRAT-4			◆			
YCAT/PHAI		◆	◆			

Notes: Batería-III = Batería third edition—*Woodcock Muñoz Pruebas de Aprovechamiento*; DAB-3 = Diagnostic Achievement Battery, third edition; KTEA-II = Kaufman Tests of Educational Achievement, second edition; Key Math = Key Math Diagnostic Arithmetic Tests, third edition; TEMA 2 = Test of Mathematical Abilities, second edition; WRAT-4 = Wide Range Achievement Test, fourth edition; PHAI = *Pruebas de Habilidades Académicas Iniciales*; YCAT = Young Children's Achievement Test; PIAT-R/NU = Peabody Individual Achievement Test—Revised/Normative Update; WIAT-III = Wechsler Individual Achievement Test, third edition; WJ-III Achieve = Woodcock Johnson Tests of Achievement, third edition—Normative Update.

to further assess the individual's working memory (e.g., Geary et al., 2004; Geary, Hoard, Byrd-Craven, Nugent, & Numtee, 2007; Proctor, 2012), and processing speed (Geary et al., 2007; Swanson & Sachse-Lee, 2001), as well as their previous (i.e., crystallized) knowledge (Parkin & Beaujean, 2012).

Math Reasoning/Application

Math reasoning is the application of the calculation skills to everyday situations, represented in word problems and often incorporating concepts and knowledge of money, measurement, and time, as well as calculation algorithms. To successfully complete math reasoning tasks, the student must be able to understand what the task is asking, tapping into language abilities and contextual knowledge, and then, using problem-solving skills (i.e., fluid ability), determine how to solve the problem and what information is relevant. If math reasoning items are not read to the student, then the task is confounded by reading level. Finally, as with calculation, the individual must retrieve and apply the appropriate algorithm. For students who have difficulty in math reasoning, but not with calculation, additional assessment of the comprehension/prior knowledge components, as well as fluid abilities, may be important to understanding the difficulties (Fuchs et al., 2012; Parkin & Beaujean, 2012; Proctor, 2012).

Math Fluency

Math fluency is a measure of math fact automaticity and has been identified as a barrier to math achievement (Stickney, Sharp, & Kenyon, 2012). In effect, when the speed and accuracy of retrieval of math knowledge is low, students exhibit lower math achievement. Further, it has been suggested that poor math fluency is a marker for mathematical learning disability (Mazzocco, Devlin, & McKenney, 2008), and may be related to deficits in phonological awareness and rapid naming (Hecht, Torgesen, Wagner, & Rashotte, 2001). Moreover, improvement of math automaticity can produce large gains in math achievement (Stickney et al., 2012).

Math fluency is usually tested by having the student complete basic calculation items, and determining the number of items completed correctly within or under time constraints. For the WIAT-III, three separate tasks and scores are generated for addition, subtraction, and multiplication. In contrast, the WJ-III Achieve task incorporates all three operations in random fashion within the same task. Noted already, phonological awareness and rapid naming are associated with proficiency, and low math fluency may warrant further consideration of these underlying processes. Notably, research suggests that math fluency is independent of reading fluency (Petrill et al., 2012).

Mathematics Achievement and English Language Learners

The Batería-III provides Spanish-language equivalents to the math calculation and math fluency tests on the WJ-III Achievement battery. For young children, the PHAI also includes a measure of math achievement. Because the assessment of calculation skills involves reduced language demands, the student usually does not need to be given these tests in more than one language; however, certain math notations and operations are not taught in the same way in some Spanish-speaking countries. Thus, mathematics symbols may look unfamiliar to a non-native English speaker. Because math reasoning involves a language component, the student's proficiency in their home language and in English, as well as the language of math instruction, should be considered (Rhodes, Ochoa, & Ortiz, 2005).

Linking Assessment to Intervention

Individualized assessment of specific academic skills is most likely to occur after attempts to address difficulties in the classroom have not been successful. When done well, individual assessment and examination of the student's PSW can inform intervention, rather than test results solely being used as a component of eligibility or diagnosis. Increasingly, there is emphasis on the use of research-based practices when developing intervention plans (IDEIA, 2004). In an educational context, an evidence-based intervention (EBI) refers to a program or intervention aimed at improving outcomes, with the emphasis on the research base (Cook, Tankersley, & Landrum, 2009; Spencer, Detrich, & Slocum, 2012). Some EBIs have been found to be effective in group, classroom, or school wide implementation (see Evidence-Based Intervention Network; http://ebi.missouri.edu). For example, suggestions for writing curricula and instructional components that have been identified to improve written language (Malecki, 2008) would be most amenable to a class-wide implementation. One EBI approach to class-wide implementation that can incorporate evidence-based practices is class-wide peer tutoring.

Class-Wide Peer Tutoring: An EBI Class-Wide Peer Tutoring Overview

Class-Wide Peer Tutoring (CWPT) is one such EBI that has been implemented and is well researched. CWPT was developed by researchers at the Juniper Gardens Children's Project at the University of Kansas (KU), with several variations developed based on the original CWPT model. Variations include the Peer-Assisted Learning Strategies (PALS; Fuchs, Fuchs, Mathes, & Simmons, 1997), the Classwide Student Tutoring Teams (CSTT; Maheady, Sacca, & Harper, 1987) and Total Class Peer Tutoring (Lo & Cartledge, 2004). Consistent with CWPT, each of the models includes: (a) content that is determined by teachers, (b) individualization of materials for students at varying levels of ability, (c) teacher monitoring and facilitation, (d) the ability to actively engage all students in the class at one time, and (e) "highly structured and evidence-based instructional components delivered by well-trained peers" (Maheady, Mallette, & Harper, 2006, p. 70). Differences include: (a) how peer partners and/or teams are formed, (b) how long students work together, and (c) whether tutor/tutee roles are reciprocal (Maheady et al., 2006).

CWPT Format and Benefits

CWPT uses a reciprocal tutoring format in which students work in dyads (or triads, in the case of an uneven number of students) to explicitly learn and review material covered by their teacher. Each student has an equal amount of time to serve as the tutor and tutee during each tutoring session. During training, students learn to present content material to their peer partner, encourage and praise correct responses, and initiate error correction for incorrect responses. Fidelity of implementation checks and satisfaction surveys (for students and teachers) are a routine part of CWPT procedures. The game-style format includes students being able to earn points individually for working cooperatively with their peer partner, correctly awarding points for correct responses, and using the error correction procedure. Points are also awarded for correct responses, with total points determined at the end of each session. Whether or not teachers incorporate the use of teams and team points, students are often motivated by being able to earn points. The use of rewards (e.g., applause from classmates, stickers, extra computer time) is often part of the CWPT format. While CWPT typically involves an entire classroom of students, it is flexible enough to be implemented with a smaller group within the classroom. Results of weekly pre- and post-tests provide helpful feedback for students, teachers, and parents.

Benefits of CWPT for students include: (a) being paired with a peer partner for one-to-one instruction, (b) opportunities for error correction, (c) increased time spent on academic behaviors, (d) increased positive social interactions between students, (e) decreased off-task and disruptive behaviors, (f) improved social skills while learning academic content, and (g) increased academic confidence. Benefits for teachers include: (a) it can be used with teachers' current curricula, (b) it can be implemented in 30- to 40-minute blocks of time, (c) it helps with classroom management, and (d) data obtained from assessments can guide instruction.

Research Base for CWPT

Research conducted on the efficacy of CWPT includes students in pre-kindergarten through high school. Although the majority of the research has focused on its implementation in elementary schools, some focus on middle and high school students (Bowman-Perrott, Greenwood, & Tapia, 2007; Kamps et al., 2008; Neddenriep, Skinner, Wallace, & McCallum, 2009). Most of the research has taken place in general education classrooms (Greenwood, 2002); however, special education classrooms (Harper, Mallette, Maheady, Parkes, & Moore, 1993), alternative school classroom settings (Bowman-Perrott, 2009), and group homes (Mayfield & Vollmer, 2007) have served as settings for CWPT implementation. CWPT has been shown to be effective for students without disabilities, students at risk for disabilities, and those identified with disabilities. Specifically, students with learning disabilities (Veerkamp, Kamps, & Cooper, 2007), emotional and behavioral disorders (Bowman-Perrott, 2009), and autism (Kamps, Barbetta, Leonard, & Delquadri, 1994) have benefitted from CWPT implementation. In addition, ELLs, as well as their native English-speaking peers, have benefitted from CWPT (Kourea, Cartledge, & Musti-Rao, 2007; Madrid, Canas, & Ortega-Medina, 2007). Findings from longitudinal CWPT studies revealed that participation in CWPT resulted in: (a) fewer dropouts, (b) fewer referrals to special education, (c) increased academic gains, and (d) increased academic engagement. CWPT studies have been included in peer tutoring literature reviews (e.g., Mastropieri, Spencer, Scruggs, & Talbott, 2000), as well as meta-analyses of group design (Rohrbeck, Ginsburg-Block, Fantuzzo, & Miller (2003), and single-case research design studies (Bowman-Perrott et al., 2013).

Based on the accumulation of research, student outcomes have been shown to be greater with the use of CWPT than with traditional teacher-led instruction (Greenwood, Maheady, & Carta, 1991). Effective instructional features (i.e., frequent opportunities to respond, increased time on-task, and regular and immediate feedback) that are empirically linked with increased academic achievement (Delquadri, Greenwood, Whorton, Carta, & Hall, 1986; Greenwood, Terry, Arreaga-Mayer, & Finney, 1992) may contribute to its success. Additionally, the use of multiple modalities (reading, writing, hearing, and talking about content material) helps students learn academic content.

Class-Wide Peer Tutoring in the Content Areas

CWPT promotes students' active engagement with the curriculum, encourages repeated practice, and serves as an approach "for increasing class-wide response opportunities" (Delquadri et al., 1986, p. 540). Research on CWPT procedures has focused primarily on basic skills areas, such as reading (Oddo, Barnett, Hawkins, & Musti-Rao, 2010) and spelling (Sideridis et al., 1997), with some emphasis on math (Hawkins, Musti-Rao, Hughes, Berry, & McGuire, 2009), social studies (Bell, Young, Blair, & Nelson, 1990), and science (Bowman-Perrott et al., 2007; Kamps et al., 2008). As a teaching strategy, it has proven effective for improving students' test performance and improvement in accuracy (e.g., Kamps et al., 1994). CWPT and similar programs are sufficiently flexible in terms of content to be used in addressing skill development across academic skills areas.

Conclusion

Academic assessment must consider background information, previous intervention history, and current levels of functioning in relation to the academic skill sets and demands of the curriculum. It is important that the measures used are not only psychometrically adequate, but also are selected with regard to the hypothesized areas of deficit. Composite scores, while provided on most major batteries, are not sufficient to tailor targeted intervention plans. All academic subskills should be considered in the academic areas in which the student is struggling, so that the PSW can be determined and associated deficit cognitive processes identified (Flanagan, Fiorello, & Ortiz, 2010). Considerably more research is needed in the area of specific academic skills assessment and ELLs with psychometrically strong measures.

The information gleaned from the academic assessment is used as part of the data-based decision-making not only for eligibility purposes, but for selection of EBI. It is important to note that EBIs area only supported for the specific skills for which the evidence exists; implementation of an EBI that addresses other than the deficit skill or process is not likely to yield the desired outcome. Approaches such as CWPT may be beneficial in improving the skills of all children, including those with specific skill deficits. Moreover, regardless of the intervention, it is important to engage in ongoing progress monitoring as part of data-based decision-making to determine whether the intervention is having the intended effect.

References

Alvarado, C. G. (2010). *Bilingual special education evaluation of culturally and linguistically diverse individuals using Woodcock tests.* Retrieved from http://educationeval.com/articles.html

Alvarado, C. G., & The Bilingual Special Education Network of Texas. (2011). *Best practices in the evaluation of students who are culturally and linguistically diverse, revised 2011.* Retrieved from http://educationeval.com

American Educational Research Association, American Psychological Association, & National Council on Measurement in Education (AERA, APA, & NCME). (1999). *Standards for educational and psychological testing.* Washington, D. C.: Author.

Batsche, G. M., Castillo, J. M., Dixon, D. N., & Forde, S. (2008). Best practices in linking assessment to intervention. In A. Thomas & J. Grimes (Eds.), *Best practices in school psychology V* (Vol. 2, pp. 177–194). Bethesda, MD: National Association of School Psychologists.

Bell, K., Young, K. R., Blair, M., & Nelson, R. (1990). Facilitating mainstreaming of students with behavioral disorders using classwide tutoring. *School Psychology Review, 19,* 564–573.

Bowman-Perrott, L. (2009). Classwide Peer Tutoring: An effective strategy for students with emotional and behavioral disorders. *Intervention in School and Clinic, 44,* 259–267.

Bowman-Perrott, L. J., Davis, H., Vannest, K. J., Williams, L., Greenwood, C. R., & Parker, R. (2013). Academic benefits of peer tutoring: A meta-analytic review of single-case research. *School Psychology Review, 42,* 39–55.

Bowman-Perrott, L. J., Greenwood, C. R., & Tapia, Y. (2007). The efficacy of CWPT used in secondary alternative school classrooms with small teacher/pupil ratios and students with emotional and behavioral disorders. *Education and Treatment of Children, 30*(3), 65–87.

Brigance, A. H., & Messer, P. (1984). *Brigance diagnostic assessment of basic skills–revised, Spanish edition.* North Billerica, MA: Curriculum Associates.

Brown, V. L., Hammill, D. D., & Wiederholt, J. L. (2009). *Test of reading comprehension, fourth edition.* Austin, TX: Pro-Ed.

Brown-Chidsey, R. (2008). The role of published norm-referenced test in problem-solving-based assessment. In R. Brown-Chidsey (Ed.), *Assessment for intervention: A problem-solving approach* (pp. 247–264). New York, NY: Guilford.

Brown-Chidsey, R., Davis, L., & Maya, C. (2003). Sources of variance in curriculum-based measures of silent reading. *Psychology in the Schools, 40,* 363–378.

Bryant, B., Wiederholt, J. L., & Bryant, D. P. (2004). *Gray diagnostic reading tests, second edition.* Austin, TX: Pro-Ed.

Carrow-Woolfolk, E. (2011). *Oral and written language scales, second edition. Examiner's manual.* Torrance, CA: Western Psychological Services.

Clark, B., Baker, S., & Chard, D. (2008). Best practices in mathematics assessment and intervention with elementary students. In A. Thomas & J. Grimes (Eds.), *Best practices in school psychology V* (Vol. 2, pp. 453–463). Bethesda, MD: National Association of School Psychologists.

Compton, D. L., Fuchs, L. S., Fuchs, D., Lambert, W., & Hamlett, C. (2012). The cognitive and academic profiles of reading and mathematics learning disabilities. *Journal of Learning Disabilties, 45,* 79–95.

Compton, D. L., Olson, R. K., DeFries, J. C., & Pennington, B. F. (2002). Comparing the relationships among two different versions of alphanumeric rapid automatized naming and word level reading skills. *Scientific Studies of Reading, 6,* 343–368.

Connolly, A. J. (2007) *KeyMath-3 diagnostic assessment: Manual forms A and B.* Minneapolis, MN: Pearson.

Cook, B. G., Tankersley, M., & Landrum, T. J. (2009). Determining evidence-based practices in special education. *Exceptional Children, 75,* 365–383.

Cooter Jr., R. B., Flynt, E. S., & Cooter, K. S. (2007). *Comprehensive reading inventory: Measuring reading development in regular and special education classrooms.* Upper Saddle River, NJ: Pearson.

Crosson, A. C., & Lesaux, N. K. (2010). Revisiting assumptions about the relationship of fluent reading to comprehension: Spanish speakers' text-reading fluency in English. *Reading and Writing, 23,* 475–494. doi: 10.1007/s11145–009–9168–8

Delquadri, J., Greenwood, C. R., Whorton, D., Carta, J. J., & Hall, R. V. (1986). Classwide Peer Tutoring. *Exceptional Children, 52,* 535–542.

Ehri, L. C. (2005). Learning to read words: Theory, findings, and issues. *Scientific Studies of Reading, 9,* 167–188.

Flanagan, D. R., Fiorello, C. A., & Ortiz, S. O. (2010). Enhancing practice through application of Cattell-Horn-Carroll theory and research: A "third method" approach to specific learning disability identification. *Psychology in the Schools, 45,* 739–760.

Flippo, R. F., Holland, D. D., McCarthy, M. T., & Swinning, E. A. (2009). Asking the right questions: How to select an informal reading inventory. *Reading Teacher, 63*(1), 79–83.

Floyd, R. G., Evans, J. J., & McGrew, K. S. (2003). Relations between measures of Cattell-Horn-Carroll (CHC) cognitive abilities and mathematics achievement across the school-age years. *Psychology in the Schools, 40,* 155–171.

Fuchs, L. S., Compton, D. L., Fuchs, D., Powell, S. R., Schumacher, R. F., Hamlett, C. L., et al. (2012). Contributions of domain-general cognitive resources and different forms of arithmetic development to pre-algebraic knowledge. *Developmental Psychology.* Advance online publication. doi: 10.1037/a0027475

Fuchs, L. S., & Fuchs, D. (2002). Curriculum-based measurement: Describing competence, enhancing outcomes, evaluating treatment, effects, and evaluating treatment nonresponders. *Peabody Journal of Education, 77*(2), 64–84.

Fuchs, L. S., Fuchs, D., Hosp, M. K., & Jenkins, J. R. (2001). Oral reading fluency as an indicator of reading competence: A theoretical, empirical, and historical analysis. *Scientific Studies of Reading, 5,* 239–256.

Fuchs, D., Fuchs, L. S., Mathes, P. G., & Simmons, D. C. (1997). Peer-assisted learning strategies: Making classrooms more responsive to diversity. *American Educational Research Journal, 34,* 174–206.

Fuchs, D., Hale, J. B., & Kearns, D. M. (2011). On the importance of a cognitive processing perspective: An introduction. *Journal of Learning Disabilities, 44,* 99–104.

Geary, D. C., Hoard, M. K., Byrd-Craven, J., & DeSoto, M. (2004). Strategy choices in simple and complex addition: Contributions of working memory and counting knowledge for children with mathematical disability. *Journal of Experimental Child Psychology, 88,* 121–151.

Geary, D.C., Hoard, M. K., Byrd-Craven, J., Nugent, L., & Numtee, C. (2007). Cognitive mechanisms underlying achievement deficits in children with mathematical learning disability. *Child Development, 78,* 1343–1359.

Greenwood, C. R. (2002). Classwide Peer Tutoring programs. In M. R. Shinn, H. M. Walker, & G. Stoner (Eds.), *Interventions for academic and behavior problems: 2. Preventative and remedial programs* (pp. 611–649). Washington, DC: National Association for School Psychologists (NASP).

Greenwood, C. R., Maheady, L., & Carta, J. J. (1991). Peer tutoring programs in the regular education classroom. In G. Stoner, M. R. Shinn, & H. M. Walker (Eds.), *Interventions for achievement and behavior problems* (pp. 179–200). Washington, DC: National Association for School Psychologists (NASP).

Greenwood, C. R., Terry, B., Arreaga-Mayer, C., & Finney, D. (1992). The ClassWide Peer Tutoring program: Implementation factors that moderate students' achievement. *Journal of Applied Behavior Analysis, 25,* 101–116.

Hale, J. B., & Fiorello, C. A. (2004). *School neuropsychology: A practitioner's handbook.* New York: Guilford Press.

Hammill, D., & Larsen, D. (2009). *Test of written language, fourth edition.* Austin, TX: Pro-Ed.

Harper, G. F., Mallette, B., Maheady, L., Parkes, V., & Moore, J. (1993). Retention and generalization of spelling words acquired using a peer-mediated instructional procedure by children with mild handicapping conditions. *Journal of Behavioral Education, 3,* 25–38.

Hawkins, R. O., Musti-Rao, S., Hughes, C., Berry, L., & McGuire, S. (2009). Applying a randomized interdependent group contingency component to classwide peer tutoring for multiplication fact fluency. *Journal of Behavioral Education, 18,* 300–318.

Hecht, S. A., Torgesen, J. K., Wagner, R. K., & Rashotte, C. A. (2001). The relations between phonological processing abilities and emerging individual differences in mathematical computation skills: A longitudinal study from second to fifth grades. *Journal of Experimental Child Psychology, 79,* 192–227.

Hresko, W. P., Herron, S. R., Peak, P. R., & Hicks, D. L. (2012). *Test of early written language* (3rd ed.). Austin, TX: Pro-Ed.

Hresko, W. P., Peak, P., Herron, S., & Bridges, D. (2000). *Young children's achievement test.* Austin, TX: Pro-Ed.

Individuals with Disabilities Education Improvement Act. (2004). Pub. L. No. 108-446, 118 Stat. 2647.

Johns, J. L., & Daniel, M. C. (2010). *Spanish reading inventory.* Dubuque, IA: Kendall Hunt.

Joshi, R. M., & Aaron, P. G. (2000). The component model of reading: Simple view of reading made a little more complex. *Reading Psychology, 21,* 85–97.

Kamps, D. M., Barbetta, P. M., Leonard, B. R., & Delquadri, J. (1994). Classwide Peer Tutoring: An integration strategy to improve reading skills and promote peer interactions among students with autism and general education peers. *Journal of Applied Behavioral Analysis, 27*(1), 49–61.

Kamps, D. M., Greenwood, C., Arreaga-Mayer, C., Veerkamp, M. B., Utley, C., Tapia, Y., et al. (2008). The efficacy of classwide peer tutoring in middle schools. *Education and Treatment of Children, 31,* 119–152.

Kaufman, A., & Kaufman, N. (2004a). *Kaufman test of educational achievement, second edition.* Minneapolis, MN: Pearson.

Kaufman, A., & Kaufman, N. (2004b). *Kaufman test of educational achievement, second edition—brief.* Minneapolis, MN: Pearson.

Kendeou, P., Papadopoulos, T. C., & Spanoudis, G. (2012). Processing demands of reading comprehension tests in young readers. *Learning and Instruction, 22,* 354–367.

Ketterlin-Geller, L. R., Baker, S. K., & Chard, D. J. (2008). Best practices in mathematics instruction and assessment in secondary settings. In A. Thomas & J. Grimes (Eds.), *Best practices in school psychology V* (Vol. 2, pp. 465–475). Bethesda, MD: National Association of School Psychologists.

Kieffer, M. J. (2012). Early oral language and later reading development in Spanish-speaking English language learners: Evidence from a nine-year longitudinal study. *Journal of Applied Developmental Psychology, 33,* 146–157.

Kourea, L., Cartledge, G., & Musti-Rao, S. (2007). Improving the reading skills of urban elementary students through total class peer tutoring. *Remedial and Special Education, 28,* 95–107.

LaBerge, D., & Samuels, S. J. (1974). Toward a theory of automatic information processing in reading. *Cognitive Psychology, 6,* 293–323.

Larsen, S., Hammill, D., & Moats, L. (1999). *Test of written spelling* (4th ed.). Austin, TX: Pro-Ed.

Lo, Y., & Cartledge, G. (2004). Total class peer tutoring and interdependent group-oriented contingency: Improving the academic and task related behaviors of fourth-grade urban students. *Education and Treatment of Children, 27,* 235–262.

Madrid, L., Canas, M., & Ortega-Medina, M. (2007). Effects of team competition versus team cooperation in classwide peer tutoring. *Journal of Educational Research, 100,* 155–160.

Maheady, L., Mallette, B., & Harper, G. F. (2006). Four classwide peer tutoring models: Similarities, differences, and implications for research and practice. *Reading & Writing Quarterly, 22,* 65–89. doi:10.1080/10573560500203541

Maheady, L., Sacca, M. K., & Harper, G. F. (1987). Classwide student tutoring teams: The effects of peer mediated instruction on the academic performance of secondary mainstreamed students. *The Journal of Special Education, 21,* 107–121.

Malecki, C. (2008). Best practices in written language assessment and intervention. In A. Thomas & J. Grimes (Eds.), *Best practices in school psychology V* (Vol. 2, pp. 477–488). Bethesda, MD: National Association of School Psychologists.

Markwardt, F. C. (1998). *Peabody individual achievement test – revised, normative update.* Circle Pines, MN: American Guidance Service, Inc.

Mastropieri, M. A., Spencer, V., Scruggs, T. E., & Talbott, E. (2000). Students with disabilities as tutors: An updated research synthesis. *Advances in Learning and Behavioral Disabilities, 15,* 247–279.

Mather, N., Wendling, B. J., Naglieri, J. A., & Goldstein, S. (2009). *Practitioner's guide to assessing intelligence and achievement.* Hoboken, NJ: Wiley.

Mayfield, K. H., & Vollmer, T. R. (2007). Teaching math skills to at-risk students using home-based peer tutoring. *Journal of Applied Behavior Analysis, 40,* 223–237. doi: 10.1 901/jaba.2007. 108–05

Mayes, S. D., Calhoun, S. L., & Lane, S. E. (2005). Diagnosing children's writing disabilities: Different tests give different results. *Perceptual and Motor Skills, 101,* 72–78.

Mazzocco, M. M. M., Devlin, K. T., & McKenney, J. L. (2008). Is it a fact? Timed arithmetic performance of children with mathematical learning disabilities (MLD) vary as a function of how MLD is defined. *Developmental Neuropsychology, 33,* 318–344.

McCrimmon, A. W., & Climie, E. A. (2011). Review of Test of Written Language—Fourth Edition. *Journal of Psychoeducational Assessment, 29,* 592–596.

McLoughlin, J. A., & Lewis, R. B. (2008). *Assessing students with special needs* (7th ed.). Upper Saddle River, NJ: Merrill/Pearson.

Muñoz-Sandoval, A. F., Cummins, J., Alvarado, C. G., & Ruef, M. L. (1998). *Bilingual Verbal Ability Tests.* Itasca, IL: Riverside.

Muñoz-Sandoval, A. F., Woodcock, R. W., McGrew, K. S., & Mather, N. (2005). *Batería III Woodcock-Muñoz: Pruebas de aprovechamiento.* Itasca, IL: Riverside Publishing.

National Institute of Child Health and Human Development (NICHD). (2000). *Report of the National Reading Panel. Teaching children to read: An evidence-based assessment of the scientific research literature on reading and its implications for reading instruction* (NIH Publication No. 00-4769). Washington, DC: U.S. Government Printing Office.

Neddenriep, C. E., Skinner, C. H., Wallace, M. A., & McCallum, E. (2009). Classwide Peer Tutoring: Two experiments investigating the generalized relationship between increased oral reading fluency and reading comprehension. *Journal of Applied School Psychology, 25,* 244–269.

Newcomer, P. (2001). *Diagnostic achievement battery examiner manual.* Austin, TX: Pro-Ed.

Nilsson, N. L. (2008). A critical analysis of eight informal reading inventories. *The Reading Teacher, 61,* 526–536.

Nunes, T., Bryant, P., Barros, R., & Sylva, K. (2012). The relative importance of two different mathematical abilities to mathematical achievement. *British Journal of Educational Psychology, 82,* 136–156.

Oddo, M., Barnett, D. W., Hawkins, R. O., & Musti-Rao, S. (2010). Reciprocal peer tutoring and repeated reading: Increasing practicality using student groups. *Psychology in the Schools, 47,* 842–858. doi: 10.1002/pits.20508

Ortiz, S. O. (2008). Issues unique to English language learners. In R. J. Morris & N. Mather (Eds.), *Evidence-based interventions for students with learning and behavioral challenges* (pp. 321–739). New York, NY: Routledge.

Parkin, J. R., & Beaujean, A. A. (2012). The effects of Wechsler Intelligence Scale for Children—fourth edition cognitive abilities on math achievement. *Journal of School Psychology, 50,* 113–128.

Paris, S. G., & Carpenter, R. D. (2003). FAQs about IRIs. *The Reading Teacher, 56,* 578–580.

Petrill, S., Logan, J., Hart, S., Vincent, P., Thompson, L., Kovas, Y., & Plomin, R. (2012). Math fluency is etiologically distinct from untimed math performance, decoding fluency, and untimed reading performance: Evidence from a twin study. *Journal of Learning Disabilities, 45,* 371–381.

Pierangelo, R., & Giuliani, G. A. (2012). *Assessment in special education: A practical approach* (4th ed.). New York, NY: Pearson.

Proctor, B. (2012). Relationships between Cattell-Horn-Carroll (CHC) cognitive abilities and math achievement within a sample of college students with learning disabilities. *Journal of Learning Disabilities, 45,* 278–287.

Quirk, M., & Beem, S. (2012). Examining the relations between reading fluency and reading comprehension for English language learners. *Psychology in the Schools, 49,* 539–553.

Ramos, J., Hresko, W., & Ramos, M. (2006). *Prueba de Habilidades Académas Iniciales.* Austin, TX: Pro-Ed.

Rhodes, R. L., Ochoa, S. H., & Ortiz, S. O. (2005). *Assessing culturally and linguistically diverse students: A practical guide.* New York, NY: The Guilford Press.

Riccio, C. A., Imhoff, B., Hasbrouck, J. E., & Davis, G. N. (2004). *Test of phonological awareness in Spanish.* Austin, TX: Pro-Ed.

Rohrbeck, C. A., Ginsburg-Block, M. D., Fantuzzo, J. W., & Miller, T. R. (2003). Peer-assisted learning interventions with elementary school students: A meta-analytic review. *Journal of Educational Psychology, 95,* 240–257.

Samuels, S. J. (2006). Toward a model of reading fluency. In S. J. Samuels & A. E. Farstrup (Eds.), *What research has to say about fluency instruction* (pp. 24–46). Newark, DE: International Reading Association.

Shinn, M. R. (2008). Identifying and validating academic problems in a problem-solving model. In R. Brown-Chidsey (Ed.), *Assessment for intervention: A problem-solving approach* (pp. 219–246). New York, NY: Guilford.

Sideridis, G. D., Utley, C., Greenwood, C. R., Delquadri, J., Dawson, H., Palmer, P., et al. (1997). Classwide peer tutoring effects on the spelling performance and social interactions of students with mild disabilities and their typical peers in an integrated instructional setting. *Journal of Behavioral Education, 7,* 435–462.

Spencer, T. D., Detrich, R., & Slocum, T. A. (2012). Evidence-based practice: A framework for making effective decisions. *Education and Treatment of Children, 35,* 127–151.

Stickney, E. M., Sharp, L. B., & Kenyon, A. S. (2012). Technology-enhanced assessment of math fact automaticity: Patterns of performance for low- and typically achieving students. *Assessment for Effective Intervention, 37,* 84–94.

Swanson, H. L., & Sachse-Lee, C. (2001). Mathematical problem-solving and working memory in children with learning disabilities: Both executive and phonological processes are important. *Journal of Experimental Child Psychology, 79,* 294–321.

Tannenbaum, K. R., Torgesen, J. K., & Wagner, R. K. (2006). Relationships between word knowledge and reading comprehension in third-grade children. *Scientific Studies of Reading, 10,* 381–399.

Valencia, S. W., Smith, A. T., Reece, A. M., Li, M., Wixson, K. K., et al. (2010). Oral reading fluency assessment: Issues of construct, criterion, and consequential validity. *Reading Research Quarterly, 45,* 270–291.

Veerkamp, M. B., Kamps, D. M., & Cooper, L. (2007). The effects of classwide peer tutoring on the reading achievement of urban middle school students. *Education and Treatment of Children, 30*(2), 21–51.

Verhoeven, L., & van Leeuwe, J. (2008). Prediction of the development of reading comprehension: A longitudinal study. *Applied Cognitive Psychology, 22,* 407–423.

Wagner, R., Torgesen, J., & Rashotte, C. (1999). *Comprehensive test of phonological processing.* Austin, TX: Pro-Ed.

Wechsler, D. (2009). *Wechsler individual achievement test, third edition.* San Antonio, TX: Pearson.

Wiley, H., & Deno, S. L. (2005). Oral reading and maze measures as predictors of success for English learners on a state standards assessment. *Remedial & Special Education, 26,* 207–214.

Wilkinson, G. S., & Robertson, G. J. (2006). *Wide range achievement test* (4th ed.). Lutz, FL: Psychological Assessment Resources.

Williams, R., Ari, O., & Santamaria, C. (2011). Measuring college students' reading comprehension ability using cloze tests. *Journal of Research in Reading, 34,* 215–231. doi: 10.1111/j.1467–9817.2009.01422.x

Woodcock, R. W. (2011). *Woodcock reading mastery tests-third edition.* Minneapolis, MN: Pearson.

Woodcock, R. W., McGrew, K. S., & Mather, N. (2007a). *The Woodcock Johnson, third edition – tests of achievement, normative update.* Rolling Meadows, IL: Riverside.

Woodcock, R. W., McGrew, K. S., & Mather, N. (2007b). *The Woodcock Johnson, third edition – tests of cognitive ability, normative update.* Rolling Meadows, IL: Riverside.

Woodcock, R. W., & Muñoz-Sandoval, A. F. (2011). *Woodcock-Muñoz language survey-revised normative update.* Rolling Meadows, IL: Riverside.

Group Tests of Academic Achievement

Steven G. Little and Angeleque Akin-Little

The *No Child Left Behind* (No Child Left Behind [NCLB], 2002) legislation mandated that every child in every public and charter school in the country be tested in reading and math in Grades 3 through 8 and at least once in Grades 10 to 12. Further, science assessments must be administered at least once during Grades 3 to 5, 6 to 9, and 10 to 12. Additionally, states must ensure that districts administer tests of English proficiency to all limited-English-proficient students. Students may also undergo state assessments in other subject areas (e.g., history, geography, writing skills) based on state requirements; however, NCLB only requires assessments in reading/language arts, math, and science. While most school districts have conducted group assessments for decades, the needs for group academic assessments have increased since the inception of NCLB.

Post NCLB, each state has developed their own set of academic standards (see http://www.education.com/reference/article/Ref_edu_table/ for links to each state's standards), but all are based on requirements provided in NCLB and other federal regulations. States must assess all students at select grade levels in order to receive federal school funding, but the act does not assert a national achievement standard (standards are set by each individual state) or a national test (test is determined by each state) (NCLB, 2002). These and other "high-stakes tests" provide the need for well developed, reliable, and valid measures. As each state has the responsibility of choosing an established test or to develop their own measure, it is impossible to review all of the possible tests in this chapter. Instead the intent of this chapter is to (a) present arguments in favor, notably few in number in the academic literature, and against high-stakes academic tests, and (b) review selected published group academic assessment batteries that have been used in states and districts throughout the country.

High-Stakes Testing

High-stakes tests are designed with one main goal in mind, to increase student learning (Amrein & Berliner, 2002). Others have purported high-stakes tests help guide curriculum, give parents an increased role in their child's education, and even to help condition children to test anxiety so that they will be better prepared for future high-stakes tests (Munoz, 2006). The academic literature, however, has focused mainly on the negative aspects of such testing. Berliner (2011) identified curriculum narrowing as the "most pernicious" aspect of the high-stakes testing movement.

Curriculum narrowing, that is, focusing on curricular areas to be tested (i.e., reading and math) at the expense of other curricular areas, reduces participation in creative and enjoyable activities for both teachers and students, restricts thinking skills, hinders achievement in later grades because of the narrow curriculum in lower grades, and compromises the construct validity of the measures (Berliner, 2011). Berliner also pointed out that achievement gains in the United States were actually greater before high-stakes testing became national policy. Similarly, Scot, Callahan, and Urquhart (2009) coined the term "Paint-by-Number Teachers and Cookie-Cutter Students" to describe how the accountability movement associated with high-stakes testing is counter to best practice in meeting the needs of some students.

Wu (2010) examined a number of the large-scale assessments used throughout the world and concluded that the assessment methodologies do not always meet the objectives of the assessments. She stated that there is a lack of critical statistical evaluation of the assessment results and that conclusions are being made without sufficient statistical rigor. Specifically, she discussed three main sources of error in large-scale assessment: measurement error at the individual student level, error due to the sampling of students (for group results), and item sampling error due to the selection of common items for equating. She identified sampling of items, the delivery of the test, and a lack of sampling rigor (e.g., sampling coverage and sample size) as the current weakest links in high-stakes achievement testing. She concluded that simply implementing an assessment program does not necessarily produce results that are sufficient to produce and support valid inferences.

Group Assessment Batteries

While many states have designed their own tests to measure student progress associated with and mandated by NCLB, other states have adopted norm-referenced tests designed by outside authors and/or organizations. In addition, individual school districts may adopt their own testing program separate from NCLB requirements in order to track student progress. The *Stanford Achievement Test, 10th edition (Stanford 10); Iowa Tests of Basic Skills (ITBS)*; and *Metropolitan Achievement Tests, 9th edition (MAT 9)*, are three of the more commonly used group achievement test batteries in the United States and will be reviewed in more detail below.

Stanford Achievement Test, 10th edition. The *Stanford 10* (Harcourt Assessment, 2003) is a group-administered test of educational achievement for students in Grades K to 12 and measures student achievement in reading, language, spelling, listening, mathematics, science, and social science. It can be administered as either a Full-Length Battery or an Abbreviated Battery. Braille and large-print editions are also available. The *Stanford 10* provides several types of scores, including raw scores, scaled scores, individual percentile ranks, stanines, grade equivalents, Normal Curve Equivalents (NCEs), Achievement/Ability Comparisons (AACs), group percentile ranks and stanines, content cluster and process cluster performance categories, and performance standards. The publisher (Pearson Education, 2011) also provides alignment to the Common Core State Standards. Scores are provided for the following content areas: Sounds and Letters, Word-Study Skills, Word Reading, Sentence Reading, Reading Comprehension, Total Reading, Mathematics, Mathematics Problem Solving, Mathematics

Procedures, Total Mathematics, Language, Spelling, Listening to Words and Stories, Listening, Environment, Science, and Social Science.

According to the publisher, administration of the *Stanford 10* requires no special training. Directions for administration are straightforward and easy for school staff or faculty to understand. Tests can be scored locally or can be sent to the publisher for offsite scoring and reporting. Use of calculators is permitted, but not required, for the Mathematics Problem Solving/Mathematics subtest, but may not be used on the Mathematics Procedures subtest. The publisher also provides a tool they call The Lexile Framework®, which allows teachers to match students to specific texts. It defines and sequences books and other reading materials in terms of difficulty and provides a way to link students' reading achievement to that scale.

The standardization sample closely follows the 2000 U.S. Census figures for geographic region, socioeconomic status, urban-rural, and ethnicity. According to Morse (2005), reliability estimates from full-length subtests are sufficient to make judgments about individual examinees. However, there are some exceptions, which include some abbreviated-length subtests, language prewriting, and some full-length subtests (e.g., Environment). However, estimates of reliability are high enough in all cases to make judgments about groups. Further, Carney (2005) concluded that reliability and validity appear to be satisfactory.

Iowa Tests of Basic Skills. The *Iowa Tests of Basic Skills Forms A and B* (*ITBS*) is a group-administered, norm-referenced battery of achievement tests for students in grades K–8 (ages 5 to 14). It is designed to measure growth in school achievement, specifically vocabulary, reading comprehension, language, mathematics, social studies, science, and sources of information. The three main purposes of the *ITBS* are: (a) to obtain information that can support instructional decisions made by teachers in the classroom, (b) to provide information to students and their parents for monitoring the student's growth from grade to grade, and (c) to examine yearly progress of grade groups as they pass through the school's curriculum (Engelhard, 2005).

The tests are ordered by levels corresponding to age and grade levels. The *ITBS* is available in Complete, Core, and Survey batteries, with the number of items and content areas varying across levels and batteries. For example, the total number of items in the Complete Battery varies from 146 items for Level 5 to 515 items for Level 14, with the Core and Survey Batteries having fewer items. Content areas vary by level with the following scores being available for the Complete Battery: Level 5 (Vocabulary, Word Analysis, Listening, Language, Mathematics, Reading Words, Reading Profile Total, and Core Total), Level 6 (same as Level 5, with the addition of Reading Comprehension and Reading Total), Levels 7 and 8 (Vocabulary, Word Analysis, Reading Comprehension, Reading Total, Listening, Spelling, Language, Math Concepts, Math Problems, Math Computation, Math Total, Core Total, Social Studies, Science, Sources of Information, Composite, Reading Profile Total, Survey Battery Total), and Levels 9 to 14 (Vocabulary, Reading Comprehension, Reading Total, Spelling, Capitalization, Punctuation, Usage and Expression, Language Total, Math Concepts and Estimation, Math Problem Solving and Data Interpretation, Math Computation, Math Total, Core Total, Social Studies, Science, Maps and Diagrams, Reference Materials, Sources of Information Total, Word Analysis [Level 9 only], Listening [Level 9 only], Composite, Reading Profile Total [Level 9 only], and Survey Battery Total). Raw scores, percent-correct scores, grade equivalents scores, developmental standard scores, percentile ranks, stanines, and normal curve equivalents are available.

In his *Mental Measurement Yearbook* review of the *ITBS*, Engelhard (2005) indicated that the *ITBS* is "as good as it gets" for a comprehensive, norm-referenced achievement test battery for elementary school students (Grades K to 8). He indicated that it is a well stan-dardized achievement test battery that has extensive evidence regarding its reliability and validity. Lane (2005) concurred with Engelhard, stating the reliability of the *ITBS* is "very respectable," and indicated that there is adequate support for validity. She did, however, cau-tion school districts to make sure that the content of the ITBS corresponds to the school's curriculum. Overall, the *ITBS* seems to be a good measure of student achievement in the elementary school grades.

Metropolitan Achievement Tests (MAT). The *Metropolitan Achievement Tests, Eighth Edi-tion* is a comprehensive measure of academic achievement in reading, mathematics, language arts, science, and social studies for students in grades K–12. Scores are provided for Sounds and Print, Reading Vocabulary, Reading Comprehension, Total Reading, Mathematics, Mathematics Concepts and Problem Solving, Mathematics Computation, Total Mathemat-ics, Language, Spelling, Science, Social Studies, and the Complete Battery. Tests can be hand or machine scored, and scores include scaled scores, national and local percentile ranks and stanines, grade equivalents, and normal curve equivalents.

The standardization sampling of the *MAT*, while expansive, is in need of additional details of the sampling and weighting process (Harwell, 2005). Four national research programs provided normative data for the *MAT*, including one sample that consisted of approximately 80,000 students from 151 school districts stratified by SES, urban-rural, and ethnicity. Har-well's concerns regarding the standardization sampling involve a lack of information on the sampling of school districts, which led the publisher to employ a weighting process that included the random duplication or deletion of some student records. While Harwell con-cluded that the weighting process was generally good, there was an overrepresentation of students from rural classrooms in one normative sample.

With regard to reliability, internal consistency reliability coefficients (KR20 and KR21) by subtest and by level as well as estimates of the Standard Error of Measurement are provided. According to Lukin (2005), the majority of the reliability coefficients are within an accept-able range (.8 to .9), with lower estimates associated primarily with lower grade levels (K–2) or the battery's short-form battery. In addition, test-retest reliability is reported in the test manual's appendix, although no information on how these data were collected is provided. While details of the collection process are lacking, Lukin concluded that the coefficients are within an acceptable range (.7 to .9). The lowest test-retest coefficients are associated with Social Studies, Science, or supplemental scores (research or thinking skills). The focus of validity reports on the *MAT* is with content-related validity, with Harwell (2005) concluding that there is a strong case in support of the content validity of the test. The publisher also notes that there is the need for a close match of *MAT* content with the local curriculum for the test to be used in a specific district or school. Lukin also reported that validity data provided are generally supportive of the tests validity. These data include completion rates, p-values, biserial correlations, progression of scaled scores, and correlations with other measures.

While both Harwell (2005) and Lukin (2005) wrote in support of the technical charac-teristics of the *MAT*, both had concerns with the lack of important information provided by the publisher. As detailed above, the lack of description of samples, designs, and statistical methods employed makes it difficult to draw firm conclusions about reliability and validity. While both Harwell and Lukin expressed concern over these deficiencies, both concluded that it appears to be more a problem of a lack of reporting than a major liability of the test. It appears that the *MAT8* is a viable group-administered test of academic achievement for school-age children.

Conclusions

The three tests reviewed in this chapter; the *Stanford Achievement Test* (10th ed.), the *Iowa Tests of Basic Skills,* and the *Metropolitan Achievement Tests* (8th ed.) all appear to be viable group tests of academic achievement for a local education agency (LEA). The LEA should, however, closely examine the test to verify a good match to the local curriculum. As the United States and many other Western countries have increased the use of tests such as these to monitor student progress, great concern has been given to the misuse of these tests and the subsequent effect these tests may have on the curriculum (e.g., curriculum narrowing; Berliner, 2011). All three tests appear to be psychometrically sound instruments, but the tests alone will not necessarily lead to what is best for all students. The potential for abusing the results of these tests exists, and schools must be cautious in interpreting these instruments, while at the same time legislators must be thoughtful with regard to legislation mandating the use of these and other potentially high-stakes tests. The danger lies not with the test, but with the use of the test results.

References

Amrein, A., & Berliner, D. (2002). High-stakes testing and student learning. *Education Policy Analysis Archives, North America.* Retrieved from http://epaa.asu.edu/ojs/article/view/297

Berliner, D. (2011). Rational responses to high stakes testing: The case of curriculum narrowing and the harm that follows. *Cambridge Journal of Education, 41,* 287–302.

Carney, R. N. (2005). Review of the Stanford Achievement Test, Tenth Edition. In R. A. Spies & B. S. Plake (Eds.), *The sixteenth mental measurements yearbook.* Lincoln, NE: Buros Institute of Mental Measurements.

Engelhard, G. (2005). Review of the Iowa Tests of Basic Skills, Forms A and B. In R. A. Spies & B. S. Plake (Eds.), *The sixteenth mental measurements yearbook.* Lincoln, NE: Buros Institute of Mental Measurements.

Harcourt Assessment (2003). *Stanford Achievement Test, Tenth Edition.* San Antonio, TX: Author.

Harwell, M. R. (2005). Review of the Metropolitan Achievement Tests, Eighth Edition. In R. A. Spies & B. S. Plake (Eds.), *The sixteenth mental measurements yearbook.* Lincoln, NE: Buros Institute of Mental Measurements.

Lane, S. (2005). Review of the Iowa Tests of Basic Skills, Forms A and B. In R. A. Spies & B. S. Plake (Eds.), *The sixteenth mental measurements yearbook.* Lincoln, NE: Buros Institute of Mental Measurements.

Lukin, L. E. (2005). Review of the Metropolitan Achievement Tests, Eighth Edition. In R. A. Spies & B. S. Plake (Eds.), *The sixteenth mental measurements yearbook.* Lincoln, NE: Buros Institute of Mental Measurements.

Morse, D. T. (2005). Review of the Stanford Achievement Test, Tenth Edition. In R. A. Spies & B. S. Plake (Eds.), *The sixteenth mental measurements yearbook.* Lincoln, NE: Buros Institute of Mental Measurements.

Munoz, R. (2006). *Make it or break it: High stakes testing pros and cons.* Retrieved from http://www.education.com/magazine/article/high-stakes-testing-pros-cons/

No Child Left Behind (NCLB) Act of 2001 (2002). Pub. L. No. 107-110, § 115, Stat. 1425.

Pearson Education. (2011). *A study of the Stanford Achievement Test Series, Tenth Edition (Stanford 10): Alignment to the Common Core State Standards.* Retrieved from http://education.pearsonassessments.com/hai/images/PDF/Stanford_10_Alignment_to_Common_Core_Standards.pdf

Scot, T. P., Callahan, C. M., & Urquhart, J. (2009). Paint-by-number teachers and cookie-cutter students: The unintended effects of high-stakes testing on the education of gifted students. *Roeper Review, 31,* 40–52.

Wu, M. (2010). Measurement, sampling, and equating errors in large-scale assessments. *Educational Measurement: Issues and Practice, 29,* 15–27.

7

Norm-Referenced Assessment and Bilingual Populations

Amanda B. Clinton and Pedro Olvera

It is well known that ethnic diversity in the United States has been on the rise for decades and that this trend is anticipated to continue in the upcoming years (U.S. Census Bureau, 2010a). As the number of individuals from diverse backgrounds increases, so does the number of U.S. residents who speak a language other than English in the home (Shin & Kominski, 2010). Naturally, students enrolled in the public school system in the United States reflect these demographic shifts. As such, our classrooms are more linguistically and culturally diverse than ever.

Bilingual and bicultural children in the United States are a heterogeneous group. More than 460 languages other than English are presently spoken in the United States, the most common being Spanish (79.2%), Vietnamese (2%), Hmong (1.6%), Cantonese (1%), and Korean (1%) (Kindler, 2002). Many of the students who are characterized as English Language Learners (ELLs) in the school system immigrated to the United States as children or adolescents, while others were born in the United States to parents who speak a language other than English at home. As a result, some ELLs learned two languages simultaneously, while others may have established their native language, and subsequently learned English. The number of children who struggle in this second language learning process have been shown to be related to demographic characteristics, such as age, socioeconomic status, citizenship status, and race/ethnicity (U.S. Department of Education [USDE], 2012). Almost twice as many children from households below or at the poverty line struggled with English, and those who were non-U.S. citizens demonstrated four times the likelihood of having language difficulties; the majority of these youngsters being identified as Hispanic (USDE, 2012).

According to the U.S Department of Education's National Center for Education Statistics, the percentage of school-aged children speaking a language other than English at home rose from 4.7 to 11.2 million in the 30-year period between 1980 and 2009 (USDE, 2012). Specifically, the percentage of school-aged children (those between the ages of 5 and 17) who are English Language Learners (ELLs) doubled from 10% to 21% during the past three decades, and now comprises approximately 43% of the overall school population. Although the number of school-aged children identified as experiencing difficulty with English language learning has decreased from 41% in 1980 to 24% in 2009 (USDE, 2010), a significant percentage continues to struggle.

The aforementioned statistical and demographic data support the need for school psychologists to understand the implications of bilingualism and biculturalism in relation to the use of standardized assessment for children enrolled in the public school system. In addition to recognizing issues related to testing in a child's second language, school psychologists must specifically understand how contextual factors, such as immigration and poverty, impact youngsters in terms of learning and behavior. This chapter addresses normative and second language acquisition processes, experiential factors that have been established as important for ELL students, and, later, specific norm-referenced measures and their uses and limitations for this population.

Language Acquisition: Native Language Acquisition

A series of generally predictable skills are involved in learning to talk and, later, learning to read in one's native language. Feldman (2011) explained that babies babble using all possible sounds across languages. However, as they become accustomed to hearing particular words and sounds, those elicited by infants increasingly reflect what they hear in their particular language environment. By about age 1, children begin speaking their first words and are focused on the phonemes related to the language that surrounds them. From this point, toddlers progress to two word combinations and, later, telegraphic speech (i.e., "I drink juice"), as the child's vocabulary becomes increasingly complex in their native language. Around age 3, children are capable of adding plurals (s) and past tense (-ed) to words. By age 5, the average child possesses the basic rules of language, although subtleties such as double entendre may be difficult for them. By age 8, even complex language usage is mastered.

Second Language Acquisition

Young children commonly acquire two languages with both relative ease and native fluency when they are exposed to the languages simultaneously, as in the case of bilingual first language acquisition (when they are exposed to "two" languages simultaneously). Additionally, many bilingual children are readily able to master a second language subsequent to establishing their first. Naturally, learning a second language—similar to learning one's first language—is a process that includes normative errors. These types of linguistic mistakes are not indicative of disability, but rather of learning acquisition processes.

When second language acquisition is sequential, it is not uncommon for the language learner to apply knowledge of their native language (L1) to the learning process of their second language (L2). In some cases, however, children acquire a second language directly, with lesser degrees of mapping from L1 to L2. Typical second language learning incorporates systemic and rule-governed errors (Paradis, 2005; Paradis, Rice, Crago, & Marquis, 2008). One frequent example is the tendency to apply regular past tense patterns to irregular verbs (Xu & Pinker, 1995), or confusion regarding regular and irregular plurals. An example of the former would be a statement such as, "He *eated*" instead of, "He *ate*." In terms of normative errors in irregular plural usage, an example would be "two *fishes*" instead of "two *fish*." Since bilingual children frequently experience inconsistent exposure to their L1 and L2, these types of normative errors may be more frequent than in monolingual children (Gathercole, 2007; Paradis, 2010).

In order to adequately evaluate the bilingual child, it is important to determine their dominant language. Determining language proficiency in L1 and L2 can present a particular challenge, because students may communicate well informally yet experience difficulty with academics in one or both languages.

Basic Interpersonal Communication (BICS; Cummins, 1981). Second language learners typically acquire socially oriented and context-embedded language within 6 months to 2 years from their initial exposure. The ability to converse with relative ease in one's L2, or mastery of Basic Interpersonal Communication (BICS), is facilitated by the environment in which conversation occurs and allows for a degree of flexibility in terms of vocabulary and usage. Engaging in verbally oriented social interactions is distinct from language usage in an academic context.

Cognitive Academic Language Proficiency (CALP; Cummins, 1981). In contrast to BICS, Cognitive Academic Language Proficiency (CALPS) is based on more technical terminology and demands significant grammatical fidelity from the speaker. CALPS may require 5–7 years to acquire. Since CALPS is rarely context embedded and is often content laden, such as teaching lectures presented in the classroom, it is considerably more challenging. CALPS is typically the area of interest in terms of school-based referrals for bilingual students and, therefore, must be determined prior to administering norm-referenced assessment measures (Olvera & Gomez-Cerrillo, in press).

Semilingualism

Children who demonstrate low literacy in both their native language and their second language may be defined as "semilingual" (Clinton, in press; Escamilla, 2006). Another term utilized to indicate the same meaning is "bi-illiteracy," which has been described as a "concept that implies low levels of literacy" in both one's native and second languages (Escamilla, 2006 p. 2330). Assessment of a semilingual child typically presents a highly complicated set of circumstances—such as immigration, low parental education levels, and poverty—that have impacted overall linguistic and, in all likelihood, cognitive development. In terms of formal assessment, semilingual children are often particularly challenging, because they do not possess a dominant language per se, but show limited vocabulary and usage in both their L1 and their L2.

Cross-Language Transfer

A child who is literate in his or her native language may be able to apply semantic or syntactic information from their L1 to the process of learning their L2, a phenomenon called cross-linguistic transfer (Kaushanskaya & Marian, 2007). Generally, the second language learner experiences a learning benefit on L2 acquisition from his or her native language knowledge in the form of cross-language transfer contributions. This process is considered bidirectional in that structural aspects, as well as specific components—such as vocabulary—of both the L1 and L2 contribute to the enrichment of the other (Paradis, Nicoladis, Crago, & Genesee, 2011; Sparks, Patton, Ganschow, & Humbach, 2012). Some research suggests an enhanced effect when the child's second language is more transparent, such as Spanish or Dutch, while their first language is more opaque, such as English (DeSousa, Greenop, & Fry, 2011; Sun-Alperin & Wang, 2011; van der Leij, Bekebrede, & Kotterink, 2010).

The bilingual child's language learning experience and literacy across languages varies widely and is distinct from that of monolingual children. Often, an ELL student will speak his/her parents' native tongue at home, learn some English from friends and the media within their community environments, and receive academic instruction predominantly in English at school. For this reason, the child may speak the family language fluently, but lack writing and spelling knowledge in this language. Furthermore, in cases where parents speak another language at home and cannot provide corrective support nor assist with homework, ELL children actually have less exposure to English overall than monolingual children. The degree to which one language transfers to another varies, but is typically greater when the child is highly literate in his or her L1 and the family environment facilitates L1 literacy (Sparks et al., 2012).

Semilingualism and Cross-language Transfer. It is recognized that native language literacy influences second language learning, and, in turn, that poor literacy in L1 can impact L2 learning. Research indicates that an insufficiently enriched L1 learning environment results in distinct growth patterns for both a child's native and acquired language (Gutiérrez-Clellen, Simon-Cereijido, & Sweet, 2012). For the school psychologist who plans to utilize norm-referenced assessment measures, determining a dominant language is important. However, in the case of semilingualism, this may not be possible. This situation is even further complicated if the child is a recent immigrant who is struggling with a new school system and distinct curriculum, has limited prior schooling or poor quality of previous schooling, and has low literacy at home. This is not uncommon for Spanish-dominant children learning English in the United States, and may place them at a particular disadvantage.

Critical Contextual Factors

Contextual factors that must be considered when assessing bilingual students include those related to family history and language use in addition to immigration, acculturation, poverty, and age/learning history. Since bilingual students are diverse not only in terms of race/ethnicity but broader experience and this larger context impacts English language learning.

Poverty

The notion of critical periods for language learning states that children are particularly sensitive to acquiring the sounds and cues related to language early in life (Feldman, 2011). Evidence suggests that sensitive periods for language learning exist for both one's native language and second language (Shafer & Garrido-Nag, 2007). Extreme environmental deprivation has a clear negative impact on brain development (Bos, Fox, Zeanah, & Nelson, 2009; Rymer, 1994; Veltman & Browne, 2001), yet even less severe circumstances may negatively impact L1 development and, in turn, present the potential for incomplete L2 development (Gutierrez-Clellan et al., 2012).

Family and School Context

In addition to linguistic aspects of language acquisition, other factors are critical to developing fluency in a second language, such as relationships between caregivers and children and academic experience. Studies have demonstrated relationships between home literacy environment and a child's later language development (de Jong & Leseman, 2001; Roberts, Jurgens, & Burchinal, 2005; Sénéchal & LeFevre, 2002). Positive, language-rich interactions between mothers or teachers and children can facilitate linguistic development (Pan, Rowe, Singer, & Snow, 2005; Quiroz, Snow, & Zhao, 2010).

Educational experience is also critical in relation to language development in the bilingual child. In cases where poverty was a concern in a bilingual child's past, it is not unlikely that he or she attended schools where resources and teacher preparation may have been limited. The lack of comprehensive literacy programs is considered critical to closing the literacy gap between rich and poor (Wamba, 2010), for which reason the lack of high-quality, language-based education is significant.

Upon enrolling in schools in the United States, bilingual children often face stereotypes and misinformation in the public schools. Data have shown that bilingual education teachers devalue the ideas and quality of thinking in their students when the students are unable to express themselves with clarity (Escamilla, 2006). Furthermore, teachers frequently assume that bilingual students received direct instruction in specific aspects of reading, oral expression, and writing that they were not actually taught. One example is use of the accent in Spanish. In one study, bilingual education teachers working in U.S. schools reported believing children from Mexico were instructed in the use of the accent in Spanish as soon as they began learning to write. However, focus on the use of accents typically occurs in upper elementary levels (Escamilla, 2006). These assumptions result in biased interpretations about causation, and incorrect conclusions about student abilities that might negatively influence their educational experience.

Immigration

The school psychologist who assesses a bilingual child must understand the implications of immigration. According to data collected by the U.S. Department of Education (2012), most of the youngsters who demonstrate difficulties with English acquisition are those who have recently arrived in the country and do not have official legal status. These demographics are further complicated by the fact that immigration is associated with low socioeconomic status, which, in turn, is related to learning difficulties (U.S. Census, 2010b).

Immigration tends to be a very stressful process. The negative impact of stress on learning and memory as a result of the body's physiological reaction response has been documented (Pinel, 2010). When the process of perceiving an attack—or being under stress—is prolonged, such as in the case of immigrating to a new country, stress hormones negatively impact brain functioning. This may result in observations of forgetfulness, distraction, and difficulties acquiring new information. If the family's transfer was dangerous in any way, these stress factors can be even greater. In addition to stress, immigration frequently implies extended travel or transition between countries and schools. Interruptions in schooling may result in falling behind in terms of basic skills and broader content.

Acculturation

Acculturation is defined by Merriam-Webster as "the cultural modification of an individual, group, or people by adapting or borrowing traits from another culture" (http://www.merriam-webster.com). It is considered a dynamic process that is ongoing and impacts a child's functioning in their new culture as a result of affecting attitudes and beliefs (Rivera, 2008). Understanding a child's level of acculturation is a key part of the assessment process, due to the way in which it may influence their academic, social-emotional, and behavioral functioning at school. A student who is not acculturated may experience particular difficulties understanding the rules and expectations in the classroom (Jacob, Decker, & Hartshorne, 2011). Resentments resulting from feelings of isolation at school or at home as a child is inclined more toward one culture or another may also be observed (Wells, 2009). Formal assessment tools and procedures, such as those utilized by teachers in the classroom or school psychologists during an evaluation, may be unfamiliar for a child who has a low level of acculturation, as well (Blatchley & Lau, 2010; Solano-Flores, 2008).

Norm-Referenced Tests and Bilingual Assessment: Bilingual/Multi-lingual Measures

The Bilingual Verbal Ability Tests (BVAT; Muñoz-Sandoval, Cummins, Alvarado, & Ruef, 2006) were developed to assess the verbal abilities of individuals from bilingual backgrounds from ages 5 to 90+. In addition to English, the BVAT is currently available in 16 languages. The BVAT has been normed on 8,818 subjects across 100 geographically diverse regions across the United States. The norming sample is based on the 2000 U.S. Census and considers the following factors: race/ethnicity, schooling, education, and occupation.

The BVAT provides an English Language Proficiency (ELP) cluster, which is a concise measure of the individual's oral language abilities (receptive and expressive) in the English language. In addition, a measure of the individual's bilingual verbal abilities (BVA) is provided, which is a cluster of the cognitive/academic language abilities of bilinguals (Muñoz-Sandoval et al., 2006). More specifically, the BVA is a cluster of the combined oral abilities (receptive and expressive) of both languages (L1 & L2). Interpretation of the ELP and BVA proceeds in the following manner:

> For a monolingual speaker, all language ability is available in English; therefore, the BVA and English language proficiency [ELP] score are identical. For a bilingual subject, the BVA score will be greater than the [ELP] if there are language abilities available in another language that are not available in English. (Muñoz-Sandoval et al., 2006, p. 3)

The BVA provides the examiner with a comprehensive understanding of the bilingual individual's total language ability in both L1 and L2.

The BVAT is similar to the Verbal Ability/Comprehension-Knowledge (Gc) cluster of the *Woodcock-Johnson Tests of Cognitive Abilities* (3rd Edition; Garfinkel & Stansfield, 1998). The Picture Vocabulary subtest examines the individual's expressive language skills through asking him/her to name familiar and unfamiliar items presented visually. The examinee is expected to respond in single words. The Oral Vocabulary subtest, which is composed of both antonyms and synonyms, assesses the examinee's comprehension of the meaning of words that are presented verbally. The Verbal Analogies subtest assesses the ability to comprehend and verbally complete a logical word association. The examinee provides the connection amongst key words in the analogy.

The examiner first administers all three subtests in English. Next, the items that were answered incorrectly in English are then administration in the student's home language (Garfinkel & Stansfield, 1998). The administration in the home language can be undertaken by the primary or ancillary examiner, provided that they are proficient in that language. The BVAT also provides an English CALP score, which ranges from one (negligible) to five (advanced). According to Garfinkel and Stansfield, the test can be used as a tool for the unbiased placement of learners both within and outside of special education. It is also sensitive to sociolinguistic issues, allowing students to demonstrate knowledge in their home languages. Limitations to consider when using this instrument include: limitations of bilingual individuals in the norm group, control for acculturation factors, language proficiency, and type of bilingual/ESL program (Rhodes, Ochoa, & Ortiz, 2005).

Reliability for the BVAT was calculated using the split-half procedure and corrected for length by the Spearman-Brown formula. Using this procedure, subtests were reported in the high .80s and mid .90s. Another test of reliability included the alternate-form alternate procedure, for which a median reliability of .84 was demonstrated. Evidence of concurrent validity, as discussed in the publication manual, also demonstrated high levels of correlation with other similar language proficiency measures, which ranged from .82 to .87. According to the manual, content validity was accounted for in that dialectal variations and untranslatable items were omitted (Muñoz-Sandoval et al., 2006).

The *Woodcock-Muñoz Language Survey-Revised* (*WMLS-R;* Alvarado, Ruef, & Schrank, 2005) provides a comprehensive overview of the individual's CALP abilities by assessing reading, writing, listening, and comprehension in both English and Spanish. The WMLS-R is appropriate for individuals ages 2 to 90+. The WML-R was normed on 8,782 subjects across the four major regions of United States (Northeast, Midwest, South, and West). The norming sample is based on the 2000 U.S. Census and considers the following factors: region, community size, sex, race, school, type of university, education, occupation, and country of birth (Schrank, McGrew, & Dailey, 2010).

Although traditional CALP designations range from 1 to 5, the WMLS-R provides designations ranging from 1 (very negligible) to 6 (very advanced). Unlike the BVAT, which only provides a verbal assessment of CALP ability, the WMLS-R goes further by adding the reading and writing cluster, thereby providing a more comprehensive measurement of the individual's CALP abilities.

As mentioned above, the WMLS-R provides English and Spanish CALP level for the various clusters including language (oral and expression), writing, and reading. The *Broad English Ability-Total* and *Amplia habilidad en español-Total* provide the most comprehensive measure of language ability (English and Spanish), including listening, speaking, reading, writing, and language comprehension. *The Oral Language-Total* and the *Lenguaje oral–Total* provide a broad measure of language competency of listening and speaking, language development, reasoning, and comprehension of language. Of particular interest is the Applied Language Proficiency (ALP), which provides a global CALP score across all language domains and serves as a global functioning of proficiency in English and Spanish. Limitations of the WMLS-R include: administration and scoring tend to be time consuming and complex, and Spanish version is not clear about socio-economic status, gender, or geographical location of norming sample (Brown & Ochoa, 2007).

The median reliability (split half) for the WMLS-R for the seven subtests ranged from .76 to .97. The median reliability for the 11 academic indices were calculated using Mosler's procedures and a range of .88 to .98 was reported (Alvarado et al., 2005). With regards to criterion-related validity, moderate correlations with other verbal measures are demonstrated. With respect to content validity, the manual provides an outline of each subtest as well as the mode of presentation and the response manner that is required of the individual. Construct validity was demonstrated by growth curves for each subtest, which plainly revealed age progression. Correlations with the Woodcock Johnson III Achievement ranged from .83–.91.

The *Wechsler Intelligence Scale for Children-Fourth Edition Spanish* (*WISC-IV Spanish*) was developed to assess Spanish dominant individuals ages 6 to 16 who are being educated in schools in the United States (Wechsler, 2005). The Spanish version is a direct translation and adaptation of the popular English version of the Wechsler Intelligence Scale for Children-Fourth Edition (WISC-IV). With the exception of the Word Reasoning subtest, all subtests have been retained in the Spanish version. The WISC-IV Spanish has included bilingual Spanish-speaking individuals in its norming sample. According to the publication manual (Wechsler, 2005), the purpose was "to ensure that the *WISC-IV Spanish* was clinically appropriate for use with Spanish-speaking children of diverse backgrounds living in the U.S." (p. 52).

For bilingual examiners, this tool provides materials in both English and Spanish to facilitate assessment in both languages. The norming sample included 851 English Language Learners (ELLs) who had been educated in the United States for fewer than 5 consecutive years and a Spanish reliability sample of 500 individuals (Clinton, 2007). In addition to the United States, regions represented in the norming include Mexico, Cuba, Puerto Rico, and the Dominican Republic, and Central and South America. The strength of the WISC IV-Spanish is that it was created for students who recently arrived in the United States and are in the process of learning English. Caution should be given, however, because the Spanish norms are equated to the WISC-IV English norms; consequently, the WISC-IV Spanish does not have distinct Spanish norms (Braden & Iribarren, 2005).

The split-half method was employed to determine reliability of the WISC-IV Spanish. Reliability coefficients for subtests ranged from a .74 (Symbol Search) to .90 (Letter-Number Sequencing). Excluding Symbol Search and Coding, the reliability coefficients of all other subtests are above .80. The median reliability of composite scores ranged from a low of .82 (Processing Speed) to a high of .97 (Full Scale Intellectual Quotient). According to the manual, content validity for the WISC-IV Spanish is acceptable due to the recognized validity of the English version of the WISC-IV. Convergent and discriminant validity was determined according to a pattern of a priori hypotheses regarding relationships between subtests and composite scores (Clinton, 2007). Concurrent validity was established by comparing the WISC-IV Spanish with other instruments (e.g., *Universal Nonverbal Intelligence Test* FSIQ & *Clinical Evaluation of Language Fundamentals 3 Spanish*).

Non-Verbal Measures

The *Universal Nonverbal Intelligence Tests* (*UNIT;* Bracken & McCallum, 1998) is a norm-referenced nonverbal intelligence test that assesses "the general intelligence and cognitive abilities of children and adolescents from ages 5 years through 17 years who may be disadvantaged by traditional verbal and language-loaded measures" (Bracken & McCallum, 1998, p. 1). The primary constructs of the UNIT include memory (attending, organizing, encoding, and recall) and reasoning (thinking ability and problem solving), and secondary constructs include symbolic (symbolic processing and mediation) and nonsymbolic internal mediation (perception, sequencing, organization, and memory (Bracken & McCallum, 1998, p. 16). Both the symbolic and nonsymbolic constructs combine to provide a full-scale intelligence quotient (FSIQ).

The UNIT was standardized on a norm sample of 2,100 children based on the 1995 U.S. Census. The sample considered the following factors: gender, race, Hispanic origin, region, parental educational attainment, community setting, classroom placement (regular or special education), and special education program (e.g., learning and speech and language disabilities, emotional-behavioral disorders, intellectual disability, giftedness, English language learners and bilingual education, and general education).

All communication between examiner and examinee is via gesture, with the intent of minimizing all modes of language (expressive and receptive; Bracken & McCallum, 1998). The UNIT uses the nine most common gestures: head nodding (approval), head shaking ("no"), open-hand shrugging ("what is the answer"), palm rolling ("continue"), pointing ("you do it"), hand waving (choose from a series of option), stop ("stop"), and thumbs up (approval). The strengths of the UNIT include relatively short administration times (30–45 minutes) and a variety of types of activities that keep students engaged. Some students may potentially become frustrated due to the prohibition of language administration of the UNIT. Though the manual presents good evidence with regards to disability identification, no evidence of the UNIT's validity in predicting academic achievement is presented (Bandalos, 2001).

The split-half method was employed to determine the reliability of the UNIT. Reliability coefficients standardization averages for subtests ranged from .64 (Mazes) to .91 (Cube Design). The median reliability composite scores ranged from a low of .86 (Reasoning) to .93 (Full Scale Intellectual Quotient) for the Extended Battery; the Abbreviated Battery reliability of the FSIQ was at .91. Test retest stability was estimated after a three-week time interval for a sample of 197 children. After correction for restriction of range, coefficients ranged from .78 to .91 for the Standard and Extended Battery full-scale scores; the Abbreviated Battery ranged from .74 to .89 (Bracken & McCallum, 1998).

Strong evidence of the factor structure of the UNIT has been demonstrated through exploratory and confirmatory factor analysis. Strong concurrent validity has been reported in the manual. Coefficients between the *Wechsler Intelligence Scale for Children–III* (*WISC III*) and the UNIT ranged from .78 to .84. Larger variability was demonstrated between the UNIT and the *Bateria-R* (Broad Cognitive Score), ranging from .30 to .67. According to the manual, predictive validity between the UNIT and achievement (i.e., *WJ-R, WIAT,* and *PIAT*) was relatively strong (McCallum & Bracken, 2012).

Non-Verbal Indices

The *Kaufman Assessment Battery for Children-Second Edition* (*KABC-2;* Kaufman & Kaufman, 2004) is a norm-referenced assessment of mental processing and the cognitive abilities of children ages 3 years to 18 years and 11 months. It was normed on a sample of 3,025 children in 253 testing sites across the United States. The KABC-2 utilizes a dual theoretical model incorporating both the Cattell-Horn-Carroll (CHC) theory of intelligence and Luria's neuropsychological theory of processing. The factorial structure, at the index level, includes the Fluid-Crystalized Index (FCI) and the Mental Processing Index (MPI). In addition, the KABC-2 includes a Nonverbal Index (NVI). The publishers claim that the examiner may choose either theoretical approach, based on the students background and experience.

The NVI has been developed for children for whom the FCI and MPI might not be appropriate, for example, individuals who may have difficulties with hearing, speech and language impairment, autism, and/or limited English proficiency (Kaufman, Lichtenberger, Fletcher-Janzen, & Kaufman, 2005). The premise underlying the development of the NVI was to "facilitate the valid assessment of children who have difficulty understanding verbal stimuli, responding orally, or both" (Kaufman et al., 2005, p. 177). The subtests that make up the NVI can be presented with gestures and responded to without words (Kaufman & Kaufman, 2004). The KABC-2 has received criticism about the interchangeability of its theoretical frameworks, specifically the CHC and Luria models. The criticism centers around the lack of utility of linking KABC-2 test data to educational and psychological interventions (Braden & Ouzts, 2005).

Internal and test-retest reliability coefficients for the NVI were computed using the Nunnally formula. Internal reliability for ages 3–6 were .90, and .92 for ages 7–18. Test–retest reliability for ages 3–6 were .72, and .87 for ages 7–18 (Kaufman et al., 2005). Overall, the KABC-2 has satisfactory construct and criterion-related validity. Confirmatory factor analytic (CFA) studies support that the KABC-2 measures a "g" factor as well as specific factors (e.g., fluid reasoning, short-term memory, visual processing, knowledge, and long term-retrieval; Sattler, 2008). The KABC-2 also demonstrated a median correlation of .81 (range .72 to .91) with other tests of intelligence (e.g., *WJ III* & *WISC IV*). In addition, a median correlation of .73 (range .67 to .79) was obtained with academic tests. The NVI in particular correlated with math (KTEA) at a range of .65 to .67, with reading at a range of .60 with reading, and .50s to .60s with oral language (Kaufman et al., 2005, p. 177).

Conclusions

Bilingual students in the United States bring myriad uniquenesses and complexities with them in terms of life experience that influence language acquisition and school performance. Frequently, ELLs have been exposed to their native and second tongues to differing degrees, depending on their educational and family backgrounds, and these factors have the potential to significantly impact school and test performance. Stressors, such as immigration, poverty, inconsistent education, and acculturation, can further influence the way in which a child responds when engaged in formal assessment. Several norm-referenced measures may be utilized with bilingual ELL students, as previously discussed, but these findings must be interpreted with caution and within the broader context of the realities of the bilingual student.

References

Alvarado, D. G., Ruef, M. L., & Schrank, F. A. (2005). *Comprehensive manual: Woodcock-Muñoz Language Survey-Revised.* Itasca, IL: Riverside Publishing.

Bandalos, D. L. (2001). Review of the Universal Nonverbal Intelligence Test. In B. S. Plake & J. C. Impara (Eds.), *The fourteenth mental measurements yearbook* (pp. 1295–1298). Lincoln, NE: The Buros Institute of Mental Measurements.

Blatchley, L. A., & Lau, M. Y. (2010). *Culturally competent assessment of English language learners for special education services.* Retrieved from http://www.nasponline.org/publications/cq/pdf/V38N7_CulturallyCompetentAssessment.pdf

Bos, K. J., Fox, N., Zeanah, C. H., & Nelson, C. (2009). Effects of early psychosocial deprivation on the development of memory and executive function. *Frontiers in Behavioral Neuroscience, 3,* doi: 10.3389/neuro.08.016.2009

Bracken, B. A., & McCallum, R. S. (1998). *Universal Nonverbal Intelligence Test.* Itasca, IL: Riverside Publishing.

Braden, J. P., & Iribarren, J. A. (2005). Test review: Wechsler, D. (2005). Wechsler Intelligence Scale for Children, Fourth Edition, Spanish. *Journal of Psychoeducational Assessment, 25,* 292–299.

Braden, J. P., & Ouzts, S. M. (2005). Review of the Kaufman Assessment Battery for Children–Second Ed. In R. A. Spies & B. S. Plake (Eds.), *The sixteenth mental measurements yearbook* (pp. 517–520). Lincoln, NB: Buros Institute of Mental Measurements, University of Lincoln Press.

Brown, J. D., & Ochoa, S. H. (2007). Review of the Woodcock-Muñoz Language Survey-Revised. In *The seventeenth mental measurements yearbook.* Retrieved from http://www.unl.edu/buros/

Clinton, A. B. (2007). Test review: Wechsler, D. (2005). Wechsler Intelligence Scale for Children, Fourth Edition, Spanish. San Antonio, TX: Psychological Corporation. *Journal of Psychoeducational Assessment, 25,* 285–292.

Clinton, A. B. (in press). Assessment of the semi-lingual child. In A. B. Clinton (Ed.), *Integrated assessment of the bilingual child.* Washington, DC: APA.

Cummins, J. (1981). The role of primary language development in promoting educational success for language minority students. In California State Department of Education (Ed.), *Schooling and language minority students: A theoretical framework*. Los Angeles: Evaluation, Dissemination and Assessment Center, California State University.

de Jong, P. F., & Leseman, P. P. M. (2001). Lasting effects of home literacy on reading achievement in school. *Journal of School Psychology, 39,* 389–414.

De Sousa, D., Greenop, K., & Fry, J. (2011). Language transfer of spelling strategies in English and Afrikaans. *International Journal of Bilingual Education and Bilingualism, 14,* 49–67.

Escamilla, K. (2006). Semilingualism applied to the literacy behaviors of Spanish-speaking emerging bilinguals: Bi-illiteracy or emerging bi-illiteracy? *Teachers College Record, 108,* 2329–2353.

Feldman, R. (2011). *Essentials of understanding psychology* (9th ed.). New York, NY: McGraw-Hill.

Garfinkel, A., & Stansfield, C. W. (1998). *Review of the Bilingual Verbal Ability Tests.* Retrieved from the Mental Measurements Yearbook database.

Gathercole, V. M. (2007). Miami and North Wales, so far and yet so near: A constructivist account of morpho-syntactic development in bilingual children. *International Journal of Bilingual Education and Bilingualism, 10,* 224–247.

Gutiérrez-Clellan, V., Simon-Cereijido, G., & Sweet, M. (2012). Predictors of second language acquisition in Latino children with specific language impairment. *American Journal of Speech-Language Pathology, 21,* 64–77.

Jacob, S., Decker, D. M., & Hartshorne, T. S. (2011). *Ethics and law for school psychologists.* New York, NY: John Wiley & Sons, Ltd.

Kaufman, A. S., & Kaufman, N. L. (2004). *Kaufman Assessment Battery for Children: Technical manual* (2nd ed.). Circle Pines, MN: American Guidance Service.

Kaufman, A. S., Lichtenberger, E. O., Fletcher-Janzen, E., & Kaufman, N. L. (2005). *Essentials of KABC-II Assessment.* Hoboken, NJ: John Wiley & Sons.

Kaushanskaya, M., & Marian, V. (2007). Nontarget language recognition and interference in bilinguals: Evidence from eye-tracking and picture naming. *Language Learning, 57,* 119–163.

Kindler, A. L. (2002). *Survey of the states limited English proficient students and available educational programs and services: 2001–2001.* Washington, DC: Office of English Language Acquisition, Language Enhancement and Academic Achievement for Limited English Proficient Students. Retrieved from http://www.ncela.gwu.edu/files/rcd/BE021853/Survey_of_the_States.pdf

McCallum, R. S., & Bracken, B. A. (2012). The Universal Nonverbal Intelligence Test: A multi-dimensional nonverbal alternative for cognitive assessment. In D. P. Flanagaon & P. L. Harrison (Eds.), *Contemporary intellectual assessment* (pp. 357–375). New York, NY: Guilford Press.

Muñoz-Sandoval, A. F., Cummins, J., Alvarado, C. G., & Ruef, M. L. (2006). *Bilingual Verbal Ability Tests: Manual.* Rolling Meadows, IL: Riverside Publishing.

Olvera, P., & Gomez-Cerrillo, L. (in press). Integrated intellectual assessment of the bilingual student. In A. B. Clinton (Ed.), *Integrated assessment of the bilingual child.* Washington, DC: APA.

Pan, B. A., Rowe, M. L., Singer, J. D., & Snow, C. E. (2005). Maternal correlates of growth in toddler vocabulary production in low-income families. *Child Development, 76,* 763–782.

Paradis, J. (2005). Grammatical morphology in children learning English as a second language: Implications of similarities with specific language impairment. *Language, Speech, and Hearing Services in the Schools, 36,* 172–187.

Paradis, J. (2010). Bilingual children's acquisition of English verb morphology: Effects of language exposure, structure complexity, and task type. *Language Learning, 60,* 651–680.

Paradis, J., Nicoladis, E., Crago, M., & Genesee, F. (2011). Bilingual children's acquisition of the past tense: A usage-based approach. *Journal of Child Language, 38,* 554–578.

Paradis, J., Rice, J. J., Crago, M., & Marquis, J. (2008). The acquisition of tense in English: Distinguishing child's second language from first language and specific language impairment. *Applied Psycholinguistics, 29,* 689–722. doi: 10.1017/S0142716408080296

Pinel, J. P. (2010). *Biopsychology* (8th ed.). New York, NY: Pearson.

Quiroz, B., Snow, C. E., & Zhao, J. (2010). Vocabulary skills of Spanish/English bilinguals: Impact of mother-child language interactions and home language and literacy support. *International Journal of Bilingualism, 14,* 379–399. doi: 10.1177/1367006910370919

Rhodes, R. L., Ochoa, H. S., & Ortiz, S. O. (2005). *Assessing culturally and linguistically diverse students: A practical guide.* New York, NY: Guilford.

Rivera, L. M. (2008). Acculturation and multicultural assessment: Issues, trends, and practice. In L. A. Suzuki & J. G. Ponterrotto (Eds.), *Handbook of multicultural assessment: clinical, psychological, and educational applications* (3rd ed., pp. 73–91). San Francisco, CA: John Wiley & Sons, Inc.

Roberts, J., Jurgens, J., & Burchinal, M. (2005). The role of home literacy practices in preschool children's language and emergent literacy skills. *Journal of Speech, Language and Hearing Research, 48,* 345–359.

Rymer, R. (1994). *Genie: A scientific tragedy.* New York, NY: Penguin.

Sattler, J. (2008). *Assessment of children: Cognitive foundations* (5th ed.). San Diego, CA: Author.

Schrank, F. A., McGrew, K. S., & Dailey, D. E. H. (2010). Technical supplement. *Woodcock-Muñoz Language Survey–Revised Normative Update.* Rolling Meadows, IL: Riverside Publishing.

Sénéchal, M., & LeFevre, J. (2002). Parental involvement in the development of children's reading skill: A five-year longitudinal study. *Child Development, 73,* 445–460.

Shafer, V. L., & Garrido-Nag, K. (2007). The neurodevelopmental bases of language. In E. Hoff & M. Shatz (Eds.), *Blackwell handbook of language development.* Malden, MA: Blackwell Publishing.

Shin, H. B., & Kominski, R. A. (2010). *Language use in the United States: 2007, American Survey Reports.* Retrieved from http://www.census.gov/hhes/socdemo/language/data/acs/ACS-12.pdf

Solano-Flores, G. (2008). Who is given tests in what language by whom, when, and where? The need for probabilistic views of language in the testing of English language learners. *Educational Researcher, 37,* 189–199.

Sparks, R. L., Patton, J., Ganschow, L., & Humbach, N. (2012). Do L1 reading achievement and L1 print exposure contribute to the prediction of L2 proficiency? *Language Learning, 62,* 473–505.

Sun-Alperin, M. K., & Wang, M. (2011). Cross-language transfer of phonological and orthographic processing skills from Spanish L1 to English L2. *Reading and Writing, 24,* 591–614.

U.S. Census Bureau. (2010a). *2010 census shows America's diversity.* Retrieved from http://2010.census.gov/news/releases/operations/cb11-cn125.html

U.S. Census Bureau. (2010b). *Poverty status of families by family type, nativity, and U.S. citizenship status and householder: 2009.* Retrieved from http://www.census.gov/population/foreign/data/cps2010.html

U.S. Department of Education. (2010). *The condition of education 2010* (NCES 2010–013). Washington, DC: National Center for Education Statistics.

U.S. Department of Education, National Center for Education Statistics. (2012). *The Condition of Education 2011* (NCES 2011–045), Indicator 6. Retrieved from http://nces.ed.gov/fastfacts/display.asp?id=96

van der Leij, B., Bekebrede, J., & Kotterink, M. (2010). Acquiring reading and vocabulary in Dutch and English: The effect of concurrent instruction. *Reading and Writing, 23,* 415–434.

Veltman, M. W., & Browne, K. D. (2001). Three decades of child mal-treatment research: Implications for the school years. *Trauma, Violence and Abuse, 2,* 215–239.

Wamba, N. G. (2010). Poverty and literacy: An introduction. *Reading & Writing Quarterly: Overcoming Learning Difficulties, 26,* 189–194.

Wells, R. (2009). Segregation and immigration: An examination of school composition for children of immigrants. *Equity and Excellence in Education, 42,* 130–151.

Wechsler, D. (2005). *Wechsler Intelligence Scale for Children–Fourth edition Spanish.* San Antonio, TX: The Psychological Corporation.

Xu, F., & Pinker, S. (1995). Weird past tense forms. *Journal of Child Language, 22,* 531–556.

Part III
Curriculum-Based Assessment

8

The Basics of Curriculum-Based Assessment

Theodore J. Christ, Milena A. Keller-Margulis,
and Amanda M. Marcotte

Curriculum-Based Assessment (CBA) was initially conceptualized as a category of techniques used to test student performance with materials that were sampled from the local curriculum (Tucker, 1985). The rationale was that the most instructionally relevant information is that which substantially corresponds with the student's experience in the classroom. Direct observation of student performance within classroom conditions provides insight on how a student performs in the curriculum and what might be done to improve student achievement. In many ways, CBA contrasts with that of published norm-referenced tests (PNRT). PNRT include most state accountability measures, along with many individually administered tests that are used by educational diagnosticians and school psychologists. They are not designed or intended to ensure substantial overlap with the curriculum or instructional procedures that are employed locally. Instead, PNRT are generally designed to represent the broad domain of an academic subject, such as reading or mathematics. They are not designed to guide curriculum placement or help refine instructional procedures. Instead, they are often used for accountability or classification. As a result, PNRT are commonly viewed as tangential or irrelevant to daily instruction. CBA was conceptualized, in part, to fill the gap left by PNRT, with improved relevance to daily instruction and curriculum placement decisions.

This chapter provides an overview of the historical perspective on assessment. This is useful because it establishes the primary distinctions between psychometric and behavioral assessments. Because CBA was historically aligned with behavioral assessment, that perspective helps illuminate some underlying assumptions and critical features. Subsequently, the prominent methods of CBA are described. Those include Curriculum-Based Measurement (CBM), Brief Experimental Analysis (BEA), Curriculum-Based Assessment for Instructional Design (CBA-ID), Curriculum-Based Assessment Criterion Referenced (CBA-CR), and Curriculum-Based Evaluation (CBE). Finally, the IDEAL Problem-Solving Model (PSM) is presented to situate each type of CBA in context.

Historical Perspective

The evolution and development of psychology as a science substantially influenced educational assessment. Prior to the mid-1800s, the human condition was understood primarily through mystics and philosophy. There were early pioneers associated with the emerging sciences of psychology and education who postulated, and later demonstrated, that it is possible to use objective methods of observation to describe and better understand the human condition. Alfred Binet's work in France in the early 1900s is a noteworthy example. He endeavored to devise a measure of human ability so that educational resources would not be wasted on the intellectually inferior. Versions of his scales continue to be used around the world in the present day; however, we use assessments in the United States for very different purposes. We use assessments to identify those students who are at risk, and improve their chances of success. We use assessments to protect and promote the success of vulnerable populations with practices that are founded in both case law and statute (cf., Individuals with Disabilities Education Improvement Act [IDEIA], 2004; No Child Left Behind Act [NCLB], 2001). In the pursuit to improve educational outcomes, there are two fairly distinct perspectives on the development, use, and evaluation of assessments. There is the psychometric perspective and the behavioral perspective.

Psychometric Assessment

The psychometric perspective emerged in the mid-to-late 1800s when Galton and Pearson collaborated to employ correlational methods that described human attributes. There were substantial gains in the science of psychometrics throughout the twentieth century. As an extension of correlational methods, Latent Trait Theory developed as the foundation of contemporary psychometrics. A latent trait is a semi-hidden characteristic of an individual that explains—or causes—a person's performance on relevant tasks. Intelligence and domain specific abilities (e.g., reading and math) are good examples of latent traits. The magnitude of a person's reading ability might be inferred or estimated from observations of their performance on a variety of tasks. The emphasis is not on the performance of any particular task or test item. Instead, the emphasis is on generalized performance across items, which represent the underlying ability. This serves as the primary justification for the use of multiple-choice tests, which is the prominent response and scoring modality used for most PNRT. Although the trait cannot be observed directly, it is inferred using correlational methods to demonstrate a generalized underlying ability that exists in the population. For that reason, psychometric methods are considered nomothetic, which use specific instances to infer a general phenomenon. In the case of reading, a student who performs poorly on a number of reading tasks is likely to be low on an underlying trait of reading ability. A student who performs well is likely to be high on the underlying trait. This is a point of criticism, because it requires multiple levels of inference. First, it requires us to infer the underlying trait, which is not directly observable. Second, it requires us to infer that the underlying trait has instructional utility or environmental/classroom relevance. The behavioral approach to assessment does not require any such inference.

Behavioral Assessment

The behavioral perspective emerged with James in the late 1800s (with the emergence of Functionalism) and continued to develop, with notable contributions from Skinner and others. The behavioral perspective emerged as a response to both introspection and higher inference correlational methods. It is generally consistent with the popularized notion of "black box" psychology, where the phenomenon of interest is always observable. That which we cannot directly observe is put aside for purposes of assessment and hypothesis development (i.e., explanations for the cause or solutions of problems; cf., Christ & Aranas, 2014).

There are many interesting phenomenon that may exist in the recesses of the mind or brain; however, behavioral assessment limits itself to that which is directly observable. From that perspective, an underlying trait is unnecessary. The primary interest is student performance on a particular task or item. Those tasks or items for which students have success represent established skills. Those tasks or items for which students do not have success represent skills that require additional demonstration, instruction, and practice. This contrasts with the higher inference nomothetic approach inherent to the psychometric perspective. Behavior assessment places emphasis on the individual student, individual tasks, and individual situations. Rather than multiple-choice-type items, authentic performance-type tasks are used more often.

Student performances on classroom tasks are measured in metrics of frequency, rate, duration, latency, magnitude, and topography. Moreover, the primary context for observation is the naturalistic environment. In the case of students, the most natural academic environment is the classroom and the most relevant tasks and items derive from the classroom situation. In contrast with the nomothetic approach of psychometrics, behavioral assessment is an idiographic approach. The approach aims to understand specific instances and unique phenomenon, which is a student's performance on a particular task. It does not depend on correlational methods or inferences of a latent trait. For that reason, behavioral assessment is considered low inference and most relevant to evaluate individual student performance within the local curriculum.

Related Developments

The dichotomy between psychometric and behavior assessment is convenient to illustrate philosophical distinctions. CBA is indeed more closely aligned with behavioral assessment than psychometric assessment; however, psychometric concepts are often applied to assessments with behavioral origins. For example, validity and reliability are often applied to evaluate the quality of CBA metrics. The intermingling of the two approaches can create confusion, especially upon a review of the published research. CBA is not treated as a purely behavioral assessment by contemporary researchers despite its origins.

Interpretations. CBA performance is interpreted using one of a variety of references: norm-reference, criterion-reference, benchmark reference, self-reference, and goal referenced. A norm-reference interpretation defines the status of student performance relative to some peer group. CBA often depends on local norms, which might characterize performance in a student's classroom, grade, school or district. *Norm-referenced* interpretations often establish a percentile rank for student performance, such that they might approximate average performance at the 50th percentile, low performance at the 20th percentile, or high performance at the 80th percentile. Unlike PNRT, national norms are used less frequently, because they are generally less relevant to educational decisions. *Criterion-referenced* interpretations establish an absolute level of performance that is expected of all students. For example, it is common to expect students to perform basic academic tasks at a high rate of accuracy. Both oral reading accuracy and basic math fact accuracy are expected to be 95%. This criterion is independent of local or national norms.

Benchmark-referenced interpretations are a hybrid of both norms and criterion. They establish the absolute level of performance on a task that predicts success on other PNRT, such as state-wide tests. For example, there are defined rates of oral reading fluency that are highly predictive of student performance on state tests. Student performance on CBA tasks can be compared against such benchmarks to evaluate the likelihood for long-term academic success. Such benchmarks are often used to estimate if a student is at high risk, some risk, or low risk.

Finally, there are *self-referenced* interpretations. These are used to evaluate the strengths and weaknesses of students or student groups within or across academic domains. It might be used to establish that sight word accuracy is 80% and addition fact accuracy is 30% of first grade. Such comparisons might help establish instructional targets/priorities. It might also be used to compare student growth (i.e., rate of student achievement) across instructional conditions. A related concept is *goal-referenced* interpretations, which is a hybrid of criterion-referenced or benchmark-referenced with self-referenced interpretations. A goal-referenced interpretation compares student performance across time, with a goal of expected academic improvement. Students who meet their weekly or short-term goal are more likely to meet their long-term goals. There are some subtleties to these methods of interpretation, but this serves as a useful general description. Norms and benchmarking are often used for screening or problem identification. Criterion referenced and self-referenced interpretations are often used for problem analysis and instructional planning. Finally, goal-referenced interpretations are used to evaluate the quality of instructional programs or progress monitoring.

General Outcome and Specific Mastery Measurement. Fuchs and Deno (1991) delineated two paradigms for CBA: Specific Mastery Measurement (SMM) and General Outcomes Measurement (GOM). SMM is used to assess student performance in a relatively narrow domain, while GOM is used to assess performance in a relatively broad domain. GOM is useful to assess student performance continuously throughout the academic year; therefore, CBAs that are constructed as a GOM encompass those skills and stimuli that span the 9 months of an academic year. Within the context of GOM, it is expected that students are unfamiliar with some of the grade level content when assessed early in the year. For example, if two-digit by two-digit multiplication were taught in third grade, then the corresponding GOM would include that and other third-grade skills and stimuli. In contrast, SMM is useful to assess student performance for a brief period of time, which is typically defined by one or a few instructional units. A math probe comprised entirely of two-digit by two-digit multiplication problems is an example of a SMM.

The distinction between GOM and SMM is often highlighted when CBA is discussed and defined. There are benefits of each approach. GOM tends to be more predictive of PNRT, which includes state accountability measures. It also tends to be more useful for both tri-annual screening in the fall, winter, and spring, and for progress monitoring across the entire academic year. SMM tends to be more useful to isolate instructional deficits and monitor progress over brief periods of time—because it is more sensitive to instructional effects.

Other Relevant Notes. There are a few points of confusion that we seek to clarify with substantial brevity. First, the term curriculum-*based* assessment can be misleading. It has become more common to use generic stimuli that are curriculum-like rather than to sample directly from the curriculum. Generally, the relevant research supports the practice so long as many of the other tenets of CBA and behavior assessment are retained (Fuchs & Deno, 1994).

Second, there is some discussion of high- and low-stakes decisions in the literature. In general, CBA was developed to inform low-stakes decisions, but it has become increasingly relevant for higher-stakes decisions in recent years. A low-stake decision is made frequently, is easily reversed, and has fewer long-term consequences. Day-to-day classroom decisions by the teacher are of relatively low stakes, but in sum they have a substantial impact. A high-stake decision is made rarely, is difficult to reverse, and has clear long-term consequences. Special education eligibility decisions are of relatively high stakes. It is critical that users of CBA understand the research-base and interpretive guidelines when they use CBA, especially if CBA outcomes are used to guide high-stakes decisions. In general, CBA was developed to guide low-stakes decisions and, in most cases, the evidence does not clearly support the use of CBA as a primary determinant for high-stakes decisions.

Prominent Examples

There are a few prominent examples of CBA that are featured in the literature. In order of their prominence, these include Curriculum-Based Measurement (CBM), Brief Experimental Analysis (BEA), Curriculum-Based Assessment for Instructional Design (CBA-ID), Curriculum Based Assessment Criterion Referenced (CBA-CR), and Curriculum-Based Evaluation (CBE). These examples all emerged as methods that used curriculum samples, authentic performance-based tasks, and low-inference interpretations of student performance to guide instruction and curriculum placement of students. These are briefly described below with more detail provided for the more prominent examples in current practice. Each section includes a brief description of the type of CBA followed by a review of the relevant research. The sections are written for a nontechnical audience. There are relevant citations, which can be accessed for more detailed information.

Curriculum-Based Measurement

Curriculum-Based Measurement (CBM) was developed to index the level and rate of student achievement in four basic skills: reading, math, spelling, and written expression. There are several distinguishing features of CBM that make it a unique measurement strategy. First, the administration and scoring of CBM is standardized and supported by research (Deno, 2003; Fuchs, 2004; Shinn, 1989; also see the special issue of *Journal of Special Education, 41[2]*). The use of CBM provides an indication of whether the student is performing adequately in grade level material, but it was not developed to diagnose specific academic deficits. It is intended as a GOM.

As the most prominent example, CBM for reading (CBM-R) is a 1-minute administration of a grade level passage. The examiner listens to the student read aloud and records a range of errors (e.g., omissions, substitutions, mispronunciations). At the end of 1 minute, the examiner records the total number of words read and subtracts the errors observed to arrive at the words read correct per minute (WRCM). The WRCM metric functions as an indicator, or "vital sign," of general reading achievement (Deno, 2003). As is described below, CBM procedures are often featured in other types of CBA.

The measures across subjects such as math and writing are similar. They use brief, timed samples of academic behavior to characterize performance. CBM was originally developed as measures that could be constructed by the user with curriculum sampling techniques (for procedures, see Shapiro, 2011a, b). The tasks and items were literally samples from the curriculum. More recently, commercially available materials were established. They provide the benefits and convenience of established difficulty levels, demonstrated technical adequacy, and norms. Prominent examples include the Formative Assessment System for Teachers (FAST; cehd.fast.umn.edu), AIMSweb (www.aimsweb.com), and Dynamic Indicators of Basic Early Literacy Skills (DIBELS; dibels.uoregon.edu).

Research Basis

CBM is one of the more researched examples of CBA. There are decades of research that provide substantial evidence of the reliability and validity of CBM as an indicator of basic skills development. The work to support the use of CBM dates back to the early 1980s (Deno, 1985; Deno, Mirkin, & Chiang, 1982). Early studies quickly provided evidence that CBM-R was a reliable and valid assessment to differentiate between typically achieving students in general education and those with reading deficits and disabilities (Peterson & Shinn, 2002). For an early review of the technical adequacy work conducted regarding CBM-R, the reader is directed to Marston (1989). More recently, reliability studies of CBM-R have yielded results suggesting adequate levels of test-retest reliability (e.g., Hosp & Fuchs, 2005), alternate forms reliability (Espin & Deno, 1993; Christ & Ardoin, 2009), and various types of validity (Wayman, Wallace, Wiley, Ticha, & Espin, 2007).

The validity of CBM-R has been well researched using various criterion measures (e.g., Deno et al., 1982; Fuchs & Deno, 1981, 1992) as well as statewide achievement tests used for accountability purposes (e.g. Good, Simmons, & Kame'enui, 2001; Hintze & Silberglitt, 2005; Shapiro, Keller, Lutz, Santoro, & Hintze, 2006; Stage & Jacobsen, 2001). Research has also been conducted to examine the relative utility of CBM-R for diverse populations with some studies suggesting CBM-R as a non-biased tool for measuring reading skills (Hintze, Callahan, Matthews, Williams, & Tobin, 2002) and others suggesting bias (e.g., Kranzler, Miller, & Jordan, 1999). Despite this lack of consistency, CBM-R is largely considered a technically adequate tool for a variety of purposes in the educational setting. Finally, most of the work regarding CBM-R was conducted at the elementary level; however, some studies suggest that this measure can also be used with middle school students (e.g. Espin & Deno, 1995; Muyskens & Marston, 2006). For an extensive review of the contemporary technical adequacy research on CBM-R, the reader is directed to Wayman et al. (2007).

There is also research to support the technical adequacy of CBM math computation and concepts and applications CBMs (see Foegan, Jiban, & Deno, 2007, for a review), and CBM writing (see McMaster & Espin, 2007). Additionally, substantial research supports the use of CBM for various activities, including screening to identify students at-risk (Deno, 2003), progress monitoring academic growth in response to instruction or intervention (Deno, Fuchs, Marston, & Shin, 2001; Fuchs, Fuchs, Hamlett, Walz, & Germann, 1993), and instructional planning (Fuchs, Fuchs, Hamlett, Phillips, & Bentz, 1994). It is the characteristics and unique functions of CBM discussed here that make it a valuable outcome measure and type of CBA as well as a measurement tool within the other approaches to CBA.

Brief Experimental Analysis

Compared to the other CBA models discussed, BEA is the most rooted in behavioral assessment. This methodology uses functional behavioral assessment strategies to investigate the effectiveness of various interventions to facilitate selection of the best intervention. This type of approach to select instructional interventions is identified as an efficient and effective method, because it allows for the examiner to test individualized interventions. As a result, the intervention that has the best impact can be selected and used while the implementation of a less effective or overly cumbersome strategy is avoided (Martens, Eckert, Bradley, & Ardoin, 1999; Riley-Tillman, Chafouleas, & McGrath, 2004).

The general steps for conducting a BEA (Riley-Tillman et al., 2004) begin with a review of data to determine the focus for intervention and possible goals for progress. Based on these data, interventions are identified that may be appropriate for the skills problem. The third step is to establish a plan for testing each intervention, followed by the determination of what order the interventions will be administered. Next, the dependent measure, often CBM, is selected, followed by data collection to establish the baseline performance on the skill of interest. Based on this information, any necessary changes to the goal are made and then implementation of the interventions begins. The interventions are implemented in the order previously determined, and data using the dependent measure is collected after each intervention is tried. The data are then reviewed, and often depicted graphically, such that the impact the interventions had on the student's skills can be compared and the best intervention selected (Riley-Tillman et al., 2004).

The BEA approach relies on single case design principles. The foundation of BEA is determining a functional relationship between the intervention selected and the academic skill performance of the student. This is demonstrated by the student response to repeated manipulation of the intervention strategies, followed by a return to baseline. A BEA approach does deviate from what would be considered ideal single-case design procedures, because the time during which each intervention is implemented is typically too brief to allow for sufficient data to suggest a true functional relationship (Riley-Tillman & Burns, 2009).

Research Basis

The evidence to support the use of BEA began in the applied behavior analysis literature and has been extended to the academic skills literature. Research has suggested the value of this methodology for the field of school psychology (Jones & Wickstrom, 2002; Martens et al., 1999). Although BEA shares terminology and some procedural elements with functional analysis (FA), it is distinguished from the latter by the focus on interventions to address problem behaviors or skills deficits, whereas FA is designed to examine the function of a behavior (Martens et al., 1999).

There is a body of literature examining the use of BEA to address academic skills problems across a range of academic areas. For example, studies have demonstrated the use of BEA procedures to select an intervention to address oral reading fluency skills. Jones and Wickstrom (2002) used BEA procedures to compare and contrast various interventions for five elementary students, with results indicating different interventions as more effective for various participants. Eckert, Ardoin, Daly, and Martens (2002) also used BEA to determine the most effective strategy to improve oral reading fluency. The methodology in this study examined the relative effectiveness of strategies to improve performance for students with reading difficulties. BEA principles and procedures were used to guide the examination of antecedent strategies, including passage preview and repeated readings, and consequence strategies, including reinforcement and performance feedback, and whether a combination of both resulted in the greatest impact on reading performance. Using an antecedent strategy improved performance for all students; however, for most of the participants (4 out of 6 students), combining both the antecedent and one or both of the consequence strategies had the greatest impact on reading. The specific combination that was most effective for each student was identified through the BEA procedures. There are numerous other studies that have used BEA procedures to identify the most advantageous intervention to improve academic skills in reading (e.g., Daly, Martens, Dool, & Hintze, 1998; Daly, Murdoch, Lillenstein, Webber, & Lentz, 2002; Eckert, Ardoin, Daisey, & Scarola, 2000; Noell, Freeland, Witt, & Gansle, 2001) and early literacy skills (Petursdottir et al., 2009), as well as math (Carson & Eckert, 2003; Codding et al., 2009; Mong & Mong, 2012).

Curriculum-Based Assessment for Instructional Design (Instructional Assessment)

CBA for instructional design (CBA-ID) is attributed to the work of Gickling. CBA-ID is used to guide instructional planning, with a primary focus to determine whether there is a mismatch between student skills and the instruction that is occurring in the classroom. It is thought that a gap between student skills and classroom instruction is what causes and maintains student skills problems. This type of assessment approach is based on a specific subskill mastery model for sampling student skill performance. Gickling is also credited with the idea that students will learn best when the material presented is not too easy (mastery level) or too difficult (frustration level) but is just challenging enough for the student to learn and demonstrate progress. The instructional level is characterized by independent student performance at a level of 93–97% accuracy (Gickling & Thompson, 1985).

There are a number of steps associated with a CBA-ID approach that involve the use of assessment strategies to ensure that instruction delivered to students is successful (Gravois & Gickling, 2008). Historically, there are four steps to the CBM-ID process that includes first identifying the materials currently used in the classroom as the focus for the assessment (Gickling & Rosenfeld, 1995). Next, using that material, the examiner works to determine the areas of skill deficit for the student by having the student read aloud and examining fluency as well as comprehension. Decisions are then made regarding the instructional strategies and modifications required in order to achieve a match between student skills and the instructional material so that the student can make appropriate progress. Lastly, the appropriate instructional material is selected and implemented, while progress is monitored.

More recently, Gravois and Gickling (2008) suggested that instead of referring to this approach as CBA, because of confusion with other approaches such as CBM that share the term "curriculum-based," it should be referred to as instructional assessment. The process for engaging in CBA-ID includes numerous steps referred to as the instructional assessment snapshot (IA snapshot) that can be repeatedly used to gather information regarding student performance (Gravois & Gickling, 2008). The recent conceptualization of the process includes three phases (Gravois & Gickling, 2008). The first phase includes three steps, including selecting the materials for assessment, building a relationship with the target student, and determining an instructional match that includes reading to the student and assessing sight word vocabulary (Gravois & Gickling, 2008). The first phase is followed by a decision point, where the examiner determines whether the material represents an appropriate match for the student. During this step, the assessor must use knowledge of instructional principals to determine the best level of material for the student. Once this is complete, phase two begins, where the student reads aloud from text while the examiner observes fluency and the mechanisms used by the student to determine unfamiliar words. Comprehension is also examined. The second decision requires the examiner to determine which further skills to examine and where intervention is required. The final phase of the IA process is the teaching phase, where instruction is provided to the student using materials that represent an appropriate instructional match, paying close attention to the instructional design principles that will allow for success while progress is monitored (Gravois & Gickling, 2008).

Research Basis

Burns and colleagues have conducted most of the recent work on CBA-ID. Their studies suggest that the use of instructional strategies that optimize the ratio of known to unknown stimuli effectively improve engagement, learning rates, and retention. Similar results were observed in reading (Burns, 2004; MacQuarrie, Tucker, Burns, & Hartman, 2002; Szadokierski & Burns, 2008) and vocabulary (Peterson-Brown & Burns, 2011). Although limited, other work begins to establish the reliability and validity of CBA-ID procedures to guide instructional decisions (Burns, 2001; Burns, Tucker, Frame, Foley, & Hauser, 2000).

Criterion-Referenced Curriculum-Based Assessment

Criterion-referenced CBA (CR-CBA), made popular by the work and writing of Blankenship and Idol (Blankenship, 1985; Idol, Nevin, & Paolucci-Whitcomb, 1999), makes use of skills measures to determine the instructional needs of students by comparing performance to a mastery criterion typically developed based on local normative student performance. The measures used to conduct this type of CBA can vary widely, to include those that sample a variety of skills as well as those that may be narrow or focused in nature. Typically, the materials used in assessment are focused on specific skills as opposed to general outcomes or more long-term measures.

The process of conducting a CR-CBA is based on the assessment of skills from curricula presented in hierarchical fashion (Blankenship, 1985). The general steps for conducting CR-CBA are similar to CBA-ID, and are intended for use by a classroom teacher. According to Blankenship (1985), the teacher should first list the skills of interest in the order in which they will be presented. The list should be examined to ensure that it includes all the relevant skills and that the skills are presented in a meaningful order. Once this has been accomplished, the teacher should determine the objectives for each skill and construct items to assess those objectives. The result is an assessment that can be given to all students in the class. The assessment should be given prior to instruction of the specific topic and its target skills. Results of this initial assessment are reviewed to determine what skills students have mastered and whether they have the prerequisite skills for the instruction that will follow. The same assessment can be given again once instruction has occurred as well as again once time has passed to determine whether the skills have been retained (Blankenship, 1985).

The distinguishing feature of this approach is the reference group for interpreting student performance on the skills measured. Student performance is compared to a criterion that is often the level considered to be mastery using local norms. Blankenship (1985) recommended that CR-CBA measures and its evaluation process be used by teachers at the beginning of the school year to determine the skills that students need to learn in order to plan for effective instruction.

Research Basis

There is no empirical research on the use of CR-CBA procedures and whether they may be more or less beneficial than other approaches to CBA. The foundation for the adequacy of this approach rests on its content validity. These procedures for determining student needs and planning for instruction is tied directly to the content of instruction in the classroom. Although never directly examined empirically as far as the authors can tell, it is likely that this approach would have face validity because of the direct connection with classroom instruction.

Curriculum-Based Assessment for Academic Assessment

Edward Shapiro developed a model of CBA (Shapiro, 1990) that integrated several existing models for assessing the academic skill problems of students and was based on the idea of a "behavioral assessment for academic skills" (Shapiro, 2011a). This approach includes four general steps of assessment and is distinguished from other models of CBA by including an extensive assessment of the academic environment as part of the model, based on the work of Shapiro and Lentz (Shapiro & Lentz, 1985). This approach, like the others, is based on the premise that the reason for the student's difficulty must be identified through the CBA process, and that the source of a student's difficulty may partially be the environment in which learning takes place.

The first step of the Shapiro approach to CBA is largely unique to this process and is an assessment of the academic environment. This step includes a teacher interview, direct observation in academic settings in question, a student interview, and a review of the permanent work products produced by the student in the classroom. The teacher interview is conducted to determine the area(s) of academic difficulty and the relative performance of the target student relative to classroom peers but may also include the use of rating scales such as the Academic Competence Evaluation Scales (ACES; DiPerna & Elliott, 2000) and the Academic Performance Rating Scales (APRS; DuPaul, Rapport, & Perriello, 1991) to gather quantitative data.

Classroom observations are typically conducted using the Behavior Observation of Students in Schools (BOSS; Shapiro, 2003, 2011b). The results of the BOSS provide data regarding student engagement in the classroom compared to peers. After a thorough assessment of the academic environment, the referral problem is confirmed and the intensity of the problem is determined. A student interview is also conducted to gather data regarding the student's perception of the problem and to gain insight into the student behavior recorded during the observation. Finally, permanent products generated by the student that provide additional evidence regarding the academic skills deficit are reviewed.

An assessment of instructional placement is then conducted to determine the nature and intensity of the academic skills deficits. This second step of the Shapiro CBA approach includes the use of CBM procedures to survey the student's academic skills in order to confirm or disconfirm the areas of academic deficit indicated through the teacher interview in the assessment of the instructional environment. This step includes direct assessments of student skills across all academic areas. Assessments may include survey-level assessments using CBM procedures to determine the target student's instructional level. Additionally, specific skills probes may be used to gather additional information.

The outcome of the assessment for instructional placement is a determination of the instructional level of functioning and a decision regarding whether the student's skills are appropriately matched to the instruction presented in the classroom. The third step of the model is instructional modification. This step is based on the CBA-ID and CBE assessment models, in which direct assessment data are gathered to determine appropriate modifications to instruction to address the student's needs. The modifications may include general strategies such as behavioral supports as well as academic strategies and instructional modifications specific to areas of academic need. The fourth step of the Shapiro CBA model involves progress monitoring. This step requires that short- and/or long-term goals be established and the related subskill and CBM (GOM), respectively, be used to measure progress on a frequent, consistent schedule. Successful progress monitoring requires that the measure directly assess the target skill areas being addressed through intervention and that the data are gathered over time and, ideally, graphed for visual inspection of progress.

A final and essential feature of the Shapiro CBA model is not a specific step in the process, but instead is the feedback loop that is created between steps 3 and 4. Once instructional modification takes place and progress monitoring is initiated, it is essential for the progress monitoring data to be observed frequently and for data-based decision-making to occur. If the graphed progress monitoring data suggest adequate progress in response to the intervention, then a decision may be made to continue with the instructional modifications in place. If adequate progress is not evident, it may be necessary to return to step 3 of this CBA model and determine whether different or additional instructional modifications may be required. This feedback loop continues in this manner until adequate progress is observed. For a thorough discussion of the selection of progress monitoring goals and measures and the procedures for graphing and interpreting data, the reader is directed to Shapiro (2011a).

Research Basis

The research basis for the Shapiro approach to CBA is grounded in the reliability and validity evidence for the various approaches integrated into the model. Research is not published on the specific model.

Curriculum-Based Evaluation

The curriculum-based evaluation approach has been popularized by Howell and colleagues (Howell & Nolet, 2000; Howell, Hosp, & Kurns, 2008; Kelley, Hosp, & Howell, 2008; Howell & Morehead, 1987). The CBE approach is a problem-solving model for evaluating student skills using repeated measures of the subskill mastery model variety over time that allows for ongoing determinations of whether instructional efforts are impacting student performance. The steps to conduct a CBE include an initial assessment, sometimes referred to as a survey-level assessment or fact finding, then the construction of hypotheses regarding the skill difficulties, direct assessment or testing of the skills to validate the problem areas, and finally the interpretation of the results, which includes both summative and formative decision-making (Howell et al., 2008; Kelley et al., 2008).

The first step to the CBE approach is what is referred to as "fact-finding" or problem identification, and the purpose is to determine whether there is a gap between the skills the student should demonstrate and the current level of performance (Howell & Nolet, 2000). This process may include survey-level assessment, but this is not always necessary if the problem is already identified using existing data. Both formal and informal measures may be used, including norm-referenced measures and direct observations and other approaches. The second step in the process is to develop hypotheses regarding the problem and to seek possible causes for the skills deficit. The hypotheses developed during this stage provide direction regarding areas for direct, specific skills assessment during the third step or validation process. This third step includes specific skills assessment to test the hypotheses. That is, specific skills measures are used to directly evaluate student performance and determine whether the reasons hypothesized to explain the performance deficits are indeed legitimate. If not, then the examiner must return to step two of the CBE model to generate new hypotheses.

The fourth and fifth steps of the process involve decision-making at the summative and formative levels, respectively. In summative decision-making, the results of step three are evaluated for how well they represent the student's current levels of performance and are then used to develop and implement instruction. The fifth and final step of the CBE process, formative decision-making, includes all the typical progress monitoring activities, such as the use of CBMs and/or specific skills measures that are administered repeatedly and graphed for data-based decision making. Progress monitoring data should be reviewed frequently to determine whether the intervention program is having the desired impact on student skills.

Research Basis

CBE is a problem-solving approach to examining student academic skills and has been referred to as a way to determine "what to teach and how to teach" (Kelley et al., 2008). It is a process, not a specific measure, and, thus, traditional conceptualization of reliability and validity is not a reasonable way to examine CBE (Howell et al., 2008). Many of the characteristics and elements of CBE, however, are largely regarded as technically adequate. For example, as discussed above, there is an extensive body of literature to support the use of CBMs to assess student skills. These measures are typically a staple of the CBE process and can be relied on to provide a reliable and valid assessment of student skills. In addition, the use of empirically validated interventions and progress monitoring yields confidence in the adequacy of the CBE approach to skills assessment and problem-solving.

CBA Summary

This section detailed various types of CBA. There are many commonalities associated with these varied approaches, most notably their value in guiding instruction and their reliance on the problem-solving model. While most of the types of CBA are models to approach assessment, CBM is unique as it refers to specific tools used to assess skills. These are tools with unique technical adequacy that are supported by decades of careful research that continues to evolve. Also unique is the Shapiro model for CBA that integrates many of the models discussed in this section as well as including a quantitative examination of the academic environment and its impact on academic skills. Each of these approaches fits uniquely in the context of a traditional problem-solving model.

Overview of the Problem-Solving Model

The problem-solving model (PSM; Deno, 1989, as adopted from Brandford & Stein, 1984) was broadly adopted as an effective framework to guide data-based decision-making in schools. The PSM delineates a series of interrelated steps from which data-based decisions can be made, with substantial reliance on behavioral assessment and curriculum-based approaches. The sequential steps of the PSM include (1) problem identification, (2) problem certification, (3) problem analysis, (4) exploring solutions, (5) evaluating solutions, and (6) problem solution (Deno, 1989; Ysseldyke & Marston, 1999). Each step can be defined for its purpose, its intended outcome, and the data necessary for drawing conclusions. Moreover, a problem is defined as a discrepancy between what is expected and what is observed in the school and classroom context. This definition of a problem is central to PSM, because it places the identified problem (e.g., low achievement) in environmental context rather than within the student. The PSM represented a major shift in how educators viewed problems.

PSM was intended to supplant the psychometric "standard battery" and "diagnostically prescriptive" approach to understand latent trait or "within child" learning problems (Deno, 1990). That diagnostically prescriptive model for assessment relies substantially on PNRT and nomothetic assumptions. The model defines problems as though they are independent of the school and classroom context. In contrast, PSM is informed by a behavioral assessment approach designed to understand the learning problems as they occur in the context of the classroom instruction and curriculum. Therein, assessment relies substantially on curriculum-based approaches and idiographic assumptions (Deno, 1990). The PSM model incorporates a scientist-practitioner model of hypothesis formation and testing designed to support differential assessment techniques to idiosyncratically assess student problems and design intervention (Christ & Aranas, 2014).

The PSM relies on interrelated assumptions that bring educators together for a common goal—to improve the instructional environment and to promote student learning. The first assumption is that every child can and will learn. Therefore, data are gathered for the purposes of improving student learning, not for identifying why learning cannot occur. This is an enormous foundational shift in educational assessment practices from assessment for the purposes of identifying disabling conditions in struggling learners (child-centered) to understanding problems as situational. This primary assumption is related to the second. There is an eco-behavioral interaction between learners and their instructional environments, including their teachers, curricula, and instructional methods. Each variable plays a unique and important role in facilitating learning; thus, each variable is necessary to consider in the assessment process. Models of CBA are effective because they each require differentiation of assessment practices to better understand the important aspects of both the student and environment that directly impact instruction. Finally, in the PSM a problem is defined as the difference between what is expected and what is occurring. At each sequential step, questions are posed and data are gathered to explore this problem definition and to operationalize how current student performance and expected levels of performance are related to one another.

Problem Identification

The first step in the PSM is *problem identification*. The purpose of this first step is to examine the equation defining what is expected and what is occurring. Problem identification involves a critical process of identifying the variables that contribute to the problem definition and data collection procedures for quantifying these variables. Problem identification begins with a referral regarding a target student in need of a change in instructional programming. From this referral question, operational targets are identified. Operational targets are defined as behaviors that are clearly defined so as to be directly and reliably measured. When selecting targets for assessment and intervention, problem-solvers choose ones that are alterable and linked to meaningful outcomes, such that when altered, meaningful changes occur for the student. Once targets are identified, data are gathered to quantify both the expectations and the student's observed behaviors so as to draw comparisons. Data collection activities will vary, depending on the model of CBA used. However, each model will include gathering data to evaluate a student's skills, quantify expectations, and summarize the differences between the two.

CBM is particularly useful for the problem-identification step of the PSM because it can be used to quantify student performance in specific content areas. Commercially available materials have normative references to help define expectations via a peer reference group. CBM can also provide an estimate of grade-level instructional materials, which can be used to describe a discrepancy in student performance.

CBE procedures are also commonly used for problem identification; however, in this model, expectations are typically defined by curricular objectives. Use of the CBE approach requires gathering data regarding instructional expectations and conducting task analyses from which hypotheses regarding prerequisite skills are formulated. Data are then gathered to assess whether the target student has the knowledge and skills to perform the expected objectives.

CBA-ID methods would make use of data to examine differences in students' instructional level and the level of the instructional materials that are being used. In this model problems would be defined as differences in performance due to a variant instructional level. In contrast, CR-CBA methods make use of a specified scope and sequence, where students are assessed on their skill acquisition within the predetermined hierarchical order. In this model, the problem would be defined specifically as differences between skills obtained and the skills presented at the expected point in the sequence.

Regardless of assessment techniques used, the goal of this first step in problem-solving is a clear and measureable statement of the problem, from which goals can be set and instructional programming can be redesigned to support the attainment of those goals.

Problem Certification

The second step in the PSM, *problem certification*, directly follows the activities in problem identification. The primary goal of this phase is to determine the magnitude of the problem and the resources needed to remedy the observed problem. During this stage, problem solvers examine the data that were gathered to determine the difference between the expectations and the observed student performance. Fewer resources are needed when the difference between observed and expected performance is small. Larger differences will require more resources.

This step has evolved from its original conception where the decisions regarding what resources are needed beyond the scope of general education services would have meant the allocation of Special Education services (Shinn, Nolet & Knutson, 1990). Within a more fluid response to intervention (RTI) model, the problem certification stage now encompasses decisions along a continuum of intensity that is dependent on the magnitude of the difference between current student performance and expected performance. A small observed difference might require strategic differentiated instruction within the general education classroom, while a larger difference that may not reflect grade-level differences in performance might require supplemental instructional supports. The largest discrepancies may require supports from Special Education services.

The data gathered during the problem-identification phase are the same data evaluated during problem certification. For example, CBM data would be examined for the percentile rank of the target student or—similar to CBA-ID data—would be evaluated for the estimated discrepancy in the student's present grade level and the grade-level instructional materials. Data gathered in the problem-identification phase using CBE and CR-CBA methodology would be summarized as the discrepancy between expected skill attainment and the actual skills of the target student.

Problem Analysis

Problem *analysis* incorporates the examination of data to devise two different hypotheses (Christ & Aranas, 2014). The first is a causal hypothesis, where data is examined to determine why the problem is occurring. The second is the intended outcome of problem analysis, which is the development of a second hypothesis regarding how the problem might be resolved.

A key feature to these hypotheses is that the focus is on alterable variables, which are can be effectively manipulated. Typically, alterable variables are environmental variables that interact with attributes of an individual. The focus on alterable environmental variables represents an important shift in assessment targets. Rather than testing individual students, data collection procedures for problem solving include a broader evaluation of the environment in which the student is expected to function.

CBE provides an effective framework for collecting the data necessary for effective problem analysis. In this model, data are gathered to evaluate variables that contribute to the identified discrepancy, including instructional, curricular, environmental variables, and the characteristics of the target student. Instruction is assessed for things such as pacing, delivery, and pedagogy. Curriculum might be assessed for its organization, scope and sequence, and difficulty of content, as well as an analysis of the enabling skills necessary to access the content of the curriculum. The environment is examined for factors that influence learning, such as student-teacher ratios, routines and clarity of expectations, and space and noise in the learning setting. The learner is assessed for the skills and needs they bring to the teaching and learning relationship. Data are gathered to evaluate these variables that may impede learning and student skills that may be underdeveloped to effectively receive subsequent instruction. Similarly, the Shapiro (2011a) model for academic skills assessment takes the same approach and incorporates the use of a detailed assessment of the instructional environment or ecology to understand fully those variables impacting performance.

Unalterable variables, such as personality traits or past educational experiences, are only considered for how they specifically relate to the development of the problem for later instructional design. For example, a student who experienced a traumatic event in the first grade may exhibit academic failure in the second grade. The traumatic event cannot be altered, but may have affected the student's access to the lessons that were taught in first grade. The lack of prior knowledge may be negatively impacting the student's ability to acquire the content of the present curriculum. By examining factors that may have contributed to the cause of the problem, problem analysts can develop a second hypothesis regarding how a problem might be resolved. Hypotheses for resolving problems are most pertinent when they are based on data in low-inference decisions, relate to the variables most likely to have affected the problem, and target alterable variables directly tied to student performance outcomes and a feasible treatment plan (Christ & Aranas, 2014).

Exploring Solutions

There are two outcomes of the *exploring solutions* phase of the PSM—a quantifiable goal for improved student performance, and the selection and specification of an intervention plan. The determination of a goal and a treatment plan depend on decisions made during previous problem-solving steps. Specifically, goal setting depends on the problem definition that was described in problem identification, where a goal is a behavioral target intended to close the gap between current and expected performance. The specification of an intervention plan relies on the hypotheses derived during problem analysis.

Decisions for goal setting are focused on determining what performance improvements can be expected. Initially, one might deduce that an expected goal for a target student demonstrating a slow rate of learning would be less ambitious than what would be observed in typically developing students. However, the opposite is true. In fact, students with lower levels of performance need goals to reflect learning rates that are more ambitious than those for typically developing students. Without more ambitious expectations, the gap in performance will persist. The consequence of setting an ambitious performance target is determining an ambitious and intensive instructional program that would make attainable the goal that was set. This represents an enormous philosophical shift for educators, evolving from the primary assumption that all children can and will learn.

CBM is the most unambiguous assessment approach for setting goals for struggling learners. The nature of CBM as a standardized tool for frequent measurement allows for a streamlined approach, where performance on a test that specifically reflects the curriculum can be directly formulated into a goal. CBM technology includes normative comparisons from which goals can be set. Additionally, many forms of CBM have rates of improvement reported in the empirical literature that can guide the specification of a goal. A unique characteristic of CBM as a general outcome measure means that use of CBM for goal setting would indicate gains in overall performance in the specified content area. In contrast, mastery measurement approaches directly measure the specific subskills that were identified as instructional targets in CBA models such as CBE, CBA-ID and CR-CBA. Goals determined in these models would reflect acquisition and mastery of skills. However, these goals would not allow for an evaluation of the effect of subskill attainment on the general performance in a broader content domain. For example, a mastery measurement goal for a first-grade student struggling to acquire early reading skills might state that after a specified period of time the student would with 100% accuracy decode words that follow a closed syllable pattern. This goal might be meaningful and important, but would not indicate how acquiring this skill might improve performance in general first-grade reading material. In contrast, using a CBM model, a goal might state that over the same period of time the student would orally read a specified number of words correctly in the first-grade text. This oral reading fluency rate can be interpreted as a general indicator of improvement in first-grade reading expectations.

From problem analysis, alterable variables have been hypothesized as maintaining the observed problems. Exploring solutions involves brainstorming variations to these alterable variables so as to design an intervention. The purpose of this step is to consider all possible solutions, including the intervention materials, interventionists, time, and logistics for implementing instructional programming beyond typical classroom instruction. In addition to the program logistics, this process must also consider the magnitude of the difference between what is expected and what is occurring and the goal for performance, as that will determine the intensity of services necessary to remedy the problem.

Data gathered from a CBE framework provides evidence to develop a comprehensive instructional plan. Critical data regarding the learner helps problem-solvers specify the instructional targets, and the attentional and motivational needs of the learner. Data collected in this model would also provide evidence about environmental variables that may impede or facilitate learning. From these data, problem-solvers can match appropriate instructional materials and pedagogies to student need. Each variable assessed in a CBE model—the instruction, curriculum, and environment—can be considered and modified to facilitate student learning.

The use of a BEA approach also has great relevance for the exploring solutions stage of the PSM. The most unique and fundamental characteristic of BEA is the systematic analysis of hypothesized variables that is conducted in the model, specifically at this phase of the PSM. BEA provides an experimental framework for evaluating which alterable variables might be most salient to solving the observed problems. BEA relies on the use of single-subject alternating treatments design methodology to test and prioritize treatment components before an intervention is implemented. Most typically, this model makes use of an Instructional Hierarchy model (IH; Haring, Lovitt, Eaton, & Hansen, 1978) that specifies varying degrees of learning acquisition and the most effective instructional approaches used to address each stage (Howell & Nolet, 2000).

Daly, Martens, and Dool (1997) proposed five basic hypotheses that can be used to explain why an academic deficit is occurring. They suggest that the problem exists because of: (1) a motivational hypothesis, (2) a fluency problem, (3) an accuracy deficit, (4) a generalization problem, and (5) a skill deficit. Each hypothesis has a corresponding suggestion for remediation. For example, a fluency problem would suggest the need for more practice, while a skill deficit would suggest that the task demands are too difficult. BEA is conducted to test these hypotheses by implementing instructional components that would likely improve student performance. The instructional component that demonstrates the greatest student response is then selected for intervention implementation.

Evaluating Solutions

In the PSM, every decision is a hypothesis to be tested. The *evaluating solutions* step of the PSM is similar to the experiment part of a research study. In this step, educators evaluate whether the instructional program was effective. In the case of the PSM, effective is defined as whether the program was successful in reducing the discrepancy between expected and observed performance. More specifically, a program may be deemed effective if the student has met the goal that was set within the previous exploring solutions phase. This step not only includes judging student progress but also determining the extent to which the program was implemented as intended—the treatment integrity. Thus, evaluating solutions to determine program success is also a two-part step that includes evaluating both implementation and student-level data.

The more clear and unambiguous a treatment plan is, the more likely that an interventionist will adhere to it. Gresham (1989) presented six factors that affect implementation integrity. Among the factors are intervention complexity; the time, materials, and number of people required; and intra-interventionist factors, such as acceptability and motivation. Addressing these factors when designing an intervention will likely increase treatment integrity. Additionally, clearly specifying the intervention program and training the interventionist to those specifications will also likely increase the integrity with which a program is implemented (Perepletchikova, Treat, & Kazdin, 2007).

Regardless of how thoughtfully an intervention program is planned, it is important to assess whether it was implemented as intended. Perepletchikova et al. (2007) warned that the validity of decisions drawn from intervention studies in which there was a breakdown in the treatment threatens the validity of decisions inferred from that study. Mistaken generalizations can have serious implications in practice, too. Invalid decisions regarding the implementation of interventions in practice can result in a misallocation of resources, where resource-intensive interventions are implemented in place of less-costly options. Even more harmful is having more school-based practitioners examine response to instruction as a component for disability determination, concluding there is a lack of response to a program that was not implemented as it was designed could result in false decisions about student disabilities.

Monitoring student progress is essential to the evaluating solutions phase of the PSM. Formative assessment, the process of gathering data within an instructional phase so as to adjust instruction as a function of student learning, may involve informal data gathering practices and standardized measurement procedures. Progress monitoring is a continuous evaluation process where problem-solvers determine whether the student is making progress toward the established goal.

Progress monitoring directly depends on the decisions that were made during the goal-setting steps of exploring solutions phase of the PSM. Effective goal setting specifies the measurement materials, time period, and success criteria. For example, if goals were established using the general outcome measurement procedures involved in CBM, student progress is monitored using CBMs. If goals were set from mastery measurement models, the probes for progress monitoring would represent specific skills.

An important distinction should be made for use of the CBM model for progress monitoring. This measurement technology allows for comparisons between student levels of performance compared to the specified goal and compared to a normative student population. Importantly, CBM also allows comparisons regarding students' rates of learning. The data gathered from frequent progress monitoring can be compared to the rate of learning observed in a normative comparison group as well as to the predicted rate of learning specified by the goal. Thus, idiographic decisions can be drawn about the student's rate of learning as a function of the intervention.

Fuchs, Fuchs, McMaster and Al Otaiba (2003) suggested that in a response to instruction (RTI) model for disability determination a dual discrepancy should be observed and quantified to evidence an underlying learning disability. They suggest that students who have learning disabilities may exhibit more discrepant skills than their peers, but also a discrepant rate of learning. CBM technology allows for educators to observe and quantify these two discrepancies.

Problem Solution

The problem-solution phase brings the evaluation process full circle, resembling problem identification. Once again, the magnitude of the identified problem is examined to determine whether a discrepancy still exists between observed and expected performance. Contrary to the problem-identification stage, however, the student has received an intensified instructional program, and the current performance level can now be evaluated as a function of the instructional changes that were implemented. Evaluation of the data must include both the students' present level of performance and the rate of improvement resulting from the instructional program.

Decisions about the outcomes can include goal attainment, where supplemental instruction is no longer needed and performance is commensurate with peers. However, if by removing intensified instructional support, the student is unable to maintain performance similar to peers, then continued supplemental instructional support may be needed. Decisions about the outcomes may also include lack of goal attainment where the student requires ongoing or intensification of instruction. If a student's observed level of performance continues to be discrepant from their peers or the student is not making progress toward the goal at the rate predicted, then the instructional plan should be examined for intensification. However, if the student's rate of performance is proportionate to the goal that was set, and indicates ambitious growth, then the instructional plan should be continued.

Summary

CBA emerged as an alternative to the overuse of PNRT, which were overused and misused in education. Kaplan wrote the following in his text entitled *The Conduct of Inquiry: Methodology for Behavioral Sciences:* "I call it the law of the instrument, and it may be formulated as follows: Give a small boy a hammer, and he will find that everything he encounters needs pounding" (1964, p. 28). This is something for educators to reflect on. Neither psychometric nor behavioral measures provide a complete set of assessment solutions in education. Neither should we treat CBA or PNRT as if we were small boys with a hammer.

This chapter describes the historical and conceptual foundations of CBA, along with common examples and context for their application. It contrasts psychometric and behavioral assessment paradigms. In all honesty, the psychometric paradigm was used as a point of contrast to enhance our description and explanation of CBA. The distinctions have been blurred in the literature. The important points are, perhaps, to understand a problem in context so that it may be resolved. Some version of CBA is often the best tool for that purpose; however, there is much development that is necessary to enhance our understanding of CBAs as they are used for assessment and evaluation. Historically, they were developed to guide routine classroom decisions. They were used primarily by teachers. They are well developed for such applications. More recently, CBA data are used to guide high-stakes decisions related to retention, special education, and classroom placement. Such decisions are best guided with multiple sources of data and, perhaps, with a review of both CBA and PNRT data. Regardless of the source, the interpretation and use of data to guide educational decisions depends on professional judgment. That requires training, reflection, and an understanding of the qualities, assumptions, and intended purposes for each assessment and source of data.

References

Blankenship, C. S., (1985). Using curriculum-based assessment data to make instructional decisions. *Exceptional Children, 52,* 233–238.

Bransford, J. D., & Stein, B. S. (1984). *The ideal problem solver: a guide for improving thinking, learning, and creativity.* New York, NY: W. H. Freeman.

Burns, M. K. (2001). Measuring sight-word acquisition and retention rates with curriculum based assessment. *Journal of Psychoeducational Assessment, 19,* 148–157. doi: 10.1177/073428290101900204

Burns, M. K. (2004). Empirical analysis of drill ratio research: Refining the instructional level for drill tasks. *Remedial and Special Education, 25,* 167–173. doi: 10.1177/07419325040250030401

Burns, M. K., Tucker, J. A., Frame, J., Foley, S., & Hauser, A. (2000). Interscorer, alternate-form, internal consistency, and test-retest reliability of Gickling's model of curriculum-based assessment for reading. *Journal of Psychoeducational Assessment, 18,* 353–360. doi: 10.1177/073428290001800405

Carson, P. M., & Eckert, T. L. (2003). An experimental analysis of mathematics instructional components: Examining the effects of student-selected versus empirically-selected. *Journal of Behavioral Education, 12,* 35–54. doi: 10.1023/A:1022370305486

Christ, T. J., & Aranas, Y. (2014). Best practices in problem analysis. In A. Thomas & P. Harrison (Eds.), *Best practices in school psychology* (Vol. 2). Bethesda, MD: National Association of School Psychologists.

Christ, T. J., & Ardoin, S. P. (2009). Curriculum-based measurement of oral reading: Passage equivalence and probe-set development. *Journal of School Psychology, 47*, 55–75.

Codding, R. S., Baglici, S., Gottesman, D., Johnson, M., Kert, A. S., & Lebeeouf, P. (2009). Selecting intervention strategies: Using brief experimental analysis for mathematics problems. *Journal of Applied School Psychology, 25*, 146–168. doi: 10.1080/15377900802484661

Daly, E. J., Witt, J. C., Martens, B. K., & Dool, E. J. (1997). A model for conducting a functional analysis of academic performance problems. *School Psychology Review, 26*(4), 554–574.

Daly III, E. J., Martens, B. K., Dool, E. J., & Hintze, J. M. (1998). Using brief functional analysis to select interventions for oral reading. *Journal of Behavioral Education, 8*, 203–218. doi: 10.1023/A:1022835607985

Daly III, E. J., Murdoch, A., Lillenstein, L., Webber, L., & Lentz, F. E. (2002). An examination of methods for testing treatments: Conducting experimental analyses of the effects of instructional components on oral reading fluency. *Education and Treatment of Children, 25*, 288–316.

Deno, S. L. (1985). Curriculum-based measurement: The emerging alternative. *Exceptional Children, 52*, 219–232.

Deno, S. L. (1989). Curriculum-based measurement and special education services: A fundamental and direct relationship. In M. R. Shinn (Ed.), *Curriculum-based measurement: Assessing special children* (pp. 1–17). New York: Guildford Press.

Deno, S. L. (1990). Individual differences and individual difference. *The Journal of Special Education, 24*(2), 160.

Deno, S. L. (2003). Developments in curriculum-based measurement. *The Journal of Special Education, 37*, 184–192.

Deno, S. L., Fuchs, L. S., Marston, D., & Shin, J. H. (2001). Using curriculum-based measurement to establish growth standards for students with learning disabilities. *School Psychology Review, 30*, 507–524.

Deno, S., Mirkin, P. K., & Chiang, B. (1982). Identifying valid measures of reading. *Exceptional Children, 49*, 36–45.

DiPerna, J. C., & Elliott, S. N. (2000). *Academic Competence Evaluation Scales*. San Antonio, TX: The Psychological Corporation.

DuPaul, G. J., Rapport, M. D., & Perriello, L. M. (1991). Teacher ratings of academic skills: The development of the Academic Performance Rating Scale. *School Psychology Review, 20*, 284–300.

Eckert, T. L., Ardoin, S. P., Daisey, D. M., & Scarola, M. D. (2000). Empirically evaluating the effectiveness of reading interventions: The use of brief experimental analysis and single-case designs. *Psychology in the Schools, 37*, 463–474. doi: 10.1002/1520-6807(200009)37:5<463::AID-PITS6>3.3.CO;2-O

Eckert, T. L., Ardoin, S. P., Daly III, E. J., & Martens, B. K. (2002). Improving oral reading fluency: An examination of the efficacy of combining skill-based and performance-based interventions. *Journal of Applied Behavior Analysis, 35*, 271–281. doi: 10.1901/jaba.2002.35–271

Espin, C. A., & Deno, S. L. (1993). Performance in reading from content area text as an indicator of achievement. *Remedial and Special Education, 14*, 47–59. doi: 10.1177/074193259301400610

Espin, C. A., & Deno, S. L. (1995). Curriculum-based measures for secondary students: Utility and task specificity of text-based reading and vocabulary measures for predicting performance on content-area tasks. *Diagnostique, 20*, 121–142.

Foegen, A., Jiban, C., & Deno, S. (2007). Progress monitoring measures in mathematics: A review of the literature. *The Journal of Special Education, 41*, 121–139. doi: 10.1177/00224669070410020101

Fuchs, L. S. (2004). The past, present, and future of Curriculum-Based Measurement research. *School Psychology Review, 33*, 188–192.

Fuchs, L. S., & Deno, S. L. (1981). *The relationship between curriculum-based mastery measures and standardized achievement tests in reading* (Report No. 57). Minneapolis, MN: University of Minnesota Institute for Research on Learning Disabilities.

Fuchs, L. S., & Deno, S. L. (1991). Paradigmatic distinctions between instructionally relevant measurement models. *Exceptional Children, 57*, 488–500.

Fuchs, L. S., & Deno, S. L. (1992). Effects of curriculum within curriculum-based measurement. *Exceptional Children, 58*, 232–243.

Fuchs, L. S., & Deno, S. L. (1994). Must instructionally useful performance assessment be based in the curriculum? *Exceptional Children, 61*, 15–24.

Fuchs, L. S., Fuchs, D., Hamlett, C. L., Phillips, N. B., & Bentz, J. (1994). Classwide curriculum-based measurement: Helping general educators meet the challenge of student diversity. *Exceptional Children, 60*, 518–537.

Fuchs, L. S., Fuchs, D., Hamlett, C. L., Walz, L., & Germann, G. (1993). Formative evaluation of academic progress: How much growth can we expect? *School Psychology Review, 22*, 27–48.

Fuchs, D., Fuchs, L. S., McMaster, K. N., & Al Otaiba, S. (2003). Identifying children at risk for reading failure: Curriculum-based measurement and the dual-discrepancy approach. In H. L. Swanson, K. R. Harris, & S. Graham (Eds.), *Handbook of learning disabilities* (pp. 431–449). New York, NY: Guilford Press.

Gickling, E. E., & Rosenfeld, S. (1995). Best practices in curriculum-based assessment. In A. Thomas & J. Grimes (Eds.), *Best practices in school psychology III* (pp. 587–596). Washington, DC: National Association of School Psychologists.

Gickling, E. E., & Thompson, V. P. (1985). A personal view of curriculum-based assessment. *Exceptional Children, 52*, 205–218.

Good III, R. H., Simmons, D. C., & Kame'enui, E. J. (2001). The importance and decision-making utility of a continuum of fluency-based indicators of foundational reading skills for third-grade high-stakes outcomes. *Scientific Studies of Reading, 5*, 257–288.

Gravois, T. A., & Gickling, E. E. (2008). *Best practices in instructional assessment.* Bethesda, MD: National Association of School Psychologists.

Gresham, F. M. (1989). Assessment of treatment integrity in school consultation and prereferral intervention. *School Psychology Review, 18*(1), 37–50.

Haring, N. G., Lovitt, T. C., Eaton, M. D., & Hansen, C. L. (Eds.). (1978). *The fourth R: Research in the classroom.* Columbus, OH: Charles E. Merrill.

Hintze, J. M., Callahan, J. E., Matthews, W. J., Williams, S. A. S., & Tobin, K. G. (2002). Oral reading fluency and prediction of reading comprehension in African American and Caucasian elementary school children. *School Psychology Review, 31*, 540–553.

Hintze, J. M., & Silberglitt, B. (2005). A longitudinal examination of the diagnostic accuracy and predictive validity of R-CBM and high-stakes testing. *School Psychology Review, 34*, 372–386.

Hosp, M. K., & Fuchs, L. S. (2005). Using CBM as an indicator of decoding, word reading, and comprehension: Do the relations change with grade? *School Psychology Review, 34*, 9–26.

Howell, K. W., Hosp, J. L., & Kurns, S. (2008). Best practices in curriculum-based evaluations. In A. Thomas & J. Grimes (Eds.), *Best practices in school psychology V* (pp. 349–362). Bethesda, MD: National Association of School Psychologists.

Howell, K. W., & Morehead, M. K. (1987). *Curriculum-based evaluation for special and remedial education.* Columbus, OH: Merrill.

Howell, K. W., & Nolet, V. (2000). *Curriculum-based evaluation: Teaching and decision making* (3rd ed.). Belmont, CA: Wadsworth.

Idol, I., Nevin, A., & Paolucci-Whitcomb, P. (1999). *Models of curriculum-based assessment: A blue-print for learning* (3rd ed.). Austin, TX: Pro-Ed.

Individuals with Disabilities Education Improvement Act (IDEIA), 20 U.S.C., Pub. L. No. 108-446 § 1400 et seq. (2004).

Jones, K. M., & Wickstrom, K. F. (2002). Done in sixty seconds: Further analysis of the brief assessment model for academic problems. *School Psychology Review, 31*, 554–568.

Kaplan, A. (1964). *The conduct of inquiry: Methodology for behavioral sciences.* New York, NY: Chandler Publishing.

Kelley, B., Hosp, J. L., & Howell, K. W. (2008). Curriculum-based evaluation and math: An overview. *Assessment for Effective Instruction, 33*, 250–256. doi: 10.1177/1534508407313490

Kranzler, J. H., Miller, D. M., & Jordan, L. (1999). An examination of racial/ethnic and gender bias on curriculum-based measurement of reading. *School Psychology Quarterly, 14*, 327–342. doi:10.1037/h0089012

MacQuarrie, L. L., Tucker, J. A., Burns, M. K., & Hartman, B. (2002). Comparison of retention rates using traditional, drill sandwich, and incremental rehearsal flash card methods. *School Psychology Review, 31*, 584–595.

Marston, D. (1989). Curriculum-based measurement: What is it and why do it? In M. R. Shinn (Ed.), *Curriculum-based measurement: Assessing special children* (pp. 18–78). New York, NY: Guilford Press.

Martens, B. K., Eckert, T. L., Bradley, T. A., & Ardoin, S. P. (1999). Identifying effective treatments from a brief experimental analysis: Using single-case design elements to aid decision making. *School Psychology Quarterly, 14*, 163–181. doi: 10.1037/h0089003

McMaster, K., & Espin, C. (2007). Technical features of curriculum-based measurement in writing: A literature review. *The Journal of Special Education, 41*, 68–84. doi: 10.1177/00224669070410020301

Mong, M. D., & Mong, K. W. (2012). The utility of brief experimental analysis and extended intervention analysis in selecting effective mathematics interventions. *Journal of Behavioral Education, 21*, 99–118. doi: 10.1007/s10864-011-9143-8

Muyskens, P., & Marston, D. B. (2006). *The relationship between curriculum-based measurement and outcomes on high-stakes tests with secondary students.* Minneapolis Public Schools. Unpublished Manuscripts.

No Child Left Behind (NCLB) Act of 2001, PL 107–110 (2001).

Noell, G. H., Freeland, J. T., Witt, J. C., & Gansle, K. A. (2001). Using brief assessments to identify effective interventions for individual students. *Journal of School Psychology, 39,* 335–355. doi: 10.1016/S0022–4405(01)00072–3

Peterson, K. M. H., & Shinn, M. R. (2002). Severe discrepancy models: Which best explains school identification practices for learning disabilities. *School Psychology Review, 31,* 459–476.

Peterson-Brown, S., & Burns, M. K. (2011). Adding a vocabulary component to incremental rehearsal to enhance retention and generalization. *School Psychology Quarterly, 26,* 245–255. doi: 10.1037/a0024914

Petursdottir, A., McMaster, K., McComas, J. J., Bradfield, T., Braganza, V., Koch-McDonald, J., Rodriguez, R., & Scharf, H. (2009). Brief experimental analysis of early reading interventions. *Journal of School Psychology, 47,* 215–243. doi: 10.1016/j.jsp.2009.02.003

Riley-Tillman, T. C., & Burns, M. K. (2009). *Evaluating educational interventions: Single-case design for measuring response to intervention.* New York, NY: The Guilford Press.

Riley-Tillman, T. C., Chafouleas, S. M., & McGrath M. C. (2004). Brief experimental analysis: An assessment strategy for selecting successful interventions. *Communiqué, 32,* 10–12.

Shapiro, E. S. (1990). An integrated model for curriculum-based assessment. *School Psychology Review, 19,* 331–349.

Shapiro, E. S. (2003). *Behavioral Observation of Students in Schools–BOSS* [Computer software]. San Antonio, TX: Pearson.

Shapiro, E. S. (2011a). *Academic skills problems: Direct assessment and intervention* (4th ed.). New York, NY: Guilford Press.

Shapiro, E. S. (2011b). *Academic skills problems workbook* (4th ed.). New York, NY: Guilford Press.

Shapiro, E. S., & Lentz, F. E. (1985). Assessing academic behavior: A behavioral approach. *School Psychology Review, 14,* 325–338.

Shapiro, M. A., Keller, M. A , Lutz, J. G., Santoro, L. E., & Hintze, J. M. (2006). Curriculum-based measures and performance on state assessment and standardized tests: Reading and math performance in Pennsylvania. *Journal of Psychoeducational Assessment, 24,* 19–35. doi: 10.1177/0734282905285237

Shinn, M. R. (Ed.). (1989). *Curriculum-based measurement: Assessing special children.* New York: Guildford Press.

Shinn, M. R., Nolet, V., & Knutson, N. (1990). Best practices in curriculum-based measurement. In A. Thomas & J. Grimes (Eds.), *Best practices in school psychology II* (pp. 287–308). Washington, D. C.: National Association of School Psychologists.

Stage, S. A., & Jacobsen, M. D. (2001). Predicting student success on a state-mandated performance-based assessment using oral reading fluency. *School Psychology Review, 30,* 407–419.

Szadokierski, I., & Burns, M. (2008). Analogue evaluation of the effects of opportunities to respond and ratios of known items within drill rehearsal of Esperanto words. *Journal of School Psychology, 46,* 593–609. doi: 10.1016/j.jsp.2008.06.004

Tucker, J. A. (1985). Curriculum-based assessment: An introduction. *Exceptional Children, 52*(3), 199–204.

Wayman, M. M., Wallace, T., Wiley, H., Ticha, R., & Espin, C. A. (2007). Literature synthesis on curriculum-based measurement in reading. *Journal of Special Education, 41,* 85–120.

Ysseldyke, J. & Marston, D. (1999). Origins of categorical special education services in schools and a rationale for changing them. In D. J. Reschly, W. D. Tilly, & J. P. Grimes, (Eds.), *Special education in transition: Functional assessment and noncategorical programming.* Longmont, CO: Sopris West.

9

The Use of Technology with Curriculum-Based Measurement (CBM)

Madi Phillips, Mark R. Shinn, and Ben Ditkowsky

Curriculum-Based Measurement (CBM) is a set of short (i.e., 1–5 minutes), standardized assessments that are used to identify at-risk students and evaluate academic progress over time (Deno, 1985; Shinn, 2010). Reading, math, writing, and spelling achievement can all be measured with CBM probes (Deno, 1985; Deno, 1986, Shinn, 1989). CBM tools are used across age groups from early childhood and elementary to secondary levels (Deno, 2003; Shinn, 1998). While CBM was originally developed to monitor Individualized Education Plan (IEP) goals for Special Education students, its use has expanded to general education, at-risk, and English Language Learners (Deno, 2003; Shinn, 1998; Shinn, 2010; Shinn & Baker, 1996; Shinn, Collins, & Gallagher, 1998).

CBM: One Type of Curriculum-Based Assessment (CBA)

Curriculum-based assessment (CBA) is the broad umbrella term for tools that are direct measures of academic behaviors, developed from local curricula and used to make instructional decisions (Deno, 1993). CBM has specific features that make the tools unique from the other three models of CBA (Hintze, Christ, & Methe, 2006; Shinn, Rosenfield, & Knutson, 1989). First, CBM is a general outcomes measurement (GOM), in that it assesses overall reading and math achievement, as opposed to any specific skills (e.g., reading comprehension and addition facts; Fuchs & Deno, 1991). Second, CBM can be used for long-term measurement of basic skills. Third, CBM is standardized, and the same administration and scoring procedures are implemented in every assessment situation. Fourth, CBM is technically adequate, with more than 30 years of research supporting it (Deno, 2003; Deno 2005; Shinn, 2008).

The purpose of this chapter is to summarize the history and current use of technology in published CBM products. Specific examples of Web 2.0 products (O'Reilly, 2005, including web-driven (e.g., easyCBM and Yearly ProgressPro) and web–supported (e.g., AIMSweb and DIBELS) testing, will be presented. CBM data organization and reports within Web 2.0 products will be highlighted. Finally, the screening and frequent progress monitoring decisions using CBM technology products will be described.

History of Computer-Based CBM (CB-CBM)

The use of computers with CBM has been around for the past 25 years (Fuchs, Deno, & Mirkin, 1983; Lembke, McMaster, & Stecker, 2012). Computer software was developed in response to problems of teacher time, scoring accuracy, and data analysis when monitoring the reading, math, and spelling progress of students in their classrooms (Fuchs, Fuchs, & Hamlett, 1994). The original software stored, graphed, and analyzed CBM data for teachers (Fuchs, Fuchs, Hamlett, & Hasselbring, 1987; Fuchs, Deno, & Mirkin, 1983). Early results of using CB-CBM indicated that teachers experienced a decrease in overall progress monitoring efficiency but an increase in satisfaction. Teachers *perceived* as more efficient the use of computer software to summarize their data once they collected it through paper-pencil procedures (Fuchs, Fuchs, Hamlett, & Hasselbring, 1987). The researchers pinpointed the inefficiency in the CB-CBM graphing procedures, but teachers experienced an increase in efficiency when analyzing student performance.

The next revision in computer software included the addition of generating, administering, and scoring CBM probes (Ferguson & Fuchs, 1991; Fuchs, Hamlett, Fuchs, Stecker, & Ferguson, 1988). Findings indicated that teachers using CB-CBM spent significantly less time in measurement and evaluation when reading, math, and spelling data were collected by computer software. However, *students* spent more time in measurement and evaluation using CB-CBM. Again, teachers were more satisfied when using CB-CBM to generate, administer, and score reading, math, and spelling probes as compared to paper-pencil procedures (Fuchs, Hamlett, Fuchs, Stecker, & Ferguson, 1988). Additionally, CB-CBM scoring accuracy was significantly higher and produced greater scoring stability than were paper-pencil administration and scoring procedures (Ferguson & Fuchs, 1991). Using computer software to generate, administer, and score CBM probes provided teachers more time for planning with accurate assessment data.

CBM results can be used to plan instruction for students who are not making progress (Fuchs & Fuchs, 2001; Fuchs, Fuchs, & Hamlett, 1992). A skills analysis component was added to CB-CBM software to support teachers in their planning of *what* to teach students who are not progressing in reading, math, or spelling (Fuchs, & Fuchs, 1990; Fuchs, Fuchs, & Hamlett, 1989; Fuchs, Fuchs, Hamlett, & Allinder, 1991). For reading, teachers who used CB-CBM that included a diagnostic analysis of their students' written retell results wrote more detailed instructional plans and effected higher achievement (Fuchs, Fuchs, & Hamlett, 1989). For math computation, similar results occurred, with teachers writing more specific instructional plans and significantly higher student achievement than did students for whom teachers did not have a diagnostic analysis option (Fuchs & Fuchs, 1990). Similarly, teachers who used CB-CBM with spelling skill analysis feedback identified a greater number of skills they were going to remediate and effected higher student achievement (Fuchs, Fuchs, Hamlett, & Allinder, 1991). Additionally, the teachers who had the diagnostic analysis option became more proficient at identifying phonetic errors independently than did teachers without that option.

Even with all of the technological advances in administration, scoring, data analysis, and instructional recommendations, the use of CBM still requires ongoing support to ensure fidelity (Fuchs & Fuchs, 1990; Fuchs & Fuchs, 2001; Fuchs, Fuchs, & Hamlett, 1989). Ensuring that teachers monitor students' progress frequently, make program modifications when students aren't progressing, and use the data for instructional planning are all tasks that benefit from ongoing teacher support.

While the CB-CBM skills analysis component assists teachers with *what* to teach, researchers evaluated the implementation of an expert system that would support teachers with *how* to teach (Fuchs & Fuchs, 1991; Fuchs, Fuchs, & Hamlett, 1993; Fuchs, Fuchs, & Hamlett,

1994). Expert systems were designed to support instructional design (Fuchs & Fuchs, 2001). Outcomes of CB-CBM with an expert system component depended on the instructional area. The most favorable results were found in the area of math (Fuchs, Fuchs, Hamlett, & Stecker, 1991). Teachers who had access to the expert systems implemented a more varied set of instructional strategies, and student achievement was significantly higher than outcomes for students whose teachers did not have access to expert systems.

On the other hand, in the area of reading, although teachers using expert systems incorporated more reading skills and utilized more instructional methods when they had access to the information (Fuchs, Fuchs, Hamlett, & Ferguson, 1992), student achievement was not significantly different from other students whose teachers utilized CBM for their progress-monitoring tool. Similar results were found in the area of spelling, where CB-CBM with an expert system produced the least favorable results (Fuchs & Fuchs, 1991, 2001). Specifically, achievement levels of students, working with teachers both with and without the option of expert system, were similar. Expert systems did not appear to alter teacher choices about how to reteach spelling skills.

Previous research had focused on the special education teacher monitoring the progress of individual students on their caseload (Fuchs & Fuchs, 2001). Next, the use of CB-CBM with instructional recommendations was applied to general education teachers and classrooms that included students with learning disabilities (Fuchs, Fuchs, Hamlett, Phillips, & Bentz, 1994). Results indicated that teachers utilizing CB-CBM with instructional recommendations in their classrooms designed better evidence-based instructional programs and effected great math achievement for their students than did teachers who did not utilize CB-CBM.

Web-Based CBM (WB-CBM)

Web-based CBM (WB-CBM) applies interactive, Web 2.0 technology requiring access to the Internet, but doesn't use locally installed software or applications (Goo, Watt, Park, & Hosp, 2012; Lembke et al., 2012). The momentum of Response to Intervention (RTI), use of technology, and increased accountability (i.e., passage of No Child Left Behind, 2002) in the schools encouraged widespread implementation of WB-CBM with all students (Goo et al., 2012). WB-CBM has become essential, as RTI components include screening an entire school population, progress monitoring all students three times a year, and engaging in more frequent progress monitoring for those students who are at-risk (Shinn, 2008). According to the U.S. Department of Education (2010), schools have both the hardware and Internet access to assess students using WB-CBM. These results can be used to predict the instructional areas of focus to meet the achievement requirements for NCLB (2002).

WB-CBM products fall into two categories, web-driven and web-supported. Web-driven products allow students to sit at a computer terminal for CBM administration and scoring. Web-supported products require a trained educator to administer and sometimes score the CBM probes. Both sets of products store, graph, and analyze CBM data.

The potential benefits of the use of Web 2.0 technology for collection, storage, and analysis of CBM is enormous. Well-programmed software can be more efficient, effective, and consistent than procedures managed by people. Over the years, CBM and technology have grown together. This section will highlight three ways in which CBM have been integrated with Web 2.0 technology. First, Web 2.0 has the potential benefit of efficiency in administration, and scoring through technology-driven testing. Second, Web 2.0 has the potential to improve school efforts with data organization and reporting. Finally, Web 2.0 has the potential to remove test administrator error with technology-supported testing.

Numerous commercially available products of evidence-based web-supported and web-driven CBM have been published (see http://www.rti4success.org/toolschartsLanding for more information). The distinction between web-supported and web-driven products is that web-supported products require a face-to-face administration of assessments, whereas web-driven products provide direct service to students through an online application of assessment and scoring. Next, four commercially available products, two from each category, will be reviewed.

Web 2.0 CBM Tools and Assessment Schedules

Early literacy measures from AIMSweb, DIBELS Net, and easyCBM are very similar. All are web supported; none is administered by a computer. DIBELS offers some of the earliest measures of early literacy with First Sound Fluency (FSF). When FSF is administered, students are orally presented with a word and are asked to produce the first sound(s). FSF is appropriate for students in pre-school and early kindergarten. AIMSweb, DIBELS Net, and easyCBM measure Phoneme Segmentation. Phoneme Segmentation requires a student to say the phonemes in a word after an examiner orally presents the whole word. While DIBELS does not recommend the use of this measure in the fall at the beginning of the school year, both AIMSweb and easyCBM indicate that a fall administration of Phoneme Segmentation is appropriate. All three systems offer measures of Letter Naming Fluency (LNF), in which students are presented with a list of letters presented in a random order and asked to name as many as they can in 1 minute. AIMSweb, DIBELS Net, and easyCBM recommend the use of LNF in fall, winter, and spring of kindergarten, as well as fall of grade 1. As for early measures of alphabetic understanding, AIMSweb and easyCBM have measures of Letter Sound Fluency (LSF) that are similar to LNF, except that students are asked to state the most common sound of letters rather than naming them. Both AIMSweb and DIBELS Net have a later measure of alphabetic understanding. Nonsense Word Fluency (NWF) is recommended from mid-kindergarten to mid-first grade. easyCBM has a measure of Word Reading Fluency (WRF) appropriate for kindergarten through third grade. The recommended schedule from the publishers for the assessment of early literacy is presented in Table 9.1.

AIMSweb, DIBELS Net, easyCBM, and Yearly ProgressPro (YPP) contain CBM tools for measuring general reading achievement. AIMSweb, DIBELS Net, and easyCBM present students with a reading passage and standardized directions asking the student to read aloud for 1 minute. At the end of the minute, the number of words read correctly and errors are recorded. For each of the Web 2.0 products, only web-supported applications record student scores, though easyCBM has been working on the development of a web-driven application (easyCBM

Table 9.1 Recommended Schedule for Assessment of Early Literacy Skills

Season	FSF[3]			PSF[2,3] PS[4]			LNF[2,3,4]			LSF[2,4]			NWF[2,3]			WRF[4]		
	F	W	S	F	W	S	F	W	S	F	W	S	F	W	S	F	W	S
K	3	3	–	2, 4	2, 3, 4			2, 3, 4			2, 4		2	2, 3		4		
1st[1]	–	–	–	2, 3, 4	–		–	–	–	–	–	–	2, 3		–	4		
2nd[1]	–	–	–	–	–		–	–	–	–	–	–	–	–	–	4		
3rd[1]	–	–	–	–	–		–	–	–	–	–	–	–	–	–	4		

Notes: [1]Yearly ProgressPro is not listed in this table because it continually assesses skills sampled from across the curriculum of the grade level. [2] AIMSweb; [3] DIBELS Next; [4] easyCBM; FSF = First Sound Fluency; PSF/PS = Phoneme Segmentation Fluency; LNF = Letter Naming Fluency; LSF = Letter Sound Fluency; NWF = Nonsense Word Fluency; WRF = Word Reading Fluency.

2012). Although Reading-CBM has a long-standing record of technical adequacy for measuring general reading achievement, concerns about face validity have driven publishers to offer to consumers additional measures. For the purpose of evaluating the quality of the DIBELS Oral Reading Fluency (DORF) score, DIBELS creators have developed the Retell Fluency parameter. Once students finish reading the DORF passage, a test administrator asks them to tell about what they have just read. The results of the Retell Fluency are then taken into account as part of the DIBELS composite score. YPP samples reading items from across the curriculum to ensure the overall validity of its reading measure. In addition, YPP provides a web-driven MAZE task, while AIMSweb and DIBELS Net provide a web-supported one. The MAZE assessment tool is a reading passage where every seventh word is replaced with a multiple-choice option of the correct word and two distractors. Students choose the word from among the three choices that best fits with the rest of the passage. easyCBM provides a web-driven multiple-choice reading comprehension measure for grades 2 through 8. Students are required to read a passage and answer 20 multiple-choice items, which are later broken down into specific categories of reading comprehension. The recommended schedule from the publishers for the assessment of general reading and comprehension is presented in Table 9.2.

Table 9.2 Recommended Schedule for Assessment of General Reading and Comprehension

Season	Sampled Reading	R-CBM[2], DORF[3], PRF[4]			Retell[3]			MAZE DAZE[3]			MCRC[4]		
		F	W	S	F	W	S	F	W	S	F	W	S
K		−	−	−	−	−	−	−	−	−	−	−	−
1st[1]		4	2, 3, 4	2, 3, 4	−	3	3	−	−	−	−	−	−
2nd	1	2, 3, 4	2, 3, 4	2, 3, 4	3	3	3	−	−	−	4	4	4
3rd	1	2, 3, 4	2, 3, 4	2, 3, 4	3	3	3	1, 2, 3	2, 3	2, 3	4	4	4
4th	1	2, 3, 4	2, 3, 4	2, 3, 4	3	3	3	2, 3	2, 3	2, 3	4	4	4
5th	1	2, 3, 4	2, 3, 4	2, 3, 4	3	3	3	2, 3	2, 3	2, 3	4	4	4
6th	1	2, 3, 4	2, 3, 4	2, 3, 4	3	3	3	2, 3	2, 3	2, 3	4	4	4
7th	1	2, 4	2, 4	2, 4	−	−	−	2	2	2	4	4	4
8th	1	2, 4	2, 4	2, 4	−	−	−	2	2	2	4	4	4

Notes: [1]Yearly ProgressPro samples skills from the domains of word analysis, spelling, reading vocabulary, passage comprehension, and language; [2]AIMSweb; [3]DIBELS Next; [4]easyCBM; R-CBM = Reading Curriculum-Based Measurement; DORF = DIBELS Oral Reading Fluency; PRF = Passage Reading Fluency; MAZE and DAZE are multiple-choice cloze passages; MCRC = Multiple-Choice Reading Comprehension.

Table 9.3 Recommended Schedule for Assessment of Language Arts

Season	Sampled Language Arts	S-CBM[2]			WE-CBM[2]		
		F	W	S	F	W	S
K		–	–	–	–	–	–
1st[1]		2	2	2	–	–	–
2nd	1	2	2	2	2	2	2
3rd	1	2	2	2	2	2	2
4th	1	2	2	2	2	2	2
5th	1	2	2	2	2	2	2
6th	1	2	2	2	2	2	2
7th	1	2	2	2	2	2	2
8th	1	2	2	2	2	2	2

Notes: Of the four selected products, AIMSweb provides CBM measures for Writing and Spelling, [1] Yearly ProgressPro samples skills from the domains of word analysis, spelling, reading vocabulary, passage comprehension, and language.

In the area of Language Arts, only AIMSweb and YPP provide measures. While YPP samples items across the grade-level curriculum, AIMSweb includes measures of spelling and written expression. The recommended schedule provided by the publishers for the assessment of language arts for AIMSweb and YPP is presented in Table 9.3.

Web-driven application of CBM is most apparent in the area of mathematics. AIMSweb and easyCBM each have suites of CBM for both early numeracy and mathematics that have the ability to provide web-supported diagnostic assessment. YPP and easyCBM have web-driven applications in mathematics, each with diagnostic item breakdowns and summaries. While the YPP tool is based on the sampling of skills from the annual curriculum, easyCBM has multiple measures of mathematics skill mastery that vary by grade level. Although DIBELS does not yet have measures of early numeracy or mathematics, there is an indication that measures are forthcoming. The recommended schedule for the assessment of early numeracy and mathematics is presented in Table 9.4.

Web 2.0 Universal Screening Decisions

The Web 2.0 tools that have been reviewed in this chapter provide methods not only for data collection and storage, but also for analysis and interpretation. Although the measures provided by the publishers of YPP and DIBELS Next are different, both of these systems identify students who are struggling, based on a fixed expectation or criterion reference. One concern about using criterion reference is that the proportion of students identified for additional assistance will undoubtedly be related to the performance of the district. easyCBM takes a different approach than do DIBELS Net and YPP, relying on a normative approach. AIMSweb leaves the question of how to identify at-risk students to the consumer, providing both normative and criterion-referenced options.

The primary purpose of universal screening within an RTI framework is to discriminate between students who are likely to be successful in the core curriculum and those who are likely to struggle without intervention. Web 2.0 products summarize and interpret the data

Table 9.4 Recommended Schedule for Assessment of Numeracy and Mathematics

Measure	K	1st	2nd	3rd	4th	5th	6th	7th	8th
Sampled across the mathematics scope and sequence			1	1	1	1	1	1	1
Oral Counting	2								
Number Identification	2								
Quantity Distribution	2								
Missing Number	2								
Math Computation		2	2	2	2	2	2	2	2
Math Concepts and Applications		2	2	2	2	2	2	2	2
Math Benchmark	4	4	4	4	4	4	4	4	4
Numbers and Operations	4	4	4	4	4	4	4		
Numbers, Operations, and Algebra		4	4	4	4	4		4	
Numbers, Operations, and Ratios							4		
Numbers, Operations, Algebra, and Geometry								4	
Data Analysis, Number, Operations, and Algebra									4
Geometry, Algebra, and Measurement						4		4	
Algebra							4		4
Geometry	4	4		4					
Measurement	4		4		4				
Geometry and Measurement									4

Notes: [1]Yearly ProgressPro samples mathematics concepts and skills from across the curriculum of the grade level. [2]AIMSweb; [3]DIBELS Next; [4]easyCBM.

in different ways. For example, while DIBELS Next provides normative information (i.e., percentile ranks) and risk status is determined based on a composite score. The composite score is generated using a combination of scores from required measures. easyCBM provides normative information, comparing students to a sample from Washington and Oregon. Graphical reports provide a norm referent, with an indication that scores below the 20th percentile are an indication of concern, however, specific interpretation is left to the consumer. AIMSweb allows the user to select from a norm or criterion reference, and then provides recommendations based on that selection. YPP provides information about the skill accuracy from across the grade-level curriculum, and instructional recommendations. Specific examples of how universal screening is conducted and summarized with different Web 2.0 solutions will be discussed.

Universal Screening with easyCBM

After assessing all students on a particular measure, teachers can access information about the specific tests their students have taken. A bar chart representing student performance provides a visual of how student skills cluster at the time of the assessment. The easyCBM Teacher's Manual (easyCBM Teacher's Manual, 2012) recommends that when students in a class "clump together," it is likely that teachers can meet the instructional

Summary

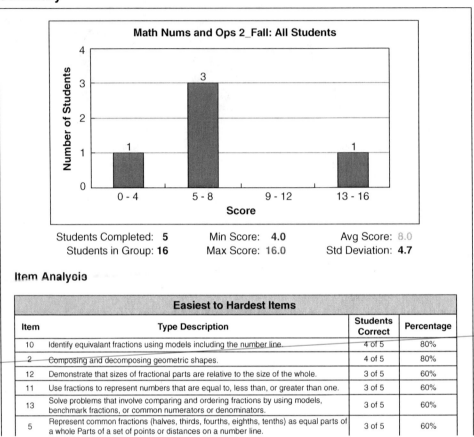

Figure 9.1 Math Nums and Ops 2_Fall: All Students

needs of their students with whole-group instruction. However, when a few students score significantly lower (or higher) than their peers, teachers may need to investigate opportunities to differentiate instruction to better meet student needs. Some of the measures include item analyses that are organized from easiest to most difficult, including the item number, type, and the percentage of students who answered the item correctly as shown in Figure 9.1.

Universal Screening with DIBELS Net

After assessing all students on the battery of DIBELS Next measures, teachers can obtain several graphical reports. DIBELS Net reports provide local normative information, but the hallmark of DIBELS Net reports is the consistent reference to expected benchmarks of performance (i.e., criterion reference). These benchmark performance levels represent the goal for a grade level in green, the cut point for at risk performance in red, and identification of some risk depicted in yellow. One example report available from DIBELS Net is the student Benchmark Assessment History Report in Figure 9.2. This report contains an individual student's performance on each measure included in the recommended DIBELS Next Battery. The report shows the expectations for the grade level as colored ranges by benchmark period, and the normative performance of students in the grade level, depicted by a "box plot." Finally, the individual student level performance on each measure is represented as a dot within the box plot.

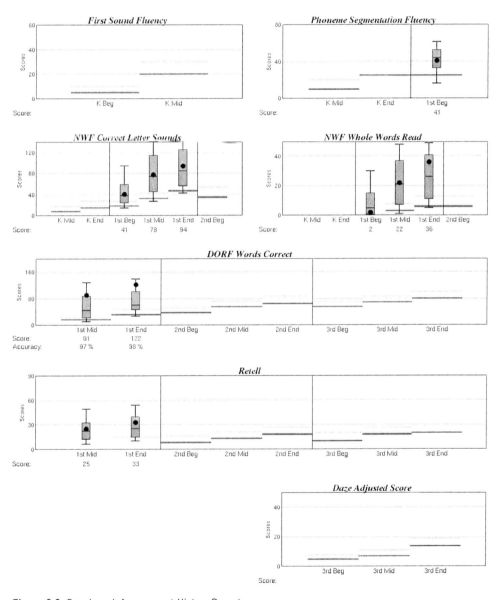

Figure 9.2 Benchmark Assessment History Report

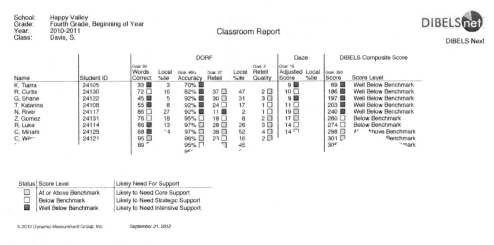

© 2012 Dynamic Measurement Group, Inc.   September 21, 2012

Figure 9.3 Classroom Report

In addition to graphical reports, teachers can access a variety of comprehensive color-coded summaries describing individual student performance, as shown in Figure 9.3. DIBELS Net reports provide a variety of scores including raw scores, local percentiles, raw growth scores, color-coded representations of whether a student is on track on each measure, and a composite score linked to a criterion-referenced performance description.

Universal Screening with AIMSweb

One of the greatest strengths of AIMSweb is the flexibility of the system. AIMSweb allows the user to determine how to evaluate universal screening data. A consumer can examine scores through a norm reference perspective, a preset criterion reference, or a custom set of criterion referenced "cut scores." After assessing all students in a grade, the teacher can generate a variety of reports with information about students relative to peers (i.e., norm reference) or relative to standards (i.e., criterion reference), or both. In addition, reports may include raw scores, local normative scores, district normative scores, and comparisons to state or national data. One example of an AIMSweb classroom report is shown in Figure 9.4.

AIMSweb also provides the user with the ability to customize norm sets according to demographic variables, such as ethnicity, English language proficiency, and economic status. Figure 9.5 shows the report options available to consumers when they want to disaggregate their normative data.

Alternatively, AIMSweb allows the user to evaluate scores based on accuracy or even growth percentiles. Both AIMSweb and DIBELS Next use the same red, yellow, and green color-coding heuristic to identify a student's at-risk level. Similar to DIBELS Next, AIMSweb provides instructional recommendations when a single score or multiple scores are entered into the system.

Class Distribution by Scores and Percentile
Red River Valley District SAMPLE - Jefferson Elementary SAMPLE
Grade 3 - (Diane Hambly - Homeroom) Winter 2003-2004
Reading - Curriculum Based Measurement

Name	Corrects	Errors	Accuracy	Performance Summary	Potential Instructional Action
Schumacher, Nels	197.0	3.0	98.5%	Well Above Average	Consider Need for Individualized Instruction
Hutton, Greg	180.0	0.0	100.0%	Well Above Average	Consider Need for Individualized Instruction
Fleeger, Sydney	179.0	1.0	99.4%	Well Above Average	Consider Need for Individualized Instruction
Darlow, Lindsay	176.0	0.0	100.0%	Well Above Average	Consider Need for Individualized Instruction
Gohman, Karina	176.0	1.0	99.4%	Well Above Average	Consider Need for Individualized Instruction
Well Above Average >= 165.0 (90th %ile)					
Scanlon, Zachary	161.0	3.0	98.2%	Above Average	Consider Need for Individualized Instruction
Ballis, Haley	145.0	3.0	98.0%	Above Average	Consider Need for Individualized Instruction
Clark, Tyler	140.0	4.0	97.2%	Above Average	Consider Need for Individualized Instruction
Above Average >= 140.0 (75th %ile)					
Connaker, Ryan	125.0	1.0	99.2%	Average	Continue Current Program
Dilts, Joey	122.0	0.0	100.0%	Average	Continue Current Program
Jensen, Kevin	113.0	1.0	00.1%	Average	Continue Current Program
Dunbar, Ellen	110.0	1.0	99.1%	Average	Continue Current Program
Mowry, Sandra	110.0	0.0	100.0%	Average	Continue Current Program
Target = 105.0					
Williams, Jessica	99.0	4.0	96.1%	Average	Continue Current Program
Odegard, Keanna	97.0	2.0	98.0%	Average	Continue Current Program
Rootkie, Derick	93.0	2.0	97.9%	Average	Continue Current Program
lynn, stacy	85.0	3.0	96.6%	Average	Continue Current Program
Braden, Hailey	77.0	2.0	97.5%	Average	Continue Current Program
Average >= 74.0 (25th %ile)					
Mackey, Darion	71.0	3.0	95.9%	Below Average	Further Assess and Consider Individualizing Program
Ames, Alex	69.0	8.0	89.6%	Below Average	Further Assess and Consider Individualizing Program
Jahnz, Carissa	64.0	2.0	97.0%	Below Average	Further Assess and Consider Individualizing Program
Nordrum-Mrst, Nate	59.0	3.0	95.2%	Below Average	Further Assess and Consider Individualizing Program
Nowling, Kari	57.0	6.0	90.5%	Below Average	Further Assess and Consider Individualizing Program
Below Average >= 49.0 (10th %ile)					
Strauss, Levi	44.0	6.0	88.0%	Well Below Average	Begin Immediate Problem Solving
Soman, Racheal	43.0	4.0	91.5%	Well Below Average	Begin Immediate Problem Solving
Hugill, Philip	24.0	4.0	85.7%	Well Below Average	Begin Immediate Problem Solving

Figure 9.4 Class Distributions by Scores and Percentile

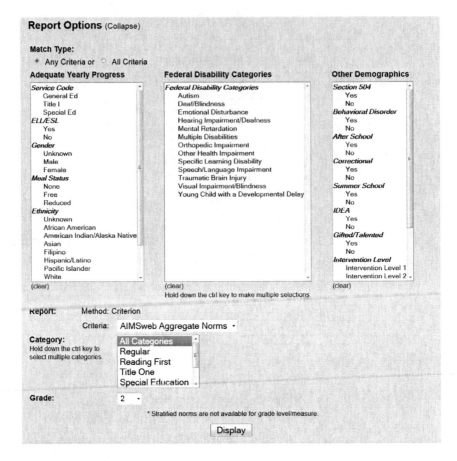

Figure 9.5 AIMSweb Report Options

Web 2.0 Frequent Progress-Monitoring Decisions

When schools allocate more resources to students beyond core instruction, then students' progress should be measured to ensure benefit. Frequent progress monitoring is the method by which educators determine whether the additional resources are making a difference. According to the AIMSweb (2012) Introductory Guide, when students receive additional Tier 2 or Tier 3 interventions, the effectiveness of the intervention should be monitored to ensure that students are being successful. Depending on both situational factors and measurement precision, progress may be monitored as often as twice a week or as infrequently as once a month.

Frequent progress monitoring is defined as the practice of testing students briefly, but often, on the skill areas in which they are receiving additional instruction, to ensure that they are making adequate progress. One requirement of frequent progress monitoring is the need for goal setting. The different Web 2.0 products recommend various goal-setting procedures, since no single agreed-on method has been determined in the research literature. Therefore, setting goals for frequent progress monitoring is a value driven activity. A criterion for a goal is determined by what an educational team values as acceptable performance in a local context.

Standards-Based Goals

When goals are standards based, a goal is selected based on what is expected for all students. This type of goal would indicate that a student who meets the expectation is likely to meet standards (e.g., grade level, school district, or state). A strength of standards-based goals is that they designate what is needed for a student to be successful, regardless of what the student can currently do. For this reason, standards-based goals are ideal in general education. Using standards-based goals can be powerful when a staff decides that students must be proficient, and the staff are willing to sacrifice typical practices, schedules, pedagogy, and materials to achieve that goal. A weakness of standards-based goals is that they can be unrealistic for some students in low-performing districts and for students with special needs.

Benchmark targets, or other standards predictive of success on high-stakes tests, are available in Web 2.0 products, peer reviewed research, or based on local program evaluations. Many general education students who have scores below the benchmark targets have goals set to criterion-reference cut scores. For example, a target in the spring of third grade is 115 Words Read Correctly (WRC) per minute; thus, all general education students in third grade who enter intervention should have a goal of 115 set for the spring of that year. Alternatively, according to the recommendations from DIBELS Net, "When monitoring a student in grade level materials, use the standard DIBELS benchmark goals and the standard timeframe in which those goals should be reached. Benchmark goals for DIBELS Next can be found on the Dynamic Measurement Group website at http://dibels.org/" (http://dibels.org/papers/ProgressMonitoringGuidelines.pdf, 2012). Similarly, AIMSweb manuals concur, in reporting "it is often appropriate to use a benchmark as the goal for a student being progress-monitored" (https://aimsweb.pearson.com/downloads/AIMSweb2.0/Aimsweb_Progress_Monitor_Guide.pdf, 2012).

Norm-Referenced Goals

A second type of goal is norm-referenced goals. This type of goal would indicate that a student who meets the expectation is likely to be successful being taught within a group of typical students. Norm-referenced goals are actually a type of standards-based goals in which the standard is the lower bound of typical for a district. This referent may be different depending on the district or the Web 2.0 product used for data collection and analysis. For example, AIMSweb sets the lower bound for typical as the 25th percentile (i.e., 2nd quartile). It would not be unheard of to set the lower bound to the 16th percentile (i.e., one standard deviation below the mean), or to split the difference, as DIBELS Net has done setting the lower bound as the 20th percentile.

AIMSweb manuals recommend setting goals for the 40th percentile rank. The rationale is that students who obtain scores in the average range relative to peers from their own district are likely to benefit from the core instruction provided in that district. At the same time, students whose performance is well below typical are more likely to struggle with core instruction in that district without intervention (AIMSweb, 2012). A strength of norm-referenced goals is that once typical is defined, a target is easy to set. Since the target is translated into a comparison to general education, this type of goal can be used to maximize Special Education compliance with the rules of Least Restrictive Environment (LRE). The recommendation for using norm-referenced goals is to set the goal for the lower bound of average (i.e., the 25th percentile); however, for some students this expectation may not be realistic. A weakness of norm-referenced goals similar to the weakness of using standard-referenced goals is that, when used dogmatically, these goals can be unrealistic for students with special needs.

Individual-Referenced Goals

Individual-referenced goals would indicate that a student who meets the expectation is making progress relative to their own level of achievement, even though it may still be substantially below either a normative or standard comparison. The goal is calculated based on the amount of growth that is expected for a student, taking into account the individual characteristics of the student and the intensity of the intervention that is being delivered. Individual-referenced goals are typically used when the amount of progress necessary to meet a normative- or standards-based goal is highly unlikely. AIMSweb provides rate of improvement (ROI) growth norms to assist an educator in determining an appropriate ROI for a student. In particular, AIMSweb refers to individual-referenced goals as ROI goals, stating "if the goal ROI for the student is so high as to be rarely observed amongst his or her peers, recognize that this goal will probably be very challenging. Similarly, a goal ROI that is commonly achieved may be insufficient for a student who will be receiving instructional intervention" (AIMSweb, 2012).

A strength of individual-referenced goals is that they are always specific to the particular student. A weakness of individual-referenced goals is that, without using a standard for expected growth, goals can be either too ambitious or too easy to attain.

In addition, individual-referenced goals require that the same measure be used during baseline and evaluation phases of the goal. This is ideal for monitoring progress within a school year, but does not work well for setting a goal in which the material being used for progress monitoring changes from baseline to evaluation phase because of scaling issues (i.e., third-grade passages are easier than fourth-grade, but more difficult than second-grade passages; and typically fifth-grade passages are easier than sixth-grade, but more difficult than fourth-grade). For students who are reading substantially below benchmark targets (i.e., students receiving Tier 3 interventions who are more that 2 years below target), an ambitious, yet realistic goal should be set. An individual student's ROI criteria should be determined by the peer group's ROI, and growth needed to close the gap between current levels of performance and typical levels of performance for students in the target student's grade level.

Progress Monitoring with easyCBM

easyCBM progress monitoring graphs track students' scores over time against four normative growth tracks. These tracks include expected linear growth for the 10th, 20th, 50th, and 90th percentiles. Both intervention lines and trend lines may be displayed on progress monitoring charts. Intervention lines delineate when instruction has changed, while trend lines describe the average growth for the student within an intervention phase. The easyCBM teacher's manual explains that this information is helpful for conducting parent conferences, Student Support Team meetings, and reviews of Individualized Education Plan (IEP) reviews (easyCBM Teacher's Manual, 2012).

Figure 9.6 is an example of an easyCBM progress monitoring graph for a student being monitored on Letter Naming Fluency (LNF). Normative growth bands are set as a watermark

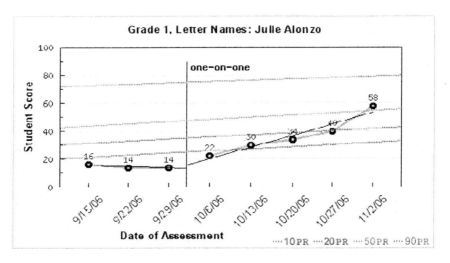

Figure 9.6 Grade 1, Letter Names: Julie Alonzo

behind the data to assist with interpretation. The earliest fall score on this chart was 16 Letter Names (LN) on 9/15. This falls below the 10th percentile of system norms. The student's performance was monitored two additional times in September, remaining below the 10th percentile, when it was decided to change to a one-on-one intervention. A vertical black line with the label "one-on-one" is indicated in early October. At this point, the scores begin to rise, as indicated by individual score icons and the trend line depicted by the sloped black line between the 10th and 20th percentiles in October, and at or above the 50th percentile by early November.

A strength of the easyCBM progress monitoring report is the large amount of data presented in a simple self-contained picture. Specifically, in this report, the teacher can easily see the range of typical scores for the period of progress monitoring. This information can assist with the interpretation regarding whether intervention is still needed. All scores are presented beside the icon, to help with precision of interpretation. Finally, a trend line is depicted to assist with the interpretation of variable data.

Progress Monitoring with DIBELS Net

According to the DIBELS Net publishers, educators should adhere to two considerations when setting goals. First, goals should be realistic, and second, goals should be ambitious. In addition, goals must include a score that the student must obtain, as well as the timeline for meeting the target. Twenty alternate forms for each grade level for each measure are available within the DIBELS Next materials. Student progress should be monitored with grade-level materials, unless the grade-level materials are too difficult for the student. For example, the DIBELS Next guidelines recommend that the student should be able to read material with at least 90% accuracy at a minimum rate of 20, 40, or 50 WRC for grades 1, 2, and 3, respectively. Specific guidelines are recommended to identify the student's appropriate progress monitoring grade level using the DIBELS Next survey, available from Cambium/Sopris West at http://www.soprislearning.com/dibelsnextsurvey/(http://dibels.org/papers/

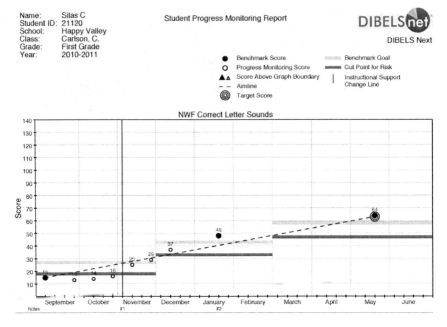

Figure 9.7 Student Progress Monitoring Report (DIBELSnet)

ProgressMonitoringGuidelines.pdf, 2012). DIBELS Net recommends using DIBELS Next benchmark goals when student progress is measured using grade-level materials.

The DIBELS Net system applies an easy to follow heuristic to evaluating progress monitoring data, the three data point rule. After a progress monitoring schedule has been set, an aimline connecting the initial score and the goal score is presented on the individual student progress monitoring graph. The aimline is used as an ongoing gauge to determine whether the student is making progress to meet the goal. When three consecutive progress monitoring data points are observed below the aimline, the indication is that the student is not making sufficient progress and the instructional program should be changed.

Figure 9.7 is an example of a progress-monitoring graph from DIBELS Net. Seasonal criterion-referenced performance bands are set as a watermark behind the data to assist with interpretation. During universal screening in the fall, the student obtained a score of 15 Letter Sounds (LS) in one minute. The score is below the at-risk expectation or red band of 18 LS for fall of first grade. From this starting point, a goal is set at or above the spring expectation of 58 LS. The goal represents a weekly increase of approximately 1.5 LS per week. In early November, a decision was made to change the intervention, as depicted by the vertical line. At winter benchmark, results indicated the student was on track toward meeting the goal, so bi-weekly progress monitoring was discontinued.

A strength of the DIBELS Net progress monitoring report is the large amount of data presented in a simple self-contained picture. In this report, the teacher or interventionist can easily see the range of expected scores for fall, winter, and spring. The aimline and target are clearly visible on the graph. Benchmark and frequent progress monitoring scores are depicted, with a simple but clear difference in presentation. Finally, all scores are presented beside the icon, to help with precision of interpretation.

Progress Monitoring with AIMSweb

AIMSweb highlights the central role that frequent progress monitoring plays in a Response to Intervention (RTI) system, as the information allows educators to evaluate the effectiveness of intervention in an RTI system. While progress monitoring with AIMSweb is a critical component of dynamically guiding intervention by providing an objective manner by which growth is considered, progress monitoring with a general outcome measure does not identify alternative treatments (AIMSweb Progress Monitoring Guide, 2012).

One way that AIMSweb is different from other Web 2.0 products is in the flexibility of the system for setting and evaluating universal screening and progress-monitoring data. Specifically, within the context of progress monitoring, AIMSweb provides the consumer with the option of targeting normative, criterion-referenced, or individually referenced goals. For example, AIMSweb provides users with local and national norms by which progress-monitoring goals can be set and data can be compared. Alternatively, AIMSweb provides an external criterion-referenced cut score to designate a degree of risk status regarding the likelihood of meeting proficiency standards on high-stakes state tests. Finally, AIMSweb provides performance-level percentile ranks and performance benchmarks for comparison to individual student growth.

In the current version of the AIMSweb system, progress is evaluated based on a comparison of the expected and observed rate of increase in scores. The AIMSweb manual for progress monitoring explains the value in examining progress monitoring graphs visually, as well as examining the individual data points around the trend line. However, the manual concludes these methods are inferior to the current use of a trend line, and the upcoming use of a projected 75% confidence interval.

In the latest update of the AIMSweb system, progress is monitored formatively with three performance labels: below, near, and above target. The distinctions are made by comparing the rate of increase in the current intervention phase to the overall expected rate of increase for the student. The progress-monitoring graph in Figure 9.8 displays two program changes. After the collection of the first eight data points, the slope (i.e., dashed line) is substantially below the expected aimline. A vertical line is presented, and another eight data points are depicted on the chart with a new slope. Although the slope in second phase of intervention increased slightly, the level of growth would make achieving the goal unlikely. A second vertical line is entered with a label of "*Program Change 2.*" The remaining data represent an increasing slope, with the eventual data above the year-end goal. In addition to the three projective status designations (i.e., below, near, and above target), the system records *goal missed* and *goal achieved* when the student's final score is entered, either below or above the goal, respectively (AIMSweb Progress Monitoring Guide, 2012).

A new feature in a future version of AIMSweb are confidence intervals embedded in the progress-monitoring graphs. A certain amount of variability in progress-monitoring scores is expected. Although the variability is expected, it makes it more difficult for educators to make defensible decisions. For example, how far below the aimline constitutes a score that is meaningfully below the aimline? How far below the goal is meaningfully below the goal? Current versions of Web 2.0 products have not presented a solution to this problem. However, a future version of AIMSweb promises confidence intervals for scores at the goal date. A confidence interval around the slope will provide additional information useful in making decisions regarding progress. A confidence interval will provide an estimated range of scores that are not different from a particular result. The appropriate use of confidence intervals marks a significant improvement in the decision-making capacity of Web 2.0 products.

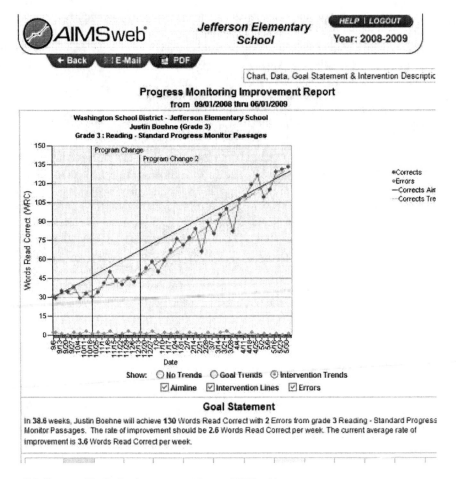

Figure 9.8 Progress Monitoring Improvement Report (AIMSweb)

Progress Monitoring with YPP

YPP represents a unique implementation of CBM. YPP is different in at least two ways from DIBELS Net, AIMSweb, and, to a different degree, easyCBM. First, YPP probes provide items sampled from grade-level curricula material rather than relying on the measurement of a single core behavior, or a small sample of representative behaviors (e.g., number of words read correctly, or number of correct digits). YPP data provides an assessment of individual students standing relative to skill mastery and retention of grade-level end-of-year goals.

Second, YPP is completely web-driven. All YPP assessment items are presented by the computer directly to the student. AIMSweb and DIBELS both have the capacity for online scoring, where administration still requires a teacher to sit with a student, but data can be directly collected by a smartphone, tablet, or computer. Some assessments on easyCBM are web driven, while other measures require a teacher to sit with the student to administer assessments.

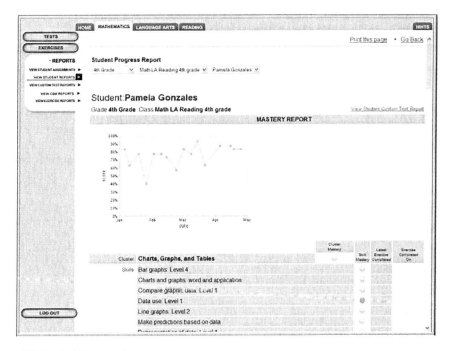

Figure 9.9 Student Progress Report

The YPP system consists of three academic components: CBM, custom measures, and instructional exercises. These three components can be used in a complimentary fashion or individually, based on the needs of the consumer. YPP is a tool that has been designed to assist educators in evaluating student progress with respect to skills and concepts that have been taught. Using this information, teachers can decide how to allocate their time for instruction and remediation. The CBM component in Figure 9.9 provides systematic testing across the entire curriculum and an automatic cumulative review of skills taught, as well as skills to be taught. A review of the data can alert educators of a lack of maintenance of skills previously mastered.

YPP reports provide a comprehensive description of student progress and areas of strength and difficulty. Educators can use these reports to determine the appropriate course of action for individuals and groups of students. YPP reports like Figure 9.10 feature the ability to "drill down" into the actual test students took to see how a student answered individual questions on CBM and custom measures.

Diagnostic reports from YPP allow educators to track student mastery of standards and retention of skills in real time. The system measures individual student, small-group, or whole-class strengths and areas of instructional need by skill, as shown in Figure 9.11.

YPP follows a criterion-referenced approach by reviewing student progress toward state and national standards at the individual student, class, school, or district levels. Using the YPP system administrators can track progress toward end-of-year expectations and use online tools to obtain demographic disaggregations of data toward meeting accountability requirements with more than 500 individual skill assessments across Grades 1–8.

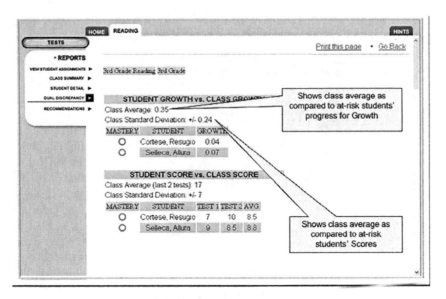

Figure 9.10 Student Growth vs. Class Growth

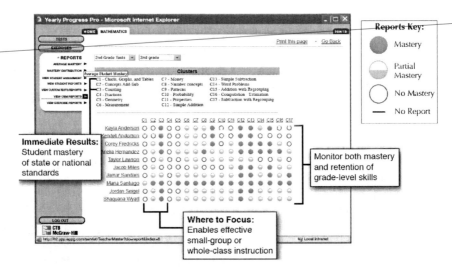

Figure 9.11 YPP Average Student Mastery Report

Summary

CBM has been around for more than 30 years. The research base supporting the use of CBM is substantial. With the passage of legislation requiring the use of data in decision-making, the need for CBM in education has never been more in demand. At the same time, the quality of the integration of CBM with computer technology has steadily increased since its creation. The availability of CBM supported by computer technology has been increasing in terms of both the level of sophistication and interactivity between the consumer and the tools. Many Web 2.0 products are available that provide educators with both the support of Internet applications and the full implementation of CBM, through web-driven applications. The example products discussed in this chapter offer a variety of measures and heuristics for how to consider the data that is collected. The review of the four Web 2.0 solutions was intended to showcase a little of the technology that is available. Each of the tools has strengths and limitations. The choice of which, if any, of these tools to use depends on the match between what the tool has to offer, and the needs and technological skill set of the consumer.

References

AIMSweb. (2012). AIMSweb introductory guide. Retrieved October 1, 2013, from http://www.aimsweb.com

AIMSweb. (2012). AIMsweb progress monitoring guide. Retrieved October 1, 2013, from https://aimsweb.pearson.com/downloads/AIMSweb2.0/Aimsweb_Progress_Monitor_Guide.pdf

Deno, S. L. (1985). Curriculum-based measurement: Emerging alternative. *Exceptional Children, 52,* 219–232.

Deno, S. L. (1986). Formative evaluation of individual student programs: A new role for school psychologists. *School Psychology Review, 15,* 358–374.

Deno, S. L. (1993). Curriculum-based measurement. In J. Kramer (Ed.), *Curriculum-based measurement* (pp. 1–23). Lincoln, NE: Buros Institute of Mental Measurements.

Deno, S. L. (2003). Developments in curriculum-based measurement. *The Journal of Special Education, 37,* 184–192.

Deno, S. L. (2005). Problem-solving assessment. In R. Brown-Chidsey (Ed.), *Assessment for intervention: A problem-solving approach* (pp. 10–40). New York, NY: Guilford Press.

DIBELS. (2012). Progress monitoring guidelines. Retrieved October 1, 2013, from http://dibels.org/papers/ProgressMonitoringGuidelines.pdf

DIBELS Next. (2012). Progress monitoring guidelines. Retrieved October 1, 2013, from http://www.soprislearning.com/dibelsnextsurvey/(http://dibels.org/papers/ProgressMonitoringGuidelines.pdf

Ferguson Jr., C. L., & Fuchs, L. S. (1991). Scoring accuracy within curriculum-based measurement: A comparison of teachers and microcomputer applications. *Journal of Special Education Technology, 11*(1), 26–32.

Fuchs, L. S., & Deno, S. L. (1991). Paradigmatic distinctions between instructionally relevant measurement models. *Exceptional Children, 57,* 488–500.

Fuchs, L. S., Deno, S. L., & Mirkin, P. K. (1983). Data-based program modification: A continuous evaluation system with computer software to facilitate implementation. *Journal of Special Education Technology, 6,* 50–57.

Fuchs, L. S., & Fuchs, D. (1990). The role of skills analysis in curriculum-based measurement in math. *School Psychology Review, 19,* 6–23.

Fuchs, L. S., & Fuchs, D. (1991). Effects of expert system advice within curriculum-based measurement on teacher planning and student achievement in spelling. *School Psychology Review, 20,* 49–67.

Fuchs, L. S., & Fuchs, D. (2001). Computer applications to curriculum-based measurement. *Special Services in the Schools, 17,* 1–14.

Fuchs, L. S., Fuchs, D., & Hamlett, C. L. (1989). Monitoring reading growth using student recalls: Effects of two teacher feedback systems. *Journal of Educational Research, 83,* 103–111.

Fuchs, L. S., Fuchs, D., & Hamlett, C. L. (1992). Computer applications to facilitate curriculum-based measurement. *Teaching Exceptional Children, 24*(4), 58–60.

Fuchs, L. S., Fuchs, D., & Hamlett, C. L. (1993). Technological advances linking the assessment of students' academic proficiency to instructional planning. *Journal of Special Education Technology, 12,* 49–62.

Fuchs, L. S., Fuchs, D., & Hamlett, C. L. (1994). Strengthening the connection between assessment and instructional planning with expert systems. *Exceptional Children, 61,* 138–146.

Fuchs, L. S., Fuchs, D., Hamlett, C. L., & Allinder, R. M. (1991). The contribution of skills analysis to curriculum-based measurement in spelling. *School Psychology Review, 20,* 443–452.

Fuchs, L. S., Fuchs, D., Hamlett, C. L., & Ferguson, C. (1992). Effects of expert system consultation within curriculum-based measurement, using a reading maze task. *Exceptional Children, 58,* 436–450.

Fuchs, L. S., Fuchs, D., Hamlett, C. L., & Hasselbring, T. (1987). Using computers with curriculum-based progress monitoring: Effects on teacher effectiveness and satisfaction. *Journal of Special Education Technology, 8*(4), 14–27.

Fuchs, L. S., Fuchs, D., Hamlett, C. L., Phillips, N. B., & Bentz, J. (1994). Classwide curriculum-based measurement: Helping general educators meet the challenge of student diversity. *Exceptional Children, 60*(6), 518–537.

Fuchs, L. S., Fuchs, D., Hamlett, C. L., & Stecker, P. M. (1991). Effects of curriculum-based measurement and consultation on teacher planning and student achievement in mathematics operations. *American Educational Research Journal, 28,* 617–641.

Fuchs, L. S., Hamlett, C. L., Fuchs, D., Stecker, P. M., & Ferguson, C. (1988). Conducting curriculum-based measurement with computerized data collection: Effects on efficiency and teacher satisfaction. *Journal of Special Education Technology, 9*(2), 73–86.

Goo, M., Watt, S., Park, Y., & Hosp, J. (2012). A guide to choosing web-based curriculum-based measurements for the classroom. *Teaching Exceptional Children, 45*(2), 34–40.

Hintze, J. M., Christ, T. J., & Methe, S. A. (2006). Curriculum-based assessment. *Psychology in the Schools, 43,* 45–56.

Lembke, E., McMaster, K. L., & Stecker, P. M. (2012). Technological applications of curriculum-based measurement in elementary setting: Curriculum-based measurement in the digital age. In C. A. Espin, K. L. McMaster, & M. M. Wayman (Eds.), *A measure of success: The influence of curriculum-based measurement on education* (pp. 125–135). Minneapolis: University of Minnesota Press.

No Child Left Behind (NCLB) Act of 2001, Pub. L. No. 107-110, § 115, Stat. 1425 (2002).

O'Reilly, T. (2005). *What is Web 2.0: Design patterns and business models for the next generation of software.* O'Reilly Media, Inc. Retrieved from http://oreilly.com/web2/archive/what-is-web-20.html

Shinn, M. R. (Ed.). (1989). *Curriculum-based measurement: Assessing special children.* New York, NY: Guilford Press.

Shinn, M. R. (Ed.). (1998). *Advanced applications of curriculum-based measurement.* New York, NY: Guilford Press.

Shinn, M. R. (2008). Best practices in curriculum-based measurement and its use in a problem-solving model. In A. Thomas & J. Grimes (Eds.), *Best practices in school psychology V* (pp. 243–262). Bethesda, MD: National Association of School Psychologists.

Shinn, M. R. (2010). Building a scientifically based data system for progress monitoring and universal screening across three tiers, including RTI using curriculum-based measurement. In M. R. Shinn & H. Walker (Eds.), *Interventions for academic and behavior problems III: Preventative and remedial approaches* (pp. 259–292). Washington, DC: National Association of School Psychologists.

Shinn, M. R., & Baker, S. K. (1996). The use of curriculum-based measurement with diverse learners. In L. A. Suzuki, P. J. Meller, & J. G. Ponterotto (Eds.), *Handbook of multicultural assessment: Clinical, psychological, and educational applications* (pp. 179–222). San Francisco, CA: Jossey-Bass.

Shinn, M. R., Collins, V. L., & Gallagher, S. (1998). Curriculum-based measurement and its use in a problem-solving model with students from minority backgrounds. In M. R. Shinn (Ed.), *Advanced applications of curriculum-based measurement* (pp. 143–174). New York, NY: Guilford Press.

Shinn, M. R., Rosenfield, S., & Knutson, N. (1989). Curriculum-based assessment: A comparison of models. *School Psychology Review, 18,* 299–316.

U.S. Department of Education. (2010). *Educational technology in U.S. public schools: Fall 2008.* National Center for Education Statistics (NCES 2010–034).

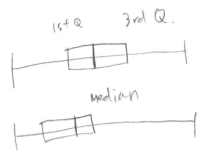

10

Responsive Assessment and Instruction Practices

Rachel Brown, Mark W. Steege, and Rebekah Bickford

Introduction

In recent years, the focus of assessment practices has shifted from assessment *of* instruction to assessment *for* instruction. A factor in the changing assessment practices is the emergence of Response to Intervention (RTI) as a support structure for all students. RTI was first formally included in federal education policy in the 2001 No Child Left Behind (NCLB) Act (No Child Left Behind [NCLB], 2001). NCLB was an update of the Elementary and Secondary Education Act (ESEA) that provides funding for support programs in U.S. schools. Additional language about RTI was included in the 2004 reauthorization of the Individuals with Disabilities Education Act (IDEIA; Individuals with Disabilities Education Improvement Act, 2004). While RTI's first formal mention was in the 21st century, it has roots that go back many more years.

History of RTI

RTI is the most recent effort to provide effective instruction for all students. Although U.S. public education has been provided, at least for some students, since colonial times, equal access to public education dates from the 1954 Supreme Court decision in the case of *Brown vs. The Board of Education of Topeka, Kansas*. In this landmark ruling, the Court decided that separate schools for Black and White children were not really "equal." This ruling triggered the desegregation of public schools and the beginning of equal access to public education by all students (Brown-Chidsey & Steege, 2010). Following the Brown decision, a national movement to grant full civil rights to African Americans began. This movement spawned efforts by other disenfranchised groups to gain equal rights as well. The women's and Indian rights movements are among those that were part of the civil rights initiatives of the 1960s and 1970s. The effort to gain the right to free public education for all students was part of the Civil Rights era. Advocates for students with disabilities worked toward passage of Public Law 94–142 in 1975. This law, initially known as the Education of the Handicapped Act

(EHA), established a federal policy granting every student, regardless of disability, access to a free appropriate public education (FAPE) in the least restrictive environment (LRE).

EHA was a major shift in U.S. education policy because it removed any option to bar a student from public school due to child-specific disability. Instead of public education being a privilege for those who could get to school and would do the work, it became a right of all children. EHA was initially designed to ensure that students with severe disabilities would be welcome in schools and have effective instruction once there. Over time, the numbers of students with more severe disabilities were overshadowed by those with so-called mild disabilities, such as Specific Learning Disability (SLD). The 1980s and 1990s saw steady increases in the numbers of students participating in special education. By 1990, when EHA was re-authorized for the second time, the majority of students participating in special education were those with mild to moderate disabilities. Due to these increases, researchers and policymakers wondered if some students identified with disabilities might have been identified in error (Benner, 1998; McLeskey & Skiba, 1990).

During the 1990s, researchers began experimenting with a way to provide special instruction (i.e., intervention) before a student was found eligible for special education (Barnett, Daly, Jones, & Lentz, 2004; Brown-Chidsey, 2005; Vaughn & Fuchs, 2003). This method was referred to as Response to Intervention (RTI) because it tested the hypothesis that the student would respond to special instruction or intervention. These researchers put forward the idea that if a student responds to instruction/intervention, the student does not have a disability. Alternatively, if the student does not respond to the instruction/intervention, then the student might have a disability. These research findings showed that when students received effective instruction prior to referral and special education, fewer students ended up needing special education (Burns, Appleton, & Stehouwer, 2005). The findings contributed to the language in NCLB that required schools to provide scientifically based general education instruction for all students in reading and math. An extension of this requirement was included in IDEA 2004, which allows school teams to use data from RTI activities as part of the process of determining if a student has a Specific Learning Disability. Most recently, the 2009 American Recovery and Reinvestment Act (ARRA) and Race to the Top initiatives required schools to show that adopted instruction practices would improve learning outcomes for all students (H.R. 1–111th Congress: American Recovery and Reinvestment Act of 2009).

In 2010, the Obama administration drafted legislation to re-authorize ESEA. The draft included many RTI-like practices, referred to as Multi-Tier Systems of Support (MTSS). MTSS is a new term for the same ideas behind RTI: providing all students with effective instruction from the beginning and then using regular assessment data to identify and support those students who need help. This chapter will provide an overview of key RTI/MTSS practices and how they can be used to implement effective assessment practices in schools. For the sake of consistency, we will use the term *responsive assessment* to describe how RTI and MTSS methods can be used to support the needs of all students.

Behavioral Foundations and Applications of Responsive Assessment

Conceptually, MTSS and RTI draw heavily on principles of applied behavior analysis (ABA). These practices also incorporate methodologies pioneered and empirically evaluated by behavior analysts. ABA is the process of systematically applying interventions based on the principles of learning theory to improve socially meaningful behaviors, and to demonstrate that the interventions employed are responsible for the improvement in behavior

(Baer, Wolf, & Risley, 1968). Baer et al. noted that ABA is "the process of applying sometimes tentative principles of behavior to the improvement of specific behaviors, and simultaneously evaluating whether or not any changes noted are indeed attributable to the process of application—and if so, to what parts of that process" (p. 91). This description is the essence of MTSS and RTI, which seek to provide students with instruction that improves the function of their school behaviors. This section provides information about the behavioral foundations the led to the emergence of responsive assessment practices.

Basically, ABA is a problem-solving process in which: (a) comprehensive assessments are conducted to understand human behavior, with the results of assessments used to design individually tailored interventions; (b) structured educational procedures and therapies are used to improve socially meaningful behaviors; and (c) objective measures are used to determine the effectiveness of those interventions. There are two major components of ABA-based educational programs: assessment and intervention.

Assessment. Within ABA-based programs, assessment plays a pivotal role. Essentially, assessment drives the delivery of interventions. In ABA, assessment is an ongoing process that occurs before, during, and after the implementation of the intervention. Assessment *before* intervention involves evaluation of the unique behaviors, needs, and characteristics of the individual, the environment, and the complex interactions between the individual and his/her environment. The results of assessment are used to design *individually tailored* intervention plans and procedures. Assessments also are conducted *during* the delivery of interventions: (a) to monitor progress, and (b) to determine the relative effectiveness of selected interventions or strategies. Sometimes, assessments are conducted *after* the intervention, to access the generality and durability of behavior change. Within ABA, analyzing program data is critical. Analyzing program data on a regular basis allows the team to evaluate clearly the efficacy of the intervention and, when necessary, to make data-based decisions regarding the modification of programs. The process for objectively evaluating the effectiveness of interventions within the field of ABA is referred to as *single-subject experimental design*.

Intervention. Interventions are those treatments, educational strategies, instructional methodologies, therapies, etc., that are implemented with the purpose of increasing adaptive behaviors and/or decreasing interfering behaviors. ABA-based programs also are characterized by the use of empirically proven interventions (i.e., evidence-based interventions). What is meant by "evidence-based"? Simply put, all ABA interventions have been "product tested." ABA interventions have been demonstrated to be clinically and scientifically sound. They have been subjected to thorough review and analysis that has demonstrated that the intervention is effective and that results are not the result of extraneous or unrelated factors. The ABA research literature includes a vast array of evidence-based interventions that can be used in schools. Matching interventions to the unique characteristics of the learner maximizes the effectiveness and efficiency of interventions. Due to the large number of options, practitioners must consider the broad range of ABA-based interventions when using assessment data to select practices to be used with individual students.

One model for conducting ABA-based responsive assessments of academic behaviors was developed by Daly and colleagues (e.g., Daly, Bonfiglio, Mattson, Persampieri, & Foreman-Yates, 2005, 2006; Daly, Murdoch, Lillenstein, Webber, & Lentz, 2002; Daly, Persampieri, McCurdy, & Gortmaker, 2005; Noell, Freeland, Witt, & Gansle, 2001). These researchers used alternating treatments designs (Steege, Brown-Chidsey & Mace, 2002) to evaluate the relative effectiveness of different reading interventions. This involved implementing several reading interventions over multiple sessions, each within a randomized order. By collecting data on reading behavior (i.e., oral reading fluency), they were able to graph each student's performance, compare the graphed data, and determine the relative effectiveness of the interventions.

Brown-Chidsey and Steege (2010) referred to the practice of trying out several interventions to see what works as "test driving" interventions. By trying out different interventions and comparing the results, teachers can identify which one(s) is most effective for an individual student. This practice is a form of responsive assessment, in that the teacher is using assessment data to respond to the student's specific need. This method is particularly useful when team members disagree as to which intervention to implement (e.g., repeated reading vs. phrase drill error correction). As shown, MTSS and RTI owe many of their core features and practices to ABA methods. By using assessments before, during, and after intervention, and by carefully analyzing the data to determine if the selected intervention is working, educators can offer truly individualized and responsive assessments for students.

Key Features of Responsive Assessment

There are three key features of responsive assessment that must be included for it to be effective. It must be preventive, formative, and universal.

Prevention Model. Responsive assessment is based on a prevention model of supporting all students. This model dates to early work by Caplan (1964) and has been adopted as a cornerstone of RTI and MTSS practices. The basic prevention model includes three levels, or tiers, of prevention: primary, secondary, and tertiary. Primary prevention refers to universal steps available to an entire population for the purpose of preventing problems. For example, the practice of vaccinating children is a form of tier 1 universal prevention, because it serves to prevent children and the adults around them from contracting certain diseases. Tier 2 prevention includes steps taken to reduce the effects of a problem early in its course and before it becomes chronic. For example, if a person develops the condition known as pre-diabetes, wherein key risk factors for diabetes, such as obesity and high blood sugar, are present, following a healthy diet, getting more exercise, and losing weight would be a tier 2 prevention program. Tier 3 prevention provides intensive treatment or programming for situations in which the problem is well established. The goal of tier 3 prevention is to mitigate the effects of the problem over the lifespan. Keeping with the pre-diabetes example above, if a person does develop diabetes, it may need to be controlled with a medication such as insulin. Taking insulin on a regular basis to treat diabetes is a form of tier 3 prevention, because it makes it possible to live with the condition but it does not make the diabetes go away. Notice that all three tiers of this prevention model have the goal of preventing later problems and making the future better.

Educators have adapted the prevention model for use in schools (Walker, Horner, Sugai, & Bullis, 1996). This adaptation includes changing the term prevention to intervention to make it clear that something specific is provided for students with higher risk factors. A graphic developed by Brown-Chidsey & Steege (2010) depicting a three-tier prevention model for RTI is shown in Figure 10.1. This figure shows three tiers of support for students in school settings. It is set up to depict both academic and behavioral supports and includes special education services in the middle, because most students with disabilities spend some or most of their school days participating in general education services. Tier 1 includes services for all students. Essentially, tier 1 is the general education curriculum. Tier 2 includes additional (i.e., supplemental) services for those students not successful with tier 1 alone. Tier 3 provides additional supplemental, or sometimes replacement, instruction for students who demonstrate the highest levels of need.

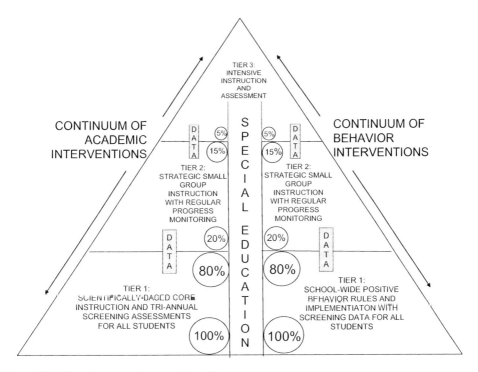

Figure 10.1 Three-tier prevention model for RTI

There are small circles in each tier of the triangle in Figure 10.1. These circles show the percentages of students expected to be successful at each tier. For tiers 1 and 2, there are circles at the bottom and top of the tiers. This is because students will enter and exit supports at these levels. All students, 100%, participate in tier 1 instruction. This is the curriculum of instruction provided by the school for all students. About 80% of students will be successful with the tier 1 instruction alone, so there is a circle showing these 80%. That leaves about 20% of students who will need additional support. These students participate in tier 2 interventions that are provided in addition to tier 1 instruction. Importantly, they receive *more* overall instruction, because that is what they need. About 15% of those who participate in tier 2 interventions will be successful with such support. That leaves about 5% of all the students in a school who will need the highly intensive supports provided at tier 3. There is no exit percentage for tier 3, because we cannot dismiss students from school just because they are still struggling. Instead, those students who still struggle after support at tiers 1, 2, and 3 are often referred for evaluation to determine if they have a disability. If a student is found to have a disability and needs special education, then an Individualized Education Program (IEP) is developed and that becomes the student's "curriculum" or program of study.

In responsive assessment, the overall decision-making process for determining which students need help is governed by student data. Notice that the lines dividing the three tiers of support have gray boxes with dotted lines around them. In these boxes is the word: *data*. This is meant to convey that decisions about which students and what types of intervention are needed must be made according to student data. Data are the doorways between the tiers. No decision about student instructional needs should be made without consulting recent, reliable, and valid data documenting student performance. This is very different from

Table 10.1 Types of Assessments Commonly Used in Schools

Type	Purpose	Example
Summative	Document what a student has learned over an extended period of time	State-mandated annual assessments in grades 3 through 8
Formative	Show the nature of a student's learning in brief incremental stages	Weekly curriculum-based measures of student progress in a specific skill
Diagnostic	Determine whether a student meets the criteria for a specific disability or condition	Comprehensive psychological evaluation that includes record review, interviews, observations, rating scales, cognitive, and/or other types of testing
Placement	Make a decision about what type of instruction would be most helpful for a student	Sequence of assessments at specific skill levels to show the student's current instructional level
Eligibility	Determine whether a student is eligible for a certain type of instructional service that is limited to students who meet certain criteria	Team meeting at which the student's assessment data are compared to eligibility requirements

traditional models of assessment that sometimes rely on numbers of students, teacher convenience, or what materials are available. Instead, responsive assessment takes the data gathered about students and uses it to identify what types of instruction students need.

Formative. Different types of assessment have been used in schools for many years. Ideally, the type of assessment is based on the types of questions it seeks to answer (Salvia & Ysseldyke, 2011). Although there are many types of assessments, Table 10.1 provides a short summary of major types used in schools. Summative assessments are the most common and have been used for years to document what students learned over a long period of time. Formative assessments are newer and provide a way to show if instruction is working at brief intervals (e.g., weekly or monthly). Diagnostic assessments are widely used as part of special education evaluation and are in-depth assessments showing if a student's behaviors match certain criteria for a diagnosis. Placement assessments are a type of instructional alignment when students complete assessments of skills at different levels to show their current skills. Finally, eligibility assessments are formal determinations of whether a student can receive certain services, such as special education. Of these types of assessments, only formative assessment provides a way to consider the effects of instruction while it is being delivered. This is because formative assessment happens over time and shows whether a student is making progress. Formative assessment is necessary for responsive practices because it allows educators to *respond* to student learning needs in a time frame that allows for instructional change.

Universal. The third major feature of responsive assessment that must be incorporated for it to be effective is universality. This means that the assessment practices must be available, as needed, for all students. While some assessments in schools are universal, not all are. Summative assessments that show whether a student met specific goals are usually universal. But, they do not help inform instruction, because if a student fails such a test there is no chance to go back and start over. In order to make assessment an instructional tool for all students, it must be used with all students in a systematic and planned way. This means that all students need to participate in universal screening assessments, so that teachers can know which students need more help. Including all students in the initial screening assessments reduces or eliminates the chance that a student might "slip through the cracks." This is very different from prior practices, when it was assumed that students were doing okay until they were not.

Universal assessments are a cornerstone for equitable access to effective instruction. Such assessments shift the responsibility for student progress away from the student alone and into a collaborative model in which students and teachers work together to create student success. And this success can only happen if teachers know which students need more help. There are very many ways that school-age students can get "off-track" and do not experience school success. Some major factors long associated with school difficulties are poverty, parent engagement, and race. However, careful analysis of student outcome data actually shows that these factors are not as important as what teachers do in the classroom (Hattie, 2008). The nature of student–teacher interactions during instruction is the single best predictor of school-learning outcomes. Given the powerful role that classroom instruction plays in student learning, it is essential that teachers have universal data about how all students are doing and which ones need more assistance.

Multi-Tier Student Supports

Given the strong benefits of using preventive, formative, and universal practices in schools, the model known as Response to Intervention (RTI) was developed. This model incorporates all of these practices into a systems-level approach to supporting all students. As noted above, this model is now known as MTSS, but the essentials remain the same. There must be responsive assessment and instruction provided universally for all students. While all the details of how to develop and implement MTSS cannot be included in one chapter, the following section outlines the core steps needed.

Responsive Assessment Practices

There are four components of responsive assessment practices in schools: core instruction, universal screening, tiered interventions, and progress monitoring. All of these steps utilize curriculum-based measures (CBM) as the primary assessment tool. Detailed information about CBM is provided in Chapter 8.

Core Instruction. This refers to the core instructional materials and practices that are used with all students in the general education curriculum. Think of this as what teachers do every day in their classrooms. Core instruction is crucial because it affects all students and is the best mechanism for ensuring effective school outcomes. Recently, the Council of Chief State School Officers (CCSSO) developed universal learning standards known as the Common Core Standards (CCS; Common Core State Standards Initiative [CCSSI], 2012). These standards are designed to offer consistency in what students will be expected to learn across schools in the United States. As of 2012, 45 states and three territories had adopted the standards. Three more states have indicated the intention to adopt the standards, with only Alaska and Texas stating the intention to use their own standards. The CCS are the first attempt by U.S. schools to adopt uniform learning goals that cut across state lines. With the implementation of the CCS, it is likely that most schools will want to use screening assessments that measure where all students are in relation to the CCS grade-level learning goals.

Universal Screening. This is the first step in providing responsive assessment. It is a process of gathering brief standardized data about every student in a school at specific times during the year. To conduct universal screenings, schools must decide what skills to measure and what assessments to use. Importantly, the skills to be measured should be the most essential outcomes that are expected of all students at each grade level. CBM is designed to measure all of the basic academic skills (Shinn, 2012). For this reason, CBMs are sometimes referred to as general outcome measures (GOM) because they tap into the very core academic skills of math, reading, spelling, and writing (Hosp, Hosp, & Howell, 2007).

The good news is that CBM accurately measures the core elements of the CCS for at least kindergarten through grade 8. And, there are many CBM tools available to schools. The National Center for Response to Intervention (NCRTI) is a virtual technical assistance center that offers comparisons of most of the available universal screening tools (National Center for Response to Intervention [NCRTI], 2012a). The NCRTI Screening Tools Chart provides a listing of numerous screening tools submitted for review by the NCRTI. Each tool is rated according to specific features, such as reliability and validity. CBM are prominent among the tools and offer an efficient way to conduct universal screenings for students in grades K through 5 or 6. Starting at the middle school level, other forms of screening can be used. Often, these are measures that can be administered with whole classes at one time such as the Group Reading Assessment and Diagnostic Evaluation (GRADE) and its math partner the GMADE (NCRTI, 2012a).

To conduct universal screening, some logistics must be considered. First, the specific screening measures to be used must be selected. As noted, these need to be aligned with the learning goals for the students at each grade level. For example, a district might decide to use the EasyCBM assessments for all kindergarten through 5th-grade students, and the GRADE and GMADE for grades 6 through 12. After selecting the specific instrument(s), the personnel who will administer the tests must be trained. This is vitally important, because test results are only as good as the accuracy of administration. Some screening assessments are administered individually, while others can be group administered. The educators who will administer the tests must know the precise and standardized rules for administration, so that the obtained results will be useful.

The decision about which personnel will administer testing is important. There are no specific rules about who should do the testing, except that it must be someone who has been adequately trained. Schools vary a great deal regarding the selection of screening personnel. In some schools, classroom teachers screen all their own students. In others, a special team of trained screening personnel do all of the screenings. In yet some other districts, all available trained adults who are able to participate—including parents, bus drivers, secretaries, and teachers' aides—conduct screenings. As stated, there is no rule about who should do the screenings, but the number of people involved may have slight effects on score accuracy. The more people who conduct the screenings, the more variable scores will be. However, this variation is small and does not appear to influence the interpretability of scores. Few studies of examiner effects have been conducted. Still, Brown-Chidsey and Gritter (2012) found that when teachers administered screening assessments, the scores were as reliable as when a district-wide team conducted the tests. It is recommended that schools carefully select and train whoever will administer the assessments and then be consistent with that choice.

In addition to training, careful planning for the dates, locations, and materials needed must be done. To provide regular updates on all students' progress, universal screening is best done three times a year. Nationally, schools typically adhere to assessment "windows" so that results can be compared to national norms. For example, fall testing is done in August or September, winter testing in December or January, and spring testing in April or May.

The reason for two different options at each "season" is that schools typically follow one of two main academic year calendars. Some schools start in August, well before Labor Day, and others start after Labor Day. The two assessment window dates give schools a range of dates from which to choose screening sessions. Ideally, screening dates are set well in advance for the entire school year. This allows teachers to know when screening will happen and when they will have results.

A detailed schedule indicating the times and places at which students will be screened is needed (Brown-Chidsey & Steege, 2010). If classroom teachers will conduct screenings of their own students, the location should be the classroom, but it may be necessary to arrange for someone to assist with the other students not being screened during that time. If others will do the screenings, then locations where screenings can be done are needed. If the selected screening measures can be administered to a whole class (e.g., GRADE), the classroom will still work. If the measures must be administered individually, then quiet spaces are needed. Examples of locations that can work include offices, libraries, or the gymnasium if there is enough space between screening stations. If the personnel doing screenings include specialists, such as school psychologists or administrators, their offices can be used.

Prior to the first screening day, the materials must be prepared. Some screening assessments are purchased in kits and will need to be opened and organized into sets. Others, such as AIMSweb and the Dynamic Indicators of Basic Early Literacy Skills (DIBELS) can be downloaded and printed from the Internet. In such cases, enough materials for all students must be copied. In addition to the specific assessment items, examiners will need a clipboard, pens, and probably a timer. By definition, all CBM items are timed, because they measure fluency. The timer function of "smart" devices such as iPhones can be used. Some screening assessments have online scoring options. For example, both AIMSweb and DIBELS have electronic versions for the individualized measures. To use online assessments, students are shown paper items, but the examiner enters the student's score during testing using a computer or tablet device, and it is automatically recorded in the data set for that school. This eliminates the need for hand-scoring and then entering student data after the screening is completed.

Sometimes, all students are in attendance on the screening dates, but not always. For this reason, it is important to create screening "make-up" dates in advance, to verify times and places when absent students can be screened. After all students' scores are collected, they must be entered into a database for analysis. Some screening measures have accompanying data entry services and systems. If no such data system comes with the screening measures, one must be created. An ideal tool for creating and managing screening data is spreadsheet software such as Microsoft *Excel* or similar products. The key is that all scores must be entered in a way that allows teachers to examine student performance individually, by class, and over time. Once all data are entered, score reports that show student performance by classroom, grade, or school can be used to determine which students need additional assistance. Importantly, the screening scores should never be used in isolation to make a decision about whether a student needs assistance. The screening scores should be used alongside other indicators of student performance, such as classroom assessment and prior performance. Taken together, the data should be used to identify those students who are struggling and need extra help.

There are two primary ways to determine which scores suggest that a student needs help: benchmark criteria or normative equivalents. Benchmarks are scores derived from the performance of a large sample of students in a given population. A benchmark criterion is a score cut-point identified as the performance level above which a student is likely to meet future learning goals. The DIBELS benchmark scores are an example of such criterion scores (DIBELS Next, 2012). Normative equivalents are also based on scores from a large sample but are organized differently. Instead of predictive analysis, normative scores are organized into a normal curve. Such scores can be organized to show what is below, average, or above-average performance for students.

Criterion benchmarks provide the most accurate way of identifying which students are most at risk for school difficulties, but not all screening measures have set benchmarks. In such cases, norms for performance can be used. For published screening assessments, national norms are available. Schools also can decide to create local norms. National norms indicate typical performance across the country, while local norms tell how prior students in the local community have done on the assessment. Ideally, both national and local norms are consulted because together they tell the most complete story about how students are doing. Often, schools will decide that all students who score below a specific percentile rank of the norms will be considered at risk. For example, the 10th or 25th percentiles might be used as indicators of students whose performance is concerning (Shinn, 2012).

Assessment of Core Curricula. After reviewing student data and examining students' levels of performance, the next question to consider is whether or not at least 80% of students in each class, grade, and school met the selected criterion for success. For example, if using national norms for reading performance, did 80% of the students obtain a score at or above the goal or benchmark score? If 80% or more of the students met the benchmark, then the universal core curriculum is achieving the desired result. But, if fewer than 80% of the students in a class, grade, or school met the goal, then it is important to examine how well the core curriculum is being implemented and what changes could be made so that 80% or more of the students will meet the goal. Recall that when using a MTSS/RTI prevention model, 80% of students should meet their grade-level goals with tier 1 instruction. The 80% rule is a cornerstone of MTSS practices because it recognizes that in any given set of students most will succeed with the general curriculum, but some will need additional help. Research and outcomes from schools where MTSS has been implemented over a long period of time have confirmed this (Burns & Gibbons, 2008). If fewer than 80% of students meet the goal, then revision of the core, tier 1, instructional program must happen before any students are provided more intensive supports.

Tiered Intervention. If 80% or more of students meet the learning goals, then the next step in data review is to identify those who need tier 2 intervention. Either those students scoring below the criterion or below a specific percentile, and for whom other data indicate a need for help, should be provided with tier 2 intervention. Such intervention includes additional instruction provided on a regular basis in the area(s) of student need. For example, if a student's screening, classroom, and prior data showed that she could not accurately provide multiplication facts for numbers through nine, then additional instruction to teach those facts should be provided. The length of time that an intervention should be provided depends on how the student does. In order to determine whether an intervention is effective, progress-monitoring data must be collected on a regular basis.

Treatment Integrity. Before reviewing progress data, it is important that the teachers reviewing the data verify that the intervention was actually implemented correctly. The accurate implementation of intervention is known as treatment integrity or treatment fidelity. Such accuracy is essential because, without it, it is impossible to know whether the outcomes observed during and after the intervention were truly the result of intervention components. Recent attention to treatment integrity has improved the tools available to evaluate and confirm whether an intervention was implemented correctly. Sanetti and Kratochwill (2012) developed a treatment integrity evaluation tool that can be used to determine whether an intervention was truly implemented as planned. Such tools are necessary as part of responsive assessment, because if the intervention was not properly put in place, it is premature to conclude that it did not work. Instead, the next step is to go back and restart the intervention as intended, collect new progress data, and then review the data to see whether different outcomes are observed. If the data show that the student improved after the intervention was correctly implemented, then it should be continued until the student meets the learning goal. As shown in Figure 10.1 and in data obtained in many schools, about 15% of students in a school will be successful as a result of tier 2 intervention.

Progress Monitoring. Progress monitoring refers to the practice of conducting brief assessments with students at regular intervals while intervention is happening. The NCRTI recommends that students participating in tier 2 interventions complete progress measures at least once a month, and that students participating in tier 3 interventions complete progress measures at least once a week. NCRTI has a tools chart of progress measures that is organized in the same manner as the one for screening assessments (NCRTI, 2012b). For a measure to be considered effective for progress monitoring, it must have enough equivalent alternate forms to be used over the time that the student participates in an intervention. If monitoring is done weekly, then there would need to be enough measures for each week of intervention. CBM is ideally suited to progress monitoring, because not only does it have alternate forms, but it is also brief to administer and sensitive to student growth over time.

Various studies have examined how long an intervention needs to be in place before it will show effects (Vaughn et al., 2009). There must be at least three data points before progress data can be interpreted (Riley-Tillman & Burns, 2009). That means that if monitoring is done monthly, it will require at least 3 months of intervention, but if monitoring is done weekly, interpretation might begin after 3 weeks. There is no rule for how long an intervention will take to show effects. A thorough treatment of how to interpret progress data is beyond the scope of this chapter, however, an excellent resource about how to interpret student data can be found in Riley-Tillman and Burns (2009). Typically, student progress data will show that the student is improving, showing no effects, or getting worse. It is less common to see worsening effects from interventions for academic skills, because once learned, students do not usually lose the skills in a short time. But, when a student shows no gains after a period of time, the data indicate that some change is needed.

When students reach the learning target, it is important not to end the intervention suddenly and expect the student to be able to maintain success without it. The student's success came about as a result of the extra support from intervention. If that support is suddenly removed, the student is likely to struggle just as before intervention. Instead, the intervention should be faded gradually, with progress monitoring maintained (Powell-Smith & Ball, 2008). When the student has shown maintenance of the skills with reduced support, then the intervention can be ended. But, some form of progress monitoring should be maintained to document that the student is successful without the supports.

Intensive Intervention and Special Education Decisions

For those students whose progress data show limited or no progress, a different intervention is needed. There is no rule about how many tier 2 interventions to try before considering a more intensive tier 3 intervention. Some districts and states require that at least two tier 2 interventions be tried before using the intense interventions typical of tier 3. In order to optimize outcomes for the student, it is important to consider what other interventions might be possible. Sometimes, benefits can be seen from adjusting the frequency, duration, and intensity of the intervention (Brown-Chidsey & Steege, 2010). For example, if the student is participating in tier 2 sessions 3 days a week, perhaps going to 5 days a week would be worth trying. If the student does not show progress after all reasonable tier 2 interventions have been tried, then a change to a tier 3 intervention is appropriate. The only real difference between tier 2 and tier 3 is the amount of time made available for instruction. Tier 2 is usually provided for 30 minutes a session, 3 to 5 days a week. Tier 3 interventions are typically 5 days a week and last for 60 minutes or more (Wanzek & Vaughn, 2008). Keep in mind that these interventions are in addition to the tier 1 core instruction already provided.

Another difference between tiers 2 and 3 is the number of students in the instruction group. Tier 2 interventions are often provided with small groups of 4 to 6 students at a time. Research has shown that small group intervention can be just as effective as one-on-one instruction (Wanzek & Vaughn, 2008). But, when a student is still struggling despite tier 2 intervention, reducing the size of the group might be effective. Very small 2 or 3 student groups or individualized instruction can be more effective, because it allows each student more time to engage with the material and practice.

Tier 3 interventions require more frequent progress monitoring than tier 2. This is because the students are at a higher risk of school failure. As noted, students participating in tier 3 interventions should complete at least weekly progress measures. The methods for interpreting the data remain the same as tier 2. For some students, the more intense supports of tier 3 provide the extra boost so that they can find school success. Nonetheless, some students do not show adequate progress as a result of tier 3. For these students, a referral for a special education evaluation is justified. When a student is still struggling despite accurately implemented interventions over a period of time, it suggests that something besides effective instruction is affecting the student's learning. For many such students, the lack of response to intervention is an indicator of a disability. Whenever a disability is suspected to be the cause of a student's learning problems, federal and state special education laws provide procedures so that the student can undergo a comprehensive evaluation. This evaluation is designed to consider all of the variables that are affecting the student's learning, and to provide information for a team to decide whether the student is eligible for special education.

IDEA provides federal rules about what states must include in special education services; however, every state has its own special education laws. For students with chronic learning difficulties such as those observed in students at tier 3, the special education category most likely to apply is Specific Learning Disability (SLD). IDEA 2004 included changed rules for the process of determining if a student has SLD. Prior to the 2004 revisions, the most commonly used method for documenting SLD was an IQ-achievement discrepancy. Due to concerns with the accuracy of this method (O'Malley, Francis, Foorman, Fletcher, & Swank, 2002), IDEA 2004 added two new ways of determining the presence of SLD. The discrepancy method was retained as an option that states could allow, but it could not be required. Notably, states were required to allow schools to utilize RTI data as part of documenting SLD. In addition, states were allowed to include other research-based methods not yet defined (IDEA, 2004).

Of these options, the RTI data method has received the most attention. Zirkel and Thomas (2010) noted that more and more states have added the RTI data option since the law was passed. Despite this growth in interest in using RTI data for SLD identification, states vary a great deal in the specific requirements for the data, and practitioners must be familiar with the laws and regulations in their states in order to use such rules accurately (Hauerwas, Brown-Chidsey, & Scott, 2013).

Case Example

Harmony Hills School District encompasses five small towns in a primarily rural and sparsely populated state. The towns range from a more prosperous bedroom community, to enclaves of high poverty and unemployment. In fact, socioeconomic status represents the primary diversity factor in the district. There are four elementary schools in the district, along with a middle school and a high school. The district has seen a steady decline in population over the years, as well as a decline in test scores and an increase in special education referrals and identifications.

These trends were accompanied by a mandate from the state department of education for all districts to employ multi-tiered systems of support in their schools. The director of student services for the Harmony Hills School District learned about MTSS in a graduate course. She recognized that the prevention measures that comprise MTSS had the potential to improve student outcomes and lower demand for special services. As such, the director earmarked a portion of the special services budget for investment in consultation and profes-sional development in MTSS.

The state mandate included a requirement to implement both MTSS for behavior and MTSS for academics. The Harmony Hills superintendent and special services director attended a series of MTSS workshops offered by the local university, and learned more about the data, systems, and practices that they would need to put in place for MTSS. The two decided to create a 5-year plan for putting all of the features of MTSS for academics and behavior in place. It was determined that the district would begin by focusing on schoolwide positive behavioral interventions and supports (SWPBIS). Harmony Hills hired someone from the university team to facilitate their process.

The first year of work began by collecting baseline data to determine which of the features of MTSS for behavior were already in place in each school. Teams were then formed in each of the schools, and charged with the task of developing a universal system of behavior support that was consistent with the culture and values of the students and staff in their respective buildings. The teams began by reviewing the results of the baseline assessment, and forming an action plan to create the elements that were not yet in place. Because the schools had very little in place to support positive behavior and prevent interfering behavior at the universal level, the action plan spanned the entire first school year.

Each team met bi-monthly with the university facilitator. The teams employed a process in which they developed plans based on the consultant's guidance, presented those plans to the rest of the school community, and then made adjustments to create a universal curriculum that the majority of the school community could endorse. While some of the schools implemented features of the curriculum as soon as they were developed, others chose to develop the whole curriculum for implementation the following year. Each of the school teams ultimately developed a unique but similar universal system of behavior prevention and support for their school.

With plans for the multi-tiered system of behavior support in place, the district turned its attention to developing MTSS for academics. The three-tier process was familiar to district employees by then. They saw the logic of employing systematic prevention and response, and teachers and administrators were eager to address the academic needs of struggling students in the same way. They recognized that they had the advantage in this phase of already having a universal system of prevention in place for academics: the academic curricula. As a result, the focus shifted in this phase from one of developing a universal system, to one of ensuring that the universal system was effective for the students in Harmony Hills schools, and that struggling students received additional support.

In this second phase of MTSS development, the district decided to focus first on literacy. A team of district literacy specialists was formed, and the members were trained in universal screening using an established system of curriculum-based measurement. A universal screening schedule was developed, and the team fanned out through the district to assess all of the students. When the results of the first screening were entered, the district used them to determine whether the universal curriculum for reading was resulting in at least 80% of the students in each school meeting benchmark expectations. They determined that the curriculum was effective in some of the schools, but not in others. The literacy team took on the role of a problem-solving team, and assessed the extent to which the curriculum was being implemented with fidelity in each of the schools. They found that some of the teachers in the district had not yet received training in the district's reading curriculum, and that some of the schools were not allotting enough time in the schedule for teachers to implement the curriculum with fidelity.

Concurrent with the development of MTSS for academics, the school teams were working to create a continuum of support for students struggling academically and behaviorally. They developed a set of criteria to evaluate the interventions currently in place. The school teams found that they had a number of interventions in place that would work well for secondary and tertiary supports and, in keeping with their goal of employing data-based decision making, decided to eliminate those interventions that did not have measurable outcomes. They coordinated the remaining supports into a continuum, and looked for gaps in their ability to address the needs of students. The elimination of non-measurable interventions allowed for the time and resources needed to create new outcomes-based interventions to fill those gaps.

The investment of time and energy by the school teams and their colleagues resulted in a workable multi-tiered system of support for students' academic and behavioral needs. While it would ultimately take the district 3 to 5 years to develop a fully functioning system, the students in the Harmony Hills school district benefitted from the district's effort immediately. Universal screening and office discipline referral data were used to determine which of the students needed support beyond the universal system. Students who were determined to be at risk for literacy and behavior problems were provided with secondary small group supports, and students with the greatest need were provided with tertiary individual supports. Students in both categories were referred to the student assistance team, which was charged with monitoring and problem-solving the students' response to intervention. A flow chart showing how the support system starts with universal screening and includes high-fidelity tier 2 support is shown in Figure 10.2. Most students are successful with tier 1 core instruction alone. Some need tier 2 supplemental support. A small number need intensive intervention and may require special education.

Jessica, a third grader, was one of the students referred for secondary support. Not only did the literacy benchmark reveal that she was not reading at the expected level, but office discipline referral data also indicated that she was engaging in minor disruptive behavior in the classroom. Jessica was included in the school's tier 2 literacy support, during which she was

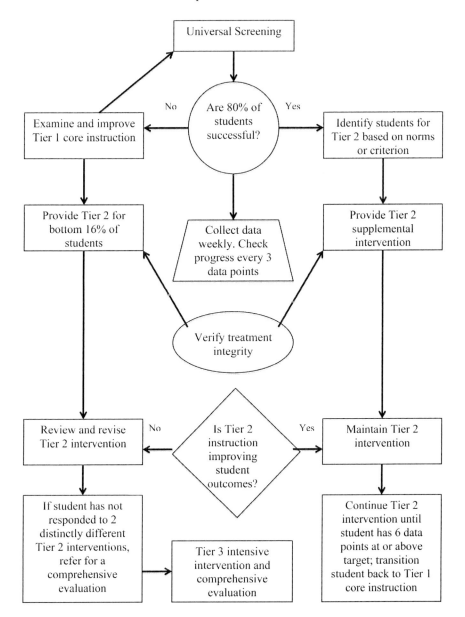

Figure 10.2 Flow chart showing system supports

provided with explicit direct instruction in phonics. This intervention occurred during the school's enrichment block, and in addition to the literacy instruction that Jessica and her class-mates already received in the classroom. In addition, she was enrolled in the school's check-in/check-out system for secondary behavior support, which provided her with pre-teaching, ongoing praise, encouragement, and corrective feedback as she went through the school day.

When the student assistance team reviewed Jessica's data, the team found that she was responding to the reading intervention at the rate necessary to meet the end-of-year benchmark. Her behavior was improving with the check-in/check-out intervention in place, but continued to interfere with her ability to access instruction in the classroom. The team reviewed the other tier 2 interventions available in the school and determined that they did not have another secondary support that would address Jessica's interfering behavior. As such, the team decided to refer Jessica to the district behavior analyst in order to determine the function of her interfering behavior and to provide her with an individual behavior support plan. The wealth of assessment data available about Jessica provided a clear summary of the steps taken to support her school success over time. The decision to consult the behavior specialist was a component of responsive assessment in that it was a response to the observed changes in Jessica's school performance over time. Her academic gains and lingering behavior difficulties showed how the school team responded to her needs in a dynamic and individual manner.

Summary

Multi-Tier Systems of Support (MTSS), also known as Response to Intervention (RTI), is a systems-based method for addressing the learning needs of all students. With origins in the Civil Rights movement as well as behavioral psychology, MTSS is a comprehensive method for utilizing prevention science to support all students. MTSS applies three tiers of prevention to school settings for the purpose of anticipating and meeting individual student needs over time. The assessment components of MTSS create responsive assessment practices that are preventive, formative, and universal. Through universal screening, verification of treatment integrity, progress monitoring, and data-based decision-making, educators can attend to the needs of all students as well as respond to individuals who need additional support.

References

Baer, D. M., Wolf, M. M., & Risley, T. R. (1968). Some current dimensions of applied behavior analysis. *Journal of Applied Behavior Analysis, 1,* 91–97.

Barnett, D., Daly III, E., Jones, K., & Lentz Jr., F. (2004). Response to intervention: Empirically based special service decisions from single-case designs of increasing and decreasing intensity. *Journal of Special Education, 38,* 66–79.

Benner, S. M. (1998). *Special education issues within the context of American society.* Belmont, CA: Wadsworth.

Brown-Chidsey, R. (2005). Scaling educational assessments to inform instruction for all students: Response to intervention as essential educational science. *Trainer's Forum, 24,* 1–4, 6–8.

Brown-Chidsey, R., & Gritter, A. (2012, February). *Comparing administration personnel: Curriculum-based measures of reading and math.* National Association of School Psychologists annual conference, Philadelphia, PA.

Brown-Chidsey, R., & Steege, M. W. (2010). *Response to intervention: Principles and strategies for effective practice* (2nd ed.). New York, NY: Guilford.

Burns, M. K., Appleton, J. J., & Stehouwer, J. D. (2005). Meta-analytic review of responsiveness-to-intervention research: Examining field-based and research-implemented models. *Journal of Psychoeducational Assessment, 23*(4), 381–394. doi: 10.1177/073428290502300406

Burns, M. K., & Gibbons, K. (2008). *Implementing response-to-intervention in elementary and secondary schools: Procedures to assure scientific-based practices.* New York, NY: Routledge.

Caplan, G. (1964). *Principles of preventive psychiatry.* New York, NY: Basic Books.

Common Core State Standards Initiative [CCSSI]. (2012). *Common standards.* Retrieved from http://www.corestandards.org/

Daly III, E. J., Bonfiglio, C. M., Mattson, T., Persampieri, M., & Foreman-Yates, K. (2005). Refining the experimental analysis of academic skills deficits: Part I. An investigation of variables that affect generalized oral reading performance. *Journal of Applied Behavior Analysis, 38,* 485.

Daly III, E. J., Bonfiglio, C. M., Mattson, T., Persampieri, M., & Foreman-Yates, K. (2006). Refining the experimental analysis of academic skills deficits: Part II. Use of brief experimental analysis to evaluate reading fluency treatments. *Journal of Applied Behavior Analysis, 39,* 323–331.

Daly III, E. J, Murdoch, A., Lillenstein, L., Webber, L., & Lentz, F. E. (2002). An examination of methods for testing treatments: Conducting brief experimental analyses of the effects of instructional components on oral reading fluency. *Education & Treatment of Children, 25*(3), 288.

Daly III, E. J., Persampieri, M., McCurdy, M., & Gortmaker, V. (2005). Generating reading interventions through experimental analysis of academic skills: Demonstration and empirical evaluation. *School Psychology Review, 34,* 395–414.

Dynamic Indicators of Basic Early Literacy Skills [DIBELS] Next. (2012). *DIBELS Next benchmark goals and composite score.* Retrieved from https://dibels.org/papers/DIBELSNextBenchmarkGoals.pdf

H.R. 1–111th Congress: American Recovery and Reinvestment Act of 2009. (2009). In www.GovTrack.us. Retrieved September 21, 2013, from http://www.govtrack.us/congress/bills/111/hr1

Hattie, J. (2008). *Visible learning: A synthesis of over 800 meta-analyses relating to achievement.* New York, NY: Routledge.

Hauerwas, L., Brown-Chidsey, R., & Scott, A. (2013). Specific learning disability and response to intervention: State-level guidance. *Exceptional Children, 80,* 101–120.

Hosp, M. K., Hosp, J. L., & Howell, K. W. (2007). *The ABCs of CBM: A practical guide to curriculum-based measurement.* New York, NY: Guilford Press.

Individuals with Disabilities Education Improvement Act of 2004, Pub. L. No.108-446, 20 U.S.C. 1400 (2004).

McLeskey, J., & Skiba, R. (1990). Reform and special education: A mainstream perspective. *Journal of Special Education, 24,* 319–326.

National Center for Response to Intervention [NCRTI]. (2012a). *Screening tools chart.* Retrieved from http://www.rti4success.org/screeningTools

National Center for Response to Intervention [NCRTI]. (2012b). *Progress monitoring tools.* Retrieved from http://www.rti4success.org/progressMonitoringTools

No Child Left Behind (NCLB) Act of 2001, 20 U.S.C.A. § 6301 *et seq.* (West 2003).

Noell, G. H., Freeland, J. T., Witt, J. C., & Gansle, K. A. (2001). Using brief assessments to identify effective interventions for individual students. *Journal of School Psychology, 39*(4), 335–355. doi: 10.1016/S0022–4405(01)00072–3

O'Malley, K. J., Francis, D. J., Foorman, B. R., Fletcher, J. M., & Swank, P. R. (2002). Growth in precursor and reading-related skills: Do low-achieving and IQ-discrepant readers develop differently? *Learning Disabilities Research and Practice, 17,* 19–35.

Powell-Smith, K., & Ball, P. (2008). Best practices in reintegration and special education exit decisions. In A. Thomas & J. Grimes (Eds.), *Best practices in school psychology V* (pp. 535–552). Bethesda, MD: National Association of School Psychologists.

Riley-Tillman, C., & Burns, M. K. (2009). *Evaluating educational interventions: Single-case design for measuring response to intervention.* New York, NY: Guilford Press.

Salvia, J., & Ysseldyke, J. E. (2011). *Assessment in special and inclusive education* (11th ed.). Boston, MA: Houghton Mifflin.

Sanetti, L. M. H., & Kratochwill, T. R. (2012). Treatment integrity assessment within a problem-solving model. In R. Brown-Chidsey & K. J. Andren (Eds.), *Assessment for intervention: A problem-solving approach* (2nd ed.). New York, NY: Guilford Press.

Shinn, M. S. (2012). Identifying and validating academic problems in a multi-tiered system of services and supports model in a time of shifting paradigms. In R. Brown-Chidsey & K. J. Andren (Eds.), *Assessment for intervention: A problem-solving approach* (2nd ed.). New York, NY: Guilford Press.

Steege, M. W., Brown-Chidsey, R., & Mace, F. C. (2002). Best practices in evaluating interventions. In A. Thomas & J. Grimes (Eds.), *Best practices in school psychology* (4th ed., pp. 517–534). Bethesda, MD: National Association of School Psychologists.

Vaughn, S., & Fuchs, L. S. (2003). Redefining learning disabilities as inadequate response to instruction: The promises and potential problems. *Learning Disabilities: Research and Practice, 18,* 137–146.Washington, DC: Author.

Vaughn, S., Wanzek, J., Murray, C. S., Scammacca, N., Linan-Thompson, S., & Woodruff, A. L. (2009). Response to early reading intervention: Examining higher and lower responders. *Exceptional Children, 75,* 165–183.

Walker, H. M., Horner, R. H., Sugai, G., & Bullis, M. (1996). Integrated approaches to preventing antisocial behavior patterns among school-age children and youth. *Journal of Emotional and Behavioral Disorders, 4*(4), 194–209.

Wanzek, J., & Vaughn, S. (2008). Response to varying amounts of time in reading intervention for students with low response to intervention. *Journal of Learning Disabilities, 41,* 126–142.

Zirkel, P. A., & Thomas, L. B. (2010). State laws for RTI: An updated snapshot. *Teaching Exceptional Children, 42*(1), 56–63.

11

Use of CBA/CBM with Culturally and Linguistically Diverse Populations

Mike Vanderwood, Catherine Tung, and Rebecca Hickey

One of the fastest-growing segments of U.S. public schools is students who are culturally and linguistically diverse (CLD; National Center for Education Statistics, 2011). These students come from racial and cultural backgrounds that are different from what is considered the mainstream. Oftentimes, English is not spoken at home, or another language is spoken in addition to English. More than 4 million English learners (ELs) reside in the United States, a majority of whom speak Spanish as their native language (Kindler, 2002). As a whole, EL students start significantly behind their non-EL peers on school entry (Rumberger & Gandara, 2004). According to a survey of 41 states, less than 20% of ELs meet state-established criteria for reading comprehension (Kindler, 2002). Due to the fact that CLD students represent a significant at-risk population, it is important for schools to use valid assessment tools in order to accurately measure their performance and to make appropriate educational decisions based on assessment data.

Several challenges concerning the validity of assessment tools for CLD students have been documented. An assessment tool is considered valid when it measures what it purports to measure. However, among the various assessment tools used in today's schools, it is unclear if the same construct is measured in mainstream students and CLD students. Specifically, success on several assessment tools that purport to measure academic achievement may actually rely heavily on knowledge of American culture or English language proficiency. In addition, a limited range of language and cultural backgrounds are represented in samples used to norm standardized assessments. In considering the increasing number of CLD students enrolling in U.S. public schools (e.g., 49.9 million in the 2007–2008 academic year), standardized assessments with norms representing the various languages spoken by those individuals are needed in order to meet their instructional needs. Among linguistically diverse students, it is often difficult to distinguish between difficulties with English language proficiency and difficulties with academics (e.g., reading; Deno, 2003). Due to the important role of reading in overall school success, the majority of the chapter will focus on research concerning a reading assessment tool (e.g., curriculum-based measurement/assessment) that shows promise in overcoming some of the aforementioned challenges. Curriculum-based measurement in the area of mathematics and writing will be discussed briefly toward the end of the chapter.

Language Development

There is a growing consensus that reading problems are best perceived as language problems, due to the reciprocal relationship between oral language and reading skills that continues throughout childhood (Fernald & Weisleder, 2011). For ELs, several experts argue that English literacy requires the development of reading skills in addition to English *academic* oral language (August & Shanahan, 2006; Cummins, 1980). To acquire academic English, EL students need explicit instruction in English that focuses on developing semantic and syntactic language skills, combined with plenty of opportunities to use academic language within the appropriate context. Students without established English academic language tend to develop significant reading comprehension deficits, even if their decoding skills are sufficiently developed (August & Shanahan, 2006).

In addition to the challenge of learning a new language, most ELs come from socioeconomically disadvantaged environments where exposure to appropriate language models is limited, and leads to entering kindergarten with a vocabulary that is half of what students from advantaged environments obtain (Hart & Risley, 1995). Yet, there are aspects of an EL's background that can cause substantial variability in how fast English is acquired. For example, the degree of language development in a student's first language mediates the English language acquisition process. It appears when ELs learn their first language, they develop knowledge about language (i.e., metalinguistic knowledge) that can be drawn upon when acquiring a second language (Cummins, 1984; Lesaux & Siegel, 2003). These ideas are encapsulated in Cummin's *linguistic interdependence hypothesis* that posits the acquisition of a second language (e.g., English) in part depends on the adequate development of a student's native language (e.g., Spanish).

Although oral language is critical for the development of reading skills, and there are clear techniques that should be implemented as part of core instruction (Echeverria, Vogt, & Short, 2008), there is very little evidence about the impact of interventions for oral language on the development of reading skills, yet this area is starting to gain more attention. There is reason to believe systematic and focused instruction of English vocabulary, listening comprehension, syntactic skills, and awareness of the components of language (i.e., metalinguistic skills) will also positively impact reading development (August & Shanahan, 2006). As support for this conclusion, Roth, Speece, and Cooper (2002) demonstrated oral language skills of English-only (EO) students measured in kindergarten were better predictors than phonological awareness skills of reading performance at the end of second grade. Therefore, for ELs, it may be important to incorporate measures of English proficiency into the assessment decision-making process, in addition to the measures we are about to describe.

Curriculum-Based Measures and CLD Students

Given the challenges facing the CLD student population presented in the previous section, it is clear that educators need tools to help them provide appropriate services and improve outcomes for students from diverse backgrounds. It is known among educators that modifying and differentiating instruction for students who are struggling can lead to improved outcomes. However, it is not always clear what area of instruction should be modified and whether the modifications lead to the desired outcomes. A problem-solving approach has been endorsed as a method that can help educators better meet the needs of students who are CLD (Rhodes, 2010). Curriculum-based assessment (CBA) is an approach to providing the information needed to improve instruction that includes either a focus on identifying the specific skills that need to be taught (e.g., Howell & Nolet, 1999), or identifying who is at risk and whether or not the support is reducing that risk (e.g., Shinn, 1998). CBA models, like Curriculum-Based Evaluation (CBE; Howell & Nolet, 1999), emphasize skill mastery and strategies that give educators ideas about "what to teach" by examining aspects of instructional delivery and instructional environment. The most well-known CBA approach, Curriculum-Based Measurement (CBM), emphasizes that the use of assessment techniques are more general in focus, often called general outcome measures (GOM; Shinn, 1998), and concentrate decision-making on "when to change" instruction. CBM tools are promoted as part of a problem solving process that places a heavy emphasis on data-based decision-making and the use of assessment tools that meet basic guidelines for reliability and validity (Deno, 2005).

In addition to the more discreet models of CBA, an integrated approach that combines a focus on the instructional environment and the use of general outcome measures has also been suggested (e.g., Shapiro, 2011). An integrated approach fits well with the recent focus on school improvement systems like Multi-Tier Systems of Support (MTSS) and derivatives of MTSS (e.g., Response to Intervention). These systems typically place a heavy emphasis on the use of assessment tools to appropriately identify students who need additional assistance and whether the assistance has an impact on student performance. Several authors suggest MTSS as an appropriate method for allocating resources for students who are CLD (Gersten et al., 2007; Vanderwood & Nam, 2008).

Although a detailed description of MTSS is beyond the scope of this chapter, it is important to understand where CBA fits and how it can be used to support school improvement. At tier 1, CBE methods can be used as part of typical instruction to identify methods of differentiation that can help students master the skills taught. CBM tools can be used for screening to identify who needs additional support and could benefit from a tier 2 intervention as well as determine whether the intervention is having the desired effect. There is fairly substantial support that CBM tools can be used with students who are native English speakers (NES) for screening and progress monitoring (Shapiro, 2011). However, as detailed more fully later in this chapter, it is inappropriate to generalize the outcomes from NES to students who are CLD (Vanderwood & Nam, 2008).

Although more research is clearly needed, there is growing consensus that assessment and intervention targets (e.g., phonemic awareness) typically used with NES are appropriate for students who are CLD (August & Shanahan, 2006). In fact, some authors suggest that with appropriately targeted interventions, ELs can grow at a faster rate than NES peers who started at a similar skill level (Lesaux & Siegel, 2003). Although ELs clearly have challenges related to language that affect reading skill development, there is no reason to believe ELs need a different type of reading assessment or intervention than NES (August & Shanahan, 2006). From an assessment perspective, it is important to assess the areas most known to influence academic outcomes. In reading, those areas are the "big five" skills of phonemic awareness, alphabetic principal, fluency, vocabulary, and comprehension (National Reading Panel, 2000). In mathematics, the targets are less clear than in reading, but do include the skills of computation, problem solving, and algebraic concepts (National Mathematics Advisory Panel, 2008).

Over the last three decades, CBM measures were developed that address these critical target skills in reading and mathematics. Although early CBM practices involved the sampling of curriculum to create assessments that were used for screening and progress monitoring, most recent approaches to CBM include the use of "standard probes" that can be used across curricula and school districts (e.g., DIBELS, AIMSweb). The standard probe approach provides several advantages, such as the ability to improve the overall psychometric properties of the measures, with the goal of improving the information that is used to help guide the problem-solving process. The standard probe approach is especially useful for discreet skills such as phonemic awareness, phonics, and math computation. By using standard probes that were developed with an external population who were followed over time, educators are able to identify the degree to which a score indicates a future probability of success or challenge. The somewhat recent use of standard CBM probes has made them absolutely essential in MTSS and other problem-solving systems.

It is important to point out that most initial research suggests that CBM measures used with native English speakers (NES) can be used equally well with ELs and students who come from culturally diverse backgrounds (Vanderwood & Nam, 2008). As discussed more fully in the next section, the challenge with interpreting the data is that most studies combine CLD students, especially ELs, into one group. However, it is clear that significant differences exist within the CLD population that could affect the overall quality of assessment tools.

Validating CBM Measures with CLD Students

One of the strengths of CBM over typically available classroom assessments is the amount of data supporting the relationship of CBM tools to critical criterion measures such as high-stakes state assessments and individualized achievement tests. For example, with NES students, there are data that suggest a strong correlation between CBM measures of early literacy skills (Fien et al., 2008), oral reading fluency (Hintze & Silberglitt, 2005), and reading comprehension (Shin, Deno, & Espin, 2000) with large-scale measures (e.g., state tests). These types of relationships provide evidence of validity and allow educators to be confident about the conclusions they make from CBM measures.

In addition to the importance of predictive validity evidence, the *Test Standards* (American Educational Research Association, American Psychological Association, National Council on Measurement in Education [AERA/APA/NCME], 1999) provide guidance about data that are needed during test development and use in educational and psychological testing. It has sections dedicated to issues that are important for students who are CLD. A major emphasis of the *Test Standards* is the concept of the "equivalence" of scores when tests are used with groups that vary on some dimension that is known to affect the construct being measured. For students who are CLD, two issues related to score equivalence are worth exploring further. First, bias is considered to be "construct-irrelevant variance that result in systematically lower or higher scores for identifiable groups of examinees" (AERA/APA/NCME, 1999, p. 76). It is important to note that according to the *Test Standards,* bias is not a mean difference between groups. Instead, bias occurs when the test scores obtained on a particular test by different subgroups has a different meaning in relation to other variables. In the context of CBM, bias would be considered to be present when scores predict with a different level of accuracy for one group (e.g., English Learners) than for another (e.g., native English speakers) on an important criterion measure (e.g., state test).

In addition to the concept of bias, the *Test Standards* also highlight the concept of equivalence related to language differences, and the need to have separate validity evidence for each "linguistic" group. For example, it may be possible that a low score on a CBM measure for an NES student may mean that the student could benefit from a specific type of reading instruction (e.g., phonics), yet the *Test Standards* caution making that same assumption for students with language differences until validity data are provided that support the conclusion. It is possible that an EL student could benefit more from additional oral language instruction than from phonics instruction. It is also possible that scores from EL students with higher levels of English proficiency have different meanings than scores from EL students with lower levels. Educators are cautioned against generalizing conclusions about the adequacy of tests when used with ELs without knowing the degree of English proficiency demonstrated by the group used for evaluating the measure (Vanderwood & Nam, 2008).

In addition to the concepts addressed in the standards, there are other sources of data, such as sensitivity and specificity that need to be examined when evaluating CBM tools used for screening and progress monitoring (Glover & Albers, 2007). Sensitivity refers to the percentage of students later found to have reading problems who were previously identified as at-risk for later reading problems. For example, after administering a fluency CBM in the beginning of the school year, three students out of 10 students were identified as at risk for later reading difficulties. However, six students fell below basic on the state testing at the end of the year, which indicates reading difficulties. Therefore, the sensitivity for this example would be 50%, shown by three out of six students later found to be at-risk who were identified as at-risk in the beginning of the school year.

Specificity is similar to sensitivity, but this term indicates the percentage of students later found not to have reading problems who had previously been identified as not at risk (Glover & Albers, 2007). In the above example, the CBM measure given at the beginning of the year indicated that four students out of 10 students were identified as not at risk for later reading problems. However, seven students scored proficient or above on the state test. Therefore, the specificity was about 57%, shown by four out of seven students later found to be not at risk who were identified as not at risk in the beginning of the school year. In order to maximize predictive accuracy, sensitivity and specificity are critical for evaluating the quality of cut scores used with CBM tools for screening purposes.

When CBM tools are used for progress monitoring, it is also important to know whether change over time can be detected by the tests (Shapiro, 2011), so that the results can be used to evaluate the impact of interventions. For example, if a CBM score does not improve over time, educators would be challenged to know whether the intervention was ineffective or whether the assessment tool lacked the ability to measure change. Therefore, it is critical to use tools that are known to be able to detect change with the group of students being monitored (e.g., third-grade English Learners with an intermediate level of English proficiency).

The concepts mentioned in this section are necessary when determining whether to use CBM with students who are CLD. As already mentioned, there is no reason to believe different concepts need to be measured for students who are CLD (August & Shanahan, 2006), yet separate evidence is needed about the specific tools used (AERA/APA/NCME, 1999). The next several sections present the research documenting what is known about using CBM tools with students who are CLD.

Early Literacy CBM and CLD Research

The most common academic area that utilizes CBM is reading. During literacy screening, educators screen the most critical skills that affect reading performance at specific grade levels. In the younger grades, early literacy skills such as phonological awareness (PA) and alphabetic principle (e.g. decoding) are the primary reading skills taught and assessed. There is fairly substantial support for the use of early literacy CBM measures as screening and progress monitoring tools for NES students. As Table 11.1 indicates, there is initial empirical

Table 11.1 Status of CBM Research with CLD Students

Type of CBM Measure	Reliability	Validity	Bias	Studies	Status of Research
Phonological Awareness	Adequate evidence	Adequate evidence		Hintze et al. (2003)	Adequate research. Research needed to explore bias.
Phonics	Adequate evidence	Adequate evidence		Fien et al. (2008); Lesaux and Siegel (2003); Fuchs, Compton et al. (2004); Fuchs, Fuchs et al. (2004), Deno et al. (1982)	Adequate research. Research needed to explore bias.
Fluency	Adequate evidence	Adequate evidence	Mixed evidence regarding bias by ethnicity and/or language status	Baker and Good (1995); Betts et al. (2006); Dominguez de Ramirez and Shapiro (2006, 2007); Englebert-Johnson (1997), Graves et al. (2005); Hintze et al. (2002); Hixson and McGlinchey (2004); Hosp et al. (2011); Johnson et al. (2009, 2010), Klein and Jimerson (2005); Kranzler et al. (1999); McMaster et al. (2006); Moore (1997); Muyskens et al. (2009); Pearce & Gayle (2009); Roehrig et al. (2008); Wiley and Deno (2005)	Adequate research. More research needed to further explore bias (especially by language proficiency)
Vocabulary	No evidence	No evidence			No research
Comprehension	Adequate evidence	Adequate evidence	Some evidence of bias against ELs	Shin et al. (2000); Silberglitt et al. (2006); McMaster et al. (2006); Wiley and Deno (2005)	Somewhat limited research
Mathematics		Weak evidence		Fuchs, Fuchs, et al. (2007)	Very limited research
Written Language	Some evidence	Weak evidence	.	Gansle et al. (2002); McMaster and Espin (2007)	Very limited research

support for use of the same early literacy CBM measures with CLD students as screening and progress monitoring measures. However, the research is limited with the EL population.

Phonological Awareness. Baker and Baker (2008) found that the best predictors of early reading in English for EL students were PA, print awareness, and alphabetic knowledge. PA is the conscious awareness of the structure of sound in speech. In a study with 30 Spanish-English bilingual first-grade students receiving reading instruction in English, Quiroga, Lemos-Britton, Mostafapour, Abbott, and Berninger (2002) demonstrated the importance of PA in learning to read. It was found that PA is significantly related to English reading skills when a student's first language is Spanish. The results also suggested that PA in the student's first language (e.g.. Spanish) predicted English reading skills.

In addition to demonstrating the critical role of PA in reading, research has supported the validity of PA curriculum based measures. In a study by Hintze, Ryan, and Stoner (2003), DIBELS phonemic segmentation fluency (PSF) task exhibited moderate to strong correlations with elision, blending words, and phonological awareness composite scores on a diagnostic assessment of PA (e.g., Comprehensive Test of Phonological Awareness—CTOPP). This relationship between PA CBM measures and well-established norm-referenced PA measure supports the use of PA CBMs (e.g., DIBELS PSF) as an initial diagnostic tool to inform reading intervention.

Phonics. Phonics, also known as alphabetic principle, is the ability to associate a letter with its sound. It is important to distinguish PA from phonics, because the two concepts are often confused. PA is the awareness of sounds in oral language, while phonics is letter-sound correspondence in printed language (Schuele & Boudreau, 2008). As Table 11.1 indicates, there is fairly limited research about phonics with ELs, yet as we do below, an argument can be made it is appropriate to use phonics CBM measures with EL students when screening.

A recent longitudinal study with ELs by Lesaux and Siegel (2003) indicted phonics skills measured in kindergarten was the best single predictor of word reading and comprehension in second grade. Similarly, Fien and colleagues (2008) also provided validity evidence for the use of phonics CBMs in screening. The participants of this study were five cohorts of about 2,400 students, which included both EL and NES students. The students were given DIBELS Nonsense Word Fluency (NWF), Oral Reading Fluency (ORF), and a group-administered norm-referenced test of overall reading proficiency (e.g., SAT-10). DIBELS NWF is a type of phonics CBM that requires students to read pseudo-words. The results indicated that the students' phonics skills (e.g., NWF scores) in kindergarten explained a moderate to large proportion of the variance in reading skills (e.g., ORF and SAT-10 scores). The stability correlations were very similar between EL and NES students, which indicates reliability. These results support the predictive validity of using phonics CBMs, such as DIBELS NWF, as a screening tool with both EL and NES students when making instructional decisions.

In addition to phonics CBMs based on pseudo-word reading, recent studies have supported phonics CBMs based on real word reading. Word Identification Fluency (WIF) is a phonics CBM task in which students have 1 minute to read individual words that are presented in lists. These lists consist of words randomly selected from high-frequency word lists. The final score is simply the number of words read correctly (Deno, Mirkin, & Chiang, 1982). The alternate test reliability of WIF was found to be 0.97 for two consecutive weeks and 0.91 for two consecutive months. When comparing NWF and WIF as a screening measure, the reliability of WIF was found to be stronger than NWF. The participants in this study included 151 at-risk first-grade students who were assessed on criterion measures of reading in the fall and spring; they were assessed on NWF and WIF once a week for 7 weeks, and twice a week for an additional 13 weeks (Fuchs, Fuchs, & Compton, 2004).

Aside from the reliability evidence supporting WIF, there is also evidence for validity. Deno, Mirkin, and Chiang (1982) provided evidence for the concurrent validity of WIF in a study with 66 students ranging from first to sixth grade. WIF was correlated with the following criterion measures: Peabody Individual Achievement Test (reading comprehension subtests) and the Stanford Diagnostic Reading Test (phonetic analysis, inferential reading comprehension, and literal reading comprehension subtests). The correlations between the first-grade WIF lists and the previous subtests were 0.76, 0.68, 0.71, and 0.75. At the sixth-grade level, the respective correlations were 0.78, 0.71, 0.68, and 0.74. These correlations provide evidence for the concurrent validity of WIF. Regarding the comparison of pseudo-word based and real-word-based phonics CBMs, Fuchs and colleagues (2004) found WIF to be a stronger screening measure than NWF in terms of concurrent and predictive validity. It was also found that WIF's utility as a progress-monitoring measure was superior to the utility of NWF.

Fluency CBM and CLD Research

The first CBM measures for reading assessed fluency, which is the accurate and automatic reading of text. These measures are typically labeled as R-CBM and are also known as ORF (Oral Reading Fluency). Due to its relatively longer history compared with CBMs in other areas, R-CBM has the most empirical research to support its reliability, validity, and utility as a screening and progress-monitoring tool with both EL and NES students.

Regarding reliability, a study with 50 bilingual EL students and 26 NES students by Baker and Good (1995) supports the reliability of R-CBM in general and across languages. Specifically, high alternate-form and point-estimate reliabilities were found for both EL and NES students. The study also provided evidence supporting the use of English R-CBM for bilingual students as a measure of reading proficiency. In another study, McMaster, Wayman, and Cao (2006) found strong alternate-form reliability and stability for oral reading fluency in a sample of 25 EL students in 8th to 12th grade.

In addition to reliability, research has supported the validity of R-CBM with ELs. In the above-mentioned study by McMaster and colleagues (2006), moderate to moderately strong validity supported the use of R-CBM as a screening tool with EL students. Moore (1997) provided additional support in the area of concurrent validity for R-CBM with EL students in a study with 316 Hispanic bilingual elementary school students. This was evidenced by moderate correlations between R-CBM (English and Spanish) and English achievement test scores. In another study, Baker and Good (1995) examined both convergent and discriminant construct validity. Evidence for convergent construct validity was indicated by a strong relationship between English R-CBM and the criterion reading measure (e.g., Stanford Diagnostic Reading Test). This same study also provided evidence of R-CBM having discriminant construct validity as evidenced by a moderate relationship between English R-CBM and the criterion language measures. In a study of 36 third- through sixth-grade students learning English at an international school in Belgium, it was found that R-CBM effectively discriminated among groups of higher- and lower-achieving students (Englebert-Johnson, 1997).

In an effort to determine whether CBM tools are sensitive to change, Graves, Plasencia-Peinado, Deno, and Johnson (2005) observed significant differences in growth on R-CBM between low/middle readers and high readers, with greater gains for the low and middle readers. This study was conducted with 77 first grade students who were taught English in a classroom with multiple languages spoken. Baker and Good (1995) also found R-CBM to be sensitive to growth among EL students. Despite data being collected over a period of only 10 weeks, Englebert-Johnson (1997) found that R-CBM revealed growth over time with EL students. Sensitivity to growth was also found in a longer study, evidenced by a gradual increase in words read correctly per minute across the year (Betts, Muyskens, & Marston, 2006).

McMaster and colleagues (2006) provided further support for R-CBM being used as a progress-monitoring tool with EL students, as evidenced by R-CBM performance increasing over time for students who received intervention. In a study with 165 first- through fifth-grade students grouped by general education and bilingual education, Dominguez de Ramirez and Shapiro (2006) found that R-CBM was sensitive to growth in both English and Spanish. A similar study by Dominguez de Ramirez and Shapiro (2007) provided further support for using R-CBM for progress monitoring in Spanish and English. This study included 68 first- through fifth-grade students in a transitional bilingual class. The above studies provide validity evidence for the use of R-CBM as a progress-monitoring tool.

The previous discussion on R-CBM focused on issues relating to the reliability and validity of R-CBM for use as a screening and progress-monitoring tool. The following discussion will focus on issues of bias in R-CBM. Various research studies examining bias as a function of ethnicity and language status will be discussed separately.

Ethnicity. Several studies explored ethnicity as a possible source of bias for using R-CBM to predict performance on high-stakes standardized tests (Hintze, Callahan, Matthews, Williams, & Tobin, 2002; Hixson & McGlinchey, 2004; Kranzler, Miller, & Jordan, 1999; Pearce & Gayle, 2009). Kranzler and colleagues (1999) examined the validity of ORF with a sample of 326 Caucasian and Black second through fifth graders. ORF passages from the school's reading textbook were administered in March. The reading comprehension portion of the California Achievement Test (CAT) was administered shortly afterward in the spring. Correlations between ORF and the CAT ranged from .51 to .63. Regression analyses were conducted for each grade, with the predictors including ORF score, gender, and ethnicity. No bias was found in second and third grade. However, bias was found in fourth and fifth grade. Specifically, ORF overestimated reading comprehension for the Black students and underestimated for the Caucasian students. From this study, grade appears to be a moderator of the presence of ethnicity bias. In the discussion, the authors state that the presence of bias should not mean the discontinued use of ORF. Instead, the authors suggest that different cut-scores may be needed for different groups in order to maximize predictive validity.

Similar to the previous study, Hintze and colleagues (2002) examined the validity of ORF with a sample of 136 Caucasian and Black second through fifth graders. Third-grade ORF passages and the reading comprehension subtest from the Woodcock Johnson Psychoeducational Battery—Revised (WJ-R) were administered during the same day. The initial results indicated that ethnicity did not affect prediction of reading comprehension scores after controlling for students' age, gender, and socioeconomic status. However, a second analysis separating the ethnic groups found a possible bias by ethnic group. It was found that age and ORF explained 58% of the variance in reading comprehension for Black students and 30% of the variance for Caucasian students. Although it was interesting that age and ORF explained much more of the variance in outcomes for Blacks than it did for Caucasians, the authors concluded that ORF generally does have bias. It is important to note some characteristics of this study that may limit the generalizability of its findings. First, ORF and the outcome measure were administered during the same day. Thus, this study does not examine predictive validity. Second, regardless of their grades, all students were administered third-grade ORF passages.

Hixson and McGlinchey (2004) examined the predictive validity of ORF with a sample of 442 Caucasian and Black fourth graders. Oral reading passages from a district basal were administered 2 weeks before the Michigan Educational Assessment Program's (MEAP) reading assessment and 4 months before the Metropolitan Achievement Tests—7th Edition's (MAT/7) total reading portion. Mixed results regarding bias by ethnicity was found depending on method of data analysis. When using simultaneous multiple regression, ORF, socioeconomic status, and ethnicity were all significant predictors of later reading outcomes on both MEAP and MAT/7. On both outcomes measures, scores of higher socioeconomic status and Caucasian students were overestimated. Scores of lower socioeconomic status and Black students were underestimated. Despite this, no evidence of bias by ethnicity or socio-economic status was found when using stepwise multiple regression.

Pearce and Gayle (2009) examined the predictive validity of ORF with a sample of 543 Caucasian and Native American third graders. DIBELS ORF was given in the winter. The reading comprehension subtest of the Dakota State Test of Educational Proficiency (DStep) given 4 months later was used as the outcome measure. The results indicated that ORF contributed 40% of the variance. Socioeconomic status contributed an additional 2%, and ethnicity contributed an additional 3%. Diagnostic accuracy analyses indicated that ORF yield high specificity and negative predictive power but lower sensitivity and positive pre-dictive power. The prevalence of false negatives was found to be higher among the Native American students.

Overall, studies examining the predictive bias of ORF by ethnicity have yielded mixed results (Hintze et al., 2002; Hixson & McGlinchey, 2004; Kranzler et al., 1999; Pearce & Gayle, 2009). Evidence of possible bias was found in some studies. However, sometimes, evidence for the presence or absence of bias was found within the same study, with differing results depending on the data analysis method used (e.g.: Hintze et al., 2002; Hixson & McGlinchey, 2004). In addition, possible moderator variables such as grade and socioeconomic status make the results of these studies less conclusive.

English Learners. Several studies examined EL status as a possible source of bias for using ORF to predict performance on high-stakes standardized tests (Hosp, Hosp, & Dole, 2011; Klein & Jimerson, 2005; Muyskens, Betts, Lau, & Marston, 2009; Roehrig, Petscher, Nettles, Hudson, & Torgesen, 2008). Two independent studies of EL students whose first language was Hmong, Somali, or Spanish established R-CBM as an appropriate screening tool. In the first study, evidence of predictive validity was provided by a moderate to moderately strong correlation between R-CBM and a high-stakes assessment (Wiley & Deno, 2005). The sec-ond study further supported the validity of R-CBM (Betts et al., 2006). Specifically, low to moderate correlations were found between fall R-CBM and later reading achievement scores, which suggests predictive validity. This study also provided concurrent validity evidence, as indicated by high correlations between spring R-CBM and reading achievement scores. Finally, it is noted that this study found predictive bias as evidenced by an under-prediction of performance among Somali students and over-prediction of performance among Hmong and Spanish students.

Klein and Jimerson (2005) examined the effect of ethnicity, gender, socioeconomic status, and home language on the concurrent and predictive validity of ORF. The participants included about 4,000 Caucasian and Hispanic first through third graders. ORF was administered in the fall and spring. The total reading score of the Stanford Achievement Test—Ninth Edition (SAT-9) administered in the spring was used as the outcome measure. After controlling for ethnicity, differences in ORF and the SAT-9 scores were found as a function of socioeconomic status and home language. Specifically, Hispanic students from low socioeconomic back-grounds scored significantly lower than did Hispanic students from higher socioeconomic backgrounds. Also, Spanish-speaking Hispanic students scored significantly lower than did English-speaking Hispanic students. For the concurrent validity analyses, significant intercept bias was found between English-speaking Caucasian students and Spanish-speaking His-panic students. For the predictive validity analyses, some evidence of bias was found between English-speaking Caucasian students and Spanish-speaking Hispanic students. Specifically,

ORF underestimated reading performance for English-speaking Caucasian students and overestimated for Spanish-speaking Hispanic students. In the discussion, the authors concluded that home language and ethnicity interact to produce bias, with neither factor alone producing bias. For example, no significant bias was found between Hispanic students who spoke Spanish and those who spoke English. Biases were also absent among English-speaking Hispanic and Caucasian students. However, the main factor contributing to bias was home language status. Mixed results were found regarding the effect of socioeconomic status.

Roehrig and colleagues (2008) examined the predictive validity of ORF as a function of ethnicity, socioeconomic status, and English learner status. The participants included 35,207 third graders from Reading First schools. DIBELS ORF was administered during four benchmark periods throughout the year. The Florida Comprehensive Assessment Test—Sunshine State Standards (FCAT-SSS) and the Stanford Achievement Test (SAT-10) administered in the spring were used as the outcome measures for reading comprehension. The results indicated that ORF predicted performance on the FCAT-SSS regardless of socioeconomic status, ethnicity, or English language learner status.

Similar to the previous studies, Hosp and colleagues (2011) examined the effect of English language learner status on the predictive validity of ORF. The participants included 3,805 first through third graders from Reading First schools. DIBELS ORF was administered during the fall, winter, and spring from the winter of first grade to the spring of third grade. The English/Language Arts portion of the Utah State Criterion-Referenced Tests (UCRTs) administered in the spring was used as the outcome measure. Receiver operating characteristic (ROC) analyses were used to calculate curves for native English speakers and ELs. Sensitivity, specificity, and overall correct classification were compared between groups. A value above .80 was considered "adequate." Overall correct classification and sensitivity were found to be generally adequate, but specificity was low for both groups. There were no significant differences between ELs and native English speakers.

Muyskens and colleagues (2009) examined the concurrent and predictive validity of ORF with a sample of ELs from different language backgrounds. The participants were 1,205 fifth-grade ELs whose native language was Spanish, Hmong, or Somali. ORF from a district basal was administered in the fall. The Minnesota Comprehensive Assessment (MCA) administered in the spring was used as the outcome measure. Regression analyses found ORF to be a significant predictor of MCA performance for all students. ROC analyses were conducted for each language group. ORF was found to predict MCA equally well for each language group. It is important to note that all participants in this study were ELs. Comparisons were made between native language groups but were not made with native English speakers.

In addition to the above studies examining language status as a possible source of bias, other studies have also touched upon this issue (Johnson, Jenkins, Petscher, & Catts, 2009; Johnson, Jenkins, & Petscher, 2010). A study by Johnson and colleagues (2009) examining the predictive validity of a variety of measures for performance on the SAT-10 in first grade found that the best predictors were the same for native English speakers and ELs. However, it was also found that lower ORF cut-scores were needed for ELs than for native English speakers in order to obtain 90% sensitivity in prediction. In another study examining the predictive validity of a variety of measures for performance on the third-grade reading performance on the Florida Comprehensive Assessment Test—Sunshine State Standards (FCAT-SSS), Johnson and colleagues (2010) found English language learner status to be included as one of the predictors among an optimal combination of factors predicting reading performance.

As a whole, the literature examining the predictive bias of ORF by EL status has yielded conflicting results. Some studies have found evidence for bias (e.g., Klein & Jimerson, 2005; Johnson et al., 2009; Johnson et al., 2010; Wiley & Deno, 2005), while others studies have found the contrary (e.g., Hosp et al., 2011; Muyskens et al., 2009; Roehrig et al., 2008). To date, it is difficult to make conclusive statements about the effect of EL status on the predictive validity of ORF. One reason for this is that studies have typically characterized ELs as a homogeneous group or, at best, as separated by native language. English language proficiency has not been considered as a source of bias. However, it is common knowledge that ELs come to school with a wide range of English language skills. According to recommendations for test standards set forth by AERA, APA, and NCME (1999), language proficiency should be considered as a part of assessment and interpretation. Some researchers have suggested that ELs may need different cut-scores than the ones used for native English speakers (Jenkins, Hudson, & Johnson, 2007).

Vocabulary and Comprehension CBM and CLD Research

There is agreement in the literature that a gap in vocabulary exists between economically disadvantaged and economically advantaged students throughout school, and that vocabulary is crucial in EL students' success (Blachowicz, Fisher, Ogle, & Watts-Taffe, 2006). Despite the importance of vocabulary, only a very limited amount of research has been done in this area connecting measures of vocabulary to critical outcomes measures.

Compared to vocabulary, more research has been done with CBM measures of reading comprehension. CBM measures that assess comprehension are commonly called MAZE tasks. For the MAZE task, words are deleted from a passage and the student must insert the appropriate word from a choice of words (Rathvon, 2004). This task is also known as a cloze-procedure assessment. One example of this type of task is the DIBELS DAZE, which gives students a choice of three words to insert in each blank throughout a grade-level passage. Although there is research supporting the use of CBM comprehension measures, a limited amount of studies have been conducted with CLD students.

A few studies have examined the adequacy of MAZE as a screening tool. Silberglitt, Burns, Madyn, and Lail (2006) examined the relationship between MAZE and a high-stakes state assessment. The participants included NES students in seventh and eighth grade. The MAZE was administered to the students 2 months before the state assessment. Correlations between MAZE and the state assessment were .54 for seventh grade and .49 for eighth grade. In comparing MAZE and R-CBM, there was no significant difference in the magnitude of their correlations with the state assessment. In another similar study, Wiley and Deno (2005) examined the relationship between MAZE and a high-stakes state assessment with a sample of 69 third- and fifth-grade students from NES and EL backgrounds. Among the EL students, 80% spoke Hmong as a first language. The results indicated that MAZE exhibited a stronger correlation with the state test among NES students than among EL students (e.g., .73 vs. .52–.57). Regarding the predictive power of MAZE compared to ORF, it was found that MAZE explained additional variance beyond ORF for NES students but not for EL students. The authors concluded that MAZE becomes more useful as a predictor of future reading performance when students get older and more proficient in English. However, MAZE is still a less useful predictor when compared to ORF. These above studies provide some validity evidence for the use of MAZE as a screening tool.

A small number of studies have examined the adequacy of MAZE as a progress-monitoring tool. In one study of MAZE with 43 second-grade NES students, Shin and colleagues (2000) provided evidence for reliability, validity, and sensitivity to growth. MAZE was found to have adequate alternate-form reliability (e.g., mean of 0.81). Additionally, improvement on the MAZE was positively related to reading performance on a standardized reading test, which indicated validity. In regards to sensitivity to growth, MAZE was found to be able to capture improvement of performance over the year and differences in growth rate. Thus, this study supported the use of the MAZE task as a progress-monitoring tool with NES students. In another study, MAZE was also found to exhibit validity (moderate to moderately strong) and sensitivity to growth (McMaster et al., 2006). However, beyond these studies, little evidence exists that supports MAZE as an adequate progress-monitoring tool.

Mathematics and Written Language CBM and CLD Research

In comparison to the area of reading, a drastically lower amount of research has been conducted with CBM in the areas of math and written language. CBM measures in math are used to measure general math competence (e.g., early numeracy skills, math computation, and math problem solving). Regarding the validity of these measures, there are currently no math CBM measures with a validity coefficient over 0.60. This evidence of only low to moderate validity may be due to the low degree of match between the content of math CBMs and standardized tests of math. For example, standardized tests of math may be measuring more than just math skills (e.g., also measuring reading skills). In a study of 225 NES students followed from first grade to second grade, it was suggested that multi-skill screeners in math, which test a range of difficulty levels and math domains, may provide a stronger indication of math outcomes (Fuchs et al., 2007) than probes that are focused on one set of skills. Further, findings from this study suggest that multi-skill CBM computation tasks have a greater relationship to second-grade outcomes than do CBM number identification or counting tasks. Overall, there is a significant lack of research regarding the use of math CBM measures with students who are CLD.

Similar to the status of math CBM, a limited amount of research has been conducted with CBM measures of written language. Despite the importance of written language for communication and careers, public education places little emphasis in this area in comparison to reading. Regarding written language CBM, there are various methods that have been explored in the scoring of these measures. The primary scoring methods include examining total words written or correct letter sequences. However, other methods that may be utilized include holistic approaches, use of long words, use of punctuation, words spelled correctly, total punctuation marks, or words in complete sentences. The lack of emphasis on written language in the schools is mirrored in the written language CBM literature, which contains little research among NES students and no research among CLD students. Gansle, Noell, VanDerHeyden, Naquin, and Slider (2002) examined various methods of scoring written language CBM to determine the methods with the greatest predictive validity. This study included 185 NES students in third and fourth grade. The results indicated that the following methods exhibited the greatest predictive validity for third grade: correct punctuation, total punctuation, and words in correct sequences. However, these validity values are still relatively inadequate, ranging from 0.31 to 0.36.

In another study, McMaster and Espin (2007) reviewed the research on the psychometrics of written expression CBM. The studies included in the review were primarily comprised of NES students. The review compared studies from the Institute for Research on Learning Disabilities (IRLD), elementary studies, and secondary studies. Among the IRLD studies, moderate to strong criterion validity was found for various methods of scoring writing. The reliability was higher across grades than within grades. It was lower for low-achieving students and students with learning disabilities. Among the elementary studies, only a few studies examined test-retest or alternate-form reliability. One of these studies reported weak alternate-form reliability. In comparison with the IRLD studies, the elementary studies found lower criterion validity. The elementary studies also used less direct measures of written expression than did the IRLD studies. In contrast to the elementary studies, the secondary studies found higher internal and alternate-form reliabilities, which were mostly at or above 0.70. Directly contradicting the IRLD studies, various methods of scoring were shown to be insufficient for secondary students. Overall, the review concluded that there is some evidence supporting the use of written language CBM in screening. However, these measures are inadequate for progress monitoring.

Recommendations and Future Research

The purpose of this chapter was to review the psychometric evidence for using CBMs with students who are culturally and linguistically diverse. As the *Test Standards* (AERA/APA/NCME, 1999) point out, validity is the most fundamental aspect of test evaluation and requires a connection between the evidence collected and the use of the test. In this chapter, we targeted using CBMs in early literacy, reading, and math for the purposes of screening and progress monitoring with CLD students in K–12 settings. Before recommendations can be provided, it is important to first understand the limitations about our current knowledge of using CBM with students who are CLD. First, the studies reviewed for this chapter were almost exclusively focused on EL students, and primarily Spanish-speaking EL students. As already mentioned, almost all studies treated the EL group as though they are homogenous and would perform and respond in a similar manner. Although there are data that suggest CBM measures can adequately predict future reading performance for ELs, there is also reason to believe there may be a need for separate cut scores for ELs with varying English proficiency (Johnson et al., 2009).

Second, most studies with students who are CLD focused on grades K–6, with almost no evidence provided examining the use of CBMs in high school settings. Relatedly, the third challenge is that most of the validity evidence is focused on measures of oral reading fluency and early literacy. There is very little validity evidence for using math and written language CBMs with the CLD student population for screening and progress monitoring. Fourth, the impact of cultural variability is significantly under-examined in the CBM literature, and what is available provides somewhat mixed results (e.g., Hosp et al, 2011; Kranzler et al., 1999).

Although there are clear limitations that affect our ability to make conclusions, Table 11.2 provides five recommendations that are supported by our review. First, CBM tools can be and should be used with the CLD K–6 student population for screening and progress monitoring. This recommendation is made in part because other options with more evidence of validity do not exist, and there is a clear need for early identification and evaluation of interventions for students coming from CLD backgrounds. Yet, as our second recommendation indicates, additional sources of data must be used to validate conclusions made based on CBM scores. This recommendation applies to all students, but given the variability in CLD students' academic performance, convergent data are absolutely essential and must be routinely used when interpreting CBM scores.

Our third recommendation builds on recommendations we have made elsewhere (Vanderwood & Nam, 2008) and is supported by recent research (Johnson et al., 2009). ELs

Table 11.2 Recommendations for Using CBM with Students Who Are CLD

---

1. CBM should be used with students who are CLD, regardless of their language and cultural background, for screening and progress monitoring.

2. CBM scores should be validated with other measures and interpreted within the context of the student's background and previous learning experiences.

3. Consideration should be given to using lower "cut scores" for screening with students who have limited English language proficiency.

4. When possible, CBM norms for reading skills developed for EL students with different levels of English proficiency should be used instead of norms for NES.

5. Rates of improvement and growth standards developed for NES can be used with students who are CLD.

---

should not be treated as one homogenous group and, as already stated, it appears there may be a need for cut-scores based on English language proficiency. This recommendation is connected to our fourth, suggesting the use of separate norms created for students at varying levels of English proficiency. Students who are considered at the beginning stage of acquiring English language proficiency should probably be compared to similar students when attempting to understand how their reading skills compare to their peers. Obviously, if separate norms are available, multiple comparisons could be made, including comparison to NES students. Our final recommendation is substantially different than three and four. Progress monitoring research suggests it is appropriate and most likely beneficial to keep expectations high for students who are CLD when they receive interventions and using NES rates of improvement and growth standards should lead to more frequent modifications and improvement of intensive interventions.

Finally, it is clear from our review of the CBM research with CLD populations there is a substantial amount of research needed in the areas of vocabulary, reading comprehension, math, and writing. In fact, even the early literacy and oral reading fluency research domains have questions that still need to be addressed in order to accurately identify who needs support and when interventions should be changed. There is also a need to more clearly conceptualize bias research with CLD populations and measures of acculturation and language should be integrated into these studies.

References

American Educational Research Association, American Psychological Association, National Council on Measurement in Education (AERA/APA/NCME). (1999). *Standards for educational and psychological testing.* Washington, DC: American Psychological Association.

August, D., & Shanahan, T. (2006). *Executive Summary: Developing literacy in second language learners: Report of the National Literacy Panel on language-minority children and youth.* Hillsdale, NJ: Lawrence Erlbaum Associates.

Baker, S. K., & Baker, D. L. (2008). English learners and response to intervention: Improving quality of instruction in general and special education. In E. L. Grigorenko (Ed.), *Educating individuals with disabilities: IDEA 2004 and beyond* (pp. 249–272). New York: Springer.

Baker, S. K., & Good, R. (1995). Curriculum-based measurement of English reading with bilingual Hispanic students: A validation study with second graders. *School Psychology Review, 24,* 561–579.

Betts, J., Muyskens, P., & Marston, D. (2006). Tracking the progress of students whose first language is not English towards English proficiency: Using CBM with English language learners. *MinneTESOL/WITESOL Journal, 23,* 15–37.

Blachowicz, C. L. Z., Fisher, P. J. L., Ogle, D., & Watts-Taffe, S. (2006). Vocabulary: Questions from the classroom. *Reading Research Quarterly, 41,* 524–539.

Cummins, J. (1980). The construct of language proficiency in bilingual education. In J. E. Alatis (Ed.), *Georgetown University round table on languages and linguistics.* Washington, DC: Georgetown University Press.

Cummins, J. (1984). Wanted: A theoretical framework for relating language proficiency to academic achievement among bilingual students. In C. Rivera (Ed.), *Language proficiency and academic achievement.* Clevedon: Multilingual Matters.

Deno, S. L. (2003). Developments in curriculum-based measurement. *Journal of Special Education, 37,* 184–192.

Deno, S. L. (2005). Problem-solving assessment. In R. Chidsey-Brown (Ed.), *Problem-solving-based assessment for educational intervention.* New York, NY: Guilford Press.

Deno, S. L., Mirkin, R. K., & Chiang, B. (1982). Identifying valid measures of reading. *Exceptional Children, 49,* 36–45.

Domínguez de Ramírez, R., & Shapiro, E. S. (2006). Curriculum-based measurement and the evaluation of reading skills of Spanish-speaking English language learners in bilingual education classrooms. *School Psychology Review, 35,* 356–369.

Domínguez de Ramírez, R., & Shapiro, E. S. (2007). Cross-language relationship between Spanish and English oral reading fluency among Spanish-speaking English language learners in bilingual education classes. *Psychology in the Schools, 44,* 795–806.

Echevarria, J., Vogt, M. E., & Short, D. J. (2008). *Making content comprehensible for English learners: The SIOP model.* New York, NY: Pearson.

Englebert-Johnson, S. R. (1997). *A comparison of English as a foreign language, learning disabled, and regular class pupils on curriculum based measures of reading and written expression and the pupil rating scale revised.* Unpublished doctoral dissertation, University of Minnesota, Minneapolis.

Fernald, A., & Weisleder, A. (2011). Early language experience is vital to developing fluency. In S. B. Newman & D. K. Dickenson (Eds.), *Handbook of early literacy research* (Vol. 3, pp. 3–19). New York, NY: Guilford Press.

Fien, H., Baker, S. K., Smolkowski, K., Mercier Smith, J. L., Kame'enui, E. J., & Thomas Beck, C. (2008). Using nonsense word fluency to measure reading proficiency in kindergarten through second grade for English learners and native English speakers. *School Psychology Review, 37,* 391–408.

Fuchs, L. S., Fuchs, D., & Compton, D. L. (2004). Monitoring early reading development in first grade: Word identification fluency versus nonsense word fluency. *Exceptional Children, 71,* 7–21.

Fuchs, L. S., Fuchs, D., Compton, D. L., Bryant, J. D., Hamlett, C. L., & Seethaler, P. M. (2007). Mathematics screening and progress monitoring at first grade: Implications for responsiveness to intervention. *Exceptional Children, 73,* 311–330.

Gansle, K. A., Noell, G. H., VanDerHeyden, A. M., Naquin, G. M., & Slider, N. J. (2002). Moving beyond total words written: The reliability, criterion validity, and time cost of alternate measures for curriculum-based measurement in writing. *School Psychology Review, 31,* 477–497.

Gersten, R., Baker, S. K., Shanahan, T., Linan-Thompson, S., Collins, P., & Scarcella, R. (2007). *Effective literacy and English language instruction for English learners in the elementary grades: A practical guide* (NCEE Report No. 2007-4011). Washington, DC: National Center for Education Evaluation and Regional Assistance, Institute of Education Sciences, U.S. Department of Education. Retrieved from http://ies.ed.gov/ncee/wwc/pdf/practiceguides

Glover, T., & Albers, C. (2007). Considerations for evaluating universal screening assessments. *Journal of School Psychology, 45,* 117–135.

Graves, A. W., Plasencia-Peinado, J., Deno, S. L., & Johnson, J. R. (2005). Formatively evaluating the reading progress of first-grade English learners in multiple-language classrooms. *Remedial and Special Education, 26,* 215–225.

Hart, B., & Risley, R. T. (1995). *Meaningful differences in the everyday experience of young American children.* Baltimore, MD: Paul H. Brookes.

Hintze, J. M., Callahan, J., Matthews, W., Williams, S., & Tobin, K. (2002). Oral reading fluency and prediction of reading comprehension in African American and Caucasian elementary school children. *School Psychology Review, 31,* 540–553.

Hintze, J. M., & Silberglitt, B. (2005). A longitudinal examination of the diagnostic accuracy and predictive validity of R-CBM and high-stakes testing. *School Psychology Review, 34,* 372–386.

Hintze, J. M., Ryan, A. L., & Stoner, G. (2003). Concurrent validity and diagnostic accuracy of the Dynamic Indicators of Basic Early Literacy Skills and the Comprehensive Test of Phonological Processing. *School Psychology Review, 32,* 541–556.

Hixson, M. D., & McGlinchey, M. T. (2004). The relationship between race, income, and oral reading fluency and performance on two reading comprehension measures. *Journal of Psychoeducational Assessment, 22,* 351–364.

Hosp, J. L., Hosp, M. A., & Dole, J. K. (2011). Potential bias in predictive validity of universal screening measures across disaggregation of subgroups. *School Psychology Review, 40,* 108–131.

Howell, K. W., & Nolet, V. (1999). *Curriculum-Based Evaluation: Teaching and decision making* (3rd ed.). Belmont, CA: Wadsworth.

Jenkins, J., Hudson, R., & Johnson, E. (2007). Screening for at-risk readers in a response to intervention framework. *School Psychology Review, 36,* 582–600.

Johnson, E. S., Jenkins, J. R., & Petscher, Y. (2010). Improving the accuracy of a direct route screening process. *Assessment for Effective Intervention, 35,* 131–140.

Johnson, E. S., Jenkins, J. R., Petscher, Y., & Catts, H. (2009). How can we improve the accuracy of screening instruments? *Learning Disabilities Research & Practice, 24,* 174–185.

Kindler, A. L. (2002). *Survey of the states' limited English proficient students and available educational programs and services: 2000–2001 summary report.* Washington, DC: National Clearinghouse for English Language Acquisition.

Klein, J., & Jimerson, S. (2005). Examining ethnic, gender, language, and socioeconomic bias in oral reading fluency scores among Caucasian and Hispanic students. *School Psychology Quarterly, 20,* 23–50.

Kranzler, J., Miller, M., & Jordan, L. (1999). An examination of racial/ethnic and gender bias on curriculum-based measurement in reading. *School Psychology Quarterly, 14,* 327–342.

Lesaux, N. K., & Siegel, L. S. (2003). The development of reading in children who speak English as a second language. *Developmental Psychology, 39,* 1005–1019.

McMaster, K. L., & Espin, C. (2007). Technical features of curriculum-based measurement in writing: A literature review. *The Journal of Special Education, 41,* 68–84.

McMaster, K. L., Wayman, M. M., & Cao, M. (2006). Monitoring the reading progress of secondary-level English learners: Technical features of oral reading and maze tasks. *Assessment for Effective Intervention, 31,* 17–31.

Moore, L. M. (1997). *An evaluation of the efficacy of curriculum based measurement reading measures in the assessment of Hispanic children.* Unpublished doctoral dissertation, Indiana University of Pennsylvania, Indiana, PA.

Muyskens, P., Betts, J., Lau, M., & Marston, D. (2009). Predictive validity of curriculum-based measures in the reading assessment of students who are English language learners. *California School Psychologist, 14,* 11–21.

National Center for Education Statistics. (2011). *The condition of education 2009* (NCES Report No. 2011-003). Washington, DC: U.S. Department of Education. Retrieved from http://nces.ed.gov/programs/coe

National Mathematics Advisory Panel. (2008). *Foundations for success: The final report of the National Mathematics Advisory Panel.* Washington, DC: U.S. Department of Education.

National Reading Panel. (2000). *Teaching children to read: An evidence-based assessment of the scientific research literature on reading and its implications for reading instruction.* Washington, DC: National Institute of Child Health and Human Development.

Pearce, L., & Gayle, R. (2009). Oral reading fluency as a predictor of reading comprehension with American Indian and White elementary students. *School Psychology Review, 38,* 419–427.

Quiroga, T., Lemos-Britton, Z., Mostafapour, E., Abbott, R. D., & Berninger, V. W. (2002). Phonological awareness and beginning reading in Spanish-Speaking ESL first graders: Research into practice. *Journal of School Psychology, 40,* 85–111.

Rathvon, N. (2004). *Early reading assessment: A practitioner's handbook.* New York, NY: Guilford Press.

Rhodes, R. L. (2010). Implementing the problem-solving model with culturally and linguistically diverse students. In G. G. Peacock, R. A. Ervin, E. J. Daly III, & K. W. Merrell (Eds.), *Practical handbook of school psychology: Effective practices for the 21st century* (pp. 566–578). New York: Guilford Press.

Roehrig, A., Petscher, Y., Nettles, S., Hudson, R., & Torgesen, J. (2008). Accuracy of the DIBELS oral reading fluency measure for predicting third grade reading comprehension outcomes. *Journal of School Psychology, 46,* 343–366.

Roth, F. P., Speece, D. L., & Cooper, D. H. (2002). A longitudinal analysis of the connection between oral language and early reading. *The Journal of Educational Research, 95,* 259–272. doi:http://dx.doi.org/10.1080/00220670209596600

Rumberger, R. W., & Gandara, P. (2004). Seeking equity in the education of California's English learners. *Teachers College Record, 106,* 2032–2056.

Schuele, C., & Boudreau, D. (2008). Phonological awareness intervention: Beyond the basics. *Language, Speech & Hearing Services in Schools, 39,* 3–20.

Shapiro, E. S. (2011). *Academic skills problems: Direct assessment and intervention* (4th ed.). New York, NY: Guilford Press.

Shin, J., Deno, S. L., & Espin, C. (2000). Technical adequacy of the maze task for curriculum-based measurement of reading growth. *The Journal of Special Education, 34,* 164–172.

Shinn, M. R. (Ed.). (1998). *Advanced applications of Curriculum-Based Measurement.* New York, NY: Guilford Press.

Silberglitt, B., Burns, M., Madyn, N., & Lail, K. (2006). Relationship of reading fluency assessment data with state accountability test scores: A longitudinal comparison of grade levels. *Psychology in the Schools, 43,* 527–535.

Vanderwood, M. L., & Nam, J. E. (2008). Best practices in assessing and improving English language learners' literacy performance. In A. Thomas & J. Grimes (Eds.), *Best practices in school psychology V* (Vol. 5, pp. 1847–1858). Washington, D.C.: NASP.

Wiley, H. I., & Deno, S. L. (2005). Oral reading and maze measures as predictors of success for English learners on a state standards assessment. *Remedial and Special Education, 26,* 207–214.

Part IV
Specific Academic
Interventions and Issues

12

Evidence-Based Reading Decoding Instruction

Clayton R. Cook, Elizabeth Holland, and Tal Slemrod

Reading is undoubtedly the most critical academic skill for students to acquire in order to thrive in school. Reading is the building block for learning in content courses (mathematics, science, social studies) and eventually parlays into one's ability to successfully participate in civic life. There are two essential phases to reading. The first phase involves the process of *learning how to read,* while the scond phase involves *reading to learn.* Logically, individuals who do not achieve success in the first phase will by default experience difficulty in the second phase. Although all reading instruction ultimately aims for success in the second phase, *reading to learn,* this chapter focuses exclusively on the first phase: *learning how to read.*

Literacy rates are currently higher than at any other time in the history of American education; however, significant numbers of students still do not acquire sufficient reading skills to be used as an effective tool to learn (Aud et al., 2010). For example, up to 32 million adults in the United States—roughly 15%—read below a 5th-grade level. This indicates that these individuals do not read with enough proficiency to secure employment that affords middle-class living (Aud et al., 2010). Reading failure can lead to school failure, which ultimately has damaging consequences with regard to students' self-concept, social interactions, and pursuit for post-secondary education experiences, including securing a fulfilling and rewarding occupation (Reschly, 2010; Stanovich, 1986).

When taking a closer look at the students who are struggling to read—38% nationally—it becomes evident that the vast majority lives in poverty or enters school with limited academic readiness. Of these students, 95% are considered instructional casualties or ABT (i.e., ain't been taught), which suggests that instruction is at the heart of their deficit; it is not a within-child pathological condition (e.g., learning disability). Indeed, research has shown that only a small proportion of students who struggle to read actually have dyslexia (i.e., reading disability). In light of this research, it is imperative that schools provide high-quality reading instruction and make available remedial reading instruction for those students who struggle to read.

Students who begin school with limited exposure to oral language and background experiences are likely to be the most at-risk for reading failure. As a result, these children often have limited exposures to the sounds associated with spoken language, knowledge of the alphabet, familiarity with print, a general sense of the purpose of reading, and vocabulary to call on when encountering words in print. Students who (a) come from low socioeconomic conditions, (b) are English language learners, or (c) have speech and hearing impairments are also clearly at increased risk of reading failure. However, even students who come from higher socioeconomic conditions and have literate parents who model reading throughout the preschool ages experience difficulties learning to read. Regardless of the reason underlying a child's reading struggles, when effective instruction is rendered, research has repeatedly shown that reading deficits and the achievement gap can be effectively addressed (Clay, 1987; Torgesen et al., 2001; Velluntino et al., 1996).

Reading represents the ability to crack the code of written language to construct the meaning behind text. It represents a multi-faceted skill that depends on range of factors, including oral language, background knowledge and experience, sight word recognition, ability to decode unfamiliar words, reading fluency, and comprehension strategies (Stanovich, 1989). In order to read English with proficiency, students must learn the associations between the 44 sounds of spoken English (the phonemes) and the 26 letters of the alphabet. Children must learn that written words are comprised of letters and that these letters correspond to particular sounds. In turn, they must also be able to understand that written words and their sounds map onto spoken language. When this is achieved, the alphabetic principle has been mastered and students are prepared to become more accurate and fluent readers, which will allow them to increasingly utilize reading as a tool to learn.

Hoover and Gough's (1990) *simple view of reading* (SVRM) stipulates that reading comprehension is a function of one's linguistic comprehension and decoding (i.e., word recognition) skills. The SVRM formula has been supported and validated by a number of research studies. Understanding the formula can help educators with assessing reading weaknesses and providing appropriate instruction to improve success. The SVRM represents reading comprehension by the following formula:

Decoding (D) x Language Comprehension (LC) = Reading Comprehension (RC)

From the SVRM, one can dissect problems with reading comprehension as stemming from (a) a deficiency in decoding (i.e., deciphering word recognition), (b) a deficiency in linguistic comprehension (i.e., oral language), or (c) deficiencies in both decoding and linguistic comprehension. As one can see, decoding plays a critical role in being able to read with comprehension. Other researchers have expanded the Simple View to include reading fluency (Adlof, Catts, & Little, 2006). Therefore, the expanded Simple View states that if there are deficits in Decoding (D), Language Comprehension (LC), or Fluency (F), then Reading Comprehension (RC) will likely be impaired. The expanded SVRM formula argues that strong reading comprehension cannot occur unless decoding skills, oral language comprehension, and reading fluency abilities are all strong. From this model, it is clear that educators must teach students to decode proficiently as early as possible. When students can decode fluently, their reading comprehension will be commensurate to their language comprehension. In tandem with decoding instruction, students must be provided with ongoing vocabulary and conceptual knowledge across a variety of content areas to develop the necessary language comprehension abilities to be competent readers.

Based on SVRM, interventions for struggling readers are effective only when they addresses the student's specific weakness, which may be the result of decoding, language comprehension, or both ($D \times LC = RC$).

- When LC = 0: Interventions focused on repeated exposure to English language, developing content knowledge, and/or vocabulary instruction will benefit struggling readers only when they have a weakness in language comprehension.
- When D = 0: Interventions focused on explicit instruction on phonemic awareness, phonics, and sight word recognition will be imperative to improve decoding and ultimately reading comprehension.
- When F = 0: Interventions focused on providing students with repeated opportunities to orally read passages and receive corrective feedback is essential to increase automaticity and fluency, so cognitive and attentional resources can be devoted to comprehension.

Reading decoding skills, fluency, and reading comprehension are the foundational skills of literacy. Without decoding skills, students are not able to recognize words and correspondingly make meaning out of text, so it is imperative that educators have deep knowledge of the basic components of reading decoding. The foundational skills needed for students to develop reading decoding skills are language development, familiarity with print, phonemic awareness, phonics, sight word recognition, and fluency. All these components comprise decoding and should be explicitly and systematically taught and developed for students to be successful. While humans have an innate predisposition for language (Chomsky, 1986), learning to read is not as instinctive. Hence, deliberate instruction that focuses on teaching students how to read is an essential aspect of schooling. The aim of this chapter is to outline the necessary foundational skills for reading decoding that must comprise any sound reading program.

Reading is a complex process that involves reciprocally related skills such as oral language, reading decoding, word recognition, and comprehension strategies (Stanovich, 1986). Weakness anywhere in this interrelated system can spell trouble for growth in the other foundation skills, and for reading development. Unfortunately, many reading instructional programs have been dictated by unfounded trends such as whole word approaches that were popularized in education. A whole word approach assumes that skills such as phonics and phonemic awareness are not necessary in reading curricula and that learning to read is similar to learning to speak. However, the research is clear and the National Reading Panel report demonstrates the importance of teaching children reading decoding skills, such as letter-sound correspondences, blending, and pronunciation (National Institute of Child Health and Human Development [NICHD], 2000; Nicholson, 1991).

Purpose of This Chapter

The purpose of this chapter is to describe effective reading decoding instruction that establishes the critical skills necessary for reading comprehension. Decoding is an essential literacy skill in order to pronounce unfamiliar words and ultimately read with fluency. When students can decode words with ease and speed, greater cognitive energy can be devoted to understanding the underlying meaning behind the text (i.e., reading comprehension). This chapter will unpack the various elements that comprise effective decoding, including language, familiarity with print, phonemic awareness, phonics, sight word recognition and fluency. However, before delving into a discussion of each of these elements, a brief discussion of the critical role of effective explicit, direct instruction is provided.

Explicit Direct Instruction

Project Follow Through represents the largest educational study ever conducted, and was initiated in the 1970s during President Lyndon Johnson's administration, to evaluate and identify the most effective instructional methods to teach core academic skills. The study lasted until 1995 and cost nearly $1 billion to operate and involved more than 20,000 students nationwide. The findings provided conclusive evidence that out of 21 instructional methods, explicit direct instruction was unanimously the most effective method to teach a wide range of academic skills, including reading.

Direct instruction, also referred to as explicit direct instruction, is a teacher-led instructional approach that is one of the most effective methods to teach students core academic skills (Kroesbergen & Van Luit, 2003). It can be a scripted or an improvised approach, but it is a systematic, step-by-step instructional format that elicits active student participation and mastery at each step. It generally involves a brisk pace of instruction and involves both whole and small groups of students. Students are provided numerous opportunities to respond to instruction and to receive feedback based on their performance. Explicit, direct instruction also includes continuous modeling by teachers, followed by more limited teacher involvement, and then fading teacher involvement as students begin to master the material and demonstrate independent performance of the target skill (Maccini & Gagnon, 2000). The following components represent key features of explicit, direct instruction:

- Teacher-led instruction
- Lesson objectives that are clear and communicated in language students are able to understand (i.e., comprehensible input)
- An instructional sequence that begins with a description of the skill to be learned (*Tell*), followed by modeling of examples and non-examples of the skill (*Show*), shared practice (*We do*), and independent demonstration of the skill (*You do*)
- Instructional activities that are differentiated and matched to students' skill levels to the maximum extent practicable
- Provision of a high level of student engagement through the use of:
    - Frequent opportunities to respond individually, with partners and in small groups
    - Random selection of students to respond to questions or provide input
    - Choral response methods in which all students respond in unison to strategic teacher-delivered questions

Ineffective instruction does not elicit a high level of academic engagement. Students are often asked to listen to the teacher lecturing, with minimal opportunities to respond to the teacher presenting the lesson (ineffective *I do* phase). Next, students are directed to independent seatwork, which often entails the completion of worksheets (ineffective *You do* phase). In turn, independent seatwork is frequently coupled with minimal to no feedback based on performance (Hayling, Cook, Gresham, State, & Kern, 2008). Using this practice, it is quite possible that failing grades can be earned based on lack of worksheet completion, despite the student having learned the material (false negative for standards mastery) and, alternatively, passing grades can be earned by copying worksheets and tests from others (false positive for standards mastery). Together, these ineffective instructional practices are associated with poor academic progress and high levels of off-task and noncompliant behavior.

In contrast, explicit direct instruction has a high level of engagement from all students, follows a brisk pace, and possesses repeated feedback (Meyer, 1984; Stein & Goldman, 1980). Students are actively engaged when the lesson is being given through the teacher requiring responses from every student (choral responding, hold up card with answer, tell your partner; effective *I do* phase). Following the lesson, the teacher uses techniques for joint and collaborative practice that is not independent practice yet, but rather is within structured small groups or teams (effective *We do* phase). After the *We do* phase, the teacher provides an independent practice activity that has been thoughtfully developed and which includes written products, completion of a computerized activity, or completion of a hands-on activity to allow students to develop skill fluency (effective *You do* phase). The independent practice is followed up with performance-based feedback so students are provided with either praise for correct responding or corrective information to support learning. Following success, students are pronounced ready for a skill acquisition assessment, which can consist of a written test or quiz, student demonstration of a skill, or oral interviews with the teacher. Evaluation consists of analyzing whether a skill has or has not been learned (i.e., a grade-level standard demonstrated). If it has not, re-teaching based on error analysis occurs and the student retakes the assessment until skill proficiency is reliably demonstrated.

Language as the Foundation for Reading

A logical question to ask with respect to reading decoding is: What are children being asked to decode? The simplest answer to this question is that children are being asked to decode language in written form. In order to read, children must be able to decode written words and map these words onto their existing and expanding language system. As a result, language is the most important developmental milestone achieved during childhood, because it is not only central for communication, but it also translates into being able to read with comprehension. Unfortunately, language is often an underrepresented feature of early childhood and elementary school programs (Gersten et al., 2007; Stubbs, 1976).

The preschool years represent a particularly critical period of learning language, but the process never ends as individuals continue to develop and progress in their ability to understand and express language (Hoff & Shatz, 2009). Without language, children's future success is compromised, as it can trigger a cascade of negative outcomes including reading and writing deficits, school failure, and ultimately school dropout (O'Connor, Bocian, Beebe-Frankenberger, & Linklater, 2010). Indeed, research has demonstrated a strong causal link between language development and performance in reading and writing, and even the presence of social-emotional problems (Benner, Nelson, & Epstein, 2002; Berninger, Abbott, Thomson, & Raskind, 2001; Tomblin, Zhang, Buckwalter, & Catts, 2000).

As children enter school, they are expected to use their language skills as tools for learning, meeting, and negotiating social demands. In addition, language is a necessary condition for reading, as demonstrated in the *Simple View of Reading Model* depicted earlier. Without language, there can be no reading, because reading itself represents the ability to recognize and understand language in written form. Given that language is central and necessary for the development of proficient reading, it is important to consider various methods of improving language.

Language Exposure and Modeling. Children develop their language skills through interactions with more advanced communicators, such as parents, siblings, and teachers. Language development is a social process that entails exposing children to words and modeling appropriate, mature use of language. The more children are talked to and with, the more likely their language will develop. Exposure and modeling are important features to enhance both receptive and descriptive aspects of language. Research has shown that the average child from a welfare family hears about 3 million words a year versus 11 million from a professional family (Hart & Risley, 1995). This discrepancy in language exposure, in turn, leads to decreased school readiness to acquire early literacy and numeracy skills (Reschly, 2010; Stanovich, 1989). In turn, the decreased school readiness comprises a child's ability to acquire early literacy and numeracy skills, which contributes to the widening of the achievement performance gap for low-income students.

It has been shown that adults are more likely to interact verbally with children who have more advanced language than with those whose language development is lagging (Kontos & Wilcox-Herzog, 1997; La Paro, Pianta & Stuhlman, 2004). This is troubling, considering that those children whose language development is lagging need more interaction, while those who actually need less get more. The ultimate aim for educators is to expose children to as much language as possible throughout their tenure in education in order to build their students' vocabularies and background knowledge necessary to become self-sufficient learners. Perhaps the most effective form of exposing and modeling language is descriptive talk. Descriptive talk entails labeling objects, tasks, or actions as one interacts with others, solves problems, or simply comments on an observation. Early childhood teachers need to expose children to language in ways that ensure that their language continues to develop, their vocabulary increases, and their grammar becomes more complex.

Vocabulary Instruction. The National Reading Panel (2002) stated, "Teaching vocabulary will not guarantee success in reading, just as learning to read words will not guarantee success in reading. However, lacking either adequate word identification skills or adequate vocabulary will ensure failure" (Biemiller, 2005). Children must be able to understand spoken words if they are ultimately going to be able to understand the meaning conveyed in text. Vocabulary instruction is generically defined as the systematic and explicit process of teaching the knowledge of words and word meanings. Vocabulary instruction is designed so children are able to learn words that enable them to be able to (a) participate in increasingly demanding conversations successfully, and (b) read more sophisticated text with comprehension (Kamil & Hiebert, 2005). Effective vocabulary instruction is about developing child-friendly definitions of words in language the students already possess, providing students with numerous opportunities to process the meaning of words at a deeper level, and creating opportunities for students to use words (Beck, McKeown, & Kucan, 2013). When effective vocabulary instruction represents an important aspect of language arts instruction, students' language and reading comprehension skills are likely to increase.

Intellectual-Cultural Experiences. Intellectual-cultural experiences represent a collection of cultural, artistic, worldly, and historic experiences that have been linked to increased intelligence, language, and school performance (Gottfried, Gottfried, Bathurst, & Guerin, 2004). The more students experience the world in diverse ways, the greater likelihood that initial schemas are established so connections can be drawn between new words or concepts derived from language. Prior experiences that focus on building background knowledge help students better comprehend texts than when compared to students with less rich background knowledge (Anderson & Pearson, 1984; Duke & Pearson, 2002). Moreover, intellectual-cultural experiences provide a solid basis for language development that translates into better scholastic performance (Bjorklund, 2011).

Familiarity with Print and Letter Naming

Whitehurst and Lonigan (1998) coined the term *emergent literacy* to represent the "skills, knowledge, and attitudes that are presumed to be developmental precursors to conventional forms of reading and writing and the environments that support these developments (e.g., shared book reading)." Children who regularly are afforded the experience of having someone read to them are more likely to have a firm notion of printed words and also greater awareness of the process of reading; that is, they are likely to have better emergent literacy. These concepts, referred to as concepts of print, are important for success in learning to read, and children who have had limited preschool experiences with printed language must be taught them (Adams, 1990; O'Connor, 2007). Therefore, experiences and environmental factors have a tremendous impact of the early literacy development of children. Indeed, environmental factors such as the number of books in a household have been shown to be an independent predictor of school readiness and later reading development (Beals, DeTemple, & Dickinson, 1994; Crain-Thoreson & Dale, 1992). They may realize that the print on a page is the source of the text information needed for reading or know that a reader looks at print from left to right.

What, then, does a parent or educator have to do to increase a child's familiarity with print? The first step is to have books, magazines, and other literature within the child's environment, so children continuously have opportunities to see and interact with printed materials. The next step is to read books aloud with children in order to develop their awareness of the general act and purpose of reading. The more time children spend reading with adults or peers, the more familiar they will be with the process of reading (Beck & McKweon, 2001). Karen Stoiber from the University of Wisconsin-Milwaukee is leading the Promoting Early Attainment of Early Reading and Language Skills (PEARLS) Project in which she is advancing the notion of familiarity of print to another level by developing strategies that not only have adults read aloud to children, but engage them in lively, passionate recitations that capture their attention and bring stories to life.

In addition to familiarity with print, research findings consistently show that one aspect of emergent reading that has a strong correlation with reading success is letter knowledge (Adams, 1990; Durrell, 1980; Ehri, 1983). The invention of the alphabet has served as one of the most significant contributions to the social history of humankind, as it has allowed for written communication and the creation and preservation of historical records. Knowledge of letter names and the different ways of visually depicting letters represents an orthographic skill. Children need to develop the concept that printed words are composed of letters, and these letters have corresponding names and sounds. While instructing children to learn letter names does not solely result in reading success (Jenkins, Bausell, & Jenkins, 1972), it can lead to the formation of memories about the basic structure or shapes of letters and serve as a mnemonic technique for recalling letter-sound associations or phonics (Adams, 1990).

Letter naming fluency has been shown to be a good predictor of reading performance and can be readily achieved via systematic instruction (Daly, Chafouleas, & Skinner, 2005). The goal of letter naming instruction is to increase children's accuracy in letter identification and naming. Once accuracy has been established, then instruction moves toward improving naming fluency, which represents how quickly and accurately a child can identify and name letters. Letter naming fluency is typically established via repeated practice opportunities and emphasis is placed on the speed of recall. Constant time delay (CTD) is a useful strategy to increase letter naming fluency (Wolery, Ault, & Doyle, 1992).

CTD is an instructional technique that was introduced in the early 1970s and has since been shown to build accuracy and fluency in numerous skills for students with and without disabilities. CTD is a prompt-fading strategy that sets students up for success through systematic, predictable, near-errorless instruction. With CTD prompting, one fades instructional prompts by inserting a delay between giving an instruction (e.g., showing a student a flash card with the letter "a" on it) and stepping in and prompting the appropriate response (e.g., "The letter on the flash card is "a." What is the letter?").

Together, familiarity with print and letter naming combine to help set the stage for adequate decoding. These skills alone do not lead to proficient decoding. Rather, when they are combined with other early literacy skills, children are able to understand and apply the alphabetic principle, which refers to understanding that each symbol (letter) corresponds to basic sounds in speech and these sounds can be used to decode written words. The following section discusses a key literacy skill in the development of the alphabetic principle—phonemic awareness.

Phonemic Awareness Instruction

For children to master the ability to decode written words, research has shown that they need to be able to detect and manipulate the sounds in spoken language (Vaughn & Linan-Thompson, 2004). Children who are able to master this skill are more likely to respond positively to subsequent literacy instruction and eventually become competent readers than those who do not (Juel, 1988; O'Connor & Bell, 2004). This precursor literacy skill is called *phonemic awareness*. Snow, Burns, and Griffin (1998) defined phonemic awareness as:

> A general appreciation of the sounds of speech as distinct from their meaning. When that insight includes an understanding that words can be divided into a sequence of phonemes, this finer-grained sensitivity is termed phonemic awareness. (p. 51)

Phonemic awareness is subsumed under the concept of *phonological awareness,* which refers to a broader understanding of the sound structure of language. Phonemic awareness instruction in and of itself helps increase children's receptivity to subsequent reading instruction, including instruction that targets phonics, fluency, and spelling (Chard, Simmons, & Kame'enui, 1998; Ryder, Tunmer, & Greaney, 2008). Research findings have consistently indicated that impairments in phonemic awareness represent a deficit in cognitive processing that impedes the acquisition of proficient reading for both students with and without disabilities (Fletcher et al., 1994; Scarborough, 2009). Without phonemic awareness, children tend to struggle to understand what letters stand for and how they directly relate to the sounds associated with words in spoken language (Liberman, 1973).

Phonemic awareness is more strongly associated with reading achievement at the end of first grade than is IQ, vocabulary, or socioeconomic status of the family (O'Connor & Jenkins, 1999). The development of phonemic awareness does not come naturally for many children. Without explicit instruction in phonemic awareness, research has shown that roughly 25% to 50% of children fail to develop this crucial early literacy skill (Adams, 1990; Juel, 1988). Fortunately, phonemic awareness can be developed through explicit instruction, and doing so significantly enhances students' reading and spelling development. Phonemic awareness instruction involves identifying (detecting onset or ending sounds), segmenting (splitting spoken words into constituent sounds), blending (combining the sounds together to produce whole words), and manipulating (adding, deleting, or substituting sounds).

Phonemic awareness instruction represents a series of oral activities. Therefore, there is often no print involved in phonemic awareness instruction, considering that its main goal is to teach children how to detect and manipulate sounds in spoken language. The progression of phonemic awareness development is depicted in Figure 12.1. As one can see, the subskills are ranked from least to most complex. At the bottom of the continuum is the basic ability to compare words and recognize similarity and dissimilarity in sound. On the other end of the phonemic awareness continuum is the subskill related to deleting (e.g., "What word do you have if you took off the sound /s/ from the word /spot/?") and manipulating (e.g., "What word do you have if you changed the sound /b/ in /bug/ to /m/?") phonemes in spoken words. Phoneme deletion and manipulation is a more complex process, because it involves altering the sound structure of spoken words and deriving new words with new meanings. The purpose of phonemic awareness instruction is to assist children with progressing through this developmental sequence of less to more complex skills in order to process, identify, and

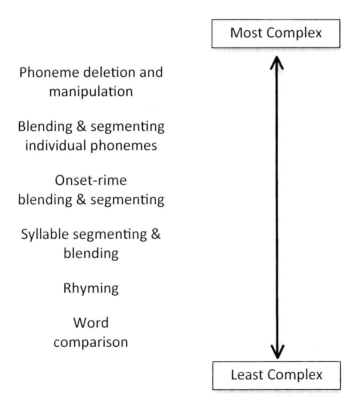

Figure 12.1 Phonemic Awareness Development

208 • Specific Academic Interventions and Issues

manipulate basic sound units in spoken words. These phonemic awareness skills set the foundation for later reading and interact in a synergistic way with knowledge of letter-sound associations to create effective reading decoding and word recognition skills. The following is a list of specific instructional activities that are designed to address particular aspects of phonemic awareness.

- **Isolation**
  - **Tell**—Phoneme isolation is saying individual sounds you hear in a word.
  - **Show**—Teacher: "For example, if I asked you what is the very first sound in boy? You would say, /b/"
  - **Do**—Teacher: "Now it's your turn, I want you to say the first sound in the word I say. Ready, here you go":
    - **Girl**
    - **Boat**
    - **Dog**
    - **Pig**
    - **Fish**
- **Categorization**
  - **Tell**—Categorization is choosing the words in a group that have similar/same or different sounds. It is important to pay close attention to what you hear because this allows us to categorize the words as similar or different.
  - **Show**—Teacher: "I'm going to say several words and the goal is to say which ones are similar and which one is different. For example, if the words were: Sad, silly, big, I would say that Sad and Silly are the same because they begin with /s/, and I would say Big is different because it starts with a /b/. Big does not belong."
  - **Do**—Teacher: "Now it's your turn. Remember the goal is to figure out which words are the same and which word is different from the group of words I'm going to say aloud. Ready, here you go."
    - Sack, cat, shove
    - Milk, butter, bug
    - Sick, good, grab
- **Phoneme segmentation**
  - **Tell**—Phoneme segmentation is a fancy way of saying breaking apart spoken words into different sounds. This means that we have to first listen to the word and then figure out what are the different sounds that go together to create the word.
  - **Show**—Teacher: "I'm going to show you how to break apart words into different sounds. When I do this, you will be able to see that a word I say has different sounds that add together to create the word. For example, if I want to say the sounds of the word *clock*, I would say /k/ /l/ /o/ /ck/. Can you hear the sounds /k/ /l/ /o/ /ck/ in the word clock. Let me show you how to segment or break apart another word."
  - **Do**—Teacher: "Now it's your turn. The goal is to listen to the word first and then break apart the word by saying all the sounds you hear. I will first say the word and then you will have three seconds to figure out the sounds. Ready, here you go."
  - What are the sounds in "cat"? /k/ /a/ /t/
    - Mat
    - Bag
    - Truck

- **Phoneme manipulation**
  - **Tell**—Phoneme manipulation means we are going to alter the words by changing the first, middle, or last sound in a word. This means that we have to first listen to the word and then figure out what are the different sounds that go together to create the word.
  - **Show**—Teacher: "I'm going to show you how to break apart words into different sounds. For example if I want to change the word, 'cat,' I can change the /k/ sound to /h/. The new word I end up with is 'hat' instead of 'cat.' This is because I changed the /k/ sound to the /h/ sound."
  - **Do**—Teacher: "Now, it's your turn. Listen to each word, follow my directions, and try your best to say the new word."
    - Say fan . . . Now change the /f/ to /k/ . . . Say the new word.
    - Say goat . . . Now change the /g/ to /b/ . . . Say the new word.

Phonics Instruction

Some people argue that sight word reading, in which students attempt to read by whole word sight recognition alone, is advantageous, given the frequency of words that are not phonetically based (Goodman, 2005; Weaver, 1990). This approach, however, has not proved to be effective for many students and does not provide the foundational skills necessary for mastery of alphabetic principle and overall literacy (Ryder et al., 2008). Most struggling readers rely on only one reading strategy when attempting to decode words, such as quickly making predictions about words based on the use of context or pictorial cues. To become a skilled reader, children must develop a wider array of strategies to call upon when systematically decoding and recognizing words. Skilled reading ultimately occurs when students can discriminate between the different sounds they hear in spoken language (phonemic awareness) and understand that sounds correspond to letters or collections of letters within the alphabet (phonics). Further, while letter names are important, research has revealed that teaching should focus on the sounds letters make by themselves and in combination with other letters, since letter names alone do not assist in developing spelling, writing, and decoding (Vellutino, Fletcher, Snowling, & Scanlon, 2004; Wagner & Torgesen, 1987).

Children learn to read by identifying all the letters in a word, not just initial or ending letters, and the sounds that correspond to the identified letters. A critical aspect of reading decoding instruction is to teach children to understand that the identities, order, and corresponding sounds of letters are essential to pronounce whole words and recognize them as part of their listening vocabulary. One of the main hurdles encountered by children who struggle to read is the ability to master letter-sound correspondences of the English written language system (Vellutino et al., 2004). As a result, research has provided robust support for teaching children how to sound out words by learning letter-sound associations and applying this knowledge when encountering words in text (Foorman, Brier, & Fletcher, 2003; Vaughn et al., 2009).

In its simplest expression, phonics refers to the system by which symbols (i.e., letters) represent sounds in an alphabetic writing system. Phonics instruction represents the process of teaching the associations between letters or groups of letters and their pronunciations (phonemes), so children develop the capability to independently sound out words. Mastery of sound-symbol relations is, therefore, the central feature of phonics instruction, which is designed to provide readers and writers with the necessary tools to decode and spell unfamiliar words. Therefore, one of the primary goals of reading decoding instruction is to teach letter-sound associations and spelling patterns.

Solely relying on applying phonetic skills letter-by-letter can result in inaccurate decoding and an inability to recognize or appropriately pronounce the word. As a result, children must also learn how to apply phonics skills to particular letter combinations in order to correctly pronounce and recognize words in print, such as consonant digraphs (th, ch, ck) and vowel diphthongs (oa, ea, ie, oo). For example, if one sounds out the word "soap" letter-by-letter (/s/ /o/ /a/ /p/), the result would be saying a word that is not included in the English language. Instead, appropriate instruction would entail teaching the diphthong "oa" and corresponding long /o/ sound it makes. In so doing, the child would be able to accurately decode the word as /s/ /oa/ /p/, as well as other words containing the same diphthong (e.g., boat, float, load). Phonics instruction should be sequential in that letter sounds that are easier to produce and frequently encountered letter patterns (e.g., short vowels, single-letter consonants) are taught first before attempting more difficult letter sounds and letter patterns.

The best way to teach phonics is via explicit, systematic direct instruction. This means developing clear objectives and teaching according to a pre-planned sequence of phonetic skills rather than teaching particular aspects of phonics as they are encountered naturally or in texts. The above section on explicit, direct instruction directly applies to phonics. In addition to explicit, direct instruction, there are some other basic recommendations for phonics instruction: (a) start teaching letter sounds as soon as possible, (b) avoid alphabetical order, (c) use cumulative introduction, (d) teach short vowel sounds initially and then move to long vowels, and (d) integrate letter sounds with phonological awareness activities (Ball & Blachman, 1991; Carnine et al., 1998; O'Connor & Jenkins, 1995).

One of the most effective instructional methods to teach phonics is segment to spell (SPS). O'Connor and Jenkins (1995) developed SPS to teach children the alphabetic principle using a combination of phonemic awareness and phonics-based instructional activities. When using SPS, one can integrate an assortment of identification, blending, segmenting, and substitution instructional activities. Figure 12.2 depicts the basic template for SPS, which

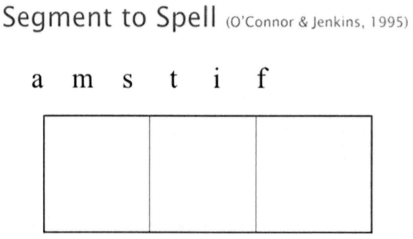

Figure 12.2 Segment to Spell

is perhaps best used when combined with letters children can manipulate by grabbing, placing, and moving around. Below is an example SPS script:

- "We are going to begin with the word 'rat.' Say 'rat.'"
  - [Student(s) says /rat/.]
- "Say all the sounds in 'rat.' Beginning with the first sound."
  - [Student(s) says /r/, then /a/, and last /t/.]
- "Good job. In the word 'rat,' what's the first sound?"
  - [Student(s) says /r/.]
- "Spell 'rat' on your table with your letters."
  - [Student(s) spells rat by grabbing the letters and putting them on the page.]
- "Now look up here. Did you spell it this way?"
  - [Teacher spells out the word.]
- "Spell 'rat' with me: 'r'-'a'-'t'. Did you spell it 'r'-'a'-'t'? Change the spelling if you want to."
  - [Student(s) checks work against the overhead.]
- "Watch me sound out the word 'rat' letter-by-letter."
  - [Touch under each letter and say the sounds /r/ /a/ /t/.]
- "Now, read it with me."
  - [Touch under each letter and encourage students to read along with you.]
  - [Student(s) says the sounds and then reads the word with the teacher.]
- "What did we spell?"
  - [Wait for student(s) to say the word 'rat.']
- "Now, let's take away the letter 't' from rat and replace it with the letter 'm.'"
  - [Student(s) grabs the letter 't' and replace it with the letter 'm.']
- "Let's see how we changed the word. What sound does the letter 'm' make?"
  - [Student(s) says the sound /m/.]
- "If we add the /m/ sound to the rest of the letters lets see what we end up with? Let's sound out letter by letter."
  - [Student(s) says /r/, then /a/, and last /m/.]
- If we say it all together what word do we have?"
  - [Student(s) blends all the sounds together /r/ /a/ /m/ and says the word 'ram.']

Sight Word Instruction

Sight words refer to a set of words that are instantly recognized, without the need for a student to apply phonics skills to sound them out. When sight words are identified, readers can recognize their pronunciation and meaning automatically, without the use of extra attention or effort in figuring out the word (LaBerge & Samuels, 1974). These words no longer make use of phonics, because immediate recollection and pronunciation of the word have been established due to repeated exposures. As such, automatic word recognition and fluent text reading allow children to focus their mental resources on the meaning of the text instead of decoding individual words, providing an important underpinning for the more sophisticated comprehension demands of texts used in the middle and upper grades (Spear-Swerling, 2011). Often, this is due to a combination of repeated encounters with words in naturalistic ways and good phonics instruction that results in the ability to decode words rapidly and with ease.

Along with effective phonemic awareness, phonics, and fluency, sight word recognition is a key aspect to successful reading decoding, and is an imperative piece to facilitate reading comprehension. Research literature has consistently supported the inclusion sight word recognition skills as a part of reading instruction (Honig, Diamond, Gutlohn, & Cole, 2008; LaBerge & Samuels, 1974; Moyer, 1982). The goal of sight word instruction is to help children develop a considerable store of words they recognize readily by sight. Some of the sight words will be phonetically irregular (e.g., of), which means that sight word instruction should also include explicit talk about which parts of the word are decodable and which are not. For example, the word "said" is phonetically regular in its initial and final sounds, /s/ and /d/, and irregular in the middle sound.

Students who struggle with decoding and site word recognition are likely to fall further behind in academic tasks and courses that require a heavy dose of reading (Lyon & Fletcher, 2001). Unless decoding and sight word recognition skills are remediated, there is a greater likelihood of these students of being disengaged in the classroom, exhibiting increased disruptive behaviors, and experiencing school failure (Cook, Dart, Collins, Restori, Vance, & Fitts, 2013). This challenge may be compounded if students are English Language Learners (ELL), where even the basic sight words are new and unrecognizable in either text or speech. Struggling readers need word repetition in a variety of contexts to develop an extensive sight word bank. For example, students need to encounter them in readings, engage in activities in which they construct sight words with manipulables, and have numerous opportunities to write them down through journaling, spelling, or other writing assignments.

Various interventions to assist student learning can be implemented around sight word instruction, including peer-tutoring interventions, small group activities, and whole-class instruction. It is best to begin with high-frequency words, which are words that are most frequently encountered in a variety of texts (e.g., newspapers, fictional stories, the web, etc.). Dolch (1948) and Fry (1980) lists represent popular sources for obtaining lists of high frequency words that can be used to teach sight words. These lists can be used to design a variety of lesson plans around the topic of teaching sight words. Specific recommendations for sight word instruction are as follows:

- *Development of a word wall or word bank* (Schulman & Payne, 2000). Words can either be depicted on a large chart for the entire class to see (Word Wall), or they can be collected in a personal journal of words for individual exposure and use (Word Bank). Both these strategies promote awareness of high-frequency words and their correct spelling.
- *Selection of key words to share with others* (Vukelich, Christie, & Enz, 2002). The teacher has each child pick a favorite word they would like to learn to read and write it on an index card. Children then share their words with the entire class, to create a collection of key words.
- *Incremental rehearsal* is an academic intervention that is used to address issues of poor retention and increase fluency of retrieval of basic facts (Joseph, 2006). Typically, 10 known and 10 unknown sight words are written onto index cards and interspersed with one another. Students then practice saying the sight words, until all words are known. If the student is unable to say a sight word correctly, the teacher or partner says the word and then has the student say it three times.
- *Word games* using high frequency words list.
  - Word sorts are games in which each sight word is written on two cards, shuffled, and laid face down. Students then match words, but must be able to say the word before earning a point.

- Bingo game using sight words instead of numbers.
- Go Fish game using words instead of cards. Each student takes a turn asking whether the other student has a particular word. Once a pair is obtained, the student is awarded a point.

Fluency Instruction

Although the ability to decode words accurately is critical to reading, the rate at which a student reads is equally as important to ensure that the student will be able to comprehend what was read. Put simply, if the student is unable to recognize and read words with ease and speed, the overall meaning of the text will likely be lost. On the other hand, if the student is able to recognize, decode, and read words rapidly and easily, the student will be able to remember what was read and relate ideas to existing schemas or background experiences.

The relationship between reading decoding and comprehension is best portrayed in Perfetti's (1985) verbal efficiency model (VEM), depicted in Figure 12.3. According to Perfetti's VEM, both decoding and comprehension consume attentional resources, which presents challenges considering there are limited amounts of attention to divide between these processes. To the extent there are more attentional resources consumed by decoding, there are fewer attentional resources available for the process of comprehension. In essence, children who acquire fluent decoding skills free up attentional resources that can be better devoted to comprehending the meaning behind text. On the other hand, children who have dysfluent decoding have to devote a significant amount of their attention to this process, which means comprehension suffers. Struggling readers' slow word recognition drains them of the very attentional resources needed to comprehend the meaning underlying text.

The amount of practice required for fluency and automaticity in reading varies greatly. However, research has revealed that the typical child needs numerous exposures to words in isolation and in text before automaticity and fluency are established. It is also critical that children read text at their independent reading level (i.e., with 95% accuracy), and that the text provides specific practice in the literacy skills being learned. Given these considerations,

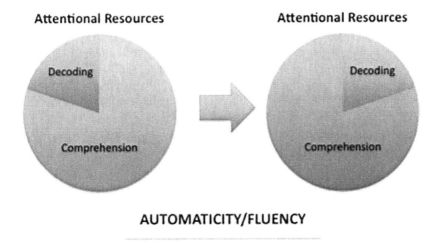

Figure 12.3 Automaticity/Fluency

the best method of teaching reading fluency is Guided Oral Repeated Reading with Feedback (GORRF; Rasinski, Blachowicz, & Lems, 2006).

Most GORRF procedures involve a more competent reader, such as a teacher, parent, or peer, reading a passage aloud to model fluent, accurate reading, followed by the student rereading the same text aloud several times while receiving feedback. It is important for the text to be at the student's independent reading level, which is defined as decoding independently 95% of the words correctly. Typically, GORRF involves reading the same text three to five times before moving on to a different passage. Examples of specific techniques that involve GORRF procedures include:

- The student reads with a peer partner. Each partner takes a turn reading to the other. A more fluent reader can be paired with a less fluent reader to model fluent reading. The more fluent reader can provide feedback and encouragement to the less fluent reader. Students of similar reading skills can also be paired, particularly if the teacher has modeled fluent reading and the partner reading involves practice.
- An adult reads with the student by modeling fluent reading and then asking the student to read the same passage aloud with encouragement and feedback by the adult.
- A student listens to a tape or recording on a computer of a fluent reader reading text at the student's independent level. The student then reads into a microphone and practices reading along with the tape until the student is able to read fluently.
- Readers' theater format that has students read scripts and rehearse a play to prepare for a performance. Students reread the scripts and receive feedback, which provides an opportunity to improve fluency skills.

Numerous commercial products are available for purchase, which explicitly focus on teaching reading fluency. For example, Six Minute Solution©, Great Leaps©, Read Naturally©, Peer-Assisted Learning Strategies©, HELPS Program©, and Elements of Reading Fluency© are all products that can be purchased for use. There is also the HELPS Program©, which was developed by Dr. John Begeny as a free evidence-based reading decoding and fluency program for schools with limited fiscal resources. Although these pre-packaged products can help streamline instruction, it is not necessary to have one of them to deliver reading fluency instruction effectively. Regardless of the curriculum used, it is critical to ensure the key instructional elements associated with high quality fluency instruction are implemented, which are repeated readings at the student's independent reading level coupled with performance-based feedback. Moreover, it is important to recognize that reading fluency is like any other skill that requires a person to coordinate a series of smaller actions into a unified process, meaning that it is practice that enables the person to ultimately develop proficiency and expertise (Kuhn & Stahl, 2003).

Conclusion

The basis of all reading is language, but in order to connect written text to one's existing oral language system, one needs to also acquire proficiency in decoding and recognizing words. This chapter has outlined the components necessary to effectively teach decoding and word recognition skills. School policies mandating systematic, explicit instruction targeting reading decoding are founded on years of evidence that demonstrate that effective teaching can alleviate or significantly reduce the risk for reading failure (Blachman et al., 2004; Denton,

Foorman, & Mathes, 2003; Foorman et al., 2006; Mathes et al., 2005; Vellutino et al., 1996). This is especially true for at-risk children, including second language learners, children who lack school readiness, children of poverty, and children with dyslexia, who are most dependent on good instruction to overcome their disadvantages (Lyon, Fletcher, Torgesen, Shaywitz, & Chhabra, 2004). In this way, effective reading decoding instruction plays a key role in the prevention and remediation of school failure, as well as ensures that students are able to acquire reading as a skill to learn.

References

Adams, M. J. (1990). *Beginning to read: Thinking and learning about print.* Cambridge, MA: MIT Press.

Adlof, S. M., Catts, H. W., & Little, T. D. (2006). Should the Simple View of Reading include a fluency component? *Reading and Writing: An Interdisciplinary Journal, 19,* 933–958.

Anderson, R. C., & Pearson, P. D. (1984). A schema-theoretic view of basic processes in reading comprehension. In P. D. Pearson, R. Barr, M. L. Kamil, & P. Mosenthal (Eds.), *Handbook of reading research* (pp. 255–291). New York, NY: Longman.

Aud, S., Hussar, W., Planty, M., Snyder, T., Bianco, K., Fox, M., Frohlich, L., Kemp, J., & Drake, L. (2010). *The condition of education 2010* (NCES 2010–028). Washington, DC: National Center for Education Statistics, Institute of Education Sciences, US Department of Education.

Ball, D. L., & Blachman, B. A. (1991). Does phoneme awareness training in kindergarten make a difference in early word recognition and developmental spelling? *Reading Research Quarterly, 26,* 49–66.

Beals, D. E., DeTemple, J. M., & Dickinson, D. K. (1994). Talking and listening that support early literacy development of children from low-income families. In D. K. Dickinson (Ed.), *Bridges to literacy: Children, families, and schools* (pp. 241–263). Cambridge, MA: Blackwell.

Beck, I. L., & McKeown, M. G. (2001). Text talk: Capturing the benefits of read-aloud experiences for young children. *Reading Teacher, 55,* 10–20.

Beck, I. L., McKeown, M. G., & Kucan, L. (2013). *Bringing words to life: Robust vocabulary instruction.* New York, NY: The Guilford Press.

Benner, G., Nelson, J., & Epstein, M. (2002). Language skills of children with EBD. *Journal of Emotional and Behavioral Disorders, 10,* 43–56.

Berninger, V. W., Abbott, R. D., Thomson, J. B., & Raskind, W. H. (2001). Language phenotype for reading and writing disability: A family approach. *Scientific Studies of Reading, 5,* 59–106.

Biemiller, A. (2005). Size and sequence in vocabulary development: Implications for choosing words for primary grade vocabulary instruction. In E. H. Hiebert & M. L. Kamil (Eds.), *Teaching and learning vocabulary: Bringing research to practice* (pp. 223–242). Mahwah, NJ: L. Erlbaum Associates.

Bjorklund, D. F. (2011). *Children's thinking.* Belmont, CA: Wadsworth.

Blachman, B. A., Schatschneider, C., Fletcher, J. M., Francis, D. J., Clonan, S. M., Shaywitz, B. A., et al. (2004). Effects of intensive reading remediation for second and third graders and a 1-year follow-up. *Journal of Educational Psychology, 96,* 444–461.

Chard, D. J., Simmons, D. C., & Kame'enui, E. J. (1998). Word recognition: Research bases. In D.C. Simmons & E. J. Kame'enui (Eds.), *What reading research tells us about children with diverse learning needs: Bases and basics* (pp. 141–168). Mahwah, NJ: Erlbaum.

Chomsky, N. (1986). *Knowledge of language: Its nature, origin, and use.* New York, NY: Praeger.

Clay, M. M. (1987). Learning to be learning disabled. *New Zealand Journal of Educational Studies, 22,* 155–173.

Cook, C. R., Dart, E., Collins, T., Restori, A.,Vance, M., & Fitts, P. (2013). Co-occurring reading and behavior problems: Transactional relationship or not? Implications for intervention. *Behavioral Disorders, 54,* 65–79.

Crain-Thoreson, C., & Dale, P. S. (1992). Do early talkers become early readers? Linguistic precocity, preschool language, and emergent literacy. *Developmental Psychology, 28,* 412–429.

Daly, E. J., Chafouleas, S., & Skinner, C. H. (2005). *Interventions for reading problems: Designing and evaluating effective strategies.* New York, NY: Guilford Press.

Denton, C., Foorman, B., & Mathes, P. (2003). Perspective: Schools that beat the odds. *Remedial and Special Education, 24,* 258–261.

Dolch, E. W. (1948). *Problems in reading.* Champaign IL: Garrard.

Duke, N. K., & Pearson, D. (2002). Effective practices for developing reading comprehension. In A. E. Farstrup & S. J. Samuels (Eds.), *What research has to say about reading instruction* (pp. 205–237). Newark, DE: International Reading Association.

Durrell, D. D. (1980). Commentary: Letter name values in reading and spelling. *Reading Research Quarterly, 16,* 159–163.

Ehri, L. C. (1983). A critique of five studies related to letter-name knowledge and learning to read. In L. M. Gentile, M. L. Kamil, & J. Blanchard (Eds.), *Reading research revisited* (pp. 143–153). Columbus, OH: C. E. Merrill.

Fletcher, J. M., Shaywitz, S. E., Shankweiler, D. P., Katz, L., Liberman, Y., Stuebing, K. K., Francis, K. J., Fowler, A. E., & Shaywitz, B. A. (1994). Cognitive profiles of reading disability: Comparisons of discrepancy and low achievement definitions. *Journal of Educational Psychology, 86,* 6–23.

Foorman, B. R., Brier, J. I., & Fletcher, J. M. (2003). Interventions aimed at improving reading success: An evidence-based approach. *Developmental Neuropsychology, 24,* 613–639.

Foorman, B. R., Schatschneider, C., Eakin, M. N., Fletcher, J. M., Moats, L. C., & Francis, D. J. (2006). The impact of instructional practices in Grades 1 and 2 on reading and spelling achievement in high poverty schools. *Contemporary Educational Psychology, 31,* 1–29.

Fry, E. (1980). The new instant word list. *The Reading Teacher, 34,* 284–289.

Gersten, R., Baker, S. K., Shanahan, T., Linan-Thompson, S., Collins, P., & Scarcella, R. (2007). *Effective literacy and English language instruction for English learners in the elementary grades: A practice guide* (NCEE 2007–4011). Washington, DC: National Center for Education Evaluation and Regional Assistance, Institute of Education Sciences, U.S. Department of Education. Retrieved from http://ies.ed.gov/ncee

Goodman, K. (2005). Making sense of written language: A lifelong journey. *Journal of Literacy Research, 37,* 1–24.

Gottfried, A. W., Gottfried, A. E., Bathurst, K., & Guerin, D. W. (2004). *Gifted IQ: Early Developmental Aspects—The Fullerton Longitudinal Study.* New York, NY: Springer.

Hart, B., & Risley, T. R. (1995). *Meaningful differences in the everyday experience of young American children.* Baltimore, MD: P. H. Brookes.

Hayling, C. C., Cook, C., Gresham, F. R., State, T., & Kern, L. (2008). An analysis of the status and stability of the behaviors of students with emotional and behavioral difficulties: A classroom direct observation study. *Journal of Behavioral Education, 17,* 24–42.

Hoff, E., & Shatz, M. (2009). *Blackwell handbook of language development.* Chichester, UK: Blackwell Publishing Ltd.

Honig, B., Diamond, L., Gutlohn, L., & Cole, C. L. (2008). *Teaching reading sourcebook.* Novato, CA: Academic Therapy Publications.

Hoover, W. A., & Gough, P. B. (1990). The simple view of reading. *Reading and Writing: An Interdisciplinary Journal, 2,* 127–160.

Jenkins, J. R., Bausell, R. B., & Jenkins, L. M. (1972). Comparison of letter-name and letter-sound training as transfer variables. *American Educational Research Journal, 9,* 75–86.

Joseph, L. M. (2006). Incremental rehearsal: A flashcard drill technique for increasing retention of reading words. *The Reading Teacher, 59,* 803–807.

Juel, C. (1988). Learning to read and write: A longitudinal study of fifty-four children from first through fourth grade. *Journal of Educational Psychology, 80,* 437–447.

Kame'enui, E. J., & Carnine, D. W. (1998). *Effective teaching strategies that accommodate diverse learners.* Upper Saddle River, NJ: Prentice Hall.

Kamil, M. L., & Hiebert, E. H. (2005). The teaching and learning of vocabulary: Perspectives and persistent issues. In E. H. Hiebert & M. L. Kamil (Eds.), *Teaching and learning vocabulary: Bringing research to practice* (pp. 1–23). Mahwah, NJ: Erlbaum.

Kontos, S., & Wilcox-Herzog, A. (1997). Teachers' interactions with children: Why are they so important? *Young Children, 52,* 4–12.

Kroesbergen, E. H., & Van Luit, J. E. (2003). Mathematics interventions for children with special educational needs. *Remedial & Special Education, 24,* 97.

Kuhn, M. R., & Stahl, S. A. (2003). Fluency: A review of developmental and remedial practices. *Journal of Educational Psychology, 95,* 3–21.

La Paro, M., Pianta, R. C., & Stuhlman, M. (2004). The classroom assessment scoring system: Findings from the prekindergarten year. *Elementary School Journal, 104,* 409–426.

LaBerge, D., & Samuels, S. J. (1974). Toward a theory of automatic information processing in reading. *Cognitive Psychology, 6,* 293–323.

Liberman, Y. (1973). Segmentation of the spoken word and reading acquisition. *Bulletin of the Orton Society, 23,* 65–77.

Lyon, G. R., & Fletcher, J. M. (2001). Early warning system. *Education Matters, 1,* 2–29.

Lyon, G. R., Fletcher, J. M., Torgesen, J. K., Shaywitz, S. E., & Chhabra, V. (2004). Preventing and remediating reading failure: A response to Allington. *Educational Leadership, 61,* 86.

Maccini, P., & Gagnon, J. C. (2000). Best practices for teaching mathematics to secondary students with special needs. *Focus on Exceptional Children, 32,* 1–22.

Mathes, P. G., Denton, C. A., Fletcher, J. M., Anthony, J. L., Francis, D. J., & Schatschneider, C. (2005). The effects of theoretically different instruction and student characteristics on the skills of struggling readers. *Reading Research Quarterly, 40,* 148–182.

Meyer, L. A. (1984). Long-term academic effects of the direct instruction project follow through. *Elementary School Journal, 84,* 380–394.

Moyer, S. B. (1982). Repeated reading. *Journal of Learning Disabilities, 15,* 619–623.

National Reading Panel (U.S.), Widmeyer Communications, & National Institute of Child Health and Human Development (U.S.). (2002). *Teaching children to read.* Washington, DC: National Institute of Child Health and Human Development, National Institutes of Health.

National Institute of Child Health and Human Development (NICHD). (2000). *Report of the National Reading Panel: Teaching children to read: An evidence-based assessment of the scientific research literature on reading and its implications for reading instruction.* Washington, DC: National Institute of Child Health and Human Development, National Institutes of Health.

Nicholson, T. (1991). Do children read words better in context or in lists? A classic study revisited. *Journal of Educational Psychology, 83,* 444–450.

O'Connor, R. E. (2007). *Teaching word recognition: Strategies for students with learning difficulties.* New York, NY: Guilford Press.

O'Connor, R. E., & Bell, K. M. (2004). Teaching students with reading disability to read words. In A. Stone, C. Silliman, B. Ehren, & K. Apel, (Eds.), *Handbook of language and literacy: Development and disorders* (pp. 479–496). New York, NY: Guilford Press.

O'Connor, R. E., Bocian, K., Beebe-Frankenberger, M., & Linklater, D. (2010). Responsiveness of students with language difficulties to early intervention in reading. *The Journal of Special Education, 43,* 220–235.

O'Connor, R. E., & Jenkins, J. R. (1995). Improving the generalization of sound/symbol knowledge: Teaching spelling to kindergarten children with disabilities. *Journal of Special Education, 29,* 255–275.

O'Connor, R. E., & Jenkins, J. R. (1999). The prediction of reading disabilities in kindergarten and first grade. *Scientific Studies of Reading, 3,* 159–197.

Perfetti, C. A. (1985). *Reading ability.* New York, NY: Oxford Press.

Rasinski, T. V, Blachowicz, C., & Lems, K. (Eds.). (2006). *Fluency instruction: Research-based best practices.* New York, NY: Guilford Press.

Reschly, A. L. (2010). Reading and school completion: Critical connections and Matthew effects. *Reading and Writing Quarterly, 26,* 67–90.

Ryder, J., Tunmer, W., & Greaney, K. (2008). Explicit instruction in phonemic awareness and phonemically based decoding skills as an intervention strategy for struggling readers in whole-language classrooms. *Reading and Writing, 21,* 349–369.

Scarborough, H. (2009). Connecting early language and literacy later reading (dis)abilities: Evidence, theory and practice. In F. Fletcher-Campbell, G. Reid, & J. Soler (Eds.), *Approaching difficulties in literacy development: Assessment, pedagogy and programmes* (pp. 23–38). Los Angeles, CA: Sage Publications.

Schulman, M. B., & Payne, C. C. (2000). *Guided reading: Making it work.* New York, NY Scholastic Professional Books.

Snow, C. E., Burns, M. S., & Griffin, P. (1998). *Preventing reading difficulties in young children.* Washington, DC: National Academy Press.

Spear-Swerling, L. (2011). Phases in reading words and phonics interventions. In R. E. O'Connor & P. F. Vadasy (Eds.), *Handbook of reading interventions* (pp. 63–87). New York, NY: Guilford Press.

Stanovich, K. E. (1986). Matthew effects in reading: Some consequences of individual differences in the acquisition of literacy. *Reading Research Quarterly, 21,* 360–406.

Stanovich, K. E. (1989). Learning disabilities in broader context. *Journal of Learning Disabilities, 22,* 287–291.

Stein, C. L., & Goldman, J. (1980). Beginning reading instruction for children with minimal brain dysfunction. *Journal of Learning Disabilities, 13,* 219–222.

Stubbs, M. (1976). *Language, schools and classrooms.* London: Methuen.

Tomblin, B. J., Zhang, X., Buckwalter, P., & Catts, H. (2000). The association of reading disability, behavioral disorders, and language impairment among second-grade children. *Journal of Child Psychology and Psychiatry, 41,* 473–483.

Torgesen, J. K., Alexander, A. W., Wagner, R. K., Rashotte, C. A., Voeller, K. S., & Conway, T. (2001). Intensive remedial instruction for children with severe reading disabilities: Immediate and long-term outcomes from two instructional approaches. *Journal of Learning Disabilities, 34,* 33–58.

Vaughn, S., & Linan-Thompson, S. (2004). *Research-based methods of reading instruction, grades K-3.* Alexandria, VA: Association for Supervision and Curriculum Development.

Vaughn, S., Wanzek, J., Murray, C. S., Scammacca, N., Linan-Thompson, S., & Woodruff, A. L. (2009). Response to early reading intervention: Examining higher and lower responders. *Exceptional Children, 75,* 165–183.

Vellutino, F. R., Fletcher, J. M., Snowling, M. J., & Scanlon, D. M. (2004). Specific reading disability (dyslexia): What have we learned in the past four decades? *Journal of Child Psychology and Psychiatry, 45,* 2–40.

Vellutino, F. R., Scanlon, D. M., Sipay, E. R., Small, S. G., Pratt, A., Chen, R., et al. (1996). Cognitive profiles of difficult-to-remediate and readily remediated poor readers: Early intervention as a vehicle for distinguishing between cognitive and experiential deficits as basic causes for specific reading disability. *Journal of Educational Psychology, 88,* 601–638.

Vukelich, C., Christie, J. F., & Enz, B. (2002). *Helping young children learn language and literacy.* Boston, MA: Allyn and Bacon.

Wagner, R. K., & Torgesen, J. K. (1987). The nature of phonological processing and its causal role in the acquisition of reading skills. *Psychological Bulletin, 101,* 192–212.

Weaver, C. (1990). *Understanding whole language.* Portsmouth, NH: Heinemann.

Whitehurst, G. J., & Lonigan, C. J. (1998). Child development and emergent literacy. *Child Development, 69,* 848–872.

Wolery, M., Ault, M. J., & Doyle, P. (1992). *Teaching students with moderate to severe disabilities: Use of response prompting strategies.* White Plains, NY: Longman.

13

Interventions for Developing Reading Comprehension

Christine E. Neddenriep

Learning to read is arguably the most emphasized skill in schools today. Educators, researchers, political figures, parents, and many other individuals invest time and resources to ensure children learn to read. Such individuals may become very concerned when a child struggles to learn to read, as we know children who demonstrate poor reading skills at the end of third grade are likely to continue to struggle with reading throughout their education (Good, Simmons, & Smith, 1998). In fact, the gap between good readers' and poor readers' skills continues to widen as these students get older, making the challenge to help the poor readers catch up more difficult even as early as the end of first grade (Good et al., 1998; Juel, 1988; Stanovich, 1986). Sadly, the effects of early reading failure multiply and predict negative outcomes academically, socially, and emotionally for children (Reschly, 2010; Terras, Thompson, & Minnis, 2009). Researchers have examined an abundance of instructional strategies designed to develop early literacy skills, as these skills form a necessary *foundation* for reading success (National Early Literacy Panel, 2008). Yet, the essence of learning to read and the reason children are taught to decode, to read fluently, and to understand words is to achieve the greater goal of taking away meaning from the written text (Durkin, 1993). In other words, the goal of reading is to understand what the author is conveying through words.

Being able to understand what one reads is an essential skill in the world today, and increasingly a prerequisite for employment (Snow, Burns, & Griffin, 1998). The individual who cannot comprehend written text is at a great disadvantage. The U.S. economy now demands a higher level of literacy achievement, and the requisite level is likely to continue to increase in the future (RAND Reading Study Group [RRSG], 2002).

Given the increased requirements, one might ask how current students' comprehension skills line up with these demands. The most recent results from the 2011 National Assessment of Educational Progress (NAEP) Reading Assessment, a national measure of reading achievement, indicate that only 34% of fourth-grade students are at or above a "proficient" level and 67% are at or above a "basic" level of reading. In other words, by NAEP definitions, one in three fourth-grade students appear to lack the requisite reading comprehension skills fundamental to proficient work at their grade level (National Center for Education Statistics

[NCES], 2011). National student reading achievement scores have remained stubbornly stable over time across grade levels despite the significant and continual improvement in math scores of the same students (NCES, 2011). Similarly, reading scores of high school students have failed to show growth over the past 20 years, with the reading achievement of twelfth-grade students having regrettably decreased by four points since 1992 (National Center for Education Statistics [NCES], 2009).

Given these national statistics, action is required to ensure students acquire reading comprehension skills. To address this, this chapter will provide a background context for understanding what reading comprehension is and how and why it varies across individuals. Further, why reading comprehension is important as well as how, when, and where to teach reading comprehension strategies will be explained. Finally, a discussion of evidence-based reading comprehension strategies used before, during, and after reading to ensure understanding will be presented, as well as a case study to illustrate implementation and evaluation of an intervention.

Understanding Reading Comprehension
What Is Reading Comprehension?

Various definitions of reading comprehension have been proposed. Key elements of these definitions describe reading comprehension as a complex, multifaceted task requiring active and purposeful thinking to create meaning from text (Durkin, 1993; National Institute of Child Health and Human Development [NICHHD], 2000). The act of comprehending requires give-and-take between the individual and the text. Individuals purposefully read and meaningfully connect their background knowledge with the text, asking and answering questions and taking away a unique understanding of the content.

Reading comprehension is frequently referred to as the invisible curriculum—meaning these are strategies that students are expected to implicitly master, given their individual initiative and the opportunity to read. As well, these skills are not necessarily taught within the classroom, as educators have traditionally viewed reading comprehension as the expected result of effective early reading instruction (Neufeld, 2005). Given the complex, multifaceted nature of the task, however, the act of merely reading alone has been found to be inadequate for reading comprehension (Pressley & Wharton-McDonald, 1997). Explicit strategy instruction is essential (NICHHD, 2000).

What Factors Influence Reading Comprehension?

Reading comprehension can vary depending on the reader, the text, and the question type (Eason, Goldberg, Young, Geist, & Cutting, 2012; RRSG, 2002). The following sections will discuss these differing influences.

Reader. When making recommendations about how to teach students to understand what they read, one should recognize the differing skills, abilities, and competencies students possess that play a role in comprehension. Background information and worldly knowledge are exceedingly important to reading comprehension (Hirsh, 2003).

Background knowledge. As children read, they connect their background knowledge to the words in the text building links to fill in informational gaps left unspoken by the author (McNamara & Kintsch, 1996). Filling in these gaps results in a complete mental depiction of the text and improves literal and inferential comprehension (Brandao & Oakhill, 2005).

Research has shown that the more prior knowledge individuals possess the better they comprehend (Taft & Leslie, 1985), and having sufficient prior knowledge can make up for having poor reading ability allowing for comprehension (Recht & Leslie, 1988). Background knowledge has been found to be especially beneficial for comprehending expository text, the more complex content found in social studies and science classes (Best, Floyd, & McNamara, 2008). However, possessing the information alone has been found to be insufficient for comprehension. Individuals must actively relate what they know to the texts they are reading (Cain, Oakhill, Barnes, & Bryant, 2001). Thus, they must ask themselves what they know about that topic and how it might help them to understand what they are reading.

Vocabulary. In addition to background knowledge, sufficient word knowledge is necessary for fluent reading and serves as an essential tie to comprehension (Joshi, 2005). Specifically, the depth, or the richness of word knowledge uniquely contributes to reading comprehension over and above the skill of reading efficiently and accurately (Nation, Cocksey, Tayler, & Bishop, 2010; Ouellette, 2006; Riedel, 2007). This relationship is described as strong, positive, and reciprocal—an ever-increasing knowledge of words facilitates greater understanding of what is read; and, as the individual reads more challenging text, their knowledge of word meanings grows (NICHHD, 2000; Stahl & Fairbanks, 1986).

As early as second grade, deficits in vocabulary knowledge can inhibit reading; and, beginning in third grade, children require an increasingly large vocabulary to comprehend grade-level material (Biemiller & Slonim, 2001). By analyzing representative reading material from the classrooms of children in grades three through nine, researchers have found these materials to contain approximately 88,500 distinct words (Nagy & Anderson, 1984). This number is staggering. Whereas children may be able to decode and correctly identify these words, they likely do not understand the word's meaning in context if they do not have prior knowledge of the word. Recognizing the word in context is not enough for comprehension; children must understand the word's meaning in order to comprehend (Biemiller, 2006).

Differences in children's vocabulary knowledge at a young age are striking, and these deficits continuously impact children as they progress in school. Differences prior to the age of four primarily reflect variation in the total number of words spoken in the home by parents. Hart and Risley (1995) found that young children from families of lower socioeconomic status (SES) heard 8 million words less per year than children from families of higher SES. As well, they found that young children from families of lower SES acquire words at a much slower rate than do children from families of higher SES, resulting in a significant gap upon entering school.

In school, this gap persists. By the end of second grade, children have acquired approximately 5,200 root words; however, the children in the lower vocabulary quartile know 2,000 fewer root words than do children in the average quartile and 4,100 fewer root words than do the children in the highest vocabulary quartile (Biemiller & Slonim, 2001). This gap cannot be closed implicitly by simply having students read more, as children typically learn the meanings of only five to 15 words out of approximately 100 words they encounter in text (Swanburn & de Glopper, 1999). Text comprehension is improved if the written word is a known word within the student's spoken vocabulary. Thus, explicit vocabulary instruction is essential to close the gap and increase the likelihood of students understanding what they read.

Reading fluency. Vocabulary contributes both to reading fluency and to reading comprehension. Reading fluency—the ability to read efficiently, accurately, and with expression is necessary to comprehend, but reading fluency alone is not enough to ensure understanding (Pikulski & Chard, 2005). Whereas many students who have become proficient in reading fluently at third grade will continue to develop sufficient reading comprehension skill, others will not. Correlations describe the relationship between oral reading fluency and reading comprehension as moderate to strong (Martson, 1989; Neddenriep, Hale, Skinner, Hawkins, & Winn, 2007; Riedel, 2007), demonstrating a fairly robust association but not a causal one. This positive correlation is explained theoretically by automaticity theory—as decoding becomes effortless and reading occurs with ease, cognitive resources are accessible for connecting the words with individuals' background knowledge and creating meaning from text (LaBerge & Samuels, 1974). Fluent readers also take the initiative to read more challenging and varied content. As a result, they are more likely to come into contact with more unfamiliar words, thereby increasing both vocabulary and comprehension (Beck, McKeown, & Kucan, 2002). Reading fluency, therefore, serves as a necessary foundation for future growth.

Higher-order cognitive abilities. To comprehend, students need the foundational skills discussed above. These reading skills are typically emphasized in elementary reading programs, and teachers frequently target them effectively for intervention. As students progress and encounter more complex text, higher-order cognitive abilities are increasingly required (Cain, Oakhill, & Bryant, 2004; Eason et al., 2012). These abilities include: (1) working memory, the ability to keep information available for short-term use; (2) inferring meaning from text; (3) planning and organizing; (3) reasoning; and (4) metacognition, the ability to monitor and check for understanding when reading. Across studies, these abilities consistently distinguish children with strong reading comprehension skills from those with weak reading comprehension skills (Cain et al., 2001; Cain et al., 2004; Cain, Oakhill, & Lemmon, 2004). Readers who effectively use these abilities successfully bring together information from across the text and combine it with their knowledge to understand the whole content. These abilities may be more or less important given the nature of the text read and the type of question answered. Discussion regarding the role of text and question type follows.

Text. The structure of text differs depending on the type of content. Within the early elementary school curriculum, children develop phonemic awareness, decoding skills, and begin to develop reading fluency through reading connected text—primarily narrative stories (NICHHD, 2000). These stories have a predictable structure. This structure is also referred to as story grammar (Dimino, Gersten, Carnine, & Blake, 1990). The author introduces the setting of the story, the main characters, initiating events, and sets up a conflict or a problem to be resolved. Recognizing this predictable pattern helps readers to understand and make sense of the plot. Generally, narrative text is easier to comprehend, relying more on reading words accurately than on use of higher-order cognitive abilities (Best et al., 2008).

Beyond third grade, children begin to additionally read expository texts—nonfiction material about animals, science, history, crafts, or even how to make and keep friends. The structure of the expository text is much more varied and complex differing with the content area (RRSG, 2002). As well, expository text is more likely to contain unfamiliar vocabulary specific to the content area. When reading expository texts, readers identify important points, the logical order of the text, and the conclusion to facilitate comprehension. Students also learn to infer relationships within the text, such as cause-and-effect, compare-and-contrast, and problem-solution. As such, comprehension of expository text has been found to be more dependent on world knowledge (Best et al., 2008) and require higher-order cognitive abilities, such as inferring meaning, reasoning, planning, and organizing (Eason et al., 2012). These abilities differ depending on question type, as well.

Question type. When referring to comprehension questions, two types are frequently cited—literal and inferential. Literal comprehension questions typically ask who, what, where, and when; the answers to these questions are generally found in the text. Inferential questions may require analysis or synthesis of content, asking how or why; or, they may require more hypothetical thinking asking what if. Answers to inferential questions require thinking beyond the text. As a result, literal comprehension questions are predictably easier to answer than are inferential questions: Literal questions require looking back to the text to recall information, whereas inferential questions require integration of information from the text with background information (Brandao & Oakhill, 2005; Eason et al., 2012). Stronger readers generally recognize when the text is sufficient to answer the question and when use of their background information in conjunction with the text is necessary to infer meaning. Accordingly, responding to inferential questions requires the higher-order thinking abilities of inferring meaning, reasoning, planning, and organizing (Eason et al., 2012).

Why Is Reading Comprehension Important?

Reading comprehension is the "essence" of reading (Durkin, 1993), an essential skill for success not only in school but also in all areas of life (Reschly, 2010). Our educational system expects that students are able to decode fluently and to comprehend material with challenging content (Alvermann, 2002); as such, reading is required in a variety of subject areas, including math, history, science, and geography. Failure to develop adequate reading comprehension skills predicts negative outcomes academically (RRSG, 2002). As well, lack of success in reading in elementary school is associated with behavior problems and the delay of social skills development in later years (Malecki & Elliott, 2002; Terras et al., 2009). Furthermore, difficulty with reading is one of the primary reasons why students are recommended for grade retention or are referred for special education evaluation, events that are consistently linked to dropping out of school and being unemployed (Reschly, 2010). Clearly, deficits in reading comprehension put children at increased risk for a variety of negative outcomes. To prevent these deficits, reading comprehension strategies must be taught.

How Are Reading Comprehension Strategies Taught?

Comprehension strategies are specific procedures that call readers' attention to their understanding of text (NICCHD, 2000). Researchers have found that good readers continually use strategies to track their understanding of text, to identify when they fail to understand, and to relate text to their prior knowledge (Boulware-Gooden, Carreker, Thornhill, & Joshi, 2007). Students' strategy use is an intentional process of choosing the most appropriate strategy and exercising it as needed. This explanation aligns well with the definition of reading comprehension. If comprehension is an active, complex, and intentional process, then it seems logical that comprehension strategy use would be similar.

Whereas strong readers use a variety of strategies they have learned through trial and error and the practice of reading, weaker readers do not. All readers can be taught to use these strategies by explicitly demonstrating their use in the context of reading and learning (Santa, 2000). Students do not learn comprehension strategies simply by reading assigned text and responding to comprehension questions. Effective strategy instruction requires a direct explanation of the strategy, modeling of the strategy paired with extensive practice opportunities, and application across a variety of text (NICHHD, 2000). Explicitness of strategy instruction is linked to improved learning outcomes, especially for low-achieving students (Manset-Williamson & Nelson, 2005).

As an example, a teacher wants to teach the strategy of comprehension monitoring. The teacher is instructing students in literature and reading Shakespeare. The teacher would first explain why the strategy is important and when to use it. The teacher might explain that Shakespeare wrote differently for poetic and dramatic purposes. He arranged words in an atypical order, he omitted some words, and he also used some unusual words. As a result of the explanation, students expect the text to be unusual, and they recognize the importance of reading carefully to check for understanding.

The teacher would next model how to use the strategy by reading aloud to the class while thinking out loud. For example, a teacher reads aloud a passage from *Julius Caesar* and demonstrates how to stop when something is not clear, "Friends, Romans, countrymen, lend me your ears; I come to bury Caesar, not to praise him." The teacher then models how to clarify the information using the strategy (Santa, 2000). For example, the teacher might say out loud, "Mark Antony appears to be appealing to the crowd to listen to him as he speaks at his friend, Caesar's funeral." Thus, the students directly see and hear an example of how and when the strategy can be used. The key is to model the strategy aloud for the students enough times that it makes sense and students feel confident attempting to use it.

The third step is to provide guided practice (NICHHD, 2000). At this time, students have an opportunity to work in groups or with partners to try the strategy using the same think-aloud narration. Working with peers allows students to practice and critique the strategy used, to give and to receive feedback while being closely monitored and supported by the teacher. Talking about the process is critical to understanding and using it (Santa, 2000).

Finally, the students are given the opportunity to repeatedly practice applying the strategy to various passages of text. Students should be given ample time to practice using the strategy and to identify when to use the strategy before instruction proceeds to a new strategy. Providing numerous examples of how and when the strategy can be applied with guided support is essential before allowing independent practice (RRSG, 2002).

When and Where Are Reading Comprehension Strategies Taught?

When and where should reading comprehension instruction occur in schools to maximize its effectiveness? Instruction should start early and occur in all relevant classes, not just during reading or English class. What is meant by early? Typically, reading comprehension is emphasized in the later elementary grades once word recognition is established. However, comprehension of text should be integrated into early reading instruction and begin as early as preschool, with support and development of oral language, vocabulary, and listening comprehension (RRSG, 2002).

In later elementary school, reading comprehension instruction is commonly found in reading classes. Textbook publishers provide reading comprehension materials to support reading instruction (Santa, 2000). However, reading comprehension is less likely to be found in classrooms where teachers are focused on content. This lack of direct comprehension instruction was initially observed in social studies classrooms in grades three through six (Durkin, 1978–1979). Within these classrooms, little reading comprehension instruction was observed; teachers were observed to assess comprehension by merely asking questions. More recent observations of classrooms have yielded similar results finding that teachers may mention a strategy and suggest students use it but fail to tell students how and why to use the strategy (Neufeld, 2005; Pressley, Wharton-McDonald, Mistretta-Hampston, & Echevarria, 1998). This observation is unfortunate, given that classes such as science and the social sciences are ideal settings for instruction. These classes provide a clear purpose for comprehension (e.g., How do Presidents differ in their decision-making styles?), which serves as a foundation for conceptual understanding permitting application and extension of theories across subject areas (e.g., How can Freudian theory of psychoanalysis explain presidential decision-making styles?).

Reading Comprehension Interventions

We have established that effective readers use a variety of intentional strategies to understand what they are reading, never relying on a single method. These strategies can be explicitly taught to struggling readers to improve their grasp of the text. Reading comprehension interventions provide readers with a plan to approach the content, methods to use while reading, and techniques to reflect on what has been read to ensure understanding of both narrative and expository text. Figure 13.1 outlines these reading comprehension strategies and organizes them by type of content and time of use. These strategies are discussed in more detail within the following sections. We have also established that certain

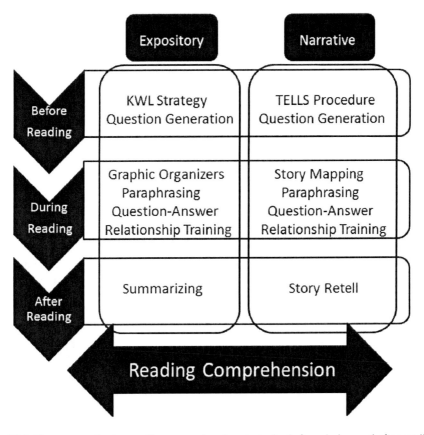

Figure 13.1 The process of using reading comprehension strategies before, during, and after reading to support understanding of expository and narrative text

skills need to be in place prior to reading to increase the likelihood readers understand what they are reading. Instructional strategies to teach these essential skills are reviewed first.

Prereading Strategies

Choose texts at an instructional level. In order to read and understand text, the content must be appropriately challenging (i.e., not too difficult and not too easy). This appropriate degree of challenge is referred to as a student's instructional level, a level at which instruction can most easily proceed. Instructional criteria have been described in terms of both speed and accuracy (Deno & Mirkin, 1977; Gickling & Armstrong, 1978). For students in third through sixth grades, text is at an instructional level if the student correctly reads between 70 and 100 words in 1 minute and the student accurately recognizes 93% to 97% of the words (Gickling & Thompson, 1985). For independent reading, the student should be able to accurately recognize 97% or more of the words in the text and should be able to read more than 100 words correctly in 1 minute. Texts should be carefully chosen with these criteria in mind.

Teach prerequisite skills. As previously mentioned, fluency and word knowledge are foundational skills for reading comprehension. If deficits exist in these areas, instructional strategies should be implemented to increase these skills.

Fluency interventions. Several reading interventions have been found to effectively increase reading fluency, as well as comprehension including repeated readings (O'Shea, Sindelar, & O'Shea, 1985; Sindelar, Monda, & O'Shea, 1990), listening while reading (Rose, 1984; Rose & Beattie, 1986), and phrase drill error correction (O'Shea, Munson, & O'Shea, 1984). The repeated readings strategy ensures sufficient practice by having the student repeatedly read aloud short, meaningful passages (e.g., 100 words) three to four times to an adult. This technique has been found to increase both fluency and comprehension of passages repeatedly read as well as passages not previously read (Therrien, 2004). Similarly, within the listening while reading intervention, the teacher or a more competent peer reads an instructional-level passage aloud and the student follows along silently. The student then reads the passage. Modeling has been found to be especially helpful in improving comprehension, as it allows the student to focus on the content prior to reading (Chard, Vaughn, & Tyler, 2002). Finally, within phrase drill error correction, the student reads the passage to an adult; the adult follows along and underlines errors. The teacher then shows the student the error words. The teacher says each error word correctly and prompts the student to reread correctly each phrase/sentence containing the error word three times: "This word is 'relaxing.' What word? Yes, 'relaxing.' Now read this phrase with the word 'relaxing' three times—'the relaxing music . . .'" This strategy is especially beneficial as it provides accurate practice within connected text. This accurate practice increases the likelihood of reading the word correctly in subsequent text, as opposed to merely practicing the word in isolation (Daly & Martens, 1994). This strategy is also recommended as a component within repeated reading interventions (Chard et al., 2002).

Key word interventions. In order for students to comprehend text, they must possess knowledge of the words: all of the words must be familiar to a child if spoken or read to them (Biemiller, 2006). Word identification is not sufficient. Preteaching these words increases reading comprehension. Most commonly, students are taught content vocabulary by the assignment of a word list; students are then expected to look up the definitions of these words, write the definitions, and use the words in sentences. Unfortunately, this is an ineffective use of students' time, as it only supports definitional knowledge (Rupley, 2005). Several evidence-based strategies exist to preteach vocabulary such that students make meaningful connections with their background knowledge and draw associations that support their learning and retention of new vocabulary.

Word webs or semantic maps. Word webs or semantic maps provide a visual illustration of the meaning of a word and its relationship to other concepts (Schwartz & Raphael, 1985). Word webs can be used to introduce words prior to reading expository or narrative text. To construct a word web, three questions are asked: "What is it?" "What is it like?" "What are some examples of it?" Students then respond to those questions as they complete the word web. If we used reading comprehension strategies as an example, we might say that reading comprehension strategies are procedures for understanding (a general descriptor). When we ask, "What is it like?" we are asking the student to identify properties of the concept that distinguish it from other similar ideas. Examples of properties might include knowledge of text, monitoring for understanding, and relating text to background knowledge. Some examples of reading comprehension strategies might include paraphrasing, story mapping, and question generation. A teacher may also ask for nonexamples, requiring the student to distinguish between the example and the nonexample. See Figure 13.2 for the example word map illustrating the concept, reading comprehension strategies. Similarly, semantic maps help to illustrate the relationship between current concepts and previously known words (Rupley, 2005). Thus, using the example of reading comprehension strategies, a semantic

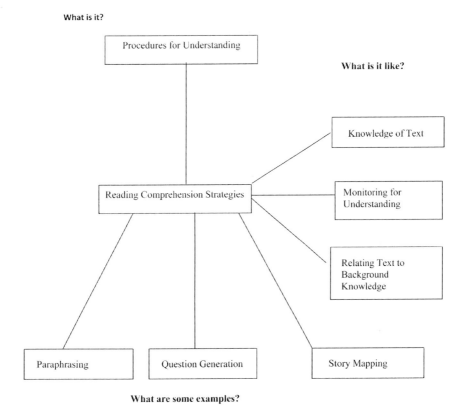

Figure 13.2 Word map example

map may illustrate the relationship between reading fluency, vocabulary, background information, and reading comprehension strategies. The map may further detail properties and examples of each concept.

Word sorts. A word sort is an activity in which students are given a list of 10 to 20 key vocabulary words from a reading selection and are asked to organize them into categories. They are asked to complete the task in small groups of four to five students and may be provided 10 to 15 minutes to do so. The sorting task affords students the opportunity to clarify their understanding of key concepts by requiring them to identify similarities and differences as they compare and contrast the words. In doing so, they recognize common relationships between core concepts and establish meaningful connection to their background knowledge (Beck et al., 2002; Templeton, Bear, Invernizzi, & Johnston, 2009).

A sort can be closed or open. For a closed word sort, the teacher provides students with the categories into which they will sort the vocabulary words (e.g., democratic government and autocratic government). For an open word sort, the categories are not given. Students are instructed to suggest categories for organizing the words. An open sort requires a greater level of analysis in distinguishing the characteristics among the words. Once the sorting is complete, a whole class discussion occurs, with each group presenting their word list for one of the categories. Students are expected to support their sorting of terms by identifying the common features of the categories and how each specific word meets these criteria. The students are creating a definitional rule for the category. The sorting can be done with words chosen from both narrative and expository text.

The word sort strategy is based on the word study approach (Bear, Invernizzi, Templeton, & Johnston, 2012), which provides students with a structured opportunity to discover common sounds, spelling patterns, and meanings. This approach has been shown to increase both phonemic awareness as well as spelling skill (Joseph, 2000; 2002). Adapting this analysis and categorization approach to understanding the meanings of words is a logical extension especially to preteach vocabulary in the content areas (Harmon, Hedrick, & Wood, 2005).

Peer-mediated constant time delay. A third way to preteach key words is to use the constant time delay (CTD) procedure. CTD provides an evidence-based method to increase content-area vocabulary knowledge in a peer tutoring format (Wannarka, Ruhl, & Kubina, in press). To implement this procedure, teachers select five to seven words from an assigned reading that are likely to be unfamiliar to the majority of students. These words should be key words that are essential to understanding the meaning of the content. Each word is written on one side of an index card and a simple definition is written on the back (no more than six words in length). Teachers provide each pair of students with a set of index cards. The student who is the tutor first reads the set of words, followed by the definition. The student repeats the word and definition. The tutor immediately corrects errors by providing the definition. Students switch roles and do the same. Next, the tutor provides the word followed by a pause up to 5 seconds. The 5-second pause allows the student time to respond. The tutor provides immediate feedback for each definition—praise for correct definitions and restating the definition correctly for errors. Students again switch roles, following the practice of the words. Students are directed to continue to practice the words until students define them with 100% accuracy. This strategy has been found to contribute to mastery of words in a shorter amount of time and with fewer errors than other similar practice methods (Hughes & Fredrick, 2006; McDonnell, Johnson, Polychronis, & Risen, 2002).

Teach prereading strategies. Prereading strategies are those methods used prior to reading to encourage reading in a more active and purposeful way. These strategies provide a structure for previewing the specific type of text read and prompt students to ask questions, which increases their awareness of and understanding of the text. These approaches also increase students' awareness of background knowledge they possess that is relevant to what they are reading. By recalling this information, readers have a basis for connecting new information to prior information. As well, these approaches teach students to generate higher-level questions, increasing their self-assessed understanding of the text.

TELLS procedure. The TELLS procedure (Idol-Maestas, 1985) is a prereading strategy used with narrative text. Prior to reading a story, students complete a TELLS worksheet which provides a structure for previewing the text (T, Title; E, Examine; L, Look; L, Look; S, Setting). Prior to using the worksheet, teachers model the use of the TELLS procedure. Teachers first ask students to read the title and to ask, "What do you think it is about?" By doing so, they are prompting students to make predictions, an inference about the author's intentions. Next, students are taught to examine the text, skimming the pages of the story for hints about the story. These hints may be found in the pictures, the text structure, or subtitles. Teachers may ask students, "What did you find?" Third, students are taught to look for important words that may be repeated within the text or printed in bold. Teachers prompt students to write them down and to ask, "What do they mean?" Fourth, students are taught to look for unfamiliar words—words they do not know. Teachers again prompt the students to write the words down and to ask, "What do they mean?" Finally, students are taught to scan the text for hints about the setting of the story—time and place. By reminding the students that these clues are likely to be at the beginning of the story, the teacher is reinforcing the student's knowledge of the story structure. Following the completion of the TELLS worksheet and using the information they have learned, students are asked to make a prediction about the story. The TELLS procedure thus incorporates asking and answering questions, making predictions, preteaching vocabulary, and activating background information as well as using knowledge of narrative text structure to enhance understanding. The TELLS procedure has been shown to increase comprehension for students using the procedure (Idol-Maestas, 1985; Ridge & Skinner, 2011). A shortcoming of this strategy is that some research indicates the strategy does not persist over time and does not transfer well to the reading of new stories.

KWL procedure. The KWL strategy is a student-centered strategy designed to activate students' background knowledge prior to reading expository text (Ogle, 1986). A chart is used with three columns. In the column labeled "K" the student brainstorms and records, "What I know about the topic." In the column labeled "W" the student records multiple ideas of, "What I want to know." In the column labeled "L" the student records, "What I learned." The final column is to be completed after reading the passage, as a check to ensure that the student's questions were answered. This strategy is especially useful in improving comprehension of expository text, as it helps students to recognize what they know as foundational knowledge and to monitor their learning to ensure that gaps are filled through reading the passage. Learning may extend beyond the reading if questions are left unanswered by the text. This technique has been effectively applied by elementary, secondary, and post-secondary teachers in a variety of subject areas (e.g., sciences, social studies, technology; Fritz, 2002; Jared & Jared, 1997; Shelley, Bridwell, Hyder, Ledford, & Patterson, 1997).

Question generation. One of the distinguishing characteristics of an engaged, self-directed learner is their tendency to ask a variety of questions (King, 1994). These questions provide a purpose and a guide for the learning process, such that comprehension is improved (NICHHD, 2000). The benefits of question generation are based on the premise that students learn how to answer questions better when they practice generating questions. Students may generate questions of various difficulty levels, such as factual questions taken directly from the text; conceptual questions, requiring an understanding/organization of concepts within the text; and, questions inferred or requiring elaboration from the text.

By teaching students to generate questions, their understanding of the conceptual quality of the question and the information required to answer the question improves. As well, their awareness of text increases such that their understanding of the text is enhanced (Davey & McBride, 1986; Taboada & Guthrie, 2006). For example, teaching a student to generate a story specific question such as, "Who is the main character?" teaches the student that each story has a primary figure around which the story develops, and information about the main character is usually described at the beginning of the story. By asking the question, readers are primed to recognize that information when reading. Similarly, teaching a student to ask a conceptual question frequently found in expository texts helps the student to look for how ideas interrelate and are categorized (e.g., "How are sleep and hibernation related?"). By teaching children to ask inferential questions, they recognize the need to go beyond the current text to access their background information in answering the question (e.g., "Why is it adaptive for some animals to hibernate in the winter and not for others?").

When children are trained to generate questions, their comprehension improves on the material read (both expository and narrative), and they effectively use the skill to improve comprehension of new material (Rosenshine, Meister, & Chapman, 1996). In addition, students trained to generate questions ask higher-level inferential questions, and they more accurately self-assess their understanding of what they are reading (Davey & McBride, 1986). One might ask whether question generation simply activates background knowledge. Question generation has been shown to uniquely contribute to reading comprehension above and beyond that of background information, such that question generation improves reading comprehension for individuals with less background information and those with more background information (Taboada & Guthrie, 2006).

Strategies During Reading

Strategies used while reading promote active monitoring of comprehension. These strategies provide a structure so that students distinguish essential from nonessential information in the text and organize the information to demonstrate how concepts and ideas relate. These approaches teach students the relationships between questions and answers, such that students ask and answer higher-level questions and recognize when the text is insufficient to answer the question. These strategies also prompt students to restate in their own words what they have read, which increases their self-assessed understanding of the text.

Story maps. A story map provides a visual representation of the essential elements of a story. As mentioned previously, narrative stories have a predictable pattern, referred to as story grammar (Dimino et al., 1990). Stories take place during a specific time and place; the author introduces characters who encounter a problem; events occur around a problem; and the problem is resolved. The story map illustrates each of these predictable elements and the relationships between the key concepts. By prompting students to use a story map, their attention is actively directed toward the text and comprehension and recall of the story is improved. Story maps have been effectively used with both elementary and secondary students with and without learning disabilities (Boulineau, Fore, Hagan-Burke, & Mack, 2004; Gardill & Jitendra, 1999). This strategy has also been shown to maintain gains over time and to transfer to the comprehension of novel stories read, as well.

As with other reading comprehension strategies, the use of the story map must be explicitly taught. A teacher first explains the essential elements of story grammar using a story map prepared in advance. Each element is specifically taught. The teacher then models the completion of a story map by thinking aloud while reading a story. Guided practice is then provided, encouraging students to read and reread the story to complete the story map accurately. The teacher immediately discusses and corrects errors to ensure accurate understanding. Additional story maps are provided to encourage students' independent practice.

Graphic organizers. Similar to story maps, graphic organizers provide a visual structure for organizing and relating main ideas and concepts. These visuals are used specifically with expository text and may include maps, webs, charts, clusters, outlines, or Venn diagrams. As discussed earlier, the structure of expository text is more complex. Readers must identify main points, organize the text, and draw conclusions to facilitate comprehension. Graphic organizers direct students' attention to important parts of expository text, helping students to organize the information and to make connections between parts of one text or multiple texts (Kim, Vaughn, Wanzek, & Wei, 2004). In addition, the organization may support readers in connecting their existing knowledge with the text, which is essential for understanding expository text (Best et al., 2008). Use of graphic organizers has resulted in increased reading comprehension for elementary and secondary students with and without learning disabilities (Gajria, Jitendra, Sood, & Sacks, 2007; Kim et al., 2004). However, maintenance of gains over time and transfer to newly read text has been limited for students with learning disabilities (Gajria et al., 2007; Kim et al., 2004).

In addition to providing structures visually to organize concepts and ideas, graphic organizers also reference key words specific to the type of text organized (Baker, Gersten, & Grossen, 2002). These key words are found within the text. Identifying these key words helps students to recognize the organizational structure of the text and the appropriate type of graphic organizer to visually represent the information (Neufeld, 2005). For example, descriptive text may be organized around key words, such as first, second, third, next, and finally. Identifying these key words helps students to put these ideas in order. Similarly, text comparing and contrasting ideas may include key words such as similarly, in contrast, as well as, and on the other hand. A text organized around a problem and solution may contain words such as cause, effect, leads to, and as a result. Students as young as second grade have been taught to use graphic organizers with key words to effectively comprehend expository text read as well as newly read text (Williams, Stafford, Lauer, Hall, & Pollini, 2009). As with story maps, teachers must explicitly model the use of graphic organizers and provide guided practice with immediate feedback.

Paraphrasing. Another effective strategy for increasing comprehension while reading is paraphrasing. Paraphrasing requires students to actively monitor their understanding by restating what they have read in their own words. It can be used with both expository and narrative text. Research shows that paraphrasing increases both students' recall of text as well as their understanding of main ideas. More specifically, the RAP paraphrasing strategy (Schumaker, Denton, & Deshler, 1984) has been effectively used to increase reading comprehension and recall of text in students as young as third grade (Hagaman, Casey, & Reid, 2012; Hagaman & Reid, 2008). RAP is an acronym identifying the three steps in the strategy. The first step is to Read the paragraph silently. Students are directed to think about what the words mean. After reading the paragraph, the second step is to Ask, "What were the main ideas and details of this paragraph?" Students are taught that the main idea is typically stated in the first sentence or expressed through the repetition of key words. They are also encouraged to reread the paragraph to help them find the main ideas and the details related to the main idea. The third step is to Paraphrase, to put the main idea and details in their own words. Doing so helps the student to remember the information and to connect it with their own knowledge. Students are prompted to give at least two details related to the main idea. Paraphrasing is effectively taught through modeling, guided practice, and feedback.

Question-Answer Relationship Training (QAR). QAR (Raphael & Au, 2005) is based on the idea that strong readers recognize what a question is asking, and the source of information needed to answer the question. QAR makes this often-hidden process more obvious to students by teaching them a common language to use across grades and subject areas. Students are first taught that information for answering questions comes either from the text or from the students' knowledge or experiences. This distinction is labeled as "in the book" versus "in my head," respectively. Questions that can be answered by looking "in the book" can be further distinguished as "right there" questions or "think and search" questions. "Right there" questions are literal questions that typically use the same words in text as those found in the question. Strategies required include recall and looking to the text for those similar words to locate the question. "Think and search" questions are also answered by information found in the text, but the questions are worded differently than the text and require students to bring together information from across the reading to answer the question. "In my head" questions are inferential questions for which the answers are not directly written in the text. They can be further distinguished as "author and me" questions and "on my own" questions. "Author and me" questions require students to think about what they have read and to connect clues from the reading with their own ideas, background information, and experience. "On my own" questions are answered exclusively using the students' ideas and experiences.

Students are progressively taught to recognize, generate, and answer these types of questions using preselected text and questions across multiple sessions. Teaching needs to be explicit by first introducing the students to the concept of question-answer relationships using several short passages to demonstrate the relationships. Teachers should provide the text, questions, answers, and the QAR label for each question. They should then think aloud and model the reason for why the label was appropriate. Students are then provided with practice by asking students to identify the QARs, to answer to the question, and to identify the strategy they used for finding the answer. Within the primary grades, students can learn to reliably distinguish between the "right there" and the "think and search" questions (Raphael & McKinney, 1983).

As students progress, the length of passages and the variety of reading materials may be increased. Fourth-grade general education students clearly distinguish among the four QAR questions (Raphael & Wonnacott, 1985). Generating questions in QAR is shown to improve students' ability to identify important information from the text, to monitor comprehension, to see relationships within text, to retell information learned, and to answer questions in students with and without disabilities (RRSG, 2002; Simmonds, 1992).

Strategies after Reading

Strategies used after reading are those strategies that prompt readers to continue to think about and reflect on what they have read. Good readers frequently reread parts of the text that were left unclear as they check for understanding. They also connect what they have read to their background knowledge as they summarize the main points or retell events within an expository or narrative text read (Pressley & Wharton-McDonald, 1997).

Story retell. Story retell is a strategy that more actively engages students in reading and extends learning by prompting them to recall what happened in a story that was heard or read (Morrow, 1986). Story retell has been associated with increases in literal and inferential comprehension, expressive vocabulary, and the number of story elements retold in children's stories (Gambrell, Koskinen, & Kapinus, 1991; Gambrell, Pfeiffer, & Wilson, 1985; Morrow, 1985; 1986). Whereas retell can be done orally or in written form, oral retell has been shown to be more efficient than written (Schisler, Joseph, Konrad, & Alber-Morgan, 2010).

To ensure accuracy of retells and to provide immediate feedback, the strategy can be implemented in a peer-tutoring format. Teachers assign students to pairs with similar reading levels for approximately four training sessions. Students are told that they will be reading a passage and paying attention to the most important ideas of the story. Students then read the passage silently. Teachers may then introduce an outline that includes prompting questions (e.g., Who are the main characters? What is the problem? How is the problem solved?). By the teacher providing these prompts, students are more likely to include more of the essential details with greater complexity within their retells (Morrow, 1986). Teachers prompt the students to write down their responses to the questions. Students then work in pairs to retell all the important ideas in the story. Pairs should reverse the order of retelling across sessions.

Summarizing. Summarizing is the process of determining the main points of a passage and restating it in one's own words. Good summaries are concise (20 words or less) and include key concepts and ideas. Looking for these key points forces students to delete unimportant items and get the "gist" of the text. Writing summaries has been shown to improve reading comprehension of expository text in students with and without disabilities (Armbruster, Anderson, & Ostertag, 1987; Bean & Steenwyk, 1984; Gajria & Salvia, 1992). Given the evidence base, the summary strategy is frequently incorporated within multi-strategy instructional programs as an essential component (e.g., Concept-Oriented Reading Instruction; Guthrie, McRae, & Klauda, 2007; Reciprocal Teaching; Palincsar & Brown, 1984; Transactional Strategy Instruction; Pressley & Wharton-McDonald, 1997).

In teaching students to write summaries, teachers may give students a checklist to evaluate the quality of their summaries. Prior to using the checklist, the teacher must teach the student to use it by modeling the strategy, providing guided practice, and offering feedback regarding performance. The checklist may include the following questions: Does the summary state the main idea? Is the main idea stated first? Does the summary give only the most important information? Is the summary brief with unimportant and redundant information deleted? Is the summary written clearly? (Boss & Vaughn, 2002). Offering this self-assessment tool provides students the opportunity to regulate their learning.

Case Study

The following case study illustrates the use of a reading comprehension intervention to improve understanding of expository text. Specifically, this case study incorporates the assessment of reading comprehension rate and the evaluation of Question-Answer Relationship Training to improve understanding of social studies and science text.

Jenny is a fourth-grade student at Jefferson Elementary School. Her teacher, Mrs. Jones, sought the consultation of the school psychologist, Mr. Thomas, as she noticed that Jenny read fluently in fourth-grade text; however, she had difficulty comprehending what she read. Specifically, Jenny read a median of 95 words correct per minute with two errors in the fall of fourth grade, putting her at low risk for reading difficulties. With regard to reading comprehension, Mrs. Jones had observed that Jenny had more difficulty understanding what she read in science and social studies text than she did with literature or math text. Given that Jenny was reading fluently in fourth-grade text, Mr. Thomas, the school psychologist, offered to assess Jenny's reading comprehension rate in literature, science, and social studies text. Several studies have begun to investigate the validity of reading comprehension rate as a more sensitive and valid indicator of reading comprehension (e.g., Neddenriep, Hale, Skinner, Hawkins, & Winn, 2007). Reading comprehension rate reflects comprehension accuracy as a rate measure. This rate measure is calculated by dividing the percentage of comprehension questions answered correctly by the time in seconds to read the passage. The quotient is then multiplied by 60 seconds, resulting in the percentage of a passage comprehended per minute. Reading comprehension rate is assessed by using 400-word passages from the *Timed Readings* series (Spargo, 1989), which contains 10 multiple-choice comprehension questions—five literal and five inferential. Mr. Thomas used passages from *Timed Readings in Literature, Social Studies, and Science* to assess Jenny's reading comprehension rate in each. In literature passages, Jenny comprehended 28% of the passage per minute; however, in social studies and science she comprehended 14.25% and 17.35%, respectively. As a result, Mr. Thomas confirmed that Jenny's rate of understanding of literature text was more similar to her peers, and her comprehension of science and social studies was discrepant from her understanding of literature. Mr. Thomas collected two additional data points, determining her rate of understanding in science and social studies text to establish a stable baseline. After Jenny completed the baseline assessment, Mr. Thomas asked her to tell him how she had answered the questions. In listening to her responses, he noticed that Jenny had difficulty understanding what the question was asking and what information was necessary to answer the question. She frequently indicated that she had guessed.

Given these observations, Mr. Thomas recommended that Mrs. Jones implement Question-Answer Relationship Training, first in science class and then in social studies class. Mr. Thomas assisted Mrs. Jones in preparing science and social studies passages of sufficient length, reading comprehension questions, and the QAR labels for each question. Per recommended procedures described previously, Mrs. Jones introduced the concept of QAR in science and taught Jenny and the students in her class to distinguish among the four QAR questions. Mrs. Jones modeled her thinking aloud and provided the reason for why the label was appropriate. She then provided practice by asking students to identify the QARs, to answer the questions, and to identify the strategy they used for finding the answer. She provided this guided practice with feedback over the next four school days. After one week of training in science, Mr. Thomas again assessed Jenny's reading comprehension rate in science and also continued to assess her reading comprehension rate in social studies text not previously read. While training continued in science over the next 5 weeks, Mr. Thomas continued to assess Jenny's progress in both science and social studies weekly. He graphed her data so that he and Mrs. Jones could determine if the intervention was improving Jenny's ability to understand what she read in science. Once they had collected sufficient data to determine that an increase in reading comprehension rate had corresponded with the implementation of the QAR procedure in science, Mrs. Jones then implemented the QAR procedure in social studies. Mr. Thomas continued to evaluate Jenny's response to intervention in both science and social studies weekly, using a multiple baseline design. By introducing the intervention at different times across two different content areas, Mr. Thomas was able to determine that the change in reading comprehension rate coincided with the introduction of the intervention to that content area and was, therefore, due to the intervention. This method is referred to as a multiple baseline design across settings (Riley-Tillman & Walcott, 2007). See Figure 13.3 displaying the graphed data.

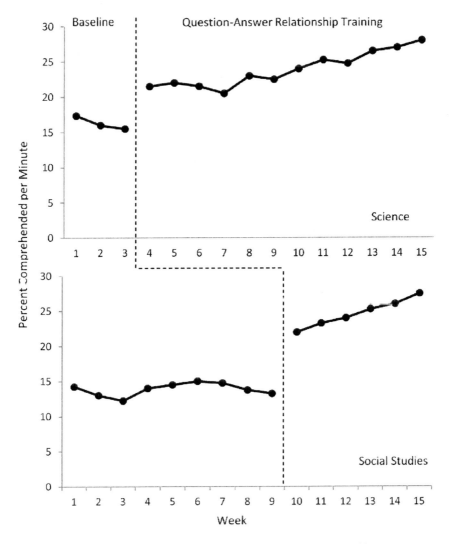

Figure 13.3 Jenny's response to Question-Answer Relationship Training across subject areas

Conclusions and Recommendations

Reading comprehension is a complex, multifaceted task that is dependent on many skills and abilities. Word knowledge, background information, fluency, and higher-order cognitive skills are essential to the development of reading comprehension. Their presence alone, however, does not ensure the development of reading comprehension. Strong readers effectively use a variety of strategies before, during, and after reading to actively engage with the text, to generate questions about the reading, to identify when they fail to understand, and to relate text to their prior knowledge. All readers benefit from explicit instruction in these strategies, such that the process of comprehension is engaged in intentionally with the reader monitoring their understanding and using strategies to guide their thinking appropriate to the nature of the text and type of questions asked. The explicit nature of instruction is especially important for students with learning disabilities (Gersten, Fuchs, Williams, & Baker, 2001).

If comprehension is an active, complex, and intentional process, then it seems logical that educators would consciously engage in a concerted effort to develop these skills throughout students' academic careers. Whereas comprehension instruction may typically start in the primary grades once word reading is established, the research suggests that instruction may begin as early as preschool with the development of oral language, vocabulary, and listening comprehension that are essential to the development of comprehension. The research also suggests that strategy instruction may occur at the same time students are developing word-reading skill. Many early literacy curricula incorporate reading comprehension strategies with word-reading instruction, as students learn to preview a text by looking at the pictures, to make predictions, and to retell what they have read (e.g., Paths to Early Literacy Success; Mathes, Allor, Torgesen, & Allen, 2001). As well, instruction should occur in all content area classes (e.g., math, social studies, science, health, etc.). These courses are the ideal setting for instruction, as there is a clear purpose for comprehension—conceptual understanding is essential for students' application of the skill in the setting in which students will continually use the skill.

Effective strategy instruction in the content areas involves more than solely teaching strategies. Research suggests that strategies are more likely to be used and understood when they are taught within the process of reading and learning. Multiple strategies should be taught for use before, during, and after reading. Sufficient time should be devoted to directly teaching each strategy, providing a rationale for why the strategy is useful, modeling the use of the strategy while reading the text, providing guided practice opportunities, and offering sufficient opportunity for independent practice with feedback so that the strategy is used accurately. Practice opportunities with feedback may be efficiently provided within peer-tutoring formats. As well, peers may model higher-level thinking, generate alternative questions, and offer unique background knowledge individual to their experience. Effective strategy instruction engages the learner such that they are motivated to read and persist in reading. Engaging the student may be accomplished by selecting text that is at an instructional level and providing choice of materials to read, as appropriate.

The research offers a range of comprehension strategies to employ with a solid empirical base. However, there are still limitations within the literature on which to extend the research. The current database is largely founded on small sample sizes, short interventions, and short-term comprehension gains. As well, some of the research is anecdotal from classroom observations. Further research is needed on a larger scale that demonstrates a causal relationship between the intervention and the change in comprehension, and assesses maintenance and generalization of these gains to newly read materials. As well, some strategies have been shown to be effective with typical students, but not with students with learning disabilities. Additional research is needed with a range of students, including students with learning disabilities and students who are English Language Learners. Finally, as we more intentionally support students' comprehension in the content areas, future research should evaluate the effectiveness of these strategies with secondary students in differing content areas.

Large-scale research is important to demonstrate "what works" with regard to reading comprehension strategies, as well as "when it works." Establishing an intervention's efficacy and effectiveness is key to building an evidence-base of interventions that can be generalized to the school setting (Detrich, Keyworth, & States, 2007). Additional examples of interventions implemented in the schools and continuously progress monitored are essential in making defensible conclusions about an individual student's response to intervention (Riley-Tillman & Burns, 2009). The case study in this chapter illustrates the effectiveness of an intervention for an individual student across subject areas. Both types of research are needed to further our understanding of reading comprehension interventions that are effective, efficient, acceptable, and easily incorporated within instruction to benefit all children.

References

Alvermann, D. E. (2002). Effective literacy instruction for adolescents. *Journal of Literacy Research, 34,* 189–208.

Armbruster, B. B., Anderson, T. H., & Ostertag, J. (1987). Does text structure/summarization instruction facilitate learning from expository text? *Reading Research Quarterly, 22,* 331–346.

Baker, S., Gersten, R., & Grossen, B. (2002). Interventions for students with reading comprehension problems. In M. R. Shinn, H. M. Walker, & G. Stoner (Eds.), *Interventions for academic and behavior problems II: Preventive and remedial approaches* (pp. 731–754). Bethesda, MD: National Association of School Psychologists.

Bean, T. W., & Steenwyk, E. L. (1984). The effect of three forms of summarization instruction on sixth graders' summary writing and comprehension. *Journal of Reading Behavior, 16,* 297–306.

Bear, D. R., Invernizzi, M. A., Templeton, S., & Johnston, F. (2012). *Words their way: Word study for phonics, vocabulary, and spelling instruction* (5th ed.). Boston, MA: Pearson.

Beck, I. L., McKeown, M. G., & Kucan, L. (2002). *Bringing words to life: Robust vocabulary instruction.* New York, NY: Guilford Press.

Best, R. M., Floyd, R. G., & McNamara, D. S. (2008). Differential competencies contributing to children's comprehension of narrative and expository texts. *Reading Psychology, 29,* 137–164. doi:10.1080/02702710801963951

Biemiller, A. (2006). Vocabulary development and instruction: A prerequisite for school learning. In D. K. Dickinson & S. B. Neuman (Eds.), *Handbook of early literacy research* (Vol. 2, pp. 41–51). New York, NY: Guilford Press.

Biemiller, A., & Slonim, N. (2001). Estimating root word vocabulary growth in normative and advantaged populations: Evidence for a common sequence of vocabulary acquisition. *Journal of Educational Psychology, 93,* 498–520. doi: 10.1037//0022–0663.93.3.498

Boss, C. S., & Vaughn, S. (2002). *Strategies for teaching students with learning and behavioral problems.* Needham Heights, MA: Allyn and Bacon.

Boulineau, T., Fore, C., Hagan-Burke, S., & Mack D. (2004). Use of story-mapping to increase the story-grammar text comprehension of elementary students with learning disabilities. *Learning Disability Quarterly, 27,* 105–121.

Boulware-Gooden, R., Carreker, S., Thornhill, A., & Joshi, R. M. (2007). Instruction of metacognitive strategies enhances reading comprehension and vocabulary achievement of third-grade students. *The Reading Teacher, 61,* 70–77. doi: 10.1598/RT.61.1.7

Brandao, A. C. P., & Oakhill, J. (2005). "How do you know this answer?" Children's use of text data and general knowledge in story comprehension. *Reading and Writing, 18,* 687–713. doi: 10.1007/s11145–005–5600-x

Cain, K., Oakhill, J. V., Barnes, M. A., & Bryant, P. E. (2001). Comprehension skill, inference making ability and their relation to knowledge. *Memory Cognition, 29,* 850–859.

Cain, K., Oakhill, J., & Bryant, P. (2004). Children's reading comprehension ability: Concurrent prediction by working memory, verbal ability, and component skills. *Journal of Educational Psychology, 96,* 31–42. doi: 10.1037/0022–0663.96.1.31

Cain, K., Oakhill, J., & Lemmon, K. (2004). Individual differences in the inference of word meanings from context: The influence of reading comprehension, vocabulary knowledge, and memory capacity. *Journal of Educational Psychology, 96,* 671–681.

Chard, D. J., Vaughn, S., & Tyler, B. (2002). A synthesis of research on effective interventions for building reading fluency with elementary students with learning disabilities. *Journal of Learning Disabilities, 35,* 386–406.

Daly III, E. J., & Martens, B. K. (1994). A comparison of three interventions for increasing oral reading performance: Application of the instructional hierarchy. *Journal of Applied Behavior Analysis, 27,* 459–469.

Davey, B., & McBride, S. (1986). Effects of question-generation training on reading comprehension. *Journal of Educational Psychology, 78,* 256–262.

Deno, S. L., & Mirkin, P. K. (1977). *Data-based problem modification: A manual.* Reston, VA: Council for Exceptional Children.

Detrich, R., Keyworth, R., & States, J. (2007). A roadmap to evidence-based education: Building an evidence-based culture. *Journal of Evidence-Based Practices for Schools, 8,* 26–44.

Dimino, J., Gersten, R., Carnine, D., & Blake, G. (1990). Story grammar: An approach for promoting at-risk secondary students' comprehension of literature. *The Elementary School Journal, 91,* 19–32.

Durkin, D. (1978–1979). What classroom observation reveals about reading comprehension instruction. *Reading Research Quarterly, 14,* 481–533.

Durkin, D. (1993). *Teaching them to read* (6th ed.). Boston, MA: Allyn and Bacon.

Eason, S. H., Goldberg, L. F., Young, K. M., Geist, M. C., & Cutting, L. E. (2012). Reader–text interactions: How differential text and question types influence cognitive skills needed for reading comprehension. *Journal of Educational Psychology.* doi: 10.1037/a0027182

Fritz, M. (2002). Using a reading strategy to foster active learning in content area courses. *Journal of College Reading and Learning, 32,* 189–194.

Gajria, M., Jitendra, A. K., Sood, S., & Sacks, G. (2007). Improving comprehension of expository text in students with LD: A research synthesis. *Journal of Learning Disabilities, 40,* 210–225.

Gajria, M., & Salvia, J. (1992). The effects of summarization instruction on text comprehension of students with learning disabilities. *Exceptional Children, 58,* 508–516.

Gambrell, L. B., Koskinen, P. S., & Kapinus, B. A. (1991). Retelling and the reading comprehension of proficient and less-proficient readers. *Journal of Educational Research, 84,* 356–363.

Gambrell, L., Pfeiffer, W., & Wilson, R. (1985, March/April). The effects of retelling upon reading comprehension and recall of text information. *Journal of Educational Research, 78,* 216–220.

Gardill, M. C., & Jitendra, A. K. (1999). Advanced story map instruction: Effects on the reading comprehension of students with learning disabilities. *The Journal of Special Education, 28,* 2–17.

Gersten, R., Fuchs, L. S., Williams, J. P., & Baker, S. (2001). Teaching reading comprehension strategies to students with learning disabilities: A review of research. *Review of Educational Research, 71,* 279–320.

Gickling, E. E., & Armstrong, D. L. (1978). Levels of instructional difficulty as related to on-task behavior, task completion, and comprehension. *Journal of Learning Disabilities, 11,* 559–566.

Gickling, E. E., & Thompson, V. P. (1985). A personal view of curriculum-based assessment. *Exceptional Children, 52,* 205–218.

Good III, R. H., Simmons, D. C., & Smith, S. B. (1998). Effective academic interventions in the United States: Evaluating and enhancing the acquisition of early literacy skills. *Educational and Child Psychology, 15,* 56–70.

Guthrie, J. T., McRae, A., & Klauda, S. L. (2007). Contributions of concept-oriented reading instruction to knowledge about interventions for motivations in reading. *Educational Psychologist, 42,* 237–250.

Hagaman, J. L., Casey, K. J., & Reid, R. (2012). The effects of the paraphrasing strategy on the reading comprehension of young students. *Remedial and Special Education, 33,* 110–123. doi: 10.1177/0741932510364548

Hagaman, J. L., & Reid, R. (2008). The effects of the paraphrasing strategy on the reading comprehension of middle school students at risk for failure in reading. *Remedial and Special Education, 29,* 222–234. doi: 10.1177/0741932507311638

Harmon, J. M., Hedrick, W. B., & Wood, K. D. (2005). Research on vocabulary instruction in the content areas: Implications for struggling readers. *Reading and Writing Quarterly, 21,* 261–280. doi: 10.1080/10573560590949377

Hart, B., & Risley, T. R. (1995). *Meaningful differences in the everyday experience of young American children.* Baltimore, MD: Brookes.

Hirsch Jr., E. D., (2003). Reading comprehension requires knowledge of words and the world. *American Educator, 27,* 10–29.

Hughes, T. A., & Fredrick, L. D. (2006). Teaching vocabulary with students with learning disabilities using classwide peer tutoring and constant time delay. *Journal of Behavioral Education, 15,* 1–23.

Idol-Maestas, L. (1985). Getting ready to read: Guided probing for poor comprehenders. *Learning Disability Quarterly, 8,* 243–254.

Jared, E. J., & Jared, A. H. (1997, March). Launching into improved comprehension: Integrating the KWL model into middle level courses. *The Technology Teacher, 56*(6), 24–31.

Joseph, L. M. (2000). Developing first graders' phonemic awareness, word identification, and spelling: A comparison of two contemporary phonic approaches. *Reading Research and Instruction, 39,* 160–169.

Joseph, L. M. (2002). Facilitating word recognition and spelling using word boxes and word sort phonic procedures. *School Psychology Review, 31,* 122–129.

Joshi, R. M. (2005). Vocabulary: A critical component of reading comprehension. *Reading and Writing Quarterly, 21,* 209–219. doi: 10.1080/10573560590949278

Juel, C. (1988). Learning to read and write: A longitudinal study of 54 children from first through fourth grades. *Journal of Educational Psychology, 80,* 437–447.

Kim, A., Vaughn, S., Wanzek, J., & Wei, S. (2004). Graphic organizers and their effects on the reading comprehension of students with LD: A synthesis of research. *Journal of Learning Disabilities, 37,* 105–118.

King, A. (1994). Autonomy and question asking: The role of personal control in guided student-generated questioning. *Learning and Individual Differences, 6,* 163–185.

LaBerge, D., & Samuels, S. J. (1974). Toward a theory of automatic information processing in reading. *Cognitive Psychology, 6,* 293–323.

Malecki, C. K., & Elliott, S. N. (2002). Children's social behaviors as predictors of academic achievement: A longitudinal analysis. *School Psychology Quarterly, 17,* 1–23.

Manset-Williamson, G., & Nelson, J. M. (2005). Balance, strategic reading instruction for upper-elementary and middle school students with reading disabilities: A comparative study of two approaches. *Learning Disability Quarterly, 28,* 59–74.

Martson, D. B. (1989). A curriculum-based measurement approach to assessing academic performance: What it is and why do it. In M. R. Shinn (Ed.), *Curriculum-based measurement: Assessing special children* (pp. 18–78). New York, NY: Guilford Press.

Mathes, P. G., Torgesen, J. K., & Allen, S. (2001). *Peer assisted literacy strategies for first-grade readers: First-grade PALS.* Longmont, CO: Sopris West.

McDonnell, J., Johnson, J. W., Polychronis, S., & Risen, T. (2002). Effects of embedded instruction on students with moderate disabilities enrolled in general education classes. *Education and Training in Mental Retardation & Developmental Disabilities, 37,* 363–377.

McNamara, D. S., & Kintsch, W. (1996). Learning from texts: Effects of prior knowledge and text coherence. *Discourse Processes, 23,* 247–288.

Morrow, L. (1985). Retelling stories: A strategy for improving young children's comprehension, concept of story structure, and oral language complexity. *Elementary School Journal, 85,* 647–661.

Morrow, L. M. (1986). Effects of structural guidance in story retelling on children's dictation of original stories. *Journal of Reading Behavior, 18,* 138–152. doi: 10.1080/10862968609547561

Nagy, W. E., & Anderson, R. C. (1984). How many words are there in printed school English? *Reading Research Quarterly, 19,* 304–330.

Nation, K., Cocksey, J., Tayler, J. S. H., & Bishop, D. V. M. (2010). A longitudinal investigation of early reading and language skills in children with poor reading comprehension. *Journal of Child Psychology and Psychiatry, 51,* 1031–1039. doi: 10.1111/j.1469–7610.2010.02254.x

National Center for Education Statistics (NCES). (2009). *The nation's report card: Grade 12 reading and mathematics 2009 national and pilot state results* (NCES 2011–455). Washington, DC: National Center for Education Statistics, Institute of Education Sciences, U.S. Department of Education.

National Center for Education Statistics (NCES). (2011). *The nation's report card: Reading 2011* (NCES 2012–457). Washington, DC: National Center for Education Statistics, Institute of Education Sciences, U.S. Department of Education.

National Early Literacy Panel. (2008). *Developing early literacy: Report of the National Early Literacy Panel.* Washington, DC: National Institute for Literacy. Retrieved from http://www.nifl.gov/earlychildhood/NELP/NELPreport.html

National Institute of Child Health and Human Development (NICHHD). (2000). *Report of the National Reading Panel. Teaching children to read: An evidence-based assessment of the scientific research literature on reading and its implications for reading instruction* (NIH Publication No. 00-4769). Washington, DC: U.S. Government Printing Office.

Neddenriep, C. E., Hale, A. D., Skinner, C. H., Hawkins, R. O., & Winn, B. (2007). A preliminary investigation of the concurrent validity of reading comprehension rate: A direct, dynamic measure of reading comprehension. *Psychology in the Schools, 44,* 373–388.

Neufeld, P. (2005). Comprehension instruction in content area classes. *International Reading Association, 59,* 302–312. doi:10.1598/RT.59.4.1

Ogle, D. M. (1986). K-W-L: A teaching model that develops active reading of expository text. *The Reading Teacher, 39,* 564–570.

O'Shea, L. J., Munson, S. M., & O'Shea, D. J. (1984). Error correction in oral reading: Evaluating the effectiveness of three procedures. *Education and Treatment of Children, 7,* 203–214.

O'Shea, L. J., Sindelar, P. T., & O'Shea, D. J. (1985). The effects of repeated readings and attentional cues on reading fluency and comprehension. *Journal of Reading Behavior, 17,* 129–141.

Ouellette, G. P. (2006). What's meaning got to do with it: The role of vocabulary in word reading and reading comprehension. *Journal of Educational Psychology, 98,* 554–566. doi: 10.1037/0022–0663.98.3.554

Palincsar, A. S., & Brown, A. L. (1984). Reciprocal teaching of comprehension-fostering and comprehension-monitoring activities. *Cognition and Instruction, 1,* 117–175.

Pikulski, J. J., & Chard, D. J. (2005). Fluency: Bridge between decoding and reading comprehension. *The Reading Teacher, 58,* 510–519.

Pressley, M., & Wharton-McDonald, R. (1997). Skilled comprehension instruction and its development through instruction. *School Psychology Review, 26,* 448–466.

Pressley, M., Wharton-McDonald, R., Mistretta-Hampston, J., & Echevarria, M. (1998). The nature of literacy instruction in ten grade-4/5 classrooms in upstate New York. *Scientific Studies of Reading, 2,* 159–194.

RAND Reading Study Group (RRSG). (2002). *Reading for understanding. Toward an R&D program in reading comprehension.* Santa Monica, CA: RAND Corporation.

Raphael, T. E., & Au, K. H. (2005). QAR: Enhancing comprehension and test taking across grades and content areas. *International Reading Association, 59,* 206–221. doi: 10.1598/RT.59.3.1

Raphael, T. E., & McKinney, J. (1983). An examination of 5th and 8th grade children's question answering behavior: An instructional study in metacognition. *Journal of Reading Behavior, 15*, 67–86.

Raphael, T. E., & Wonnacott, C. A. (1985). Heightening fourth grade students' sensitivity to sources of information for answering comprehension questions. *Reading Research Quarterly, 20*, 282–296.

Reschly, A. L. (2010). Reading and school completion: Critical connections and Matthew effects. *Reading and Writing Quarterly, 26*, 67–90. doi: 10.1080/10573560903397023

Recht, D. R., & Leslie, L. (1988). Effect of prior knowledge on good and poor readers memory of text. *Journal of Educational Psychology, 80*, 16–20.

Riedel, B. W. (2007). The relation between DIBELS, reading comprehension, and vocabulary in urban first-grade students. *Reading Research Quarterly, 42*, 546–567. doi: 10.1598/RRQ.42.4.5

Ridge, A. D., & Skinner, C. H. (2011). Using the TELLS prereading procedure to enhance comprehension levels and rates in secondary students. *Psychology in the Schools, 48*, 46–58. doi: 10.1002/pits.20539

Riley-Tillman, T. C., & Burns, M. K. (2009). *Evaluating educational interventions: Single-case design for measuring response to intervention*. New York, NY: Guilford Press.

Rose, T. L. (1984). The effects of two prepractice procedures on oral reading. *Journal of Learning Disabilities, 17*, 544–548.

Rose, T. L., & Beattie, J. R. (1986). Relative effects of teacher-directed and taped previewing on oral reading. *Learning Disability Quarterly, 9*, 193–199.

Rosenshine, B., Meister, C., & Chapman, S. (1996). Teaching students to generate questions: A review of the intervention studies. *Review of Educational Research, 66*, 181–221.

Rupley, W. H. (2005). Vocabulary instruction for the struggling readers. *Reading and Writing Quarterly, 21*, 239–260. doi: 10.1080/10573560590949368

Santa, C. M. (2000). The complexity of comprehension. *Reading Today, 17*(4), 30–32.

Schisler, R., Joseph, L. M., Konrad, M., & Alber-Morgan, S. (2010). Comparison of the effectiveness and efficiency of oral and written retellings and passage review as strategies for comprehending text. *Psychology in the Schools, 47*, 135–152. doi: 10.1002/pits.20460

Schumaker, J. B., Denton, P. H., & Deshler, D. D. (1984). *The paraphrasing strategy*. Lawrence, KS: University of Kansas.

Schwartz, R. M., & Raphael, T. E. (1985). Concept of definition: A key to improving students' vocabulary. *The Reading Teacher, 39*, 198–205.

Shelley, A. C., Bridwell, B., Hyder, L., Ledford, N., & Patterson, P. (1997). Revisiting the K-W-L: What we knew; what we wanted to know; what we learned. *Reading Horizons, 37*, 233–242.

Simmonds, E. P. M. (1992). The effects of teacher training and implementation of two methods of improving the comprehension skills of students with learning disabilities. *Learning Disabilities Research and Practice, 7*, 194–198.

Sindelar, P. T., Monda, L. E., & O'Shea, L. J. (1990). Effects of repeated readings on instructional- and mastery-level readers. *Journal of Educational Research, 83*, 220–226.

Snow, C. E., Burns, S. M., & Griffin, P. (1998). *Preventing reading difficulties in young children*. Washington, DC: National Academy Press.

Spargo, E. (1989). *Time readings*. Providence, RI: Jamestown.

Stahl, S., & Fairbanks, M. (1986). The effects of vocabulary instruction: A model-based meta-analysis. *Review of Educational Research, 56*, 72–110.

Stanovich, K. E. (1986). Matthew effects in reading: Some consequences of individual differences in the acquisition of literacy. *Reading Research Quarterly, 21*, 360–406.

Swanburn, M. S. L., & de Glopper, K. (1999). Incidental word learning while reading: A meta-analysis. *Review of Educational Research, 69*, 261–285.

Taboada, A., & Guthrie, J. T. (2006). Contributions of student questioning and prior knowledge to construction of knowledge from reading information text. *Journal of Literary Research, 38*, 1–35.

Taft, M. L., & Leslie, L. (1985). The effects of prior knowledge and oral reading accuracy on miscues and comprehension. *Journal of Reading Behavior, 17*, 163–179.

Templeton, S., Bear, Dr. R., Invernizzi, M., & Johnston, F. (2009). *Vocabulary their way: Word study with middle and secondary students*. Boston, MA: Pearson.

Terras, M. M., Thompson, L. C., & Minnis, H. (2009). Dyslexia and psycho-social functioning: An exploratory study of the role of self-esteem and understanding. *Dyslexia, 15*, 304–327. doi: 10.1002/dys.386

Therrien, W. J. (2004). Fluency and comprehension gains as a result of repeated reading. *Remedial and Special Education, 25*, 252–261.

Wannarka, R., Ruhl, K., & Kubina, R. (in press). Using peer-mediated constant time delay to teach content area vocabulary to middle school students with disruptive behavior. *Journal of Evidence-Based Practices for Schools*.

Williams, J. P., Stafford, K. B., Lauer, K. D., Hall, K. M., & Pollini, S. (2009). Embedding reading comprehension training in content-area instruction. *Journal of Educational Psychology, 101*, 1–20. doi: 10.1037/a0013152

14

Linking Classroom Assessment to Written Language Interventions

Linda H. Mason and Anne Mong Cramer

Recent initiatives for improving academic outcomes for all students, such as the Common Core State Standards (CCSS, 2012) have prompted attention to writing in both assessment and intervention literature. Students are expected to end schooling prepared for writing in college and the workplace, demonstrated by: (a) writing arguments, informative/explanatory text, and narrative text; (b) writing with clarity and cohesion to meet task, purpose, and audience; (c) planning and revising, editing, or rewriting; (d) using technology for production, publication, and collaboration; (e) writing both short and longer responses to demonstrate understanding of subject matter; (f) using and integrating multiple sources while avoiding plagiarism; (g) gathering evidence from text to support writing; and (h) writing in both short and extended time frames. Given the specificity of initiatives and the "shared responsibility" within schools (CCSS, 2012, p.4), it is essential that all teachers understand how formative writing assessment for process skills and written expression can be used to inform writing instruction that ensures student progress towards meeting standards (Graham, Harris, & Hebert, 2011).

Accurate evaluation of students' process skill mastery and skill application during written expression, for instructional, diagnostic, and remediation purposes, should drive classroom assessment (Huot & Neal, 2006). Formative assessment measures, such as curriculum-based measurement, that examine core writing components such as fluency, syntactic maturity, vocabulary, content, and writing mechanics (e.g., transcription skills, spelling, and sentence development) should occur frequently, immediately after instruction and in weeks following, to ensure that skills are maintained (Benson & Campbell, 2009). Students' ability to "introduce a topic or text clearly" for opinion and informative writing (CCSS, 2012, for example, can be assessed systematically within the context of handwriting, spelling, and sentence writing instruction. Clearly, students who are unable to write legible (i.e., sentences with unreadable handwriting or multiple misspellings) and clearly written sentences (i.e., sentences with poor syntax) do not have the emerging skills required for expressing ideas about a topic or text in writing.

Alternatively, formative assessments for benchmarking written expression development provide evidence of students' process skill application specific to genre and task. Benchmark assessment rubrics and writing prompts should be scaffolded for developmental/grade level to support reliable and valid evaluation of what students need in terms of intervention (Sermis, Burstein, & Leacock, 2006). Teachers should adopt and alternate longer and shorter handwritten or keyboarded assessments (e.g., paragraph or essay responses), to reduce student's time in assessment as well as to assess students' ability to address task and purpose (Graham et al., 2011). Assessment rubrics inform instruction by evaluating a students' ability to demonstrate knowledge and express ideas by (a) including the primary traits for the genre in writing, (b) organizing text, and (c) attending to audience and task purpose.

Intervention, developed based on assessment of students' process and written expression skills, will be described in this chapter. As noted previously, assessment with a focus on process skills should occur systematically and include balancing assessment for new and previously taught skills. Formative benchmark assessment, with a focus on applied skills for genre specific skills such as opinion, informative, and narrative writing, should be developmentally suitable and distributed across tasks. Writing assessment and intervention is no longer limited to the language arts or English classroom, but shared across disciplines.

Intervention for Writing Skills

Many students have difficulty writing and will require intensive skill-based intervention to meet standards (Graham & Harris, 2003; Mason & Graham, 2008). Struggling writers, unfortunately, are often expected to plan and write short and extended responses prior to mastering handwriting, spelling, and sentence construction skills. Students with these skill deficits tend to ignore critical writing processes, and therefore, are often categorized as poor writers despite having acceptable written content (Graham, 2006). Handwriting, spelling, and sentence writing are best assessed through frequent (e.g., weekly) formative assessment (Graham, 1999; Saddler, 2012). The ultimate goal, of course, is that benchmark assessments will provide evidence that students can apply writing skills to more complex writing tasks.

Handwriting and Spelling

Best practice for handwriting and spelling includes providing students' with individualized, frequent, short lessons for skill deficit remediation. During the course of handwriting instruction, generally provided in kindergarten through third grade, teachers should evaluate students' use of materials such as pencil grip and paper placement, legibility of letter formation, and handwriting speed. Typically, spelling assessment and instruction is integrated within a test-study-test approach where students are tested, provided instruction for misspelled words, and retested (Mason, Harris, & Graham, 2013).

Ninety-seven percent of surveyed elementary teachers believe that handwriting instruction is important (Graham et al., 2008); however, 12% of these same teachers indicate being unprepared to teach handwriting. Effective handwriting instruction for students struggling with writing should include explicitly teaching students to (a) form letters through teacher-led modeling, (b) compare and contrast letter features, (c) use facilitative supports such as marks for paper placement and grip molds for pencils, (d) independently evaluate and improve their handwriting, and (e) improve handwriting fluency (Graham, 1999). Letter formation should be taught in isolation, followed by application in context (Troia, 2006).

Spelling is one of the most pervasive of writing difficulties and the one most difficult to remediate (Darch, Eaves, Crowe, Simmons, & Conniff, 2006; Moats, 2009). Given the multiple skills needed to spell well, effective instruction for spelling difficulties should include explicit instruction for phonological awareness, useful spelling rules, phonics skills application, and irregular word spelling (Wanzek et al., 2006). Graham (1983, 1999) suggested that for struggling learners, word study strategies such as the Five-Step Word study strategy (say the word; write and say the word, check the word; trace and say the word; write the word from memory and check; repeat the five steps) should be used for distributive practice. Students should be taught to spell words they use in their writing; prior to teaching a word, students should know the word's meaning. Maintenance and generalization should be supported by continual review of previously learned words and integration of spelling words with students' reading and writing (Mason, Harris, & Graham, 2013).

One program, the CASL Handwriting/Spelling Program for young writers, includes assessment and instructional practices in a program that addresses both handwriting and spelling (Graham & Harris, 2012; Graham, Harris, & Fink, 2000; Graham, Harris, & Fink-Chorzempa, 2002). Students skills are developed by instruction for (a) writing the letters of the alphabet, (b) handwriting fluency, (c) knowledge of sound/letter combinations, (d) spelling patterns involving long and short vowels, and (e) words commonly used when writing. Results for CASL instruction across the randomized control trial studies indicated significant improvement in students' handwriting and spelling with effect sizes (ES) ranging from 0.54 to 1.46. The CASL handwriting and spelling program for first grade is available online at no cost at http://www.specialed.ccsu.edu/nicoll-senft/handwriting%20and%20Spelling%20Manual%20saved.rtf.

Sentence Writing

Saddler (2012) noted that sentences can be scored using analytic scoring procedures (e.g., grammatical correctness, punctuation, capitalization, and use of target structures) and/or a more subjective score, effectiveness (e.g., clarity and directness of meaning, rhythmic appeal, and intended audience). Teachers should be cautioned to avoid scoring according to sentence length as this measure provides little diagnostic information. Formative assessment, directly linking sentence-writing exercises to skills learned, is recommended.

Given the negative effect grammar instruction (e.g., punctuation and capitalization rule instruction, sentence diagraming) has on student performance ($ES = -0.32$; Graham & Perin, 2007), disaggregating what should be taught for improving students' syntactic skills is important. Unlike traditional grammar instruction, sentence construction instruction has a moderate positive effect ($ES = 0.50$; Graham & Perin, 2007), resulting in improved written text quality (Nippold, 2004). Both Strategy Instruction Model (SIM) sentence writing (Schmidt, Deshler, Schumaker, & Alley, 1988) and sentence combining instruction (Saddler, Behforooz, & Asaro, 2008; Saddler & Graham, 2005) have been established as effective methods for improving students' sentence writing abilities.

In SIM sentence writing instruction, students learn to write four sentence types by first selecting one of 14 different sentence formulas to apply to simple, compound, complex, and compound-complex sentence structures, and then explore and write words to fit the formula. A mnemonic, PENS (Picks, Explores, Noted, Subject), is used to help students remember the steps. Students check their work to make sure a complete sentence has been written (Schmidt, Deshler, Schumaker, & Alley, 1988). See crl@ku.edu and information regarding SIM instruction in the next sections for more detail.

Sentence combining instruction should be presented in a developmental sequence in terms of syntactical constructions (Saddler, 2012). Sentence combining focuses instruction for writing six different sentence types: compound sentences; sentences with adjective or adverb modifiers; sentences connected with coordinating or subordinating conjunctions; sentences that contain a modifying clause; appositives (i.e., two phrases referring to the same noun); and sentences that contain possessive nouns. The following multiple sentences— "Dick walked to the mall," and "Jane walked to the mall," for example—can be combined as "Dick and Jane walked to the mall." Sentence combining instruction should be explicit with: (a) the purpose and benefits of sentence combining established; (b) teacher modeling the procedures while talking out loud while providing examples and non-examples; (c) guided group, peer, and individual practice; and (d) application to the students' writing. Saddler's 2012 text, *Teacher's Guide to Effective Sentence Writing*, provides description of instruction and includes reproducible materials.

Intervention for Written Expression

Prior to CCSS (2012), when evaluating students' written papers, the function of the writing assignment varied across disciplines. In English classes, for example, multiple processes such as planning, drafting, revising, editing, and publishing resulted in refined benchmark style products. In other disciplines, conversely, the function of writing may have served as a writing to learn evaluation tool to establish students' present level of experience or knowledge of a topic, exploration and levels of inquiry, knowledge summarization, or ability to develop new questions. Often, these writing to learn activities did not serve as writing benchmark assessment; students' attention was not directed to process skills, but to substantive characteristics, such as content, clarity, and cogency. Given the focus, as noted in CCSS (2012), for writing as shared and meaningfully applied across academic areas, writing to learn activities can and should also serve as formative benchmark assessments. Knowledge about the writing process and effective writing instruction is, therefore, most important across content and disciplines (Graham, Harris, & Hebert, 2011). Fortunately, evidence-based intervention has been established across disciplines (e.g., Mason, Benedek-Wood, Kubina, & Wood, 2012).

Strategy instruction as a written expression intervention has demonstrated the largest effects (*ES* = 0.82) for improving students' writing (Graham & Perin, 2007). More specifically, research in strategy instruction for struggling writers provides foundational principles for what works in improving students' written expression performance. Four foundational models of effective written expression intervention, to be described in the next section, have been proven effective across disciplines for a wide range of learners. Self-Regulated Strategy Development (SRSD), the model with the largest research-base, will be described in detail. Specific Strategy Instruction Model (SIM) and SRSD strategies for improving students' benchmark skills in writing narrative, informative, and opinion/persuasive papers, and for revision, will then be highlighted.

Evidence-Based Strategy Instructional Models

Effective strategy instruction follows an explicit instructional model (see Archer & Hughes, 2011). Effective strategy instruction pacing is criterion based, recursive, and scaffolded to support a smooth transition of responsibility for strategy use from teacher to student. Teacher-supported guided practice and student-independent practice builds fluency, reducing processing demands and allowing for more focus on higher-level idea generation (Mason & Kubina, 2011). When students are fluent in the implementation of writing strategies, assessment through writing is more likely to reflect what students know about the content, reducing concern that the assessment of their understanding is limited by their writing skills.

Englert et al.'s (1991) landmark randomized control trial study with fourth- and fifth-grade students established the effectiveness of an integrated approach, Cognitive Strategy Instruction in Writing (CSIW), for teaching text structure strategies for writing explanation and comparison/contrast expository essays (*ES* = 0.52 for writing quality). Using an explicit instructional model, students were taught to use the POWER (Plan, Organize, Write, Edit, and Revise) strategy and think sheets for strategic self-questioning to evaluate their writing throughout the writing process (i.e., planning, composing, revising, and editing). Peer conferencing and group activities supported dialoguing and collaboration.

Wong and colleagues also examined dialoguing and strategy instruction with eighth- and ninth-grade students with learning disabilities and English language learners (Wong et al., 1994). Intervention components included (a) explicit explanation and modeling for an opinion essay planning strategy, (b) peer collaborative practice in planning an essay, (c) teacher evaluation of planning, (d) individual writing the essay on a computer, (e) student-teacher conferencing, (f) pair revision for content, and (g) individual error-monitoring. The intervention had a positive and strong impact on the quality of students' writing (*ES* = 1.52 to 3.50). Both Englert et al. (1991) and Wong et al. (1994) established the advantages for imbedding instructional conversations for feedback during explicit writing instruction. Additional critical principles for effective writing instruction include (a) teaching self-regulation, (b) fostering participation in a writing community, and (c) teaching in meaningful contexts.

The Strategy Instruction Model (SIM) focuses on improving writing outcomes with the goal of teaching students to apply learned strategies to grade-level task (Schumaker & Deshler, 2003). The SIM instructional sequence includes eight stages of strategy acquisition: (1) pretest students' skills and establish a purpose and goals for learning; (2) describe how each strategy step facilitates learning and describe when to use the strategy; (3) teacher-led modeling by thinking out loud each step of strategy application for the targeted skill; (4) practice activities that enable the students to memorize the strategy steps; (5) controlled practice—practice is scaffolded by increasing task difficulty only after easier tasks are mastered; (6) advanced practice—practice in grade-level contexts; (7) post-test and obtain commitment for generalization; (8) generalization—application of learned strategies in the general education classroom. Generalization is supported by both administrators and general education teachers by providing (a) orientation for opportunities for generalization; (b) students with numerous opportunities to generalize (with feedback); (c) adaptation to help students learn to modify the strategy to meet demands in different settings; and (d) periodic probes to evaluate maintenance of skills. SIM instruction for high-school-aged students has been established as effective in numerous single subject design studies. Professional development is a critical component of SIM instruction; therefore, SIM instructional materials are available only in conjunction with professional development provided by certified SIM Professional Developers. Information regarding SIM training can be located at University of Kansas, Center for Research on Learning's (KU-CRL) director of professional development at crl@ku.edu. Further information including newsletters, videotapes/DVDs, and CDs that can be ordered is found at www.kucrl.org/.

Self-Regulated Strategy Development (SRSD). SRSD instruction supports independent, self-regulated performance in writing, as validated in more than fifty studies over the past thirty years. The model, developed by Harris and Graham (1992), promotes imbedding cognitive strategies with self-regulated learning to support efficient, successful completion of complex tasks (Harris, Graham, MacArthur, Reid, & Mason, 2011). A meta-analysis focused on

SRSD instruction for students with learning disabilities noted strong effect sizes ($ES = 1.15$) for 20 experimental studies (Graham, 2006). Since 2005, the SRSD research base has expanded and strengthened even more, including studies examining SRSD for struggling learners (e.g., Harris, Graham, & Mason, 2006) and students with emotional and behavioral disorders, attention deficit hyperactivity disorder, and autism spectrum disorders (Taft & Mason, 2011).

SRSD instruction weaves strategy acquisition and students' self-regulated learning. Self-regulation, used throughout the writing process, helps writers to be more reflective about their writing ability, gives them tools for managing distracting and negative thoughts, encourages strategy ownership, and supports strategy modification as the need arises (Mason, Harris, & Graham, 2011). The first procedure, goal setting, begins prior to learning a writing strategy, when students establish a goal to work with the teacher and to do their best to learn a new strategy. As students begin to learn the strategy basics, additional goals, such as enhancing genre-specific elements or including sentence and vocabulary variety, may be added. After goal setting, students are encouraged to reflect on and self-monitor (the second self-regulation procedure) progress in meeting goals. Progress is generally charted and graphed to show improvement over time. When goals are only partially met, students monitor their work, redirecting efforts to the specific area in need of attention. Self-instruction is the third SRSD self-regulation component. Students learn to support writing by talking to themselves throughout the writing process. The teacher assists students in developing personal self-instructions for problem definition; focus of attention and planning; strategy use, self-evaluation and error correcting; coping and self-control; and self-reinforcement. The fourth self-regulation procedure, self-reinforcement is supported by (a) the students' visual representation of progress through self-monitoring, representing goal achievement and (b) self-reinforcement through positive self-instruction. In addition to self-regulation, six stages of strategy acquisition provide a framework for SRSD instruction that can be effectively applied to teaching a variety of different strategies.

Develop pre-skills and background knowledge. Instruction begins with developing the terminology of the specific text structure being taught. Throughout discussion, the teacher establishes the students' background knowledge. For example, instruction in a persuasive strategy might begin with a discussion of the meaning of the words *strategy* and *persuade.* First, students may describe how strategies are used in other parts of their lives, such as winning video game levels. Students may also describe times they tried to persuade a parent, and then describe their success. Students and the teacher may discuss examples of persuasion seen and heard every day in advertising, political debates, or negotiations with parents, teachers, and friends.

Discuss it. In the "discuss it" stage, the teacher introduces the strategy, emphasizing the specific components of planning, writing, and/or revising process and the critical elements contained in the text structure to be taught. Students are shown the graphic organizers and materials associated with the strategy, as the teacher explains how the strategy is useful and will improve the quality and efficiency of the students' writing. In this stage, students may compare their previous writing papers to the criteria established for the current strategy. The teacher reassures students that strategy instruction will help their writing become better, once they have learned the trick. Students begin to memorize the mnemonic associated with the strategy in this stage.

Model it. The heart of strategy instruction is modeling (Association for Supervision and Curriculum Development [ASCD], 2002). During modeling, the teacher explicitly models using the strategy, self-regulation procedures, and all instructional materials so that students can see how a good writer works through the writing process. During modeling, the teacher should verbalize what is usually reserved for internal self-talk, so that students are able to hear the inner thoughts of a competent writer. Teachers model each strategy step as they actually plan, write, revise, and edit a paper.

Memorize it. Memorization begins when students are first introduced to the strategy in the "discuss it" stage. Repeated practice with memorization builds fluency, increases fidelity in applying the strategy, and reduces dependency on printed materials. Most students are able to memorize a strategy relatively quickly, but for those who find memorization too challenging, printed mnemonic sheets and organizers can be maintained.

Guided practice. During guided practice, teachers work collaboratively with students, gradually fading teacher support and shifting responsibility to the student writer. Guided practice should be repeated until students demonstrate mastery of the strategy. During guided practice, teachers should carefully observe students' performance for gaps in understanding and correct strategy use. Previously taught lessons can be revisited as necessary to build students' writing skills. During guided practice, teachers help students self-evaluate their writing, count critical elements, and graph results. Students are generally motivated by graphing and are proud of themselves when critical element counts increase with each new composition.

Independent practice. During independent practice, students work independently while teachers monitor for consistent performance and reteach, as needed. This phase of instruction is a good time to emphasize generalization of the new strategy into other subjects and writing areas. It is also the time to celebrate students' growth and progress.

SRSD instruction can be seen in both elementary and middle school classrooms in the video *Teaching Students with Learning Disabilities: Using Learning Strategies* (ASCD, 2002). Online interactive tutorials on SRSD are available at http://iris.peabody.vanderbilt.edu/pow/chalcycle.htm. Lesson plans and student support materials for elementary students (grades 1 through 3) can be found online at http://hobbs.vanderbilt.edu/projectwrite/. Thorough description of instructional components and complete lesson plans and reproducible organizers are also available in two texts: *Powerful Writing Strategies for All Students* (Harris, Graham, Mason, & Friedlander, 2008) and *Powerful Strategies for Improving Reading and Writing in Content Areas* (Mason, Reid, & Hagaman, 2012).

Initiatives for Written Expression

CCSS (2012) identifies writing standards for three text structures across kindergarten through twelfth-grade levels—narrative, informative, and opinion/persuasive text. Each text structure has unique characteristics or critical elements that readers expect to see in a particular type of writing. For example, narrative texts follow a story line and generally include characters, settings, sense of time, and so on. Informative texts explain concepts and contain facts and details, often have a clear sequence, and may include cause and effect relationships. Persuasive texts include the author's position, reasons and explanations, counterarguments, and conclusions. All of these text structures can be meaningfully applied to all academic areas. Strategy instruction that specifically addresses the three genres for short and longer writing assignments is highlighted next.

Benchmarking Skills—Writing Paragraphs

Paragraph writing is both a process skill, for example, when paragraphs make up a larger writing project such as an essay or report, and a benchmark skill, when evaluated as writing "routinely over . . . shorter time frames (a single sitting or a day or two) for a range of tasks, purposes, and audiences" (e.g., CCSS, 2012, p. 21). Interventions for improving students' short constructed response writing (i.e., paragraphs) have been validated in both SIM and SRSD instruction.

The SIM paragraph writing strategy (Schumaker & Lyerla, 1991) focuses instruction for paragraphs that list or describe or demonstrate sequence, compare/contrast, or demonstrate cause and effect. The mnemonic SLOW CaPS (Show the type of paragraph in the first sentence; List the type of details you plan to write about; Order the details; Write the details in complete sentences and cap off the paragraph with a Concluding, Passing, or Summary sentence) is used to facilitate strategy step memorization. In a single-subject design study with secondary students, Moran, Schumaker, and Vetter (1981) found SIM instruction effective for improving structural elements written in a paragraph. See http://www.kucrl.org/sim/strategies/paragraph.shtml for professional training information.

Mason and colleagues established the effectiveness of a one-to-one tutoring model for teaching quick writes (i.e., short responses often used in secondary content classes) (Mason, Benedek-Wood, & Valasa, 2009). SRSD for persuasive quick writing has been validated for secondary students in single subject study (e.g., Mason, Kubina, & Taft, 2009; Mason, Kubina, Valasa, & Mong Cramer, 2010) and one quasi-experiment study (Mason, Kubina, Kostewicz, Mong Cramer, & Datchuk, 2012) with large effects ($ES = 1.04$ to 1.33). The mnemonic POW (Pick my idea, Organize my notes, Write and say more) and TREE (Topic sentence; Reasons three or more—include a counter reason and refute; Explain reasons; Ending sentence) facilitates strategy step application. In each study, after students learned to write a quick write with all TREE elements, structured practice for writing the quick write in a 10-minute time frame was provided. SRSD for quick writing for the POW+TREE strategy and POW+TIDE (Topic sentence, Ideas, Details, Ending sentence) for informative writing have been evaluated in secondary middle school classrooms. Preliminary evidence indicates that SRSD for whole group instruction, in inclusive science classrooms, is also effective (Benedek-Wood, Mason, Wood, & Kubina, 2012; Mason, Kubina et al., 2012). Complete lessons and materials for POW+TREE and POW+TIDE quick writing are available in *Powerful Strategies for Improving Reading and Writing in Content Areas* (Mason, Reid et al., 2012).

Benchmarking Skills—Writing and Revising Essays

Novice and struggling writers tend to combine all phases (planning, writing, revising) in one step, trying to get their ideas out on paper, resulting in disorganized, ineffective writing (Englert, Mariage, & Dunsmore, 2006). Fortunately, a number of strategies have been validated as effective in improving students' writing for general and genre-specific tasks. Therrien and colleagues (Therrien, Hughes, Kapelski, & Mokhtari, 2009), for example, found large effects ($ES = 1.69$ for strategy-specific improvement) for SIM instruction in improving essay test writing performance of 42 seventh- and eighth-grade students. Students were taught a six-step writing strategy, ANSWER (Analyze the action words in the question, Notice the requirements of the question, Set up an outline, Work in detail, Engineer your answer, Review your answer). It is important to remember, as one looks at strategies such as ANSWER and the strategies to be described next, that it is not the individual strategy mnemonic or strategy steps that improve writing, but evidence-based strategy instruction as detailed earlier in this chapter.

Narrative text. Most children are introduced to narrative text at an early age through storybooks. Good narrative text includes interesting characters engaged in some type of activity in a vivid setting. Narrative text generally has a sense of time and place, a clear beginning, a series of events that often includes a problem, and an ending that brings a satisfying resolution to the problem. Kindergarteners may recognize narrative text structure based on the antics of Winnie-the-Pooh (Milne, 1926), while older readers may identify elements of narrative structure as they reflect on the Harry Potter stories (Rowling, 1999). While narrative structure may be familiar in reading, additional support is often needed to help students translate their story ideas into written text. Additionally, students should be taught that narratives extend beyond the land of make-believe to include nonfiction texts such as personal narratives, biographies, and historical narratives.

One well-tested SRSD narrative strategy for story writing, POW (Pick my idea, Organize my notes, Write and say more) + WWW, What = 2, How = 2 (Who, When, Where, What does the main character do or want to do? What happens next? How does the main character or other characters feel? How does the story end?) can be taught to both young developing writers and struggling adolescents (e.g., Asaro-Saddler & Saddler, 2010; Harris et al., 2006). Students use a graphic organizer with the mnemonic to guide idea generation and organization during planning, then use their written plan for composing a story. Students are encouraged to write and say more during writing; after writing, students self-monitor and graph performance in writing a story with the seven strategy elements. SRSD for C-Space (Characters, Setting, Problem, Action, Conclusion, Emotion) is an effective, evidence-based narrative-writing strategy that can be used for fiction or nonfiction and is applicable to a variety of age and ability levels (MacArthur, Schwartz, & Graham, 1991). Like WWW, What = 2, How = 2 instruction, students plan before writing, make notes for the six strategy elements, use an organizer during composing, write and say more, and self-monitor and graph performance. Lesson plans and support materials for WWW, What = 2, How = 2 for story writing for elementary students (grades 1 through 3) can be found online at http://hobbs.vanderbilt.edu/projectwrite/ See Harris et al. (2008) for complete lesson plans and materials for both narrative writing strategies for stories, and Mason, Reid, and Hagaman (2012) for C-SPACE for writing biographies.

Informational Text. Informational text structures for reporting knowledge are more complex than narrative structures. Organization is critical if the author is to achieve the goal of transferring knowledge and understanding to the reader. SRSD for the PLAN strategy (Pay attention to the prompt, List the main ideas, Add supporting Ideas, Number your ideas) is a general strategy that pairs effectively with a variety of genre specific strategies (De La Paz & Graham, 1997). De La Paz (1999), for example, combined PLAN & WRITE (Work from your plan to develop your thesis statement, Remember your goals, Include transition words, Try to use different kinds of sentences, Exciting, interesting, $100,000 words) for writing informative text. During instruction, students are provided think sheets to develop and improve paragraph writing, sentence writing, and vocabulary usage. De La Paz and colleagues describe how PLAN & WRITE has been used effectively to promote fluency in expository writing, which further functioned as preparation for statewide assessments (De La Paz, Owen, Harris, & Graham, 2000). See Harris et al. (2008) for complete lesson plans and materials.

Students' text comprehension is improved when they write about what they read (Graham & Hebert, 2010). One two-part strategy, SRSD for TWA (Think before reading, think While reading, and think After reading; Mason, 2004) and PLANS (Pick goals, List ways to meet goals, And, make Notes, Sequence notes; Graham, MacArthur, Schwartz, & Page-Voth, 1992), supports students during reading for information, writing notes for what has been read, and writing an informative paper (Mason, Dunn Davison, Hammer, Miller, & Glutting, 2012; Mason, Hickey Snyder, Sukhram, & Kedem, 2006). The TWA strategy is a nine-step reading comprehension strategy designed to support self-regulation, comprehension, and vocabulary development while reading. Before reading, students activate their background knowledge by considering what they know and generate questions about what they would like to learn from the reading. During reading, students use a note-taking graphic organizer to record main ideas and supporting details, and are encouraged to self-monitor reading speed and understanding, and to reread sections that are confusing. During reading, students answer the "What I want to learn" questions generated earlier. After reading, students think about what they read, review their notes for main ideas and details, and retell the highlights from the reading. The PLANS component incorporates a goal setting component that supports students in planning, supplementing, and organizing their notes from the reading prior to writing an informative retell of what was learned. TWA+PLANS lessons also include mini-lessons to support vocabulary and sentence growth. See Harris et al. (2008) and Mason, Reid et al. (2012) for complete TWA+PLANS lesson plans and materials.

Persuasive Text. The art of persuasion requires one to present a convincing argument and to present and refute counter positions. Arguments must be supported with sound logic and explained with sufficient detail to be persuasive. Opinion and persuasive writing requires an intricate balance, a balance situated within the complexities of writing.

SRSD for the POW + TREE strategies has been effectively adapted to meet the needs of young elementary students (e.g., Graham, Harris, & Mason, 2005; Harris et al., 2006) and students in secondary settings (e.g., Mastropieri et al., 2012). For young writers, the TREE steps are adjusted to meet students' developmental level (Topic sentence—Tell what you believe, Reasons—three or more, Ending- Wrap it up right, and Examine—Do I have all my parts?). As noted in the description of POW + TREE for quick writing, mature authors are encouraged to consider the opposing viewpoint, include a counterargument, and refute that argument with an appropriate explanation. Writing prompts should be carefully considered to assist students in focusing on the task of learning the process of writing persuasively by writing personal opinions before writing for academic-specific topics. Lesson plans and support materials for elementary students (grades 1 through 3) can be found online at http://hobbs.vanderbilt.edu/projectwrite/ and in Harris et al. (2008) for older elementary students.

SRSD for the STOP (Suspend judgment, Take a position, Organize ideas, Plan and write more) and DARE (Develop the topic, Add ideas, Reject, Ending) strategy guides writers to consider both sides of an argument during the planning process (De La Paz & Graham, 1997). Students are taught to (a) Suspend judgment by listing reasons for each side of a position before deciding on a premise, (b) Take a position after evaluating the listed ideas, (c) Organize ideas from strongest to weakest or most important to least important, and (d) Plan and write more while writing the essay. The DARE component focuses the writer's attention on specific critical elements of the persuasive argument by teaching students to develop a strong topic sentence, add logical supporting ideas, reject possible arguments for the other side, and end with an effective, convincing conclusion. For students who have difficulty developing a position, STOP helps students in deliberating the decision process and keeping reasons organized. See Harris et al. (2008) and Mason, Reid et al. (2012) for complete STOP and DARE lesson plans and materials.

Revision and Editing. Many writers integrate revision and editing into a single process after a rough draft has been written. Writing mechanics, especially for struggling writers, should not be dismissed, as these writers often have so many spelling and sentence-level errors in syntax, capitalization, and punctuation that meaning is completely overshadowed. One well-supported approach, SIM for the COPS (Capitalization and communication,

Organization and layout, Punctuation and Paragraphing, Spelling and Sentence Structure) editing strategy, provides students a method for reviewing and editing writing (Schumaker et al., 1981). The COPS mnemonic checklist prompts students to the rules associated with each step. For example, for capitalization section, question prompts include, "Did you capitalize the first word in each sentence?" "Did you capitalize each proper noun?" and so on. In the area of communication, questions focus the students' attention to the clarity of ideas and vocabulary use. The COPS strategy is a powerful editing tool and has been combined with other strategies, such as Berry and Mason's (2012) SRSD for POW+TREE+COPS instruction for improving General Educational Development (GED) writing test outcomes with adult learners.

Often, however, struggling writers edit for writing mechanics, such as spelling, capitalization, and punctuation, ignoring content-level revision. As noted above, writing mechanics are important; however, revision should focus on clarifying and enhancing content meaning, resulting in improving the quality (MacArthur & Graham, 1987; MacArthur et al., 1991). For struggling writers, identifying contextual weaknesses in writing is particularly problematic. Researchers speculate that this may be the result of a cognitive disconnect between what the writer intends to write, and what is actually written (MacArthur et al., 1991). MacArthur and colleagues further ventured that when writers read their own work, the writer's mind fills in missing and ambiguous details not present in the written text. Fortunately, two solutions, peer revision instruction and technology for revision, assist students in improving writing at the revision stage. In fact, the positive effects of peer-assisted learning and technology for writing are well documented in the literature (Graham & Perin, 2007).

Peer revision. For peer revision to be effective, teachers must teach student editors how to provide appropriate support and feedback to peers, and then carefully monitor student interactions for accuracy (Greenwood, Carta, & Kamps, 1990). Evidence suggests that over time and peer editing practice, authors begin to internalize and apply peer editors' feedback when writing paper drafts (Stoddard & MacArthur, 1993). Peer revising is effective for all grade levels. In fact, young first-grade students have been successful in using peer editing checklists, writers' portfolios, and questionnaires to make meaningful contributions to content and simple mechanical edits for peers' work (Jasmine & Weiner, 2007).

One strategy, the Student Editor Strategy, assists students in increasing revising knowledge for improving overall writing quality (MacArthur et al., 1991; MacArthur, Graham, Schwartz, & Schafer, 1995; Stoddard & MacArthur, 1993). The Student Editor Strategy for revision is approached in two phases, substantive change and mechanical change. Student pairs follow a reciprocal five-step procedure during peer editing: (a) authors read their paper aloud to their editors, (b) the editor discusses what they liked best about their partner's paper, (c) the editor rereads the paper silently, (d) the editor makes editing suggestions to the author, and (e) the editor discusses the editing suggestions with the author. Stoddard and MacArthur (1993) identified four guiding revision questions: (1) Parts—Does it have a good beginning, middle and ending? (2) Order—Does it follow a logical sequence? (3) Details—Where could more details be added? and (4) Clarity—Is there any part that is hard to understand? Following peer conferencing, each author reviews the editor's suggestions, making substantive changes. In a second peer conference, students discuss the substantive changes made and edit one another's paper for mechanical errors.

Morris Kindzierski (2009) tested a peer revision checklist for students with emotional and behavioral disorders: (a) Does the paper have an interesting beginning, middle, and ending sentence? (b) Is it easy to understand? (c) Does it have interesting and different words? (d) Is it clear and well organized? (e) Is it boring? and (f) Does it have correct spelling and punctuation? Peer editors reciprocally evaluated each other's writing. The editor asks the writer to orally evaluate their work using the questions on the checklist, and then the editor selects two of the six areas in need of improvements, making suggestions for how the author might improve their essay. After instruction, Morris Kindzierski reported decreased antisocial verbal exchanges between students.

Technology for revision. Multiple features included in standard word processing programs may help students produce better-written products by facilitating efficient revision during and after drafting. MacArthur (2006) noted that two meta-analyses on the effects of word processing (Bangert-Drowns, 1993; Goldberg, Russell, & Cook, 2003) found moderate improvements for word processing on length and quality of compositions. Findings noted: (a) word processing is more powerful when included in the context of writing instruction, (b) greater effect sizes were found for struggling writers when compared to typically achieving peers, and (c) results were significantly stronger for students who had typing skills in excess of 20 words-per-minute, while poor typists had significantly lower scores. Based on these findings, students who are competent typists may be at a disadvantage when using pencil and paper during writing assessment. Unfortunately, research on the effects of word processing suggests that while writers are more likely to make revisions when using a word processor, the changes are superficial and do not change meaning (MacArthur, 2006).

When considering the many benefits of built-in editing features in software, it is important to remember that it is the student's choice to accept or reject recommendations. If the student struggles with reading and spelling, they may have trouble making the correct choice for replacing misspelled words, or they may not recognize inaccurate or auto-correct substitutions. MacArthur, Graham, Haynes, and De La Paz (1996) examined the effects of spell checkers on the writing outcomes of students with learning disabilities, identifying several limitations. First, spell checkers do not flag inappropriate or misspelled words if the incorrect version of a word exists in a dictionary; therefore, homonyms, and other real words, though incorrect in the context of an author's sentence, will not be flagged for correction. In MacArthur et al.'s (1996) study, this type of error accounted for 37% of the errors in middle school students' writing. In 25% of the errors, the student's attempt to spell a word was so far from the correct spelling that the spell checker did not supply the correct word in the list of suggested substitutions. Although technology may not be a solution for all weak spellers, evidence does suggest that providing explicit instruction in how to effectively utilize spell checkers does promote success (McNaughton, Hughes, & Ofiesh, 1997).

Conclusions

In summary, writing assessment should include frequent formative assessment for evaluating students' basic skills in handwriting, spelling, and sentence and paragraph development. Formative benchmark assessments should be given across disciplines to evaluate students' basic skill application and ability to write to genre specific tasks. Intervention, based on students' needs as noted in assessment, should include evidence-based instruction for basic skill development as well as for improving students' written expression throughout the writing processes of planning, composing, revising, and editing. It is critical that teachers not rely on strategies and technology to replace instruction. Best practice includes explicit strategy instruction supported by a collaborative writing environment for teacher and peer feedback, and by teaching students processes for self-regulating the writing process.

References

Archer, A. L., & Hughes, C. A. (2011). *Explicit instruction: Effective and efficient teaching.* New York, NY: Guilford Press.

Asaro-Saddler, K., & Saddler, B. (2010). Planning instruction and self-regulation training: Effects on writers with autism spectrum disorder. *Exceptional Children, 77,* 107–124.

Association for Supervision and Curriculum Development (ASCD). (2002). *Teaching students with learning disabilities: Using learning strategies.* Retrieved from http://shop.ascd.org/Default.aspx?TabID=55&ProductId=1553

Bangert-Drownes, R. L. (1993). The word processor as an instructional tool: A meta-analysis of word processing in writing instruction. *Review of Educational Research, 63,* 69–93.

Benedek-Wood, E., Mason, L. H., Wood, P., & Kubina, R. M. (2012). *Effects of SRSD for quick writing instruction in four inclusive science classrooms.* Manuscript in preparation.

Benson, B. J., & Campbell, H. M. (2009). Assessment of student writing with curriculum-based measurement. In G. A. Troia (Ed.), *Instruction and assessment for struggling writers* (pp. 337–357). New York, NY: Guilford Press.

Berry, A., & Mason, L. H. (2012). The effects of self-regulated strategy development on the writing of expository essays for adults with written expression difficulties: Preparing for the GED. *Remedial and Special Education, 33,* 124–136.

Common Core State Standards Initiative. (2012). Retrieved from http://www.corestandards.org

Darch, C., Eaves, R. C., Crowe, D. A., Simmons, K., & Conniff, A. (2006). Teaching spelling to students with learning disabilities: A comparison of rule-based strategies versus traditional instruction. *Journal of Direct Instruction, 6,* 1–16.

De La Paz, S. (1999). Self-regulated strategy instruction in regular education settings: Improving outcomes for students with and without learning disabilities. *Learning Disabilities Research and Practice, 14,* 92–106.

De La Paz, S., & Graham, S. (1997). Strategy instruction in planning: Effects on the writing performance and behavior of students with writing difficulties. *Exceptional Children, 63,* 167–181

De La Paz, S., Owen, B., Harris, K., & Graham, S. (2000). Riding Elvis's motorcycle: Using Self-Regulated Strategy Development to PLAN and WRITE for a state writing exam. *Learning Disabilities Research & Practice, 15,* 101–109.

Englert, C. S., Mariage, T. V., & Dunsmore, K. (2006). Tenets of sociocultural theory in writing instruction research. In C. A. Macarthur, S. Graham, & J. Fitzgerald (Eds.), *Handbook of writing research* (pp. 208–221). New York, NY: Guilford Press.

Englert, C. S., Raphael, T. E., Anderson, L. M., Anthony, H. M., Stevens, D. D., & Fear, K. L. (1991). Making writing strategies and self-talk visible: Cognitive strategy instruction in writing in regular and special education classrooms. *American Educational Research Journal, 28,* 337–372.

Goldberg, A., Russell, M., & Cook, A. (2003). The effect of computers on student writing: A meta-analysis of studies from 1992–2002. *Journal of Technology, Learning and Assessment, 2,* 1–51.

Graham, S. (1983). Effective spelling instruction. *Elementary School Journal, 83,* 560–567.

Graham, S. (1999). Handwriting and spelling instruction for students with learning disabilities: A review. *Learning Disability Quarterly, 22,* 78–98.

Graham, S. (2006). Strategy instruction and the teaching of writing: A meta-analysis. In C. MacArthur, S. Graham, & J. Fitzgerald (Eds.), *Handbook of writing research* (pp. 187–207). New York, NY: Guilford Press.

Graham, S., & Harris, K. R. (2003). Students with learning disabilities and the process of writing: A meta-analysis of SRSD studies. In L. Swanson, K. R. Harris, & S. Graham (Eds.), *Handbook of research on learning disabilities* (pp. 383–402). New York, NY: Guilford.

Graham, S., & Harris, K. R. (2012). Retrieved from http://www.specialed.ccsu.edu/nicoll-senft/handwriting%20 and%20Spelling%20Manual%20saved.rtf

Graham, S., Harris, K. R., & Fink, B. (2000). Is handwriting causally related to learning to write? Treatment of handwriting problems in beginning writers. *Journal of Educational Psychology, 92,* 620-633.

Graham, S., Harris, K. R., & Fink-Chorzempa, B. (2002). Contributions of spelling instruction to the spelling, writing, and reading of poor spellers. *Journal of Educational Psychology, 94,* 669-686.

Graham, S., Harris, K. R., & Hebert, M. (2011). *Assessing writing.* Report prepared for the Carnegie Corp. of New York, NY.

Graham, S., Harris, K. R., & Mason, L. H. (2005). Improving the writing performance, knowledge, and self-efficacy of struggling young writers: The effects of self-regulated strategy development. *Contemporary Educational Psychology, 30,* 207–241.

Graham, S., Harris, K. R., Mason, L. H., Fink, B., Moran, S., & Saddler, B. (2008). Teaching handwriting in the primary grades: A national survey. *Reading and Writing: An Interdisciplinary Journal, 21,* 49–69.

Graham, S., & Hebert, M. A. (2010). *Writing to read: Evidence for how writing can improve reading. A Carnegie Corporation time to act report.* Washington, DC: Alliance for Excellent Education.

Graham, S., MacArthur, C., Schwartz, S., & Page-Voth, V. (1992). Improving the compositions of students with learning disabilities using a strategy involving product and process goal setting. *Exceptional Children, 58,* 322–334.

Graham, S., & Perin, D. (2007). A meta-analysis of writing instruction. *Journal of Educational Psychology, 99,* 445–476.

Greenwood, C. R., Carta, J. J., & Kamps, D. M. (1990). *Teacher- versus peer-mediated instruction: A review of educational advantages and disadvantages.* Sussex, UK: Wiley Ltd.

Harris, K. R., & Graham, S. (1992). Self-regulated strategy development: A part of the writing process. In M. Pressley, K. Harris, & J. Guthrie (Eds.), *Promoting academic competence and literacy in schools.* San Diego, CA: Academic Press.

Harris, K. R., Graham, S., MacArthur, C., Reid, R., & Mason, L. H. (2011). Self-regulated learning processes and children's writing. In B. Zimmerman & D. Schunk (Eds.), *Handbook of self-regulation of learning and performance* (pp. 187–201). Danvers, MA: Routledge.

Harris, K. R., Graham, S., & Mason, L. H. (2006). Self-regulated strategy development for 2nd-grade students who struggle with writing. *American Educational Research Journal, 43,* 295–340.

Harris, K. R., Graham, S., Mason, L. H., & Friedlander, B. (2008). *Powerful writing strategies for all students.* Baltimore, MD: Brooks Publishing Co., Inc.

Huot, B., & Neal, M. (2006). Writing assessment: A techno-history. In C. MacArthur, S. Graham, & J. Fitzgerald (Eds.), *Handbook of writing research* (pp. 417–432). New York, NY: Guilford Press.

Jasmine, J., & Weiner, W. (2007). The effects of writing workshop on abilities of first grade students to become confident and independent writers. *Early Childhood Education Journal, 35,* 131–139.

MacArthur, C. A. (2006). The effects of new technologies on writing and writing processes. In C. A. Macarthur, S. Graham, & J. Fitzgerald (Eds.), *Handbook of writing research* (pp. 248–262). New York, NY: Guilford Press.

MacArthur, C. A., & Graham, S. (1987). LD students composing under three methods of text production: Handwriting, word processing, and dictation. *Journal of Special Education, 21,* 22–42.

MacArthur, C., Graham, S., Haynes, J., & De La Paz, S. (1996). Spelling checkers and students with learning disabilities: Performance comparisons and impact on spelling. *Journal of Special Education, 30,* 35–57.

MacArthur, C. A., Graham, S., Schwartz, S. S., & Schafer, W. D. (1995). Evaluation of a writing instruction model that integrated a process approach, strategy instruction, and word processing. *Learning Disability Quarterly, 18,* 278–291.

MacArthur, C., Schwartz, S., & Graham, S. (1991). Effects of a reciprocal peer revision strategy in special education classrooms. *Learning Disability Research and Practice, 6,* 201–210.

Mason, L. H. (2004). Explicit self-regulated strategy development versus reciprocal questioning: Effects on expository reading comprehension among struggling readers. *Journal of Educational Psychology, 96,* 283–296.

Mason, L. H., Benedek-Wood, E., Kubina, R., & Wood, P. (2012). *SRSD for quick writing instruction in the middle school science classroom.* Manuscript in preparation.

Mason, L. H., Benedek-Wood, E., & Valasa, L. (2009). Quick writing for students who struggle with writing. *Journal of Adolescent and Adult Literacy, 53,* 313–322.

Mason, L. H., Dunn Davison, M., Hammer, C. S., Miller, C. A., & Glutting, J. (2012). Knowledge, writing, and language outcomes for a reading comprehension and writing intervention. *Reading and Writing: An Interdisciplinary Journal.* Published online first, July 28, 2012. doi 10.1007/s11145–012–9409–0

Mason, L. H., & Graham, S. (2008). Writing instruction for adolescents with learning disabilities: Programs of intervention research. *Learning Disabilities Research and Practice, 23,* 103–112.

Mason, L. H., Harris, K. R., & Graham, S. (2011). Self-regulated strategy development for students with writing difficulties. *Theory in Practice, 50,* 20–27.

Mason, L. H., Harris, K. R., & Graham, S. (2013). Strategies for improving student outcomes in written expression. In M. Tankersley & B. Cook (Eds.), *Effective practices in special education* (pp. 86–97). Upper Saddle River, NJ: Pearson.

Mason, L. H., Hickey Snyder, K., Sukhram, D. P., & Kedem, Y. (2006). Self-regulated strategy development for expository reading comprehension and informative writing: Effects for nine 4th-grade students who struggle with learning. *Exceptional Children, 73,* 69–89.

Mason, L. H., & Kubina, R. M. (2011). Developing writing fluency for adolescents with disabilities. *Assessment and Intervention: Advances in Learning and Behavioral Disabilities, 24,* 295–319.

Mason, L. H., Kubina, R. M., Kostewicz, D., Mong Cramer, A., & Datchuk, S. (2013). *Improving quick writing performance of middle school struggling learners. Contemporary Educational Psychology, 38,* 236–246.

Mason, L. H., Kubina, R., & Taft, R. (2011). Developing quick writing skills of middle school students with disabilities. *Journal of Special Education, 44,* 205–220.

Mason, L. H., Kubina, R. M., Valasa, L. L., & Cramer, A. M. (2010). Evaluating effective writing instruction of adolescent students in an emotional and/or behavioral support setting. *Journal of Behavioral Disorders, 35,* 140–156.

Mason, L. H., Reid, R., & Hagaman, J. (2012). *Building comprehension in adolescents: Powerful strategies for improving reading and writing in content areas.* Baltimore, MD: Brooks Publishing Co., Inc.

Mastropieri, M. A., Scruggs, T. E., Cerar, N. I., Allen-Bronaugh, D., Thompson, C., Guckert, M., Leins, P., Hauth, C., & Cuenca-Sanchez, Y. (2012). Fluent persuasive writing with students with emotional disturbance: Developing arguments and counterarguments. *Journal of Special Education.* doi: 10.1177/0022466912440456

McNaughton, D., Hughes, C., & Ofiesh, N. (1997). Proofreading for students with learning disabilities: Integrating computer use and strategy use. *Learning Disabilities Research and Practice, 12,* 16–28.

Milne, A. A. (1926). *Winnie-the-Pooh.* London, UK: Methuen & Co., Ltd.

Moats, L. (2009). Teaching spelling to students with language and learning disabilities. In G. A. Troia (Ed.), *Instruction and assessment for struggling writers* (pp. 269–289). New York, NY: Guilford Press.

Moran, M. R., Schumaker, J. B., & Vetter, A. F. (1981). *Teaching a paragraph organization strategy to learning disabled adolescents* (Research Rep. No. 54). Lawrence, KS: Institute for Research in Learning Disabilities.

Morris Kindzierski, C. M. (2009). "I like it the way it is!": Peer-revision writing strategies for students with emotional behavioral disorders. *Preventing School Failure, 54,* 51–59.

Nippold, M. (2004). Research on later language development: International perspectives. In R. Berman (Ed.), *Language development across childhood and adolescence* (pp. 1–8). Philadelphia, PA: John Benjamins Publishing Co.

Rowling, J. K. (1999). *Harry Potter and the sorcerer's stone.* New York, NY: Scholastic.

Saddler, B. (2012). *Teacher's guide to effective sentence writing.* New York, NY: Guilford Press.

Saddler, B., Behforooz, B., & Asaro, K. (2008). The effects of sentence-combining instruction on the writing of fourth-grade students with writing difficulties. *Journal of Special Education, 42,* 79–90.

Saddler, B., & Graham, S. (2005). The effects of peer-assisted sentence-combining instruction on the writing performance of more and less skilled young writers. *Journal of Educational Psychology, 97,* 43–54.

Schmidt, J. L., Deshler, D. D., Schumaker, J. B., & Alley, G. R. (1988). Effects of generalization instruction on the written language performance of adolescents with learning disabilities in the mainstream classroom. *Reading, Writing, and Learning Disabilities, 4,* 291–309.

Schumaker, J. B., & Deshler, D. D. (2003). Can students with LD become competent writers? *Learning Disabilities Quarterly, 26,* 129–141.

Schumaker, J. B., Deshler, D. D., Nolan, S., Clark, F. L., Alley, G. R., & Warner, M. M. (1981). *Error monitoring: A learning strategy for improving academic performance of LD adolescents* (Research Rep. No. 34). Lawrence, KS: University of Kansas.

Schumaker, J. B., & Lyerla, K. D. (1991). *The paragraph writing strategy: Instructor's manual.* Lawrence, KS: The University of Kansas Center for Research on Learning.

Sermis, M. D., Burstein, J., & Leacock, C. (2006). Application of computer in assessment and analysis of writing. In C. MacArthur, S. Graham, & J. Fitzgerald (Eds.), *Handbook of writing research* (pp. 187–207). New York, NY: Guilford Press.

Stoddard, B., & MacArthur, C. A. (1993). A peer editor strategy: Guiding learning-disabled students in response and revision. *Research in the Teaching of English, 27,* 76–103.

Taft, R., & Mason, L. H. (2011). Examining effects of writing interventions: Spotlighting results for students with primary disabilities other than learning disabilities. *Remedial and Special Education, 32,* 359–370.

Therrien, W. J., Hughes, C., Kapelski, C., & Mokhtari, K. (2009). Effectiveness of a test taking strategy on students' with learning disabilities achievement on essay tests. *Journal of Learning Disabilities, 42,* 14–23.

Troia, G. A. (2006). Writing instruction for students with learning disabilities. In S. Graham, C. A. MacArthur, & J. Fitzgerald (Eds.), *Best practices in writing instruction* (pp. 324–336). New York, NY: Guilford Press.

Wanzek, J., Vaughn, S., Wexler, J., Swanson, E. A., Edmonds, M., & Kim, A. (2006). A synthesis of spelling and reading interventions and their effects on the spelling outcomes of students with LD. *Journal of Learning Disabilities, 39,* 528–543.

Wong, B. Y. L., Butler, D. L., Ficzere, S. A., Kuperis, S., Corden, M., & Zelmer, J. (1994). Teaching problem learners revision skills and sensitivity to audience through two instructional modes: Student-teacher versus student-student interactive dialogues. *Learning Disabilities Research & Practice, 9,* 78–90.

Instructional Resources

Process Skills

Center for Accelerating Student Learning (CASL). http://www.specialed.ccsu.edu/nicoll-senft/handwriting%20and%20Spelling%20Manual%20saved.rtf

Saddler, B. (2012). *Teacher's guide to effective sentence writing.* New York, NY: Guilford Press.

Strategy Instructional Model (SIM)

Kansas University Center for Research on Learning:
http://www.kucrl.org/.edu
http://www.kucrl.org/sim/strategies/paragraph.shtml

Self-Regulated Strategy Development (SRSD)

Association for Supervision and Curriculum Development (ASCD). (2002). *Teaching students with learning disabilities: Using learning strategies.* Retrieved from http://shop.ascd.org/Default.aspx?TabID=55&ProductId=1553
Harris, K. R., Graham, S., Mason, L. H., & Friedlander, B. (2008). *Powerful writing strategies for all students.* Baltimore, MD: Brooks Publishing Co., Inc.
Mason, L. H., Reid, R., & Hagaman, J. (2012). *Building comprehension in adolescents: Powerful strategies for improving reading and writing in content areas.* Baltimore, MD: Brooks Publishing Co. Inc.
Vanderbilt University:
http://hobbs.vanderbilt.edu/projectwrite.
http://iris.peabody.vanderbilt.edu/pow/chalbycle.htm.

15

Mathematics Interventions

Robin S. Codding and Ryan J. Martin

Introduction: Importance of Mathematics

Besides representing one of the fundamental three "Rs" taught and learned in school, mathematics knowledge is necessary for everyday life. Mathematics understanding is utilized in simple trips to the grocery store, required for nearly all forms of employment, underscores acquisition of items, such as homes and cars, is involved in daily life tasks, such as cooking, permits us to maintain and understand personal health, is prevalent in social media, and is fundamental to the development of technology that we utilize on an hourly basis (National Research Council [NCR], 2001; Patton, Cronin, Bassett, & Koppel, 1997). Competence in mathematics is increasingly critical, as evidenced by employment data suggesting that development in mathematics, science, and engineering careers will likely outpace general job growth (National Mathematics Advisory Panel [NMAP], 2008). Compelling research has suggested that although prerequisite reading, mathematics, and attention skills upon school entry all predict later school achievement, the most significant of these predictors is mathematics (Duncan et al., 2007). Unfortunately, it also appears that challenges with mathematics in preschool or during the kindergarten year persist through intermediate grades, without intervention (Morgan, Farkas, & Wu, 2009). Until recently, less attention has been paid to mathematics instruction and intervention, and it is possible that such directly provided school-based mathematics experiences may substantially impact student outcomes (NCR, 2001).

The focus on mathematics competency, or proficiency, within education integrates the following five elements: (a) conceptual understanding, (b) procedural fluency, (c) strategic competence, (d) adaptive reasoning, and (e) productive disposition (NCR, 2001). Conceptual understanding might be defined as knowledge of math concepts, principles, and ideas, such as the commutative property (i.e., $2 + 5 = 5 + 2$), place value according to the base-10 system, and doubles with other sums ($7 + 8 = 7 + 7 + 1$). Procedural fluency is the notion that students use algorithms, mnemonics, mental math, and other procedures appropriately and efficiently. Included herein is the importance of automatic recall of basic facts (NMAP, 2008).

Strategic competence refers to mathematical problem solving via visual or mental representation. Adaptive reasoning reflects, "logical thought, reflection, explanation and justification" (NCR, 2001, p. 116). Finally, productive disposition is the motivation to engage in, provide effort toward, and belief about mathematics learning. A central tenet associated with this definition of proficiency is that each of these elements is mutually dependent (NCR, 2001; NMAP, 2008). For example, the use of effective procedures permits enhanced conceptual understanding of more complex ideas (NCR, 2001; NMAP, 2008; Fuchs et al., 2006; Geary, Hoard, Byrd-Craven, & DeSoto, 2004; Geary, Bailey, & Hoard, 2009). However, knowledge of procedures without conceptual understanding or adaptive reasoning may lead to inefficient problem solving and errors.

Empirically Supported Instruction and Intervention Practices in Mathematics

Evidence-based practice (EBP) refers to the integration of the best available intervention research, clinical expertise, and context within which the intervention will be utilized (American Psychological Association Presidential Task Force on Evidence-Based Practice, 2006). This requires that interventionists be familiar with the most recent evidence supporting treatment strategies, as well as be able to analyze the intervention match within the local context (e.g., school, classroom, instructional quality) and according to student skills (Burns, Codding, Boice, & Lukito, 2010; Gickling, Shane, & Croskery, 1989; Kratochwill & Shernoff, 2004). An important caveat in the pursuit of EBP is that interventionists make data-based decisions founded on the utility, feasibility, and effectiveness of recommended treatment strategies within their own setting (Kratochwill & Shernoff, 2004). The focus of the present chapter is to describe one aspect of EBP: the available evidence associated with intervention strategies that can be used with students at risk for and with mathematics challenges. A number of intervention strategies in the areas of early numeracy, computation fluency, and mathematics problem solving have been supported within the extant literature and reflect national recommendations. The organization of this chapter will be as follows. First, we will describe general recommendations of the NMAP (2008) report for mathematics. Second, we will identify specific challenges faced by children who find mathematics difficult. Third, we will describe general instructional strategies effective for children with mathematics difficulties. Fourth, we will outline specific intervention components for inclusion in intervention packages. Finally, strategies appropriate for addressing early numeracy, computation, and word problem solving for elementary school grades will be explained.

The NMAP (2008) developed a series of recommendations in their final report for general mathematics practices according to the existing research and policy. (Interested readers are encouraged to review this report for details.) Some of the central findings and suggestions included: (a) development of a focused curriculum involving proficiency in key areas that progress in a coherent manner across elementary and secondary grades that is relatively consistent across states; (b) publication of shorter and more focused textbooks; (c) definition of algebra and development of a topic list; (d) goal for general education programming to cultivate proficiency with whole numbers, fractions, and essential elements of geometry and measurement; (e) integration of conceptual understanding, computation fluency, and problem solving skills; (f) instructional practices that combine teacher-directed and student-centered approaches; (g) use of cooperative learning strategies to improve computation skills; (h) use of formative assessment; (i) provision of explicit instruction to students with mathematics challenges; and (j) caution regarding calculators given the potential harm their use may have on mathematics learning. This report, in combination with previous recommendations from the NCR (2001) and development of curriculum focal points by the National Council of Teachers of Mathematics (2006), offers much-needed consistency regarding general instructional practices and core instructional content provided to all students in kindergarten through grade eight.

Challenges of Students with Mathematics Difficulties

Not surprising given the complex, multi-topic nature of mathematics content, mathematical difficulties appear to be multi-faceted. Bryant, Bryant, and Hammill (2000) found that special education professionals listed more than 30 different behaviors that differentiated children with weaknesses in mathematics, compared to those without weaknesses. The most commonly cited behavior was trouble solving word problems, and some of the best predictors' of mathematics challenges included procedural difficulty with multi-step problems and borrowing errors, which also reflects empirical evidence (Geary, 1993). Other studies have suggested that automatic fact retrieval and calculation fluency may represent the central feature of children with mathematics difficulties (e.g., Gersten, Jordan, & Flojo, 2005). For example, research has illustrated that students without mathematics learning disabilities recall as much as three times the number of basic facts as do their peers with learning disabilities; however, accuracy of basic fact performance is equivalent (Hasselbring, Goin, & Bransford, 1988; Gersten & Chard, 1999).

Children with mathematics learning disabilities also tend to use less-mature counting strategies, such as guessing and the sum procedure (e.g., in the problem 3 + 4, children count both numbers starting with 1), and make more counting errors than do their peers (Geary et al., 2004). That is, these children may not be familiar with the magnitude sequence of numerals and, therefore, can only determine which number comes first (e.g., 3 or 4) by counting from 1 (Baroody, Bajwa, & Eiland, 2009). A series of longitudinal studies illustrated that knowledge of and fluency with number words, numerals, and their quantities, as well as number lines, represent critical components that underlie mathematics learning (Geary, 2011; Geary et al., 2009; Jordan, Kaplan, Ramineni, & Locuniak, 2009). Difficulties in these core areas have been shown to be stable through the elementary school years (Jordan, Hanich, & Kaplan, 2003b; Jordan et al., 2009), and mathematics competency in kindergarten is highly predictive of later school achievement (Duncan et al., 2007; Jordan et al., 2009; Morgan et al., 2009).

General Instructional Features for Success

Educational practices in mathematics vary in form and approach. The same is true regarding mathematics education for students with differing abilities and aptitude. Numerous studies have attempted to examine the efficacy of practices that aim to improve mathematics outcomes for struggling students (Baker, Gersten, & Lee, 2002; Browder, Spooner, Ahlgrim-Delzell, Harris, & Wakeman, 2008; Gersten et al., 2009; Kroesbergen & Van Luit, 2003). Throughout the current literature, struggling students range in ability from those with low achievement in mathematics or those at risk of failure (Baker et al., 2002), to students with cognitive disabilities or learning disabilities (LD) (Browder et al., 2008; Gersten et al., 2009), as well as students participating in special education programs (Kroesbergen & Van Luit, 2003). Mathematics instruction for struggling students often incorporates many of the methods and practices that are efficacious with students from the general population. However, meta-analytic findings regarding mathematics instruction provide evidence for certain instructional practices that tend to be well-suited for special populations and lead to positive outcomes with these students. For example, explicit/direct instruction has been one of the most thoroughly investigated practices for struggling students, and has also demonstrated the most consistent positive results. In Baker, Gersten, and Lee's (2002) meta-analysis, explicit/direct instruction produced moderate to strong effect sizes for low-achieving students at risk for failure in mathematics. In a similar meta-analysis of mathematics instruction for students with LD, Gersten et al. (2009) also found strong effect sizes for explicit/direct instruction independent of other practices. Specifically for the learning of basic skills, Kroesbergen and Van Luit (2003) found direct instruction to be effective with children in special education programs. Another form of instruction has also demonstrated positive results among struggling students. Systematic instruction often mimics direct/explicit instruction, but involves prompting and feedback procedures for specific target skills as a key component (Browder et al., 2008). In a meta-analysis of instructional practices for students with severe cognitive disabilities, Browder et al. (2008) found systematic instruction to be an evidence-based practice.

In some contexts and formats, self-instruction has demonstrated positive results with struggling students. Specifically for learning problem-solving skills, Kroesbergen and Van Luit (2003) found self-instruction to be effective for children in special education programs. Similarly, Gersten et al. (2009) found that encouraging students with LD to learn and use verbalizations to guide themselves through their work was consistently efficacious across studies, as verbalizing thinking or strategies may help students to self-regulate and avoid simple errors stemming from impulsivity. Gersten et al. (2009) also found positive effects when students with LD were taught heuristic problem solving strategies, which helped students "to organize abstract information and to remember organizational frameworks or schema" (p. 1231), and are often paired with verbalization strategies. However, the authors express a need for further research regarding the use of heuristics with LD students, as the complex nature of heuristics may, in certain contexts, provide unnecessary challenges for this population.

Another heavily researched instructional practice is peer-assisted learning. Though this practice has been found to be quite effective for the general population (Slavin & Lake, 2008), the efficacy of various peer-assisted learning practices for struggling students tends to vary by format and student disability. Baker et al. (2002) found that peer-assisted learning programs produced moderate to strong effect sizes within the domain of math computation; however, there was insufficient evidence to indicate similar effects in other domains. Conversely, Gersten et al. (2009) did not find any significant effect sizes for within-class peer-assisted learning with LD students. However, the same meta-analysis did find strong effect sizes for LD students participating in cross-age peer tutoring. The authors explain these differential effects as a function of the LD students' abilities relative to those of their peers; same-aged peers within the classroom may be more proficient in mathematics, but may lack an ability to explain or demonstrate principles in a meaningful way, whereas older children may have better-developed skills in instructional support (i.e., prompting, fading) and thus appear to be more likely to help LD students improve.

Performance feedback is often a crucial component of the learning process, and its application to mathematics instruction has been investigated in a multitude of forms. A number of studies have investigated academic outcomes as they relate to providing teachers, students, and parents with data regarding students' mathematics performance. Gersten et al. (2009)

found that providing teachers with detailed student performance data produced mixed results. Special education teachers provided with such data tend to increase positive outcomes for students, compared to regular education teachers, likely due to special education teachers regularly working with performance data to set specific goals with students. However, Baker et al. (2002) found evidence for greater effect sizes when teachers were provided with student performance data that included specific recommendations to guide further instruction. Providing teachers with recommendations in addition to the student performance data appears to be a crucial component for the utility of such practice. At the student level, Gersten et al. (2009) found only marginal effects for providing performance feedback data, though limited research did indicate stronger effects when the feedback provided to students was effort related. As opposed to general performance data, effort-related data may be more motivating to students and in turn be more useful; the authors suggest this as an area requiring additional research. Across studies that provided parents with student performance data, Baker et al. (2002) found no significant effects with low-achieving students. Although providing parents with such data may not directly produce positive effects in student performance, it may be a low-cost and simple way to indirectly benefit students through parental involvement and communication.

With an increased presence of digital media in schools and classrooms, the use of Computer-Aided Instruction (CAI) in conjunction with mathematics instruction has also been examined in numerous studies (Kroesbergen & Van Luit, 2003; Slavin & Lake, 2008; Slavin, Lake, & Groff, 2009). There are several practical applications of CAI technology in the mathematics classroom. First, CAI programs can be used as a means to teach various lessons or to demonstrate new concepts. Also, CAI can be used to provide both teachers and students with performance feedback data, which may identify areas of strength and weakness, as well as students' general progress. Evidence for the efficacy of CAI programs is mixed among current literature, and tends to vary by its implementation. Slavin and Lake's (2008) best-evidence syntheses found modest effect sizes for CAI programs at the elementary level and weak effect sizes for CAI programs used in middle/high school settings (Slavin et al., 2009). Studies tended to demonstrate more positive outcomes if the CAI programs were used in conjunction with or as a supplement to regular classroom instruction (Slavin & Lake, 2008; Slavin et al., 2009), and when implementation was limited to 30 minutes of weekly instruction time (Slavin & Lake, 2009). The findings of Slavin and Lake (2008) and Slavin et al.'s (2009) best-evidence syntheses are limited, in that many of the included studies of CAI were conducted in the 1980s and 1990s and featured CAI programs that are outdated and/or no longer commercially available. Nevertheless, Kroesbergen and Van Luit (2003) demonstrated the potential efficacy and utility of these programs in a meta-analysis. Although classrooms using CAI programs tended to have lower overall effect sizes than did classrooms using other interventions; a number of included studies paired CAI with direct instruction and produced positive effects. In these cases, although it is difficult to attribute positive effects to CAI programs independent of direct instruction (a practice with demonstrated efficacy), Kroesbergen and Van Luit's (2003) findings confirm the notion that CAI is less effective than teacher-led instruction, but can prove to be a valuable tool if used in conjunction with the general curriculum.

Common Intervention Features for Struggling Students

Identification of core intervention components is important to facilitate the development of novel mathematics treatments, particularly since fewer standard protocol interventions are available through clearinghouses and publishing companies (Fuchs, Fuchs, Powell et al.,

Table 15.1 Core Treatment Components

1. Explicit Instruction
2. Self-Instruction: Verbalize Math Thinking
3. Concrete-Visual-Abstract Representation of Number Concepts
4. Opportunities for and Sequence of Practice
5. Progress Monitoring and Performance Feedback
6. Motivation

2008; NMAP, 2008). Table 15.1 provides a list of common intervention features identified through literature summaries as being generally effective (Fuchs, Fuchs, Powell et al., 2008; Baker et al., 2002; Bryant & Bryant, 2008; Gersten et al., 2009; NMAP, 2008; NCR, 2001; Swanson, 2009; Swanson & Sachse-Lee, 2000). While none of these six components has illustrated effectiveness in isolation, combinations of these elements have resulted in improved skill proficiency for children with difficulty in mathematics (Fuchs, Fuchs, Powell et al., 2008; Gersten et al., 2009; Swanson, 2009).

Explicit instruction has been found to be necessary, albeit not sufficient, to facilitate the acquisition of basic skills for children with mathematics challenges (Baker et al., 2002; Fuchs, Fuchs, Powell et al., 2008; Gersten et al., 2009; Swanson, 2009; Swanson & Sachse-Lee, 2000). Explicit instruction includes teacher presentation of advance organizers and demonstration of specific skills and/or strategies in small, sequential steps with many examples. This methodology also incorporates guided practice with a gradual shift to independent practice using teacher-modeled steps and followed with frequent corrective feedback. Review and maintenance checks are used to ensure mastery of previously learned skills.

Self-instruction is considered to be a self-regulation or meta-cognitive strategy and tends to include self-questioning, think-alouds to model problem-solving steps, and simple heuristics such as "Say, Ask, Check," which reminds students to read the problem, ask themselves questions about the process of reading a problem, and check their work for each step (Kroesbergen & Van Luit, 2003; Montague, 2008). The purpose of self-instruction is to provide and model the use of visual and verbal prompts to provide a mechanism for students to monitor their own problem solving (Goldman, 1989). Verbalizing thinking may be particularly important to encourage the self-regulation of students who struggle with mathematics during the problem-solving process (Gersten et al., 2009; Swanson, 2009). Therefore, interventionists should encourage and model conversations that permit students to communicate how they are going to approach solving various mathematics problems or explain correct answers (Gersten et al., 2009). Strategy steps for different problem types are stated aloud in action terms, such as "read the problem first, next find the bigger number," and proceeded by students repeating and completing each step (Kroeger & Kouche, 2006; Tournaki, 2003). In small intervention groups, think aloud procedures could be modeled by interventionists and practiced by students using choral responding. In their seminal work, Meichenbaum and Goodman (1971) also suggested modeling of and practice with self-statements such as, "work slowly and follow the steps," to help students focus attention on the task, prevent impulsive responding, and manage frustration.

Strategic use of visual representation along with concrete manipulatives and practice with numerals has been shown to be an important element of treatment packages (Flores, 2009, 2010; Gersten et al., 2009; Mercer & Miller, 1992; Miller & Mercer, 1993; Swanson, 2009). Although the use of manipulatives, such as counters, chips, and blocks, to illustrate early mathematics concepts is not new, current recommendations suggest that the same mathematics concept be illustrated sequentially using concrete examples, visual representation, and abstract numerical symbols (Baroody, Bajwa et al., 2009). For example, Mercer and Miller (1992) found that students with mathematics learning disabilities benefited from independent practice of number combinations with concrete manipulatives an average of three times before practicing the same concept using visual displays such as pictures of objects, tally marks, number-lines, strip diagrams, and/or ten frames. Once students achieve accuracy independently solving problems using visual representations, practice with the numerals is initiated (Flores, 2010). A critical aspect of this progression is that use of manipulatives is brief and faded in order to advance toward visual representations, which serve as an intermediate step, and then abstract symbols (i.e., numerals).

Surprisingly, recent traditions in curricula and instruction have moved away from providing sufficient opportunities for practice to facilitate mastery of concepts and cumulative review to ensure retention of previously learned skills (Daly, Martens, Barnett, Witt, & Olson, 2007; NMAP, 2008). However, the extant literature supports such carefully constructed practice opportunities (Baroody, Eiland, & Thompson, 2009; Codding, Burns, & Lukito, 2011; Fuchs, Fuchs, Powell et al., 2008; Daly et al., 2007; Burns, VanDerHeyden, & Jiban, 2006; Powell, Fuchs, Fuchs, Cirino, & Fletcher, 2009; Swanson, 2009). In fact, one of the best predictors of mathematics competency maintenance in adulthood is quantity of school-based rehearsal and practice (Bahrick & Hall, 1998). Rather than focus on grade-level concepts, it is important to first identify missing foundational and prerequisite skills, and focus on building mastery in those areas (Gersten et al., 2009; Swanson, 2009). Development of effective practice opportunities requires that students be presented with material that matches their instructional level. In mathematics, this means that students should perform skills with approximately 70% to 85% accuracy, 14 to 31 digits correct per minute (grades 2 and 3), or 24 to 49 digits correct per minute (grades 4 and 5) (Burns et al., 2006; Gickling & Thompson, 1985). Practice should be sequenced systematically in small sets and according to student progress (Baroody, Eiland et al., 2009; Fuchs, Fuchs, Powell et al., 2008; Martens & Eckert, 2007). Conducting a survey level assessment using curriculum-based assessment-instructional design (Gickling & Havertape, 1981) is one way that interventionists can identify students' instructional levels on a pre-determined skill hierarchy (Burns et al., 2010). Practice sessions are generally brief but frequent and are constructed with both skills in isolation (e.g., flash cards) as well as application of component skills in context (e.g., word problems) (Daly et al., 2007; Fuchs, Fuchs, Craddock et al., 2008). Practice sessions are structured to incorporate modeling, immediate feedback on performance, and reinforcement for effort (Codding, Burns, et al., 2011; Daly et al., 2007).

Formative assessment, or progress monitoring, was a clear recommendation offered by the NMAP (2008), given the robust effect that distributing precise student performance data to teachers has on mathematics achievement (Fuchs, Fuchs, Hamlett, & Stecker, 1991. Formative assessment in mathematics requires that mastery measures, which evaluate specific skills targeted for intervention, and more generalized grade-level measures be evaluated daily, weekly, or monthly in order to examine immediate and generalized treatment effects (Hosp & Ardoin, 2008; Gersten et al., 2009). Providing students with their progress monitoring data or asking students to track their own performance may serve to improve engagement in the learning process (Codding, Chan-Iannetta, George, Ferreira, & Volpe, 2011; Codding, Chan-Iannetta, Palmer, & Lukito, 2009; Gersten et al., 2009).

Preliminary research supports incorporation of motivation strategies to encourage students' active engagement in mathematics activities (Gersten et al., 2009; NMAP, 2008). Interventionists may incorporate reinforcement for putting effort towards, persisting with, and accurately completing tasks (Gersten et al., 2009). Reinforcement might consist of specific praise for effort (e.g., "I like how you are making sure to follow each problem solving step") (Schunk & Cox, 1986), tokens or points that are later exchanged for prizes from a treasure chest (Fuchs et al., 2005; Fuchs, Fuchs, Craddock et al., 2008), and/or goal setting (Schunk, 1985; Fuchs et al., 1997; Codding, Chan-Iannetta, et al., 2009; Codding, Chan-Iannetta, et al., 2011).

Early Numeracy Conceptual Basis

A commonly described but evolving construct that underlines mathematical learning is number sense (Berch, 2005; Gersten & Chard, 1999). Number sense may be generally summarized as the understanding of numerals and their meaning, fluent and flexible use of numbers, proficiency with quantity comparisons, and mental representation of numbers (Gersten et al., 2005; Kalchman, Moss, & Case, 2001). Early numeracy competencies necessary for learning require that students recognize the relationship between numerals (e.g., 6), number words (e.g., "six"), and the quantities they represent, as well as fluently work with these representations (Geary, 2011). Number sense is acquired both formally and informally, with most children understanding basic counting principles such as 1:1 correspondence between verbal labels and objects as well as stable-order (i.e., verbal labels, or tags, have a stable rank order; "one, two, three") and cardinality (i.e., knowing the last number counted in an array represents the total number of items) prior to school entry (Gelman & Gallistel, 1978). Preschool-age children also are able to automatically recognize the number of items in a set when presented with, for example, an array of dots (•••) and can estimate which number array is larger (•••• vs. ••) (Baroody & Gatzke, 1991). Therefore, some students entering school understand numerical quantity comparisons as well as the distance between the numbers (5 is 3 bigger than 2); others may only know 5 is greater than 2; and still others may know how to use counting strategies to solve problems (Gersten & Chard, 1999; Siegler, 1988).

Two central elements of number sense with implications for school-based interventions are strategic counting and magnitude comparison (Gersten, Clarke, & Jordan, 2007). Given that children with mathematical challenges often use immature counting strategies, such as guessing or lining up two sets of items and counting all the objects from one, it is important that children learn what Siegler (1988) labeled as back-up counting strategies. One such strategy, the min or counting on strategy, is an essential form of counting in which children, when presented with a problem such as 4 + 1 = , recognize the larger quantity (4) and count up by the other addend (1). When the problem is presented in the reverse order, 1 + 4 = , children recognize that it is simpler to begin counting from 4. Use of the min strategy requires children to master problem solving strategies, recognize the number of items in a set, and provide the appropriate number word label (Gersten & Chard, 1999; Baroody, Bajwa, et al., 2009). The decomposition strategy, also known as doubles + 1, encourages children to use their knowledge of previously learned doubles facts (e.g., 2 + 2 = 4) to solve problems such as 2 + 3 (e.g., = 2 + 2 + 1; Woodward, 2006). Strategic counting provides a foundation for the commutative (e.g., 4 + 5 = 5 + 4) and associate (e.g., [2 + 6] + 1 = 2 + [6 + 1]) laws and likely facilitates automaticity with number combinations (Baroody, Bajwa, et al., 2009; Jordan et al., 2003a).

Magnitude comparison builds on the foundational informal skill subitizing (i.e., automatic recognition of a quantity of objects) and results in discrimination of two sets of objects or pictures of objects. Children subsequently learn to connect numerals to the object or pictorial representation of it, understanding, for example, that 8 is bigger than 4, and later are able to determine that 8 is 4 greater than 4 (Gersten & Chard, 1999). Numerical quantity discrimination among numbers that are farther apart (9 vs. 1) results in greater accuracy initially than those that are closer together (3 vs. 4), which is a phenomena known as the distance effect (Wilson, Dehaene, Dubois, & Fayol, 2009). Researchers postulate that by age 6, children assemble their knowledge of counting principles and magnitude comparison into a mental number line (Geary, 2011; Kalchman et al., 2001). The mental number line is consequently conceptualized as a central "big idea" for whole number knowledge (Gersten & Chard, 1999; Jordan, Kaplan, Olah, & Locuniak, 2006). Numerical magnitude representations in pre- and elementary school-age children are correlated with performance on a range of numerical competencies, including use of sophisticated counting strategies, and predict performance on arithmetic combinations (Booth & Seigler, 2008). As students' progress through early schooling more mental number line representations are generated (e.g., counting by 2s or 5s) and double-digit number combinations begin to be conceptualized using number lines for tens and ones (Kalchman et al., 2001). According to Siegler and Ramani (2009), accurate rank order number line estimates of numbers 0 to 100 and 0 to 1,000 occur in second and fourth grades, respectively.

Research-Supported Interventions

There is a paucity of research evaluating interventions that improve symbolic and non-symbolic aspects of early number sense in the beginning school years. Some evidence has suggested that interventions be introduced mid-kindergarten in order to appropriately capture the students most in need of additional support. Some children who begin their schooling experience with low number knowledge have been shown to make moderate gains by mid-year, which resulted in higher first-grade achievement (Jordan, Kaplan, Locuniak & Ramineni, 2007). Existing interventions are delivered in four different formats: (a) individual tutoring, (b) small group tutoring, (c) computer-assisted, or (d) a combination of small group tutoring and computer-assisted. Curriculum content for these interventions ranges from emphasis on numerical representations on number lines to comprehensive presentation of key early number concepts and number combinations using a variety of approaches.

Numeracy Recovery (Dowker, 2001) is an individualized intervention designed for 6- and 7-year-olds, according to performance on a numeracy screener. The intervention was designed to be administered by classroom teachers once weekly for 30 minutes per session which is accomplished by folding other school professionals, such as teaching assistants, into the classroom to work with students not receiving the intervention. Intervention concepts include basic counting principles, written numeral practice, place value, word problems, translation between concrete, verbal, and abstract representations, derived fact strategies, estimation, and automatic recall of basic facts. Core concepts are delivered and practiced through the use of counters, verbalization, object sorting and recording, exposure to and practice with the same problem delivered in different forms, sequenced presentation of a small set of basic facts, and number games. Preliminary research evidence found that students who received this treatment package for 30 weeks demonstrated improvement on three different standardized tests (Dowker, 2007).

The majority of examined treatment approaches utilize a small group-tutoring format. *Number Worlds* (Griffin, 1998, 2004) can be implemented in small groups with 4 to 5 students and also includes a classroom supplement, with the length of implementation varying between 15 and 60 minutes, depending on grade level and format. Although this intervention package encompasses kindergarten to grade 8, we will discuss the content only through second grade. The curriculum is developmentally sequenced and includes 30 interactive games, verbal prompts, think alouds, and a variety of visual representations (e.g., thermometer, dial, number line, group of objects, dot patterns). Each component strives to build foundational number sense skills, such as magnitude comparison and strategic counting, practice of numerical positions on different number lines, as well as adding and subtracting. Research has demonstrated students who receive *Number Worlds* improve their number knowledge, strategy use, and generalization of these skills in kindergarten, all of which were retained in first grade. A consideration for use of this program is that training for teachers is intensive and these preliminary positive results were accomplished with researcher collaboration.

Number Rockets (Fuchs et al., 2005; Fuchs, Fuchs, & Hollenbeck, 2007) is a treatment package designed for first through third grades that includes small group tutoring and computer practice. Treatment sessions are designed to be 40 minutes in length, provided three times weekly for 20 weeks. Thirty minutes of each session are devoted to tutoring in groups of two to three students, and 10 minutes at the end of each session is reserved for individual computer practice using a program called Math FLASH (Fuchs, Hamlett, & Powell, 2003). A sequence of 17 scripted topics is included using a combination of explicit and strategy instruction as well as concrete-representation-abstract formats. Mastery of delivered skills is assessed daily and the first day of each new topic incorporates cumulative review of prior content. To ensure engagement in the program, points are awarded for appropriate behavior and traded for prizes. The Math FLASH program targets fact families and requires students to automatically recall basic facts. Research findings illustrated improved performance on computation, concepts and application, and story problems tasks for at-risk first-grade students in the experimental group, which exceeded performance of the at-risk control students.

Bryant and colleagues (i.e., Bryant et al., 2011; Bryant, Bryant, Gersten, Scammacca, & Chavez, 2008; Bryant, Bryant, Gersten, Scammacca, Funk, Winter et al., 2008) have also designed an intervention to address the needs of first-grade students determined to be at risk for mathematics difficulties, using recommendations from the National Research Council (2001), NCTM focal points (2006), and the NMAP (2008). The intervention package is delivered 4 days weekly for 25 minutes across 19 total weeks in small groups of three to five students. Intervention content includes: (a) counting sequence and principles; (b) number knowledge including magnitude and quantity comparison, order, and sequence; and (c) part-whole relations, as well as combining and separating sets and basic facts. Instruction incorporates the explicit instruction, verbalized thinking, strategic counting (i.e., counting on, doubles + 1, make 10 + more, fact families), visual representation, progress monitoring, reinforcement, as well as daily practice and warm-up exercises. Students receiving the treatment package outperformed students in the comparison group on place value, number sequences, number combinations (adding and subtracting), and computation.

Many of these individualized and small group interventions incorporate the general recommended treatment elements (see Table 15.1) described in the collective literature, such as explicit and strategy instruction, visual representations, think alouds, practice and cumulative review, progress monitoring, as well as reinforcement for engagement. Other common features that reflect research in early numeracy are: (a) the combination of number sense activities with practice to encourage basic fact recall (Pellegrino & Goldman, 1987; Gersten & Chard, 1999), and (b) direct instruction of strategy use such as the min (counting on) and doubles + 1 (Siegler, 1988).

Another set of studies has focused intervention delivery on magnitude representations of the number line, a treatment aspect included in many of the previously discussed intervention packages. Predominately, these interventions have used number games to illustrate and instruct basic number concepts, given evidence suggesting that young children who played more board games at home and/or with friends and relatives were more proficient with number line estimation tasks, number identification, magnitude comparison, and counting (Ramani & Siegler, 2008).

Siegler and Ramani (2009) created *The Great Race*, which encourages direct instruction of number lines in the form of board games designed in a linear, horizontal format. The horizontal box is divided into equal squares of different colors that are consecutively numbered from 1 to 10. Each child receives a player piece and begins their turn with a spinner divided into two sections labeled with the numerals 1 and 2 to indicate whether they move either one or two spaces along the game board. This game requires practice with strategic counting, number identification, and the connection with number line representations. Preliminary evidence for this treatment has been illustrated with preschool students. Four 15- to 20-minute sessions led to improvements in preschool proficiency for magnitude comparison, number line estimation, counting, and number identification, when compared to children who did not play the game.

The number race adaptive game software program follows the same conceptual basis as *The Great Race* and has been used with 7- to 9-year-old students (Wilson et al., 2009; Wilson, Dehaene, Pinel, Revkin, Cohen, & Cohen, 2006). Students are presented with a task such as number comparison, for which they are required to choose the larger of two quantities of treasures presented symbolically (i.e., numerals or number word) or non-symbolically (i.e., dot arrays). Following their selection, students receive feedback in all three formats: numeral, number word, and dot array. The program varies in difficulty level by alternating numerical distance (e.g., decreasing difference between dot arrays and numerals from large to small), time permitted for response selection, and conceptual complexity (e.g., decrease ratio of non-symbolic to symbolic information; adding and subtracting quantities).

Computation Conceptual Basis

A robust finding in the literature is that automatic recall of number combinations appears to be a hallmark indicator of students experiencing challenges in mathematics (Geary, 2011; Gersten et al., 2005; Jordan, Hanich, & Kaplan, 2003b; NMAP, 2008). For example, Jordan, Kaplan, Locuniak, and Ramineni (2007) illustrated that early number skills at kindergarten entry along with growth in quantitative skills across the first 1.5 years of school explained 66% of the variance in first-grade mathematics achievement. Of those early number skills, competence with simple arithmetic tasks appeared to be critical. This is consistent with other research demonstrating that poor addition facts at the end of kindergarten predict learning disabilities by the end of third grade (Mazzocco & Thompson, 2005). Earlier work suggested that a unifying feature of children with mathematics learning disabilities and those with combined mathematics and reading disabilities is lack of computation fluency (Gersten et al., 2005; Jordan et al., 2003b).

Students without basic fact fluency may be less able to grasp underlying mathematics concepts or access higher-level mathematics curricula (Gersten & Chard, 1999). Because conscious attention toward multiple tasks simultaneously is challenging, students that have to direct more cognitive resources to retrieving the solution to 5 + 8 may experience interference with higher-order thinking or problem solving (Barrouillet & Fayol, 1998; Dahaene, 1997). Evidence also exists to suggest that students with low number combination fluency may exhibit greater anxiety for mathematics tasks than will students with more fluent skills (Cates & Rhymer, 2003). Whether it is the additional effort required, anxiety, or a combination of the two, collectively this evidence suggests that students without number combination fluency may engage in less frequent practice with mathematics content and complete fewer mathematics-related tasks (Billington, Skinner, & Cruchon, 2004; Skinner, Belfiore, Mace, Williams-Wilson, & Johns, 1997).

Fluency refers to high rates of accurate responding, suggesting that students have previously been exposed to conceptual instruction and activities that build basic skill acquisition (Haring & Eaton, 1978; Rivera & Bryant, 1992). Fluency is the second stage of skill development, following acquisition (stage one) and preceding generalization (stage three). Strategies to enhance fluency differ from those designed to increase accurate computational performance (Burns et al., 2010; Codding et al., 2007). Explicit instruction containing modeling and error correction are commonly used components for building accurate responding, as are using number lines, concrete and visual representations, and strategic counting (Gersten et al., 2009, Stokes & Baer, 1977). These strategies are effective for helping students understand concepts that underlie number combinations, such as quantity discrimination, counting, and mental use of number lines (Gersten et al., 2005; Poncy, Skinner, & O'Mara, 2006). However, once students have attained accuracy, continued use of these strategies could be counterproductive for building fluency, as students may become strategy dependent (Poncy et al., 2006). Enhancing fluency requires that productive practice opportunities are designed to: (a) be brief, (b) be timed, (c) be novel, (d) provide immediate performance feedback, and (e) support engagement with reinforcement (Daly et al., 2007; Rivera & Bryant, 1992). Fluency-building activities should include drill with a range of facts presented in isolation and in context of previously learned items (e.g., worksheet format) in order to ensure maintenance and generalization of skills (Codding, Burns et al., 2011; Haring & Eaton, 1978). Self-managed practice opportunities are also effective ways to improve fluency (Codding, Hilt-Panahon, Panahon, & Benson, 2009; Codding, Burns, et al., 2011).

There is some evidence to suggest that determining whether skill performance falls within the frustration or instructional levels according to curriculum-based assessment is useful for intervention selection (Burns et al., 2010; Codding et al., 2007; Rhymer et al., 2002). For students with skills falling in the frustration range (acquisition stage of skill development), a more intensive treatment plan that offers repeated strategic practice with individual facts, practice with self- or teacher-directed modeling, and self-monitoring appears to be more effective (Burns et al., 2010; Codding et al., 2007; Codding, Archer, & Connell, 2010). For students with skills in the instructional range (fluency stage of skill development), more simplistic options, such as timed practice and reinforcement applied contingent on improved performance, may be viable alternatives.

Research-Supported Interventions

The interventions listed below will assist with developing automaticity with number combinations. Each of these strategies offers direct practice on fact retrieval and has evidence of effectiveness in isolation or combined with other components. Common considerations when using these interventions is to introduce new facts in small sets of no more than 10, use of fact families, and definition of a specific performance criterion for mastery that is achieved prior to introducing new facts (Hasselbring, Lott, & Zydney, 2005; Stein, Silbert, & Carnine, 1997; Woodward, 2006). In order to provide an appropriate target starting point for students, it will be useful to conduct a survey level assessment using either Curriculum-Based Assessment for Instructional Design (Gravois & Gickling, 2002) or Curriculum-Based Evaluation (Howell & Nolet, 2000). Although evidence suggests that direct practice opportunities with basic facts is necessary to promote automaticity (Powell et al., 2009; Tournaki, 2003), some evidence also suggests that incorporating doubling strategies ($6 \times 7 = 6 \times 6 + 1$) and visual representation via number lines or arrays along with explicit practice results in greater retention and maintenance (Fuchs, Powell et al., 2010; Woodward, 2006).

Taped Problems. This intervention was developed by McCallum, Skinner, and Hutchins (2004) and requires students to listen to an audiotape that presented problems and answers using varying time-delay procedures (no delay to 4-s delay). Students are given a worksheet that contains the problems (without the answers) in identical order and are instructed to "beat the tape" by writing an answer to the problem prior to the audio recording. The progressive delay sequence was used in order to prevent students from using inefficient strategies to solve problems and to encourage automatic mental retrieval. Active treatment ingredients include immediate feedback and frequent opportunities to respond (Bliss et al., 2010). This strategy has been adapted for class-wide use, and a variation has been developed that adds contingent reinforcement to the treatment package (McCallum, Skinner, Turner, & Saecker, 2006; McCleary et al., 2011; Miller, Skinner, Gibby, Galyon, & Meadows-Allen, 2011; Windingstad, Skinner, Rowland, Cardin, & Fearrington, 2009). Evidence has suggested it might not be as effective with students in the acquisition stage of skill development and that it requires less instructional time than other similar strategies, making it an efficient option (Mong & Mong, 2012; Poncy, Skinner, & Jaspers, 2007).

Cover-Copy-Compare. Cover-Copy-Compare (CCC) is a student self-managed intervention that offers a series of brief learning trials using the following sequence of five steps: (a) look at the problem with the answer, (b) cover the stimulus problem with the answer, (c) record the problem and answer, (d) uncover the problem with the answer, and (e) compare the response to the modeled answer (Skinner, McLaughlin, & Logan, 1997). Variation of these procedures have included verbally stating the problem and answer in lieu of writing it (Skinner, Bamberg, Smith, & Powell, 1993; Skinner et al., 1997; Skinner, Ford, & Yunker, 1991), or both writing and stating the problem and answer aloud (Skinner et al., 1993). The more common alternative, called Model-Cover-Copy-Compare (Grafman & Cates, 2010; Ozaki, Williams, & McLaughlin, 1996), includes an additional step where students copy the stimulus problem. Required materials are minimal and include: (a) specially designed worksheets that contain math facts with the problem and answer along with space next to each problem for student recording, and (b) an index card for covering the model problem. Training typically requires that the process be demonstrated for students, and guided practice is used to ensure that students are following the procedures correctly. However, once students have demonstrated appropriate use of the intervention, students can use this intervention independently.

Key intervention components of CCC include modeling, errorless learning, practice, and immediate feedback. This intervention has yielded moderate to large effect sizes across studies (Codding, Hilt-Panahon et al., 2009; Joseph et al., 2012), with the largest effects yielded when the intervention is combined with goal setting and feedback or reinforcement (Bolich, Kavon, McLaughlin, Williams, & Urlacher 1995; Codding, Chan-Iannetta et al., 2009; Skinner et al., 1993). One study also suggested that this intervention is more effective with students whose skills were in the acquisition stage of skill development (Codding et al., 2007).

Explicit Timing. This simple procedure provides students with timed opportunities to practice basic facts. The premise of this intervention is based on the notion that students who are in the proficiency stage of learning (instructional skill level) benefit from repeated opportunities to practice in novel and interesting ways (Daly et al., 2007; Rivera & Bryant, 1992). Students are provided with a mathematics assignment and required to mark their progress in one-minute intervals, either until they complete the assignment or until the designated time for the task is finished (e.g., 10 minutes of total practice; Codding et al., 2007; Van Houten & Thomson, 1976). By requiring students to briefly stop and circle or underline the problem that was completed during each of these short time intervals, immediate feedback on fluency is provided and progress becomes more salient to the student (Rhymer et al., 2002; Van Houten & Thompson, 1976). Evidence has suggested that this intervention increases rates of correctly completed problems, with mixed evidence on whether this treatment maintains accurate performance (Codding et al., 2007; Rhymer, Henington, Skinner, & Looby, 1999; Rhymer et al., 2002; Van Houten & Thompson, 1976). Explicit timing may be more effective at increasing rates of responding while maintaining accuracy when the task is single-digit number combinations as compared to complex number combinations (e.g., 3 × 3 digit multiplication; Rhymer et al., 2002).

Incremental Rehearsal. Providing practice of basic mathematics facts in isolation often through the use of flashcards, otherwise known as drill, is a key aspect of building proficient responding, particularly for those in the acquisition stage of skill development (Burns et al., 2010; Codding, Burns, et al., 2011; Haring & Eaton, 1978). Traditional drill often requires that a sequence of items, usually all unknown facts, be presented, after which students provide oral responses and receive error correction and feedback. Another form of flashcard practice is the *Drill Sandwich* (Coulter & Coulter, 1989). The Drill Sandwich follows the same procedure, but includes a 1:1 mixture of known and unknown facts, thereby employing a critical element of practice—a sequence of appropriately matched skills (Burns et al., 2006). Incorporating some known items is useful, perhaps even necessary, for increasing students' academic engagement and preference for the activity (e.g., Skinner, Fletcher, Wildmon, & Belfiore, 1996). A more recent variation in drill procedures has been developed, Incremental Rehearsal (IR), which includes a progression of known to unknown facts beginning with the presentation of one known and one unknown item and ending with presentation of 90% known and 10% unknown facts (Burns, 2005). Data in the area of reading has illustrated that IR may result in greater retention and generalization of material than the Drill Sandwich and traditional flash card methods (MacQuarrie, Tucker, Burns, & Hartman, 2002; Nist & Joseph, 2008), but that traditional drill methods may be more efficient (Skinner, 2008; Volpe, Mulé, Briesch, Joseph, & Burns, 2011). Preliminary research on IR in mathematics has shown it to be effective for improving multiplication fact fluency and accuracy (Burns, 2005; Codding et al., 2010).

Computer Assisted Instruction. *Math FLASH* (Fuchs et al. 2003) is a computer-assisted program focusing on fact families (e.g., $1 + 3 = 4, 3 + 1 = 4, 4 - 1 = 3, 4 - 3 = 1$) that range in difficulty according to mastery of pre-requisite material. Student performance levels are stored in the program, and cumulative review of previously mastered facts is incorporated. A math fact and corresponding answer are flashed on the screen for 1 to 2 seconds before disappearing. At that time, students are required to type the fact with the answer using the computer keyboard. When correct, the typed fact remains on the screen, the program says the fact aloud, and applause and points are awarded. Accumulation of five points translates into virtual prizes that are stored in a treasure chest at the bottom of the screen (Fuchs et al., 2007). When incorrect, the typed fact disappears and the program states the correct problem and answer, which also appears on the screen. The duration of time that the fact remains on the screen is manipulated to provide more time for students who commit more errors. Overall performance feedback at the end of 10-minute sessions are presented in terms of the number of correct items and the level of mastery attained. This program has illustrated effectiveness for improving automaticity as part of treatment packages across first and third grades (Fuchs et al., 2007; Powell et al., 2009).

Word-Problem Solving Conceptual Basis

Word-problem solving is one of the most common forms of mathematical problem solving (Jonassen, 2003), and, as noted earlier, appears to be the most challenging for students, according to teacher report (Bryant et al., 2000). Word-problem solving requires integration of many aspects of mathematics knowledge: (a) understanding mathematics language, (b) identifying relevant information, (c) disregarding irrelevant information, (e) creating a mental representation, (f) developing a plan to solve the problem, and (g) employing the appropriate procedural strategies to carry out the plan (Desoete, Roeyers, & De Clercq, 2003). Historically, curricula have limited instruction of word-problem solving to the identification of key terms or syntax rather than understanding the underlying structure of the word problem itself (Jitendra, Griffin, Deatline-Buchman, & Sczesniak, 2007). In meta-analysis evaluating methods for facilitating word-problem solving, Xin and Jitendra (1999) examined the effectiveness of three techniques: representation techniques, strategy instruction, and computer-assisted instruction. Results suggested that computer-assisted instruction that utilized strategy or representation techniques as well as representation techniques yielded large effects, whereas strategy instruction resulted in moderate effect sizes. The authors also found that benefits of these interventions were larger for simple, compared to complex, problems.

Research-Supported Interventions

Strategy training refers to the use of heuristics and self-regulation techniques such as verbal modeling, prompting, cueing, and self-questioning to facilitate mathematical problem solving (Montague, 2008). For example, Case, Harris, and Graham (1992) taught students a five-step strategy: (a) read the problem; (b) look for the key words and circle them, (c) draw the problem using pictures, (d) write the corresponding math problem in sentence format, and (e) write the answer. Instruction of this strategy is incorporated within a six-stage sequence that begins with instruction on the skills and knowledge needed to apply these strategies, think alouds to demonstrate the use of the strategies, memorization of strategies and self-regulation statements, guided practice, and progress monitoring (Montague, 2008). Cassel and Reid (1996) used a similar sequence of instructional steps and incorporated a nine-step heuristic with the name FAST DRAW. In this sequence students are also required to re-read the problem, recheck the operation, and check their work.

Representation techniques include the use of diagramming, manipulatives, verbalization, and mapping. Recently researchers have expanded on one aspect of representation known as mapping, or schema-based instruction (SBI), to directly teach underlying structures of word problems to students at risk or with learning disabilities in mathematics. Using the word problem classification system developed by Carpenter and Moser (1984), SBI teaches students to recognize whether they are presented with a change, combine, or compare problem. Change problems include beginning, change, and ending information and often provide a situation where an initial quantity is presented that is either increased or decreased (Jitendra, Griffin, Deatline-Buchman, & Sczesniak 2007). Group problems involve part-part-whole relations and compare problems include compared, referent, and difference information. Any of the three pieces of information from each problem type may be missing, and the problem can be solved using the remaining two pieces of given information. Once students identify the problem type, they use a corresponding diagram to translate the problem from words into numerical sentences that are then solved. In this way, SBI facilitates the translation of word problems into the mental representations, as well as combines conceptual understanding with procedural knowledge. Explicit modeling of strategy steps, explanation, and elaboration with "think-alouds" and practice are also used. Research on SBI at the elementary level has illustrated that SBI must be strategically faded to promote independent use by students (Jitendra, Griffin, et al., 2007), and is considerably more effective for at-risk students when paired with SBI classroom instruction (Fuchs, Fuchs, Craddock et al., 2008). A recent study also illustrated that not only did SBI improve word-problem solving of second graders, compared with conventional word-problem instruction, but also facilitated the translation of word problems to algebraic equations (Fuchs et al., 2010). When comparing SBI to strategy instruction, the evidence is mixed, with one study favoring SBI (Jitendra, Haria et al., 2007) and another finding that both interventions were equally effective (Griffin & Jitendra, 2009). According to Fuchs, Fuchs, Craddock et al. (2008), systematic motivation that encourages persistence, contemplation and generation of different solutions, as well as rewards students for engaging in self-regulation activities, is a necessary addition to SBI when used in a small-group tutoring format. The following three programs specifically use SBI to teach word-problem solving.

Hot Math Tutoring. This tutoring program (Fuchs et al., 2007; Fuchs et al., 2004; Fuchs et al., 2002) was designed for grade three as a small-group tutoring or supplemental class-wide program. The program is intended for use two to three times weekly for about 30 minutes each session over a total of 13 weeks. Explicit and schema-based instruction is used. For example, posters illustrate problem-solving steps, teachers' model four different problem-solving types, and peer pairs solve partially completed and uncompleted problems, followed by independent practice. Cumulative review, transfer of skills, scaffolding, self-regulation strategies, manipulatives, and rewards are all incorporated (Fuchs et al., 2007; Fuchs, Fuchs, Powell et al., 2008).

Solving Math Word Problems (Jitendra, 2007). This program is appropriate for students in grades one through eight, and includes two variations: (a) addition and subtraction, and (b) multiplication and division. Units are organized around four problem-solving types, and sessions range from 30 to 60 minutes each. The program can be implemented in small groups or individually. Students are taught to identify the problem-solving schema and represent word problems using the appropriate diagram. A four-step strategy, FOPS, is taught to students: (a) Find the problem type, (b) Organize using the diagram, (c) Plan to solve the problem, and (d) Solve the problem (Jitendra, 2007). Direct modeling of the problem-solving process is provided using think-alouds, and scaffolding is used so that students gradually attain more independence with problem solving. Progress monitoring measures are incorporated into the program.

Pirate Math (Fuchs, Fuchs, Powell et al., 2008). This program is designated for use with third-grade students and can be implemented individually or using small-group tutoring. The program consists of both basic word-problem solving as well as direct computation practice organized into four units. The first unit teaches counting strategies for basic mathematics facts, two-step computation procedures, and solving algebraic equations. The remaining three units provide explicit instruction on three problem-solving types using schema-based instruction. Each treatment session is 25 to 30 minutes in length, for approximately 16 sessions.

Conclusion

Although packaged treatment programs for addressing mathematics challenges are currently limited, a convincing body of literature exists to define the specific treatment components that can produce improvements in the areas of number sense, number combination fluency, and word problems. Coupled with carefully designed assessments to screen for risk and develop interventions according to specific skill weaknesses, an appropriate treatment match can be found to improve mathematics learning.

References

American Psychological Association Presidential Task Force on Evidence-Based Practice. (2006). Evidence-based practice in psychology *American Psychologist, 61*(4), 271–285. doi: 10.1037/0003–066X.61.4.271

Bahrick, H. P., & Hall, L. K. (1998). Lifetime maintenance of high school mathematics content. In M. Lawton & T. A. Salthouse (Eds.), *Essential papers on the psychology of aging* (pp. 296–324). New York, NY: New York University Press.

Baker, S., Gersten, R., & Lee, D. (2002). A synthesis of empirical research on teaching mathematics to low-achieving students. *The Elementary School Journal, 103,* 51–73.

Baroody, A. J., Bajwa, N., & Eiland, M. (2009). Why can't Johnny remember the basic facts? *Developmental Disabilities Research Reviews, 15,* 69–79. doi: 10.1002/ddrr.45

Baroody, A. J., Eiland, M., & Thompson, B. (2009). Fostering at-risk preschoolers' number sense. *Early Education and Development, 20,* 80–128. doi: 10.1080/10409280802206619

Baroody, A. J., & Gatzke, M. S. (1991). The estimation of set size by potentially gifted kindergarten-age children. *Journal of Research in Mathematics Education, 22,* 59–68.

Barrouillet, P., & Fayol, M. (1998). From algorithmic computing to direct retrieval: Evidence from number and alphabetic arithmetic in children and adults. *Memory & Cognition, 26,* 355–368.

Berch, D. B. (2005). Making sense of number sense: Implications for children with mathematical disabilities. *Journal of Learning Disabilities, 38,* 333–339. doi: 10.1177/00222194050380040901

Billington, E. J., Skinner, C. H., & Cruchon, N. M. (2004). Improving sixth-grade students perceptions of high-effort assignments by assigning more work: Interaction of additive interspersal and assignment effort on assignment choice. *Journal of School Psychology, 42,* 477–490. doi: 10.1016/j.jsp.2004.08.003

Bliss, S. L., Skinner, C. H., McCallum, E., Saecker, L. B., Rowland-Bryant, E., & Brown, K. S. (2010). A comparison of taped problems with and without a brief post-treatment assessment on multiplication fluency. *Journal of Behavioral Education, 19,* 156–168. doi: 10.1007/s10864–010–9106–5

Bolich, B., Kavon, N., McLaughlin, T. F., Williams, R. L., & Urlacher, S. (1995). The effects of copy, cover, compare procedure and a token economy on the retention of basic multiplication facts by two middle school students with ADD and ADHD. *B.C. Journal of Special Education, 19,* 1–10.

Booth, J. L., & Siegler, R. S. (2008). Numerical magnitude representations influence arithmetic learning. *Child Development, 79,* 1016–1031. doi: 10.1111/j.1467–8624.2008.01173.x

Browder, D. M., Spooner, F., Ahlgrim-Delzell, L., Harris, A. A., & Wakeman, S. (2008). A meta-analysis on teaching mathematics to students with significant cognitive disabilities. *Exceptional Children, 74,* 407–432.

Bryant, B. R., & Bryant, D. (2008). Introduction to the special series: Mathematics and learning disabilities. *Learning Disability Quarterly, 31,* 3–8.

Bryant, D. P., Bryant, B. R., Gersten, R., Scammacca, N., & Chavez, M. M. (2008). Mathematics intervention for first- and second-grade students with mathematics difficulties: The effects of tier 2 intervention delivered as booster lessons. *Remedial and Special Education, 29*, 20–32.

Bryant, D., Bryant, B. R., Gersten, R. M., Scammacca, N. N., Funk, C., Winter, A., & Pool, C. (2008). The effects of Tier 2 intervention on the mathematics performance of first-grade students who are at risk for mathematics difficulties. *Learning Disability Quarterly, 31*, 47–63.

Bryant, D., Bryant, B. R., & Hammill, D. D. (2000). Characteristic behaviors of students with LD who have teacher-identified math weaknesses. *Journal of Learning Disabilities, 33*, 168–177. doi: 10.1177/002221940003300205

Bryant, D., Bryant, B. R., Roberts, G., Vaughn, S., Pfannenstiel, K., Porterfield, J., & Gersten, R. (2011). Early numeracy intervention program for first-grade students with mathematics difficulties. *Exceptional Children, 78*, 7–23.

Burns, M. K. (2005). Using incremental rehearsal to increase fluency of single-digit multiplication facts with children identified as learning disabled in mathematics computation. *Education & Treatment of Children, 28*, 237–249.

Burns, M. K., Codding, R. S., Boice, C., & Lukito, G. (2010). Meta-analysis of acquisition and fluency math interventions with instruction and frustration level skills: Evidence for a skill-by-treatment interaction. *School Psychology Review, 39*, 69–83.

Burns, M. K., VanDerHeyden, A.M., & Jiban, C. (2006). Assessing the instructional level for mathematics: A comparison of methods. *School Psychology Review, 35*, 401–418.

Carpenter, T. P., & Moser, J. M. (1984). The acquisition of addition and subtraction concepts in grades one through three. *Journal for Research in Mathematics Education, 15*, 179–202. doi: 10.2307/748348

Case, L. P., Harris, K. R., & Graham, S. (1992). Improving the mathematical problem-solving skills of students with learning disabilities: Self-regulated strategy development. *The Journal of Special Education, 26*, 1–19. doi: 10.1177/002246699202600101

Cassel, J., & Reid, R. (1996). Use of a self-regulated strategy intervention to improve word problem-solving skills of students with mild disabilities. *Journal of Behavioral Education, 6*, 153–172. doi: 10.1007/BF02110230

Cates, G.L., & Rhymer, K. N. (2003). Examining the relationship between mathematics anxiety and mathematics performance: An instructional hierarchy perspective. *Journal of Behavioral Education, 12*, 23–34.

Codding, R. S., Archer, J., & Connell, J. (2010). A systematic replication and extension using incremental rehearsal to improve multiplication skills: An investigation of generalization. *Journal of Behavioral Education, 19*, 93–105.

Codding, R. S., Burns, M. K., & Lukito, G. (2011). Meta-analysis of mathematic basic-fact fluency interventions: A component analysis. *Learning Disabilities Research & Practice, 26*, 36–47. doi: 10.1111/j.1540–5826.2010.00323.x

Codding, R. S., Chan-Iannetta, L., George, S., Ferreira, K., & Volpe, R. (2011). Early number skills: Examining the effects of class-wide interventions on kindergarten performance. *School Psychology Quarterly, 26*, 85–96.

Codding, R. S., Chan-Iannetta, L., Palmer, M., & Lukito, G. (2009). Examining a class-wide application of cover-copy-compare with and without goal setting to enhance mathematics fluency. *School Psychology Quarterly, 24*, 173–185.

Codding, R. S., Hilt-Panahon, A., Panahon, C., & Benson, J. (2009). Addressing mathematics computation problems: A review of simple and moderate intensity interventions. *Education and Treatment of Children, 32*, 279–312.

Codding, R. S., Shiyko, M., Russo, M., Birch, S., Fanning, E., & Jaspen, D. (2007). Comparing mathematics interventions: Does initial level of fluency predict intervention effectiveness? *Journal of School Psychology, 45*, 603–617.

Coulter, W. A., & Coulter, E. M. (1989). *Curriculum-based assessment for instructional design: Trainer's manual.* (Unpublished training manual available from Directions and Resources, P.O. Box 57113, New Orleans, LA 70157)

Dahaene, S. (1997). *The number sense: How the mind creates mathematics.* New York, NY: Oxford University.

Daly, E. J., Martens, B. K., Barnett, D., Witt, J. C., & Olson, S.C. (2007). Varying intervention delivery in response to intervention: Confronting and resolving challenges with measurement instruction and intensity. *School Psychology Review, 36*, 562–581.

Desoete, A., Roeyers, H., & De Clercq, A. (2003). Can offline metacognition enhance mathematical problem solving? *Journal of Educational Psychology, 95*(1), 188–200.

Dowker, A. (2001). Numeracy recovery: A pilot scheme for early intervention with young children with numeracy difficulties. *Support for Learning, 16*, 6–10. doi: 10.1111/1467–9604.00178

Dowker, A. (2007). What can intervention tell us about arithmetical difficulties? *Educational and Child Psychology, 24*, 64–82.

Duncan, G. J., Dowsett, C. J., Claessens, A., Magnuson, K., Huston, A.C., Klebanov, P., et al. (2007). School readiness and later achievement. *Developmental Psychology, 43*, 1428–1446.

Flores, M. M. (2009). Teaching subtraction with regrouping to students experiencing difficulty in mathematics. *Preventing School Failure, 53*, 145–152.

Flores, M. M. (2010). Using the concrete-representational-abstract sequence to teach subtraction with regrouping to students at risk for failure. *Remedial and Special Education, 31,* 195–207. doi: 10.1177/0741932508327467

Fuchs, L. S., Compton, D. L., Fuchs, D., Paulsen, K., Bryant, J. D., & Hamlett, C. L. (2005). The prevention, identification, and cognitive determinants of math difficulty. *Journal of Educational Psychology, 97,* 493–513. doi: 10.1037/0022–0663.97.3.493

Fuchs, L. S., Fuchs, D., Craddock, C., Hollenbeck, K. N., Hamlett, C. K., et al. (2008). Effects of small-group tutoring with and without validated classroom instruction on at-risk students' math problem solving: Are two tiers of prevention better than one? *Journal of Educational Psychology, 100,* 491–509.

Fuchs, L. S., Fuchs, D., Hamlett, C. L., Hope, S. K., Hollenbeck, K. N., Capizzi, A. M., & Brothers, R. L. (2006). Extending responsiveness-to-intervention to math problem-solving at third grade. *Teaching Exceptional Children, 38,* 59–63.

Fuchs, L. S., Fuchs, D., Hamlett, C. L., & Stecker, P. M. (1991). Effects of curriculum-based measurement and consultation on teacher planning and student achievement in mathematics operations. *American Educational Research Journal, 28,* 617–641.

Fuchs, L. S., Fuchs, D., & Hollenbeck, K. N. (2007). Extending responsiveness to intervention to mathematics at first and third grades. *Learning Disabilities Research & Practice, 22,* 13–24. doi: 10.1111/j.1540–5826.2007.00227.x

Fuchs, L. S., Fuchs, D., Karns, K., Hamlett, C. L., Katzaroff, M., & Dutka, S. (1997). Effects of task-focused goal on low-achieving students with and without learning disabilities. *American Educational Research Journal, 34,* 513–543.

Fuchs, L. S., Fuchs, D., Powell, S. R., Seethaler, P.M., Cirino, P. T., et al. (2008). Intensive intervention for students with mathematics disabilities: Seven principles of effective practice. *Learning Disabilities Quarterly, 31,* 79–92.

Fuchs, L. S., Hamlett, C. L., & Powell, S. R. (2003). Math Flash [computer program] (Available from L. S. Fuchs, 328 Peabody, Vanderbilt University, Nashville, TN 37203)

Fuchs, L. S., Powell, S. R., Seethaler, P.M., Cirino, P. T., Fletcher, J. M., Fuchs, D., & Hamlett, C. L. (2010). The effects of strategic counting instruction, with and without deliberate practice, on number combination skill among students with mathematics difficulties. *Learning and Individual Differences, 20,* 89–100. doi: 10.1016/j.lindif.2009.09.003

Geary, D. C. (1993). Mathematical disabilities: Cognitive, neuropsychological, and genetic components. *Psychological Bulletin, 114,* 345–362. doi: 10.1037/0033–2909.114.2.345

Geary, D. C. (2004). Mathematics and learning disabilities. *Journal of Learning Disabilities, 37,* 4–15.

Geary, D. C. (2011). Cognitive predictors of achievement growth in mathematics: A 5-year longitudinal study. *Developmental Psychology, 47,* 1539–1552. doi: 10.1037/a0025510

Geary, D. C., Bailey, D. H., & Hoard, M. K. (2009). Predicting mathematical achievement and mathematical learning disability with a simple screening tool: The number sets test. *Journal of Psychoeducational Assessment, 27,* 265–279. doi: 10.1177/0734282908330592

Geary, D. C., Hoard, M. K., Byrd-Craven, J., & DeSoto, M. (2004). Strategy choices in simple and complex addition: Contributions of working memory and counting knowledge for children with mathematical disability. *Journal of Experimental Child Psychology, 88,* 121–151. doi: 10.1016/j.jecp.2004.03.002

Gelman, R., & Gallistel, C. R. (1978). *The child's understanding of number.* Cambridge, MA: Harvard University Press.

Gersten, R., & Chard, D. (1999). Number sense: Rethinking arithmetic instruction for students with mathematical disabilities. *Journal of Special Education, 33,* 18–28.

Gersten, R., Chard, D. J., Jayanthi, M., Baker, S. K., Morphy, P., & Flojo, J. (2009). Mathematics instruction for students with learning disabilities: A meta-analysis of instructional components. *Review of Educational Research, 79,* 1202–1242. doi: 10.3102/0034654309334431

Gersten, R., Clarke, B. S., & Jordan, N. C. (2007). *Screening for Mathematics Difficulties in K-3 Students.* Portsmouth, NH: RMC Research Corporation, Center on Instruction.

Gersten, R., Jordan, N. C., & Flojo, J. R. (2005). Early identification and interventions for students with mathematics difficulties. *Journal of Learning Disabilities, 38,* 93–304.

Gickling, E. E., & Havertape, S. (1981). *Curriculum-based assessment (CBA).* Minneapolis, MN: School Psychology Inservice Training Network.

Gickling, E. E., Shane, R. L., & Croskery, K. M. (1989). Developing math skills in low-achieving high school students through curriculum-based assessment. *School Psychology Review, 18,* 344–356.

Gickling, E., & Thompson, V. (1985). A personal view of curriculum-based assessment. *Exceptional Children, 52,* 205–218.

Goldman, S. R. (1989). Strategy instruction in mathematics. *Learning Disability Quarterly, 12,* 43–55.

Grafman, J. M., & Cates, G. L. (2010). The differential effects of two self-managed math instruction procedures: Cover, copy, and compare versus copy, over, and compare. *Psychology in the Schools, 47,* 153–165.

Gravois, T. A., & Gickling, E. E. (2002). Best practices in curriculum-based assessment. In A. Thomas & J. Grimes (Eds.), *Best practices in school psychology* IV (Vol. 2, pp. 885–898). Bethesda, MD: National Association of School Psychologists.

Griffin, C. C., & Jitendra, A. K. (2009). Word problem-solving instruction in inclusive third-grade mathematics classrooms. *The Journal of Educational Research, 102,* 187–201. doi: 10.3200/JOER.102.3.187–202

Griffin, S. (1998). Math readiness: What is it? How can families make sure kids will have it? *Transition, 28,* 18–19.

Griffin, S. (2004). Building number sense with number worlds: A mathematics program for young children. *Early Childhood Research Quarterly, 19,* 173–180.

Haring, N. G., & Eaton, M. D. (1978). Systematic instructional technology: An instructional hierarchy. In N. G. Haring, T. C. Lovitt, M. D. Eaton, & C. L. Hansen (Eds.), *The fourth R: Research in the classroom* (pp. 23–40). Columbus, OH: Merrill.

Hasselbring, T. S., Goin, L., & Bransford, J. (1988). Developing math automaticity in learning handicapped children: The role of computerized drill and practice. *Focus on Exceptional Children, 20*(6), 1–7.

Hasselbring, T. S., Lott, A., & Zydney, J. (2005). *Technology-supported math instruction for students with disabilities: Two decades of research and development.* Retrieved from http://www.cited.org/library/resourcedocs/Tech-SupportedMathInstruction-FinalPaper_early.pdf

Hosp, J. L., & Ardoin, S. P. (2008). Assessment for instructional planning. *Assessment for Effective Intervention, 33,* 69–77. doi: 10.1177/1534508407311428

Howell, K. W., & Nolet, V. (2000). *Curriculum-based evaluation: Teaching and decision making* (3rd ed.). Belmont, CA: Wadsworth.

Jitendra, A. K. (2007). *Solving math word problems. Teaching students with learning disabilities using schema-based instruction.* Austin, TX: Pro-Ed,

Jitendra, A. K., Griffin, C. C., Deatline-Buchman, A., & Sczesniak, E. (2007). Mathematical word-problem solving in third-grade classrooms. *The Journal of Educational Research, 100,* 283–302. doi: 10.3200/JOER.100.5.283–302

Jitendra, A. K., Haria, P., Griffin, C. C., Leh, J., Adams, A., & Kaduvettoor, A. (2007). A comparison of single and multiple strategy instruction on third-grade students' mathematical problem solving. *Journal of Educational Psychology, 99*(1), 115–127. doi:10.1037/0022-0663.99.1.115

Jonassen, D. H. (2003). Designing research-based instruction for story problems. *Educational Psychology Review, 15,* 267–296. doi: 10.1023/A:1024648217919

Jordan, N. C., Hanich, L., & Kaplan, D. (2003a). A longitudinal study of mathematical competencies in children with specific mathematics difficulties versus children with comorbid mathematics and reading difficulties. *Child Development, 74,* 834–850.

Jordan, N. C., Hanich, L. B., & Kaplan, D. (2003b). Arithmetic fact mastery in young children: A longitudinal investigation. *Journal of Experimental Child Psychology, 85,* 103–119. doi: 10.1016/S0022–0965(03)00032–8

Jordan, N. C., Kaplan, D., Locuniak, M. N., & Ramineni, C. (2007). Predicting first-grade math achievement from developmental number sense trajectories. *Learning Disabilities Research & Practice, 22,* 36–46. doi: 10.1111/j.1540–5826.2007.00229.x

Jordan, N., Kaplan, D., Olah, L. N., & Locuniak, M. N. (2006). Number sense growth in kindergarten: A longitudinal investigation of children at risk for mathematics difficulties. *Child Development, 77,* 153–175.

Jordan, N. C., Kaplan, D., Ramineni, C., & Locuniak, M. N. (2009). Early math matters: Kindergarten number competence and later mathematics outcomes. *Developmental Psychology, 45,* 850–867. doi: 10.1037/a0014939

Joseph, L., Konrad, M., Cates, G., Vajcner, T., Eveleigh, E., & Fishley, K. M. (2012). A meta-analytic review of the cover-copy-compare and variations of this self-management procedure. *Psychology in the Schools, 49,* 122–136.

Kalchman, M., Moss, J., & Case, R. (2001). Psychological models for the development of mathematical understanding: Rational numbers and functions. In S. M. Carver, D. Klahr, S. M. Carver, & D. Klahr (Eds.), *Cognition and instruction: Twenty-five years of progress* (pp. 1–38). Mahwah, NJ: Lawrence Erlbaum Associates Publishers.

Kratochwill, T. R., & Shernoff, E. S. (2004). Evidence-based practice: Promoting evidence-based interventions in school psychology. *School Psychology Review, 33,* 34–48.

Kroeger, S. D., & Kouche, B. (2006). Using peer-assisted learning strategies to increase response to intervention in inclusive middle math settings. *Teaching Exceptional Children, 38*(5), 6–13.

Kroesbergen, E. H., & Van Luit, J. E. H. (2003). Mathematics intervention for children with special needs: A meta-analysis. *Remedial and Special Education, 24,* 97–114.

MacQuarrie, L. L., Tucker, J. A., Burns, M. K., & Hartman, B. (2002). Comparison of retention rates using traditional, drill sandwich, and incremental rehearsal flash card methods. *School Psychology Review, 31,* 584–595.

Martens, B. K., & Eckert, T. L. (2007). The instructional hierarchy as a model of stimulus control over student and teacher behavior: We're close but are we close enough? *Journal of Behavioral Education, 16,* 83–91.

Mazzocco, M. M., & Thompson, R. E. (2005). Kindergarten predictors of math learning disability. *Learning Disabilities Research & Practice, 20*(3), 142–155. doi:10.1111/j.1540-5826.2005.00129.x

McCallum, E., Skinner, C. H., & Hutchins, H. (2004). The taped-problems intervention: Increasing division fact fluency using a low-tech self-managed time-delay intervention. *Journal of Applied School Psychology, 20*, 129–147. doi: 10.1300/J370v20n02_08

McCallum, E., Skinner, C. H., Turner, H., & Saecker, L. (2006). The taped-problems intervention: Increasing multiplication fact fluency using a low-tech, class-wide, time-delay intervention. *School Psychology Review, 35*, 419–434.

McCleary, D. F., Aspiranti, K. B., Skinner, C. H., Foster, L. N., Luna, E., Murray, K., & Woody, A. (2011). Enhancing math fact fluency via taped problems in intact second- and fourth-grade classrooms. *Journal of Evidence-Based Practices for Schools, 12*, 179–201.

Meichenbaum, D. .H., & Goodman, J. (1971). Training impulsive children to talk to themselves: A means of developing self-control. *Journal of Abnormal Psychology, 77*, 115–126.

Mercer, C. D., & Miller, S. P. (1992). Teaching students with learning problems in math to acquire, understand, and apply basic math facts. *RASE: Remedial & Special Education, 13*, 19–35, 61. doi: 10.1177/074193259201300303

Miller, K. C., Skinner, C. H., Gibby, L., Galyon, C. E., & Meadows-Allen, S. (2011). Evaluating generalization of addition-fact fluency using the Taped-Problems Procedure in a second-grade classroom. *Journal of Behavioral Education, 20*, 203–220.

Miller, S., & Mercer, C. D. (1993). Mnemonics: Enhancing the math performance of students with learning difficulties. *Intervention in School and Clinic, 29*, 78–82.

Mong, M. D., & Mong, K. W. (2012). The utility of brief experimental analysis and extended intervention analysis in selecting effective mathematics interventions. *Journal of Behavioral Education, 21*(2), 99–118

Montague, M. (2008). Self-regulation strategies to improve mathematical problem solving for students with learning disabilities. *Learning Disability Quarterly, 31*, 37–44.

Morgan, P. L., Farkas, G., & Wu, Q. (2009). Kindergarten predictors of recurring externalizing and internalizing psychopathology in the third and fifth grades. *Journal of Emotional and Behavioral Disorders, 17*, 67–79.

National Council of Teachers of Mathematics. (2006). *Curriculum focal points*. Retrieved from http://www.nctm-media.org/cfp/focal_points_by_grade.pdf

National Mathematics Advisory Panel (NMAP). (2008, March). *Foundations for success: The final report of the National Mathematics Advisory Panel*. Washington, DC: U.S. Department of Education. Retrieved from http://www.colonialsd.org/colonial/lib/colonial/national_math_panel_highlights_march_2008.doc

National Research Council (NCR). (2001). *Adding it up: Helping children learn mathematics* (free executive summary). J. Kilpatrick, J. Swafford, & B. Findel (Eds.). Mathematics Learning Study Committee, Center for Education, Division of Behavioral and Social Sciences and Education. Washington, DC: National Academy Press. Retrieved from http://www.nap.edu/catalog/9822.html

Nist, L., & Joseph, L. M. (2008). Effectiveness and efficiency of flashcard drill instructional methods on urban first-graders' word recognition, acquisition, maintenance, and generalization. *School Psychology Review, 37*, 294–308.

Ozaki, C., Williams, R. L., & McLaughlin, T. E. (1996). Effects of a copy/cover/compare drill and practice procedure for multiplication facts mastery with a sixth grade student with learning disabilities. *B.C. Journal of Special Education, 20*, 65–73.

Patton, J. R., Cronin, M. E., Bassett, D. S., & Koppel, A. E. (1997). A life skills approach to mathematics instruction: Preparing students with learning disabilities for the real-life math demands of adulthood. *Journal of Learning Disabilities, 30*, 178–187.

Pellegrino, J. W., & Goldman, S. R. (1987). Information processing and elementary mathematics. *Journal of Learning Disabilities, 20*, 23–32, 57. doi: 10.1177/002221948702000105

Poncy, B. C., Skinner, C. H., & Jaspers, K. E. (2007). Evaluating and comparing interventions designed to enhance math fact accuracy and fluency: Cover copy, and compare versus taped problems. *Journal of Behavioral Education, 16*, 27–37.

Poncy, B. C., Skinner, C. H., & O'Mara, T. (2006). Detect, practice, and repair: The effects of a classwide intervention on elementary students' math-fact fluency. *Journal of Evidence-Based Practices for Schools, 7*, 47–68.

Powell, S. R., Fuchs, L. S., Fuchs, D., Cirino, P. T., & Fletcher, J. M. (2009). Effects of fact retrieval tutoring on third-grade students with math difficulties with and without reading difficulties. *Learning Disabilities Research & Practice, 24*, 1–11. doi :10.1111/j.1540–5826.2008.01272.x

Ramani, G. B., & Siegler, R. S. (2008). Promoting broad and stable improvements in low-income children's numerical knowledge through playing number board games. *Child Development, 79*, 375–394. doi: 10.1111/j.1467-8624.2007.01131

Rhymer, K. N., Henington, C., Skinner, C. H., & Looby, E. (1999). The effects of explicit timing on mathematics performance in second-grade Caucasian and African American students. *School Psychology Quarterly, 14,* 397–407. doi: 10.1037/h0089016

Rhymer, K. N., Skinner, C. H., Jackson, S., McNeill, S., Smith, T., & Jackson, B. (2002). The 1-minute explicit timing intervention: The influence of mathematics problem difficulty. *Journal of Instructional Psychology, 29,* 305–311.

Rivera, D. M., & Bryant, B. R. (1992). Mathematics instruction for students with special needs. *Intervention in School & Clinic, 28,* 71–86.

Schunk, D. H. (1985). Participation in goal setting: Effects on self-efficacy and skills of learning-disabled children. *The Journal of Special Education, 19,* 307–317.

Schunk, D. H., & Cox, P. D. (1986). Strategy training and attributional feedback with learning-disabled students. *Journal of Educational Psychology, 78,* 201–209. doi: 10.1037/0022–0663.78.3.201

Siegler, R. S. (1988). Strategy choice procedures and the development of multiplication skill. *Journal of Experimental Psychology: General, 117,* 258–275. doi: 10.1037/0096–3445.117.3.258

Siegler, R. S., & Ramani, G. B. (2009). Playing linear number board games—but not circular ones—improves low-income preschoolers' numerical understanding. *Journal of Educational Psychology, 101,* 545–560. doi: 10.1037/a0014239

Skinner, C. H. (2008). Theoretical and applied implications of precisely measuring learning rates. *School Psychology Review, 37,* 309–314.

Skinner, C. H., Bamberg, H. W., Smith, E. S., & Powell, S. S. (1993). Cognitive copy, cover, and compare: Subvocal responding to increase rates of accurate division responding. *Remedial and Special Education, 14,* 49–56.

Skinner, C. H., Belfiore, P. J., Mace, H. W., Williams-Wilson, S., & Johns, G. A. (1997). Altering response topography to increase response efficiency and learning rates. *School Psychology Quarterly, 12,* 54–64. doi: 10.1037/h0088947

Skinner, C. H., Fletcher, P. A., Wildmon, M., & Belfiore, P. J. (1996). Improving assignment preference through interspersing additional problems: Brief versus easy problems. *Journal of Behavioral Education, 6*(4), 427–436. doi:10.1007/BF02110515

Skinner, C. H., Ford, J. M., & Yunker, B, D. (1991). A comparison of instructional response requirements on the multiplication performance of behaviorally disordered students. *Behavioral Disorders, 17,* 56–65.

Skinner, C. H., McLaughlin, T. E., & Logan, P. (1997). Cover, copy, and compare: A self-managed academic intervention effective across skills, students, and settings. *Journal of Behavioral Education, 7,* 295–306.

Slavin, R. E., & Lake, C. (2008). Effective programs in mathematics: A best evidence synthesis. *Review of Educational Research, 78,* 427–515.

Slavin, R. E., Lake, C., & Groff, C. (2009). Effective programs in middle and high school mathematics: A best-evidence synthesis. *Review of Educational Research, 79,* 839–911.

Stein, M., Silbert, J., & Carnine, D. (1997). *Designing effective mathematics instruction: A direct instruction approach.* Upper Saddle River, NJ: Prentice-Hall.

Stokes, T. F., & Baer, D. M. (1977). An implicit technology of generalization. *Journal of Applied Behavior Analysis, 10,* 349–367.

Swanson, H. L. (2009). Science-supported math instruction for children with math difficulties: Converting a meta-analysis to practice. In S. Rosenfield & V. Berninger (Eds.), *Implementing evidence-based academic interventions in school settings* (pp. 85–106). New York, NY: Oxford University Press.

Swanson, H. L., & Sachse-Lee, C. (2000). A meta-analysis of single-subject design intervention research for students with learning disabilities. *Journal of Learning Disabilities, 33,* 114–136.

Tournaki, N. (2003). The differential effects of teaching addition through strategy instruction versus drill and practice to students with and without learning disabilities. *Journal of Learning Disabilities, 36,* 449–458.

Van Houten, R., & Thompson, C. (1976). The effects of explicit timing on math performance. *Journal of Applied Behavior Analysis, 9,* 227–230.

Volpe, R. J., Mulé, C. M., Briesch, A.M., Joseph, L. M., & Burns, M. K. (2011). A comparison of two flashcard drill methods targeting word recognition. *Journal of Behavioral Education, 20,* 117–137. doi: 10.1007/s10864-011-9124-y

Wilson, A. J., Dehaene, S., Dubois, O., & Fayol, M. (2009). Effects of an adaptive game intervention on accessing number sense in low-socioeconomic-status kindergarten children. *Mind, Brain, and Education, 3,* 224–234. doi: 10.1111/j.1751–228X.2009.01075.x

Wilson, A. J., Dehaene, S., Pinel, P., Revkin, S. K., Cohen, L., & Cohen, D. (2006). Principles underlying the design of "The Number Race," an adaptive computer game for remediation of dyscalculia. *Behavioral and Brain Functions, 2,*19. doi:10.1186/1744-9081-2-19

Windingstad, S., Skinner, C. H., Rowland, E., Cardin, E., & Fearrington, J. Y. (2009). Extending research on a math fluency building intervention: Applying taped problems in a second-grade classroom. *Journal of Applied School Psychology, 25,* 364–381.

Woodward, J. (2006). Developing automaticity in multiplication facts: Integrating strategy instruction with timed practice drills. *Learning Disability Quarterly, 29,* 269–289.

Xin, Y. P., & Jitendra, A. K. (1999). The effects of instruction in solving mathematical word problems for students with learning problems: A meta-analysis. *The Journal of Special Education, 32,* 207–225.

16

Occasioning Behaviors That Cause Learning

Kathryn E. Jaspers, Christopher H. Skinner, Erin E. C. Henze,
Sara J. McCane-Bowling, and Emily F. Rowlette

Often, when we think of enhancing academic achievement or skills, we focus on what the educator needs to do to teach, as opposed to what the student needs to do to learn (Lindgren & Suter, 1985). In order to learn, students must engage in active, accurate, academic (AAA) responding. Researchers have shown that increasing rates of AAA responding can enhance learning at the acquisition, fluency or automaticity building, and maintenance stages of skill development (Greenwood, Delquadri, & Hall, 1984; Ivarie, 1986; Skinner, Fletcher, & Henington, 1996; Skinner & Shapiro, 1989). High rates of responding allow educators to program generalization and discrimination by providing multiple examples of stimuli that should occasion the target response, and similar stimuli that should not occasion the target response, sometimes referred to as non-exemplars (Skinner & Daly, 2010). Finally, students engaged in high rates of AAA responding cannot engage in many incompatible inappropriate behaviors (Skinner, Pappas, & Davis, 2005; Skinner, Williams, & Neddenriep, 2004).

Many have recognized the relationship between AAA responding and skill development and have addressed this concern by allocating more time for AAA responding. For example, more time has been allocated at the end of formal education (e.g., many school psychology programs now average more than 6 years, and across many campuses undergraduate education is becoming a 5-year process), or at the beginning of our formal education (e.g., increasing kindergarten from half a school day to a whole school day, preschool). Once our formal education begins, time is often re-allocated to allow students to "catch up" with their peers or specific criteria. This time many come from summer recess (e.g., extended school year, summer school) or from within the typical school day (Skinner, McCleary, Poncy, Cates, & Skolits, 2013). For example, time may be re-allocated from art, music, and recess so that students can receive response-to-intervention (RTI) remedial reading service (Hughes & Dexter, 2011; Skinner, 2010).

Time re-allocation strategies may prove effective for remedying problems; however, there are often costs (Skinner, Belfiore, & Watson, 1995/2002). There are costs in terms of resources associated with providing services such as RTI and summer school (Skinner, 2010). Re-allocation of student time from one activity to another also has costs. It may seem appropriate to some to re-allocate time from music, art, or recess to remedy reading skill deficits;

however, students learn many social skills when they have the opportunities to interact in semi-structured or less-structured environments, such as recess. Many in society will benefit from our ability to develop and nurture skilled musicians and artists, and influencing children to appreciate the arts may enhance their quality of life immeasurably (Skinner, 2008). A third concern is that we may eventually find that there is no more time to re-allocate. This concern seems to be more common, as parents and children become involved in so many different structured, scheduled activities (Melman, Little, & Akin-Little, 2007) and teachers are challenged to develop more skills in students at a younger age.

Perhaps the biggest cost associated with enhancing skill development by re-allocating more time is that such procedures discourage our search for better learning and skill development procedures (Skinner et al., 2013). Even if time were not scarce, waiting for students to fall behind and then applying remedial procedures has costs. Students who fall behind their peers are often stigmatized, particularly when given a label. Furthermore, in the process of falling behind, students often become discouraged and disillusioned with education, educators, and themselves. Consequently, developing new strategies and procedures that prevent students from needing remedial services by enhancing their learning or skill-development rates (i.e., more learning in a fixed amount of time) is a better alternative than trying to find more time to apply current procedures that caused them to fall behind in the first place.

Allow for Responding

When asked to respond, there are instances when students cannot respond. In some cases, this is caused by skill deficits; they do not have the prerequisite skills needed to respond. In other instances, failure to respond is a function of other factors, some of which are very easy to work around. Next, we will address issues related to failure to engage in AAA responding following teacher-delivered instruction, assuming that teacher-delivered group instruction is designed to cause early acquisition, and assignments that follow teacher instruction are designed to enhance acquisition, build fluency or automaticity, and promote maintenance, generalization, and discrimination.

Materials

One reason that students cannot respond is that they have failed to bring materials needed to respond (e.g., no pencil, left workbook at home). This could be seen as a "teachable moment" and educators may be tempted to allow students to experience "natural consequences" as they sit in their seats unable to respond (e.g., unable to complete independent seatwork assignment in their workbook). Given that learning and skill development is contingent on responding, educators should not let natural consequences prevail. Instead, educators should keep extra material on hand for such instances, so that all students have the opportunity to engage in AAA responding. Concerns over shaping responsibility should be addressed in a manner that does not retard academic skill development (Skinner & McCleary, 2010).

Attention to Directions/Instructions

It is not uncommon for teachers to become frustrated with having to repeat simple directions because some students were not paying attention. When a student raises his hand to ask a question like "what page are we supposed to be on?" educators may once again find themselves presented with a teachable moment. Again, because engaging in AAA responding is required for learning, educators must repeat the simple direction so that students can *get to the doing* (i.e., engage in AAA responding). When students cannot engage in AAA responding because they did not pay attention to a lesson that was designed to allow them to acquire the ability to respond, educators are faced with a can't-do problem. These instances are a bit different than instances of not paying attention to simple directions, in that repeated failure to pay attention during instruction can result in serious skill deficits because they prevent or limit students' post-instruction AAA responding (Saecker et al., 2008).

Attention During Instruction

Several strategies can be used to enhance attention during instruction. One strategy focuses on transitions from one activity (e.g., independent language arts seatwork) to a new activity (e.g., teacher-led math instruction). Even teachers with many years of experience have difficulty managing transitions (Buck, 1999; Campbell & Skinner, 2004; Codding & Smyth, 2008; Connell & Carta, 1993; Yarbrough, Skinner, Lee, & Lemmons, 2004). Class-wide activity transitions require all students to stop doing something, attend to directions/instructions for the next activity, and begin the next activity (Dawson-Rodriques, Lavay, Butt, & Lacourse, 1997; Fudge, Reece, Skinner, & Cowden, 2007). Efficient activity transitions should take little time and effort and decrease the probability of students engaging in inappropriate behaviors (Fudge et al., 2008). Particularly in elementary schools, activity transitions occur frequently and evidence suggests they are rarely efficient, with 20%–39% of the school day spent in transitions (Carta, Atwater, Schwartz, & Miller, 1990; Codding & Smyth, 2008). These 1 to 2 hours per day spent transitioning reduce the time available for educators to teach and students to learn (Carta, Greenwood, & Robinson, 1987; Fudge et al., 2007; Gettinger & Seibert, 2002).

When an educator begins to provide teacher-led instruction, those still engaged in other activities are less likely to attend to instructions, which may prevent early acquisition and the students' ability to engage in AAA responding that follow teacher-led instruction. Consequently, educators find themselves having to repeat instructions/directions so that those who were not attending can benefit from the time allotted for AAA responding. While we support this re-teaching, a better strategy would be to secure students' attention prior to beginning teacher-led instruction and maintain their attention throughout instruction (Saecker et al., 2008).

Color Wheel Procedures. Color Wheel (CW) procedures were developed by educators/researchers (i.e., Drs. Gina Scale, Deb Dentis, and Edward Lentz) as a component of a comprehensive classroom management system that would be applied across all students and grade levels at a laboratory school serving students with emotional and behavioral disorders. CW procedures involve several stimuli, including posted rules, the wheel itself, and verbal cues delivered by the teacher. The color wheel can be constructed from inexpensive materials (cardboard, construction paper, tack) and is posted in the front of the class where the teacher frequently delivers class-wide directions/instructions. Like a traffic light, the color wheel contains three colors (red, yellow, and green), indicating current behavioral expectations. The wheel is always "on," with the displayed color indicating a specific set of rules or behavioral expectations that are currently in place. Thus, with the CW procedure there are three sets of classroom rules: red rules, yellow rules, and green rules, which are summarized in Table 16.1 (Skinner, Scala, Dendas, & Lentz, 2007; Skinner & Skinner, 2007).

Table 16.1 CW Posted Classroom Rules

Red Rules	Yellow Rules	Green Rules
1. Desk clear	1. Raise hand to leave seat	1. Use inside voices
2. Seat in seat ("in area"—good for floor activities)	2. Raise hand to speak (not "no talking")	2. Respect others
3. Eyes on speaker	3. Eyes on speaker or work (not "on-task")	3. Hands and feet to self
4. No talking		4. Follow all directions
5. No hand raising (ready position)	4. Follow directions	
	5. Hands and feet to self	

Red rules are used when a teacher needs all students' undivided attention. Teachers are encouraged to use red for every activity transition, in order to influence students to cease their current activity and attend to instruction for the next activity. The yellow rules are designed to set behavioral expectations for many different academic activities, including independent seatwork, academic games, tests, teacher-led instruction, and peer presentations. The green rules are designed for free time, cooperative academic projects, fine arts, and other activities where teachers want to encourage more spontaneous interactions. All three sets of rules are taught to the students and posted next to the wheel (Skinner et al., 2007).

There are specific, repeatable, and predictable procedures for transitioning from one activity to another and one set of rules to another. Specifically, before the class stops their current activity, they are given two warnings, a 2-minute (e.g., "The color wheel is going to red in 2 minutes") and a 30-second warning (Kern & Clemens, 2007). After the warning time has elapsed, the teacher turns the wheel to red and faces the students who, if they are following the red rules, are in their seat with their desk clear (no materials to distract their attention), looking at the teacher, and not talking or even allowed to raise their hand to speak. The teacher then *quickly* communicates with the students. Speed is important, because red rules are the most difficult to follow, and the more time the class spends on red, the more likely someone is to break the rules. For example, with all students paying attention, the teacher may praise the group for following red rules and instruct the students that after she turns the color wheel to yellow they are to take out some scrap paper, a pencil, and their math text and turn to page 76. After turning the wheel to yellow, some students may raise their hand and let the teacher know that they need something to be able to complete the next task (e.g., sharpen their pencil, forgot their textbook). Additionally, the teacher may need to address other concerns (e.g., to go to the bathroom). After dealing with these issues all at once, teacher-led instruction can begin without interruption and without having to repeat, re-direct, re-instruct, or reprimand. Other, more subtle CW procedures and a rationale for each procedure are summarized in Table 16.2 (Skinner et al., 2007).

Researchers have found that CW procedures increased on-task behavior (i.e., attending to teacher-led instruction or independent seatwork) across all students in second- and fourth-grade classrooms (Fudge et al., 2007; Fudge et al., 2008). Others found evidence that these procedures can reduce out-of-seat behavior (Choate, Skinner, Fearrington, Kohler, & Skolits, 2007). Saecker et al. (2008) found that applying CW procedures reduced the number of times a teacher had to repeat directions or instructions. Researchers who have combined CW procedures with group rewards also found evidence that CW procedures reduced inappropriate behaviors (Below, Skinner, Skinner, Sorrell, & Irwin, 2008; Hautau, Skinner, Pfaffman,

Table 16.2 CW Procedures and Procedure Rationales

Procedure	Rationale
1. Teach the students the rules. Read/recite frequently (McIntosh et al., 2004).	Students must know rules. Repeating and reciting rules may serve as antecedent stimuli for rule-following behavior.
2. Post wheel and written rules next to each other near where group directions/instructions are typically delivered.	All three stimuli visible at the same time makes it easier for students to know and follow the rules. Also, having the wheel close allows the teachers to change it after finishing delivering instructions/directions.
3. Write rules using your own colloquialisms (seat-in-seat) and make them brief.	Child learning and understanding is critical, not language used. Briefly worded rules allow for rapid recitation.
4. Fade warnings, recitations and praise as year goes on, but do not stop, as you may need to rehearse a bit as new students enter the room.	At some point, too much repetition and recitation is unnecessary.
5. Use red frequently, for almost every activity transition, so that you can clearly communicate with the class.	Establishing transition routines is important, and consistency helps some students behave appropriately.
6. Almost always transition using red. Do not go from yellow to green. Instead go from yellow to red to green.	You want to make it clear that one activity has ended before beginning another activity.
7. Keep brief time on red. Do not teach or provide lectures (academic) on red.	You want to occasion rule-following behavior. The longer you are on red, the more likely someone will break a rule.
8. After quick directions/instruction on red, turn back to yellow and respond to raised hands.	You may have a child who needs immediate attention (e.g., really, really has to go to the bathroom).
9. DO NOT USE RED AS PUNISHMENT.	You want to occasion rule following. It is unlikely that the entire class misbehaved and deserves punishment, so those who behaved well may resent this punishment and break red rules.
10. Praise students for rule-following behavior. Do not say something like, "Well, it is about time you grow up and behave! Why haven't you been doing this all along?"	The goal of CW is rule following and praising rule following is likely to increases this behavior and enhance the quality of the classroom environment.
11. You may use time on green as a group reward (all or none of the students get the time on green).	Time on green allows students to engage in preferred behaviors and, therefore, can be a powerful and efficient reward for each student.
12. You, not the students, turn the wheel.	Many students will take directions from adults but not peers. Also, although the wheel cost little to make, it does take time to make the wheel and children may accidentally destroy it.

Foster, & Clark, 2008); however, another study suggested that additional rewards may not be necessary, as CW procedures seemed to be effective without the addition of group-oriented rewards (Kirk et al., 2010).

Interspersing Active Responding. While CW procedures may help capture students' attention, interspersing active student responding during teacher-led instruction may help maintain students' attention. There are numerous ways to accomplish this goal. Perhaps the simplest is to apply recitation procedures (e.g., ask the class questions and call on students to answer). While recitation procedures are simple, there are several recommendations that may maximize student attention and enhance learning.

First, during teacher-led instruction, questions should be directed to the entire class so that all students are encouraged to try to cognitively respond and raise their hand. Teachers should never call on a specific student prior to asking a question, because the student's class-mates may not try to respond. The next issue is deciding how long to wait before calling on a student to answer the question. Wait-time length (i.e., time after the question is asked until a student is called on to answer) depends upon the question and the students in the classroom. When the teacher asks a fact, the wait time should be short, because students either know it or they do not. However, when responses require more thought, reasoning, or sequential steps, more time should be provided (Riley, 1986; Rowe, 1974). Across the entire class, some students will need more time to come up with answers than will others; however, teach-ers should not extend wait times too long, as they reduce time for instruction and learning (Black, Forbes, Yaw, & Skinner, 2013).

While teachers may call on only one student, response card technology can be used to enhance the probability that all students will respond to a question. For example, a teacher could ask a question during a science lesson and then have the students write the answer on Mylar boards. Students would then be asked to simultaneously display their written answer by holding them over their head facing the teacher (Gardner, Heward, & Grossi, 1994). Simultane-ous verbal responding (i.e., choral responding) can also allow all students in a class to respond to questions. More high-tech procedures can also be used by asking all students to respond using clickers or computers. There are several advantages associated with applying response card technology, as opposed to calling on one student to answer questions. When all students respond, teachers can use their responses as feedback to guide future instruction. For exam-ple, specific erroneous responses may cue an instructor to reteach (with a focus on clarifying specific confusion), engage in error correction techniques (Grskovic & Belfiore, 1996), or move on to the next concept (Heward, 1994). Furthermore, research on student responding suggests that more or higher rates of overt, active, academic responding is likely to enhance students' attention to teacher instruction and student learning (Carnine, 1976; Darch & Gersten, 1985; Gardner et al., 1994; Hawkins, Skinner, & Oliver, 2005; Robinson & Skinner, 2002).

Choosing to Respond

Assuming students engage in AAA responding because they (1) have the pre-requisite skills, perhaps learned from teacher-led instruction; (2) know what is expected (e.g., paid attention to directions); and (3) have materials needed to respond (e.g., worksheets or Mylar boards), they may still choose to do something else. Furthermore, because this choice is continuous, at any moment in time they can choose to stop their AAA responding and engage in another behavior (McCurdy, Skinner, Grantham, Watson, & Hindman, 2001). While many human behavior theorists, scientists, and philosophers have focused on factors influencing choice or motivation, behaviorists are less likely to focus on within-student characteristics (e.g., the student is oppositional-defiant) that influence choice, and more likely to focus on other, perhaps more malleable factors that may influence choice (Malone, 1990).

Assignment Choice, Effort, and Interspersal

Providing students with options and allowing them to choose academic assignments can result in increased independent work production and academic engaged time, and decreased problem behaviors, such as disruptions or off-task behavior (Dunlap et al., 1994; Kern et al., 1998). However, there are several reasons why caution is needed when providing students with assignment options. When given the choice of two behaviors and all else is held constant, people are more likely to choose the behavior that requires the least effort (Friman & Poling, 1995; Hawthorn-Embree, Taylor, Skinner, Parkhurst, & Nalls, in press). Consequently, when given an option of two assignments, students are more likely to choose the assignment that requires the least amount of effort to complete. Because learning typically requires effort, students may choose to engage in the assignment that causes the least amount of learning.

Interspersal Procedures. Students perceive assignments as less effortful if they are interspersed with more discrete tasks (e.g., math computation problems) that are quicker and easier to complete (Billington & DiTommaso, 2003; Billington & Skinner, 2002). The interspersal technique, which involves interspersing tasks that are briefer and easier within an assignment, has been used as an alternative method to traditional drill and practice. Interspersal techniques include both substitutive and additive interspersal (Cates, 2005). Substitutive interspersal involves removing target tasks (e.g., a 3-digit by 2-digit multiplication problem) and substituting briefer and easier tasks (a 1-digit by 1-digit problem). When applying additive interspersal procedures, no target problems are removed from intact assignments; rather, briefer and easier tasks are added and interspersed among the longer target tasks.

Students may be more likely to choose to work on substitutive interspersal assignments because they require less effort to complete than target assignments (Skinner, 2002). However, researchers on substitutive interspersal ratios suggest that, because they require less effort to complete, they may also occasion less learning. Roberts, Turco, and Shapiro (1991) investigated the effects of four known to unknown ratios on students' reading of vocabulary words: 90/10, 80/20, 60/40, and 50/50. In this study, the 50/50 ratio resulted in the greatest number of new words learned; however, a limitation of this study is that ratios with greater than 50% unknown problems were not investigated. In a follow-up study, Roberts and Shapiro (1996) found that when comparing known to unknown ratios of 20/80, 50/50, and 80/20, the ratios with greater percentage of unknown words resulted in greater levels of learning. Additional research on ratios of known to unknown tasks resulted in support for traditional drill and practice (i.e., all unknown or target problems) when compared known to unknown ratios of 3:3 and 18:6 in both spelling (Cates et al., 2003) and word reading (Joseph & Nist, 2006).

Others have altered flashcard assignments using a procedure known as incremental rehearsal, so that much of the one-to-one instructional time is spent responding to words that students already know how to read. Such procedures may increase the probability that students will choose to do the assignment, because they reduce the amount of difficult or challenging tasks assigned per learning minute and, in some instances, enhance reinforcement for accurate responding. Furthermore, two meta-analyses suggest that these procedures enhance learning (Burns, 2004; Burns, Zaslofsky, Kanive, & Parker, 2012). Despite these findings, we do not recommend applying most incremental rehearsal procedures, because so much student time is allotted to known tasks (e.g., known words), and researchers have found evidence that if that time were re-allocated to unknown tasks, learning can be accelerated (Cates et al., 2003; Forbes, Black, Yaw, & Skinner, 2013; Nist & Joseph, 2008; Skinner, 2008).

Whereas substitutive interspersal can involve watering down the curricula, additive interspersal involves adding more tasks that are brief and easy, rather than replacing target items with the brief and easy tasks. In these instances, the assignments are not reduced. Furthermore, if the interspersed tasks require very little time, this procedure does not reduce rates of responding to target items (Skinner, 2002; Wildmon, Skinner, McCurdy, & Sims, 1999; Wildmon, Skinner, & McDade, 1998; Wildmon, Skinner, Watson, & Garrett, 2004). The other advantage to interspersing very brief tasks is that brief tasks typically require less effort (Billington & DiTommaso, 2003; Hawthorn-Embree et al., in press).

Though most additive interspersal research has been completed with mathematics (see Skinner, 2002), researchers have also found that interspersing easier tasks may be effective for other assignments that are composed of discrete tasks, such as language arts worksheets (Meadows & Skinner, 2005) and grammar assignments (Teeple & Skinner, 2004). Researchers have shown that additive interspersal procedures are effective with elementary school (McCurdy et al., 2001), middle school (Billington, Skinner, & Cruchon, 2004), high school (Johns, Skinner, & Nail, 2000), and college students (Billington, Skinner, Hutchins, & Malone, 2004). Furthermore, researchers have found that additive interspersal procedures can influence numerous outcomes, including students' perceptions of assignments, assignment preference and choice, and their academic engagement.

Perceptions. Numerous researchers have found that altering math computation assignments by interspersing additional brief math computation problems causes students to rate the assignment as requiring less time and effort to complete (Billington & Skinner, 2006; Skinner, 2002; Skinner, Fletcher, Wildmon, & Belfiore, 1996; Skinner, Robinson, Johns, Logan, & Belfiore, 1996). Researchers have also tested the strength of the interspersal procedure. For example, Cates et al. (1999) found that college students ranked an assignment with 20% (e.g., 12 as opposed to 10) more long, high-effort computation problems (e.g., $597 \times 84 = $ _____) as requiring less effort than control assignments when additional brief problems (e.g., $3 \times 2 = $ _____) were added to the longer assignment. In a follow-up study, Cates and Skinner (2000) found that students receiving remedial mathematics instruction would rate an assignment with 14 high-effort problems as requiring less effort than a similar assignment with 10 high-effort problems, when a brief problem was added to the assignment with 14 high-effort problems. Other researchers found similar results when they manipulated effort within problems, as opposed to number of problems (Billington, Skinner, & Cruchon, 2004; Billington, Skinner, Hutchins et al., 2004). Research on students' perceptions of assignments is important, as it facilitates our understanding of why additive interspersal works; however, it is useful only as much as it results in changes in students' choice to engage in assignments.

Preference and Choice. In both an individual study (Skinner, Hall-Johnson et al., 1999) and a meta-analysis of interspersal research (Skinner, 2002), researchers found a linear relationship between problem completion rate and likelihood that students would select an assignment for homework. Billington and Skinner (2006) found similar results with respect to effort and time perceptions: the greater the difference in problem completion rates across the two assignments, the more likely students were to choose to work on the assignment with the interspersed brief problems. This caused researchers to hypothesize that each completed discrete problem served as a reinforcer. As one way to cause people to choose to engage in higher effort tasks is to enhance rates of reinforcement for that task, this hypothesis may explain why Cates and Skinner (2000) found that high school students with weak math skills (they were placed in remedial math) were more likely to choose to complete a worksheet with 14 three-digit by two-digit math problems plus additional one-digit by one-digit problem interspersed every third problem, over a control sheet with only 10 three-digit by two-digit problems.

Engagement. In addition to improvements in assignment perceptions, preference, and choice, additive interspersal techniques result in greater endurance over time and academic engagement. McCurdy et al. (2001) found increased levels of academic engagement in an elementary student when they altered workbook assignments by adding and interspersing brief math tasks. Although they used substitutive interspersal procedures (i.e., they watered down the curricula by replacing target task with easier task), Calderhead, Filter, and Albin (2006) found that their procedure increased on-task behavior. Montarello and Martens (2005) found that three of their four participants maintained a higher rate of digits correct per minute toward the end of a 10-minute assignment during interspersal conditions, when compared to a no-interspersal condition, with the fourth participant showing no difference between conditions. Students not only demonstrated greater work completion rates, but the rates were also better maintained throughout the class period; thus they displayed greater endurance.

Ratios. Cates and Dalenberg (2005) compared different ratios (1:1, 1:3, 1:5) of easy/brief to target, high-effort problems within interspersal assignments. Because students were spending so much time on the brief problems, they found that college students completed significantly fewer problems when the target to interspersed ratio was 1:1. Furthermore, students did not rate the 1:5 interspersal assignments as less time consuming than the control assignments. In a follow-up study with middle-school students, Cates and Erkfritz (2007) found that students did not perceive differences between the 1:5 interspersal condition and a control condition with only target problems. Together with earlier research on 1:3 ratios, these studies provide support for a 1:3 easy-to-target problem ratio. However, these recommended ratios may not generalize to other tasks, especially when the time required to complete the interspersed and higher-effort tasks is much different than the computation assignment investigated in these studies (Skinner, 2002; Wildmon et al., 1999).

Other Assignment Alteration Procedures

Researchers have investigated several other assignment alteration procedures that may enhance the probability of students choosing to engage in academic work. Again, we will avoid focusing on procedures that may reduce learning, because they reduce assignment demands.

Brief Sheets. One assignment alteration procedure was initiated by a practitioner and graduate student who wanted to know if they could apply the additive interspersal procedure to a student (with intellectual disabilities) whose independent math seatwork included only adding 0 or 1 to number no larger than 3 (e.g., 2 + 1 = __). This student would receive an assignment with about 30 such problems, 6 rows of 5 problems on each sheet. He would often start the assignment, but after finishing a few problems, he would quit, fold his arms, and glare at the teacher. This situation does not lend itself to interspersal procedure, because it is difficult to come up with a briefer task or math problem than those targeted (Wallace, Cox, & Skinner, 2003). Even if briefer problems could be applied, the additive interspersal procedure may not have worked, because it is based on an assumption that the student has a history of reinforcement for assignment completion. Specifically, if assignment completion has been reinforced, then stimuli that precede assignment completion (completed discrete task) should be conditioned reinforcers. Therefore, enhancing rates of task competition by interspersing additional briefer tasks enhances rates of reinforcement (Skinner, 2002).

While the student's learning history may not have allowed Wallace et al. (2003) to apply additive interspersal procedures, researchers decided that they would provide a learning history that would result in reinforcement for assignment completion. Each day, the teacher used a paper cutter to cut each 30-problem assignment into six brief assignments with five problems each. After the student was given the brief assignment, he completed all the problems and raised his hand. The teacher approached to pick up his assignment and said, "You finished one assignment, give me one high five," and then the teacher slapped the student's raised hand one time as she placed the next brief assignment on the student's desk. When he finished that assignment, procedures were repeated, but two fives were given for two assignments completed. After a few days, the student was completing all 30 problems. Additionally, the student was experiencing a new learning history, one where assignments were completed and assignment completion was reinforced.

Partial Assignment Completion (PAC). Recently researchers began investigating the partial assignment completion (PAC) effect, another strategy that may influence the probability of students finishing assignments (Hawthorn-Embree, Skinner, Parkhurst, O'Neil, & Conley, 2010). This research is based on gestalt and behavioral theories that incomplete or interrupted tasks or assignments are aversive, which may increase the probability that students will choose to complete those tasks or assignments. Although research on this effect is emerging, it appears that students may be more likely to choose to work on an assignment that they have already begun; however, the PAC effect is not very powerful (Hawthorn-Embree, Skinner, Parkhurst, & Conley, 2011). Regardless, educators can take advantage of PAC effects by requiring students to start assignments, even when there is only enough time left in the day or class period to complete just a small portion of the assignment (Hawthorn-Embree et al., in press).

Alter Response Topography. Another strategy that may enhance the AAA responding rates and learning rates is to alter response topography. Some responses take more effort than others. For example, researchers altered traditional cover, copy, and compare procedures; after students looked at and covered a math fact problem and answer, instead of having students write the problem and answer they were instructed to state it aloud or to themselves (Skinner, Bamberg, Smith, & Powell, 1993; Skinner, Belfiore, Mace, Williams-Wilson, & Johns, 1997; Skinner, Ford, & Yunker, 1991).

Increasing Rates of AAA Responding

If AAA responding causes learning, then allotting more time for AAA responding is not the only general strategy for enhancing learning. Another strategy would be to enhance AAA responding rates or the number of AAA responses made in a fixed period of time. One way to enhance AAA responding rates is to alter the response topography to a more efficient form. Again, returning to the cover, copy, and compare studies, Skinner et al. (1997) found that altering responding from written to verbal almost tripled AAA responding rates, which cause more learning in a fixed period of time.

Other procedures that we have previously discussed also increase AAA responding rates class wide. For example, during recitations asking the question and then calling on someone (as opposed to calling on someone and then asking the question), increases the number of students who respond to the question in a fixed period of time. Therefore, in a class of 20 students, if three questions are asked per minute, AAA responding could be 60 per minute. Response cards and clickers can accomplish the same goals.

Explicit Timing

Other procedures that have been used to enhance students' rates of responding during independent seatwork often include elements of explicit timing. Explicit timing, a procedure in which students are told they are being timed while completing an academic assignment

(Rhymer et al., 2002), has been shown to improve students' academic performance during independent seatwork (Evans-Hampton, Skinner, Henington, Sims, & McDaniel, 2002; Rhymer et al., 2002; Rhymer, Henington, Skinner, & Looby, 1999; Rhymer, Skinner, Henington, D'Reaux, & Sims, 1998; Van Houten, Hill, & Parsons, 1975; Van Houten, Morrison, Jarvis, & McDonald, 1974; Van Houten & Thompson, 1976). For example, Van Houten and Thompson (1976) implemented the explicit timing intervention during second-grade students' independent mathematics seatwork. They announced each 1-minute interval that passed and instructed students to circle the last problem they finished. They found that student rates of responding and accuracy levels increased under the explicit timing condition, as opposed to a control situation when students completed the exercises but did not know they were being timed.

Rhymer et al. (1999) compared the explicit-timing procedure to a control condition with no overt timing in African American and Caucasian second-grade students completing addition and subtraction problems. They found no cross-group differences, but both groups completed more problems per minute during the explicit timing condition (i.e., increased response rates), and accuracy remained consistent, with no increase across either condition. In two other studies, researchers found evidence that explicit-timing procedures enhance rates of responding, but accuracy of those responses may be influenced by problem difficulty and skill development. Specifically, on more difficult problems, students with stronger skills may be more likely to show an increase in accuracy when explicitly timed than will those with weaker skills (Rhymer et al. 1998; Rhymer et al., 2002).

While many researchers are concerned that prompting higher rates of responding during independent seatwork could cause students to rush and make more errors, researchers have found that such procedures either have no effect on accuracy or enhance accuracy. Though it is far from certain what explains these inconsistent findings, research on pacing suggests that increasing rates of responding may increase students' on-task levels or attention to tasks (Carnine, 1976; Darche & Gersten, 1985). Therefore, enhancing students' rates of responding may enhance accuracy on tasks that require high levels of sustained attention (Robinson & Skinner, 2002). For example, Hawkins et al. (2005) read sequential multi-step math problems to students (e.g., $3 \times 7 + 9 - 22 \times 8 - 59 =$ ____), with a brief pause between reading sequential operations. During one condition, students were allowed to use paper and pencil to perform each step. Under the other condition, they could not use paper and pencil until it was time to write their final answer. Researchers manipulated rates of responding via the application of the additive interspersal procedure (i.e., they interspersed additional brief, easy problems). Results showed that increasing rates of responding on the written work had no impact on accuracy, but caused a large increase in accurate responding on the work that had to be done cognitively (i.e., without paper/pencil). Hawkins et al. (2005) suggested that increasing rates of responding could enhance accuracy on tasks that require high levels of sustained attention.

Reinforcement for Higher Rates of High Effort AAA Responding

One reason many educators advocate developing basic academic skills to the point of automaticity or fluency (i.e., so that they can be performed with little time and require few cognitive resources) is that speed of responding typically correlates with effort (Skinner, 1998). Consequently, those with strong academic skills may be more likely to choose to engage in assigned academic tasks than might those with weaker academic skills. As engaging in academic assignments is often required to enhance skill development, this phenomenon can cause a downward spiral in those who are already behind (e.g., those with skill deficits). As they continue to choose not to engage in assigned work, they fall farther behind, making it less likely that they develop their skills and choose to respond to more advanced, higher-effort tasks. At the same time, those who require little effort to respond continue to choose to respond to more advanced tasks, enhancing their skill development, which causes larger and larger differences in skill-development levels among fluent and dysfluent students (Binder, 1996; Skinner, 1998; Stanovich, 1986).

Researchers have shown that one way to influence students to choose to engage in higher-effort academic responding is to enhance the reinforcement for such responding (e.g., Mace, McCurdy, & Quigley, 1990; Neef, Mace, & Shade, 1993; Neef, Mace, Shea, & Shade, 1992; Neef, Shade, & Miller, 1994). Reinforcement for AAA responding can be strengthened by providing higher-quality reinforcers. For example, pizza may be a higher-quality reinforcer than is liver. Additionally, providing higher rates of reinforcement for academic responding can increase the probability of students choosing to engage in AAA responding. Consider the *brief sheets* intervention described earlier (Wallace et al., 2003). By breaking one math assignment into six, the student raised his hand and was reinforced every time he completed a five-problem assignment. Under typical conditions he would only be reinforced after completing 30 problems, something he rarely did, perhaps because it required too much effort for the amount and frequency of reinforcement received. Finally, providing more immediate reinforcement can increase the probability of students choosing to engage in AAA responding. For example, immediately after a student finishes an assignment, providing praise and a gold star would be more likely to influence AAA responding than would providing the same praise and star the following school day after the assignment was graded.

Independent Group-Oriented Rewards. Educational environments are social structures; therefore, it comes as no surprise that most of the reward structures (i.e., contingencies) are designed to be fair. In general, fair means the application of independent group-oriented contingencies. These contingencies are considered fair because the same rules (if you do X, then you get this consequence) apply to everyone. Perhaps because they are used in most legal systems, independent group-oriented punishments are easiest to describe. For example, any student who brings a gun to school is suspended for a year. Additionally, some high-stakes consequences for academic behaviors (e.g., report card grades) are also applied using independent groups. Specifically, in most instances, the targeted behaviors (e.g., test performance, all get the same test), criteria (e.g., 80–89% correct), and consequences (e.g., letter grade of B) are the same for everyone (group aspect of the contingency). The independent aspect of the contingency is that each student gets access to consequences contingent on his or her own behavior or performance. Letter grades are the most obvious and formal contingencies for academic behaviors (e.g., in college syllabi contingencies—target behavior, criteria, and consequence in the form of grades—are often detailed enough to be considered a contract). However, teachers provide many other incidental reinforcers for academic behaviors that cause learning (e.g., completing an assignment, paying attention in class, answer a recitation question) and for performance on tasks that reflect learning (e.g., exams), including praise, gold stars, or allowing students who finish their work to engage in preferred behaviors.

Unfortunately, the use of traditional reinforcement procedures may not be powerful enough to cause students with weak academic skills to choose to work on academic assignments. Specifically, the reinforcement for completing an assignment at a criteria level (e.g.,

B or better) is not worth the amount of effort (given their weak skills) required to choose to engage in target academic behaviors. One alternative is to provide them with different tasks, criteria, or stronger reinforcement. While such strategies are acceptable and often required when working with exceptional children (e.g., individual education plans are developed), in general-education classrooms such procedures are often considered unfair. For example, consider how a parent may react if his or her child received a low grade and did not qualify for a scholarship, while another child whose performance was identical received a higher grade (i.e., different criteria across group members). Also, consider how a child would react if he did not earn access to an ice cream party, but another child who had easy assignments did meet the criteria for earning the ice cream (Skinner, Skinner, & Burton, 2009; Skinner, Skinner, Skinner, & Cashwell, 1999).

Interdependent Group-Oriented Rewards. Fortunately, there are alternatives available that allow educators to enhance reinforcement for students with weaker skill deficits. Interdependent group contingencies have been effective across a variety of behaviors, academic skills, settings, and populations (Little, Akin-Little, & Newman-Eig, 2010; Pappas, Skinner, & Skinner, 2010; Popkin & Skinner, 2003; Sharp & Skinner, 2004; Skinner, Cashwell, & Skinner, 2000). With interdependent group-oriented contingencies all students in a group receive access to a reward, based on the group as a whole meeting some criterion (Litow & Pumroy, 1975).

Group-oriented criteria could include averages (e.g., class average, randomly select five assignments and average them), high score, low score (e.g., if all scores above 70%), amount of work completed (e.g., if 20 of the 25 students turn in homework), and cumulative criteria (e.g., when the class spells 10,000 words on spelling exams, carrying the data across weeks, we will have a popcorn party). Staying with our last example, the students who were already doing well in spelling have the opportunity to earn additional reinforcement. The chance to earn a popcorn party may provide enough additional reinforcement for weaker spellers to try their best. Even if they do not meet the criteria for praise, any improvement will contribute to the group earning the popcorn party. Also, if the weaker spellers are given a different set of words (i.e., easier words), their peers are less likely to complain, because this modification in their curricula enhances the probability of all students earning the additional reward, the popcorn party (Skinner et al., 2009).

Applying rewards in an all-or-none fashion allows educators to apply inexpensive activity rewards (e.g., listening to music during independent seatwork) that are difficult to apply to some and not all students. When all or none earn awards, concerns about belittling and stealing rewards are mitigated. Finally, and perhaps most importantly, when the entire class earns a reward, everyone gets to share the glory; consequently, students who rarely earn rewards for their academic behaviors get to experience success (Skinner, Cashwell, & Dunn, 1996).

Many of the challenges associated with layering additional interdependent group-oriented rewards onto current independent group-oriented contingencies can be addressed by using unknown or randomly selected components (Skinner & Watson, 1993). Not all rewards may be reinforcers for every student in the group. Rather than informing students of the rewards, rewards can be written down on a slip of paper and randomly selected when criteria are met. Therefore, not all rewards have to be powerful reinforcers for all students, as long as some in the pool are reinforcing to each student.

When setting a criterion, we do not want to use one that is too high (they may give up) or too low (we may not get their best effort). In most instances with group-oriented criteria, all students are encouraged to do their best. For example, if the criterion is a class average of 90% on an exam, no one is sure how well they have to do for the group to meet the average; consequently, everyone may try their best. Randomly selecting criteria can also achieve this goal. To encourage students to do their best across tasks, researchers have also randomly selected academic target behaviors. When additional reinforcement may be delivered contingent on your performance on X, Y, or Z, and you perform poorly on X, you may still put forth a lot of effort on Y and Z, because these target behaviors may be randomly selected and rewards delivered based on the group's performance on these tasks (Kelshaw, Sterling-Turner, Henry, & Skinner, 2000; Skinner, Skinner, & Sterling-Turner, 2002).

Popkin and Skinner (2003) provided an excellent example of how to apply interdependent group-oriented contingencies with randomly selected components when they worked with a class of five students with serious emotional disturbances. Students were allowed to suggest group rewards that were inexpensive, that most students would enjoy, and that required little time. After being approved by the teacher, they were written on slips of paper and placed into a container. During the course of the study, students could continue making suggestions for rewards. Criteria were also randomly selected from slips of paper that included percent scores (e.g., 85%) and a target behavior (e.g., spelling). Initially, all 30 slips targeted spelling, and students were told that the teacher would randomly select a slip of paper at the end of the day and if the class average spelling scores met or exceeded the criterion, she would select a reward. Students always had at least one spelling assignment or test per day, but students did not have the same assignments or grade-level curricula. After a few weeks, 30 more slips of paper were added that had math written on them, along with similar criteria. Finally, 30 more slips of paper were added with English written on them and similar criteria. Thus, in the final phase, the teacher would randomly select from a slip of paper with spelling, math, or English written on it, along with a criterion, and if the class met the criterion, she randomly selected a reward (e.g., play a game).

Table 16.3 provides a summary of the results, and several things are worth noting. First, the students showed meaningful improvements in their performance, as evidenced by their letter grade increases. Prior to beginning the study the teacher was not sure if the work was too difficult. Clearly, it was not too difficult. In fact, it may have been too easy. Second, no students complained that peers had easier work than they did. Third, by starting with one target behavior and adding new ones, the contingency was faded, not by reducing reward strength, but rather by requiring more work for the same reward (first just spelling, then spelling and math, and finally, spelling, math, and English).

Table 16.3 Average Percent Correct and Letter Grades on Daily Assignment for Baseline and Intervention Phases Across Academic Content Areas and Students

Student	Spelling		Mathematics		English	
	Baseline X-Grade	Intervention X-Grade	Baseline X-Grade	Intervention X-Grade	Baseline X-Grade	Intervention X-Grade
One	93.3 A	97.7 A	68.4 D	89.8 A	85.6 B	98.0 A
Two	69.0 D	92.3 A	64.7 D	86.6 B	80.2 B	92.0 A
Three	26.2 F	96.3 A	72.4 C	86.1 B	72.9 C	90.0 A
Four	90.7 A	98.5 A	58.0 F	80.4 B	86.8 B	100.0 A
Five	0.00 F	89.5 A	63.7 D	84.0 B	87.7 B	79.0 C
Class	62.2 D	96.2 A	66.6 D	86.6 B	85.7 B	93.3 A

One side effect was noted as the teacher explained that she now had a lot more work to grade. However, other side effects that may have occurred include students complaining that a classmate received access to the reward, even though the classmate did not do any work. Also, teachers may have concerns with this unpreventable side effect. The best reaction to these complaints is to first admit this negative side effect. Second, teachers and students can be reminded of other rewards and consequences that are delivered solely on each student's own behavior (e.g., letter grades). Finally, a response that works remarkably well with students is to agree and suggest that we should cease running these additional rewards programs. The same response is also useful when group members complain because a difficult randomly selected criterion was selected. Complaining quickly ceases because these additional group reward programs can only result in students earning extra rewards (Skinner et al., 2009).

A more serious potential side effect is when the group does not earn a reward and blames it on a particular student. This is potentially very harmful, as students who rarely get access to rewards for academic behaviors are now being punished. One way to avoid this is to always base rewards on non-public behaviors. Alternatively, random selection of target behaviors (randomly select five tests) without letting students know whose tests were selected can also accomplish this goal. Cumulative, as opposed to all-or-nothing, criteria can help address this problem. For example, if the criterion is 10,000 total words spelled correctly on spelling test, then each student's test is a chance to contribute to the goal and no students hurt progress.

Summing Up

Students who have the prerequisite skills to engage in AAA responding but just need a bit more (materials, instruction, directions) should be given the bit more. We build schools, train and pay teachers, and establish systems to pay for all this so that students can engage in AAA responding. Then, we tell students and their parents that learning is critical. If learning is so important, certainly we should not prevent it from occurring because a student forgot a pencil or was not paying attention when the teacher informed them which page their assignment was on (Skinner & McCleary, 2010).

Providing students *can* engage in AAA responding, they may still choose to engage in many competing alternative behaviors, sometimes because the desired tasks take so much effort. While making academic assignments easier may increase the probability of students choosing to do assignments, when this involves watering down the curricula, such procedures can also reduce learning rates (Cates et al., 2003; Nist & Joseph, 2008; Skinner, 2010). Other assignment alteration strategies, such as interspersing additional brief tasks, applying response card technology, using brief sheets, or altering response topographies, may enhance the probability of students choosing to do the work, without reducing rates of responding to target tasks (e.g., Cates & Skinner, 2000; Skinner, 2002; Wallace et al., 2003).

Finally, researchers can increase the probability of students choosing to engage in high-effort academic tasks by enhancing reinforcement for choosing to engage in such tasks (Neef et al., 1994). Although typical independent group-oriented contingencies have limitations, interdependent group-oriented rewards can be used to enhance the probability of students choosing to engage in assigned academic work (Skinner et al., 2004). Such procedures can be applied using inexpensive group activity rewards. Additionally, because they may enhance cooperative behavior among students and allow some students who rarely earn rewards for academic behaviors, to do just that, educators should consider applying these class-wide procedures more frequently. While these procedures may have little impact on the strong performers, they may cause those with weaker skills to choose to engage in AAA responding.

References

Below, J. L., Skinner, A. L., Skinner, C. H., Sorrell, C. A., & Irwin, A. (2008). Decreasing out-of-seat behavior in a kindergarten classroom: Supplementing the Color Wheel with interdependent group-oriented rewards. *Journal of Evidence-Based Practices for Schools, 9,* 33–46.

Billington, E., & DiTommaso, N. M. (2003). Demonstrations and applications of the matching law in education. *Journal of Behavioral Education, 12,* 91–104.

Billington, E. J., & Skinner, C. H. (2002). Getting students to choose to do more work: Evidence of the effectiveness of the interspersal procedure. *Journal of Behavioral Education, 11,* 105–116.

Billington, E. J., & Skinner, C. H. (2006). Reducing perceptions of time required to complete math assignments by adding problems to assignments: A meta-analysis of the additive interspersal procedure. *Journal of Behavioral Education, 15,* 183–190.

Billington, E. J., Skinner, C. H., & Cruchon, N. M. (2004). Improving sixth-grade students' perceptions of high-effort assignments by assigning more work: Interaction of additive interspersal and assignment effort on assignment choice. *Journal of School Psychology, 42,* 477–490.

Billington, E. J., Skinner, C. H., Hutchins, H. M., & Malone, J. C. (2004). Varying problem effort and choice: Using the interspersal technique to influence choice towards more effortful assignments. *Journal of Behavioral Education, 13,* 193–207.

Binder, C. (1996). Behavioral fluency: Evolution of a new paradigm. *The Behavior Analyst, 19,* 163–197.

Black, M. P., Forbes, B. E., Yaw, J. S., & Skinner, C. H. (2013, February). *A comparison of sight-word learning rates across three computer-based interventions.* Presented at the annual meeting of the National Association of School Psychologists, Seattle, WA.

Buck, G. H. (1999). Smoothing the rough edges of classroom transitions. *Intervention in School and Clinic, 34,* 224–235.

Burns, M. K. (2004). Empirical analysis of drill ratio research: Refining the instructional level for drill tasks. *Remedial and Special Education, 25,* 167–175.

Burns, M. K., Zaslofsky, A. F., Kanive, R., & Parker, D. C. (2012). Meta-analysis of incremental rehearsal using phi coefficients to compared single-case and group designs. *Journal of Behavioral Education, 21,* 185–202.

Calderhead, W. J., Filter, K. J., & Albin, R. W. (2006). An investigation of incremental effects of interspersing math items on task-related behavior. *Journal of Behavioral Education, 15,* 53–67.

Campbell, S., & Skinner, C. H. (2004). Combining explicit timing with interdependent group contingency program to decrease transition times: An investigation of the timely transitions game. *Journal of Applied School Psychology, 20*(2), 11–28.

Carnine, D. W. (1976). Effects of two teacher presentation rates on off-task behavior, answering correctly, and participation. *Journal of Applied Behavior Analysis, 9,* 199–206.

Carta, J. J., Atwater, J. B., Schwartz, I. S., & Miller, P. A. (1990). Applications of ecobehavioral analysis in study of transitions across early education settings. *Education and Treatment of Children, 13,* 298–316.

Carta, J. J., Greenwood, C. R., & Robinson, S. L. (1987). Application of an ecobehavioral approach to the evaluation of early intervention programs. *Advances in Behavioral Assessment of Children and Families, 3,* 123–155.

Cates, G. L. (2005). A review of the effects of interspersing procedures on the stages of academic skill development. *Journal of Behavioral Education, 14,* 305–325.

Cates, G. L., & Dalenberg, A. E. (2005). Effects of interspersing rate on student preferences for mathematics assignments, *Journal of Behavioral Education, 14,* 89–103.

Cates, G. L., & Erkfritz, K. N. (2007). Effects of interspersing rates on students' performance on and preferences for mathematics assignments: Testing the discrete task completion hypothesis. *Psychology in the Schools, 44,* 615–625.

Cates, G. L., & Skinner, C. H. (2000). Getting remedial mathematics students to prefer homework with 20% and 40% more problems: An investigation of the strength of the interspersing procedure. *Psychology in the Schools, 37,* 339–347.

Cates, G. L., Skinner, C. H., Watkins, C. E., Rhymer, K. N., McNeill, B. S., & McCurdy, M. (1999). Effects of interspersing additional brief math problems on student performance and perception of math assignments: Getting students to prefer to do more work. *Journal of Behavioral Education, 9,* 177–193.

Cates, G. L., Skinner, C. H., Watson, T. S., Meadows, T. J., Weaver, A., & Jackson, B. (2003). Instructional effectiveness and instructional efficiency as considerations for data-based decision-making: An evaluation of interspersing procedures. *School Psychology Review, 32,* 601–616.

Choate, S. M., Skinner, C. H., Fearrington, J., Kohler, B., & Skolits, G. (2007). Extending the external validity of the Color Wheel procedures: Decreasing out-of-seat behavior in an intact, rural, 1st-grade classroom. *Journal of Evidence-Based Practices for Schools, 8,* 120–133.

Codding, R. S., & Smyth, C. A. (2008). Using performance feedback to decrease classroom transition time and examine collateral effects on academic engagement. *Journal of Educational & Psychological Consultation, 18,* 325–345.

Connell, M., & Carta, J. (1993). Building independence during in-class transitions: Teaching in-class transitions skills to preschoolers with developmental delays through choral-response-based self-assessment and contingent praise. *Education and Treatment of Children, 16,* 160–174.

Darch, C., & Gersten, R. (1985). The effects of teacher presentation rate and praise on LD students' oral reading performance. *British Journal of Educational Psychology, 55,* 295–303.

Dawson-Rodriques, K., Lavay, B., Butt, K., & Lacourse, M. (1997). A plan to reduce transition time in physical education. *Journal of Physical Education Recreation and Dance, 68,* 30–34.

Dunlap, G., dePerczel, M., Clarke, S., Wilson, D., Wright, S., White, R., & Gomez, A. (1994). Choice-making to promote adaptive behavior for students with emotional and behavioral challenges. *Journal of Applied Behavior Analysis, 27,* 505–518.

Evans-Hampton, T. N., Skinner, C. H., Henington, C., Sims, S., & McDaniel, C. E. (2002). An investigation of situational bias: Conspicuous and covert timing during curriculum-based measurement of mathematics across African American and Caucasian students. *School Psychology Review, 31,* 529–539,

Forbes, B, E,, Black, M P., Yaw, J. S., & Skinner, C. H. (2013, February). *A comparison of traditional drill and interspersal flashcard intervention technique.* Presented at the annual meeting of the National Association of School Psychologists, Seattle, WA.

Friman, P. C., & Poling, A. (1995). Making life easier with effort: Basic findings and applied research on response effort. *Journal of Applied Behavior Analysis, 28,* 583–590.

Fudge, D. L., Reece, L., Skinner, C. H., & Cowden, D. (2007). Using multiple classroom rules, public cues, and consistent transition strategies to reduce inappropriate vocalization: An investigation of the Color Wheel. *Journal of Evidence-Based Practices for School, 8,* 102–119.

Fudge, D. L., Skinner, C. H., Williams, J. L., Cowden, D., Clark, J., & Bliss, S. L. (2008). The Color Wheel classroom management system: Increasing on-task behavior in every student in a second-grade classroom. *Journal of School Psychology, 46,* 575–592.

Gardner III, R., Heward, W. L., & Grossi, T. A. (1994). Effects of response cards on student participation and academic achievement: A systematic replication with inner-city students during whole-class science instruction. *Journal of Applied Behavior Analysis, 27,* 63–71.

Gettinger, M., & Seibert, J. K. (2002). Best practices in increasing academic learning time. In A. Thomas (Ed.), *Best practices in school psychology IV* (pp. 773–787). Bethesda, MD: National Association of School Psychologists.

Greenwood, C. R., Delquadri, J., & Hall, R. V. (1984). Opportunity to respond and student academic performance. In W. Herward, T., Heron, D. Hill, & J. Trap-Porter (Eds.), *Behavior analysis in education* (pp. 58–88). Columbus, OH: Charles E Merrill.

Grskovic, J. A., & Belfiore, P. J. (1996). Improving the spelling performance of students with disabilities. *Journal of Behavioral Education, 6,* 343–354.

Hautau, B. L., Skinner, C. H., Pfaffman, J., Foster, S., & Clark, J. C. (2008). Extending the external validity of the Color Wheel: Increasing on-task behavior in an urban, kindergarten classroom. *Journal of Evidence-Based Practices for Schools, 9,* 3–17.

Hawkins, J., Skinner, C. H., & Oliver, R. (2005). The effects of task demands and additive interspersal ratios on fifth-grade students' mathematics accuracy. *School Psychology Review, 34,* 543–555.

Hawthorn-Embree, M. L., Skinner, C. H., Parkhurst, J., & Conley, E. (2011). An initial investigation of the partial-assignment completion effect on students' assignment choice behavior. *Journal of School Psychology, 49,* 433–442.

Hawthorn-Embree, M., Skinner, C. H., Parkhurst, J., O'Neil, M., & Conley, E. (2010). Assignment choice: Do students choose briefer assignments or finishing what they started? *School Psychology Quarterly, 25,* 143–151.

Hawthorn-Embree, M. L., Taylor, E. P., Skinner, C. H., Parkhurst, J., & Nalls, M. L. (in press). Replicating and extending research on the partial assignment completion effect: Is sunk cost related to partial assignment completion strength? *Psychology in the Schools.*

Heward, W. L. (1994). Three "low-tech" strategies for increasing the frequency of active student response during group instruction. In R. Gardner III, D. M. Sainaito, J. O. Cooper, T. E. Heron, W. L. Heward, J. W. Eshleman, & T. A. Grossi (Eds.), *Behavior analysis in education* (pp. 283–320). Pacific Grove, CA: Brooks/Cole.

Hughes, C. A., & Dexter, D. D. (2011). Response to intervention: A researched-based summary. *Theory into Practice, 50*, 4–11.

Ivarie, J. J. (1986). Effects of proficiency rates on later performance of a recall and writing behavior. *Remedial and Special Education, 7*, 25–30.

Johns, G. A., Skinner, C. H., & Nail, G. L. (2000). Effects of interspersing briefer mathematics problems on assignment choice in students with learning disabilities. *Journal of Behavioral Education, 10*, 95–106.

Joseph, L. M., & Nist, L. M. (2006). Comparing the effects of unknown-known ratios on word reading learning versus learning rates. *Journal of Behavioral Education, 15*, 69–79.

Kelshaw, K., Sterling-Turner, H. E., Henry, J., & Skinner, C. H. (2000). Randomized interdependent group contingencies: Group reinforcement with a twist. *Psychology in the Schools, 37*, 523–533.

Kern, L., & Clemens, N. H., (2007). Antecedent strategies to promote appropriate classroom behavior. *Psychology in the Schools, 44*, 65–75.

Kern, L., Vorndran, C. M., Hilt, A., Ringdahl, H. E., Adelman, B. E., & Dunlap, G. (1998). Choice as an intervention to improve behavior: A review of the literature. *Journal of Behavioral Education, 8*, 151–169.

Kirk, E. R., Becker, J. A., Skinner, C. H., Fearrington, J. Y., McCane-Bowling, S. J., Amburn, C., Luna, E., & Greear, C. (2010). Deceasing inappropriate vocalizations using group contingencies and Color Wheel procedures: A component analysis. *Psychology in the Schools, 47*, 931–943.

Lindgren, H. C., & Suter, W. N, (1985). *Educational psychology in the classroom* (2nd ed.). Monterey, CA: Brooks/Cole.

Litow, L., & Pumroy, D. K. (1975). A brief review of classroom group oriented contingencies. *Journal of Applied Behavior Analysis, 8*, 341–347.

Little, S. G., Akin-Little, A., & Newman-Eig, L. M. (2010). Effects on homework completion and accuracy of varied and constant reinforcement within an interdependent group contingency system. *Journal of Applied School Psychology, 26*, 115–131.

Mace, F. C., McCurdy, B., & Quigley, E. A. (1990). A collateral effect of reward predicted by matching theory. *Journal of Applied Behavior Analysis, 23*, 197–205.

Malone, J. C. (1990). *Theories of learning: A historical approach.* Belmont, CA: Wadsworth.

McCurdy, M., Skinner, C. H., Grantham, K., Watson, T. S., & Hindman, P. M. (2001). Increasing on-task behavior in an elementary student during mathematics seatwork by interspersing additional brief problems. *School Psychology Review, 30*, 391–400.

McIntosh, K., Herman, K., Sandford, A., McGraw, K., & Florence, K. (2004). Teaching transitions: Techniques for promoting success between lessons. *Teaching Exceptional Children, 37*, 32–38.

Meadows, S. F., & Skinner, C. H. (2005). Causing students to choose more language arts work: Enhancing the validity of the additive interspersal procedure. *Journal of Behavioral Education, 14*, 227–247.

Melman, S., Little, S. G., & Akin-Little, K. A. (2007). Adolescent overscheduling: The relationship between levels of participation in scheduled activities and self-reported clinical symptomology. *The High School Journal, 90*, 19–30.

Montarello, S., & Martens, B. K. (2005). Effects of interspersed brief problems on students' endurance at completing math work. *Journal of Behavioral Education, 14*, 249–266.

Neef, N. A., Mace, F. C., & Shade, D. (1993). Impulsivity in students with serious emotional disturbance: The interactive effects of reinforcer rate, delay, and quality. *Journal of Applied Behavior Analysis, 26*, 37–52.

Neef, N. A., Mace, F. C., Shea, M. C., & Shade, D. (1992). Effects of reinforcer rate and reinforcer quality on time allocation: Extension of matching theory to educational settings. *Journal of Applied Behavior Analysis, 25*, 691–699.

Neef, N. A., Shade, D., & Miller, M. S. (1994). Assessing the influential dimensions of reinforcers on choice in students with serious emotional disturbance. *Journal of Applied Behavior Analysis, 27*, 575–583.

Nist, L., & Joseph, L. M., (2008). Effectiveness and efficiency of flash card drill instructional methods on urban first-graders' word recognition, acquisition, maintenance, and generalization. *School Psychology Review, 37*, 294–308.

Popkin, J., & Skinner, C. H. (2003). Enhancing academic performance in a classroom serving students with serious emotional disturbance: Interdependent contingencies with randomly selected components. *School Psychology Review, 32*, 282–295.

Rhymer, K. N., Henington, C., Skinner, C. H., & Looby, E. J. (1999). The effects of explicit timing on mathematics performance in second-grade Caucasian and African-American students. *School Psychology Quarterly, 14*, 397–407.

Rhymer, K. N., Skinner, C. H., Henington, C., D'Reaux, R. A., & Sims, S. (1998). Effects of explicit timing on mathematics problem completion rates in African-American third-grade elementary children. *Journal of Applied Behavioral Analysis, 31*, 673–677.

Rhymer, K. N., Skinner, C. H., Jackson, S., McNeill, S., Smith, T., & Jackson, B. (2002). The 1-minute explicit timing intervention: The influence of mathematics problem difficulty. *Journal of Instructional Psychology, 29*, 305–311.

Riley, J. P. (1986). The effects of teachers' wait-time and knowledge comprehension questioning on science achievement. *Journal of Research in Science Teaching, 23*, 335–342.

Roberts, M. L., & Shapiro, E. S. (1996). Effects of instructional ratios on students' reading performance in a regular education classroom. *Journal of School Psychology, 34*, 73–91.

Roberts, M. L., Turco, T. L., & Shapiro, E. S. (1991). Differential effects of fixed instructional ratios on students' progress in reading. *Journal of Psychoeducational Assessment, 9*, 308–318.

Robinson, S. L., & Skinner, C. H. (2002). Interspersing additional easier items to enhance mathematics performance on subtests requiring different task demands. *School Psychology Quarterly, 17*, 191–205.

Rowe, M. (1974). Wait-time and rewards as instructional variables, their influence on language, logic and fate control: Part one-Wait time. *Journal of Research in Science Teaching, 17*, 469–475.

Saecker, L., Sager, K., Williams, J. L., Skinner, C. H., Spurgeon, S., & Luna, E. (2008). Decreasing teacher's repeated directions and students' inappropriate talking in an urban, fifth-grade classroom using the Color Wheel procedures. *Journal of Evidence Based Practices for Schools, 9*, 18–32.

Sharp, S. R., & Skinner, C. H. (2004). Using interdependent group contingencies with randomly selected criteria and paired reading to enhance class-wide reading performance. *Journal of Applied School Psychology, 20*, 29–46.

Skinner, C. H. (1998). Preventing academic skills deficits. In T. S. Watson & F. Gresham (Eds.), *Handbook of child behavior therapy: Ecological considerations in assessment, treatment, and evaluation* (pp. 61–83). New York, NY: Plenum.

Skinner, C. H. (2002). An empirical analysis of interspersal research evidence, implications, and applications of the discrete task completion hypothesis. *Journal of School Psychology, 40*, 347–368.

Skinner, C. H. (2008). Theoretical and applied implications of precisely measuring learning rates. *School Psychology Review, 37*, 309–314.

Skinner, C. H. (2010). Applied comparative effectiveness researchers must measure learning rates: A commentary on efficiency articles. *Psychology in the Schools, 47*, 166–172.

Skinner, C. H., Bamberg, H., Smith, E. S., & Powell, S. (1993). Subvocal responding to increase division fact fluency. *Remedial and Special Education, 14*, 49–56.

Skinner, C. H., Belfiore, P. J., Mace, H. W., Williams-Wilson, S., & Johns, G. A. (1997). Altering response topography to increase response efficiency and learning rates. *School Psychology Quarterly, 12*, 54–64.

Skinner, C. H., Belfiore, P. J., & Watson, T. S. (2002). Assessing the relative effects of interventions in students with mild disabilities: Assessing instructional time. *Journal of Psychoeducational Assessment, 20*, 345–357. (Reprinted from *Assessment in Rehabilitation and Exceptionality, 2*, 207–220, 1995.)

Skinner, C. H., Cashwell, C., & Dunn, M. (1996). Independent and interdependent group contingencies: Smoothing the rough waters. *Special Services in the Schools, 12*, 61–78.

Skinner, C. H., Cashwell, T. H., & Skinner, A. L. (2000). Increasing tootling: The effects of a peer-monitored group contingency program on students' reports of peers' prosocial behaviors. *Psychology in the Schools, 37*, 263–270.

Skinner, C. H., & Daly, E. J. (2010). Improving generalization of academic skills: Commentary on the special series. *Journal of Behavioral Education, 19*, 106–115.

Skinner, C. H., Fletcher, P. A., & Henington, C. (1996). Increasing learning rates by increasing student response rates: A summary of research. *School Psychology Quarterly, 11*, 313–325.

Skinner, C. H., Fletcher, P. A., Wildmon, M., & Belfiore, P. J. (1996). Improving assignment preference through interspersal: Problem completion rates versus easy problems. *Journal of Behavioral Education, 6*, 427–437.

Skinner, C. H., Ford, J. M., & Yunker, B. D. (1991). A comparison of instructional response requirements on the multiplication performance of behavior disordered students. *Behavior Disorders, 17*, 56–65.

Skinner, C. H., Hall-Johnson, K., Skinner, A. L., Cates, G., Weber, J., & Johns, G. (1999). Enhancing perceptions of mathematics assignments by increasing relative rates of problem completion through the interspersal technique. *Journal of Experimental Education, 68*, 43–59.

Skinner, C. H., & McCleary, D. F. (2010). Academic engagement, time on task, and AAA responding. In A. Canter, L. Z. Paige, & S. Shaw (Eds.), *Helping children at home and school-III: Handouts for families and educators* (pp. S3H1–S3H3) Bethesda, MD: National Association of School Psychologists.

Skinner, C. H., McCleary, D. F., Poncy, B., C., Cates, G. L., & Skolits, G. J. (2013). Emerging opportunities for school psychologists to enhance our remediation procedure evidence base as we apply response to intervention. *Psychology in the Schools, 50,* 272–289.

Skinner, C. H., Pappas, D. N., & Davis, K. A. (2005). Enhancing academic engagement: Providing opportunities for responding and influencing students to choose to respond. *Psychology in the Schools, 42,* 389–403.

Skinner, C. H., Robinson, S. L., Johns, G. A., Logan, P., & Belfiore, P. J. (1996). Applying Herrnstein's matching law to influence students' choice to complete difficult academic assignments. *Journal of Experimental Education, 65,* 5–17.

Skinner, C. H., Scala, G., Dendas, D., & Lentz, F. E. (2007). The color wheel: Implementation guidelines. *Journal of Evidence-Based Practices for Schools, 8,* 134–140.

Skinner, C. H., & Shapiro, E. S. (1989). A comparison of a taped-words and drill interventions on reading fluency in adolescents with behavior disorders. *Education and Treatment of Children, 12,* 123–133.

Skinner, C. H., & Skinner, A. L. (2007). Establishing an evidence base for a classroom management procedure with a series of studies: Evaluating the Color Wheel. *Journal of Evidence-Based Practices for Schools, 8,* 88–101.

Skinner, C. H., Skinner, A. L., & Burton, B. (2009). Applying group-oriented contingencies in classrooms. In K. A. Akin-Little, S. G. Little, M. Bray, & T. Kehle (Eds.), *Behavioral interventions in schools: Evidence-based positive strategies* (pp. 157–170). Washington, DC: APA Press.

Skinner, C. H., Skinner, C. F., Skinner, A. L., & Cashwell, T. H. (1999). Using interdependent contingencies with groups of students: Why the principal kissed a pig. *Educational Administration Quarterly, 35,* 206–820.

Skinner, C. H., Skinner, A. L., & Sterling-Turner, H. E. (2002). Best practices in utilizing group contingencies for intervention and prevention. In A. Thomas & J. Grimes (Eds.), *Best practices in school psychology* (4th ed., pp. 817–830). Washington, DC: National Association of School Psychologists.

Skinner, C. H., & Watson, T. S. (1993). Lotteries in the classroom. *Legends, 15*(1), 2–3. (Reprinted in *The Florida Psychology in the Schools Newsletter,* (1995), *21*(2), 11–12; and the *Behavioral School Psychologist Digest,* (1997) *1*(4), 7–9.)

Skinner, C. H., Williams, R. L., & Neddenriep, C. E. (2004). Using interdependent group-oriented reinforcement to enhance academic performance in general education classrooms. *School Psychology Review, 33,* 384–397.

Stanovich, K. E. (1986). Matthew effects in reading: Some consequences of individual differences in the acquisition of literacy. *Reading Research Quarterly, 21,* 360–406.

Teeple, D. F., & Skinner, C. H. (2004). Enhancing grammar assignment perceptions by increasing assignment demands: An extension of interspersal research. *Journal of Emotional and Behavioral Disorders, 12,* 120–127.

Van Houten, R., Hill, S., & Parsons, M. (1975). An analysis of a performance feedback system: The effects of timing and feedback, public posing, and praise upon academic performance and peer interaction. *Journal of Applied Behavior Analysis, 12,* 581–591.

Van Houten, R., Morrison, E., Jarvis, R., & McDonald, M. (1974). The effects of explicitly timing and feedback on compositional response rate in elementary school children. *Journal of Applied Behavior Analysis, 7,* 547–555.

Van Houten, R., & Thompson, C. (1976). The effects of explicit timing on math performance. *Journal of Applied Behavior Analysis, 9,* 227–230.

Wallace, M. A., Cox, E. A., & Skinner, C. H. (2003). Increasing independent seatwork: Breaking large assignments into smaller assignments and teaching a student with retardation to recruit reinforcement. *School Psychology Review, 23,* 132–142.

Wildmon, M. E., Skinner, C. H., McCurdy, M., & Sims, S. (1999). Improving secondary students' perceptions of the "dreaded mathematics word problem assignment" by giving them more word problems. *Psychology in the Schools, 36,* 319–325.

Wildmon, M. E., Skinner, C. H., & McDade, A. (1998). Interspersing additional brief easy problems to increase assignment preference on mathematics reading problems. *Journal of Behavioral Education, 8,* 337–346.

Wildmon, M. E., Skinner, C. H., Watson, T. S., & Garrett, L. S. (2004). Enhancing assignment perceptions in students with mathematics learning disabilities by including more work: An extension of interspersal research. *School Psychology Quarterly, 19,* 106–120.

Yarbrough, J. L., Skinner, C. H., Lee, Y. J., & Lemmons, C. (2004). Decreasing transition times in a second grade classroom: Scientific support for the timely transitions game. *Journal of Applied School Psychology, 20,* 85–108.

17

Increasing Instructional Efficacy:
A Focus on Teacher Variables

Kathleen Lynne Lane, Wendy Peia Oakes,
Holly Mariah Menzies, and Kathryn Germer

In recent years, we have seen a shift in how teachers support K–12 students with diverse learning, behavioral, and social needs. Rather than subscribing to a "wait-to-fail" model in which teachers wait until a student has a clear discrepancy between current and desired levels of performance before providing individualized supports to remediate deficits, many school systems have moved toward a systems approach for assisting students. Essentially, school-site teams are embracing the concepts of *prevention* and *search-and-serve* specified in the Individuals with Disabilities Education Improvement Act (IDEIA, 2004) by building tiered systems of support. There are several types of three-tiered models, such as Response to Intervention (RTI) emphasizing academic performance (Fuchs & Fuchs, 2006), positive behavior interventions and supports (PBIS) emphasizing behavioral and social performance (Sugai & Horner, 2002), and comprehensive, integrated, three-tiered (CI3T) models focusing on academic, behavioral, and social performance (Lane, Oakes, & Menzies, 2010). These multi-tiered systems of support typically include three levels of prevention: primary (tier 1, for all), secondary (tier 2, for some), and tertiary (tier 3, for a few), offering graduated support according to students' specific needs. These models provide a coordinated, data-informed system of increasingly intensive assistance focusing on (a) preventing the development of learning and behavior problems from occurring in the first place with tier 1 supports, and (b) responding efficiently with students whose performance suggest tier 2 (e.g., small group instruction targeting goal-setting and self-management skills; Oakes, Lane, Cox, Magrane, Jenkins, & Hankins, 2012) or tier 3 (e.g., functional assessment-based interventions; Umbreit, Ferro, Liaupsin, & Lane, 2007) supports are warranted.

In these models, there are several critical components, three of which we highlight here (Lane & Walker, 2012). First, it is important to use reliable and valid tools and procedures for determining which students need additional support. In the academic domain, curriculum-based measures such as AIMSweb (Pearson Education, 2010; see American Institutes for Research for a review of available measures, www.rti4success.org) are administered in fall, winter, and spring to *all* students, to ensure they are progressing as anticipated throughout the school year. Those below established benchmarks are provided supplementary support (e.g., tier 2 or 3) over and above tier 1 instruction to get the student back on track, so to speak, so they continue to progress at the desired level and rate of growth. Similarly, behavior screening tools (e.g., BASC-2 Behavior and Emotional Screening Scale, BASC-2 BESS; Kamphaus & Reynolds, 2007; and the Student Risk Screening Scale, SRSS; Drummond, 1994) are also available for administration in fall, winter, and spring to look for any student whose behavior deviates substantially from the norm, indicating it may impede a student's ability to access instructional experiences. As with academic-screening data, behavior-screening data can be analyzed (ideally in conjunction with academic data; Kalberg, Lane, & Menzies, 2010) to inform instruction. For example, a fifth-grade student performing below benchmark in reading on AIMSweb and who scores in the elevated risk range on the BASC-2 BESS may benefit from a repeated readings intervention to build fluency (Strong, Wehby, Falk, & Lane, 2004), as well as a self-monitoring intervention to help the student stay engaged in the supplemental intervention (Menzies, Lane, & Lee, 2009).

Second, and related to the first point, is determining whether students are indeed non-responsive, by making sure the primary prevention plan is in place with sufficient integrity (Bruhn, Lane, & Hirsch, in press). By collecting treatment integrity data we can be more confident in the decisions we make regarding responsiveness. For example, if the same student noted above is in a classroom where the primary prevention reading program is being implemented with low fidelity (<80%) and the school-wide PBIS is not being implemented (e.g., PBIS tickets are not being distributed with behavior specific praise when students meet school-wide expectations), then tier 2 or tier 3 supports may not be necessary. In this case, intervention efforts should focus on improving tier 1 implementation.

Third, and the focus of this chapter, while we certainly agree student-centered, evidenced-based tier 2 and tier 3 efforts are highly important for supporting students (Tankersley & Cook, 2013), we also think it is necessary to consider teacher-level variables before focusing on student-level supports. Instructional techniques teachers use to promote engagement and management are implicitly part of tier 1 practices. However, there are instances when teachers may benefit from additional support in these strategies and practices if they are not being implemented with sufficient fidelity. In some cases, the techniques were not addressed in teacher preparation programs, thereby requiring initial instruction. In other instances teachers may simply drift away from using the practices as part of regular school practices, requiring support in revisiting these techniques. In both circumstances, teachers can be supported through high-quality practice-based professional development offerings that include coaching and performance feedback (Ball & Cohen, 1999; Grossman & McDonald, 2008).

This recommendation is to first consider teacher-level variables rather than beginning with student-level intervention efforts. It is easy to think of students' behavior as something separate from the academic work we present to them; however, good instructional planning is integral to providing educational experiences that promote students' engagement and enhance their motivation to participate in school work. And when students are eager to take part in the academic life of the classroom, they are much less likely to display behavior challenges. This is why effective instructional techniques are a critical component of tier 1 practices. Of course, there will always be classroom management issues, but similar to effective instructional techniques; there are low-intensity behavioral strategies that can be used to address these as well. Consistently integrating instructional and behavioral strategies that maximize and encourage participation of all students in a classroom may be of sufficient power to prevent the need for intensive, individualized supports, such as behavior contracts (Downing, 2002) and self-monitoring (Menzies et al., 2009). While we definitely endorse the full scope of supports—from low- (e.g., proximity; Kerr & Valenti, 2009) to high-intensity (e.g., functional assessment-based interventions, Germer et al., 2012), we encourage teachers to heed the advice of researchers dedicated to PBIS work: work smarter, not harder, by beginning with the simplest change necessary to achieve the objective at hand (Sugai & Horner, 2002).

Purpose

The intent of this chapter is to introduce instructional strategies and practices that increase instructional efficacy. We focus on two key areas: (a) differentiating curriculum to enhance motivation and increase engagement, and (b) implementing low-intensity behavioral supports to strengthen positive instructional experiences. We consider how differentiation of content, process, and products promotes student access to instruction and offers a variety of ways for students to demonstrate what they are learning (Tomlinson, 2005). Then, we introduce a series of low-intensity, teacher-delivered behavioral supports to enhance learning. These include: proximity (Kerr & Valenti, 2009), high rates of opportunities to respond (Conroy, Sutherland, Snyder, & Marsh, 2008), behavior-specific praise (Sutherland, 2000), choice (Kern, Manteegna, Vorndran, Bailin, & Hilt, 2001), and high-probability request sequences (Mace et al., 1988).

Differentiating Curriculum to Enhance Motivation and Increase Engagement

There is a large body of literature on the topic of differentiating instruction for all types of students. We view this literature as critical to supporting desirable student behavior, as its focus is to promote student engagement and motivation. One of the most promising aspects of this work is that it can be used in general education classrooms where students vary widely in their abilities. In this chapter, we discuss Tomlinson's (1999) three dimensions of differentiation—content, process, and product—as a way to think about instructional delivery that makes content both accessible and engaging.

Content

The first instructional decision focuses on *what* to teach. Recently, many states have adopted the Common Core State Standards in English language arts and mathematics, which specify the knowledge and skills students are expected to acquire at each grade level. These standards were developed by the Council of Chief State School Officers and the National Governors Association Center for Best Practices (2011) (NGA Center), in collaboration with other stakeholders, to provide shared standards nationwide. States and school districts also publish content standards for other subject areas, such as science, history, the arts, technology, and physical education.

Yet, many content-related decisions still must be made when addressing curriculum. Tomlinson (2001) provides several approaches for determining which parts of the curriculum to focus on, one of which is called *concept-based teaching*. In this approach, teachers use essential concepts and principles to guide student learning. For example, in a unit on the American Revolution, the concept of cooperation could be used as a tool to focus on, connect, and analyze various events. How were Americans forced to work together rather than as separate colonies? How did the colonists work with nations such as France and Spain to gain support for the revolution? Concept-based teaching automatically highlights which aspects of the curriculum are most important to teach. This is in contrast to emphasizing rote memorization of definitions, dates, and events or moving through all content on a chronological timeline. Students are more likely to remember concept-based information, because it requires that they connect facts to broader ideas. It also creates a framework of meaning where students are able to plug in other related information as they learn it. In classes such as U.S. History where each year adds additional content, it is impossible to meaningfully teach all available content. Focusing on concepts helps teachers to choose salient, critical information that affords great meaning for students, providing them with opportunities to have a deeper understanding of the subject matter (Gersten, Baker, Smith-Johnson, Dimino, & Peterson, 2006). In addition, concept-based teaching emphasizes higher-order skills, such as analyzing, comparing, making judgments, and synthesizing information. This approach is more effective than through the entire curriculum.

Curriculum compacting is another method for differentiating content (Reis & Renzulli, 1992). Using this technique, teachers can assess students' knowledge about a subject (essentially a pre-test) to determine their level of knowledge or skill. Students who have mastered a given topic (e.g., how to find the derivative of polynomials) can be excused from a particular lesson (or set of lessons) and provided a learning opportunity appropriate to their current levels of performance. This allows them to access new concepts rather than revisit material they already know. Such strategies are particularly useful for students who have extensive content knowledge or skills sets in a specific area. Adjusting the curriculum to be more interesting and rigorous can enhance students' motivation, often resulting in a high level of academic engagement and, subsequently, increased academic performance (Lepper, 1988).

Tomlinson (2001) offers other suggestions for content differentiation: (a) using varied materials such as media (e.g., YouTube videos), computer applications, magazines, simulation activities, and field trips; (b) developing learning contracts in which teachers and students agree on the content to be studied and how it will be approached, with defined goals and activities; (c) mini-lessons, which involve short, focused lessons to enable enrichment for students needing to extend the depth of their knowledge and remediation for students who need another opportunity to learn the content covered as a whole class; and (d) other support systems, ranging from graphic organizers, advanced organizers, study guides, peer partners, and adult mentors. While it is beyond the scope of the chapter to explain these in full, we encourage the interested reader to learn more about these strategies, with a goal of increasing student engagement and improving academic performance for all learners.

Process

Another aspect of differentiation is to examine *process,* namely the instructional activities teachers develop to assist students in mastering concepts, skills, and knowledge. Tomlinson (2001) refers to this as creating a "sense-making activity" (p. 79) for students. In other words, what will students do to learn the material? If the lesson objective is to identify "bigger" and "smaller," some children will learn the concept by seeing graphic representations of big and small, others will learn by having the opportunity to classify items as either big or small, and still others may learn best by creating or choosing their own big and small objects. In addition, the teacher might offer a whole group lesson where she explains the concept to everyone and then students work in pairs to identify big and small objects. Each of these activities offers a different way to learn the concept: visually or kinesthetically, and independently or collaboratively. Ideally, students will have several differentiated opportunities to work with the new ideas, skills, or concepts.

Another way to differentiate process is to have simultaneous activities available, such as cooperative learning groups, computer-assisted instruction, or independent writing activities. Students can be directed to the appropriate type of activity based on their interests, skills, or readiness. In some grades, the activities can be set up as learning centers (e.g., listening to an audio book, or creating a graphic organizer) where students work either independently or collaboratively with their peers. When differentiating process activities, it important to consider students' learning preferences, interests, and skill sets to ensure that the activities are motivating. By motivating, we mean activities are constructed to create interest, incorporate choice, and are challenging enough to stretch students intellectually (Deci & Ryan, 1985)— points we will discuss more fully in subsequent sections.

We do want to stress the importance of skill level when differentiating instruction. Students are less likely to fully engage in tasks perceived as too easy or too difficult. Students experience the greatest academic growth when instruction is in their zone of proximal development (Vygotsky, 1978). Finding the delicate balance between instructional tasks that are challenging—yet, not too challenging—can be daunting, particularly when students vary widely in their academic, behavioral, and instructional skills sets.

To skillfully differentiate instruction, teachers need mechanisms for (a) becoming familiar with students' strengths and weaknesses, as well as (b) identifying students who may require alternative methods of accessing instruction. Academic screening tools such as AIMSweb (Pearson Education, 2010) and behavior screening tools such as the BASC-2 BESS (Kamphaus & Reynolds, 2007) can be helpful with both these objectives. Screening tools provide reliable, valid data and offer a systematic, universal method for detecting students who may require more than traditional tier 1 programming.

Product

The final area we address for differentiation is product—the tangible evidence of what a student understands about a given topic, concept, or skill. Essentially, products are the mechanisms by which students "show what they know." Products are the vehicles for engaging deeply in the material taught, an opportunity to interact with the concepts introduced over an extended period of time. For example, students learning a foreign language could create products that range from creating a YouTube video in which the student gives directions for making *crème brûlée* (see http://www.youtube.com/watch?v = Hy5LOxhGDJg) to writing an original short story—both in the foreign language. Both tasks are challenging, intrinsically motivating depending on the students' interest, and allow the teacher to evaluate the student's skill.

In our experience as K–12 classroom teachers of general and special education students, we have seen the pride students experience when developing and completing such products. Recalling one event, an eighth-grade student with a specific learning disability who often struggled with work-completion issues worked for several weeks on a five-paragraph expository essay. After completing the final peer editing steps, he turned in the essay with a word count printed in bold on the front page (2,106 words). When asked about this addition to the title page, he smiled and replied, "I know we don't need it, but I never thought I could write so many words! I thought you should know."

Products are far more than a culminating activity for an instructional unit. Differentiation of products offers another opportunity for motivating and engaging students through various learning activities. To ensure the final products allow students creative license but are still consistent with the intended learning outcomes, we encourage teachers to consider the following guidelines noted in Lane, Menzies, Bruhn, and Crnobori (2011). First, determine the key expectations for the assignment. What are the concepts and skills students must demonstrate? This must be determined at the onset of the instructional unit to help establish a clear vision for both the teacher and the student. Second, incorporate choice in the selection of products to again improve motivation and engagement in this potentially meaningful learning experience (see Box 17.1). Use some class time to brainstorm possibilities for what these products might include, with attention to issues of timing. Such projects are an excellent opportunity to develop self-determined behaviors, such as decision-making, goal-setting, and self-regulation (Carter, Lane, Crnobori, Bruhn, & Oakes, 2011), because they require students to plan, make timelines, set incremental goals, and the like. Third, once students select the product to be developed (which ideally would not be the same product for every student as it should be based on individual interest), work with students to develop a structure for the core elements required to meet the initial goals of and expectations for the product (Tomlinson, 2001). For example, in the YouTube video noted above, what would the teacher like to see? An introductory title slide? Evidence of editing skills? Particular vocabulary? Pronunciation? A rubric is highly useful in clarifying grading guidelines, to ensure the teacher and students are clear on what is expected. In other words, we want students to experience success with any product generated and be likely to put forth strong effort on comparable assignments in the future. Therefore, we want to clarify the goals, incorporate choice, and offer a structure to ensure expectations are met.

Box 17.1

Why do I like my new gym class? I like it because there are realistic expectations and there are choices on what we can do in class. We can choose to participate in the group activity or we can spend time walking around the track. In my last gym class, the teachers had such unrealistic expectations for students that it wasn't possible for all of us to meet their goals. For example, we all had heart rate monitors that had to get to a certain level for each student, but the equipment did not work consistently and teachers did not adjust their expectations for those students who had problems with the equipment.
    Katie, 13 years old, 8th grade

Planning for Differentiation

When deciding how to put all the elements of differentiation together, using a planning model such as the *Big Ideas* framework (Coyne, Kame'enui, & Carnine, 2007; Simmons & Kame'enui, 1996) can be a helpful first step. It suggests considering the following six elements when preparing a lesson or unit: (1) big ideas, (2) conspicuous strategies, (3) mediated scaffolding, (4) strategic integration, (5) judicious review, and (6) primed background knowledge. The first three elements help a teacher to determine the most important concepts to focus on, the best strategies for teaching them, and the level of support various students will need to master the information or skill. Then a teacher creates opportunities to use (strategic integration) and practice (judicious review) the new knowledge meaningfully. Finally, finding ways to help students build on prior skills to learn and use the new material "primes" their background knowledge. Differentiation is especially pertinent to the first three elements. "Big ideas" is where you differentiate around content, and both "conspicuous strategies" and "mediated scaffolding" are where differentiation of process and product can occur. Using a planning framework can help avoid having differentiation become a series of instructional events that are not coherently focused.

Collectively, differentiation of content, process, and products provides positive, meaningful instructional experiences for students by addressing their interests, learning preferences, and skill levels. Such techniques empower teachers to support students in (a) being more motivated to participate in instructional tasks, (b) being more fully engaged academically (and consequently less disruptive), and (c) experiencing improved academic outcomes as a result of being fully engaged in meaningful, challenging lessons.

Relation to Motivation and Engagement

In considering these facets of differentiation, we focused on these three points (content, process, and product; Tomlinson, 2001) with a look toward enhancing students' achievement motivation (Dev, 1997). In brief, creating learning opportunities that are in and of themselves enjoyable and rewarding (Aldermann, 1999; Pintrich & Schunk, 2002) will foster and develop students' *intrinsic* motivation. When students are intrinsically motivated, they are eager to participate and are willing to be fully engaged in learning. In many of the examples discussed previously, it becomes clear how these instructional elements and/or techniques foster intrinsic motivation. First, lessons can be constructed to offer students choices, empowering them to become more autonomous and self-determined in their own learning (referred to as *control;* Deci & Ryan, 1985; Ormrod, 2000; Stipek, 1993). Second, teachers can create learning experiences that stretch the learner slightly beyond what they think they are capable of achieving, ensuring tasks are neither too easy or too difficult (referred to as *challenge;* Cooper, Heron, & Heward, 2007; Lepper, 1988; Stipek, 1993; Umbreit, Lane, & Dejud, 2004). Third, by developing lessons that incorporate the element of surprise or novelty, or that diverge from what is typically expected, teachers can elicit students' interest (*curiosity,* Stipek, 1993). Finally, teachers can provide a rationale, or help students see the "big picture," for why a particular learning activity is worth the investment of their time; otherwise they may see lessons as a series of unrelated and perhaps tedious set of tasks (*contextualization;* Lepper, 1988). Collectively, these have been referred to as *The 4 Cs:* instructional elements enhancing intrinsic motivation: *control, challenge, curiosity,* and *contextualization* (Lane et al., 2011), derived from the work of experts in classroom motivation.

We certainly support—and encourage—using reinforcement systems grounded in applied behavior analytics to motivate students and increase the future probability of students being fully engaged in instructional activities, particularly for students who are extrinsically motivated (e.g., those who engage in given tasks to access [or avoid] various rewards, such as teacher attention, tangibles, or sensory experiences; Cooper et al., 2007; Umbreit et al., 2007). Yet, we feel it is equally important to consider how instructional strategies can be used to develop students' intrinsic motivation. To this end, we stress the importance of employing a balance between extrinsic and intrinsic motivation, with an overarching goal of helping students to become academically engaged in meaningful, interesting, challenging, and relevant lessons, to ultimately improve overall achievement. In addition to differentiating curriculum to enhance motivation, increase engagement, and support increased academic performance, behavioral supports can be used to facilitate these goals. In the following sections, we shift to low-intensity behavioral supports, many of which can be used during instruction.

Implementing Low-Intensity Behavioral Supports to Enhance Instructional Experiences

In addition to examining instructional and curricular processes to improve students' behavior, teachers can use a variety of simple strategies to help students remain engaged and on task. We discuss several of them here, including proximity, high rates of opportunities to respond, behavior-specific praise, choice, and high-probability request sequences. Strategically employing these techniques takes both knowledge and skill on the teacher's part. While it is true there are certain dispositional elements that make one a good teacher (e.g., patience, flexibility), it also requires considerable pedagogical expertise. The most expert teachers use these techniques within a rich curriculum and as part of effective instruction. Skilled teachers also consider each student's individual personality when deciding which strategies will promote academic and behavioral success. It is this orchestration of many elements that makes a teacher successful with even difficult students.

Proximity

Moving closer to stand near a student who is daydreaming, bothering another student, or playing around makes intuitive sense and, indeed, the mere presence of the teacher is often enough to help a student refocus his or her energies and get back to work. While proximity is a frequently used and fundamental behavior management strategy (Kerr & Valenti, 2009), there are several factors teachers should consider when using physical proximity to cue a student to on-task behavior.

First, a teacher must continually monitor the entire classroom, even while working with individual students or delivering a lesson. Identifying, *before* there is a problem, the student who would benefit from having you closer is essential in cueing the student early, so that proximity is a reminder, not a challenge or a punishment. The teacher who constantly, and subtly, communicates her awareness of what students are doing (Kounin, 1977), and whether she approves of their actions, is what is so powerful in helping a student remain focused on the assigned task. An early reminder provides a student the opportunity to make a good choice, rather than creating a scenario where the student needs to be reprimanded. A reprimand is more likely to result in hurt feelings or an escalation of negative behavior, whereas a reminder can prevent these (Colvin, 2004). An experienced teacher often knows before the student himself that he is veering off track. Another advantage of using proximity is that it is a silent cue that does not necessarily draw attention to the student or away from instruction. This minimizes or eliminates any disruption in the flow of classroom activities.

There are two important caveats when using proximity. The first is that it should not be interpreted by the student as a challenge. Rushing quickly to a student's desk or moving too far into his or her personal space can be interpreted as threatening. Similarly, it is not necessary to frown or use negative body language. Use neutral or friendly cues to keep students on task. Reminding students about good behavior, as opposed to communicating displeasure, is the more effective strategy. Then the focus is on prompting the desired behaviors rather than a reactive, punishment-based approach. This is not to say there are never consequences for misbehavior, but proximity is a cueing or a redirection strategy, not a punishment (Cooper et al., 2007).

The second consideration is when students intentionally misbehave to get the teacher's attention. In this case, proximity may only promote the behavior one is trying to eliminate. Some students purposely engage the teacher as a way to remain off task or to avoid the work at hand. A teacher must know the students well enough to decide when proximity will be effective or if a different strategy is needed.

High Rates of Opportunities to Respond

Opportunities to respond (OTR) is a technique for structuring a lesson so students respond frequently, and accurately, to questions about the material (Greenwood, Delquadri, & Hall, 1984). Many classrooms are dominated by interactions where the teacher calls on a single student at a time. While sometimes appropriate, this instructional mode is characterized by a slower pace, as the teacher must wait to hear the student's response and then provide feedback. While all students are supposed to be listening and benefitting from these interactions, less-motivated students may use it as an opportunity to be off task. The format also limits the active participation of large numbers of students, as only a few can be called on during a class period. Students with behavioral issues are already less likely to engage in academic activities or to be called on by the teacher, leaving them with scarce occasions for successful participation. Use of OTR both enhances learning and manages behavior because it promotes active participation in academic activities, which is incompatible with maladaptive behavior.

When using an OTR approach, the teacher's goal is to elicit frequent, accurate participation—approximately four to six responses per minute, with an 80% accuracy rate when learning new material. If the activity is practice of known material, the rate should be higher, with eight to 12 responses per minute at 90% accuracy (Sutherland & Wehby, 2001). A variety of response formats can be used with OTR, including choral responding, a gestural movement such as "thumbs up or down," or marking answers on individual white boards or on cell phones. When using OTR, teachers should do the following (Conroy et al., 2008): Increase the rate of instructional talk to include repeated verbal or visual (or both) types of prompting; present information that cues students to the correct answer (e.g., "This is an A. What letter is this?"); use modifications that accommodate students' level of functioning; use adequate wait time to allow students to respond; and provide corrective feedback, error correction, and progress monitoring (p. 27).

OTR is a rapid-paced, feedback-rich instructional technique that maximizes student participation in a lesson. The pace and frequent feedback work to diminish maladaptive behaviors by leaving little time for off-task behavior, while at the same time making it possible for students to participate with a high level of success. Equally important is that the format can diminish the anxiety students may feel about offering a wrong answer. Choral responding allows students to participate in a way that the teacher can quickly and easily evaluate student understanding without drawing attention to incorrect responses. Even when the response mode is not choral, the stakes are lowered because the overall number of opportunities to participate, and subsequently the number of opportunities to answer correctly is increased.

Several studies have demonstrated the advantages of using OTR. Not only does it decrease disruptive behavior, but it increases the number of correct responses as well (Haydon & Hunter, 2011; Sutherland, Alder, & Gunter, 2003). It is effective in general education settings as well as with students with emotional and behavioral disorders (EBD; Sutherland & Wehby, 2001). For example, a study conducted by Haydon, Mancil, and Van Loan (2009) in a general education science room showed that the disruptive behavior of a female student was reduced when the teacher increased OTRs with choral responding. The number of questions the student answered correctly also increased. Another study (Christle & Schuster, 2003) that took place in a fourth-grade general education class during mathematics showed similar results. When the teacher switched from a hand-raising procedure to the use of response cards, students participated more and had more correct answers on the weekly math quiz. The technique has worked equally well with students who have severe behavioral issues. In a study of eight children with emotional and behavioral disorders (Sutherland et al., 2003), students raised the average percentage of time on task from 55% to 79%, in addition to decreasing their disruptive behavior and increasing the number of correct responses.

Behavior-Specific Praise

Behavior-specific praise (BSP) can be used to create a learning environment where students are offered instructive and supportive feedback. Teachers spend a fair amount of time throughout the school day providing students with information about their performance, sometimes in regard to academic work and other times as encouragement to pay attention or refrain from problem behaviors. This feedback is maximized when students clearly understand what prompted the praise, but teachers often give general or non-behavior-specific praise (NBSP) when they use comments such as "good work" or "great job." In these cases, the student may not be sure exactly what the teacher is referring to, or may even believe the praise to be insincere if it does not appear to be connected to a particular action. BSP is a praise statement directly linked to the behavior it describes. So, instead of "good job," a teacher would say, "Thank you for putting away your materials so quickly and quietly." This cues students to the behaviors they should demonstrate, while at the same time making them feel good because the teacher has noticed their work or effort (Cooper et al., 2007). Students will more clearly understand the connection between their actions and desirable consequence. BSP is remarkably powerful for a simple technique and has been shown to increase compliance and on-task behavior, and to decrease disruptive behavior (Musti-Rao & Haydon, 2011; Sutherland, 2000).

Although straightforward, it can be difficult to increase a teacher's use of BSP. Teachers are more likely to rely on NBSP or to use reprimands at a much greater rate than praise (Gorman-Smith, 2003). The following suggestions can help teachers improve their use of BSP (see Musti-Rao & Haydon, 2011, for a complete description of these steps). First is to increase self-awareness of how often one is using the technique. Self-monitoring by taking a frequency count throughout the day (or within a particular time period) will provide a basis of comparison over time. Second, it can help to choose a target student or a target behavior. This reminds the teacher to use BSP whenever she encounters the targeted behavior or the targeted student engaging in a desirable classroom behavior. Similarly, one can focus on particular areas of the classroom and rotate through them with the aim of using BSP (e.g., dividing the room into quadrants or moving from the front of the room to the back). Use of a cueing device is also an easy option with technology such as smartphones. Setting an alarm to vibrate at regular intervals (or using an app that performs the function) is a reminder to use BSP. Finally, one can ask a peer or administrator to observe and provide feedback on one's usage of BSP. This can be extremely effective, because it also provides the opportunity to discuss a variety of issues related to using BSP with a knowledgeable colleague.

BSP is an effective technique that requires little advance planning or preparation to implement. It encourages on-task behavior (Sutherland, Wehby, & Copeland, 2000) while promoting a classroom climate that focuses on the positive rather than relying on reactive techniques such as reprimands. This is critical when working with students who have higher rates of non-compliance, as they are likely to react adversely to a reprimand, thus escalating negative interactions (Van Acker, Grant, & Henry, 1996).

Choice

As we discussed previously, incorporating choice into students' instructional experiences can be very effective to support desired behavior and academic engagement (Dunlap, Foster-Johnson, Clarke, Kern, & Childs, 1995; Kern, Delaney, Clarke, Dunlap, & Childs, 2001; Kern & Manz, 2004). In the absence of differentiated instruction, the school day can be perceived as long and tedious, characterized by some students as "like prison," in the sense there is limited opportunity for choice and independence. Yet, skillful teachers are able to incorporate choice into classroom activities. Incorporating choice (e.g., choice in the order instructional activities are completed [process] and choice in how they "show what they know" [products]), communicates to students that teachers value and respect students' interests, preferences, and abilities (see Box 17.2).

Box 17.2

Why did I like my AP AB Calculus class? The teacher differentiated the workload for different students. He trusted us to do the work we thought was necessary to understand the topic he taught. For example, you could do the homework problems for extra practice if you were struggling with topic. But, if you felt as though you mastered the topic, you did not have to do the homework. The consequence for not studying when you should have done additional practice was as follows: your test grade would reflect a poor decision and you could adjust your study plans for the next unit.
    Nathan, 16 years old, 11th grade

Several interesting studies have been conducted demonstrating how the introduction of choice is associated with fewer behavior problems and higher levels of engagement in instructional tasks. For example, Dunlap et al. (1995) conducted a study with students with EBD involving choice. Results indicated that allowing students to choose six out of eight options for assignments they wanted to complete resulted in lower levels of disruptive behavior. Similarly, Kern and colleagues (2001) showed that simply being allowed the option to choose which assignment to complete first resulted in increased on-task behavior and decreased problem behavior. In this study, students did not avoid or escape any task. They were still required to complete all tasks, but could determine for themselves the order of task completion.

Not only have studies shown improved behavior, but evidence also suggests improved academic performance. For example, Cosden, Gannon, and Haring (1995) also demonstrated that giving students options from 10 activities (e.g., answering science questions, writing assignments, or work problems) resulted in improved rates of accuracy relative to the no-choice condition.

High-Probability Request Sequences

High-probability request (HPR) sequences can be used to increase a student's compliant and appropriate responding when delivered prior to an instruction with which the student is unlikely to comply (Mace et al., 1988). HPR sequences consist of two parts: (a) the rapid presentation of several instructions to which the student typically complies (high-probability, or high-p, requests) immediately followed by (b) a single instruction to which the student typically does not comply (low-probability, or low-p, request). For example, an elementary school teacher might use the following HPR sequence with a student who is typically non-compliant when instructed to begin an independent reading activity: (1) "Get your book" (high-p), (2) "Open to page 15" (high-p), (3) "Point to the dog" (high-p), and (4) "Start reading" (low-p). Behavior-specific praise of the student's appropriate response immediately follows *each* successive request. HPR sequences can also be embedded in written tasks. For example, a high school geometry teacher might create a worksheet with three to five straight-forward computations of the area of a circle (high-p requests) followed by an instruction to write a two-column proof for the area of a circle (low-p request).

The applied behavior analytic principles of behavioral momentum (Mace et al., 1988) and response generalization (Horner, Day, Sprague, & O'Brien, 1991) are often cited in explanations of the efficacy of HPR sequences in increasing compliance. A series of high-p requests each followed by behavior specific praise functions to build a momentum for compliant responding prior to the presentation of the low-p request. Analogous to how a sprinter continues to run even after he has crossed the finish line, compliant responding is strengthened through the rapid presentation of high-p requests and consequently maintains following the low-p request.

Effective implementation of HPR sequences relies on the accurate identification of high-p and low-p requests. Just as how the thought of participating in the teachers versus students volleyball match makes one teacher smile with anticipation and another cringe with dread, high-p and low-p requests vary depending on the individual student. As a general guideline, requests to which a student responds accurately at least 80% of the time are high-p requests (Davis & McLaughlin, 2013). A teacher should identify a variety of high-p requests across instructional activities and task demands so the HPR sequence can be randomized. Repeating the same high-p requests weakens the effectiveness of HPR sequences increasing compliance (Davis & Reichle, 1996). Conversely, requests to which a student responds less than 50% of the time are low-p requests (Davis & McLaughlin, 2013). Although a student typically does not comply with these requests, is it imperative that their noncompliance results from a performance, rather than acquisition, deficit. No matter how much behavioral momentum for compliant responding an HPR sequence generates, a student is unable to comply with a request if he or she does not know the appropriate response.

Summary

These strategies—proximity, high rates of opportunities to respond, behavior-specific praise, choice, and high-probability request sequences—are relatively low-cost investments with respect to teacher time and effort. We offer this collective set of behavioral supports as feasible (socially valid) and effective techniques for increasing instructional efficacy from a behavioral perspective. These are by no means an exhaustive list, and we encourage teachers to consider incorporating not only these practices but also others. For example, we encourage teachers to also explore instructive feedback by providing clear, supportive information about a student response (not necessarily corrective) in an effort to provide more efficient learning for students. Even though the interaction between teacher and students is brief (e.g., the teacher smiles and says, "Yes, that is how you derive the formula"), students do retain the new, supplemental, or repeated information (Werts, Wolery, Holcombe, & Gast, 1995). Also, we recommend learning about other behavioral techniques, such as differential reinforcement schedules for increasing desired behaviors and reducing undesirable behaviors which build upon the information mentioned for behavior specific praise (e.g., differential reinforcement of incompatible behaviors and differential reinforcement of lower rates of behavior; Cooper et al., 2007).

Concluding Thoughts

Our goal in writing this chapter was to introduce instructional strategies and practices that increase instructional efficacy. First, we focused on differentiating curriculum to enhance motivation and increase engagement. We provided an overview of differentiation of content, process, and products, with the intent of empowering teachers with the information needed to increase student access to instruction and to provide students with a variety of ways to demonstrate what they are learning (Tomlinson, 2005). Next, we shifted to low-intensity behavioral supports teachers can employ to establish positive instructional experiences for all learners. While there is a multitude of behavior techniques derived from principles of applied behavior analytics, we focused on low-intensity, teacher-delivered behavioral supports to support learning. Specifically, we introduced proximity (Kerr & Valenti, 2009), high rates of opportunities to respond (Conroy et al., 2008), behavior-specific praise (Sutherland, 2000), choice (Kern et al., 2001), and high-probability request sequences (Mace et al., 1988).

We are hopeful this information will be useful and manageable for teachers working within the context of multi-tiered systems of prevention. As we discussed in this chapter, there is a range of options available before moving forward with more resource-intensive supports for students needing tier 2 or tier 3 interventions. For professionals interested in implementing some of these instructional strategies and practices that increase instructional efficacy and the behavioral supports noted, we offer a few recommendations listed as follows.

Recommendations

1. When students are not responding to primary prevention efforts, we encourage teachers to first consider teacher-related variables to address, rather than look at every problem or challenge as a "within-child" concern. In many instance, it will be far more efficient—both in terms of teacher-time and potential breadth of impact—for teachers to first shift their own behaviors rather than beginning with individual behavioral supports for students.

2. When reviewing the literature to look for instructional and behavioral strategies to reduce problem behavior, increase academic engagement, and improve academic performance, we recommend picking strategies with sufficient evidence to support that the strategy or practice is effective in your context (Tankersley & Cook, 2013). Instructional time is simply too precious to spend on strategies and practices not likely to yield the desired outcome, be it higher rates of academic engagement, increased work completion, or improvements in oral reading skills. We recommend the practice guides published by the U.S. Department of Education, Institute of Education Sciences as a resource.

3. When considering implementing any of the ideas mentioned in this chapter, we encourage you to be patient—with yourself as the teacher and with your students. We have tremendous respect for the complexity of the classroom and for teachers for being committed to working so diligently to support learning. These strategies will work, but do take time to acquire and master. Try selecting one strategy to focus on for a given period of time (e.g., commit to increasing your rate of behavior specific praise for a one-week period). As the strategy becomes incorporated into your natural instructional flow, select a new strategy to focus on.

4. When possible, seek high-quality professional development offerings to support you in revisiting these practices or learning them for the first time. We recommend practice-based professional development that moves beyond information sharing and incorporates opportunity to practices skills taught with the support of coaching and performance feedback from other professionals (Ball & Cohen, 1999; Grossman & McDonald, 2008).

We offer the strategies discussed in this chapter as respectful suggestions to teachers faced with the formidable task of educating students with increasingly diverse academic, behavioral, and social needs. Effective implementation of one or several of the strategies discussed in this chapter may provide sufficient support to negate the need for resource-intensive secondary or tertiary interventions for students with additional needs. Given the demands placed on teachers in a typical day, we offer these strategies in hope of supplementing and reinforcing existing skills and expertise to maximize instructional efficacy.

References

Alderman, M. K. (1999). *Motivation for achievement: Possibilities for teaching and learning.* Mahwah, NJ: Lawrence Earlbaum Associates.

American Institutes for Research, National Center on Response to Intervention. (n.d.). *Screening tools chart.* Retrieved from http://www.rti4success.org/screeningTools

Ball, D. L., & Cohen, D. K. (1999). Developing practice, developing practitioners: Toward a practice-based theory of professional education. In L. Darling-Hammond & G. Sykes (Eds.), *Teaching as a learning profession: Handbook for policy and practice* (pp. 3–31). San Francisco, CA: Jossey-Bass.

Bruhn, A., Lane, K. L., & Hirsch, S. (in press). *A review of secondary interventions conducted within multi-tiered models of behavioral prevention. Journal of Emotional and Behavioral Disorders.*

Carter, E. W., Lane, K. L., Crnobori, M. E., Bruhn, A. L., & Oakes, W. P. (2011). Self-determination interventions for students with and at risk for emotional and behavioral disorders: Mapping the knowledge base. *Behavioral Disorders, 36,* 100–116.

Christle, C. A., & Schuster, J. W. (2003). The effects of using response cards on student participation: Academic achievement, and on-task behavior during whole-class, math instruction. *Journal of Behavioral Education, 12,* 147–165.

Colvin, G. (2004). *Managing the cycle of serious acting out behavior.* Eugene, OR: Behavior Associates.

Conroy, M. A., Sutherland, K. S., Snyder, A. L., & Marsh, S. (2008). Classwide interventions: Effective instruction makes a difference. *Teaching Exceptional Children, 40*(6), 24–30.

Cook, B., & Tankersley, M. (Eds.). (2013). *Effective practices in special education.* Boston, MA: Pearson.

Cooper, J. O., Heron, T. E., & Heward, W. L. (2007). *Applied behavior analysis.* Upper Saddle River, NJ: Pearson Education.

Cosden, M., Gannon, C., & Haring, T. G. (1995). Teacher-control versus student-control over choice of task and reinforcement for students with severe behavior problems. *Journal of Behavioral Education, 5,* 11–27.

Council of Chief State School Officers & the National Governors Association Center for Best Practices. (2011). *Common Core State Standards Initiative.* Washington, DC: Author.

Coyne, M., Kame'enui, E., & Carnine, D. (2007). *Effective teaching strategies that accommodate diverse learners.* Upper Saddle River, NJ: Pearson Merrill Prentice Hall.

Davis, C. A., & McLaughlin, A. (2013). Strategies to improve compliance. In K. L. Lane, B. G. Cook, & M. G. Tankersley (Eds.), *Research-based strategies for improving outcomes in behavior* (pp. 46–58). New York, NY: Pearson.

Davis, C. A., & Reichle, J. (1996). Variant and invariant high-probability requests: Increasing appropriate behaviors in children with emotional-behavioral disorders. *Journal of Applied Behavior Analysis, 29,* 471–482.

Deci, E. L., & Ryan, R. M. (1985). *Intrinsic motivation and self-determination in human behavior.* New York, NY: Plenum Press.

Dev, P. C. (1997). Intrinsic motivation and academic achievement: What does their relationship imply for the classroom teacher? *Remedial and Special Education, 18,* 12–19.

Downing, J. A. (2002). Individualized behavior contracts. *Intervention in School and Clinic, 37,* 168–172.

Drummond, T. (1994). *The Student Risk Screening Scale (SRSS).* Grants Pass, OR: Josephine County Mental Health Program.

Dunlap, G., Foster-Johnson, L., Clarke, S., Kern, L., & Childs, K. (1995). Modifying activities to produce functional outcomes: Effects on the problem behaviors of students with disabilities. *Journal of the Association for Persons with Severe Handicaps, 20,* 248–258.

Fuchs, D., & Fuchs, L. (2006). Introduction to response to intervention: What, why, and how valid is it? *Reading Research Quarterly, 41,* 93–99.

Germer, K. A., Kaplan, L. M., Giroux, L. N., Markham, E. H., Ferris, G., Oakes, W., & Lane, K. L. (2012). A function-based intervention to increase a second-grade student's on-task behavior in a general education classroom. *Beyond Behavior, 20,* 19–30.

Gersten, R., Baker, S. K., Smith-Johnson, J., Dimino, J., & Peterson, A. (2006). Eyes on the prize: Teaching complex historical content to middle school students with learning disabilities. *Exceptional Children, 72,* 264–280.

Gorman-Smith, D. (2003). Effects of teacher training and consultation on teacher behavior toward students at high risk for aggression. *Behavior Therapy, 34,* 437–452.

Greenwood, C. R., Delquadri, J., & Hall, R. V. (1984). *Opportunity to respond and student academic performance.* Kansas City, KS: University of Kansas, Juniper Gardens Children's Project.

Grossman, P., & McDonald, M. (2008). Back to the future: Directions for research in teaching and teacher education. *American Educational Research Journal, 45,* 184–205.

Haydon, T., & Hunter, W. (2011). The effects of two types of teacher questioning on teacher behavior and student performance: A case study. *Education & Treatment of Children, 34,* 229–245.

Haydon, T., Mancil, G., & Van Loan, C. (2009). Using opportunities to respond in a general education classroom: A case study. *Education and Treatment of Children, 32,* 267–278.

Horner, R. H., Day, H. M., Sprague, J. R., & O'Brien, M. (1991). Interspersed requests: A nonaversive procedure for reducing aggression and self-injury during instruction. *Journal of Applied Behavior Analysis, 24,* 265–278.

Individuals with Disabilities Education Improvement Act of 2004, 20 U.S.C. 1400 et seq. (2004). (reauthorization of Individuals with Disabilities Act 1990).

Kalberg, J. R., Lane, K. L., & Menzies, H. M. (2010). Using systematic screening procedures to identify students who are nonresponsive to primary prevention efforts: Integrating academic and behavioral measures. *Education and Treatment of Children, 33,* 561–584.

Kamphaus, R. W., & Reynolds, C. R. (2007). *BASC™-2 Behavior and Emotional Screening System (BASC™-2 BESS).* San Antonio, TX: Pearson.

Kern, L., Delaney, B., Clarke, S., Dunlap, G., & Childs, K. (2001). Improving the classroom behavior of students with emotional and behavioral disorders using individualized curricular modifications. *Journal of Emotional and Behavioral Disorders, 9,* 239–247.

Kern, L., Mantegna, M. E., Vorndran, C. M., Bailin, D., & Hilt, A. (2001). Choice of task sequence to reduce problem behaviors. *Journal of Positive Interventions, 3,* 3-10.

Kern, L., & Manz, P. (2004). A look at current validity issues of school-wide behavior support. *Behavioral Disorders, 30,* 47–59.

Kerr, M., & Valenti, M. W. (2009). Controls from within the classroom: Crises or conversations? *Reclaiming Children & Youth, 17*(4), 30–34.

Kounin, J. (1977). *Discipline and group management in classrooms.* New York, NY: Holt, Rinehart, & Winston.

Lane, K. L., Menzies, H., Bruhn, A., & Crnobori, M. (2011). *Managing challenging behaviors in schools: Research-based strategies that work.* New York, NY: Guilford Press.

Lane, K. L., Oakes, W. P., & Menzies, H. M. (2010). Systematic screenings to prevent the development of learning and behavior problems: Considerations for practitioners, researchers, and policy makers. *Journal of Disabilities Policy Studies, 21,* 160–172.

Lane, K. L., & Walker, H. M. (2012). The connection between assessment and intervention: How does screening lead to better interventions? In B. Bateman, M. Tankersley, & J. Lloyd (Eds.), *Issues in special education.* Chapter submitted for review.

Lepper, M. (1988). Motivational considerations in the study of instruction. *Cognition and Instruction, 5,* 289–309.

Mace, F. C., Hock, M. L., Lalli, J. S., West, B. J., Belfiore, P., Pinter, E., & Brown, D. K. (1988). Behavioral momentum in the treatment of noncompliance. *Journal of Applied Behavior Analysis, 21,* 123–141.

Menzies, H., Lane, K. L., & Lee, J. M. (2009). Self-monitoring strategies for use in the classroom: A promising practice to support productive behavior for students with emotional or behavioral disorders. *Beyond Behavior, 18,* 27–35.

Musti-Rao, S., & Haydon, T. (2011). Strategies to increase behavior-specific teacher praise in an inclusive environment. *Intervention in School and Clinic, 47,* 91–97.

Oakes, W. P., Lane, K. L., Cox, M., Magrane, A., Jenkins, A., & Hankins, K. (2012). Tier 2 supports to improve motivation and performance of elementary students with behavioral challenges and poor work completion. *Education and Treatment of Children, 35,* 547–584

Ormrod, J. A. (2000). *Educational psychology: Developing learners* (3rd ed.). Upper Saddle River, NJ: Pearson.

Pearson Education. (2010). AIMSWeb. San Antonio, TX: Author.

Pintrich, P. R., & Schunk, D. H. (2002). *Motivation in education: Theory, research, and applications* (2nd ed.). Upper Saddle River, NJ: Pearson.

Reis, S., & Renzulli, J. (1992). Using curriculum compacting to challenge the above-average. *Educational Leadership, 50,* 51–57.

Simmons, D., & Kame'enui, E. (1996). A focus on curriculum design: When children fail. *Focus on Exceptional Children, 28,* 1. Retrieved from Academic Search Premier database.

Stipek, D. J. (1993). *Motivation to learn: From theory to practice* (2nd ed.). Boston, MA: Allyn and Bacon.

Strong, A. C., Wehby, J. H., Falk, K. B., & Lane, K. L. (2004). The impact of a structured reading curriculum and repeated reading on the performance of junior high students with emotional and behavioral disorders. *School Psychology Quarterly, 33,* 561–581.

Sugai, G., & Horner, R. H. (2002). The evolution of discipline practices: School-wide positive behavior supports. *Child & Family Behavior Therapy, 24,* 25–50.

Sutherland, K. S. (2000). Promoting positive interactions between teachers and students with emotional/behavioral disorders. *Preventing School Failure, 44,* 110–115.

Sutherland, K. S., Alder, N., & Gunter, P. L. (2003). The effect of varying rates of opportunities to respond to academic requests on the classroom behavior of students with EBD. *Journal of Emotional and Behavioral Disorders, 11,* 239–248.

Sutherland, K. S., & Wehby, J. H. (2001). Exploring the relationship between increased opportunities to respond to academic requests and the academic and behavioral outcomes of students with EBD: A review. *Remedial and Special Education, 22,* 113–21.

Sutherland, K. S., Wehby, J. H., & Copeland, S. R. (2000). Effect of varying rates of behavior-specific praise on the on-task behavior of students with EBD. *Journal of Emotional and Behavioral Disorders, 8,* 2–8.

Tomlinson, C. A. (1999). *The differentiated classroom: Responding to the needs of all learners.* Alexandria, VA: Association for Supervision and Curriculum Development.

Tomlinson, C. A. (2001). *How to differentiate instruction in mixed-ability classrooms.* Upper Saddle River, NJ: Pearson Education, Inc.

Tomlinson, C. A. (2005). *An educator's guide to differentiating instruction.* Boston, MA: Houghton-Mifflin.

Umbreit, J., Ferro, J., Liaupsin, C., & Lane, K. (2007). *Functional behavioral assessment and function-based intervention: An effective, practical approach.* Upper Saddle River, NJ: Prentice-Hall.

Umbreit, J., Lane, K. L., & Dejud, C. (2004). Improving classroom behavior by modifying task difficulty: The effects of increasing the difficulty of too-easy tasks. *Journal of Positive Behavior Interventions, 6,* 13–20.

U.S. Department of Education, Institute for Education Sciences. (n.d.). *What works clearinghouse practice guides.* Retrieved from http://ies.ed.gov/ncee/wwc/

Van Acker, R., Grant, S. H., & Henry, D. (1996). Teacher and student behavior as a function of aggression. *Education and Treatment of Children, 19,* 316–334.

Vygotsky, L. S. (1978). *Mind in society.* Cambridge, MA: Harvard University Press.

Werts, M., Wolery, M., Holcombe, A., & Gast, D. (1995). Instructive feedback: Review of parameters and effects. *Journal of Behavioral Education, 5,* 55–75.

18

Standards-Based Assessment

Tom Nicholson

This chapter will focus on the Common Core State Standards (CCSS) and, in particular, the English Language Arts (ELA) standards. The CCSS represent the latest in a history of massive attempts in the United States to write commonly agreed-upon standards for the key discipline areas of Language Arts and Mathematics (CCSSO, 2010a, 2010b). The chapter will start with a definition of standards, explain what the new CCSS is, look at the positives and negatives of CCSS, and end by comparing them with and end by comparing them with similar efforts to introduce standards for reading, writing, and mathematics in both New Zealand and Australia.

The chapter will argue that there are many positives about the CCSS. An outsider coming to the CCSS website is awestruck in terms of the work that has gone into the standards. It has been a massive project and there will be many pluses. The most important plus is that they will provide consistency of standards across the nation's schools. Another plus is that they are more egalitarian than are standardized tests for assessing achievement because, in theory, everyone should be able to meet the standards. The downside is that the sheer number of CCSS may be mental overload for the average teacher and student. In contrast, the New Zealand and Australian standards for each grade level are far fewer and the old adage of "keep it simple" may be a much more practical approach than the present CCSS in the United States.

Looking at the systems in place in the three countries, it is only in New Zealand that teachers are expected to assess whether or not their students have achieved the expected "standard" at each grade level. Teachers in New Zealand are struggling to assess whether students are above, at, or below the national standard in reading, writing, and mathematics. In contrast, in Australia and the United States, an external body does the assessment so that teachers do not have to do anything except wait to see the results. Which way is better, to empower teachers to make their own decisions about the achievement of their pupils or to give that power to someone else?

This chapter will argue that it is better to empower teachers and to give them a sense of what it means to be reading, writing, speaking, listening, and doing mathematics at grade level. Standards-based assessment will not achieve its vision unless it starts at the end rather than the beginning, so that teachers know what kind of reader/writer/mathematician they are trying to construct. It is also important to empower teachers to make their own assessments of whether they have achieved the vision. Teachers need freedom to implement standards and assess them. How else will they be able to make the classroom boat go faster? We want the teacher to be thinking about the standard, to be saying, "I think James is doing well at the moment and he will be at the national standard in reading, writing, and math at the end of the year." In contrast, when someone else does the assessing, the results are probably more accurate, but the teacher might feel disconnected with the process of assessment, and engage in a lot of anxious but unnecessary activity preparing for and predicting what will be in the test. As Hattie (2009) put it, "indeed my own 5-year-old in his North Carolina school had to spend 40 minutes a week learning how to fill in bubble sheets in anticipation of the next year's testing regime" (p. 4).

Visions, Aspirations, and High-Stakes Testing

A standards-based assessment system has the vision that it is possible to close the achievement gap. Unlike a standardized test, where half the pupils who sit the test will pass and half will fail, a standards-based assessment sets a level that in theory it is possible for all pupils to pass. It has a vision that everyone, rich or poor, needs to meet the same standards and there is no double standard, one for the rich and one for the poor.

Standards are aspirational, in that governments can set the standards at a higher level if that is what they want to do, or make it less aspirational by setting the standards at a lower level. If the standards are set at a higher level, this may reflect the desire of the government to create a more academic education system. Standards at a lower level might fit with a government goal of equity to give more success to those pupils who might otherwise fail to achieve the standard if it was set too high.

In most countries, setting standards by itself, though a worthy thing to do, does not seem to have teeth if teachers are not required to meet the standards. As a result, standards usually come with a requirement that schools must meet the standards. The results for schools may be published in newspapers, e.g., these schools are Exemplary (93% or above), these are Recognized (80–92%), these are Acceptable (67–79%), and these are Unacceptable (below 67%). In New Zealand, newspapers publish the percent of pupils in each school who are above the standard, at the standard, below the standard, and well below the standard. The government website does not compare schools, but allows parents to look up the results for their school. The Australian website is similar.

In education, however, schools are nowadays not only asked to teach to academic standards but policymakers also want to know whether or not schools are meeting those standards. In countries where these results are made public, there is huge opposition from teachers. Standards in many places have become a smoking gun. They have turned into "high-stakes" assessment: "There is so much wrapped up in schooling and seemingly so much at stake, that schools can become emotional cauldrons and the policies that shape them hotly contested" (Polesel, Dulfer, & Turnbull, 2012, p. 3).

The issue, then, is that the introduction of standards, followed with testing of those standards across schools, and comparing schools and states in whether or not they meet the standards, opens the way for warring factions to argue their case that the standards are either fair or unfair. So the issue is not so much about the idea of standards as about using those standards as a way of comparing schools.

What Are "Standards"?

A standard in the education world is a benchmark that describes the type of task that students expect to achieve to meet the demands of the curriculum at each point in their schooling. The aim is to make those demands very clear and explicit so that the pupils, parents, and teachers know what to aim for. If they meet the standard, the belief is that they are on track for success in terms of high school graduation.

The word "standard" derives from the French word *estendart*, meaning "to extend," or in Old English, "to stand." Pearson (1993, p. 458) tried to pin down the essence of a standard by using a dictionary definition, explaining that the dictionary has numerous meanings for standard (e.g., a "standard" can refer to a plant, such as a standard rose) but that some are very relevant to education, as in:

1. Something that is established by authority, custom, or general consent as a model or example to be followed
2. A definite level or degree of quality that is proper or adequate for a specific purpose
3. A carefully thought-out method of performing a task
4. Any measure by which one judges a thing good, authentic, or adequate

Synonyms include: criterion, gauge, yardstick, touchstone, and test.

Among the above four definitions, Pearson (1993) thought that definition 1 was about vision, the idea of stating who we are and where we want to be, whereas definitions 2 and 4 were about testing, that is, about finding out whether we have met the standard. Definition 3 was about how we might operationalize the standard. For example, the modern "standard" for getting married seems to be as follows: start with a "wow" entrance to the wedding venue, like arriving in a helicopter or on a horse. After that, have a "wow" reception in the most-expensive or weirdest place possible, with magicians, singers, bands, and everything else you can think of to make it different.

The online OED gives similar explanations to the Merriam-Webster. A standard can be:

a. A level of quality or attainment
b. Something used as a measure, a norm, or a model
c. A flag (used in the military)

Definitions 1 and 2 in the OED fit with the idea of vision, of what we stand for and want to be. The metaphor of a flag in definition 3 makes sense if we think of a flag as something that stands for our core values.

The History of Standards

Pearson and Hiebert (2013) explained, "standards have become a staple of the American school and curriculum since they first entered the reform scene in the early 1990s" (p. 1). The aim was to "develop a clear statement of what students should know and be able to do at various developmental levels" (p. 1), so that they would be armed with the knowledge and skills they would need to graduate from high school, go to college, and enter the world of work.

Standards have been high on the agenda of policymakers since at least the late 1980s (Pearson, 1993, 2013). The idea of standards has appeal in that it is more descriptive than a test score. It does more than say, for example, that your child is reading or writing or doing math at grade 4 level. It is also saying that these are the texts that your child can read and write, and this is the sort of math problem that your child can solve. Standards seem to be transparent, to be specific and clear. They may be clear but as we shall see later, assessing the standards can be very unclear.

A standard also reflects what society thinks is the "right" level of achievement. We often hear in the media that "standards are slipping" in regard to something, whether it is the quality of news reporting, or the driving skills of our teenagers, or the penalties for crime—or educational achievement. Standards are an opportunity to set the level of achievement to which our society aspires.

A downside is that in recent times, the impetus to "raise standards" is linked to the idea that standards have been slipping. For example, National Assessment of Educational Progress (NAEP) results in 1994 placed California as second to last of the 50 states in reading (Louisiana was last, and that would not have been a surprise given the low socioeconomic status of that state, but it was a surprise that California was next to last). The poor performance of California might have been the result of factors unrelated to education, such as the increased number of immigrants flooding into that state at the time, but this was not how the media explained it (Purcell-Gates, 2009). There was much public concern that standards were "slipping." Hattie (2009, p. 1) explained what happened during that time and afterwards:

> After a tide of negative reports about schooling in the United States, that country looked to national standards to dramatically improve its system. The first President Bush introduced Goals Education 2000, which was picked up by his successor President Clinton. But despite much haggling and blue-ribbon committees, the policy was gaining little, if any, traction, and the second President Bush, realizing that these national standards would be merely words with no effect, proclaimed, on his third day in office, that standards without measurement were not worth the words—hence the policy: "No Child Left Behind" (NCLB), in which individual states set their own standards and measures. Now, President Obama says he has the answer to the current malaise about NCLB—he announced recently that the problem with NCLB is that there are 50 standards and 50 tests, and his solution is to have one set of national standards and one national test.

These standards have now been developed and have been accepted by 46 states and District of Columbia. They are called the Common Core State Standards (CCSS), which we will now explain.

The Common Core State Standards (CCSS)

The CCSS cover grades K–12. They aim to set out standards needed to make American students career and college ready. The writers of these documents have also looked at standards in countries such as the United Kingdom, Singapore, Australia, and New Zealand, so as to make the CCSS standards consistent with global standards. The website has two main documents explaining the standards (http://www.corestandards.org/). The first document is *Common Core State Standards for English Language Arts **and** Literacy in History/Social Studies, Science, and Technical Subjects* (CCSSO, 2010a). The second is *Common Core State Standards for Mathematics* (CCSSO, 2010b).

The CCSS website for English Language Arts (ELA) has an appendix with exemplars of texts (fiction and nonfiction) across the grades K–12. In addition, it has an appendix of writing exemplars across the grades K–12—http://www.corestandards.org/the-standards. Another appendix on the website explains the research behind the CCSS, and yet another explains how the standards apply to English language learners and to students with disabilities. Two features of the English Language Arts standards are: (1) that they are not just about reading and writing, but also include listening and speaking—whereas in Australia and New Zealand the focus is more on reading and writing; and (2) that they link to content area outcomes of school, including history/social sciences, science, and the technical subjects. The CCSS in English Language Arts aims to lift the quality and complexity of what students read and write. In Mathematics, the standards are designed to give depth and rigor, to avoid a curriculum that is "a mile wide and an inch deep" (introduction to CCSS mathematics document, CCSSO, 2010b, p. 3).

Pearson and Hiebert (2013) note other different features of CCSS. First, there is an emphasis on close and critical reading, especially the idea of deep analysis of the text and verifying inferences by citing evidence from the text. Second, there is an emphasis on building disciplinary knowledge by reading social studies and history texts, and science and technical texts. Third, there is a focus on using technology to meet the standards, accessing print and nonprint media, using digital texts and the Internet. In writing, there is a focus on building keyboard skills. Fourth, there is an emphasis on giving students texts that have substance, that have complexity. Students need to read "grade-level text" that is defined in both quantitative (the suggestion is to use Lexile calibration) and qualitative analysis of the demands of the text.

Pearson and Hiebert (2013) explain that another positive is that the CCSS are not driven in a top–down way by the federal government, but by the National Governors Association Center for Best Practices (NGA) and the Council of Chief State School Officers (CCSSO). The new standards, which 46 states and the District of Columbia have now adopted, set out standards from K–12 that will enable students to have sufficient knowledge and skills to be "college ready" and be able to take their place as effective citizens. The standards cover maths and the language arts (reading and writing and oral language), as well as literacy in the subject areas. Along with the common core standards, the federal government is investing (about $350 million as of Fall 2012) (Pearson, 2013) in assessments to measure whether students meet the standards.

The CCSS documents have a vision of what it means to be an accomplished reader, as stated in their introduction (CCSSO/NGA, 2010a, p. 3; see Pearson, 2013). To paraphrase this vision, the hope is that students who meet the standards will:

a. Understand and enjoy complex literature
b. Read critically and carefully
c. Engage widely and deeply with high-quality texts
d. Reason cogently and expect to see evidence, which is essential to citizenship

Another positive for CCSS is that it does not mandate exactly how to meet the standards. The document says, "the Standards leave room for teachers, curriculum developers, and states to determine how those goals should be reached and what additional topics should be addressed" (CCSSO/NGA, 2010a, p. 4; also see Pearson, 2013).

Themes and Anchor Standards

The CCSS has a basic structure of themes, anchor standards, and then specific standards for each grade (see Figure 18.1). For example, in English Language Arts for Reading, there are four themes: (1) key ideas and details, (2) craft and structure, (3) integration of knowledge,

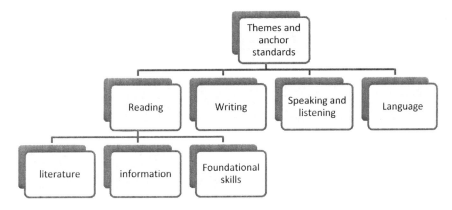

Figure 18.1 Themes and anchor standards for English

and (4) range of reading/ level of complexity. For the theme of key ideas and details in Reading, there are three anchor standards: (1) read closely, (2) find central ideas, and (3) analyze the development of characters, events, and ideas. For writing, the four themes are: (1) text types and processes, (2) production and distribution of writing, (3) research to build and present knowledge, and (4) range of writing. For writing, for the theme of text types and processes, there are three anchor standards: (1) write arguments to support claims, (2) write clear and accurate nonfiction texts, and (3) write fiction that is well structured. For speaking and listening, there are two themes (comprehension/collaboration and presentation of knowledge) and six anchor standards. For language, there are three themes (conventions, knowledge of language, and vocabulary) and six anchor standards. In Reading, the themes and anchor standards are specific for literature and information text at each grade. There are four foundational skills: (1) concepts about print, (2) phonemic awareness, (3) phonics, and (4) fluency.

If I Were a Grade 4 Teacher, How Many Standards Would I Have to Meet?

The standards for grade 4 (as an example) include 10 standards for literature (fiction) and 10 standards for informational text, plus two standards for "foundational skills" that cover phonics/word recognition and fluency. In addition, there are 10 writing standards, six speaking/listening standards, and six language standards. In total, at grade 4, there are 44 English Language Arts standards.

In contrast, in Mathematics at grade 4, there are 28 standards, spread across five strands:

1. Operations and algebraic thinking (5 standards)
2. Number and operations in base 10 (6 standards)
3. Number and operations—fractions (7 standards)
4. Measurement and data (7 standards)
5. Geometry (3 standards)

This number of 28 math standards is a lot less than the 44 standards at grade 4 level for language arts.

The Number of Standards Across All Grades

When you look at the total package of standards for language and literacy across all the grades, there are 44 language arts standards for each grade across 11 grade groupings (K–8 plus grades 9–10 and 11–12)—with 46 standards at kindergarten, due to initial standards for phonological awareness and concepts about print. That is a total of 11 grade groups × 44 standards = 484 standards.

Then there are standards to cover language and literacy across the discipline areas of history/social science and science/technical subjects at grades 6–12. There are 60 standards across three grade groupings covering reading (10 standards in grades 6–8, 9–10, and 11–12) and the same pattern in writing, for a total of 120 standards across reading and writing in the discipline areas. This adds up to a staggering 604 standards for English Language Arts from grades K–12 (484 plus 120). Is it too much?

For math, the number of standards varies across the grades, depending on whether new topics are introduced, for example, fractions are introduced in grade 4. Kindergarten and grade 1 each have 21 standards, grade 2 has 30 standards, grade 3 has 22 standards, grade 4 has 28 standards, and so on. There are certainly not as many standards for maths as there are for the language arts.

Positives of the Common Core State Standards

A recent survey of parents found that about half thought that the standards would make America more competitive globally and would improve education, though 40% thought the standards would not make much difference. In addition, 75% of parents agreed that the standards would bring more consistency in the quality of education across the states (Bushaw & Lopez, 2012). This suggests several positives for the standards:

a. Vision. The common core standards sets out a vision of what could be achieved.
b. Teacher empowerment. The standards explain that teachers are free to choose how they will achieve the standards.
c. Consistency. There is now just one set of standards across nearly all the States—replacing the chaos of every state setting its own standards—this gives consistency.
d. Quality. The fact there are agreed standards will make it easier to achieve the goal of having students leave high school career and college ready, and equipped for citizenship.
e. Global competitiveness. The standards are intended to make students more able to compete successfully on the world stage.
f. The standards have a vision of the accomplished reader that most teachers would agree with.
g. The standards are specific, not vague.
h. The standards set targets and goals.

Negatives of the Common Core State Standards

There are several possible negatives that apply to the CCSS:

a. The standards are not based on any particular theory of reading, writing, speaking, listening, or mathematics. Nor are they based on any particular level of evidence. The common core standards are a result of consensus among knowledgeable professionals (Pearson, 2013).

b. Parents think that the new common core standards will not change anything, will not make a difference (Bushaw & Lopez, 2012).

c. The emphasis on English Language Arts and Mathematics might narrow the curriculum and give less time for other school subjects, and will create a de-facto national curriculum.

d. Standards will be followed by national assessments of standards and this may result in "high-stakes" assessment where schools can be punished for not achieving the standards.

e. The results of standards-based assessment might be published on the Internet by the government, with comparisons of schools who do well and not so well, as has happened in the United Kingdom, Australia, and New Zealand.

f. The standards will be expensive to implement.

g. The standards may be the thin edge of a wedge to national testing and a "pick a bubble" testing regime.

National Standards in New Zealand

In 2009, the New Zealand government published Reading and Writing Standards for Years 1–8 and the Mathematics Standards for Years 1–8 (see Ministry of Education, 2009a and 2009b—and website—http://nzcurriculum.tki.org.nz/National-Standards). Schools must implement the standards and each school each year must assess their own pupils and report the results to the Ministry of Education, with compulsory reporting starting in 2011.

Why introduce common standards across schools? The reason was that although there was a national curriculum, it was vague about what represented an adequate achievement benchmark at each grade level. In addition, every school used different assessment systems. There was no common national assessment of achievement that applied to all schools. There were 2,500 different "islands" (or schools) that all did their own thing. A student might go from one school to the next, thinking they were at a particular level, but the next school would assess differently and they would find they were not at that level. There was complete lack of consistency across schools, and this was problematic in terms of equity.

The National Standards approach in New Zealand is different to CCSS in the United States, in that there are not as many standards specified for each grade level. Another difference is that it is not associated with national testing, as in other countries. There is no external test of achievement that is related to the standards. Instead, each school assesses its own pupils according to criteria associated with the standards.

The New Zealand national standards documents are each about 55 pages in total, to cover years 1–8. This includes the exemplars themselves. The reading and writing document gives one or two reading and writing illustrative examples at each year level, with further examples on the Ministry website. In mathematics, there are up to nine illustrative examples at each year level.

The New Zealand standards are exemplar based, in that at each grade (or year) level, the documents give an example of the kind of text a student needs to be able to read, or a piece of writing that they could write, or a math problem that they could solve. The national standards require pupils to be able to read the text aloud at 90% accuracy or better up to the end of year 3, as part of the decision whether or not the pupil can read the text with understanding. There are also other criteria the student must meet to decide if the student is reading

Table 18.1 National Standards Criteria for Comprehension at End of Year 3 (Pupils Nearly Eight Years Old)

Text feature	Years 1 and 2	Year 3 and 4	Years 5 and 6	Years 7 and 8
Settings and contexts	Familiar, concrete settings and contexts	Some unfamiliar	Some abstract ideas	Complex, sophisticated, abstract ideas
Text structure content	One main structure and simple storyline	One main structure but more than one story line	Two or more text types in the one article	Non-continuous and mixed text types
	Mostly explicit, but some implicit content— simple inferences	A mix of explicit and implicit content— simple inferences	More complex inferences	Complex inferences, irrelevant information that has to be ignored

Table 18.2 National Standards Criteria for Comprehension at End of Year 5 and 6 (Pupils Nearly Ten and Eleven Years Old)

Characteristics of texts

1. Abstract ideas, in greater numbers than in texts at earlier levels, accompanied by concrete examples in the text that help support the students understanding
2. Some ideas and information that are conveyed indirectly and require students to infer by drawing on several related pieces of information in the text
3. Some information that is irrelevant to the identified purpose for reading [that is, some competing information], which students need to identify and reject as they integrate pieces of information in order to answer questions
4. Mixed text types [for example, a complex explanation may be included as part of a report]

with understanding. After the end of year 3, the assumption is that oral reading accuracy will routinely be at 90% accuracy or better, and there is no need to assess this. A brief summary of the comprehension criteria are shown in Table 18.1. (Dymock & Nicholson, 2012)

The general criteria are more elaborate for end of year 5–6 comprehension, as shown in Table 18.2. (Dymock & Nicholson, 2012)

Figure 18.2 is an annotated national standards exemplar showing what pupils should be able to read at the end of year 5 (9-10 years of age). The full text of the exemplar, called "Drought," is in Figure 18.3 (Frater, 2010). This exemplar, along with other annotated exemplars of the reading and writing standards, is located on the Ministry of Education's website, (http://litera cyonline.tki.org.nz/Literacy-Online/Student-needs/National-Standards-Reading-and-Writing/National-Standards-illustrations/Year-5/Drought-Reading).

As can be seen in the exemplar, it is assumed that the pupil can decode the text with at least 90% accuracy. In addition, the teacher will assess whether or not the pupil meets other criteria such as ability to connect to her own prior knowledge, to make inferences, to integrate and evaluate information, and so on.

There are similar national standards exemplars for writing. A writing exemplar for Year 6 (10-year-old level) is in Figure 18.4. It is a fictional "conversation" between Captain Cook and Christopher Columbus (http://literacyonline.tki.org.nz/Literacy-Online/Student-needs/National-Standards-Reading-and-Writing/National-Standards-illustrations/Year-6/A-Conversation-Writing).

Other national standards examples are in McLachlan, Nicholson, Fielding Barnsley, Mercer, & Ohi (2013), and in Dymock and Nicholson (2012).

BY THE END OF YEAR 5

ILLUSTRATING THE READING STANDARD

"Drought" *School Journal,* Part 3 Number 2, 2010   *Noun frequency level: 9–10*

By the end of year 5, students are required to use a variety of fiction and non-fiction texts to locate, evaluate, and integrate information and ideas in order to meet the reading demands of the curriculum, drawing on the knowledge, skills, and attitudes described for the end of year 5 in the Literacy Learning Progressions. The curriculum tasks will also involve the students in generating their own questions as well as answering questions from the teacher.

The students in a year 5 class are involved in a health inquiry into how people respond to and cope with difficult circumstances. They are identifying ways to express feelings about loss and grief and are building on the key competencies of managing self and relating to others.

"Drought" is told through the eyes of a girl whose rural community is dealing with a drought. Her mother has died some time before, and she lives alone with her father. An underlying tension builds throughout the story, paralleling the community's desperate need for rain with the father's need to come to terms with the death of his wife.

The teacher chose "Drought" because the text is a first-person narrative that provides opportunities for the students to make connections with the characters' sense of loss, to identify how this loss affects the characters, and to find out how they deal with it. The abstract ideas of loss and grief are conveyed indirectly, which requires students to make inferences and to integrate information within the text.

The following example illustrates aspects of the task and text and demonstrates how a student engages with both task and text to meet the reading demands of the curriculum. A number of such examples would be used to inform the overall teacher judgment for this student.

Every classroom window's open – even the doors – yet I'm drowning in sweat.

> The student locates information to understand that a drought is part of the setting of the story. She makes connections to her own knowledge of droughts and experiences of hot weather. She integrates information within the first page to infer that the situation in the story (the drought and its consequences) is very serious and affects all aspects of the narrator's daily life.

But all I see is a swimming pool – deep ... cold ... blue. I open my eyes to a dusty playing field and a square of dead grass. Drought. The dreaded word that flashes on our TV screen night after night along with pictures of sheep with their ribs poking through.

With support, the student locates, evaluates, and integrates information about Dad to understand that while Dad is physically tired, he is also not his usual self in other ways. She infers that Dad may also be overworking because he is unhappy about his wife's death.

I wait for him to tell me to use my imagination – but I guess it was Mum who said things like that. Dad still hasn't eaten anything, and there are big black bags under his eyes. He drives the town's only water tanker, and he's worked every day for weeks.

This time the story comes, but the drought in the story is Dad's. Like the ever-blue sky, he's holding back tears. From time to time, a small cloud drifts by, but he blinks it away.

> The student integrates the idea of Dad "holding back tears" with the statement "The moment they burst, Dad cries" and relates it to her earlier evaluation about how Dad isn't coping. She connects the need for Dad to let go with the need for the rain to come. The student discusses the abstract idea of "drought" and, with support, relates the idea of an emotional drought (Dad's) to the physical drought affecting the community.

Then one night, he falls into such a deep sleep, a cloud creeps by without him noticing.

Fat white clouds at first, then grey ones, then black – and the blackest clouds are bursting with rain. The moment they burst, Dad cries.

> The student notices how the final paragraph reflects what happened in the story that came to the girl – more and more clouds are coming, so the drought could end. This also gives the girl a positive action to take for her father. The student evaluates this low-key but positive ending and judges it to be effective and moving for this story.

The moon's up now, and the sky's littered with stars. As I stand awhile, thinking about the story, a wisp of cloud passes in front of the moon. Then, as more and more clouds start to block out the stars, I run inside and wake Dad.

> The student refers to the purpose for reading, and with teacher support, connects the scenario in the text with her own experiences or other situations she has read about, such as when people have been involved in a disaster or tragedy. She concludes that it's often useful for people to find a way to express their grief or worry (perhaps by crying or perhaps in a creative way – like the girl's cloud story).

Figure 18.2 National Standards Reading Exemplar "Drought"

Drought

by Adrienne Frater

Ms Frost wipes a drip of sweat from her brow. "I want you to write a story about drought." She fans her face with a maths book. Drought! In this weather! I swallow my groan. Every classroom window's open – even the doors – yet I'm drowning in sweat. I flop across my desk like a dead fish.

"You can plan your story this afternoon and make a start on it tonight for homework." Ms Frost's face is so red it looks like she's been running a marathon.

I lick my lips, pick up my pen, close my eyes, and wait for ideas. But all I see is a swimming pool – deep ... cold ... blue. I open my eyes to a dusty playing field and a square of dead grass. Drought. The dreaded word that flashes on our TV screen night after night along with pictures of sheep with their ribs poking through. And to think Ms Frost expects us to write about it.

2

Figure 18.3 "Drought" text

"Do we write fact or fiction?" Miri asks.

Ms Frost doesn't answer right away. Her eyes flick up to the blue of the sky, which stares down on a row of limp trees. "Whatever," she says and takes a swig from her water bottle. A few pens scratch, but like mine, most remain still. Pete's and Miri's sighs whistle down my neck.

Miri's my best friend, and Pete lives next door. Since Mum died, I've been staying over at Pete's house until Dad gets home from work.

Figure 18.3 (Continued)

"Drought!" moans Miri when the bell sets us free.

"Drought!" moans Pete, scuffing his toes in the dust. "Anyone for a swim?"

The school pool's been dry for weeks, but we're lucky: Pete's farm has a creek. Most summers, the swimming hole's deep enough to jump into, but this year, it's so shallow his mum lets us swim there alone. Miri and I change behind the willows. We dart from patch of shade to patch of shade yelling "Yee-ha!"

Pete's already sprawled on his back in the creek. "Having a mud bath?" I yell.

Splat! A mud pie hits my left shoulder. *Splosh!* Miri gets Pete on the nose. *Splat ... splosh ... splotch!* We roar and scream like the crowd at a rugby match when someone scores a try. Then we rinse off in the trickle of water. The swim that wasn't a swim doesn't cool me down, but it sure keeps my mind off the dreaded story.

4

Figure 18.3 (Continued)

"I've got to write a story for homework," I tell Dad as I take a mouthful of limp lettuce.

"No sweat," he says, shoving his food around on his plate. "You write beaut stories."

"Not about drought."

I wait for him to tell me to dig deep. I wait for him to tell me to use my imagination – but I guess it was Mum who said things like that. Dad still hasn't eaten anything, and there are big black bags under his eyes. He drives the town's only water tanker, and he's worked every day for weeks. Dad yawns a giant yawn, and his head nearly falls into his plate. "I'll do the dishes," I say.

Figure 18.3 (Continued)

I dump the plates in the sink and start on our once-a-day dishes. We no longer use the dishwasher. We have a brick in the loo. We don't water the garden, and we take two-minute showers. I clank the last plate onto the draining rack and leave the dishes to dry. I guess I could write about the brick in the loo and the once-a-day dishes. I wipe down the bench and leave Dad asleep at the table.

My bedroom's a hot box. I fling open the windows and switch on my precious fan. I get so close it nearly chops off my nose. Then I flop on my bed and stare at the ceiling. After a time, the ceiling turns pink, then red, then lemon, and for the first time that day, I feel I can breathe. I get up and sit at my desk. I open my exercise book to a blank page. I pick up my pen and, trying not to think of Dad asleep at the table, or Mum dying, or the skinny sheep, I close my eyes.

This time the story comes, but the drought in the story is Dad's. Like the ever-blue sky, he's holding back tears. From time to time, a small cloud drifts by, but he blinks it away. Each time he does this, his sadness grows deeper. All he does is get up and go to work and come home and go to bed. Then one night, he falls into such a deep sleep, a cloud creeps by without him noticing. Then another comes, and another, and another. Fat white clouds at first, then grey ones, then black — and the blackest clouds are bursting with rain. The moment they burst, Dad cries.

6

Figure 18.3 (Continued)

Figure 18.3 (Continued)

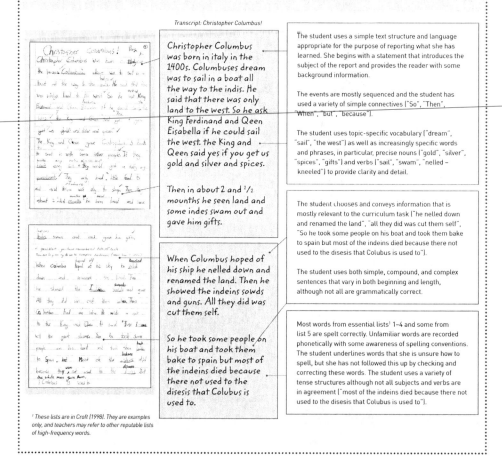

BY THE END OF YEAR 4

ILLUSTRATING THE WRITING STANDARD

Christopher Columbus!

By the end of year 4, students are required to create a variety of texts in order to think about, record, and communicate experiences, ideas, and information across the curriculum. To meet the standard, students draw on the knowledge, skills, and attitudes for writing described in the Literacy Learning Progressions for students at this level.

This example is placed at "By the end of year 4" because it demonstrates that the student is meeting the writing demands of the curriculum at level 2. The student has used a simple text structure to respond to the task, has included mostly relevant content (with some detail), has attempted complex sentences (with some errors), and has chosen some specific nouns, verbs, and adjectives to convey ideas and information.

As part of a social studies unit, the students in this year 4 class are inquiring into the ways in which explorers of the past affected the places they went to and the people they met. The class shared the stories of several explorers, and students chose one explorer to research further. The class developed a series of questions to guide their research and they took notes as they researched, which they then used to report on the changes that their chosen explorer caused.

The following example illustrates aspects of the task and text and demonstrates how a student engages with both task and text to meet the writing demands of the curriculum. A number of such examples would be used to inform the overall teacher judgment for this student.

Transcript: Christopher Columbus!

Christopher Columbus was born in italy in the 1400s. Columbuses dream was to sail in a boat all the way to the indis. He said that there was only land to the west. So he ask King Ferdinand and Qeen Eisabella if he could sail the west. the King and Qeen said yes if you get us gold and silver and spices.

Then in about 2 and ¹/₂ mounths he seen land and some indes swam out and gave him gifts.

When Columbus hoped of his ship he nelled down and renamed the land. Then he showed the indeins sowds and guns. All they did was cut them self.

So he took some people on his boat and took them bake to spain but most of the indeins died because there not used to the disesis that Colubus is used to.

The student uses a simple text structure and language appropriate for the purpose of reporting what she has learned. She begins with a statement that introduces the subject of the report and provides the reader with some background information.

The events are mostly sequenced and the student has used a variety of simple connectives ("So", "Then", "When", "but", "because").

The student uses topic-specific vocabulary ("dream", "sail", "the west") as well as increasingly specific words and phrases, in particular, precise nouns ("gold", "silver", "spices", "gifts") and verbs ("sail", "swam", "nelled – kneeled") to provide clarity and detail.

The student chooses and conveys information that is mostly relevant to the curriculum task ("he nelled down and renamed the land", "all they did was cut them self", "So he took some people on his boat and took them bake to spain but most of the indeins died because there not used to the disesis that Colubus is used to").

The student uses both simple, compound, and complex sentences that vary in both beginning and length, although not all are grammatically correct.

Most words from essential lists[1] 1–4 and some from list 5 are spelt correctly. Unfamiliar words are recorded phonetically with some awareness of spelling conventions. The student underlines words that she is unsure how to spell, but she has not followed this up by checking and correcting these words. The student uses a variety of tense structures although not all subjects and verbs are in agreement ("most of the indeins died because there not used to the disesis that Colubus is used to").

[1] These lists are in Croft (1998). They are examples only, and teachers may refer to other reputable lists of high-frequency words.

Figure 18.4 National Standards Writing Exemplar

The Problem of League Tables

The national standards results for each school first appeared on the New Zealand government's Education Counts website in 2012. You go to the website if you Google "Education Counts NZ," click on the link at the top of the page to "National Standards," which takes you to the school site where you enter the name of the school you are interested in. If you do that, you can download and read the school's report of their own assessment of their pupils in terms of the national standards. Schools must report the percentages of pupils achieving at, above, below, or well below the standard for reading, writing, and math. For example, a high-achieving school might report that 50% of their pupils are at the national standard in reading, writing, and mathematics, 45% are above, 5% are below, and none are well below.

Some of the arguments against the reporting of national standards results for each school on the Ministry website have been set out by the New Zealand Assessment Academy, which consists of a group of academics who specialize in assessment (Johnston, 2012):

1. The data can be used to publish league tables of results that compare schools, with some schools, especially those in poverty areas, being "named and shamed" for their poor results.
2. The data are not reliable in that there is no way of knowing whether schools have assessed their pupils accurately.
3. The data will misrepresent schools from disadvantaged areas that are more likely to have large numbers of students reading, writing, or doing math below the standards.
4. The data only show "point in time" results, they do not show the amount of progress that pupils have made.
5. The data will lead to a narrowing of the curriculum as schools focus on passing the standards and avoid subjects that are not assessed, such as art and music.

At this time, the Ministry's national standards data are most vulnerable to the criticism that teachers are unable to assess correctly what is "at," "above," or "below" the standard. Even the New Zealand Prime Minister John Key called the recently published national standards data "ropey." Why are the data ropey? The reason is a lack of moderation of assessments across schools. Ministry of Education research supports this. A Ministry-sponsored survey of 100 schools (Ward & Thomas, 2012) asked teachers to assess a asked teachers to assess a piece of writing or a math piece of work and to decide whether or not the exemplar was at the national standard. They found that teachers varied widely in their ability to assess pupils. In writing, they ranged from 3% accuracy to 95% accuracy. In the writing example, the piece of year-4 writing was "above" the national standard, but only 3% of teachers marked it that way and 97% gave it a lower rating of "at the standard." On a positive note, you could say that teachers were in the right direction—they did rate the writing as passable. In math, teacher judgments ranged from 18% correct to 90%.

Ward and Thomas (2012) found that only one-third of teachers in their survey checked with teachers in other schools about the reliability of their assessments, and when they did check, it was mainly for writing. More than 70% of teachers relied on their professional judgments, but the study found also that most teachers consulted the national standards documents as well as other teachers to make their "overall teacher judgments" (OTJs) about the reading, writing, and math levels of each student. This suggests that the main area of weakness is the lack of between-school moderation of OTJs.

The Situation in Australia

Australia does not have a separate national standards website. Standards are built into their national curriculum (http://www.australiancurriculum.edu.au/). The national curriculum website explains what standards are expected of pupils from years Foundation-Year 10 for English, mathematics, science, and history. The website has work samples for each subject, including videos to watch of students completing certain standards (e.g., conducting an interview) or responding to questions relating to the standards (e.g., in their foundation year, showing if they understand concepts about print).

There has been national assessment in Australia since 2008. The Australian national assessment website gives achievement results for every school in the country (if you Google "My School Australia"—http://www.myschool.edu.au/). The national test is called NAPLAN (National Assessment Programme for Literacy and Numeracy). It assesses achievement of every pupil in the country on an annual basis at Years 3, 7, and 9, in reading, writing, language (spelling, grammar, punctuation), and mathematics. Their website is http://www.naplan.edu.au/. The NAPLAN assessments in Australia are based on the Australian Curriculum.

Where to From Here?

Where to from here? We have to have standards. We are surrounded by standards. They affect both the high and low performers (Pearson, 1993). Every year, even at the high end of the achievement market, students have hurdles (standards) to get over, for example, sitting entry exams to university, competing to pass the standards to get into law or medical schools. The reality of standards is also in sport, competing to achieve a qualifying mark or speed to get entry into finals or championships. At the low end, we are faced with standards even to get a driving license, and there is much pressure to keep raising the driving license standards to improve the appalling crash rates on our roads.

In almost every job, there are standards that must be passed. For example, employees who work in retail outlets must meet certain standards. The level of service at one retail franchise should be similar to the next, if staff training meets the same standards.

A positive argument for standards is that, in principle, everyone can achieve the standards. It is not a bell curve, where half pass and half fail. The standards are achievable. In principle, a student can be above the standard even in a poorly perceived school. If they are above the standard, then they have achieved at the same level as a student in a highly perceived school. If you pass common standards for your subjects at high school, for example, even if your school is in the poorest town in the country, then you are college ready. It should not matter whether you attended Struggletown High or Eton College, because the standards you sat for and passed will be the same in both places.

The major advantage of having common standards across the whole country is that it signals equity. That is, when you do pass the standard, that pass standard will (in theory) be the same whether you come from the wrong or right side of the tracks, whether you are a plumber or a hair stylist in the worst or best part of town. The nice thing about the common core standards in the United States is that they will apply to all, or nearly all of the states, so that there is consistency across the country.

This is what the national standards are about in New Zealand, as well. The country is in the early stages of this process and the data are "ropey," but this should improve with better moderation across schools. If we do not have standards that are widely accepted, then we will always have inequity. The search to be at a "standard" that has global currency suggests that standards should be even wider than at the national level. They should be at an international level.

On the debit side, the argument against standards is that it replaces teacher creativity and leads to a McDonaldization of the curriculum, where each school delivers the same product. Another negative is that some schools will look bad even if it is not their fault, because they are located in a low-socioeconomic area. National standards means that some pupils will be "below" the standards and others will be "at" or "above," and this means that there will be winners and losers. Pearson (1993) writes:

> I know of no way to eliminate completely the harmful potential impact of standards. If standards exist and if meeting them or failing to meet them bears consequences for individuals, then some students will experience the "joy of victory" and others the "agony of defeat." Perhaps the best we can hope for is to make the standards completely transparent so that everyone will be able to see what we mean by them. By opening our values to public scrutiny, we permit evaluation of their potential for harm; standards and assessments that are left unseen and unstated are more likely to be arbitrary and harmful. (p. 470)

Conclusion

When we compare the U.S. Common Core State Standards (CCSSO, 2010a, 2010b) with the Australian or New Zealand standards, the contrast in terms of the number of standards is huge. In English Language Arts alone, the CCSS has nearly 500 standards. This seems way too many. Teachers may get weighed down by all of these standards.

It seems strange that there are so many standards when there are simpler frameworks that could be used. In reading, for example, there is Project Read (Calfee & Patrick, 1995) which seems to be a wonderful example of a simple model for teaching decoding skills (Nicholson, 2005), vocabulary (Nicholson & Dymock, 2010), and comprehension (Dymock & Nicholson, 2012).

Another problematic aspect is that the CCSS does not give a clear picture of what a grade-level reader or writer or math student is like. The CCSS specifies lots of standards, like boxes to be ticked off, but it is hard to see the complete picture. The Australian standards are fewer than the CCSS, but it is still hard to see the complete picture. In contrast, the New Zealand standards start at the end, with a vision of what students at each grade level should be able to read, write, or calculate. It is a complex picture, but at least you can see it.

The CCSS provides all the pieces needed to build a house—but where is the house? It would be better if the teacher had a sense of what the house looked like and had the power to assess whether or not she has built a house, and not just a list of parts needed to build the house. At each grade level, the house will be different, with a simple house in the early years and more complex ones later.

Standards-based assessment often seems like a list of components to build the house, with the hope that if you check off all the parts as "done," you have built the "house"—i.e., a pupil who can read, write, and do math at their grade level. This seems the wrong way to go about it—instead, it would be better to show teachers what kind of house they are supposed to build (as in the New Zealand national standards), and then verify if this has been achieved during the school year. If there are pupils struggling, then check the parts to find out which ones are missing (e.g., phonics, grammar, text structure, inferences, etc.) and attend to these.

To summarize, this chapter has argued that more is less and that standards only make sense if they paint a clear picture of what they want our pupils to become, and if teachers have some ownership of them and have to figure out a way to achieve them for each pupil in their class. It may be that we need to have national assessment—for complete accuracy— but we also need teacher assessment to give ownership at the classroom level and to enable teachers to be builders rather than clerks who simply check off standards as achieved or not achieved.

Special note about the author—I was a member of an independent advisory group to provide expert advice to the New Zealand government on National Standards for Reading, Writing, and Mathematics. This talk represents just my own views, not those of the advisory group.

Author note

Thanks to Adrienne Frater and her agent Richards Literary Agency for permission to reprint the text of Drought, from the *New Zealand School Journal* (2010, part3, number 2, pages 2–17) and to Learning Media for permission to reprint the illustrations. Thanks also to Learning Media for permission to reprint two national standards exemplars, a reading exemplar on the text "Drought" and a writing exemplar on a meeting between Captain Cook and Christopher Columbus.

References

Bushaw, W. J., & Lopez, S. J. (2012). Public education in the United States: A nation divided. *Phi Delta Kappan, 94*(1), 9–25.

Calfee, R. C., & Patrick, C. L. (1995). *Teach our children well: Bringing K-12 education into the 21st century.* Stanford, CA: Stanford Alumni.

CCSSO/NGA. (2010a). *Common Core State Standards for English language arts & literacy in history/social studies, Science, and Technical Subjects.* Washington, DC: Council of Chief State School Officers & National Governors Association. Retrieved from www.corestandards.org

CCSSO/NGA. (2010b). *Common Core State Standards for mathematics.* Washington, DC: Council of Chief State School Officers & National Governors Association. Retrieved from www.corestandards.org

Dymock, S. J., & Nicholson, T. (2012). *Teaching reading comprehension. The what, the how, the why.* Wellington, New Zealand: NZCER Press.

Frater, A. (2010). Drought. *School Journal, 3*(2), 2–17.

Hattie, J. (2009). *Horizons and whirlpools: The well travelled pathway of national standards.* Unpublished paper, The University of Auckland

Johnston, M. (2012, October 5). Publishing national standards may do more harm than good. *NZ Herald.* Retrieved from http://www.nzherald.co.nz/education/news/article.cfm?c_id=35&objectid=10838391

McLachlan, C., Nicholson, T., Fielding Barnsley, R., Mercer, L., & Ohi, S. (2013). *Literacy in early childhood and primary: Issues, challenges, solutions.* Melbourne, AU: Cambridge University Press.

Merriam-Webster. (1983). *The Merriam-Webster dictionary.* Springfield, MA: G&C Merriam.

Ministry of Education (2009a). *The New Zealand curriculum reading and writing standards for years 1–8.* Wellington: Learning Media.

Ministry of Education (2009b). *The New Zealand curriculum mathematics standards for years 1–8.* Wellington: Learning Media.

Nicholson, T. (2005). *Phonics handbook.* Chichester, England: Wiley.

Nicholson, T., & Dymock, S. (2010). *Teaching reading vocabulary.* Wellington, New Zealand: NZCER Press.

Pearson, P. D. (1993). Standards for the English language arts: A policy perspective. *Journal of Reading Behavior, 25*, 457–475.

Pearson, P. D. (2013). Research foundations for the Common Core State Standards in English language arts. In S. Neuman & L. Gambrell (Eds.), *Reading instruction in the age of Common Core State standards* (pp. 237–262). Newark, DE: International Reading Association.

Pearson, P. D., & Hiebert, E. H. (2013). Understanding the Common Core State Standards. In L. Morrow, T. Shanahan, & K. K. Wixson (Eds.), *Teaching with the Common Core Standards for English language arts: What educators need to know* (Book 1: Grades PreK-2; Book 2: Grades 3–5). New York, NY: Guilford Press.

Polesel, J., Dulfer, N., & Turnbull, M. (2012). *The experience of education. The impacts of high stakes testing on school students and their families.* Sydney, AU: Whitlam Institute.

Purcell-Gates, V. (2009). The irrelevance—and danger—of the simple view. In J. Soler, F. Fletcher-Campbell, & G. Reid (Eds.), *Understanding difficulties in literacy development: Issues and concepts* (pp. 67–76). London, UK: Sage.

Ward, J., & Thomas, G. (2012). *National standards: School monitoring and evaluation project, 2011.* Wellington, NZ: Ministry of Education.

List of Contributors

Angeleque Akin-Little, PhD, Akin-Little & Little Behavioral Psychology Consultants PLLC—Angeleque Akin-Little is president of a behavioral psychology consulting company based in northern New York. She has previously served on the faculty of universities in the United States and New Zealand, has published extensively in the school psychology literature, served on several editorial boards of major school psychology journals, and served as Secretary of Division 16 (School Psychology) of the American Psychological Association. She is a Fellow of the APA and is a licensed psychologist in New York, California, and New Zealand. She is also a board-certified behavior analyst. Her research interests involve behavioral interventions, the effects of extrinsic reinforcement on intrinsic motivation, and the use of trauma-focused CBT with children post-natural disaster.

Vincent C. Alfonso, PhD, Fordham University—Vincent C. Alfonso is Professor in the Graduate School of Education at Fordham University. He is president of Division 16 of the American Psychological Association and New York delegate to the National Association of School Psychologists. Dr. Alfonso primarily publishes articles, books, and book chapters on assessment.

Rebekah Bickford, PsyD, University of Southern Maine—Dr. Bickford is Assistant Clinical Research Professor of Educational and School Psychology at the University of Southern Maine. She earned her doctorate in school psychology at the University of Southern Maine in 2012. Her research includes classroom consultation, the impact of teacher praise on student well-being, and novel applications of Positive Behavioral Interventions and Supports.

Lisa Bowman-Perrott, PhD, Texas A&M University—Dr. Bowman-Perrott is an Assistant Professor in the Special Education Program at Texas A&M University. Her research interests are academic and behavioral interventions for students with or at risk for emotional and behavioral disorders, including peer tutoring.

Rachel Brown, PhD, NCSP, University of Southern Maine—Dr. Brown is Associate Professor of Educational and School Psychology at the University of Southern Maine. She earned her doctorate in school psychology at the University of Massachusetts in 2000. Prior to that, she taught general and special education for 10 years. Her research interests are Response to Intervention, curriculum-based measurement, and effective academic instruction.

Theodore J. Christ, PhD, University of Minnesota—Dr. Christ is an Associate Professor in the Educational Psychology Department at the University of Minnesota. He is also the Director of the Formative Assessment System for Teachers (FAST; fast.cehd.umn.edu) and Co-Director of the Research Institute for Problem Solving (RIPS). Dr. Christ is engaged in research to develop, evaluate, and improve assessments that are used to enhance data-based decisions, problem solving, and response to intervention. Dr. Christ has numerous publications and national presentations on topics related to Curriculum-Based Measurement, data-based decision-making, and Direct Behavior Rating. He is the principal and co-principal investigator of multiple projects funded through the Institute of Education Sciences and Office of Special Education Programming. Dr. Christ received the 2008 Lightner Witmer Early Career Award from Division 16 of the American Psychological Association for outstanding early career scholarship.

Amanda B. Clinton, PhD, University of Puerto Rico, Mayagüez—Dr. Amanda Clinton is an Associate Professor of Psychology at the University of Puerto Rico, Mayagüez. Her primary research interests are bilingualism and learning disabilities, cultural adaptation, social emotional development, and effective pedagogy for minority students.

Robin S. Codding, Ph.D., University of Massachusetts, Boston—Robin S. Codding is Associate Professor of School Psychology at the University of Massachusetts, Boston. Her research interests include school-based interventions and procedural integrity, with special focus on mathematics assessment and intervention. Dr. Codding has been author or co-author of more than 35 articles and book chapters, and was the 2010 co-recipient of the Lightner Witmer Early Career Scholar Award from the Division 16 of the American Psychological Association.

Clayton R. Cook, Ph.D., University of Washington—Dr. Clayton Cook is an Assistant Professor in the College of Education at the University of Washington in Seattle. He received his PhD from the University of California, Riverside, and subsequently went on to do his internship at Boys Town in Omaha, Nebraska. Dr. Cook has published numerous peer-reviewed articles and three books on the topic of students with or at risk for academic, emotional, and behavioral disorders and the application of RTI practices for these students.

Anne Mong Cramer, Ph.D., Indiana University of Pennsylvania—Dr. Cramer is an Assistant Professor at Indiana University of Pennsylvania, and is co-coordinator of the Early Childhood Special Education dual certification program. She teaches courses in literacy, classroom management, and child development. Her research interests include peer-mediated learning, literacy development in struggling learners, and placement transitions for students with special learning needs.

Andrea Dennison, SSP, Texas A&M University—Andrea Dennison is a PhD candidate in School Psychology at Texas A&M University. Her research focuses on multi-systemic variables that impact the academic and psychological functioning of culturally and linguistically diverse students.

Ben Ditkowsky, PhD, Barrington (IL) Community Unit School District 220—Dr. Ditkowsky received his PhD from the University of Oregon in 2002. He is currently working as a district administrator in Barrington Community Unit School District 220. In the past, Ben has worked as a district administrator, an educational consultant, an external evaluator for the Northern Region of the Illinois ASPIRE grant, a behavior specialist, and as a teacher in both special and general classrooms. In addition, Ben maintains MeasureEffects.com, a website that provides free educational tools and templates to assist educators with analysis and display of achievement and behavioral data.

Shauna G. Dixon, MS, EdM—Shauna Dixon has graduate degrees in Mind, Brain, and Education from Harvard Graduate School of Education, and School Psychology from St. John's University, where she is pursuing her doctoral degree. Ms. Dixon's efforts are designed to show how advances in neuroscience can impact educational and school psychology practice and policy.

Dawn P. Flanagan, PhD, St. Johns University—Dr. Flanagan is Professor of Psychology at St. John's University in Queens, New York, and Clinical Assistant Professor at Yale Child Study Center, Yale University, School of Medicine, in New Haven, Connecticut. She is a widely published author and serves as an expert witness, learning disability consultant, and test and measurement consultant and trainer for organizations both nationally and internationally. She recently published *Essentials of Cross-Battery Assessment, 3rd edition, Contemporary Intellectual Assessment: Theories, Tests and Issues—3rd Edition* and *Essentials of Specific Learning Disability Identification*. Dr. Flanagan is primary author of six online professional development programs on learning disabilities and is co-editor of the forthcoming book, *Essentials of Planning, Selecting, and Tailoring Interventions for the Unique Learner*. She is a fellow of the American Psychological Association and a diplomate of the American Board of Psychological Specialties.

Kristin A. Gansle, PhD, Louisiana State University—Dr. Gansle is an Associate Professor in the School of Education, in Special Education Programs, at Louisiana State University, Baton Rouge, LA. Her recent research interests include value-added assessment of teacher preparation programs, correlates of quality teacher preparation programs, and educational assessment and intervention.

Kathryn Germer, MEd, Nashville, TN—Kathryn Germer received her MEd from Peabody College of Vanderbilt University in May 2013 and plans to pursue a teaching position serving students with severe disabilities. Her research interests include the design, implementation, and evaluation of functional assessment-based interventions within comprehensive, integrated, three-tiered (CI3T) models of prevention.

Erin E. C. Henze, PhD, University of Detroit Mercy—Dr. Henze received her PhD from the University of Tennessee in 2008. She is currently Assistant Professor of Psychology at the University of Detroit Mercy and is a certified School Psychologist and Licensed Psychologist. Her research interests include development and evaluation of psychoeducational interventions for school-aged children, teaching practices at the college level, and supervision and training issues in School Psychology.

Rebecca Hickey, University of California, Riverside—Rebecca is a doctoral student in the APA-accredited School Psychology program at the University of California, Riverside. Her research interests include academic assessment and intervention, and consultation.

Elizabeth Holland, MAT, University of Washington—Elizabeth Holland holds an Ed.S. degree in School Psychology from the University of Washington and is a Nationally Certified School Psychologist. She is currently a Ph.D. student at the University of Washington and has a longstanding interest in reading interventions. She is also a former public school teacher with a Masters of Arts in Teaching from the University of Puget Sound and has worked with students with reading disabilities for over 10 years.

Kathryn E. Jaspers, PhD, University of Houston—Clear Lake—Dr. Jaspers received her PhD in School Psychology from The University of Tennessee, and she practiced as a school psychologist before joining the faculty at UHCL in 2011. Her interests include academic interventions, consultation, and measurement of intervention efficiency, maintenance, and generalization.

Milena A. Keller-Margulis, PhD, University of Houston—Milena A. Keller-Margulis is Assistant Professor of School Psychology at the University of Houston. Her research interests include the technical adequacy and practical utility of curriculum-based measurement, as well as the scaling-up of response to intervention implementation in schools.

Kathleen Lynne Lane, PhD, University of Kansas—Kathleen Lynne Lane is a Professor in the Department of Special Education at the University of Kansas. She earned her master's degree and doctorate in education from the University of California, Riverside. Dr. Lane's research interests focus on school-based interventions (academic and behavioral) with students at risk for emotional and behavioral disorders (EBD), with an emphasis on systematic screenings to detect students with behavioral challenges at the earliest possible juncture. She has designed, implemented, and evaluated comprehensive, integrated, three-tiered (CI3T) models of prevention in elementary, middle, and high school settings to prevent the development of learning and behavior challenges, and responding to existing instances. She is the co-editor of *Remedial and Special Education*. Dr. Lane has co-authored five books and published 120 refereed journal articles and 23 book chapters.

Steven G. Little, PhD, Walden University—Steven Little is currently a Professor in the Clinical Psychology program at Walden University. He has served on the faculty at universities in the United States and New Zealand, including as Professor of Educational Psychology and Director of the Educational Psychology Program at Massey University in Auckland, New Zealand. He has published more than 100 articles and book chapters. He is a former President of the Division of School Psychology of the American Psychological Association (APA) and a Fellow of the American Psychological Association. He is a licensed psychologist in New York, California, and New Zealand, and a board-certified behavior analyst (BCBA-D). He was the 2009 Jack Bardon Award winner for Lifetime Service to the profession of School Psychology given by Division 16 of the APA.

Amanda M. Marcotte, PhD, University of Massachusetts at Amherst—Amanda Marcotte is an assistant professor in the School Psychology Program at the University of Massachusetts Amherst, where she teaches courses on academic assessment and interventions for children. Her research interests are in the areas of educational practices designed to prevent academic and behavioral problems in schools. She has conducted research on methods of formative assessment for reading comprehension problems, and is currently investigating various measures of emergent literacy skills.

Ryan J. Martin, University of Massachusetts, Boston—Ryan J. Martin is a doctoral student in the school psychology program at the University of Massachusetts, Boston. His research interests include mathematics assessment and intervention, as well as parent implementation of home-based interventions.

Linda H. Mason, PhD, The University of North Carolina at Chapel Hill—Dr. Linda H. Mason is a Professor at The University of North Carolina at Chapel Hill. Dr. Mason conducts research in literacy for students with special needs. She is on eight editorial boards, including *Reading Research Quarterly, Journal of Educational Psychology,* and *Exceptional Children.* Dr. Mason has two co-authored books, *Powerful writing strategies for all students* and *Building comprehension in adolescents: Powerful strategies for improving reading and writing in content areas.* Dr. Mason was awarded the Council for Exceptional Children-Division of Research Distinguished Early Career Award in 2011, and a Fulbright Scholarship to teach at the University of Szeged, Hungary, in Fall 2011.

Sara J. McCane-Bowling, PhD, The University of Tennessee at Chattanooga—Dr. Bowling received her PhD in 2007 from the School Psychology program at the University of Tennessee (Knoxville). She currently works as an Assistant Professor for the University of Tennessee at Chattanooga and primarily teaches coursework for their NASP-approved School Psychology program. She has published and presented on various topics, including curriculum-based measurement, academic intervention, and positive behavior intervention and supports.

Holly Mariah Menzies, PhD, California State University, Los Angeles—Dr. Menzies is faculty in the Division of Special Education and Counseling at California State University, Los Angeles. She is the program coordinator for the mild/moderate disabilities program.

Christine E. Neddenriep, PhD, University of Wisconsin–Whitewater—Christine Neddenriep is an Associate Professor of Psychology and Coordinator of the School Psychology Program at the University of Wisconsin–Whitewater. Her areas of research interests include the implementation and evaluation of academic interventions in educational settings. She has also conducted research examining the validity of the reading comprehension rate measure.

Tom Nicholson, PhD, Massey University—Tom Nicholson is a professor in Education at Massey University in Auckland, New Zealand, teaching in human development, educational research methods, language, literacy, and cognition, writing in the classroom, and social justice and literacy, and sometimes applied behavior analysis. His research focuses on issues related to literacy and he has been a member of a government advisory team on National Standards in Reading, Writing, and Mathematics. He is a member of the Reading Hall of Fame. He is married, lives in Auckland. He likes walking, going to nice cafes, looking at art, and going to movies.

George H. Noell, PhD, Louisiana State University—Dr. Noell is a Professor of Psychology at Louisiana State University, Baton Rouge, LA. His research interests are behavioral consultation, intervention implementation, and assessment procedures that have treatment utility. He has also been actively engaged in research and policy work examining the use of quantitative data to assess and strengthen teacher preparation.

Wendy Peia Oakes, PhD, Arizona State University—Dr. Wendy Oakes is an Assistant Professor in Mary Lou Fulton Teachers College. Her research focuses on practices that improve the educational outcomes for young children with emotional and behavioral disorders through the implementation of evidence-based academic and behavioral interventions within three-tiered models of prevention and professional development for implementing these practices with fidelity. Dr. Oakes serves on the editorial board for *Remedial and Special Education* and on the executive board for the Council for Exceptional Children—Division for Research.

Pedro Olvera, Azusa Pacific University—Dr. Pedro Olvera is an Associate Professor of School Psychology at Azusa Pacific University, Los Angeles. His research interests include bilingual school psychology practices, culturally and linguistically appropriate home-school collaborative strategies, and Cattell-Horn-Carroll (CHC)/Cross-Battery assessment with English Language Learners.

Madi Phillips, PhD, National Louis University—Dr. Phillips is an Assistant Professor in the School Psychology Program at National Louis University. She has been involved as a school psychologist and consultant in multi-tiered system of support (MTSS) and Response to Intervention (RtI) implementation in Illinois and Iowa. Since coming to NLU, Madi has continued that involvement through her work on an IHE RtI grant and the Chicago Teacher Partnership Program.

Cynthia A. Riccio, PhD, Texas A&M University—Dr. Riccio is a Professor and Director of Training at Texas A&M University. Her research focuses on learning disabilities and ADHD, from a neuropsychological perspective. She has published extensively in the area of assessment.

Emily F. Rowlette, PhD, Jefferson County Schools, TN—Dr. Rowlette received her PhD in School Psychology from the University of Tennessee in 2010. She currently works as a school psychologist for a public school system in Tennessee. Dr. Rowlette's research interests include specific learning disabilities, ADHD, and academic and behavioral interventions. She is actively involved in designing and implementing the Response to Intervention program in her school district.

Mark R. Shinn, PhD, National Louis University—Dr. Shinn received his Ph.D. from the University of Minnesota in 1981. He has published two edited books on Curriculum-Based Measurement and co-edited three editions of *Interventions for Achievement and Behavior Problems,* including the 2010 third edition. *Interventions for Achievement and Behavior Problems in a 3-Tier Model,* including RTI published by the National Association of School Psychologists (NASP). Dr. Shinn also has published almost 100 professional journal articles and book chapters on CBM, progress monitoring, and problem-solving model service delivery systems. In 2003, he was awarded the APA Division 16 Jack Bardon Award for Distinguished Career Service Contributions.

Christopher H. Skinner, PhD, The University of Tennessee—Dr. Skinner received his PhD in School Psychology from Lehigh University in 1989. He is professor and program coordinator of School Psychology programs at UT. Working with his students, Dr. Skinner has published more than 200 articles and book chapters, most focused on evaluating, validating, and comparing academic and behavioral interventions. He was named APA Division 16 Senior Scientist in 2012 and in 2013 received the APA Division 25 Fred S. Keller award.

Tal Slemrod, M.S., University of Washington—Tal Slemrod is in the Special Education PhD program at the University of Washington. His research focuses on identifying effective academic and behavioral interventions for adolescents and young adults with disabilities. Specifically, he works with schools to find effective strategies for increasing access to general education curriculum for students with disabilities in the inclusive classroom.

Mark W. Steege, PhD, BCBA-D, NCSP, University of Southern Maine—Dr. Steege is Professor of Educational and School Psychology at the University of Southern Maine. He earned his doctorate in school psychology at the University of Iowa in 1986. He is an Iowa native and worked as a school psychologist there while earning his doctorate. His research interests are functional behavioral assessment, behavior analytic problem solving, and interventions for autism spectrum disorders.

Catherine Tung, University of California, Riverside—Catherine's research interests include examining techniques to improve the reliability and validity of CBM tools with English Leaners. She is conducts research and works as a school psychologist in Southern California.

Mike Vanderwood, PhD, University of California, Riverside—Dr. Vanderwood is an Associate Professor and School Psychology Program Coordinator at the University of California–Riverside. His research focuses on evaluating and improving the quality of assessment, intervention, and consultation tools used in a multi-tiered (e.g., RTI) approach to service delivery for culturally and linguistically diverse students.

Index

Note: Page numbers in *italics* indicate figures and tables.

familiarity with print 205
family and language learning 105
Five-Step Word study strategy 243
fluency: in computation and number
combination 267–8; in letter naming 205–6;
in reading, and comprehension 221–2;
in reading, instruction in *213*, 213–14; of
reading, interventions for 226
fluency, assessment of: CBM and CLD research
186–90; math 89; reading 82–3; writing 87
formative feature of responsive assessment
166, *166*
forward chaining 17–18
frequent progress monitoring: with AIMSweb
155, *156*; with DIBELS Net 153–4, *154*;
with easyCBM 152–3, *153*; overview of 150;
standards-based goals 151; Web 2.0 tools for
150–7, *158*; with YPP 156–7, *157, 158*
full individual initial evaluation 79, 80

general case framework for intervention:
contextual considerations 11–13; design issues
13–14; identifying instructional targets 8–11;
implementing 21; prompting 16–17; shaping
15; teaching discrete responses 14–15; teaching
skills requiring sequences of behavior 17–18;
teaching strategic behaviors 19–21; teaching
structured bodies of knowledge 18–19
General Outcomes Measurement paradigm for
CBA 120, 168
goal-referenced interpretations of CBA
performance 120
goals, setting: for frequent progress monitoring
151–2; for struggling learners 132
GORT-5 (Gray Oral Reading Tests-Fifth
Edition): characteristics of and task demands
52–3; content and administration features
of *60*; IDEIA SLD areas and *49*; reliability of
72–3; subtests on *35*; technical features of *63–4*
grammar instruction 243
graphic organizers 19, 231
The Great Race intervention 267
group assessment: of academic achievement
97–101; purpose of 4; universal screening 168
Group Math Assessment and Diagnostic
Evaluation 168
group-oriented rewards 291–4
Group Reading Assessment and Diagnostic
Evaluation 168
Guided Oral Repeated Reading with Feedback 214

handwriting, intervention for 242
higher-order cognitive abilities and
comprehension 222
high-frequency words 212
high-probability request sequences 311

high-stakes decisions and CBA 121
high-stakes testing 97–8, 317
Hot Math Tutoring program 272

IDEIA *see* Individuals with Disabilities
Improvement Education Act
immigration, implications of 106
implementation of intervention plans 21
incremental rehearsal 212, 270
independent group-oriented rewards 291–2
individual assessment: achievement batteries
80–1; of math skills 87–9, *88*; purpose of 3–4;
of reading skills *81*, 81–5; of specific academic
areas 79–80; of written expression 85–7, *86*
individual-referenced goals for frequent progress
monitoring 152
Individuals with Disabilities Education Act 300
Individuals with Disabilities Improvement
Education Act (IDEIA): correspondence
between achievement categories and CHC
theory 45–6, *46, 47–50,* 51; full individual
initial evaluation 79, linking assessment and
intervention and 27; SLD and 33; variation
in achievement test characteristics and task
demands 51, *52–8, 58–9*
inferential comprehension questions 222–3
informal reading inventories 83, 84–5
informational text, writing and revising 249–50
instruction: in after reading strategies 232–3;
in prereading strategies 228–30; in reading
comprehension strategies 223–5, 236–7; in
during reading strategies 230–2; for success
in mathematics 259–61; *see also* decoding
instruction, evidence-based; explicit direct
instruction; intervention; responsive
assessment and instruction practices
instructional efficacy: differentiating curriculum
to enhance motivation and engagement
302–7; implementing low-intensity behavioral
supports to enhance experiences 307–12;
overview of 300–2; recommendations for
312–13
instructional targets 8–11, *9*
intellectual-cultural experiences and reading
204–5
intensive intervention and special education
decisions 171–3
interdependent group-oriented rewards 292–4
interpretations of CBA performance 119–20
interspersal procedures for tasks 286–8
intervention: within ABA-based programs 163–4;
common features for mathematics 261–4, *262*;
tiered 170; for writing skills 241–4; for written
expression 244–52; *see also* evidence-based
intervention; general case framework for
intervention; instruction